Statistical Reasoning

Gary Smith
Fletcher Jones Professor of Economics
Pomona College

Allyn and Bacon, Inc.
Boston London Sydney Toronto

Developmental Editor: Jane Dahl

Library of Congress Cataloging in Publication Data

Smith, Gary, 1945–
   Statistical reasoning.

   Includes index.
   1. Statistics.   2. Probabilities.   I. Title.
QA276.12.S58 1985   519.2   84–16957
ISBN 0–205–08295–5

Printed in the United States of America.

10 9 8 7 6 5 4 3 2 1   90 89 88 87 86 85

The author would like to thank Addison-Wesley Publishing Company for their permission to include material (pp. 135–136, 139–140, 164–165, 483, and 663–664) take from his text *Money and Banking* (pp. 9, 180, 184, 185, 189–190, and 275–278), copyright © 1982 by Addison-Wesley Publishing Company, Inc., Reading, Massachusetts.
Additional credits appear on page 714, which constitutes a continuation of the copyright page.

For my wife, Betsy,
several standard deviations above the mean.

In the year of our Lord 1432, there arose a grievous quarrel among the brethren of a monastery over the number of teeth in the mouth of a horse. For thirteen days the disputation raged without ceasing. All the ancient books and chronicles were fetched out, and wonderful and ponderous erudition, such as was never before heard of in this region, was made manifest. At the beginning of the fourteenth day, a youthful friar of goodly bearing asked his learned superiors for permission to add a word.

Straightaway, to the wonder of the disputants whose deep wisdom he sore vexed, he beseeched then to unbend in a manner coarse and unheard of, and to look in the mouth of a horse to find an answer to their questionings. At this, their dignity being greatly hurt, they waxed exceedinging wroth; and joining in a mighty uproar, they fell upon him, hip and thigh, and cast him out forthwith. For, said they, surely Satan hath tempted this bold neophyte to declare unholy and unheard of ways of finding truth contrary to all the teachings of their fathers!

Francis Bacon (1561–1626)

Contents

Preface

H.G. Wells once wrote that "Statistical thinking will one day be as necessary for efficient citizenship as the ability to read and write." And today it is. We live in a complex society in which informed decisions require an intelligent interpretation of all sorts of statistical data and probability judgments.

Probability and statistics can help you decide which foods are unhealthful, which careers are lucrative, what car to drive, how much insurance to have, and which stocks to purchase. Businesses routinely use statistics to gauge markets, design products, schedule activities, monitor production, and even more. Government statisticians measure things ranging from unemployment to corn production to births to pollution. Each year, the tip of this statistical iceberg is published in the *Statistical Abstract*. Some of these data, such as weather patterns and crop production, help citizens and business make intelligent plans. Others, such as unemployment, inflation, and product safety tests, are used by government policy makers.

Government data also provide ammunition for election campaigns, and voters must decide whether the politicans are using or abusing statistics. In 1984, Ronald Reagan was so upset by contrary data that he used the 19th century British politican Benjamin Disraeli's immortal retort, "There are three kinds of lies—lies, damn lies, and statistics." And then President Reagan proceeded to cite some statistics of his own!

The essence of probability and statistics is thinking clearly about some important, yet unfamiliar ideas. This is why this book is titled *Statistical Reasoning*. This is not a "plug and chug" text, where the student is just given a formula and some data and told to plug in the numbers and chug out an answer. That is too easy and useless a task. At best, it gives practice at addition, subtraction, division, and multiplication; at worst, it numbs the mind and tricks one into thinking that probability and statistics are just tedious subcategories of arithmetic.

To the contrary, they are very interesting and important talents. Today, any necessary arithmetic computations can be done easily with pocket calculators or computers. It is the thinking that you must learn, and this course will help you. You will learn how to use probabilities and statistical reasoning, how to recognize the abuses of others, and how to judge the competing claims of advertisers and politicians.

The chapters rely heavily on examples to teach their lessons, since there are so many real world situations that require statistical analysis. A sampling is on the inside cover of this text, intended to whet your appetite. There are many, many more in the book itself. These will show you the breadth of probability and statistics, illustrate how the tools are used, and even teach you something about the examples themselves. The statisticians and editors who read these chapters all said they learned some interesting things from the examples—you will too.

Each chapter has a plethora of exercises, of varying type and difficulty. Some are simple computations, to reinforce the chapter material. Many are real world examples, opportunities to apply important principles. Those that are a bit more difficult are prefaced by a single bullet ●—those more difficult still have two bullets.

Several reviewers mentioned that the exercises are an absolutely essential part of this book—and so they are. You can't become proficient at racquetball just by watching, and you can't learn probability and statistics just by reading. You have to go out and try to hit a few balls yourself. You may miss a few at first; but soon you will acquire the necessary skills and experience.

I have prepared a computer disk that will do virtually all of the computations required in this course. This disk is not necessary, but it offers a nice alternative to a pocket calculator or large computer. A very good study guide has been prepared by Roy V. Erickson, of Michigan State University.

I am grateful to the Literary Executor of the late Sir Ronald A. Fisher, F.R.S., to Dr. Frank Yates, F.R.S., and to Longman Group Ltd, London, for permission to reprint Table III from their book *Statistical Tables for Biological, Agricultural, and Medical Research* (6th Edition, 1974).

Several enthusiastic, yet careful, reviewers have provided helpful suggestions and welcome encouragement:

Roy V. Erickson, Michigan State University
James Stapleton, Michigan State University
Frank W. Puffer, Clark University
George Briden, University of Rhode Island

Ronald S. Koot, The Pennsylvania State University
Mary Sue Younger, The University of Tennessee at Knoxville
Bernard Isselhardt, Rochester Institute of Technology

I thank each of you.

Many fine people at Allyn and Bacon helped turn my drafts into a book: Richard Carle, Jane Dahl, Barbara Hewes, and especially Mary Hill—the most careful and conscientious of production editors.

I welcome your comments and suggestions.

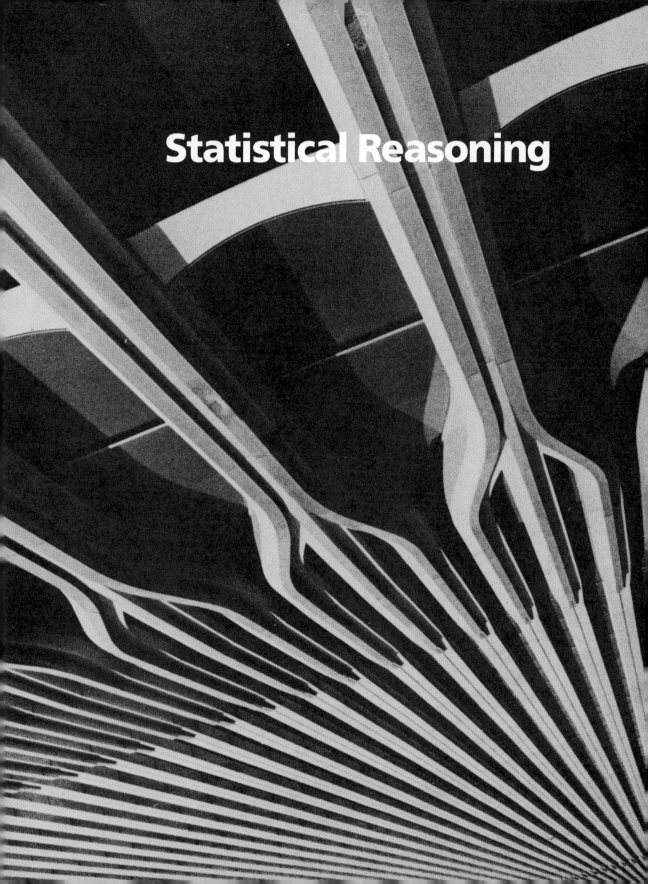

Statistical Reasoning

World Trade Center, New York
© Joel Gordon, 1981

CHAPTER 1

Introduction

Life is a school of probability.

Walter Bagehot

TOPICS

Probabilities are used to analyze uncertain situations. If it is true that only death and taxes are certain, then that leaves a lot of targets for probability analysis! When you hear that the odds are 100 to 1 that the Chicago Cubs will be in the World Series, those odds reflect a probability assessment. The Educational Testing Service applies probabilities when it calculates standardized scores on its SAT tests. Colleges use probabilities when they decide how many students to admit, how many professors to employ, and how many classrooms to build. Probabilities are involved when an army decides to attack or retreat, when a business decides to expand or contract, and when you decide whether or not to take an umbrella to school. Uncertainties are all around us, and so are probabilities.

Historically, the first rigorous application of probability theory involved games of chance, and games are still a fertile field for probability analysis. Gambling casinos use probabilities when they set payoffs for roulette, craps, and slot machines. Governments use probabilities when they set payoffs for public lotteries. Good poker players have learned probabilities from long and sometimes expensive experience. Probability calculations have been used to devise systems for winning at blackjack.[1] In recent years, backgammon has been extensively studied by mathematicians and devoted players, again using probabilities. A few years ago, probabilities were used to analyze the game of Monopoly.[2]

Probabilities are also used in gambles that don't really involve standard games of chance. When a bookie offers odds on the winner of the next Super Bowl, the next president of the United States, or the sex of a celebrity's baby, that bookie is using probabilities. These probabilities cannot be as precisely reasoned as those in roulette or craps, but it is certain that the bookie has thought very carefully about how probable the wagered event is.

Another early use of probabilities was in setting insurance rates. Consider, for example, a life insurance policy that will pay $100,000 if Mr. Jones dies. In deciding whether to offer this policy and how large a premium to charge, the insurance company would like to know how probable it is that Mr. Jones will die soon. They will use data from the experiences of other men of similar age, health, and occupation to estimate the probabilities that Mr. Jones will live another year, another 10 years, and another 50 years. Their enthusiasm for issuing the policy and the premium they charge will depend on whether Mr. Jones is 18 or 98, whether he is in good health or the recent recipient of an artificial heart, and whether he is a college professor or a soldier of fortune. Insurance companies also estimate probabilities when they offer disability insurance, medical insurance, car insurance, boat insurance, home insurance, and business insurance. They have less data to go on, but they still estimate probabilities when they offer insurance against a baseball strike or offer to insure some part of a starlet's anatomy.

1.1   PROBABILITY VERSUS STATISTICS

If an unbent coin is fairly flipped, then simple logic tells us that the probability of heads is 1/2 (one chance in two) and the probability of tails is 1/2. Similarly, in roulette, craps, and other games of chance, we can use logic alone to infer probabilities. We will begin making such inferences in the next chapter. With insurance rates, however, logic alone is not enough. Common sense tells us that a 98-year-old person is more likely to die within a year than an 18-year-old is. But how much more likely? This is where statistics come in. By examining the observed mortality rates of 18-year-olds and 98-year-olds, we may be able to estimate the respective probabilities. The use of specific data to estimate probabilities is termed **statistical inference**.

There is a close relationship between probability and statistics that can be brought out by distinguishing between a **population** and a **sample**. Most statistical data are a sample from a much larger population. To predict the outcome of a presidential election, for instance, pollsters interview a few thousand voters. The people who are polled are a sample from a population consisting of the tens of millions of people who will vote in the actual election. Statistical inference involves using the poll data to predict the outcome of the election and assess how much confidence we have in our prediction.*

Probabilities enter because there is chance involved in the selection of the people to be interviewed. Even if 52 percent of all voters favor the Democratic candidate, there is a chance that, by the luck of the draw, 51 percent of the people picked for the poll will favor the Republican candidate. Probability calculations can tell us the likelihood of such an unfortunate sampling error. This possibility of sampling error explains why poll results are given as "51 percent ± 3 percent." In this course, you will learn where the ± 3 percent comes from and exactly what it means.

In general, probabilities are used to describe anticipated outcomes. Statistical data are the observed outcomes, and statistical inference is the use of data to draw inferences about the underlying probabilities.

If an unbent coin is fairly flipped, then we anticipate that heads and tails will come up about equally often. We can say even more about the anticipated outcomes with some easy probability rules that you will soon learn. If the coin is flipped 5 times, the probability of 5 straight heads works out to be .03 (3 chances in 100). With 20 flips, the probability of 15 or more heads turns out to be .02. With 100 flips, the probability of 60 or more heads is .03. These are all probability calculations about the likelihood of forthcoming data (the outcome of the coin flips), given certain assumptions (that the coin is unbent and fairly flipped).

We can think of the forthcoming coin tosses as a sample from a hypothetical infinite population consisting of all of the outcomes, were this coin to be flipped endlessly. Probability theory tells us how often various samples (such as 16 heads

*A statistical population need not be large, but it must contain every person, place, or thing that we're interested in. If we're only interested in how the two adults in my household will vote, then my wife and I are the entire population. A sample could consist of either of us or both of us. In practice, partial samples are used when the population is too large to be analyzed completely. Thus, the distinction between a sample and the entire population usually arises in cases where the population is large.

in 20 tosses) should occur. The actual results, perhaps 52 heads and 48 tails in 100 flips, are our statistical data. An example of a statistical inference is that these particular data are consistent with our assumption that the coin is unbent and fairly flipped. If heads had come up 87 times in 100 flips, we might infer that this is too improbable a result to be consistent with our assumption that the coin is fair. The observation of 87 heads in 100 flips suggests that heads and tails are not equally likely with this particular coin. Either the coin or the coin tosser may be crooked. A more specific statistical inference is an estimate that the probability of throwing heads with this unusual coin is .87 $\pm$ .10. In this course you will learn how to calculate probabilities, scrutinize data, and draw such inferences.

Election Polls

The collection of all the people who will vote in an upcoming election is a finite population. A poll of 100 voters is a sample from this population of all voters. Probability theory tells us how often various samples should occur. For instance, if half of all voters favor candidate H and half favor candidate T, then (just as with our coin flips) there is a .03 probability that at least 60 of the 100 voters we poll will favor H. It's not very likely, but there is this slim chance of a very misleading poll result. In this course, you will learn how the chances of an inaccurate poll can be reduced by taking a larger sample. If, for example, the population of all voters is evenly divided and 400 voters are surveyed, it turns out that there is then only a .00003 probability that 60 percent or more of the sample will favor H.

In this way, probability theory tells us how often we can anticipate observing certain data, given certain assumptions about the underlying population. These observed data may be a winning streak at roulette, high sales of a new product, or a favorable election poll. Statistical inference works in the other direction, using observed data to gauge the characteristics of the underlying population. Statistical inference is used to estimate one's chances of winning a game, to project future sales, and to predict the outcome of an upcoming election. In each case, we have to allow for a margin of error because luck alone can cause the observed data to be atypical. Statistical inference tells us how to make good estimates and how much confidence we can put in our estimates. Naturally, as with the election poll between H and T, the reliability of our estimates depends on the amount of data we have. A poll of 400 people is less likely to be misleading than a poll of 100 people or 5 people. Methods of statistical inference can tell us how big a poll we need to obtain reliable estimates.

Statistical inference can also be used to confirm or discredit theories about the underlying population. One theory might be that candidate T is going to win the upcoming election. If a poll is taken and 60 percent of those polled favor candidate H, then these data cast some doubt on the theory that T is the voter's choice. The degree of doubt depends, of course, on the size of the sample. If 5 voters are surveyed and 3 favor H, this is very flimsy evidence. If 1000 voters are polled and 600 favor H, this evidence strongly discredits the theory that T will win the election.

In this course, you will learn to use probabilities to make this sort of statistical inference. You will be able to use data to test such theories as: smoking is dangerous to your health; vitamin C fights colds; Volvos last longer than Fords; and the unemployment rate influences presidential elections.

Statistical inference is very interesting and useful. It is used in election polls and unemployment surveys; in marketing tests and tests of product safety; in constructing macroeconometric forecasting models and interpreting psychological test scores; and in testing and refining scientific theories about the human body and the nature of the universe. But, as explained earlier, the foundation of statistical inference is probability—deducing the likelihood of observing various data from an assumed population. And so, starting in the next chapter, you will learn about probabilities before you learn about the details of statistical inference. But, before we begin, I want to show you a little bit of descriptive statistics and some of the tools that are repeatedly used in both probability analysis and statistical inference. **Descriptive statistics** are simple techniques for briefly describing a population or sample. For this purpose, statisticians use graphs and numerical measures of the center and spread of the data. We'll quickly run through some of these methods in the next section.

Exercises

1.1   A poll conducted shortly before the 1984 Democratic presidential primary in California found that 29 percent of those considered likely voters favored Gary Hart, 28 percent favored Walter Mondale, 11 percent favored Jesse Jackson, and 32 percent expressed no preference. From what population is the poll intended to be a sample? Why, by chance alone, might the poll results differ from the actual election results?

1.2   (*continuation*) Can you think of any other reasons why the election and poll results might differ?

1.3   (*continuation*) In the primary election itself, 38 percent voted for Hart, 35 percent for Mondale, 21 percent for Jackson, and 6 percent for others. Would the errors be more surprising if the poll had involved 50 voters or 5000 voters? Explain your reasoning.

1.4   (*continuation*) In fact, this poll surveyed 445 likely voters. If you were a pollster, why might you survey more than 50 voters? Why might you decide to survey fewer than 5000 voters?

1.2   DIAGRAMS OF FREQUENCY DISTRIBUTIONS

Statisticians use graphs to portray characteristics of a population or sample. Suppose we are on the eve of a gubernatorial election between two candidates, Mary Jones and John Martin. The population consists of all people who will vote in this election. Perhaps there are, conveniently enough, exactly 1,000,000 voters, of whom 550,000 favor Mary and 450,000 favor John. Figure 1.1 illustrates this voter distribution. On the horizontal axis is a characteristic of interest, which here is just the names of the two candidates. On the vertical axis is a measure of the distribution of voter preferences. As shown in Figure 1.1, there are two equivalent alternatives for the vertical scale. One possibility is the number of voters who prefer each candidate, the **absolute frequency**. Another possibility is the **relative frequency**, which is the fraction of all voters who prefer each candidate. Either way, the graph looks exactly the same; it is just a matter of choosing to use either the absolute number or the relative frequency. In practice, the relative frequency is used more often because it is somewhat easier to digest and interpret, the fraction being easily converted into a percentage. When we say that a candidate receives 55 percent of the vote, we can easily compare that 55 percent figure to predictions and other elections:

> The incumbent, Mary Jones, scored a decisive victory today over her challenger, John Martin. In receiving 55 percent of the votes, she improved on the 52 percent of the vote received when elected four years ago. In the big cities, especially, she ran well ahead of her earlier pace. Jones also did better than her party yesterday, which received only 48 percent of the statewide presidential vote. With her stunning victory, Jones is now being mentioned as a future vice-presidential candidate.

The data in Figure 1.1 describe the entire population of 1,000,000 voters. Were we to ask 100 of these voters who they favored, this would be a sample. The results of this particular poll might be as shown in Figure 1.2; 54 favor Mary and 46 favor John. The vertical axis shows the relative frequencies: 54/100 = .54 and 46/100 = .46. Figures 1.1 and 1.2 have a similar appearance, but it is very important that you understand the conceptual distinction between a population and a sample. The population relative frequencies in Figure 1.1 give the fractions of all voters who favor each candidate. Before the actual election, these population frequencies are unknown and are an interesting subject of speculation. When we

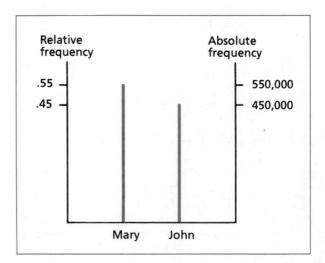

Figure 1.1   *A voter population*

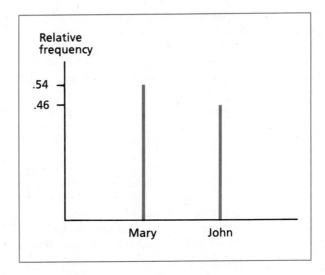

Figure 1.2   *A voter sample*

take a sample, we reach into this population and query only some of the voters. The sample relative frequencies in Figure 1.2 are the actual result of one particular poll. Another poll will query a different sample of voters and, most likely, give somewhat different results. The sample frequencies will vary from poll to poll.

> Probability theory can tell us, for an assumed population, the likely magnitudes of these sampling variations from poll to poll. Statistical inference can help us make informed judgments about the population from which the sample was drawn.

Figures 1.1 and 1.2 are examples of what statisticians call a frequency distribution or relative frequency distribution.

> A **frequency distribution** shows the fraction of a population or sample having certain characteristics.

This first example involved political preferences. Often, there are numerical units on the horizontal axis, instead of qualitative distinctions like "John" and "Mary." For instance, here are some data on household incomes in the United States in 1979:

income category	income in 1979	number of households	relative frequency
low	$0–$9,999	23,416,000	.296
middle	$10,000–$19,999	23,653,000	.299
upper	$20,000–$49,999	28,716,000	.363
high	$50,000 and over	3,243,000	.041
total		79,108,000	1.000

It is plainly impractical to list all 79,108,000 incomes. Instead, the incomes have been grouped into four categories: low ($0–$9,999), middle ($10,000–$19,999), upper ($20,000–$49,999), and high ($50,000 and up). By dividing the number of households in each category into the total number of households, we obtain the relative frequencies. For instance, the 23,416,000 households in the low-income group represent a fraction

$$\frac{23{,}416{,}000}{79{,}108{,}000} = .296$$

of the total population. If our arithmetic is correct, then the four relative frequencies should add up to 1, as they do here.

Figure 1.3 shows the relative frequency distribution of the income data. The heights of the three lines show the relative frequencies, with each relative frequency line placed in the middle of the appropriate interval. For instance, the .296 relative frequency of $0–$9,999 in household income is placed at the $5,000 point on the horizontal axis. The category "$50,000 and over" presents a special problem in that the lack of an upper limit precludes the specification of a midpoint. One possible approach, which I've taken in Figure 1.3, is just to ignore these people by omitting them from the graph. An alternative would be to use an estimate of the average income of this upper 4 percent of the households.

Bar Graphs and Histograms

Sometimes more descriptive graphics are used to display data. The lines of a simple graph may be replaced by bars; Figure 1.4 is a simple *bar chart* representation of Figure 1.3. A bar chart has the advantage of showing the width of the interval represented by a frequency. In Figure 1.3, it is not at all easy to tell which incomes

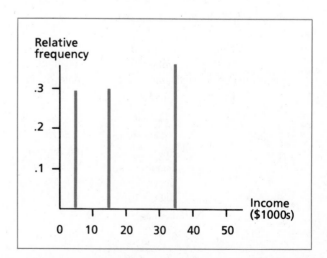

Figure 1.3 *A relative frequency diagram of U.S. income distribution, 1979*

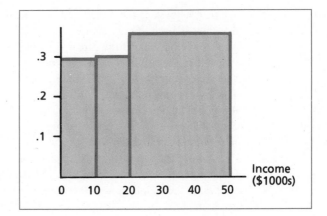

Figure 1.4   *A bar chart of U.S. income distribution, 1979*

correspond to which relative frequencies. The bars in Figure 1.4, in contrast, show very clearly that the first frequency refers to $0 to $10,000 income; the second is for $10,000 to $20,000; and the third is for $20,000 to $50,000.

Statisticians use a superficially similar, but actually quite different, graphical device, called a **histogram**. Figure 1.5 is a histogram representation of the household income data. A histogram has bars, like a bar chart, which show the width of each interval. The heights are determined differently, however, and so the bar chart in Figure 1.4 and the histogram in Figure 1.5 look quite different. As two statisticians, W. Allen Wallis and Harry Roberts, put it, "though bar charts and histograms are often confused, they have no relation except the fortuitous one that both involve bars—as do musical scores and saloons."[3]

In a simple *bar chart,* relative frequencies are shown by the *heights* of the bars. In a *histogram,* relative frequencies are shown by the *areas* inside the bars. Because the human eye gauges size by area, the bar chart in Figure 1.4 seems to

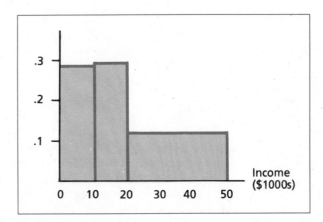

Figure 1.5   *A histogram of U.S. income distribution, 1979*

say that the bulk of the population is in the upper-income group. Yet the data show that most households are actually in the low-income and middle-income categories. The simple bar chart in Figure 1.4 is misleading because it is the area inside a bar rather than its height that catches our attention. This discrepancy between height and area occurs because the three income intervals do not have the same width. The low-income and middle-income categories each span a $10,000 interval, while the upper-income interval spans $30,000. The wider interval gives the upper-income bar a fatter base and a larger area, making it appear to hold more of the population than it really does.

A histogram corrects this optical illusion by using areas to represent relative frequencies. Let's measure income in $10,000 units. The width of the low-income interval is then 1 of these $10,000 units. A height of .296 for the low-income bar gives an area of (base)(height) = (1)(.296) = .296, as intended. What about the middle-income category? Its base is also 1 unit, because it spans the $10,000 interval from $10,000 to $20,000. A bar height of .299 gives the correct area of (base)(height) = (1)(.299) = .299. So far, the heights have just been the relative frequencies, because the first two intervals have the same 1-unit width. But matters change when we get to the upper-income category. Its base is 3 units because it spans a $30,000 interval. To make the area equal to the relative frequency, we need to set the height equal to the relative frequency divided by 3:

$$\text{area} = (\text{base})(\text{height})$$

$$.363 = (3)(\text{height})$$

implies

$$\text{height} = .363/3$$

$$= .121$$

Figure 1.5 shows the resulting histogram, which does indeed give a very different image than the bar diagram in Figure 1.4.

> If the intervals are of equal width, then a histogram is constructed in the same way as a bar chart. But, if the interval widths are unequal, then the height of a histogram block is calculated by dividing the relative frequency by the width of the interval.

Pluses and Minuses

One of the primary disadvantages of a bar chart is that its appearance is very sensitive to the largely arbitrary choice of intervals. How, exactly, did I decide where to draw the dividing lines between low, middle, and upper incomes? My particular choice was arbitrary in that there are other divisions that I could have used and there are no compelling criteria for my choice. Table 1.1 shows more detailed data on the income distribution. What if, for instance, I had put the dividing

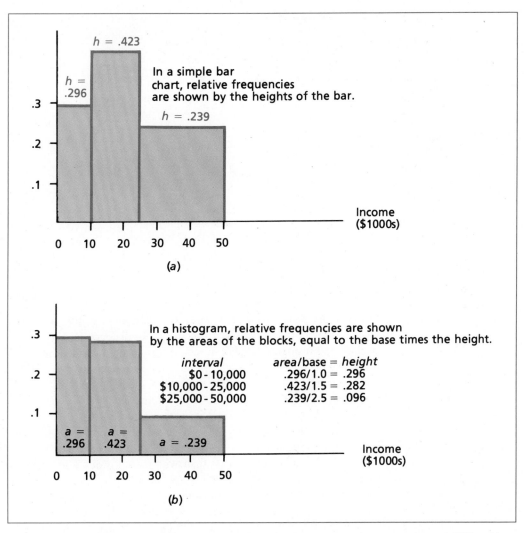

In a simple bar chart, relative frequencies are shown by the heights of the bar.

In a histogram, relative frequencies are shown by the areas of the blocks, equal to the base times the height.

interval	area/base = height
$0-10,000	.296/1.0 = .296
$10,000-25,000	.423/1.5 = .282
$25,000-50,000	.239/2.5 = .096

Figure 1.6 (a) *A bar chart and* (b) *histogram of U.S. income distribution, 1979, with revised intervals*

line between middle-income and upper-income households at $25,000 instead of $20,000? Figure 1.6 shows the consequent bar chart and histogram, along with the appropriate arithmetic. First compare Figures 1.4 and 1.6(*a*). The appearance of the bar chart is drastically altered by this innocent redefinition of the intervals. Now compare Figures 1.5 and 1.6(*b*). The histograms look pretty much the same.

Bar charts are also greatly affected by changes in the number of intervals. Why did I use three income categories? Why not four, five, or some other number? There is no compelling reason here, so I would hope that my graphs are not very

Table 1.1 *Household income, 1979*

Income in 1979	*Number of households*	*Relative frequency*
$0–$4,999	10,411,000	.132
$5,000–$9,999	13,006,000	.164
$10,000–$14,999	12,574,000	.159
$15,000–$19,999	11,099,000	.140
$20,000–$24,999	9,783,000	.124
$25,000–$34,999	12,380,000	.156
$35,000–$49,999	6,577,000	.083
$50,000 and over	3,276,000	.041
Total	79,108,000	1.000

Note: If income groups are combined, the relative frequencies are added. For instance, the income range $0–$9,999 has a relative frequency .132 + .164 = .296.

Source: U.S. Bureau of the Census, Current Population Survey, in *Statistical Abstract of the United States*. (Washington, D.C.: U.S. Government Printing Office, 1981.)

sensitive to this arbitrary choice. Bar charts are, in fact, more sensitive than histograms, and this is another reason why statisticians prefer histograms. Figure 1.7 shows the bar chart and histogram when household incomes are divided into five categories. Again, the bar chart is strikingly transformed and seems to give a brand new picture of the income distribution. The appearance of the histogram, in contrast, is little changed and the changes that do occur just convey the additional information that is provided by five intervals instead of three.

Look at the incomes from $0 to $10,000. When this income range is divided into two intervals, as in Figure 1.7(*b*), the histogram shows that there are more people with incomes of $5,000 to $10,000 than with incomes of $0 to $5,000. When these two intervals are combined, as in Figures 1.5 and 1.6(*b*), the histogram gives us an average of the two separate intervals. The same thing occurs in the $20,000 to $50,000 range, but the results are more dramatic. The two intervals in Figure 1.7(*b*) show the preponderance of people in the $20,000 to $35,000 range, while the single interval in Figure 1.5 gives an average. If there are marked variations in the number of households in adjacent income levels, then it is usually a good idea to show that variation by using more intervals.

Bar charts can be useful, especially when the intervals are of equal width. But if the interval widths vary, bar charts can paint very misleading pictures, and which misleading picture is painted depends on the essentially arbitrary selection of the intervals. Histograms, on the other hand, give reasonably accurate pictures, which are not overly sensitive to the intervals picked. The histograms in Figures 1.5, 1.6(*b*) and 1.7(*b*) all show the distribution of households across income levels reasonably well. The only real difference is that five intervals provide a little more detail than three intervals.

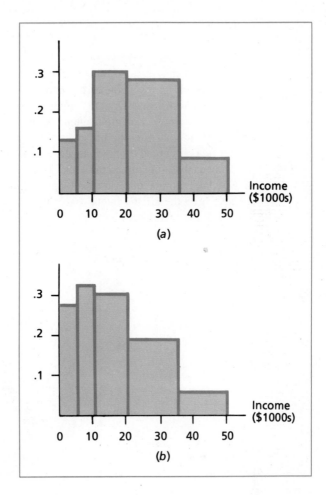

Figure 1.7   (a) *A bar chart and* (b) *histogram of U.S. income distribution, 1979, with five intervals*

Choosing Intervals

In general, histograms with only two or three intervals don't convey enough information to be worth the effort. If there are only two relative frequencies, these can be told in words as easily as pictures. A histogram is useful when there are several relative frequencies, because a picture is easier to absorb than a mass of numbers. At the other extreme, if the number of intervals gets too large, a histogram can turn into a jumble of jagged spikes, with each representing only a few observations. A rough rule of thumb is to divide the data into from five to fifteen intervals, using more intervals when you have more data. With 50 observations, five intervals is about as fine a gradation as you can have without spreading your data too thinly. With 50,000 observations, fifteen intervals could be supported. The exact number of intervals chosen is a matter of taste.

Misleading Picture Graphs

Graphic artists often use pictures instead of plain bars to enliven the bar graphs printed in newspapers and popular magazines. For example, Figure 1 shows a hypothetical comparison of the number of oranges that are produced, using two different fertilizers. Orange output is doubled using Harvey's Special Formula. This impressive accomplishment is made even more impressive by the use of oranges to construct the bar chart. Most people looking at such a chart will notice the areas occupied by the oranges, and not their heights. An orange with twice the diameter has four times the area. The visual impact of Figure 1 is that Harvey's Special Formula quadruples orange output. This dramatic impression may well have been the artist's intent, but it is still misleading.

These picturesque but exaggerated bar charts are quite common. I have seen

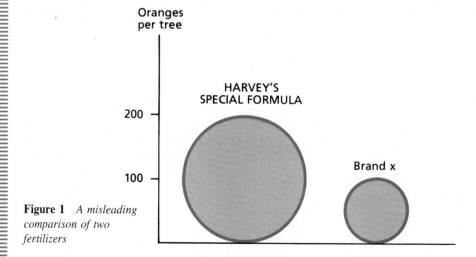

Figure 1   *A misleading comparison of two fertilizers*

The width and location of the intervals must also be chosen. The simplest decision is equally wide intervals covering all of the data. If the incomes range from $0 to $100,000 and five intervals are desired, then five $20,000 intervals are one possibility:*

$0–$20,000
$20,000–$40,000
$40,000–$60,000
$60,000–$80,000
$80,000–$100,000

*There is also a question of what to do with data right on an interval dividing line, such as a $20,000 income. Three alternatives are: (1) put them in the first interval (start the second interval at $20,000.01); (2) put them in the second interval (end the first interval at $19,999.99); and (3) alternate, putting half of the borderline data in the lower of the two intervals and half in the upper intervals.

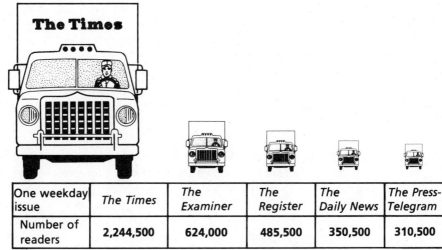

One weekday issue	*The Times*	*The Examiner*	*The Register*	*The Daily News*	*The Press-Telegram*
Number of readers	**2,244,500**	**624,000**	**485,500**	**350,500**	**310,500**

Source: Harold R. Jacobs, Mathematics: A Human Endeavor (San Francisco: W.H. Freeman, 1982), p. 562.

Figure 2   *An artist's bar chart*

charts using people, oil wells, dollar signs, and all sorts of things. Figure 2 shows one example from a newspaper advertisement boasting that "*The Times* has 2,244,500 readers every weekday—more than the next four area newspapers *combined*."[4] The height of *The Times* truck is about 3.6 times that of the nearest competitor, reflecting the fact that their circulation is 3.6 times that of *The Examiner*. But the width of *The Times* truck is also 3.6 times bigger, making the area of the truck $(3.6)^2 = 13$ times that of the nearest competitor. The circulation numbers say that *The Times* has somewhat more readers than the other four papers combined. The picture says that *The Times* dwarfs the competition. This visual image is very effective, but inaccurate.

Other choices are made for a variety of reasons. Often, the data are not evenly distributed over the entire range. There are many more people with incomes of $20,000 to $40,000 than with incomes of $60,000 to $80,000 or of $80,000 to $100,000. We may want to spend one of our five intervals distinguishing those with $20,000 and $30,000 incomes rather than separating people with $60,000 and $80,000:

$0–$20,000
$20,000–$30,000
$30,000–$40,000
$40,000–$60,000
$60,000–$100,000

Similarly, we may be more interested in seeing how many of those in the $0 to $20,000 range earn less than $10,000 than in seeing how many of those earning more than $40,000 are in the $40,000 to $60,000 range. If so, then we might choose these five intervals:

$0–$10,000
$10,000–$20,000
$20,000–$30,000
$30,000–$40,000
$40,000–$100,000

A rough rule of thumb is to choose the interval widths so that approximately equal amounts of data fall into each interval. The income intervals in Table 1.1 have this characteristic, except for the two upper-income categories, which could have been merged.

Another consideration is that some intervals may have intrinsic interest. With income data, tax brackets or the official definition of the poverty level may dictate where an interesting interval begins or ends. The next example gives another illustration of how naturally interesting boundaries may influence the choice of intervals.

Years of Schooling

Table 1.2 shows the years of schooling received by 127,882,000 U.S. citizens, who are age 25 and older. The Census Bureau has grouped these data into seven intervals to allow for natural breaks at the completion of elementary school (8 years), high school (12 years), and college (16 years). Figure 1.8 shows the relative frequency distribution.

Table 1.2   *Years of schooling for persons 25-years-old and over, 1980*

Years of schooling	*Number of persons*	*Relative frequency*
0–4	4,348,000	.034
5–7	7,545,000	.059
8	10,486,000	.082
9–11	17,776,000	.139
12	47,060,000	.368
13–15	18,927,000	.148
16 or more	21,740,000	.170
Total	127,882,000	1.000

Source: U.S. Bureau of the Census, Current Population Survey, in *Statistical Abstract of the United States*. (Washington, D.C.: U.S. Government Printing Office, 1981.)

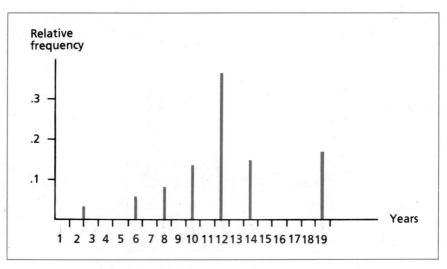

Figure 1.8 *A frequency diagram for years of schooling, 1980*

Again, we have an endpoint problem with the unbounded category "16 years or more." We could omit these people or we could put their relative frequency at a point representing the average years of schooling for people in this category. I don't know this average value, but it's difficult to ignore 17 percent of the population. So, I've just used 19 years as a "guesstimate" in Figure 1.8.

Figure 1.9 shows the corresponding bar chart and histogram. The bar chart

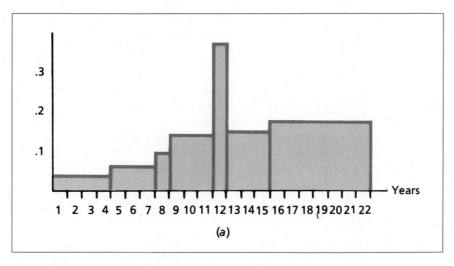

Figure 1.9a *A bar chart for years of schooling, 1980*

Figure 1.9b   *A histogram for years of schooling, 1980*

gives too much visual weight to college graduates and makes it appear that far more than a sixth of the population is in this category. The histogram puts things back into perspective. Figure 1.9(*b*) also shows the importance of the natural stopping points after 8 and 12 years of schooling. If we had more detailed data on college graduates, there would undoubtedly be another large spike at 16 years.

Exercises

1.5   The U.S. Census Bureau reported that there were 110,032,000 males and 116,473,000 females living in the United States on April 1, 1980. Calculate the relative frequencies of male and female U.S. residents and draw a relative frequency diagram.

1.6   The 1980 census found that more than half of the people in Massachusetts identified with a single ancestry group. These single-ancestry people were divided as follows:

Irish	665,119
English	459,249
Italian	430,744
French	313,557
Portuguese	190,034
Polish	161,529
other	947,003
total	3,167,235

Calculate the relative frequencies and draw a relative frequency diagram.

1.7   Construct a sample of dice rolls by rolling a standard six-sided die thirty times. Construct a table showing the absolute number and the relative frequency with which each of the six possible numbers appeared. Draw a relative frequency diagram for this sample.

1.8 The following data show the age-distribution of deaths from scarlet fever in England and Wales in 1933:[5]

age in years	number of deaths
0–1	16
1–2	69
2–3	89
3–4	74
4–5	74
5–10	213
10–15	70
15–20	27
20–30	43
30–40	23
40–50	16
50–60	12
60–70	1
70–80	2

Construct a histogram for these data.

1.9 Regroup the household income data in Table 1.1 into the following three categories:

low income:	$0–$24,999
middle income:	$25,000–$34,999
upper income:	$35,000–$49,999

Draw a bar chart and histogram using these three intervals and compare your graphs to Figures 1.4 and 1.5. Show any calculations that you find necessary in constructing these graphs. What specific differences do you notice in the appearance of this new bar chart? What specific differences do you notice in the new histogram?

1.10 Draw a bar chart and histogram for the seven income categories given in Table 1.1, omitting those earning $50,000 and over. Show any necessary calculations. Are these two graphs significantly different from Figures 1.4 and 1.5? What differences immediately catch your eye?

1.3 THE CENTER OF A DISTRIBUTION

Statisticians often use one or two summary statistics other than graphs to characterize a frequency distribution. The most common of these summary statistics are the *mode, median,* and *mean* to identify the center of a distribution. The objective is usually to describe the "average" or "typical" value of the variable in question.

The **mode** identifies the most commonplace value of the variable being analyzed. In Table 1.1, we can see that modal household income in 1979 is the $5,000–$9,999 interval. This is the "typical" household income in the sense that there are more people in this income range than in any other. However, the mode is often arbitrary in that it can be significantly altered by a simple reclassification of the intervals. If, for example, we put the $25,000–$34,999 and $35,000–$49,999

Table 1.3 *Income distribution in Smalland*

Income in 1980	Number of households	Relative frequency
$0–$500	1	.01
$500–$1000	1	.01
$1000–$1500	1	.01
.	.	.
.	.	.
.	.	.
$48,000–$48,500	1	.01
$48,500–$49,000	1	.01
$50,000,000	2	.02
Total	100	1.00

incomes into a single $25,000–$49,999 interval, then this would be the modal income interval.

In addition, the fact that some value is the mode is no guarantee that it is at all common. As an extreme example, consider the hypothetical country of Smalland. There are 100 people in Smalland, with the incomes shown in Table 1.3. The modal income is $50,000,000—yet 98 percent of the households earn less than $50,000! The mode is seldom used in practice, except to answer the very special questions that it is designed to answer: What is the most watched television show? What is the best-selling automobile? What is the most common cause of death?

The **median** is the middle value of the data. Imagine that we arrange the data from lowest value to highest value and then, starting at each end of the data, count inward. When our two counts meet in the middle, we have located the median. (If there are an even number of observations, then we split the difference between the middle two.) Half of the data are less than or equal to the median and half are greater than or equal to the median. The median household income in Smalland is $25,000. This is the center of the income distribution, in that half of the population earned more than this and half earned less.

The arithmetic **mean** is the simple average value of the data.* If there are n values

$$X_1, X_2, \cdots, X_n$$

then the mean is the sum of these values, divided by n:

$$\text{mean} = \frac{X_1 + X_2 + \cdots + X_n}{n}$$

---

*There is also a *geometric mean*, which is found by multiplying rather than adding the data. The geometric mean is used, for example, in financial calculations of compounded rates of return.

The conventional symbol for the mean is $\overline{X}$ (pronounced "X bar"). Statisticians also use a shorthand notation when several numbers are to be added up:

$$\overline{X} = \frac{\sum_{i=1}^{n} X_i}{n}$$

The Greek letter Σ (capital "sigma") signifies the summation of a set of values $X_1, X_2, \ldots, X_n$ written as X_i for i ranging from 1 to n. If the range is obvious, then the limits can be omitted:

$$\overline{X} = \frac{\sum X_i}{n}$$

or even

$$\overline{X} = \frac{\sum X}{n}$$

The average value of income in Smalland works out to be $1,024,010. The average Smallander is a millionaire! Actually, the typical Smallander is not only not a millionaire, but seldom even sees a millionaire. There are 2 multimillionaires in Smalland and 98 people earning between $0 and $50,000. This is a good example of why you should not be quick to interpret the statistical average as being "the typical value."

Another example was provided in 1984 by Lawrence Simpson, director of the University of Virginia's office of career planning. Reporting on the jobs taken by the school's 1983 graduates, he noted that

> Our highest salaries were for graduates of the Department of Rhetoric and Communications Studies, where the beginning average pay was $55,000 a year. Of course, the average height was 6'5".
>
> Thanks, Ralph.[6]

Ralph Sampson, the first player picked in that year's National Basketball Association draft, pulled up the average salary and the average height.

The mean, or average, income tells us how much each person would earn if the total income were unchanged and everyone had the same income. If people do not, in fact, earn the same income, then there may be few people or even no one earning the "average" income. It need not be the case that half of the people earn more than the average income and half earn less. As in Smalland and at the University of Virginia, the mean can be affected greatly by a few extreme observations. It is for this reason that the U.S. Census Bureau reports both the mean and median household income. In 1979, the mean household income in the United States was $19,620 while the median was $16,553. Apparently, the mean was pulled up above the median by a few people with very high incomes.

Grouped Data

If all we have are grouped data, then the mean and the median can only be approximated. Let's use the eight income intervals in Table 1.1 as an example. To calculate an average income, we need to estimate the incomes of the people within each interval. The simplest solution is to assume that everyone in an interval has an income equal to the midpoint of the interval.* Thus, the income for each group can be approximated as the product of the midpoint value and the number of households:

income interval	approximate midpoint	number of households	total income
$0– $4,999	$2,500	10,442,000	$26,105,000,000
$5,000– $9,999	$7,500	12,974,000	$97,305,000,000
$10,000–$14,999	$12,500	12,578,000	$157,225,000,000
$15,000–$19,999	$17,500	11,075,000	$193,812,500,000
$20,000–$24,999	$22,500	9,809,000	$220,702,500,000
$25,000–$34,999	$30,000	12,341,000	$370,230,000,000
$35,000–$49,999	$42,500	6,566,000	$279,055,000,000
$50,000 and over	$70,000(?)	3,243,000	$227,010,000,000
total		79,108,000	$1,571,445,000,000

For the open-ended category "$50,000 and over," we can do little more than pluck a number (such as $70,000) out of the air, one that doesn't seem especially outrageous. The estimated mean is then given by dividing total income by the number of households,

$$\overline{X} = \frac{\Sigma X}{n}$$

$$= \frac{\$1,571,445,000,000}{79,108,000}$$

$$= \$19,865$$

which is gratifyingly close to the actual mean $19,620 that the Census Bureau calculated using data for all 79 million households.

There is an equivalent way of calculating a mean with grouped data, using relative frequencies. Suppose that we were trying to find the mean income of 10 people, 7 who earn $20,000 and 3 who earn $30,000. One way is the method used previously: find the total income and then divide by the total number of people

$$\text{mean} = \frac{7(\$20,000) + 3(\$30,000)}{10} = \frac{\$230,000}{10} = \$23,000$$

Alternatively, this computation can be rearranged as

*We would get the same answer, with a little more work, if we assumed incomes were evenly distributed throughout each interval.

$$\text{mean} = \left(\frac{7}{10}\right) \$20{,}000 + \left(\frac{3}{10}\right) \$30{,}000$$

$$= \$14{,}000 + \$9{,}000 = \$23{,}000$$

That is, the mean is a *weighted average* of the incomes, with the weights being equal to the relative frequencies. To turn this rule into a mathematical formula, if there are n_i observations of income x_i, then the mean is

$$\overline{X} = \Sigma\, x_i \left(\frac{n_i}{n}\right)$$

Applying this method to the income data,

income interval	approximate midpoint x_i	relative frequency n_i/n	product $x_i(n_i/n)$
$0– $4,999	$2,500	.132	$330.00
$5,000– $9,999	$7,500	.164	$1230.00
$10,000–$14,999	$12,500	.159	$1987.50
$15,000–$19,999	$17,500	.140	$2450.00
$20,000–$24,999	$22,500	.124	$2790.00
$25,000–$34,999	$30,000	.156	$4680.00
$35,000–$49,999	$42,500	.083	$3527.50
$50,000 and over	$70,000(?)	.041	$2870.00
total			$19,865.00

we get the same $19,865 mean as before.

Now, let's estimate the median income using these grouped data. If we split 79,108,000 households down the middle, we have 39,554,000 in the lower half and 39,554,000 in the upper half. Counting in from either end of Table 1.1 puts us somewhere in the $15,000–$19,999 interval. For a more precise number, we can estimate where the median hides in this interval by assuming that incomes are evenly distributed throughout the interval. To start with, we know that the three lowest income intervals contain 35,994,000 households. To get the median 39,554,000th household, we need 3,560,000 more households out of the fourth interval, which contains 11,075,000 households. This represents about a third of the people in that interval

$$\frac{3{,}560{,}000}{11{,}075{,}000} = .321$$

If the incomes are evenly distributed, then the median income would be found about a third of the way into the interval:

$$\begin{aligned}
\text{median estimate} &= \$15{,}000 + .321(\$20{,}000 - \$15{,}000) \\
&= \$15{,}000 + \$1{,}607 \\
&= \$16{,}607
\end{aligned}$$

which is quite close to the actual median $16,553 that the Census Bureau found by having one of its giant computers count 39,554,000 households.

Midterm Scores

The nature of the mode, median, and mean, and a comparison among them can be brought out by an inspection of some relative frequency distributions. Here are some hypothetical data on midterm scores in a statistics class:

first test: 99 91 84 84 80 80 80 76 76 69 61

Figure 1.10 shows the relative frequency distribution. These scores were frankly rigged to be symmetrical with a single peak. Which score is the mode? The most common score is 80, which is the peak of the relative frequency distribution in Figure 1.10. What about the median? As there are 11 scores, we need to count in 5 from either end to locate the median. It, too, turns out to be 80. And the mean? If you add up these 11 scores and divide by 11, you will find that the data's symmetry implies that each score above 80 is balanced by a corresponding score below 80. Thus, the mean, too, is 80. These calculations are an illustration of this general principle.

If a relative frequency distribution is single peaked and perfectly symmetrical, then the mean, median, and mode coincide.

Conversely, if a relative frequency distribution has more than one peak or is asymmetrical, then the mean, median, and mode will not coincide.

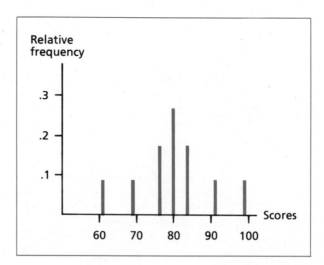

Figure 1.10 *Midterm scores*

If the mean, median, and mode do differ, then we need to bear in mind what each measures. The mean tells us the arithmetic average value; the median tells us the middle value; and the mode tells us the most common value.

Exercises

1.11   Here are some data on United Airlines' annual profit, as a percentage of its net worth:

year	profit
1972	3.1
1973	7.2
1974	12.7
1975	− 0.7
1976	2.4
1977	10.1
1978	25.6
1979	− 6.3
1980	1.8
1981	− 6.3
1982	1.0

Calculate the mean, median, and mode. Does each measure give a similar description of United Airlines' profits over this period? If they differ, which measures do you think are misleading?

1.12   Here are some midterm scores from a small honors statistics class:

$$17 \ 81 \ 82 \ 84 \ 87 \ 91 \ 93 \ 98 \ 98$$

Find the mean, median, and mode. Are their values similar or dissimilar? If they are dissimilar, which measure do you think gives a better description of how the class did on this test?

1.13   Estimate the mean and median for the scarlet-fever data in Exercise 1.8.

1.14   In estimating the average household income from Table 1.1, I assumed a $70,000 income for the households in the category "$50,000 and over." How much difference would it have made to my estimate of the mean if I had instead assumed an income of $60,000? Of $100,000?

1.15   I used a computer program to simulate 600 rolls of a single six-sided die. The results were 96 ones, 94 twos, 110 threes, 91 fours, 103 fives, and 106 sixes. Calculate the relative frequencies for this sample and draw a relative frequency diagram. What are the mean, median, and modal die numbers?

1.16   (*continuation*) I used this computer program again and, this time, obtained 111 ones, 100 twos, 93 threes, 103 fours, 90 fives, and 103 sixes. What are the mean, median, and mode for this second sample? Now combine these two 600-roll samples into one 1200-roll sample. What are the mean, median, and mode for this combined sample? Which of these three measures the center of a distribution is the least stable here? Is this a fluke, or do you think that this measure would probably be the least stable if we did experiment again?

1.4   THE SPREAD OF A DISTRIBUTION

The mean is, by far, the most commonly reported statistic. However, an average does not tell us the underlying variety that may, in fact, be of far greater interest. Sir Francis Galton once commented that

> It is difficult to understand why statisticians commonly limit their enquiries to Averages, and do not revel in more comprehensive views. Their souls seem as dull to the charm of variety as that of the native of one of our flat English counties, whose retrospect of Switzerland was that, if its mountains could be thrown into its lakes, two nuisances would be got rid of at once.[7]

For a more mundate example, imagine your state of mind a few weeks from now, when your statistics instructor hands back your midterms. You naturally will be interested in knowing how you did and, for comparison, how the class as a whole did. Perhaps, the average score turns out to be 80. That's an interesting figure to know. But you may well want to know a bit more about the scores. Did every student get 80? Or did half get 100 and half get 60? Or did most students get 100s and the rest get 0s?

The only way to know the complete distribution is to examine every single score. With a few tests, that's certainly feasible, but 300 tests would be trying. And no sane person wants to look at 79,108,000 household incomes. A starting place for organizing massive amounts of data is to sort the values into a small number of intervals. A relative frequency distribution or a histogram can then give a picture of the distribution of test scores, household incomes, or other data. However, pictures can also be difficult to digest and can, at times, be misleading. In addition, there are many occasions when pictures are just not sufficient or convenient, particularly when two sets of data, such as test scores for different classes or incomes in different years, are being compared. In these cases, statisticians use a few summary statistics to facilitate descriptions and comparisons.

While the mean, median, and mode describe the center of a distribution, other statistics gauge the spread of a distribution. One obvious choice is the **range**, which is simply the difference between the largest and the smallest values. In the 11 test scores discussed earlier,

first test: 99 91 84 84 80 80 80 76 76 69 61

the highest score is 99 and the lowest score is 61, giving a 38-point range. The professor might describe the test results by saying that, "The average score was 80, with a 38-point range from a high of 99 to a low of 61." The problem with the range is that it only looks at the extreme values, and the extremes are often atypical. In skating and diving contests, for example, the high and low scores of the judges are discarded to avoid their eccentricities.

Here is another set of 11 test scores that have a mean of 80 and a range of 38:

second test: 99 80 80 80 80 80 80 80 80 80 61

These scores are symmetrically centered at 80 with a 38-point range, from 99 to 61, the same as in the first set. But the range is now a very misleading indicator of the dispersion of the scores. Here, there are 9 students who did equally well and 2 outliers. Our common sense says that there is less dispersion in these scores than in the first test scores or in the following scores:

third test: 99 99 99 99 99 80 61 61 61 61 61

The problem with the range is that it only takes into account the spread between the two extreme values and ignores the dispersion among all the rest of the data. What we would really like is some measure of the overall or average spread of the data.

A natural attempt to measure the average spread in the data would be to compute the **deviation** of each data point from the mean and then calculate the average of these deviations. The deviation from the mean is simply each data point minus the mean. Those values greater than the mean give positive deviations; those values less than the mean give negative deviations. For the scores from the first test, as Table 1.4 shows, the average deviation about the mean turns out to be zero, which is hardly an informative statistic. In fact, the same result would have been obtained even if the data had not been symmetrical.

The average deviation from the mean is always zero.

The average deviation turns out to be zero because the positive and negative deviations from the mean offset each other. To eliminate this offsetting of positive and negative deviations, we could take the absolute value of each deviation and then calculate the *average absolute deviation,* which is the sum of the n absolute values of the deviations from the mean, divided by n. Table 1.4 shows that the average absolute deviation works out to be 6.9 for the first set of test scores. Do you think that the average absolute deviations for the second and third sets of test scores will be larger or smaller than 6.9? The actual calculations are left as Exercise 1.21, but I won't be giving anything away if I tell you that the average absolute deviation is less than 6.9 for the second test and greater than 6.9 for the third test. The average absolute deviation successfully gauges the dispersion in these data and it is easy to calculate and interpret. All in all, it is a very appealing measure of the spread of the data.

The only real problem with the average absolute deviation is that it presents formidable problems for mathematical analyses, and mathematicians love to analyze statistical measures—to see how they change as data are added, deleted, or combined. Mathematicians have developed differentiation, integration, and other powerful analytical tools, but these tools don't work very well with absolute values. It is largely for this reason that statisticians have developed another measure of the spread of the data.

Do you remember why we took absolute values in the first place? It was to keep the positive and negative deviations from offsetting each other. Another trick that accomplishes the same thing is to square each deviation from the mean. The squares of positive and negative deviations will both be positive. Then we can calculate the average squared deviation by adding up these n squared deviations and dividing by n.* The result is called the **variance**:

$$\text{variance} = \text{average squared deviation from the mean}$$

$$= \frac{\Sigma\,(X_i - \overline{X})^2}{n}$$

Table 1.4 shows the calculation of the variance for the first set of test scores. First, each deviation from the mean is calculated. Then these deviations are squared. Then the 11 squared deviations are added up and divided by 11. The result is a variance of 93.5.†

One problem with the variance is that the squaring of each deviation gives the variance a scale much larger than that of the original data. To offset this, statisticians also compute the **standard deviation**:

$$\text{standard deviation} = \text{square root of the variance}$$

Table 1.4   *Three measures of the spread of a distribution*

Test score	Deviation from mean	Absolute deviation	Squared deviation
99	19	19	361
91	11	11	121
84	4	4	16
84	4	4	16
80	0	0	0
80	0	0	0
80	0	0	0
76	−4	4	16
76	−4	4	16
69	−11	11	121
61	−19	19	361
Sum	0	76	1028
Average	0	6.9	93.5

*If the data are a small sample, statisticians generally divide by $n - 1$ rather than n. In later chapters, I will explain the reason for this curious practice.

†When, as shown here, the calculations are made step by step, there is a shortcut formula:

$$\text{variance} = \frac{\Sigma\,(X^2)}{n} - (\overline{X})^2$$

that is, the average value of X^2, minus the square of the average value of X. In practice, variances are usually calculated by a computer program or a calculator that has this formula built in.

With the exception of the scale difference, the variance and the standard deviation are interchangeable gauges of the spread of the data, in that a data set with a higher variance will also have a higher standard deviation. Although there are exceptions, it is also typically true that data with a large variance and standard deviation will also have a high average absolute deviation. The standard deviation of the first set of test scores, for instance, is $\sqrt{93.5} = 9.7$, while the average absolute deviation is 6.9. Computations of the average absolute deviation and the standard deviation both show that the second test scores are the least dispersed and that the third test scores are the most dispersed.

One final note is that these various statistical measures can be computed for either a population or a sample. Indeed, I haven't told you whether the test scores that we've been manipulating are the complete population that we are interested in or just a sample from a larger set of test scores. There is an important conceptual distinction between a population and a sample—a sample is only part (and, often, a very small part) of a population and is therefore subject to sampling error. This distinction is often reinforced by using different symbols for population statistics and sample statistics; for instance, Greek symbols are used for the former and English symbols are used for the latter:

$$\mu = \text{population mean}$$

$$\overline{X} = \text{sample mean}$$

$$\sigma = \text{population standard deviation}$$

$$s = \text{sample standard deviation}$$

But that's enough statistical formulas for now. Let's do a few more examples, and then I'll finish my explanation of what this course is all about and we can get on with the course itself.

The Profitability of Five Companies

Table 1.5 shows the annual profits (relative to net worth) for five very different companies over the ten-year period 1972–1981. These are a mass of data that is not easy to absorb. The mean and standard deviation can help summarize the data in a way that facilitates meaningful comparisons:

	annual profit, 1972–1981	
company	*mean*	*standard deviation*
American Water Works	7.61%	0.64%
Browne & Sharpe	7.62%	7.01%
Campbell Soup	13.56%	0.99%
McDonald's	20.04%	0.96%
Pan American	− 0.98%	13.46%

Table 1.5 *Five companies' profits, as a percentage of net worth*

Year	American Water Works	Brown & Sharpe	Campbell Soup	McDonald's	Pan American
1972	7.2	2.1	11.0	17.9	− 7.0
1973	6.6	5.8	13.6	19.9	− 4.7
1974	6.8	6.5	13.7	20.4	−26.7
1975	7.3	−5.4	13.1	21.0	−18.0
1976	7.8	2.3	14.3	21.0	− 2.3
1977	8.0	7.7	13.9	21.3	12.5
1978	7.7	15.2	14.2	20.4	18.3
1979	7.5	18.4	14.8	19.8	10.5
1980	8.7	16.8	14.0	19.4	10.0
1981	8.5	6.8	13.0	19.3	− 2.4

The SAT Scores of College Applicants

Table 1 shows the distribution of verbal Scholastic Aptitude Test (SAT) scores for male and female applicants for admission to Pomona College in 1982. A natural question is whether the distribution of scores is similar for males and females, and an answer is provided by a computation of the mean and standard deviation for each sex. Because these are grouped data, we will assume that everyone in each interval received the same score, equal to the interval midpoint. The details of the female computation are shown in Table 2. The means and standard deviations turn out to be

	female	male
mean	558	564
standard deviation	98	99

The average score of the male applicants is slightly higher than the average score of the female applicants. The standard deviations are virtually the same, indicating that there is the same spread in the female and male scores. Apparently, the distribution of verbal SAT scores is very similar for female and male applicants to this college.

Table 1   *Verbal SAT scores of female and male applicants for admission to Pomona College in 1982*

Verbal SAT score	Female applicants		Male applicants	
	Number	*Frequency*	*Number*	*Frequency*
750–800	9	.0096	10	.0125
700–750	48	.0511	48	.0600
650–700	114	.1213	98	.1225
600–650	157	.1670	152	.1900
550–600	186	.1979	159	.1988
500–550	187	.1989	143	.1788
450–500	105	.1117	98	.1225
400–450	87	.0926	40	.0500
350–400	20	.0213	23	.0288
300–350	17	.0181	15	.0188
250–300	5	.0053	9	.0113
200–250	5	.0053	5	.0063
Total	940	1.0	800	1.0

Table 2   *Computation of the mean and standard deviation for female applicants in Table 1*

Interval midpoint x_i	x_i^2	Frequency n_i/n	$x_i(n_i/n)$	$x_i^2(n_i/n)$
775	600,625	.0096	7.4	5750.7
725	525,625	.0511	37.0	26,840.4
675	455,625	.1213	81.9	55,256.6
625	390,625	.1670	104.4	65,242.6
575	330,625	.1979	113.8	65,421.5
525	275,625	.1989	104.4	54,831.8
475	225,625	.1117	53.1	25,202.8
425	180,625	.0926	39.3	16,717.4
375	140,625	.0213	8.0	2,992.0
325	105,625	.0181	5.9	1,910.2
275	75,625	.0053	1.5	402.3
225	50,625	.0053	1.2	269.3
Total		1.0	557.9	320,837.6
			the average value of X	average value of X^2

variance of X = (average value of X^2)   minus   (average value of X)^2

$$= 320{,}837.6 - (557.9)^2$$

$$= 9585.2$$

standard deviation of X = square root of variance = 98

American Water Works, which is the largest private water company in the United States, sells water in twenty states at prices set by regulatory commissions to give the company a "fair" rate of return. Over this ten-year period, the average annual profit rate was 7.61 percent. The small standard deviation accurately reflects the fact the company's profit rate varied little from year to year.

Brown & Sharpe earned almost exactly the same average return as American Water Works, but with a much higher standard deviation. As a manufacturer of tools and equipment, their sales and profits are sensitive to the nation's economy. For instance, they lost money during the 1975 recession, but they made a lot of money in 1979, when the economy was relatively strong. Over this ten-year period, American Water Works and Brown & Sharpe were, on the average, equally profitable, but American Water Works's profits were much more stable.

Campbell Soup is an interesting contrast; their standard deviation is almost as low as that of American Water Works, but their average profit rate is nearly double that of the first two companies. Year in and year out, they made about the same 13 percent to 14 percent profit. McDonald's (the hamburger place) has done even better, earning an average profit of 20 percent, with the same low standard deviation as Campbell Soup. This is why so many investors like McDonald's stock, and why its price per share doubled over this ten-year period (from $24 a share at the beginning of 1972 to $48 a share at the end of 1981). At the other extreme is Pan American, the second largest U.S. airline, which lost money in six of these ten years. Their profits ranged from a high of 18.3 percent to a low of -26.7 percent. The average was -0.98 percent with a whopping standard deviation of 13.46 percent. No wonder the price of its stock fell from a high of $17.80 a share in 1972 to a low of $2.40 per share in 1981.

Exercises

1.17   Here are some annual data on profits (as a percentage of net worth) for Ford, General Motors, and Winnebago (a manufacturer of motor homes):

year	Ford	General Motors	Winnebago
1972	14.7	18.7	25.0
1973	14.2	19.3	-8.9
1974	5.8	7.6	-10.3
1975	3.7	9.6	-3.7
1976	13.9	20.3	10.0
1977	19.8	21.4	4.1
1978	16.4	20.2	1.4
1979	11.2	15.2	-5.5
1980	-18.1	-4.3	-21.7
1981	-14.4	1.9	6.5

Calculate the mean and standard deviation of each of these companies' profits.

1.18   (*continuation*) Which of these three companies' stocks would you guess performed the best and the worst over this ten-year period?

1.19 Languages vary in the number of syllables in their words. Here are some relative frequencies for four different languages:[8]

number of syllables	relative frequencies			
	Arabic	English	German	Japanese
1	.23	.71	.56	.36
2	.50	.19	.31	.34
3	.22	.07	.09	.18
4	.05	.02	.03	.09
5	.00	.01	.01	.02
6	.00	.00	.00	.01
total	1.00	1.00	1.00	1.00

a. Sketch a relative frequency diagram for each of these four languages.
b. Calculate the mean, median, and mode for each of these four languages.
c. Calculate the average absolute deviation and standard deviation for each of these four languages.
d. Based on these descriptive statistics, describe (in words) the differences among these four languages.

● **1.20** Here are some U.S. household income data, for whites and blacks:

income in 1979	relative frequencies	
	white	black
$0– $4,999	.116	.257
$5,000– $9,999	.157	.234
$10,000–$14,999	.158	.167
$15,000–$19,999	.143	.118
$20,000–$24,999	.128	.087
$25,000–$34,999	.164	.092
$35,000–$49,999	.089	.037
$50,000 and over	.045	.007
total	1.000	1.000

Assume that the average income for those in the category "$50,000 and over" is $65,000 for white households and $60,000 for black households. Calculate the mean, median, and modal income for white and black households. Calculate the average absolute deviation, the variance, and the standard deviation of incomes for blacks and whites. What are the two pictures drawn by these various statistics?

● **1.21** Table 1.4 shows that the first set of test scores discussed in the text has an average absolute deviation of 6.9 and an average squared deviation (or variance) of 93.5. The standard deviation of these scores is the square root of the variance, $\sqrt{93.5} = 9.7$.

Calculate the average absolute deviation, the variance, and the standard deviation for both the second and third sets of test scores given in the text. Do these three measures agree in their assessment of which test scores have the most spread and which have the least spread?

● ● **1.22** Construct two sets of 11 test scores such that the average absolute deviation and the standard deviation disagree in their assessment of which data set has the greater spread.

1.5 THE USES AND MISUSES OF PROBABILITY AND STATISTICS

Over the years, the uses of probability and statistics have multiplied as people have recognized the prevalence of uncertainty and the power of this analysis. When Gregor Mendel first experimented with hybrid sweet peas, he used probabilities to explain his results. His experiments provided the basis for modern genetics, in which probabilities are still central. Scientists also use probability analysis to describe the movements of atoms, the decay of radioactive particles, and the life cycle of bacteria. Probabilities and statistics are used to evaluate medicines, judge the health effects of smoking, and explain longevity. One scientist has written that probability theory is now "a cornerstone of all of the sciences."[9]

Businesses use probability and statistics to gauge manufacturing precision, estimate demand, and design marketing strategies. Economists use probability and statistics to evaluate investments, describe financial markets, predict consumer spending, and formulate economic policies. Other social scientists use probability and statistics to conduct opinion polls, measure discrimination, and gauge the deterrence effects of capital punishment. Probability and statistics are used to decipher secret codes, and have even been applied to writing patterns to determine whether it was Alexander Hamilton or James Madison who authored twelve disputed Federalist Papers. (The statisticians concluded that the evidence is very strong that Madison authored at least eleven of these twelve papers.)

Probabilities and statistics abound in sports. Basketball players are told to take "high percentage shots," which are shots made from a distance and angle where a particular player has a high probability of making a basket. Football teams use detailed statistical models to evaluate prospective players. Football coaches ranging from Plano High to the Dallas Cowboys estimate their opponent's "tendencies," for instance, the plays a particular team is most likely to call when it has the ball inside its own 20-yard line on the third down with 3 yards to go for a first down. When a football coach must choose between punting, trying for a field goal, or trying for a first down, probabilities are racing through the coach's mind.

Baseball is probably the most statistical sport, starting with lifetime batting averages and running through a certain pitcher's record against Robin Yount during night games in August. Good baseball managers are continually "playing the percentages." They bring in a left-handed pitcher to face a left-handed batter. They instruct a .245 hitter to make a sacrifice bunt to advance a runner to second base. They put their good hitters at the start of the lineup and their weak hitters at the end. In the late innings, they take out a good-hitting, weak-fielding player who has just batted and bring in a weak-hitting, good-fielding player. In all of these cases and many more, the good manager is trying to use statistics to make victory more probable.

Fallible humans also misuse probabilities and statistics. We see skill where there is luck. We see psychic phenomena where there is chance. We confirm flimsy theories with coincidences. We distort and misreport data to prove our prejudices. We take foolish chances, counting on an erroneous "law of averages" to bail us out. We waste money on worthless gambling systems. We play inferior backgammon, bridge, and poker. We buy too much insurance and too many different stocks. And we neglect many important risks.

I wrote this textbook to introduce you to probability and statistics. It is not encyclopedic and it is not just a collection of arcane formulas and crunched numbers. Instead, I've tried to emphasize some important principles that you can use all your life. You don't need to memorize 250 formulas or add up 2500 six-digit numbers. You can always look up the formulas and have a computer do your arithmetic. What you really need is an understanding of what you are doing.

You will see that the world is filled with uncertainties. You will find out what probabilities are and what they can be used for. You will learn how to figure probabilities correctly and how to recognize the everyday errors in the calculations of others. You will see how data can be used and misused in estimating probabilities. You will learn why the unemployment rate is "±0.2 percent" and why an election prediction is "±3 percent." You will understand what it means to say that the evidence supports or rejects someone's theory. You will learn how to test theories yourself. You will find out what is meant by the commonplace report that researchers have found a *statistically significant relationship* between this and that. You will see why expert studies sometimes disagree and how statistical tests can be abused. By learning all of this, you will make this course one of the most interesting and useful courses that you will ever take.

Exercises

1.23 Only 10 percent of all divorces involve a woman with a college degree and only 5 percent involve a woman with eight or fewer years of education. Do these data show that a man should marry a woman who either has a lot of education or very little? What other data would you like to see before jumping to this conclusion?

1.24 Professor Robinson is contemplating job offers in San Francisco, California and Albuquerque, New Mexico. Temperature is very important to Ms. Robinson because she cannot jog or write scholarly papers when the weather is either very hot or very cold. A check of the *Statistical Abstract* reveals that, over the thirty-year period of 1941–1970, the average temperature was 56.9°F in San Francisco and 56.8°F in Albuquerque. Should Professor Robinson therefore conclude that the temperatures are quite similar in these two cities?

1.25 An old joke is that a certain economics professor left Yale to go to Harvard and thereby improved the average quality of both departments. Is this possible?

1.26 Ann Landers once wrote, "Nothing shocks me anymore, especially when I know that 50 percent of the doctors who practice medicine graduated in the bottom half of their class." (*Boston Globe,* August 14, 1976). Is Ann Landers using the mean, median, or mode to gauge doctor skills? Is there any relationship between the competency of the medical profession and the fact that 50 percent of all doctors are below average?

1.6   SUMMARY

Probabilities tell us how often we can anticipate observing certain outcomes, given certain assumptions about the underlying population. Statistical inference is the use of observed sample data to draw inferences about the characteristics of this population. For instance, probabilities tell us, if the voters are evenly divided, the chances that a poll of 400 voters will find 60 percent preferring one candidate. Statistical inference uses the observed 60 percent preference to estimate what fraction of the population prefer this candidate. Because a sample is only part of the population, this estimate must allow a margin for sampling error such as ± 5 percent.

Descriptive statistics are simple techniques for briefly describing a population or a sample. A frequency distribution shows the fraction of a population or sample that has certain characteristics. A histogram uses areas to show relative frequencies. The height of each block in a histogram is equal to the relative frequency divided by the width of the interval. In constructing histograms, the data are usually grouped so that there are between 5 and 15 intervals, with 15 intervals used only when there are thousands of observations and fewer intervals used when there are fewer data.

The mean, median, and mode are used to measure the center of a set of data. The mean is the average value of the data; the median is the middle value; and the mode is the most common value. The formula for the mean is

$$\overline{X} = \frac{\Sigma X}{n}$$

that is, the sum of the values of X, divided by the number of observations n. With grouped data, the mean can be estimated by adding up the centers of each interval, x_i, multiplied by the interval's relative frequency n_i/n,

$$\overline{X} = \Sigma \, x_i\left(\frac{n_i}{n}\right)$$

The variance and standard deviation gauge the spread of a distribution. The variance is calculated as the average squared deviation from the mean:

$$\text{variance} = \frac{\Sigma \, (X_i - \overline{X})^2}{n}$$

The standard deviation s is the square root of the variance.

REVIEW EXERCISES

1.27   A recording of the degree of cloudiness at Greenwich each day during July in the years 1890–1904 obtained the following results:[10]

degree of cloudiness	number of days
0	320
1	129
2	74
3	68
4	45
5	45
6	55
7	65
8	90
9	148
10	676

Calculate the ten relative frequencies and draw a relative frequency diagram.

1.28 Here are the distributions of math SAT scores for male and female applicants to Pomona College in 1982:

math SAT score	number of females	number of males
750–800	13	68
700–750	73	108
650–700	117	157
600–650	218	175
550–600	196	115
500–550	136	92
450–500	103	56
400–450	53	19
350–400	20	5
300–350	9	4
250–300	2	0
total	940	799

Calculate the relative frequencies and make two frequency diagrams, one for female applicants and one for males. Do you detect any differences between these two distributions?

1.29 A study of the ages at which Australian men married during the years 1907–1914 found:[11]

age	number of men	age	number of men
15–18	294	39–42	9,320
18–21	10,995	42–48	11,006
21–24	61,101	48–54	5,810
24–27	73,054	54–60	2,755
27–30	56,501	60–66	1,459
30–33	33,478	66–78	1,143
33–36	20,569	78–90	119
36–39	14,281		

Use a histogram to show the distribution of these marriage ages.

1.30   Here are some census data on the ages of the U.S. resident population in 1980:

age	number
0–4	16,344,000
5–9	16,697,000
10–14	18,241,000
15–19	21,162,000
20–24	21,313,000
25–29	19,518,000
30–34	17,558,000
35–39	13,963,000
40–44	11,668,000
45–49	11,088,000
50–54	11,709,000
55–59	11,614,000
60–64	10,086,000
65–99	25,544,000

Calculate the relative frequencies and make a frequency diagram.

1.31   (*continuation*) Now draw a bar chart and histogram for the U.S. age distribution. Show any calculations that you find necessary. In what ways, if any, does the bar chart appear to give a misleading picture of the age distribution?

1.32   (*continuation*) Now regroup the fourteen age intervals into seven intervals: 0–9, 10–19, . . . , 60–100. Draw a bar chart and histogram for these seven categories. Show any necessary calculations. Are there any striking differences between these graphs and the ones drawn in the preceding exercise?

1.33   Regroup the schooling data in Table 1.2 into the three categories: 0–11 years, 12 years, and 13–22 years. Draw a bar chart and histogram using these intervals. Show any necessary calculations. Compare your two graphs with those in Figure 1.9. Did this interval regrouping cause any major changes in the appearance of the bar chart and the histogram?

1.34   The Smalland income data in Table 1.3 consist of ninety-eight $500 intervals plus the two multimillionaires. For a bar chart, let's put the two rich households into the interval "$49,000–$100,000,000." Draw a rough sketch of the resulting bar chart and histogram. Show any necessary calculations. Which picture do you think conveys the more accurate image of Smalland's income distribution?

• **1.35**   At the end of each baseball season, newspapers publish the final batting averages for all players with at least 250 times at bat. Go to a library and find the 1984 National League batting averages. Group these averages into intervals .180–.199, .200–.219, and so on and then draw a histogram.

• **1.36**   When, if ever, will a bar chart and a histogram look the same?

• **1.37**   The U.S. household income data in Table 1.1 includes the open-ended category "$50,000 and over." Estimate the average income of this upper 4 percent of the households using the Census Bureau's calculation that the average income for all 79,108,000 households was $19,620.

• **1.38** It has been said that, "The average stockholder is a 53-year-old white woman." What does "average" mean here?

• **1.39** What is your mean speed if a. you drive 20 miles per hour for one hour and 40 miles per hour for one hour? b. you drive 20 miles per hour for twenty miles and 40 miles per hour for twenty miles?

1.40 During the week ending July 8, 1984, the most popular television show in America was ABC's 20/20. Does this mean that most people in the United States watched this show that week?

1.41 Roll a pair of standard dice twenty times, and each time record the sum of the two numbers rolled. Calculate the mean, median, and mode. Repeat this experiment five times. Which of these three measures seems to be the least stable?

• **1.42** Exercise 1.30 gives the age distribution of the U.S. population. Which age interval is the mode? Estimate the mean and the median. Now regroup these fourteen age intervals into seven intervals: 0–9, 10–19, . . . , 60–100. Show the relative frequencies for these seven age intervals. Find the modal age interval and estimate the mean and median. Did the regrouping of the data cause any substantial differences in the mean, median, or mode?

1.43 The alumni of Clareville's Class of 1919 seem to be getting younger every year. In 1984, their average age was 87; in 1985 it is 86. How can this be?

• **1.44** The U.S. Census Bureau reported that the household income data shown in Table 1.1 has a mean of $19,620 and a median of $16,553. Why do you think that the mean and the median are not the same? What, specifically, pulls the mean up above the median?

1.45 Exercise 1.29 shows the distribution of the ages of Australian men who married during the years 1907–1914. What is the modal age interval? Estimate the mean and median age at marriage.

1.46 You are going to roll a standard die twice and then calculate the mean and standard deviation for these rolls. What is

a. the largest possible mean?
b. the smallest possible mean?
c. the largest possible standard deviation?
d. the smallest possible standard deviation?

1.47 A researcher is studying data on the financial wealth of 100 professors at a small liberal arts college. Their wealths range from $200 to $200,000, with a mean of $20,004 and a median of $12,500. When putting these data into a statistical computer program, the researcher mistakenly enters $2,000,000 for the person with the $200,000 wealth. How greatly does this error affect the mean and the median?

• **1.48** Exercise 1.28 shows the math SAT scores of male and female applicants to Pomona College in 1982. Estimate the mean and standard deviation for both male applicants and female applicants. Does there seem to be any difference in the center or spread of the male and female scores?

•• **1.49** Table 1.4 shows that the average deviation from the mean of eleven symmetrical midterm scores works out to be zero. Show that the average deviation from a mean is always zero.

•• **1.50**   In our statistical calculations, we've generally assumed that the average value for an interval is at the midpoint of the interval; for example, that the average income of blacks in the $25,000–$34,999 interval is $30,000. Can you think of any statistical reason why this simple assumption may be systematically wrong? Can you think of any better way to estimate the average income of blacks in this income interval, using only the data given in Exercise 1.20? Use your new, improved procedure to estimate the average income of blacks in each of the seven closed-ended intervals given in Exercise 1.20. Now use these interval-average estimates to reestimate the average income of all black households. Is this reestimate very different from your original estimate made in Exercise 1.20?

PART **1**

Probability

Ribbon cable, computer circuit board.
© Mark Antman/The Image Works.

CHAPTER **2**

The Probability Idea

A reasonable probability is the only certainty.

E.W. Howe

TOPICS

2.1 INTRODUCTION

There are very few things in our lives that are absolutely certain. This uncertainty makes life challenging and very interesting. Think how boring it would be to know in advance everything that was going to happen to us. School, love, career, marriage, and family would all be so much less fun if the mystery were taken out. We wouldn't need elections because the winners and losers would be known beforehand. We wouldn't need much of a stock market because everyone would know what the stock prices would be tomorrow and every day after that. We wouldn't need sports events because we would already know the outcomes. How interesting do you find reruns of old football games? If the world were certain, life would be like a rerun of an old football game. We would be bored actors and actresses walking through a lifeless script.

Thankfully, life is full of uncertainties, with all of the attendant thrills and frustrations. The idea behind probabilities is to try to quantify these uncertainties. Uncertainty means that a variety of outcomes are possible. We can better understand this uncertainty and be more prepared for the possibilities if we use probabilities to describe which outcomes are likely and which are unlikely. In this chapter, you will begin to see where these probabilities come from and what they are used for. We will begin with games of chance because, when viewed from a financially safe distance, these are an ideal vehicle for introducing probability logic.

2.2 THE GAMBLING ROOTS

The first systematic analysis of probabilities seems to have been conducted by Gerolamo Cardano "Cardan" (1501–1576). In his *Liber de Ludo Aleac (Book of Games of Chance)*,[1] Cardan explained the rules of various games, philosophized on the morality of gambling, and provided tips for catching cheats.* He also set forth some carefully thought-out probability principles.

The Flip of a Coin

When a fair coin is flipped, Cardan reasoned that there are two "equally likely" outcomes: heads or tails. As these outcomes are equally likely, each has a probability of 1/2 of occurring. If we roll a fair six-sided die, there are six equally likely outcomes. Therefore, each outcome has a probability of 1/6 of occurring. What about the probability of obtaining an even number when rolling a single die? Cardan

---

*Cardan suggested that gambling was "invented" during the Trojan wars to entertain the soldiers during a ten-year siege of Palamedes.

reasoned that, as three of the six possible outcomes are even numbers, the probability must be 3/6, which reduces to 1/2. In general, if there are n equally likely outcomes and m of these outcomes are ''successes,'' then the probability of a successful outcome is m/n.

What is the probability of rolling a 5 or a 6? These are two of the six possibilities. So, the probability is 2/6, which reduces to 1/3. What is the probability of rolling a number greater than 1? Five of the six possible numbers are greater than 1, so the probability is 5/6. What is the probability of rolling a 1, 2, 3, 4, 5, or 6? These are six of the six possible outcomes, so the probability is 6/6, which reduces to 1.0. That answer, 1.0, is the largest a probability can ever be. If there are six possible outcomes, then the number of possible successes cannot be greater than six.

We can also use the idea of equally likely events to interpret probability statements. If I say that the probability of some event happening is 1/6, then we can interpret my assessment as meaning that it is as if this event were one of six equally likely possibilities. Or, even more concretely, we could say that this event is as likely to occur as is the number 3 when a fair die is rolled.

> The **classical interpretation of probabilities** is that the probability of any one of m events occurring, when there are n equally likely possible outcomes, is m/n.

The next milestone in probability theory was laid by the French mathematician Blaise Pascal in the 1600s. There is a (probably overdramatic) legend that the French nobleman Antoine Gombauld, the Chevalier de Mere, had won a considerable amount of money betting that he could roll at least one 6 in four throws of a single die. But he was losing money betting that he could roll at least one double-6 in twenty-four throws of a pair of dice. De Mere asked Pascal about this problem and, later, about other puzzling games of chance. De Mere's problem is tough and a little tricky, but you will soon be able to answer it with ease.

Pascal discussed these gambling puzzles with a number of European mathematicians, including Pierre de Fermet, and these discussions led to the first great books on the mathematical theory of probability: Christiaan Huygen's *De Ratiociniis in Ludo Aleae* (1657) and Pascal's *Treatise on Figurate Numbers* (1665). Huygens and Pascal, like Cardan before them, computed probabilities by counting the number of equally likely outcomes. However, Huygens and Pascal were much more systematic and rigorous than Cardan and were more successful in energizing other intellectuals into studying probabilities.

The underpinning of their work is the identification of equally likely outcomes. But, how do we know if two events are equally likely? Another seventeenth-century French mathematician, Pierre Laplace, argued that we should presume that two events are equally likely unless we have good reason to believe otherwise.

Laplace's Principle of Insufficient Reason states that, in the absence of compelling evidence to the contrary, we should assume that events are equally likely.

If the coin is unbent and the die is symmetrical, then we should assume each possible outcome to be equally likely. We refrain from this assumption if the coin is two-headed, the die seems unbalanced, or the thrower is disreputable.

Several Coin Flips

So far, we have only looked at easy problems such as the flip of a fair coin and the roll of a fair die. More complicated problems may involve a more careful and lengthy enumeration of the possible outcomes. Consider a coin flipped twice. The possibilities are:

> 2 heads
> 1 head and 1 tail
> 2 tails

It is tempting to apply Laplace's Principle of Insufficient Reason and assume that each of these three outcomes has a 1/3 probability of occurring. This was, in fact, the answer given by the prominent mathematician Jean d'Alembert. But that answer is wrong!

There is only one way to get two heads and only one way to obtain two tails, but there are two different ways of getting one head and one tail. We could get a head on the first flip and a tail on the second, or we could get a tail on the first flip and then a head on the second.

To enumerate the outcomes correctly, we can construct a **probability tree** to show the possibilities. On the first flip, there are two equally likely outcomes: a head or a tail. In either case, the second flip is also equally likely to be a head or a tail. If we use H for "heads" and T for "tails," then the possible outcomes are

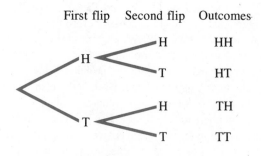

There are really four equally likely outcomes, with two involving one head and one tail. The probability of two heads is 1/4, the probability of two tails is 1/4, and the probability of one head and one tail is 2/4. The same logic would apply if we simultaneously flipped two coins, instead of flipping the same coin twice.

What about three flips? Now the probability tree looks like this:

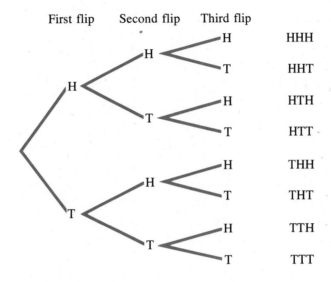

There are eight possible outcomes. By inspection, the probabilities are

event	number of successes	probability
three heads	1	1/8
two heads, one tail	3	3/8
one head, two tails	3	3/8
three tails	1	1/8
total	8	1

This logic can be extended to four flips, five flips, and more, ad nauseum.

Dice

Let's instead move on to some dice problems. If we roll two dice, what is the probability of getting double-6s? What is the probability of getting numbers that add up to 7? Which is more likely, numbers that add up to 7 or numbers that add up to 8? The classical, equally-likely procedure is to enumerate the possible outcomes shown in Table 2.1. Thus, the probabilities are as shown in Table 2.2. The probability of double-6s is 1/36. The probability of numbers that add up to 7 is 1/6, which is slightly more likely than numbers that add to 8.

Table 2.1   *Possible outcomes when two dice are rolled*

First die	Second die	Outcome	Sum of numbers
1	1	1–1	2
	2	1–2	3
	3	1–3	4
	4	1–4	5
	5	1–5	6
	6	1–6	7
2	1	2–1	3
	2	2–2	4
	3	2–3	5
	4	2–4	6
	5	2–5	7
	6	2–6	8
3	1	3–1	4
	2	3–2	5
	3	3–3	6
	4	3–4	7
	5	3–5	8
	6	3–6	9
4	1	4–1	5
	2	4–2	6
	3	4–3	7
	4	4–4	8
	5	4–5	9
	6	4–6	10
5	1	5–1	6
	2	5–2	7
	3	5–3	8
	4	5–4	9
	5	5–5	10
	6	5–6	11
6	1	6–1	7
	2	6–2	8
	3	6–3	9
	4	6–4	10
	5	6–5	11
	6	6–6	12

Table 2.2 *Probabilities when two dice are rolled*

Sum of dice	Number of successes	Probability
2	1	1/36
3	2	2/36
4	3	3/36
5	4	4/36
6	5	5/36
7	6	6/36
8	5	5/36
9	4	4/36
10	3	3/36
11	2	2/36
12	1	1/36

In some professions or pastimes, it is helpful to remember the structure of dice probabilities shown in Table 2.2. You can see that 7 has the largest probability. The probabilities then decline symmetrically as we move away from 7. A sum of 7 is more likely than a sum of 6 or 8, which are more likely than a sum of 5 or 9, and so on.

Often, we are interested in just a single probability, rather than the entire Table 2.2, and there is a shortcut logic. Suppose we want to know the probability of rolling numbers that sum to 4. First, figure out the total number of possible outcomes. The first die has six possible outcomes, and for each of these outcomes, the second die has six possible outcomes. So, there are 6(6) = 36 possibilities in all. Now, of these thirty-six possible outcomes, how many involve numbers that add up to 4? That is, how many different ways are there to roll numbers that sum to 4? Well, there's a 1 on the first die and a 3 on the second, 3 on the first and 1 on the second, or 2 on both dice. So, three possibilities out of thirty-six implies a probability 3/36, which reduces to 1/12. What about the probability of rolling numbers that add up to 5? There are four ways to roll a sum of 5: 1–4, 2–3, 3–2, and 4–1. So, the probability is 4/36, which reduces to 1/9.

Let's do one more. In many games, a special importance is attached to "doubles," with both dice showing the same number. Doubles can win a game, lose a game, give you extra moves, give you an extra roll, or get you out of jail. What is the probability of rolling doubles? By now, this should be easy for you. There are thirty-six possible outcomes and six ways to get doubles (1–1, 2–2, 3–3, 4–4, 5–5, and 6–6), so the probability of doubles is 6/36, which reduces to 1/6.

This framework is infinitely expandable. In any situation, just enumerate all the possible, equally likely outcomes and then count up the possible successes. This also grows infinitely complicated as the chain of outcomes grows longer. Remember de Mere's problem? He was interested in twenty-four throws of a pair of dice! Each pair has thirty-six possible outcomes, and each of these thirty-six possibilities has thirty-six different possibilities for the next pair. The total number of equally likely outcomes is $36^{24} = 2.25 \times 10^{37}$. It would be quite a chore to enumerate all of these possibilities. We might as well try counting the number of grains of sand on a beach. Fortunately, mathematicians have developed some probability rules that allow us to solve most problems, including de Mere's, very quickly. I'll show you a few counting tricks in the next section, but I want to save most of the rules for the next chapter.

The Dice Maker

Craps is a game of chance, and casino operators want to keep it that way. Their dice are custom-made to their specifications, milled to a ten-thousandth of an inch to form as nearly perfect a cube as possible. While cheap plastic dice are polished in a mechanical tumbler similar to those used by lapidarists, such mechanical polishing also gives them rounded edges, and casinos want their dice to have sharp, true edges on all sides.

Most casino dice are made of celluloid. The raw celluloic is "cured" over a period of time to dry it out and give it stability. Then it goes through a series of milling operations to form it into a perfect cube. Following that, shallow indentations to form the spots are made on all six sides. These indentations are filled with a white polyester resin, and the dice are then subjected to a final grinding which leaves them with smooth, even surfaces.

Some casinos order their dice made in "off" sizes, as a safeguard against "switching" by dishonest players.

Even the heat of a shooter's hands may slightly alter the size of a pair of dice. Bud Jones of Las Vegas, whose factory furnishes casinos with about 12,000 pairs of dice a month, says that dice should never be held for more than 30 days if precise sizing is desired.

Dice in most casinos are changed frequently, and many pairs of "used" dice are given to customers as souvenirs. The price of custom-made dice in quantity runs about $1.50 a pair.

Source: *Gambler's Digest,* Clement McQuaid, ed., Northfield, Illinois: Digest Books, 1971, p. 90.

Backgammon

An understanding of probabilities is one of the keys to mastering the game of backgammon. Many of the world's best players have mathematical backgrounds. The others have learned the game's probabilities through long experience.

In backgammon, you roll two dice and use each number separately to move your pieces. If you roll a 5–3, for example, you move one piece 5 spaces and one piece (possibly the same piece) 3 spaces. An added wrinkle is that doubles are moved twice. A double-6, for example, lets you move four pieces 6 spaces.

Now, consider the following commonplace problem. You want to know whether it is safer to leave a piece 1 or 2 spaces from your opponent. Is your opponent more likely to be able to hit you by moving 1 space or by moving 2 spaces?

To move 1 space, your opponent must roll a 1 on one of the dice. The possible ways are 1–1, 1–2, 1–3, 1–4, 1–5, 1–6, 2–1, 3–1, 4–1, 5–1, or 6–1. (Notice that I did not count 1–1 twice.) Altogether, there are eleven ways to roll a 1, and so the probability of being hit from 1 space away is 11/36. What about from 2 spaces away? Your opponent must roll a 2 on one die (eleven possible ways) or double-1s (one way). Altogether, there are twelve ways, making the probability 12/36. Thus it is safer to be 1 space away than 2 spaces away.

If the piece is 3 spaces away, your opponent must roll a 3 on one die (eleven ways), a 1 on one die and a 2 on the other (two ways), or double-1s (one way). The total probability is 14/36. By similar calculations, the probabilities from 4, 5, and 6 spaces away are 15/36, 15/36, and 17/36.

When the piece is more than 6 spaces away, the probabilities drop off because it takes both dice to roll a 7 or higher. As shown in Table 2.2, the probability of rolling a sum of 7 is only 6/36, or 1/6. If the piece is 8 spaces away, your opponent must roll an 8 (five ways, according to Table 2.2) or use double-2s, giving a total probability of 6/36. To hit a piece 9 spaces away, there are four ways to roll a 9, plus double-3s, for a total probability of 5/36. There are three ways to roll a 10 and two ways to roll an 11. Twelve spaces away can be hit by double-6s, double-4s, or even double-3s. The probabilities are shown in the following chart:

number of spaces away	1	2	3	4	5	6	7	8	9	10	11	12
probability of being hit	$\frac{11}{36}$	$\frac{12}{36}$	$\frac{14}{36}$	$\frac{15}{36}$	$\frac{15}{36}$	$\frac{17}{36}$	$\frac{6}{36}$	$\frac{6}{36}$	$\frac{5}{36}$	$\frac{3}{36}$	$\frac{2}{36}$	$\frac{3}{36}$

We have derived one important backgammon rule of thumb. For 6 spaces or less, the closer you are to your opponent, the less likely you are to be hit. You are much safer if you are more than 6 spaces away and, after 6 spaces, the farther away you are, the safer you are. This easy-to-remember rule is a good approximation, but is not precisely correct. Twelve spaces away, for example, is more dangerous than 11 spaces, because doubles can be moved twice.

"Careers"

In the Parker Brothers board game "Careers," there are two corner squares, labeled Hospital and Park Bench. To leave the hospital square, you must either pay half of your salary or roll a sum of 5 or less with two dice. What is the probability of rolling a sum of 5 or less? There are ten ways to do this: 1–1, 1–2, 1–3, 1–4, 2–1, 2–2, 2–3, 3–1, 3–2, or 4–1. So, the probability of rolling a 5 or less is a sickly 10/36, a little less than 1/3.

It is a bit easier to roll off the Park Bench. Here, you need to pay half of your cash on hand or else roll a 7, 11, or doubles. Let's count the ways: 1–6, 6–1, 2–5, 5–2, 3–4, 4–3, 5–6, 6–5, 1–1, 2–2, 3–3, 4–4, 5–5, or 6–6. Fourteen ways in all gives a probability of 14/36.

Exercises

2.1   Your final exam consists of ten essay questions. Four of your answers are good enough to be graded "A," four are worth a "B," and two merit only a "C." There are over 100 students in this class, so your harried instructor decides to read just one essay per exam and use that grade as the final-exam score. If each of your essays is equally likely to be read, what is the probability that your instructor will choose one of your "A" answers? One of your "B" answers? One of your "C" answers?

2.2   A random-number generator is equally likely to produce any one of the 100 numbers 0, 1, 2, . . . , 99. What is the probability that the number it generates will

a. be less than 10?
b. be odd?
c. be 99?
d. have 9 as the last digit?

2.3   In the card game Between the Sheets, each player is dealt two cards, face up. Ace is low and king is high. The player can then fold or bet that the value of a third dealt card will be between the values of the two original cards. The bet is lost if the third card is above, below, or matches the first two cards. You have been dealt two cards and there are fifty cards left in the deck. What is your probability of winning a bet if your cards are

a. a three and a nine?
b. a four and a ten?
c. a five and a queen?
d. an ace and a king?
e. a pair of jacks?

2.4   Mr. and Mrs. ZPG have decided to have two children. Let's assume that boy and girl babies are equally likely and that a baby's sex is unrelated to the sex of earlier babies. What is the probability that the ZPG's two children will be a boy and a girl?

2.5 Darryl Royal, a very successful football coach at the University of Texas, once explained why he preferred running the ball to passing it:

> When you pass, three things can happen [completion, incompletion, or interception], and two of them are bad.

Can we infer that there is a 2/3 probability that something bad will happen when the Texas football team passes the ball?

2.6 You are playing draw poker and have been dealt four spades and a heart. You discard the heart and draw a new card. What is the probability that this new card will be a spade, giving you a flush?

• **2.7** You are playing draw poker and have been dealt three spades and two hearts. You discard the two hearts. What is the probability of drawing two spades?

2.3 COUNTING PERMUTATIONS AND COMBINATIONS

How many possible five-card hands are there in the game of poker? What is the probability of three of a kind? Is a flush less likely than a straight? These are probability questions that require a careful, complex counting of the possible number of outcomes. It turns out, though, that there is a standard counting procedure that we can use to handle these and a wide variety of other problems. The logic is clearest if we develop this counting procedure in three stages.

Permutations of *n* Distinct Items

Peter, Paul, and Mary are three distinct names. A rearrangement of the order in which these names appear is called a **permutation.** How many possible orderings are there? There are six permutations:

Peter, Paul, & Mary
Peter, Mary, & Paul
Paul, Peter, & Mary
Paul, Mary, & Peter
Mary, Peter, & Paul
Mary, Paul, & Peter

We can think of an ordering as three slots into which these three names will be placed. Any one of the three names can be put into the first slot, and whichever name is put in the first slot leaves two possibilities for the second slot. Given the two names in the first and second slots, there is only one name left for the third slot. So, if there are three first-slot possibilities, each with two second-slot possibilities, and then one third-slot possibility, then there are $(3)(2)(1) = 6$ possible orderings. If there were four names (such as John, Paul, George, and Ringo), there would be $(4)(3)(2)(1) = 24$ possible orderings.

In general, the number of different permutations of n distinct items is

$$n! = n(n - 1)(n - 2) \ldots 1$$

The mathematical symbol $n!$ (''n factorial'') signifies the product of the integers from n down to 1.

As another example, consider a horse race with 10 horses and an ''exacta'' prize for anyone who can pick the exact order of finish, first through tenth place. How many possible orderings are there? Any one of 10 horses could finish first. For each of these 10 possible first-place finishers, there are 9 possible second-place horses. We have 90 first-second orderings and, for each of these, there are 8 possible third-place finishers. And so, the possibilities multiply. Overall, the number of possible orderings of ten horses is

$$(10)(9)(8)(7)(6)(5)(4)(3)(2)(1) = 3,628,800$$

If the horses are evenly matched, it will not be easy to pick the exact order of finish. In fact, if each of these 3,628,800 possible orderings is equally likely, then your probability of picking the correct ordering is only 1/3,628,800.

Permutations of r Out of n Distinct Items

Now consider a somewhat different problem. We again have n distinct items, but now we only want to use r of them. For example, in our race of 10 horses ($n = 10$), the exacta prize may be awarded for picking the first 3 places in order ($r = 3$). If so, how many different orders of finish are there? Well, any of the 10 horses could finish first, and whichever finishes first, there are still 9 possible second-place finishers. For each of these 90 first-second pairs, there are 8 possible third-place finishers. So, there are $(10)(9)(8) = 720$ possible three-horse orderings in a ten-horse race.

In general, the number of different permutations of r out of n distinct items is

$$n(n - 1)(n - 2) \ldots (n - r + 1) = \frac{n!}{(n - r)!}$$

For another example, consider the Chief Executive Officer (CEO) of a company with offices in 20 different cities. This busy CEO decides to visit 5 of these 20 offices. How many different five-office sequences are possible? The first visit could be to any of 20 offices, followed by any of 19, and so on. The total number of possible sequences is

$$(20)(19)(18)(17)(16) = 1,860,480$$

Combinations of *r* Out of *n* Distinct Items

So far, we have looked at situations where the ordering makes a difference. Visiting Boston and then New York was assumed to be different from visiting New York and then Boston in the CEO's calculation. In many cases, though, order is unimportant. The CEO may not care which office is visited first and which second, but only which 5 offices are visited. If so, by how much did we overcount in our calculations?

Well, take any 5 selected offices, say Boston, New York, Philadelphia, New Haven, and Newark; this is one five-city combination. Our permutation count included all possible sequences of these 5 cities. There are $(5)(4)(3)(2)(1) = 120$ such ordered sequences. We counted 120 permutations, while our CEO considers it just one five-city combination; the same is true of every five-city combination. In arriving at 1,860,480 as the total number of possible ordered sequences, each five-city combination was counted 120 times. To find the number of different five-city combinations, we need to divide 1,860,480 by 120:

$$\frac{(20)(19)(18)(17)(16)}{(5)(4)(3)(2)(1)} = \frac{1,860,480}{120} = 15,504$$

Ignoring the order in which they are visited, there are 15,504 combinations of 5 cities to visit. For each of these 15,504 combinations, there are 120 different orders in which these 5 particular cities could be visited. If the sequence makes a difference, then there are 1,860,480 possible five-city itineraries.

In general, if there are n cities, of which r will be selected, then there are $n!/(n - r)!$ different itineraries. This calculation takes into account the fact that each combination of r cities could be visited in $r!$ different sequences. If we do not care about the order in which the cities are visited, then there are $n!/(n - r)!r!$ different combinations of r cities.

When order is unimportant, we say that we are counting r **combinations,** rather than r permutations.

The number of different r-item combinations using n distinct items is

$$\frac{n!}{r!(n - r)!}$$

for which a shorthand notation is $\binom{n}{r}$.

A special word about $r = 0$ and $r = n$: We define $0! = 1$ so that

$$\binom{n}{0} = \binom{n}{n} = 1$$

This rule is in accordance with our common sense because, if we are going to visit no cities or every city, then there is only one possible choice.

Some Poker Hands

Card games are a fertile area for counting combinations. In five-card poker, for example, what is the probability of being dealt a royal flush: the ace, king, queen, jack, and ten of the same suit? First, let's count how many five-card hands are possible. We are taking $r = 5$ cards out of a deck of $n = 52$ distinct cards. As the order in which the cards are received is unimportant, the number of possible five-card hands is

$$\binom{52}{5} = \frac{(52)(51)(50)(49)(48)}{(5)(4)(3)(2)(1)} = 2,598,960$$

How many of these five-card hands are royal flushes? There are four, one in each suit. Therefore, if the cards are well shuffled and fairly dealt, so that every possible hand is equally likely to be dealt, then the probability of a royal flush is

$$P[\text{royal flush}] = \frac{4}{2,598,960} = .00000154$$

or a one-in-a-million shot.

What about the probability of being dealt a straight flush, other than a royal flush? You could have an ace through five, two through six, or all the way up to nine through king. There are 9 possible straight flushes in each suit, giving 36 altogether. Therefore,

$$P[\text{straight flush}] = \frac{36}{2,598,960} = .00001385$$

Let's do one more. What is the probability of being dealt four of a kind? There are 13 four-of-a-kinds and each could have any one of 48 other cards as the fifth card in the hand. Therefore, there are $13(48) = 624$ hands that contain four of a kind and

$$P[\text{four of a kind}] = \frac{624}{2,598,960} = .00024$$

Notice that these poker probabilities are inversely related to the hand's value. A royal flush is the most valuable poker hand and the least likely to occur. A straight flush beats four of a kind, and is less likely to be dealt. This is true through the complete ranking of poker hands: royal flush, straight flush, four of a kind, full house, flush, straight, three of a kind, two pairs, and a pair. In a comparison of any two of these types of poker hands, the more valuable hand is also the less probable.* I've shown you three of these probabilities already and the remainder

---

*This rule does not extend to specific hands. For example, three aces beats three kings, even though both are equally probable. Also, improbable hands are not necessarily valuable. The probability of drawing the seven of clubs, five of diamonds, four of hearts, three of spades, and two of clubs is 1/2,598,960, but this rare hand loses to any simple pair.

Table 2.3 *Five-card poker hands*

Type of hand	Number of combinations	Probability
Royal flush	4	.00000154
Straight flush	36	.00001385
Four of a kind	624	.00024
Full house	3,744	.00144
Flush	5,108	.00197
Straight	10,200	.00392
Three of a kind	54,912	.02113
Two pair	123,552	.04754
One pair	1,098,240	.42257
Other hands	1,302,540	.50118
Total	2,598,640	1.0

are given in Table 2.3. If your appetite is whetted, there are some good books that thoroughly analyze probabilities for poker, bridge, monopoly, and other complex games.[2]

Exercises

2.8 In the United States, the telephone numbers within any area code contain 7 digits. How many possible 7-digit numbers are there? (Use zeroes and allow numbers to repeat, such as 333-0202.)

2.9 Johnny has forgotten the 3-digit combination to his school padlock. He decides to try all possible combinations. How many are there? What is the probability that his first guess will be correct? (Assume that there are 39 numbers on the padlock and that numbers can be repeated.)

2.10 A television game show gives the contestant an opportunity to win a car by unscrambling the 4 digits 6789 to match the price of the car. How many possible arrangements of these 4 digits are there?

2.11 A popular magazine prints the pictures of 10 celebrities, as they look now and as they looked as babies. Prizes are given to readers who can correctly match all 10 celebrities with their baby pictures. If the match is completely random, what is the probability of winning?

2.12 The Daily Planet has printed the pictures of 10 gurgling babies. The publisher has secretly judged their cuteness, ranking the babies first through tenth. A substantial prize will be given to any reader whose rankings match those of the publisher. What are one's chances of winning if the babies are all equally cute and the reader must correctly pick

a. all 10 places in order?
b. the first 5 places in order?

c. the first 3 places in order?

d. the 5 cutest babies, not necessarily in order?

e. the 3 cutest babies, not necessarily in order?

2.13   Professor Smith likes to liven up his statistics course by telling 2 jokes during the semester. He repeats the jokes from year to year, but for the sake of variety, he has vowed never to tell the same pair of jokes twice. If Professor Smith knows 10 jokes, how many years can he last before breaking his vow?

• **2.14**   A certain store sells 31 different flavors of ice cream. How many different 3-scoop cones are possible if

a. each flavor must be different and the order of the flavors is unimportant?

b. each flavor must be different and the order of the flavors is important?

c. flavors need not be different and the order of the flavors is unimportant?

d. flavors need not be different and the order of the flavors is important?

2.4   LONG-RUN FREQUENCIES

One of the difficulties with the classical approach to probabilities is that there may be compelling evidence that the possible events are not equally likely. A life insurance company is interested in the probability of a reasonably healthy 20-year-old woman dying within a year. The possible outcomes are ''dead'' or ''alive'' after one year, but we can hardly assume these to be equally likely. What can we do?

Another probability approach was developed to handle such situations. If a coin is equally likely to come up heads or tails, then we might suppose that in a large number of coin flips, heads and tails would each come up about half the time. Indeed, we might define *probability* in this way: If we say that some event has a probability of $1/2$ of occurring, we mean that if the situation were repeated over and over, this event would occur about half of the time. Or, turning it around, if we observe an event consistently occurring half the time, we could say that its probability of occurring is $1/2$.

> The **long-run frequency interpretation of probabilities** is that if, in n (a large number of) identical situations, a certain event occurs m times, then its probability is m/n.

The life insurance company might estimate the probability of a 20-year-old woman dying within a year by looking at the experiences of millions of other women when they were 20 years old. If they had data on 10 million such women and found that 12,000 died within a year, then they might estimate the probability as $12,000/10,000,000 = .0012$, or slightly more than 1 in 1000. In fact, some thirty years after Pascal's *Treatise* appeared, the Royal Society of London published mortality tables that could be used to price life insurance.

The equally-likely and long-run frequency approaches to probability are not inconsistent with each other. They are just two different ways of thinking about probabilities. If a coin is equally likely to land heads or tails, then we expect it to land heads about half the time. One statistician, Karl Pearson, actually whiled away the hours by flipping a coin 24,000 times and carefully recording the outcomes. There were 12,012 heads and 11,988 tails, which gives a probability of heads of 12,012/24,000 = .5005. Apparently, his coin was unbent.

Pearson's experiment is dwarfed by that of a Swiss astronomer named Wolf, who rolled dice over a forty-year period, from 1850 to 1893. In one set of experiments, Wolf tossed a pair of dice, one red and the other white, 20,000 times. An economist, John Maynard Keynes, commented on the results:

> . . . the records of the relative frequency of each face show that the dice must have been very irregular, the six face of the white die, for example, falling 38% more often than the four face of the same die. This, then, is the sole conclusion of these immensely laborious experiments—that Wolf's dice were very ill made. . . .
>
> Wolf recorded altogether . . . in the course of his life 280,000 results of tossing individual dice. It is not clear that Wolf had any well-defined object in view in making these records, which are published in curious conjunction with various astronomical results, and they afford a wonderful example of the pure love of experiment and observation.[3]

The equally-likely and long-run frequency approaches are consistent with each other, but clearly they differ in how they go about obtaining probabilities. In the equally-likely method, we sit down, enumerate the possible outcomes, and meditate on their equal likelihood. In the long-run frequency method, we get up, go out, and collect some real data. The equally-likely method is most appropriate for well-structured gambling situations, where we are pretty sure that we have fair coins or fair dice and, thus, gathering data would just be a boring waste of time. The long-run frequency approach is best when we suspect that the possibilities are not really equally likely, and so we want to use some data to confirm or deny our suspicions. The long-run frequency approach is obviously needed for situations like insurance company mortality tables, where it is apparent that living and dying are not equally likely. It may also be useful in fine tuning the probabilities of events that are not quite equally likely.

Will It Be a Boy or a Girl?

Consider the probability that a newborn baby will be a boy. Laplace's Principle of Insufficient Reason suggests that we may as well assume that boy and girl babies are equally likely and, consequently, assign a probability of 1/2 to each. But, if we took the time to examine the data, we would find that boy babies slightly outnumber girl babies. During the years 1975–1979, there were 16,466,000 recorded births in the United States, of which 8,444,000 were gurgling boys and 8,022,000 were bouncing girls. With these data, the long-run frequency estimate of the probability of a boy is

$$P[\text{boy}] = \frac{8,444,000}{16,466,000} = .513$$

A Scientific Study of Roulette

Outside of the United States, roulette wheels generally have 37 slots, numbered 0, 1, 2, . . . , 36. Those used in the United States have an additional 00 slot, giving

Mendel's Genetic Theory

Gregor Mendel (1822–1884), an Austrian monk, used probabilities to explain the inheritance of various traits. Mendel's theory laid the basis for modern genetics, including the development of many remarkable hybrid plants. One of his early experiments involved the cross-breeding of sweet peas, some with yellow seeds and some with green seeds. He noticed a number of statistical regularities that he explained by postulating that there are entities, now called genes, that determine seed color and are inherited from the parent plants.

Mendel found that a crossing of purebred yellow-seeded and green-seeded plants produced plants with yellow seeds. But when these hybrids were fertilized with their own pollen, a variety of peas emerged. One-fourth had green seeds and continued to produce green-seeded plants when they were self-fertilized. One-fourth had yellow seeds and continued to produce yellow-seeded plants when they were self-fertilized. The remaining half had yellow seeds and yielded the same offspring proportions as the original hybrids.

What theory could explain these data? Mendel hypothesized that each plant has two genes, each of which could be either Y or G. Thus, a pea plant could be either YY, GG, or YG. A plant with YY genes produces yellow flowers, while a plant with GG genes produces green flowers. A plant with YG genes produces yellow seeds and, therefore, Y is said to be the dominant gene.

Probability comes in because one gene is inherited from each of the parent plants. When both parents are YY, the offspring will be YY and produce yellow flowers. When both parents are GG, the offspring will be GG, too. When a parent is YG, the offspring is equally likely to inherit the Y or the G gene. Thus, the offspring of two hybrid parents has probabilities 1/4 of being GG, 1/4 of being YY, and 1/2 of being YG—just as Mendel found in his experiments!

Matters are not always this simple. Some traits, such as hair color, depend on more than one pair of genes. Some genes, such as those for blood type, have more than two alternative kinds. And some traits, such as height, depend on environment as well as genes. However, Mendel's genetic theory is still an extraordinarily simple, yet powerful, application of probability theory.

38 slots in all. If the wheel is balanced, clean, and fair, we might expect each slot to be equally likely to catch the spun ball, but in practice, a roulette wheel usually has a few imperfections that cause some numbers to win slightly more often than others.

In the late 1800s, an English engineer, William Jaggers, took dramatic advantage of these imperfections. He paid six assistants to spend every day for an entire month observing the roulette wheels at Monte Carlo and record the numbers that won. Jaggers found that certain numbers did come up more often than others. He then proceeded to bet heavily on these numbers and, in four days, won 1.5 million francs, nearly $200,000—a fortune in the late 1800s. In the 1960s, while their fellow students were studying or protesting, a group of Berkeley students were reported to have pulled off a similar feat in Las Vegas. Nowadays, unfortunately, casinos examine and rotate their roulette wheels frequently to frustrate the long-run frequency bettors.

Exercises

2.15 In 1977, 6101 oil wells were drilled in new fields and 1004 of these discovered significant oil or gas.[4] What is the probability that a newly drilled well in 1977 was successful?

2.16 A study of monthly returns in the stock market over the 55-year period, 1926–1980, found that the return was positive in 403 months and negative in 257 months.[5] Based solely on these data, what is your estimate of the probability of a positive monthly return in the stock market?

2.17 The Swiss astronomer Wolf tossed two dice 100,000 times and found that pairs came up 16,466 times. Use these data to estimate the probability of rolling pairs. Is this empirical long-run frequency close to the theoretical probability implied by an equally-likely assumption?

2.18 A 50-year-old has to pay more for life insurance than a 20-year-old. Is this because 50-year-olds have higher incomes and can therefore afford to pay more for insurance?

2.19 The U.S. Postal Service handled 56 billion pieces of mail in 1978, of which 4.5 billion pieces were initially misdelivered and 211,203 were reported lost completely. Based on these data, what is the probability that a letter will be lost completely? Can you think of any reasons why these long-run frequency probabilities may understate or overstate the chances that the next letter you send will be misdelivered or lost?

2.20 The color of the flowers on Japanese four-o'clocks is determined by a pair of genes, each of which could be either R or W. The flower is red if the genes are RR, white if WW, and pink if RW. What are the respective probabilities of red, white, and pink flowers if

a. the parent plants are RR and WW?
b. the parent plants are RR and RW?
c. the parent plants are RW and RW?

2.21 A book recently calculated the probabilities of "being injured by various items around your house.''[6] The authors conclude that, ''As the figures show, our homes are veritable booby traps. Even your cocktail table is out to get you. These accounted for almost 64,000 injuries [in 1977], more than all ladders [62,000 injuries].'' Using data based on 74,050,000 households, they calculated that the probability of being injured by a cocktail table was 64,000/74,050,000 = .00086 and the probability of being injured by a ladder was 62,000/74,050,000 = .00084. Should we conclude that cocktail tables are indeed more dangerous than ladders? Do their probability calculations make sense?

2.5   SUBJECTIVE PROBABILITIES

The long-run frequency approach allows us to extend probabilities to events that are not equally likely. But its application is limited to situations where we have lots of repetitive data, while much of the uncertainty that surrounds us concerns virtually unique situations. There are no frequency data if the situation has never occurred before. For example, we might be keenly interested in the outcome of an upcoming presidential election. Perhaps the opposing candidates support policies that will have important effects on our lives. Decisions about buying or selling stocks, expanding or contracting a business, or even whether or not to enlist in the Army may well be affected by who you think is going to be elected president.

In 1946, the ''Wizard of Odds'' calculated presidential probabilities as follows:

> Miss Deanne Skinner of Monrovia, California, asks: Can the Wizard tell me what the odds are of the next President of the United States being a Democrat? . . . Without considering the candidates, the odds would be 2 to 1 in favor of a Republican because since 1861 when that party was founded, there have been 12 Republican Presidents and only 7 Democrats.[7]

But we can't very well predict an election winner simply by calculating the relative frequencies with which Democrats and Republicans have been elected president. In 1936, Franklin Roosevelt ran for reelection against Alf Landon. At that time, there had been 20 previous presidential contests between Republicans and Democrats, with the Republicans winning 14.* Should the 1936 forecasters have concluded that Landon had a 70 percent chance of winning? Or should they have somehow taken into account that Roosevelt was a popular president running for reelection against the unexciting Governor of Kansas?

Similarly, by 1964, the tally was 16 election victories for the Republicans and 11 for the Democrats. Did Barry Goldwater then have a 16/27 = .59 chance of thwarting Lyndon Johnson's reelection bid? Should we assume that the Republicans' odds were the same in 1964 and, four years later, in 1968 when the Republican candidate was Richard Nixon and the Democratic candidate was George

*These numbers differ from the Wizard's because he looked at presidents rather than elections. For example, Woodrow Wilson won in 1912 and 1916, and so I counted two Democratic Party victories, while the Wizard counted one Democratic president. Similarly, I ignored Chester Arthur, who became president in 1881, after James Garfield was assassinated; the Wizard counted Arthur as another Republican president.

McGovern? Clearly, the odds change from election to election, depending on the state of the nation and the personalities of the candidates.

The outcome of a presidential election is uncertain and it would be useful to quantify that uncertainty. We would like to have more than a shrug of the shoulders and sheepish "who knows?" Neither the equally-likely nor the long-run-frequency approach is satisfactory, however. The choice of president is not determined by the flip of a coin, bent or unbent, every four years.

In the same spirit, a good weather forecaster will use more than historical records and a lucky penny to predict tomorrow's weather. It would be hard to make rational plans if the forecaster simply said, "Maybe it will rain and, then again, maybe it won't." It's much more informative to hear, "There's a 90 percent chance of rain tomorrow." Similarly, a good doctor will base each prognosis on the individual patient, and not on some long-run average. To make rational decisions, the patient needs to know, "You have a 60 percent chance of surviving such an operation," and not "You will survive, unless you don't."

The same is true of many interesting situations. Who is going to win the next Super Bowl? Will this first-round draft choice be a successful pro quarterback? Will you be accepted by a certain graduate school? Will we find oil if we drill here? Is the unemployment rate going to increase or decrease? Did this person rob that bank? Will the Soviet Union attack China? Each example is uncertain and ripe for a probability assessment, but none fits into the equally-likely or long-run-frequency mold.

Bayes' Approach

In the eighteenth century, Reverend Thomas Bayes apparently wrestled with an even more challenging problem—the probability that God exists. The equally-likely and long-run-frequency approaches are useless, and yet, this is an uncertainty that is of great interest to many people, including Reverend Bayes. Such a probability is necessarily subjective. The best that any person can do is to weigh the available evidence and logical arguments and come up with a personal probability of God's existence. This idea of personal probabilities has been extended and refined by other *Bayesians,* who argue that many uncertain situations can only be analyzed by means of subjective probability assessments. Bayesians are ready, willing, and eager to assign probabilities to football games, oil drilling, war strategy, and God.

A Super Bowl Probability

These probabilities can be elicited by observing the choices people make. As I am writing this, Miami is about to play Washington in Super Bowl XVII. During a statistics class, I offered one of my students, Juan Guerra, $10 if he could correctly predict the Super Bowl winner. He chose the Washington Redskins, thereby indicating that he believed the probability of Washington winning the game to be greater than .5.

The Future Price of Gold

Horace W. Brock, an ambitious political economist, set out in late 1981 to predict the price of gold in 1987—a formidable task! He frankly admitted that he didn't know what the price would be, but aimed instead for a probability distribution. His basic tools were the economist's demand and supply curves, the statistician's probability tree, and the political scientist's knowledge of world affairs.[8]

He divided demand into ten components: private investment, large central bank investment, smaller central bank investment, electronic usage, dental usage, other industrial usage, and jewelry usage in four areas (North America, Europe, Japan, and the rest of the world). Supply was divided into three areas: communist countries, South Africa, and other western nations. For each of these demand and supply components, Brock used a probability tree to describe possible scenarios. Private investment demand, for instance, was assumed to depend on interest rates, economic growth rates, inflation rates, the value of the U.S. dollar, and the level of world anxiety. Probabilities were then attached to various combinations of events. Figure 1 shows the start of the probability tree, tracing out combinations of interest

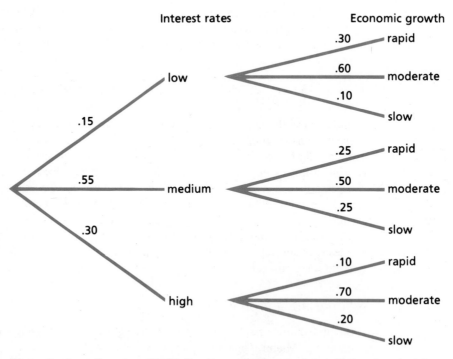

Figure 1   *A small portion of H.W. Brock's probability tree for predicting the price of gold in 1987*

Figure 2 *The price of gold in 1987 given 6 percent inflation, as forecast by H.W. Brock in 1981*

rates and economic growth. (Brock's tree kept branching to include inflation, the value of the dollar, and world anxiety.) The probabilities in the first branching of the tree (.15, .55, and .30) indicate a belief that interest rates are more likely to be high than low. The probabilities for the second branching are conditional upon the level of interest rates. In particular, if interest rates do turn out to be low, it is more likely that economic growth will be rapid.

The next stage was to "guesstimate" private investment demand at different prices under the various possible scenarios. At a price of $375, Brock's estimates of private investment demand ranged from 500 tons (if there were high interest rates, slow growth, low inflation, a strong U.S. dollar, and little world anxiety) to 1000 tons (if there were low interest rates, rapid growth, high inflation, a weak dollar, and lots of anxiety). At a price of $750 an ounce, demand drops to a range of −150 tons to 500 tons. Trees, probabilities, and quantities, were constructed for all of the components of demand and supply, and the equilibration of total demand and supply then yielded a probability distribution for the price of gold. Brock's predictions are conditional on the inflation rate; Figure 2 shows the case of a 6 percent annual inflation.

The scenarios, probabilities, demands, and supplies are, of course, all subjective. In this case, they represent Brock's distillation of eighty confidential interviews with prominent and well-informed experts including bankers, political analysts, economists, journalists, and finance ministers. His predictions may or may not prove accurate, but that's not really the point. The lesson is that since the future is uncertain, all we can hope for is a subjective probability distribution based on the kinds of considerations that Brock took into account. Most people interested in the future price of gold will think about these very same things, though much more informally. What Brock has provided is an ambitious attempt to implement a formal framework for thinking about a very tough question.

To learn more about his subjective probability assessment, I offered Juan more choices. Which of the following gambles would he prefer:

$10 if Washington wins; or
$10 if a red card is drawn from a deck containing six red cards and four black cards?

Juan chose the card draw, indicating that he believed Washington's probability of winning to be less than .6. I then offered him this choice:

$10 if Washington wins; or
$10 if a red card is drawn from a deck containing 55 red cards and 45 black cards.

Again, he chose the card draw, putting Washington's probability of winning somewhere between .50 and .55.

With further questioning, I pinned him down to a probability of .52 by finding that he was indifferent about these choices:

$10 if Washington wins; or
$10 if a red card is drawn from a deck containing 52 red cards and 48 black cards.

This student knew some facts about the two teams. Washington's record was 11–1, while Miami's was 10–2, but Miami had played a slightly tougher schedule. Miami also had one of the very best coaches in football, Don Shula, while the Redskins had a largely unknown, second-year coach, Joe Gibbs. On the other hand, Washington seemed to be an emotional team on a roll. None of these varied tidbits of information can be directly translated into a probability, but Juan subjectively weighed what he knew and came up with a personal probability of .52 for Washington winning.

> The **Bayesian interpretation of probabilities** is that an event has a subjective probability of m/n of occurring if you are indifferent between a gamble hinging on this event and a gamble hinging on the draw of a red card from a deck in which a fraction m/n of the cards are red.

Objectivist Objections

Many probability theorists are not comfortable with the Bayesian approach. They prefer objective probabilities derived from equally-likely principles or long-run frequencies. It is not scientific to pull probabilities out of the air. It is especially disturbing that subjective probabilities vary from person to person. If a coin is fair, heads and tails are equally likely. If 8,444,000 out of 16,466,00 babies born were boys, then the probability of giving birth to a boy is .513. These are scientific "facts" on which we can all agree and draw common conclusions. How can we have a scientific discourse if one person says that the probability of something is .8 while another person says that it is .4?

Bayesians respond that these subjective disagreements are all about us and should not be ignored. When Juan picked Washington to win, several other students hissed, because they believed that Miami was more likely to win. Some even wanted to make bets with Juan. It is these very disagreements that make football games so interesting. If probability analysis ignores subjective probabilities, it will miss most of life's uncertainties.

Will we find oil here? Will the unemployment rate go up or down? Will the Soviet Union attack China? These are all uncertainties about which informed and well-intentioned people disagree. Instead of ignoring these disagreements, Bayesians argue that it is better to quantify them by pinning down people's subjective probabilities.

You and I may be debating about whether or not we will find oil in a particular location. We can each present our arguments and call each other names. That might be fun, but it is certainly not enough. It would be nice to have something more than me saying "maybe there is" and you cleverly retorting "maybe not."

If we specify our subjective probabilities of finding oil, then we can see how much we really disagree. Perhaps we've been arguing viciously over a slight difference in probabilities, .48 versus .52. We can also use probabilities to calculate the expected costs and benefits of drilling, as we will see later in this book. Explicit probabilities allow us to see where we disagree about the value of drilling and by how much. Admittedly, it would be nicer to have an agreed-upon objective probability, but there isn't any here. Bayesians argue that it is better to proceed with subjective probabilities than to simply rely on vague arguments and name calling.

Can We Put Probabilities on Events That Have Already Occurred?

There is an even deeper dispute between the objectivists and the subjectivists. Theoretical objectivists adhere very strictly to the coin-flip metaphor. We can imagine God flipping a coin (albeit a slightly bent coin) to determine whether a child will be a boy or a girl. Or, more exactly, we might imagine God reaching into a bag that contains 513 boys and 487 girls. Objectivists don't like to apply probabilities to situations that can't be fit into this metaphor. For example, they would not apply a .513 probability after a child's sex has been determined, even if the baby is not yet born and the sex is not yet known by the outside world. Once the child has been conceived, it is a boy either with probability 1.0 or with probability .0. Is my own oldest child a boy? A Bayesian who doesn't know the answer would freely assign a probability of about .5. An objectivist who doesn't know would refuse to answer, protesting that this is a misuse of probabilities.

By the same logic, objectivists say that a coin has a .5 probability of landing heads before it is flipped, but not afterward. What if the coin has been flipped and then immediately covered before anyone could see whether it landed heads or tails? The strict objectivist argues that the coin is now either a head or a tail and, consequently, is no longer a fit subject for a .5 probability statement. The Bayesian, in contrast, argues that any uncertain situation is susceptible to a probability assessment. The Bayesian will hold to a .5 probability until there is some evidence of whether it is a head or a tail.

As another example, I was once asked to play the Bayesian devil's advocate in an academic objectivist-subjectivist debate. The objectivist asked me the probability that October 23, 1845 was a Tuesday. I replied, "Before or after I consult an almanac?" In the absence of any information, a Bayesian would undoubtedly say that the probability of this particular date being a Tuesday is 1/7. Once an almanac had been consulted, the probability would be revised to .0 because October 23, 1845 turns out to have been a Thursday. In this debate, the objectivist argued that 1/7 was not a proper use of probabilities. No matter how informed or ignorant I was, October 23, 1845 was a Thursday. Its probability of being a Tuesday always was and always will be zero.

This debate may seem like a lot of academic hot air about nothing and, to a large extent, it is; but the objectivists and the subjectivists do look at many things a bit differently. Think of the question, "Is there oil where we are drilling?" The Bayesian would advise using the available information to come up with a subjective probability. The strict objectivist would object that there is either oil here or there isn't, so it is not appropriate to assign any probability other than zero or one. The same thing would happen with the question, "Did this person rob that bank?" The Bayesian is willing to assign probabilities; the objectivist isn't. Throughout this book, we will see that Bayesians assign probabilities to all sorts of uncertainties, while the objectivists keep a narrower perspective.

Exercises

2.22   A business executive believes that a new dog perfume is just as likely to fail as to succeed. What is this executive's implicit probability of the product's success?

2.23   A security analyst believes that it is twice as likely that the stock market will go up rather than down during the next twelve months. What is this analyst's implicit probability of the market going up during the next twelve months? (Assume there is no chance that the market will not change at all.)

2.24   An economist says that a depression within the next five years is about as likely as drawing a red marble out of a bag containing 5 red marbles, 20 blue marbles, and 75 green marbles. What is the probability that this economist places on a depression within the next five years?

2.25   About 20 percent of the students who take the GMAT test for admission to business school score above 600. Explain why you believe that your probability of scoring above 600 on the GMAT is either larger or smaller than .20.

2.26   Explain why you either agree or disagree with this assessment:

There is really no difference between classical and Bayesian probabilities because "equally-likely outcomes" is just a subjective assumption.

2.27   What answer would you give if you were asked the probability that April 1, 1929 was a Saturday? Imagine that a friend offers the following friendly wager. You are asked to pick any day of the week and then to pick any day of the year and any year before 1950. You select Saturday and November 11, 1945. You are then offered a wager in which you win $10 if November 11, 1945 was a Saturday, but must pay $1 if it is not. Would you accept this wager? How far could the prize be reduced below $10 before you would lose interest?

• **2.28** A book recently answered the question, "What are the odds of being indicted or convicted for criminal tax activity?" by noting that, "Of the 136,718,000 tax returns of all kind filed in fiscal 1978, just 2,634 were referred for prosecution and 1,724 indictments issued."[9] Thus, they calculated the probability of being indicted as 1,724/136,718,000 = .000013. Similarly, because 1,414 people were convicted, the book concludes that the probability of being convicted of criminal tax activity is 1,414/136,718,000 = .000010.

Why are these probability calculations of dubious value? What is their correct interpretation?

2.6 SUMMARY

Probabilities are used to quantify life's uncertainties. There are three basic approaches: the enumeration of equally likely events, the computation of observed relative frequencies, and a subjective assessment based on a blending of facts and opinions.

The classical equally-likely approach was devised to handle games of chance—the roll of the dice, spin of the roulette wheel, and deal of the cards. If there are m "successes" in n possible outcomes, with each being equally likely, then the probability of a success is m/n. Sometimes we have to use the permutation and combination formulas to enumerate the possible outcomes. Suppose that we are choosing r out of n distinct items.

$$\text{When the order matters, the number of different permutations is} \quad \frac{n!}{(n-r)!}$$

$$\text{When order is unimportant, the number of different combinations is} \quad \binom{n}{r} = \frac{n!}{r!(n-r)!}$$

The frequentist approach is designed for cases where there are lots of data and the possible outcomes are apparently not equally likely. If an event has occurred m times in n (a very large number) identical situations, then its probability is m/n. For instance, 8,444,000 boys in 16,466,000 births implies an 8,444,000/16,466,000 = .513 probability of a boy.

The subjectivist approach is closely associated with Reverend Thomas Bayes. A subjective probability is based on an intuitive blending of a variety of information. Consider, for instance, the stock market. I may well resist making an equally-likely assumption or using past relative frequencies. Instead, based on what I know about the stock market and the economy, I may believe that there is a .60 probability that the stock market will go up this year. Subjective probabilities such as this obviously vary from person to person.

REVIEW EXERCISES

2.29 There are 40,000 students at Big State University (BSU). Of these 40,000 students, 5000 love BSU, 10,000 hate BSU, and 25,000 never stop to think about it. Timeweek magazine decides to do a story on BSU and sends out a reporter to interview a student. If each student is equally likely to be interviewed, what is the probability that the reporter will talk to a student who hates BSU?

Now assume that the reporter is not interested in interviewing one of the 25,000 students who have no opinion of BSU. If one of these apathetic students is accidentally selected, the reporter will just move on to another student, until one is found who either loves or hates BSU. Now what is the probability that the person interviewed will be a student who hates BSU?

2.30 A prominent mathematician, Jean d'Alembert, argued that there is a 1/3 probability of two tails when a coin is flipped twice. He reasoned that we could obtain a head on the first flip, a head on the second flip, or no heads. Therefore, the probability of two tails (no heads) is 1/3. Similarly, he reasoned that a coin flipped three times could yield a head on the first flip, a head on the second flip, a head on the third flip, or no heads. Therefore, the probability of three tails (no heads) is 1/4. Explain the flaw in d'Alembert's reasoning.

2.31 In the carnival game Under and Over Seven, the player can either predict that the sum of a pair of dice will be less than 7 or greater than 7. What is the probability that such a prediction will be correct?

2.32 Larry, Moe, and Joe are going to draw straws to decide who brings the beer. A neutral observer shows the tops of three straws and lets them pick, with the short straw losing. Joe insists on drawing last. That way, if Larry or Moe picks the short straw, Joe won't have any chance of drawing it. Is there an advantage to drawing last?

● **2.33** Galileo was asked whether the numbers on three rolled dice will sum to 9 or 10 more often. He counted the possible outcomes and provided the answer. What is the probability of rolling a 9 with three dice? What is the probability of rolling a 10? Which is more probable?

●● **2.34** A ''double-deuces'' die is a special six-sided die with two 2s and no 5s. A ''double-fives'' die has two 5s and no 2s. Construct a table showing the probabilities of rolling the sums 2, 3, . . . , 12 using two standard dice, two double-deuces dice, and two double-fives dice. In the game craps, the roller wins if the first roll is a 7 or 11 and loses if it is a 2, 3, or 12. Which set of dice is the most advantageous to the roller? Which set is least advantageous?

2.35 You are playing draw poker and have been dealt a four, five, seven, eight, and king. You discard the king and draw a new card, hoping for a six to fill your inside straight. What is your probability of success? If you are instead dealt a four, five, six, seven, and king, what is your probability of drawing either a three or eight to complete your straight?

●● **2.36** You are playing draw poker and have been dealt a pair of fours, a jack, a seven, and a three. You keep the pair and discard the other three cards. What is the probability of drawing at least one more four?

2.37 In craps, a bettor can make a ''field'' bet. The bet is lost if a 5, 6, 7, or 8 comes up on the next roll of a pair of dice. Any other number is a win. A $1 field bet gains $1 if a 3, 4, 9, 10, or 11 is rolled and gains $2 if a 2 or 12 is rolled. One author wrote that "field betting is a fascinating wager. . . . After all, how can they pass up a bargain that gives them seven numbers in their favor, compared to four in opposition?"[10]

What is the probability of winning a field bet? If you make 36 field bets and the numbers come up as frequently as they should (one 2, two 3s, and so on), how many dollars will you come out ahead?

● **2.38** (*continuation*) Explain why you agree or disagree with this advice on placing field bets:

> One of the best ways to play the field is to go along with the dice. If a field number shows up, continue field betting. Thus, if a streak occurs, players will be in on it.
>
> Or else you may attempt the opposite. When a field number comes up, stop betting and wait for a non-field number. Afterwards, bet the field again. In this way, players will be cutting down the percentage of numbers against them.[11]

● **2.39** There are three categories of professors at Metro U.:

	male	*female*	*total*
full professors	400	100	500
associate professors	100	100	200
assistant professors	150	150	300
total	650	350	1000

One of these three categories of professors is picked at random, and then one of the persons in that selected category is picked at random. What is the probability that the selected person is a male?

● **2.40** (*continuation*) If, using the data in the preceding exercise, a male is picked at random, what is the probability that the selected person is a full professor? If, in contrast, a female is picked at random, what is the probability that she is a full professor? Do these data suggest that gender and rank are related or unrelated?

● **2.41** Galileo wrote a short note on the probabilities of obtaining a sum of 9, 10, 11, or 12 when three dice are rolled. Someone else had concluded that these numbers are equally likely, because there are six ways to obtain a 9 (1–4–4, 1–3–5, 1–2–6, 2–3–4, 2–2–5, or 3–3–3), six ways to obtain a 10 (1–4–5, 1–3–6, 2–4–4, 2–3–5, 2–2–6, or 3–3–4), six ways to obtain an 11 (1–5–5, 1–4–6, 2–4–5, 2–3–6, 3–4–4, or 3–3–5), and six ways to obtain a 12 (1–5–6, 2–4–6, 2–5–5, 3–4–5, 3–3–6, or 4–4–4). Yet Galileo observed "from long observation, gamblers consider 10 and 11 to be more likely than 9 and 12." How do you think Galileo resolved this conflict between theory and observation?

●● **2.42** Here's a probability variant on three-card Monte. You are shown three cards: one black on both sides, one white on both sides, and one white on one side and black on the other. The three cards are dropped into an empty bag and you slide one out; it happens to be black on the side that is showing. The operator of the game says, "We know that this is not the double-white card. We also know that it could be either black or white on the other side. I will bet $5 against your $4 that it is, in fact, black on the other side." Can the operator make money from such bets without cheating somehow?

2.43 Explain why you think that the following strategy for winning coin tosses is sound or unsound:

> Let the other man make the call, for if you are the one who calls, the chances are 3 to 2 against you. Explanation: 7 out of 10 people will cry heads, but heads will turn up only 5 times out of 10, so if you let your opponent call, you have the greater probability of winning.[12]

2.44 Raymond Queneau wrote an unusual book of poetry, *Cent mille milliards de poemes*. This book contains only 10 pages, but each page is sliced into 14 strips, with each strip of paper containing one line of poetry. The reader can then construct a 14-line poem by taking each line from any of the 10 pages. How many lines of poetry did Queneau write? How many different 14-line poems can be constructed?

2.45 California license plates once used a number followed by a letter, followed by four more numbers. How many different license plates were possible? In 1956, California changed to a system used by several other states: three letters, followed by three numbers. If there are no forbidden combinations, how many different license plates of this type are possible? Then California also began issuing plates with three numbers followed by three letters. How many additional plates did this reversal allow? In 1978, California introduced license plates with a number followed by three letters and then three more numbers. How many different plates of this type are possible? Why do you think California keeps changing its license plate system?

2.46 A television show gives the contestant the chance to win a trip to Buffalo by guessing the price of a mystery package. The contestant is given a penny, nickel, dime, and quarter and told that a combination of some or all of these coins gives the exact price of the mystery package. How many different prices are possible?

2.47 There are 11 positions on a soccer team. A team has just been formed for children who are five to six years old, with one player's parent as coach. This inexperienced coach decides to try every child in every position to find the best possible starting lineup. How many possible lineups are there

a. if there are 11 children on the team?
b. if there are 13 children on the team?
c. if there are 13 children on the team and it is predetermined that the coach's child will start in the center-forward position?

2.48 The Morse code consists of a sequence of telegraphic "dot" or "dash" signals, with each sequence representing a letter of the English alphabet. For example, dot = E; dot-dash = A; and dot-dash-dot = R. Thus, dot dot-dash dot-dash-dot gives the message "EAR." The distress signal is dot-dot-dot dash-dash-dash dot-dot-dot = SOS. How many English letters can be represented by sequences of from one to three dot or dash signals? How long a sequence did Morse have to allow in order to include all 26 letters of the English alphabet?

●● **2.49** On a recent English test, students were given the names of four authors and the names of four novels. The students were to match each novel with the correct author. If a student just guesses randomly, what is the probability of getting all four correct? Three correct? Two correct? One correct? None correct? The teacher gives one point for a correct answer and subtracts one point for a wrong answer. Is a guesser more likely to have a positive score or a negative score?

● ● **2.50**   (For the bridge aficionado.) In a game of bridge, you and your partner have nine spades including the ace and king, but not the queen. If you play the ace and then the king, what is the probability that the queen will fall?

CHAPTER 3

Probability Rules

This branch of mathematics [probability] is the only one, I believe, in which good writers frequently get results entirely erroneous.

Charles Sanders Peirce

TOPICS

You have now seen what probabilities are and why there is a need for them. You have also seen that there is some disagreement among theoreticians about the interpretation of probabilities. Probabilities can also be treated as just another interesting mathematical problem. Many clever mathematicians have proven some useful probability theorems, without ever specifying what probabilities are and where they come from.[1] Both objectivists and subjectivists alike can consequently use these theorems to simplify their probability calculations.

3.1 VENN DIAGRAMS

We won't go through any elaborate mathematical proofs here, but we can use a simple picture to intuitively justify the theorems. Consider an uncertain situation for which there are, say, ten possible outcomes. We can number these outcomes 1, 2, . . . , 10 and then represent the outcomes by putting ten numbered points inside the box shown in Figure 3.1. Each point in this box represents a possible outcome. These sorts of figures were originated by the mathematician John Venn.

> A **Venn diagram** is a box representing the possible outcomes of an uncertain situation. It can be used to intuitively justify probability rules.

To make the exposition simpler, I'll assume that each of the ten possible outcomes is equally likely. However, the analysis also holds for events that are not equally likely.

The circle A in Figure 3.1 represents the statement, "Event 4, 5, or 6 will occur." These are three of ten equally likely possibilities, and the probability that one of these events will occur is 3/10. We can show this by writing

$$P[A] = .3$$

We can put as many or as few events as we want into a subset like A. Obviously,

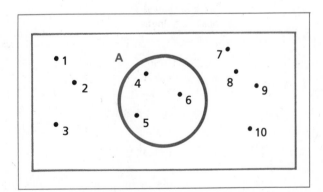

Figure 3.1 *A Venn diagram*

the probability cannot be negative or greater than one,

$$0 \leq P[A] \leq 1 \tag{3.1}$$

Venn diagrams can be used to show three useful probability theorems: the addition rule, the multiplication rule, and the subtraction rule.

Exercises

3.1 Consider the roll of a four-sided die that is numbered 1, 2, 3, and 4. Draw a Venn diagram showing these four possible outcomes. Now draw three circles showing the following rolls:

a. 1
b. an even number
c. 1 or an even number

Now draw a new Venn diagram with the numbers 1, 2, 3, and 4 and then draw three circles showing the following rolls:

d. 4
e. 4 or an even number
f. 4 and an even number

What are the probabilities of each of these six results?

3.2 One of five soldiers must go on a dangerous mission. Five pieces of paper are placed in a hat. Four are blank and one, marked with an X, determines the volunteer for this mission. The five soldiers are:

Arv, a white enlisted man
Bill, a black enlisted man
Clyde, a black drafted man
Doris, a white enlisted woman
Ernie, a white drafted man

Draw a Venn diagram, using A, B, C, D, and E to represent these five soldiers. Use circles to show the cases in which the volunteer is

a. black
b. black or drafted
c. black and drafted

Now draw a new Venn diagram and show the cases in which the volunteer is

d. black or female
e. black or male
f. black and male

What are these six probabilities?

3.2 THE ADDITION RULE

You are going to flip two coins. What is the probability of getting at least one head, either on the first flip or on the second flip? It is tempting to simply add up the probability of a head on the first flip plus the probability of a head on the second flip, but that would give .5 + .5 = 1.0, which can't be right. It is not at all certain that you will get at least one head; you may well get tails on both flips.

The error is a double counting of the case of two heads. Our .5 probability for heads on the first toss includes the case where we also get heads on the second toss, and our .5 probability for heads on the second toss also includes the case of two heads. If we add together these two .5 probabilities, we will count the two-heads case twice.

Let's list the four possible outcomes, as we have done before:

HT
HH
TH
TT

The first and second outcomes involve a head on the first flip. The second and third outcomes involve a head on the second flip. If we simply add two successful outcomes plus two successful outcomes, the second outcome, HH, is counted twice. The correct probability, counting HH only once, is 3/4.

Figure 3.2 shows a Venn diagram representation of this double-counting potential. Set A contains the outcomes in which the first flip is a head. Set B contains the outcomes in which the second flip is a head. The outcome TT is in neither set. The outcome HH is in both sets. We are interested in the probability of "A or B": the probability of a head on the first or second flip. If we simply count the two outcomes in A and the two outcomes in B and add them together to get four, we will double count the outcome HH that is in both A and B.

One way to correct this double counting is to enumerate all the possible outcomes and then count the successful ones carefully. Another way, which is often simpler, is to knowingly double count and then subtract the outcomes that are counted twice. This is the **addition rule**:

$$P[A \text{ or } B] = P[A] + P[B] - P[A \text{ and } B] \tag{3.2}$$

In this two-coin case, the probability of a head on the first flip is 1/2, the

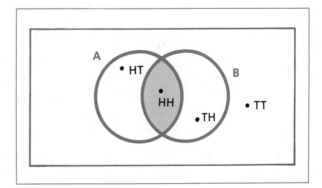

Figure 3.2 *Double counting double heads*

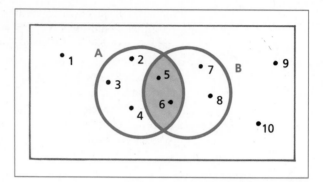

Figure 3.3 *Two overlapping sets*

probability of a head on the second flip is 1/2, and the probability of heads on both flips is 1/4. Therefore, the probability of a head on either the first or second flip is $1/2 + 1/2 - 1/4 = 3/4$.

Figure 3.3 shows another example. There are ten possible outcomes, of which five are in A and four are in B. Perhaps one of ten people is to be randomly selected to chair a committee. Group A might be people under 30 years of age, while group B is females. What is the probability that the selected person will be in either A or B? It depends on how much overlap there is—how many outcomes are included in both A and B (that is, how many of those under 30 are also female). In Figure 3.3, there are two outcomes that are in both A and B. Therefore,

$$P[A \text{ or } B] = P[A] + P[B] - P[A \text{ and } B]$$
$$= 5/10 + 4/10 - 2/10$$
$$= 7/10$$

If there are no outcomes that are in both A and B, and hence $P[A \text{ and } B] = 0$, then there is no double-counting problem. If this is the case, then A and B are said to be mutually exclusive.

A and B are **mutually exclusive** if $P[A \text{ and } B] = 0$. If A and B are mutually exclusive, then the addition rule (Equation 3.2) simplifies to

$$P[A \text{ or } B] = P[A] + P[B]$$

If, in the committee example, all five of the people under 30 were male, then A and B would be mutually exclusive. The probability of selecting someone who is female or under 30 would be $5/10 + 4/10 = 9/10$.

Figure 3.4 shows two mutually exclusive sets. These six possible outcomes might be the number that comes up when a die is rolled. Set A contains the even numbers and set B contains the number 5. Sets A and B are mutually exclusive because the outcome cannot be both even and the number 5. The probability that the number that is rolled is either even or 5 is

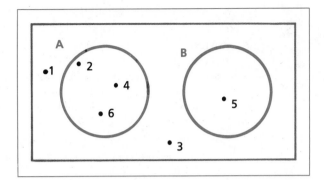

Figure 3.4 *Two mutually exclusive sets*

$$P[\text{even number or } 5] = P[\text{even number}] + P[5]$$
$$= 3/6 + 1/6$$
$$= 4/6$$

What about the probability of either an even number or a 6? Here the sets overlap because 6 is an even number.

$$P[\text{even number of } 6] = P[\text{even number}] + P[6] - P[\text{even number and } 6]$$
$$= 3/6 + 1/6 - 1/6$$
$$= 3/6$$

Let's do one more that is a little more complicated. You are playing a card game in which spades and honors (ace, king, queen, or jack) are valuable. If you draw a card from a full 52-card deck, what is the probability that it is one of these valuable cards? Think about it for a minute and see if you can figure out the answer before reading on.

Let's define A and B as follows:

A: a spade

B: an honor card

There are 13 spades and 16 honor cards (four in each of the four suits). Therefore, $P[A] = 13/52$ and $P[B] = 16/52$. Now, what is $P[A$ and $B]$? There are four cards (the ace, king, queen, and jack of spades) that are both spades and honors. So, $P[A$ and $B] = 4/52$. Our answer is

$$P[\text{space or honor}] = P[\text{spade}] + P[\text{honor}] - P[\text{spade and honor}]$$
$$= 13/52 + 16/52 - 4/52$$
$$= 25/52$$

There is nearly a 50 percent chance of drawing a card that is either a spade or an honor.

As one more example, imagine that you own a small business and have contracted to supply your product at a fixed price—$20 apiece. You like the security provided by a guaranteed customer, but you are worried about two possible catastrophes: (a) The Federal Reserve (Fed) will engineer a tight-money "credit crunch" that dries up the financing you need to buy raw materials and manufacture your product; and (b) the Fed will cause an easy-money inflation that drives up your material and labor costs and prevents you from making a profit at a price of $20 apiece. Perhaps you believe that the probability of tight money is .20 and the probability of easy money is .10. As tight money and easy money are mutually exclusive, the probability of one or the other is .20 + .10 = .30.

Exercises

3.3   You draw two cards out of a standard 52-card deck. What is the probability that one or the other of these cards is the queen of spades?

3.4   You are playing backgammon and need to roll a 1 on either of your two dice to hit your opponent. What are your chances?

3.5   A security analyst tells you that there is a .3 chance that a certain company will be bought up by Exxon and a .3 chance that it will be purchased by Mobil. What is the probability that it will be acquired by one or the other of these two companies?

3.6   You run a small business and have two big fears: (a) you will be squeezed by a credit crunch; and (b) the Environmental Protection Agency (EPA) will decide that your product is a threat to the environment. You believe that there is a .20 probability of a credit crunch, a .05 probability of a damaging EPA decision, and a .01 chance that both of these disasters will occur. What is the probability that at least one of your fears will come true?

3.3   CONDITIONAL PROBABILITIES AND INDEPENDENT EVENTS

We are sometimes interested in the probability that one of the events in A will occur, given that one of the events in B occurs. This is written as $P[A|B]$ and is called a conditional probability.

> The **conditional probability** $P[A|B]$ is the probability that A occurs, given that B has occurred.

Be careful that you don't interpret $P[A|B]$ as the probability of A divided by the probability of B:

$$P[A|B] \quad \text{is } not \quad P[A]/P[B]$$

The notation $P[A|B]$ is a special shorthand for "the probability of A, given that we know B has occurred."

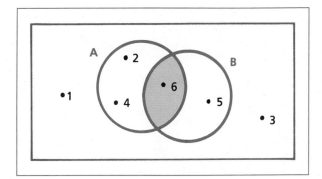

Figure 3.5 *A conditional probability*

Consider, for example, the roll of a standard six-sided die. The six possible outcomes are shown in the Venn diagram in Figure 3.5. The set A contains the even numbers 2, 4, and 6. Set B contains the numbers larger than 4. The conditional probability

$$P[A|B] = P[\text{even number}|\text{larger than 4}]$$

asks the question, "If we roll a number larger than 4, what is the probability that it is even?" To answer this question, we can think of B as a restricted-outcome space. If the number if larger than 4, then it must be either a 5 or a 6. Now, what fraction of these two outcomes are even? One-half is the answer. To obtain this answer, we compared the number of elements in both A and B (one)* with the number of elements in B (two). Given in terms of probability this translates into a ratio of the chances of both A and B happening to the chances of B happening. The conditional probability is given by this ratio of probabilities:

$$P[A|B] = \frac{P[A \text{ and } B]}{P[B]} \tag{3.3}$$

Here,

$$P[\text{even}|\text{larger than 4}] = P[\text{even and larger than 4}]/P[\text{larger than 4}]$$

$$= (1/6)/(2/6)$$

$$= 1/2$$

What about the conditional probability

$$P[B|A] = P[\text{larger than 4}|\text{even number}]$$

This probability asks the question, "If the number is even, what is the probability that it is larger than 4?" Now, we want to know the number of elements that are in both A and B relative to the number that are in A. That is,

---

*The expression "both A and B" is used here (and elsewhere) to signify the area of intersection of the two sets, not their combined areas.

$$P[B|A] = \frac{P[A \text{ and } B]}{P[A]} \tag{3.4}$$

Here,

$$P[\text{larger than 4}|\text{even}] = P[\text{larger than 4 and even}]/P[\text{even}]$$

$$= (1/6)/(3/6)$$

$$= 1/3$$

Notice the differences between Equations 3.3 and 3.4. Conditional probabilities are important, but they can be confusing. Go through this example again if you are not sure that you understand what $P[A|B]$ and $P[B|A]$ mean.

It is also important to recognize the difference between $P[A]$ and $P[A|B]$. The expression $P[A]$ asks, "Considering all possible outcomes, what is the probability that A occurs?" The expression $P[A|B]$, in contrast, asks, "Assuming that one of the outcomes in B occurs, what is the probability that A also occurs?" These two probabilities are not equal unless A and B are independent.

> A and B are **independent** if $P[A|B] = P[A]$. If $P[A|B]$ does equal $P[A]$, then $P[B|A] = P[B]$, too.

The conditional clause "given that B has occurred" means that you have this additional information that may persuade you to revise your probability of A occurring. The logic behind the concept of independence is that the knowledge that one has occurred does not alter the probability that the other has also occurred.

In the die example shown in Figure 3.5, A and B are, in fact, independent. The probability of an even number is $1/2$. If the number is larger than 4, then the probability that it is even is still $1/2$, so both $P[A]$ and $P[A|B]$ are $1/2$. Similarly, both $P[B]$ and $P[B|A]$ are $1/3$. The probability of a number larger than 4 is $1/3$, and if the number is even (2, 4, or 6), then the probability that it is larger than 4 is still $1/3$.

Age and Sex

To reinforce the ideas of conditional probabilities and independence, let's do a somewhat different example. Table 3.1 gives some 1980 Census data on age and

Table 3.1   *Age and sex in the United States*

	Males	*Females*	*Total*
Less than 25 years old	47,625,000	46,131,000	93,756,000
25 Years and older	62,408,000	70,341,000	132,749,000
Total	110,033,000	116,472,000	226,505,000

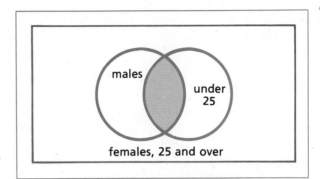

Figure 3.6   *One representation of data for age and sex in the U.S.*

sex in the United States. One possible Venn diagram that results from these data is shown in Figure 3.6.

Now imagine that we are going to reach into the United States and pick someone at random. What is the probability that this person will be a male? What is the probability that this person will be at least 25 years old? Are age and sex independent? Let's use M and F to denote male and female and use "25" and "not 25" to label age. Table 3.1 yields the following probabilities:

$$P[M \text{ and not } 25] = 47,625,000/226,505,000 = .210$$

$$P[M \text{ and } 25] = 62,408,000/226,505,000 = .276$$

$$P[F \text{ and not } 25] = 46,131,000/226,505,000 = .204$$

$$P[F \text{ and } 25] = 70,341,000/226,505,000 = .311$$

We can also see from the totals in Table 3.1 that

$$P[M] = 110,033,000/226,505,000 = .486$$

$$P[F] = 116,472,000/226,505,000 = .514$$

$$P[\text{not } 25] = 93,756,000/226,505,000 = .414$$

$$P[25] = 132,749,000/226,505,000 = .586$$

The population of the United States is 51 percent female and 59 percent at least 25 years old.

Now let's ask a trickier question. If the person picked is 25 or older, what is the probability that this person is male? Using our conditional probability rule,

$$P[M|25] = P[M \text{ and } 25]/P[25]$$

$$= .276/.582$$

$$= .474$$

Similarly, the probability that someone under 25 is a male works out to be

$$P[M|\text{not } 25] = P[M \text{ and not } 25]/P[\text{not } 25]$$

$$= .210/.414$$

$$= .507$$

These conditional probabilities compare to an overall .486 probability of being male. Therefore, age and sex are not independent. The young are predominantly male because babies are slightly more likely to be male. The old are predominantly female because auto accidents, murders, wars, and health problems give males a shorter life expectancy.

Winning Streaks

In any fair game of chance, a player will win some and lose some (or, it often seems, win some and lose many). The wins sometimes will be scattered and, at other times, will be bunched together. Many gamblers attach a great deal of significance to these runs of luck. They apparently believe that luck is some sort of infectious disease that a player catches and then takes awhile to get over. For example, Clement McQuaid, ''author, vintner, home gardener and keen student of gambling games, most of which he has played profitably,'' offers this advice:

> There is only one way to show a profit. Bet light on your losses and heavy on your wins. Many good gamblers follow a specific procedure. a. *Bet minimums when you're losing.* . . . b. *Bet heavy when you're winning.* . . . c. *Quit on a losing streak, not a winning streak.* While the law of mathematic probability averages out, it doesn't operate on a set pattern. Wins and losses go in streaks more often than they alternate. If you've had a good winning streak and a loss follows it, bet minimums long enough to see whether or not another winning streak is coming up. If it isn't, quit while you're still ahead.[2]

You will indeed show a profit if you win your big bets and lose only your small ones. But how are you to know in advance whether you are going to win or lose your next bet? Suppose you are playing craps and have won three times in a row. You know that you have been winning and you are probably excited about it, but dice have no memories or emotions. Games were invented by people. Dice don't know the difference between a winning number and a losing number. Dice do not know what happened on the last roll and do not care whether you are betting heavily or lightly on the next roll. A die is just an inanimate celluloid cube and each of the six sides is still equally likely to come up. The outcomes are independent in that the probabilities are the same, roll after roll.

Sometimes you will win four times in a row, but at least as often, you will win three in a row and then lose the fourth. Sometimes you will win five times in a row, but at least as often, you will win four in a row and then lose the fifth. You may fondly recall those rare occasions when you won four, five, or more times in a row, and you will wish that you had bet more heavily. Unfortunately, there is just no way to predict when a winning streak will begin or end. Games of chance are the classic example of independent events.

Exercises

3.7 A single six-sided die is rolled. Let A contain the odd numbers 1, 3, and 5 and let B contain the numbers larger than 3 (4, 5, and 6). What is $P[A]$? $P[B]$? $P[A|B]$? $P[B|A]$? $P[A$ and $B]$? Are A and B independent?

3.8 Use Table 3.1 to calculate $P[F|25]$ and $P[25|F]$. Explain what these probabilities mean. Use these probabilities to see whether sex and age are independent.

3.9 You flip a coin seven times. What is the probability of heads on the seventh flip, given that you've gotten heads on five of the first six flips?

3.10 Evaluate this advice for winning at craps at Las Vegas:

> First of all, try to find a hot table. Never remain at a cold one. Always make it a policy to keep looking—move around! A tip-off might be the yelling crowd where a hot roll may be taking place. Another indication usually is a lot of chips spread every which way around the table by numerous players. If the action is continuous, you'll know you've caught a good table. Keep in mind that it is far more lucrative to tag along on the tail end of a hot roll than it is to go in fresh on a cold one. And no one moving from table to table will actually catch a hot roll from the beginning. If 65 percent of a streak is caught, it's enough![3]

● **3.11** Let's pick words at random from a typical book and see if there is any pattern in the arrangements of the vowels and consonants. In particular, we'll use the words on page 76 of this chapter. Let p_1 be the probability that the first letter of a word chosen at random from that page is a vowel, and let p_2 be the probability that the second letter of a word chosen at random is a vowel. Do you think that these two events are independent? Use the words on page 76 of this chapter to calculate p_1 and p_2 and to check your theory about independence.

3.4 THE MULTIPLICATION RULE

The equations for conditional probabilities show us how to calculate $P[A|B]$ and $P[B|A]$ if we know $P[A$ and $B]$, $P[A]$, and $P[B]$. But often, we are interested in the other way around; we know $P[A|B]$ or $P[B|A]$ and want to calculate $P[A$ and $B]$. We can make this calculation by rearranging Equations 3.4 and 3.3 to obtain the **multiplication rule:**

$$P[A \text{ and } B] = P[A]P[B|A] \tag{3.5}$$

$$P[A \text{ and } B] = P[B]P[A|B] \tag{3.6}$$

For both A and B to occur, first one must occur and then, given that it has occurred, the other must occur, too. Notice that $P[A \text{ and } B]$ can be calculated in either of two ways, depending on the information at our fingertips.

Let's do an example. What is the probability of drawing two aces in a row out of a standard 52-card deck? Let A_1 stand for an ace on the first pick and A_2 for an ace on the second pick. The probability that we're after is

$$P[A_1 \text{ and } A_2] = P[A_1]P[A_2|A_1]$$

$P[A_1]$ is 4/52 because there are initially 4 aces scattered among the 52 cards. If we are lucky enough to pick an ace, then the odds of picking another ace are diminished because there will be only 3 aces left among the 51 remaining cards, $P[A_2|A_1] = 3/51$. The probability of drawing 2 aces in a row is

$$P[A_1 \text{ and } A_2] = \left(\frac{4}{52}\right)\left(\frac{3}{51}\right) = .0045$$

If we attempted this feat over and over again, we would succeed less than 5 times in every 1000 tries.

A $P[A \text{ and } B]$ question usually can be given a sequential structure and then solved by the multiplication rule. Even if we were picking two cards simultaneously, we could imagine that one was drawn slightly before the other and then use the formula given previously. The logic of an "A and B" problem is that two conditions, A and B, have to be met. The first condition will be met a certain fraction of the time. Then, a fraction of these times, the second condition will be met. Both conditions will be met only a fraction of a fraction of the time.

We can visualize this logic by thinking of a probability tree in which the branches are not equally likely. Figure 3.7 shows such a tree. Here, we need to pick two aces. We will pick the first ace 4/52 of the time and, then, 3/51 of these times we will successfully draw the second ace. Our probability of drawing two aces is a fraction 3/51 of the fraction 4/52, or (4/52)(3/51).

This logic can be extended indefinitely. Consider the probability of drawing four straight aces:

$P[A_1 \text{ and } A_2 \text{ and } A_3 \text{ and } A_4]$

$$= P[A_1]P[A_2|A_1]P[A_3|A_1 \text{ and } A_2]P[A_4|A_1 \text{ and } A_2 \text{ and } A_3]$$

$$= \left(\frac{4}{52}\right)\left(\frac{3}{51}\right)\left(\frac{2}{50}\right)\left(\frac{1}{49}\right)$$

$$= .0000037$$

If you were to try again and again, you could anticipate drawing four straight aces about four times in every 1 million tries.

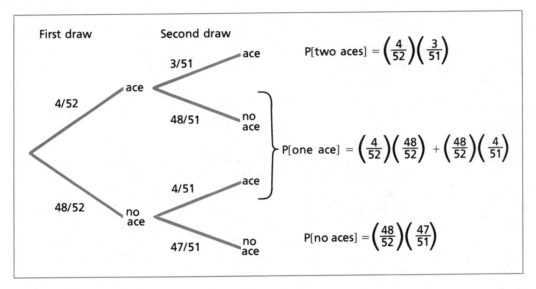

Figure 3.7 *A probability tree for two aces in a row*

These draws are not independent of each other, because the odds change as cards are taken out of the deck. If, instead, the selected card is put back into the deck and the deck is shuffled thoroughly, then the probability of picking an ace remains 4/52 on each draw. These draws are independent of each other because the probability is not affected by the outcomes of other draws. This is an example of the distinction between sampling *without* replacement and sampling *with* replacement.

> **Sampling without replacement** means that the selected item is removed and cannot be selected again.

> **Sampling with replacement** means that the selected item is replaced and can be selected again.

With replacement, the probability of picking four straight aces is

$$P[A_1 \text{ and } A_2 \text{ and } A_3 \text{ and } A_4] = P[A_1]P[A_2]P[A_3]P[A_4]$$

$$= \left(\frac{4}{52}\right)\left(\frac{4}{52}\right)\left(\frac{4}{52}\right)\left(\frac{4}{52}\right)$$

$$= .0000350$$

The odds are somewhat improved because you now may be able to draw the same ace again, but it is still a very unlikely outcome.

The Incentive to Know Slow Horses

Some racetracks offer ''superfectas'' in which a great deal of money can be won by correctly picking the first four finishers in a horse race. From time to time, there are allegations that jockeys are persuaded to slow their horses to keep them out of the top four places. Superfectas provide a considerable incentive for this chicanery because the chances of picking the first four finishers correctly are much higher if some horses can be excluded.

To illustrate the point simply, let's assume that the order of finish is completely random. If there are eight horses in the race, what is the probability of picking the first four finishers in correct order? This is a multiplication problem. You must pick first place, second place, third place, and fourth place correctly. If eight horses are equally likely to win, then the probability that your selected horse will finish first is 1/8. Now, if you get first place right, then there are seven possible second-place finishers, and the probability that your second-place pick will also be correct is 1/7. So far, so good. If you pick the first two right, then there are six horses left that could finish third, and the probability of a correct pick is 1/6. Similarly, if your first three selections are right, then you have a 1/5 chance of picking fourth place correctly, too.

Now, to put these numbers together, let ''1st'' represent the correct selection of the first-place horse, let ''2nd'' represent the correct pick of the second-place horse, and so on. Then,

P[1st and 2nd and 3rd and 4th]

Exercises

3.12   You are playing poker and have been dealt three clubs and two spades. If you discard the two spades, what are the chances of drawing two clubs to give you a flush?

3.13   What are the sucker's chances of winning this game:

> Take a small opaque bottle and seven olives, two of which are green, five black. The green ones are considered the ''unlucky'' ones. Place all seven olives in the bottle, the neck of which should be such a size that it will allow only one olive to pass through at a time. Ask the sucker to shake them and then wager that he will not be able to roll out three olives without getting an unlucky green one amongst them.[4]

3.14   You want to pick the first four finishers (in order) in an eight-horse race, and it costs $2 to make one of these four-horse picks. You decide to guarantee success by betting on all possible four-horse combinations. How much money will this ''blanket bet'' cost? If you know that three of the these eight horses will not finish among the top four, how much will a blanket bet cost?

3.15   You want to pick the first four finishers in a six-horse race. If the order of finish is random, what is your probability of success? If you can rule out one horse, what is your probability of success? Now, compare your answers with the probabilities given in the text

$$= P[\text{1st}] \, P[\text{2nd}|\text{1st}] \, P[\text{3rd}|\text{1st and 2nd}] \, P[\text{4th}|\text{1st and 2nd and 3rd}]$$

$$= \left(\frac{1}{8}\right) \left(\frac{1}{7}\right) \frac{1}{6} \left(\frac{1}{5}\right)$$

$$= .0006$$

What if you were certain that a particular horse will not be one of the first four finishers? Then, there would be only seven horses to worry about, and

$$P[\text{1st and 2nd and 3rd and 4th}] = \left(\frac{1}{7}\right) \left(\frac{1}{6}\right) \left(\frac{1}{5}\right) \left(\frac{1}{4}\right)$$

$$= .0012$$

If you can rule out one of the horses, then your probability of winning the superfecta is doubled.

What if you could rule out three horses? There would be only five horses to consider, and

$$P[\text{1st and 2nd and 3rd and 4th}] = \left(\frac{1}{5}\right) \left(\frac{1}{4}\right) \left(\frac{1}{3}\right) \left(\frac{1}{2}\right)$$

$$= .0083$$

If you know that three horses will run slow enough to lose, then your probability of winning the superfecta is fourteen times greater than when the race is fair.

for an eight-horse superfecta. Is there greater incentive to guarantee a slow horse in a six-horse or an eight-horse superfecta? If you were a statistical consultant to your state gambling commission, what recommendation could you make on the basis of these calculations?

3.16 A bag contains 4 red balls, 5 white balls, and 6 blue balls. Determine the following probabilities:

a. $P[R]$ if 1 ball is drawn.
b. $P[R \text{ or } W]$ if 1 ball is drawn.
c. $P[R, W, \text{ and } B, \text{ in that order}]$ if 3 balls are drawn without replacement.
d. $P[R, W, \text{ and } B, \text{ in that order}]$ if 3 balls are drawn with replacement.

• **3.17** (*continuation*) In the preceding exercise, what is the probability that 3 balls, drawn without replacement, will be red, white, and blue, in any order?

3.5 THE SUBTRACTION RULE

We've seen how the multiplication rule can be extended easily to a long sequence of events. The addition rule is not so easily extended. For two sets of outcomes, the addition rule is

$$P[A \text{ or } B] = P[A] + P[B] - P[A \text{ and } B]$$

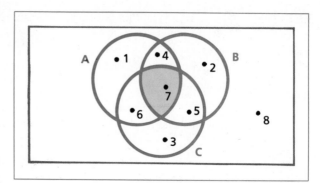

Figure 3.8 *The addition rule for three groups*

With three sets, the correction for double counting becomes more complicated. Figure 3.8 shows the relevant Venn diagram. Points 1 through 7 are representative outcomes that should each be counted once in calculating *P*[*A* or *B* or *C*]. If we simply add the three probabilities *P*[*A*], *P*[*B*], and *P*[*C*], we include the following:

probability	outcomes
P[*A*]	1, 4, 6, 7
P[*B*]	2, 4, 5, 7
P[*C*]	3, 5, 6, 7

The summation *P*[*A*] + *P*[*B*] + *P*[*C*] counts outcomes 1, 2, and 3 once; it counts outcomes 4, 5, and 6 twice; and it counts outcome 7 three times. What if we now subtract *P*[*A* and *B*], *P*[*A* and *C*], and *P*[*B* and *C*]? That will undo the double counting of outcomes 4, 5, and 6, but it will also leave outcome 7 uncounted. So, the correct rule must be

$$P[A \text{ or } B \text{ or } C] = P[A] + P[B] + P[C]$$

$$- P[A \text{ and } B] - P[A \text{ and } C] - P[B \text{ and } C]$$

$$+ P[A \text{ and } B \text{ and } C] \qquad (3.7)$$

This expression is complex but not unusable. However, as we go to more than three sets, the addition rule quickly becomes unwieldy. Fortunately, we have a subtraction rule to spare us such misery.

The **subtraction rule** is a powerful ploy based on the simple observation that the probability of something occurring is equal to one minus the probability that it does not occur.

$$P[A] = 1 - P[\text{not } A]$$

This is very useful because it often is easier to figure out the probability of something not occurring than it is to figure out the probability that it will occur.

Consider, for example, the probability of getting at least one head in three flips of a coin. This is a three-set addition problem. We want to know the probability of a head on the first flip or the second flip or the third flip. We could coerce an answer out of Equation 3.7:

$$P[H_1 \text{ or } H_2 \text{ or } H_3] = P[H_1] + P[H_2] + P[H_3]$$
$$- P[H_1 \text{ and } H_2] - P[H_1 \text{ and } H_3] - P[H_2 \text{ and } H_3]$$
$$+ P[H_1 \text{ and } H_2 \text{ and } H_3]$$
$$= \frac{1}{2} + \frac{1}{2} + \frac{1}{2} - \frac{1}{4} - \frac{1}{4} - \frac{1}{4} + \frac{1}{8}$$
$$= 7/8$$

The subtraction rule provides an easy alternative. The probability of at least one head is equal to one minus the probability of no heads, or one minus the probability of three straight tails. The probability of three straight tails is an easy multiplication rule: $(1/2)(1/2)(1/2) = 1/8$. Thus, the probability of at least one head in three flips is $1 - 1/8 = 7/8$, as simple as that.

De Mere's Problem

We're now ready to tackle de Mere's problem. De Mere was puzzled by his experience with two wagers:

1. Roll at least one 6 in four throws of a single die.
2. Roll at least one double-6 in twenty-four throws of a pair of dice.

The probability of a 6 on a single throw of a die is $1/6$. A naive calculation of the probability of a 6 with four throws would be $4/6$. This calculation is wrong because of the double-counting problem. Apparently de Mere was using it as a rough approximation to judge that the odds were in his favor, and he was winning more than half the time.

The probability of a double-6 on a single throw of a pair of dice is $1/36$. A naive calculation of the probability of a double-6 with twenty-four throws is $24/36$, which reduces to $4/6$ again. There is still a double-counting problem, but de Mere apparently believed that, as a rough approximation, the odds should be in his favor; yet, he lost this second bet more often than he won. He turned to Pascal for an explanation.

We could try to construct a probability tree and enumerate the possible outcomes, but the second bet has 36^{24} branches, which is many more than I want to draw. We could try the addition rule, but the addition rule for twenty-four sets is more complicated than I want to think about. The easy path is, of course, the subtraction rule. The desired probabilities are, with remarkable simplicity,

Matched Birthdays

In a class with 23 students, what is the probability that at least 2 students were born on the same day of the year? Surprisingly, the probability is greater than 1/2!

How would we go about figuring such a probability? This is a tough addition problem: the probability that one student has the same birthday as any of the other 22 students, plus the probability that a second student has the same birthday as any of the other students, and so on, in addition to a mind-boggling adjustment for all of the double counting. The easy alternative is, you guessed it, the subtraction rule. The probability of at least one matched birthday is one minus the probability of no matches.

It is traditional in this classic problem to ignore February 29 and to assume that all of the remaining 365 days of the year are equally likely to be a birthday. Now, pick any two students. The first has some birthday, say November 11. The probability that the second person has a different birthday is 364/365. Now add a third student. The probability of another different birthday, given that the first two didn't match, is 363/365. The probability that the first two don't match and that the third also doesn't match is the product of these probabilities:

P[1 & 2 don't match and 3 doesn't match 1 or 2]

$\quad = P$[1 & 2 don't match]

$\qquad \cdot P$[3 doesn't match 1 or 2/1 & 2 don't match]

$$= \left(\frac{364}{365}\right)\left(\frac{363}{365}\right)$$

Extending this logic, the probability that none of the 23 students' birthdays match is

$$\left(\frac{364}{365}\right)\left(\frac{363}{365}\right)\left(\frac{362}{365}\right) \cdots \left(\frac{343}{365}\right)$$

and the probability of at least one match is

$$1 - \left(\frac{364}{365}\right)\left(\frac{363}{365}\right)\left(\frac{362}{365}\right) \cdots \left(\frac{343}{365}\right) = .51$$

Analogous computations show that the probability of at least one matched birthday is .71 with 30 students, .97 with 50 students, and .9999997 with 100 students. Unless you have an unusually small class, there are probably at least two students in your statistics class who share a birthday.

1. $P[\text{at least one 6}] = 1 - P[\text{no 6s in 4 throws}]$

$$= 1 - (5/6)^4$$

$$= .518$$

2. $P[\text{at least one double-6}] = 1 - P[\text{no double-6s in 24 throws}]$

$$= 1 - (35/36)^{24}$$

$$= .491$$

De Mere's experience was consistent with the correct probabilities. The odds were with him on the first bet, but they were against him on the second bet.

The more general moral is, if you've got a problem that seems hopelessly complicated, try the subtraction rule. It just may be the trick you need.

Exercises

3.18 In the carnival game Queens, there are six cards—two kings, two queens, and two jacks. The cards are turned face down and shuffled. The player picks two cards and wins if neither card is a queen. What is the probability of winning?

3.19 A dance studio once offered $25 worth of dancing lessons to anyone with a "lucky" dollar bill containing a 2, 5, or 7 in its eight-digit serial number. What is the probability that a dollar bill will win this prize? If you have three dollar bills, what is the probability that at least one will win?

3.20 You are playing poker and have been dealt the three of clubs, the five of clubs, the seven of clubs, the jack of clubs, and the jack of spades. If you keep the pair of jacks and throw the three small clubs, what is the probability of drawing at least one more jack? If you instead keep the four clubs, what is the probability of drawing a fifth club?

• **3.21** If you are in a class with 23 students, what is the probability that at least one other person has the same birthday as <u>you</u>? What if there are 100 students in the class? 250 students? (Be careful!)

• **3.22** In a family of four people, what is the probability that at least two persons have the same astrological sign? (Assume that each of the twelve astrological signs is equally likely to contain someone's birthday.)

3.6 BAYES' THEOREM

We've discussed the conditional probabilities $P[A|B]$ and $P[B|A]$, and we've seen how they can be used via the multiplication rule to find $P[A \text{ and } B]$. Sometimes we are interested in the special problem of converting knowledge of $P[A|B]$ into a calculation of $P[B|A]$. That is, we know the probability that A will occur, given that B has occurred, but what we want to know is the probability that B will occur, given that A has occurred. For instance, we may know the probability that a test will be "positive" if we have a certain disease, but what we are interested in is the probability of disease when the test turns out "positive." We can use the multiplication rule and a bit of logic to make these sorts of conversions successfully.

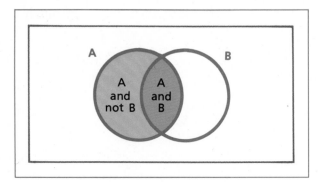

Figure 3.9 *A tricky way to calculate* P[A]

Reverend Bayes, as we saw in Chapter 2, was interested in a very special problem, using known facts to confirm the existence of God. He seemingly wanted to calculate the probability that God exists, given what we observe about the world: $P[\text{God}|\text{observations}]$. Our logic is concerned with the reverse question—the probability that we would observe what we do, if there were a god: $P[\text{observations}|\text{God}]$. Bayes' theorem tells us how to go from one conditional probability to the other.* Bayes did not prove the existence of God, but his conversion theorem has turned out to be extremely useful, nonetheless. It is also the foundation for the modern Bayesian approach to probability and statistics.

The multiplication rule, Equations 3.5 and 3.6, can be written in two ways,

$$P[A \text{ and } B] = P[A]\, P[B|A]$$

$$P[A \text{ and } B] = P[B]\, P[A|B]$$

If we substitute one equation into the other to eliminate $P[A \text{ and } B]$, we obtain **Bayes' theorem:**

$$P[B|A] = \frac{P[B]\, P[A|B]}{P[A]} \tag{3.8}$$

This equation is the vehicle for converting $P[A|B]$ into $P[B|A]$.

In practice, as we will soon see, $P[A]$ often is not immediately apparent in the kinds of questions that Bayes' theorem is designed to answer. But, with a subtle trick, $P[A]$ can be derived from information that is available. Figure 3.9 uses a

---

*We must speculate about Bayes' motives because little is known about him. He left few published writings and these do not even contain what is now called ''Bayes' theorem.'' It was Laplace[5] who actually wrote down the general rule and then labeled it ''Bayes' theorem.'' Bayes did work out some specific problems of this sort, such as using the frequency with which some event has occurred to calculate the probability that the probability of this event occurring lies in a certain range. The friend who found Bayes' major paper and had an annotated version published posthumously argued that Bayes' approach could be used ''to confirm the argument taken from final causes for the existence of the Diety.''[6] It is not certain, though that this is the usage that Bayes himself had in mind.

Venn diagram to reveal the trick. The set A consists of two parts that are shaded in grey and in color. The color portion is "A and B," which we have analyzed frequently. The remaining, grey portion of A is "A and not B," which comprises those outcomes that are in A and are not in B. The multiplication rule tells us that the probabilities of an outcome being in these two separate parts of A are given by

$$P[A \text{ and } B] = P[B]\ P[A|B]$$

$$P[A \text{ and not } B] = P[\text{not } B]\ P[A|\text{not } B]$$

Logic tells us that an outcome in A must be in one part or the other, either in "A and B" or in "A and not B," and the addition rule tells us that, because the two parts are mutually exclusive, the probability of being in one part or the other is the simple sum of the separate probabilities:

$$P[A] = P[A \text{ and } B] + P[A \text{ and not } B]$$

$$= P[B]\ P[A|B] + P[\text{not } B]\ P[A|\text{not } B] \tag{3.9}$$

Now, substituting Equation 3.9 into Equation 3.8, we obtain Bayes' theorem in its most frequently used form,*

$$P[B|A] = \frac{P[B]\ P[A|B]}{P[B]\ P[A|B] + P[\text{not } B]\ P[A|\text{not } B]} \tag{3.10}$$

A Rare Disease

Enough theory! On to an example. Consider a rare disease that can be accurately detected by a medical test. Let "disease" and "no disease" signify the presence or absence of the disease, and let "yes" and "no" represent the test results. We'll assume that only one person in a hundred has this disease:

$$P[\text{disease}] = .01$$

$$P[\text{no disease}] = .99$$

In either case, whether the person does or does not have the disease, the test gives a correct diagnosis 95 percent of the time:

$$P[\text{"yes"}|\text{disease}] = .95$$

$$P[\text{"no"}|\text{no disease}] = .95$$

It is important to recognize precisely what these conditional probabilities mean. If you have the disease, there is a 95 percent chance that the test will register "yes"

---

*Sometimes, the outcomes are divided into several sets: $B_1, B_2, \ldots, B_n$ instead of just B and "not B." If, like B and "not B," these sets include all possible outcomes, then Equations 3.9 and 3.10 can be generalized by using

$$P[A] = P[B_1]\ P[A|B_1] + P[B_2]\ P[A|B_2] + \cdots + P[B_n]\ P[A|B_n]$$

and a 5 percent chance that the test will register "no." If you do not have the disease, there is a .95 probability that the test will register "no" and a .05 probability that the test will register "yes."

Most of us are interested in the reverse question. If the test does register "yes," what is the probability that we have the disease? If the test registers "no," what is the probability that we do not have the disease? These probabilities are not .95! The probability that the test will say "yes" if you have the disease is not the same concept as the probability that you have the disease if the test does, in fact, say "yes." To go from the former to the latter, we need Bayes' theorem.

$P[\text{disease}|\text{"yes"}]$

$$= \frac{P[\text{disease and "yes"}]}{P[\text{"yes"}]}$$

$$= \frac{P[\text{disease}]\ P[\text{"yes"}|\text{disease}]}{P[\text{disease}]P[\text{"yes"}|\text{disease}] + P[\text{no disease}]P[\text{"yes"}|\text{no disease}]}$$

$$= \frac{(.01)(.95)}{(.01)(.95) + (.99)(.05)}$$

$$= .161$$

One percent of the entire population has the disease. Sixteen percent of those diagnosed "yes" have the disease. The "yes" reading makes it more likely that you have the disease, but it is still far from certain.

We can also calculate the probability of disease when the test result is negative:

$P[\text{disease}|\text{"no"}]$

$$= \frac{P[\text{disease}]P[\text{"no"}|\text{disease}]}{P[\text{disease}]P[\text{"no"}|\text{disease}] + P[\text{no disease}]P[\text{"no"}|\text{no disease}]}$$

$$= \frac{(.01)(.05)}{(.01)(.05) + (.99)(.95)}$$

$$= .0005$$

If you have not been tested, then there is a .01 probability that you have the disease. If you are tested and the results are negative, then the probability that you have the disease falls to .0005.

These results are typical of the effects of applying Bayes' theorem. We can often interpret the situation as one in which initial probabilities are revised in the light of empirical evidence. Here, the initial probability of disease is .01. After the test, this probability is either revised up to .16 or down to .0005, depending on whether the test reading is positive or negative. Academics call these initial and revised probabilities the *prior* and *posterior* probabilities.

The **prior probability** $P[A]$ is the probability assigned to A before certain data are gathered. The **posterior probability** $P[A|\text{data}]$ is the revised probability, given these observed data.

As more data are collected, the probabilities can be revised again and again. For example, in the rare-disease problem, if the first diagnosis is positive, the doctor may recommend a second test. The .16 probability of disease will then be revised further, up or down, depending on the outcome of the second test. Exercise 3.40 works out these details.

Adjusting the Weather Forecast

Your favorite television weather forecaster may pretend to be a standup comic, an underweight starlet, or an overweight turkey. Some even pretend to be meteorologists. If you pay attention to their forecasts, you will find that they make mistakes, and you may find that their mistakes are disproportionately of certain kinds. If so, you can make your own forecasts by adjusting the television forecasts.

Perhaps you live in a city where there is .01 inch of precipitation (either rain or snow) on about one out of every three days. Yet your friendly television forecaster predicts "wet" or "dry" by flipping a coin. As a result, there are a disproportionate number of "wet" forecasts. You could do better with homemade forecasts that ignored the television forecaster and just used the historical data, giving a 1/3 probability of precipitation.

A more subtle bias occurs when the forecaster is informed, but tilts the forecasts one way or the other. There are some days when the forecast is clearcut; the forecaster sticks his or her head out the window and is soaked. There are many days when the weather is very uncertain. An optimistic forecaster might invariably forecast "dry" on these iffy days, to keep the show happy and upbeat. In contrast, a pessimistic forecaster may always call the close ones "wet," to avoid the wrath of angry viewers caught in the rain without an umbrella. In either case, you can adjust these slanted forecasts to get a better estimate of the chances of precipitation.

To illustrate this adjustment, we'll consider the case of the forecaster who, "when in doubt, calls it 'wet.' " The forecaster who, "when in doubt, calls it 'dry,' " is left as an exercise at the end of the chapter. Let's say that it is dry two out of three days and that one-fourth of these dry days are so obviously going to be dry that the forecaster predicts "dry." But on three-fourths of the dry days, the weather appears sufficiently uncertain that the forecaster predicts "wet" just to be safe. Thus, $P[\text{"dry"}|\text{dry}] = .25$ and $P[\text{"wet"}|\text{dry}] = .75$, where the quotation marks signify the forecast. When it is actually going to be wet, there is only a .05 chance that this cautious forecaster will be misled into making a "dry" forecast: $P[\text{"wet"}|\text{wet}] = .95$ and $P[\text{"dry"}|\text{wet}] = .05$.

Some Guilty People Go Free

In the United States, defendants are presumed innocent until they are proven guilty "beyond a reasonable doubt." The intent is to protect the innocent fully, because it is "better to let nine guilty people go free, than to send one innocent person to prison."

For illustrative purposes, let's assume that 75 percent of all defendants brought to trial are guilty, 70 percent of all guilty defendants are convicted, and 90 percent of all innocent defendants are set free. These hypothetical numbers imply that, on the average, out of every 1000 defendants, 750 are guilty and 250 are innocent. Of the 750 who are guilty, .7(750) = 525 are convicted, while the remaining 225 go free. Of the 250 who are innocent, .9(250) = 225 go free while 25 are convicted. With these figures, it is indeed true that for every innocent person who goes to prison, nine guilty people go free (225/25 = 9).

Now let's ask two somewhat different questions. Of those who do go free, what fraction are actually guilty? Of those who are convicted, what fraction are innocent? We can find the answers in the previous data. If 225 guilty people go free and 225 innocent people go free, half of those who go free are, in fact, guilty. If 525 guilty people and 25 innocent people are convicted, 25/550 = .045 (4.5 percent) of the people convicted are, in fact, innocent. See Figure 1.

These calculations are actually an application of Bayes' rule. Here are the formulas, using "G" for guilty and "I" for innocent:

$$P[G|\text{go free}] = \frac{P[G]\,P[\text{go free}|G]}{P[G]P[\text{go free}|G] + P[I]P[\text{go free}|I]}$$

$$= \frac{.75(.3)}{.75(.3) + .25(.9)}$$

$$= \frac{.225}{.225 + .225}$$

$$= .5$$

If we are aware of this forecaster's conservative bias, how can we adjust the forecasts to obtain a more accurate weather gauge? Bayes' formula tells us how to combine the historical data with the forecaster's record to obtain revised weather probabilities:

$$P[\text{dry}|\text{"dry"}] = \frac{P[\text{dry}]\,P[\text{"dry"}|\text{dry}]}{P[\text{dry}]\,P[\text{"dry"}|\text{dry}] + P[\text{wet}]\,P[\text{"dry"}|\text{wet}]}$$

$$= \frac{(2/3)(.25)}{(2/3)(.25) + (1/3)(.05)}$$

$$= .91$$

and

$$P[\text{I}|\text{convicted}] = \frac{P[\text{I}]\ P[\text{convicted}|\text{I}]}{P[\text{I}]P[\text{convicted}|\text{I}] + P[\text{G}]P[\text{convicted}|\text{G}]}$$

$$= \frac{.25(.1)}{.25(.1) + .75(.7)}$$

$$= \frac{.25}{.25 + .525}$$

$$= .045$$

750 guilty defendants

525
convicted

225 go free

250 innocent defendants

25 convicted

225 go free

Figure 1 *Of those who go free, half are guilty!*

$$P[\text{wet}|\text{``wet''}] = \frac{P[\text{wet}]\ P[\text{``wet''}|\text{wet}]}{P[\text{wet}]\ P[\text{``wet''}|\text{wet}] + P[\text{dry}]\ P[\text{``wet''}|\text{dry}]}$$

$$= \frac{(1/3)(.95)}{(1/3)(.95) + (2/3)(.75)}$$

$$= .39$$

You can be pretty confident that the weather will be dry when the forecast is "dry," because this cautious forecaster almost never says "dry" unless dry weather is almost certain. On the other hand, the "wet" forecasts are of little value because this forecaster makes them so readily. The revised .39 probability of precipitation is not much higher than the historical 1/3 probability. The ''dry'' forecast is informative, but the ''wet'' forecast is almost worthless.

A Miracle or a Trick?

Let's do a second example. This one is a little more off the wall, but it's closer to Bayes' initial inquiry into the existence of God. We saw earlier that the probability of drawing four straight aces from a standard 52-card deck is

$$(4/52)(3/51)(2/50)(1/49) = .0000037$$

This is a very unlikely event. If some character were to walk up to you, announce that she is going to pick four aces in a row, and then do just that, you are likely to suspect some chicanery. Perhaps she is really an amateur magician performing a prepared trick. The four aces may be prearranged on top of the deck, the deck may contain 52 aces, or she may be using other gimmicks that I am pledged not to reveal. If you had any suspicions that the draw was going to be rigged, these suspicions would certainly be bolstered by the woman's success. Four aces in a row is just too improbable to attribute to luck alone.

Bayes' theorem can handle this kind of situation, too. Let's say that, as a trusting person, you are 99 percent sure that this is a random draw from a standard deck. We can write this prior probability as

$$P[\text{standard deck}] = .99$$

$$P[\text{rigged deck}] = .01$$

What are your revised probabilities, after seeing the feat performed? The probabilities of picking four aces from a standard deck and from a perfectly rigged deck are

$$P[4 \text{ aces}|\text{standard deck}] = .0000037$$

$$P[4 \text{ aces}|\text{rigged deck}] = 1.0$$

Therefore, Bayes' theorem yields the posterior probability

$$P[\text{standard deck}|4 \text{ aces}] = \frac{.99(.0000037)}{.99(.0000037) + .01(1.0)}$$

$$= .000366$$

You went in trusting, 99 percent sure that the deck was fair, but after witnessing a feat that would be miraculously improbable if the deck were fair, you are 99.96 percent certain that the deck is rigged somehow.

This example is very much in the spirit of Bayes' intended application of his theorem. You have some theory about the world, such as this being a fair deck or there being a god. You then gather evidence. If the evidence is consistent with your theory, then you are more confident that your theory is correct. If the evidence is not consistent with your theory, then you are more doubtful of the theory. This general methodological approach can be applied to virtually all of the physical and social sciences. Indeed, this is the very way science proceeds, although by more informal means. A theory is accepted as long as it is successful in explaining what we observe. When new evidence accumulates that cannot be explained by the accepted theory, then the conventional wisdom is discredited and replaced with a new theory that can explain the data. Later in this book we will look at some formal procedures for confirming or rejecting hypotheses.

Objectivist Objections

There can be no dispute about the mechanics of Bayes' theorem. Its mathematics are impeccable. Objectivists, however, are not comfortable with the way it is applied. They don't like the whole idea of applying subjective probabilities to theories. Such probabilities vary whimsically from person to person and from time to time, and even more fundamentally, theories are not a proper subject for probabilities. A theory is either correct or it is incorrect; it is not correct half of the time, with its correctness being determined by the flip of a coin.

Let's go back to the doctor's office for the disease diagnosis. This is an example where the probabilities did not seem subjective or whimsical, yet strict objectivists would balk at assigning a probability of disease to a particular person. If we were about to pick one person at random from the population, we could legitimately say that there is a .01 probability that we will pick someone who has the disease. Once the person has been selected and is in the doctor's office being diagnosed, objectivists argue that we can no longer talk about a .01 or .16 probability of this person having the disease. The person either does or does not have the disease. We can say things like, "If a person does not have the disease, there is only a .05 probability of obtaining a positive diagnosis." But, objectivists argue that we should not turn this conditional probability around. A strict objectivist will not say, "Because the diagnosis is 'yes' for Mary Morgan, there is a .16 probability that Mary has the disease."

Bayesians argue that it is precisely this latter probability that is of interest. The .16 probability is used to convey our estimate of how likely it is that Mary has the disease. The interpretation is simply, and admittedly rather cruelly put in this instance, that we are indifferent between a wager in which we win $100 if Mary turns out to have the disease and a wager in which we win $100 if a red ball is drawn from a bag containing 16 red balls and 84 black balls.

The rigged-deck example is even more discomforting to objectivists because it requires a whimsical, subjective assessment of whether a particular unexamined deck is rigged or fair. Where did that .99 probability of a fair deck come from? It was apparently plucked out of the air and has nothing to support it. It is not reliable and cannot be scientific. Bayesians respond that, as fragile as this probability is, it is necessary to answer the relevant question: Do we believe the four-ace demonstration to be a miracle or a trick? Indeed, people make such whimsical, subjective assessments all the time. Bayes' theorem just shows us how to do the arithmetic correctly.

This objectivist-subjectivist debate may still seem like a lot of academic quarreling about nothing. You will soon see that it matters very much what one thinks about scientific theories and the use of data to test and revise these hypotheses.

Exercises

3.23 Two marksmen, Billy Bob and Jimmy Bob, simultaneously shoot at an empty beer can. Billy Bob has a .5 probability of hitting the can, while Jimmy Bob has a .25 probability of a hit. One bullet hits the can. What is the probability that it was fired by Billy Bob?

3.24 A certain lie detector is 90 percent accurate in detecting truth and lies. That is, $P[\text{``truth''}|\text{truth-teller}] = .90$ and $P[\text{``lies''}|\text{liar}] = .90$, where the quotation marks indicate the machine's assessment. Of the people tested, 80 percent are truth-tellers and 20 percent are liars. If the detector registers ``truth,'' what is the probability that this person is, in fact, telling the truth? If this lie detector registers ``lies,'' what is the probability that the person tested really is a liar? How would these probabilities be altered if half the people tested are truthful and half are liars?

3.25 Econ Oil is interested in the possibility of an oil deposit under the Astrodome in Houston, Texas. The local expert believes that there is a 30 percent chance that a significant oil field will be found there. An exploratory drilling (on the fifty-yard line) is positive. Historically, such tests are 70 percent accurate: $P[\text{positive}|\text{oil}] = .7$ and $P[\text{negative}|\text{no oil}] = .7$. What should Econ's revised probability of oil be? (Is this why the football team is called the Houston Oilers?)

• 3.26 Critically evaluate the following:

A large metropolitan police department made a check of the clothing worn by pedestrians killed in traffic at night. About four-fifths of the victims were wearing dark clothes and one-fifth light-colored garments. This study points up the rule that pedestrians are less likely to encounter traffic mishaps at night if they wear or carry something white after dark so that drivers can see them more easily.[7]

• 3.27 Twenty-five percent of the designer jeans manufactured for Claudia La Claudia have imperfections. Each pair of jeans is independently examined by two inspectors before it leaves the plant. Each inspector has a .9 probability of correctly spotting an imperfect pair. Perfect pairs are never classified ``imperfect.'' What is the probability that a pair of jeans that passes inspection is actually imperfect, if

a. jeans are rejected if either or both inspectors spots a flaw?
b. jeans are rejected only if both inspectors spot a flaw?

3.7 SUMMARY

A number of rules simplify the computation of probabilities. The addition rule gives us the probability that either A or B will occur, or both:

$$\text{addition rule:} \quad P[A \text{ or } B] = P[A] + P[B] - P[A \text{ and } B]$$

The multiplication rule gives the probability that both A and B will occur:

$$\text{multiplication rule:} \quad P[A \text{ and } B] = P[A]\, P[B|A]$$
$$= P[B]\, P[A|B]$$

where $P[B|A]$ is the conditional probability that B will occur, given that A has occurred.

The subtraction rule is handy because sometimes the easiest way to find the probability that A will occur is to reason out the probability that A will not occur:

$$\text{subtraction rule:} \quad P[A] = 1 - P[\text{not } A]$$

Bayes' theorem tells us how to get from $P[A|B]$ to $P[B|A]$:

$$\text{Bayes' theorem: } P[B|A] = \frac{P[B]\, P[A|B]}{P[A]}$$

$$= \frac{P[B]\, P[A|B]}{P[B]\, P[A|B] + P[\text{not } B]\, P[A|\text{not } B]}$$

Two events are said to be mutually exclusive if $P[A \text{ and } B] = 0$. Two events are independent if $P[A \text{ and } B] = P[A]\, P[B]$. When sampling with replacement from a deck of cards, for example, the outcomes are independent. When sampling without replacement, the outcomes are not independent because the probabilities change as cards are removed from the deck.

REVIEW EXERCISES

3.28 You are playing poker and have been dealt 2 fours, 2 tens, and an ace. You discard the ace. What is the probability of picking up either another four or another ten, to make a full house?

3.29 ''When the cards are dealt in bridge, there is a 1/4 probability that I will get the ace of spades and a 1/3 probability that my partner will get it if I don't. Therefore, we have a 7/12 probability of getting the ace of spades.'' Explain why you agree or disagree with this reasoning.

3.30 Each box of Cracker Jack candy contains a small prize. Each of the 10 children at Joanna's birthday party are given a box of Cracker Jack. If there are 50 equally likely prizes, what is the probability that every child will get a different prize?

3.31   Verbally explain the difference between two events being independent and being mutually exclusive. Give an example to illustrate this distinction.

3.32   Here are some detailed data on age and sex from the 1980 U.S. Census:

age	males	females	total
under 15	26,313,000	25,069,000	51,282,000
15–24	21,412,000	21,062,000	42,474,000
25–39	25,239,000	25,799,000	51,038,000
40–59	22,197,000	23,884,000	46,081,000
over 59	14,972,000	20,658,000	35,630,000
total	110,033,000	116,472,000	226,505,000

Calculate the following probabilities: $P[M]$, $P[M|under\ 15]$, $P[M|15–24]$, $P[M|25–39]$, $P[M|40–59]$, and $P[M|over\ 59]$. Are age and sex independent? If not, what dependencies do you detect in these data?

3.33   In Exercise 2.39, we looked at the distribution of males and females among three categories of professors at Metro U. Are rank and sex independent in these data? If not, what dependencies do you detect?

• **3.34**   Explain why you think that the following system does or does not have merit:

There are many systems of all kinds but in talking to gamblers you will find the one they believe in most (and it can be used for most gambling games) is the "watch" or "patience" system. It's simple. If you are playing dice and certain bets pay even money, before you put your first stake on any of the numbers watch until one chance shows up at least three or four consecutive times and then put your first stake on the opposite chance.[8]

3.35   Pepys asked Newton which of the following three events is most likely:

a. at least one 6 when six dice are rolled,
b. at least two 6s when twelve dice are rolled, or
c. at least three 6s when eighteen dice are rolled?

Answer Pepys's question.

• **3.36**   In the game craps, a pair of dice are rolled. The roller immediately wins if a 7 or 11 comes up and loses with a 2, 3, or 12 ("craps"). If any other number comes up, then this becomes the "point" number and the dice are rolled again and again until either the point number or a 7 comes up. The roller wins if the point number comes up first and loses if a 7 is rolled first. What is the roller's probability of winning a game of craps?

• **3.37**   Cheaters sometimes sneak gimmicked dice into friendly craps games. One type of gimmicked dice is "tops and bottoms." Each of these dice contains only three different numbers, with the matching numbers on opposite ends to avoid detection. One die has a 3, 4, and 5 while the other die has a 1, 5, and 6. What is the roller's probability of winning a game of craps using these tops-and-bottoms dice?

3.38 At a certain selective college, 80 percent of the freshman class were ranked in the top quarter of their high school class. It turns out that 25 percent of the freshman class got good enough grades to make the dean's list their first year, and that 90 percent of the students on the dean's list were in the top quarter of their high school class. Of those freshmen in the top quarter of their high school class, what fraction made the dean's list their first year? What fraction of those not in the top quarter of their high school class made the dean's list their first year?

• 3.39 There are four secretaries in my department: Bob, Carol, Ted, and Alice. Their typing speed and accuracy is quite dissimilar. Bob types 40 percent of the departmental correspondence, but 25 percent of his work contains serious mistakes (transposesd words, omitted lines, and so on). Carol types 30 percent of the correspondence and 20 percent of her work has serious mistakes. Ted types 20 percent of the correspondence and 20 percent of his work has serious mistakes. Alice only types 10 percent of the correspondence, but she never makes a serious mistake.

I wrote a letter to the student newspaper, vigorously protesting the demise of the dress code. Fortunately, I decided to proofread the letter before signing it, because several of my choicest words were omitted or misplaced by the typist. What is the probability that this letter was typed by Bob? By Carol? By Ted? By Alice?

• • 3.40 This exercise extends the rare-disease example discussed in the text by considering a second test. Our given probabilities are $P[\text{disease}] = .01$, $P[\text{``yes''}|\text{disease}] = .95$, and $P[\text{``no''}|\text{no disease}] = .95$. Assume that each test is independent and that these .95 accuracy probabilities apply to each test.

a. Calculate the probability of disease given two "yes" readings, $P[\text{disease}|\text{``yes''}$ and "yes"], by directly applying Bayes' theorem.

b. Now use a two-step procedure to calculate $P[\text{disease}|\text{``yes''}$ and "yes"]. The text shows that, after one positive test, the revised probability of disease is .161. Take this value as the new prior probability going into the second test, $P[\text{disease}] = .161$. Now, use this new prior probability and Bayes' theorem to calculate a further revised probability of disease, given a "yes" reading on the second test.

c. Compare your answers to (a) and (b). What is the moral?

• 3.41 Half of the cars that come off of the assembly line at U.S. Motors have flaws in their appearance and half have flaws in their performance. These flaws are independent. There are two independent inspectors at U.S. Motors, one who checks each car's appearance and one who checks its performance. When a car is flawed, each inspector will spot the flaw 80 percent of the time and overlook the flaw 20 percent of the time. Neither inspector ever sees a flaw when there is none.

As a car comes off the assembly line, what is the probability

a. that it has flaws in its appearance and performance?
b. that it only has flaws in its appearance?
c. that it only has flaws in its performance?
d. that it is flawless?

Each car is then checked by the two inspectors. What are the probabilities

e. that a car that has flaws in both its appearance and performance will pass both inspectors?
f. that a car with flaws in both its appearance and performance will pass neither inspector?

g. that a car with an acceptable appearance but flawed performance will pass both inspectors?

h. that a car will pass both inspectors?

If you buy a car that has been passed by both of these inspectors, what is the probability that

i. it has a flawed appearance and performance?

j. only its appearance is flawed?

k. only its performance is flawed?

l. it has no flaws?

• **3.42**   Jack Cooper lives in New York City, where, throughout the year, there is at least .01 inch of precipitation on about one out of every three days. But Dr. Chuckles, Mr. Cooper's favorite weather forecaster, uses a Susan B. Anthony dollar to forecast ''wet'' or ''dry'' each day. Thus, $P[\text{''wet''}|\text{wet}] = P[\text{''wet''}|\text{dry}] = .5$. If Mr. Cooper knows Bayes' theorem and wants better forecasts, what should he use for $P[\text{wet}|\text{''wet''}]$?

How might he actually use this revised probability to make homemade forecasts that will be accurate more often than those of Dr. Chuckles? If he follows your advice, what is Jack's overall probability of making a correct forecast? What is Dr. Chuckles's probability of making a correct forecast?

• • **3.43**   (*continuation*) Mr. Smith knows nothing about weather forecasting other than it is wet in New York one-third of the time. He decides to construct a ''weather spinner'' similar to those that many professionals are rumored to use. He will draw a circle and color part of it green (''wet'') and the remainder yellow (''dry''). A free-spinning needle is then attached and spun each day to make a weather forecast. If Mr. Smith wants to maximize the probability of making a correct forecast, what fraction of the circle should be colored green? Don't just guess; try to formally derive an answer.

Mr. Smith is going to move to San Juan, Puerto Rico, where there is, on average, precipitation 199 days a year. How should he adjust his weather spinner?

3.44   A certain optimistic weather forecaster predicts ''dry and sunny'' unless there is clear evidence of imminent precipitation. When there is going to be precipitation, this is apparent one-fourth of the time and the forecaster predicts ''wet.'' The other three-quarters of the wet days, the precipitation is not certain and this optimistic forecaster predicts ''dry.'' Thus $P[\text{''wet''}|\text{wet}] = .25$ and $P[\text{''dry''}|\text{wet}] = .75$. When it is going to be dry, there is only a .01 chance that the weather will look threatening enough to provoke a ''wet'' forecast: $P[\text{''wet''}|\text{dry}] = .01$ and $P[\text{''dry''}|\text{dry}] = .99$. If, in fact, it is wet one-third of the days ($P[\text{wet}] = 1/3$), then what will be your adjusted weather probabilities $P[\text{wet}|\text{''wet''}]$ and $P[\text{dry}|\text{''dry''}]$?

• • **3.45**   Consider a deadly disease that is transmitted genetically. Let's say that the gene H is healthy, while the gene L is lethal. The genetic pair LL causes death during birth or early childhood. The genetic pairs HH and HL are both healthy, in that H is the dominant gene. But individuals with HL genes are carriers of the lethal gene who, if they marry other carriers, may have children with the lethal genetic combination LL. Unfortunately, the only way to be certain that someone is a carrier is to discover this deadly disease in their children.

If 1 percent of the adult population have HL genes and 99 percent have HH genes, what fraction of their children will have LL genes? Of those children who do not have LL genes, what fraction will be HH and what fraction will be HL?

● **3.46** (*continuation*) If a child has the lethal disease considered in the preceding exercise, then the parents must both be carriers. If these parents have another child, what is the probability that this next child, too, will have the lethal disease?

●● **3.47** (*continuation*) Many societies prohibit brother-sister marriages. One explanation is that such marriages are bad genetic risks. If two people are picked at random, what is the probability that both will be carriers of the lethal gene discovered in Exercise 3.45? If a brother and sister marry, what is the probability that they will both be carriers? How much more likely is it that a child will be LL if the parents are brother and sister?

● **3.48** Bertram's matchbox contains four matches, two of which are burnt and two of which are fresh. If we draw two matches randomly, what is the probability that we will get one burnt match and one fresh match?

● **3.49** We have three boxes, each with two drawers and a coin in each drawer. The coins are both gold in one box, both silver in another box, and one gold and one silver in the third box. A drawer is chosen at random from a randomly selected box. If the coin in this drawer is gold, what is the probability that this box's other drawer also contains a gold coin?

●● **3.50** Larry, Moe, and Curly are three prisoners, kept in separate cells. Two of them will be hanged in the morning and the third will be set free. Part of their punishment is that the prisoners do not know which two will be hanged. As each is equally likely to be set free, Curly calculates his chances to be only 1/3. Knowing some probability analysis, he says to a guard, "Look, I know that Larry or Moe is going to hang in the morning, so it can't hurt to tell me the name of one man, either Larry or Moe, who is going to be hanged." Accepting this argument, the jailer reveals that Larry will be hanged. Curly sleeps easier that night because, now that he knows that only he or Moe will live, his odds of being set free have risen from 1/3 to 1/2. Yet Curly would have reasoned in exactly the same way if the jailer had revealed that Moe would be hanged, implying that his probability of being set free goes up to 1/2 no matter who the jailer names! Whose probability logic is flawed?

CHAPTER 4

Probability Distributions

The Fairly Intelligent Fly

A large spider in an old house built a beautiful web in which to catch flies. Every time a fly landed on the web and was entangled in it the spider devoured him, so that when another fly came along he would think the web was a safe and quiet place in which to rest. One day a fairly intelligent fly buzzed around above the web so long without lighting that the spider appeared and said, "Come on down." But the fly was too clever for him and said, "I never light where I don't see other flies and I don't see any other flies in your house." So he flew away until he came to a place where there were a great many other flies. He was about to settle down among them when a bee buzzed up and said, "Hold it, stupid, that's flypaper. All those flies are trapped." "Don't be silly," said the fly, "they're dancing." So he settled down and became stuck to the flypaper with all the other flies. Moral: There is no safety in numbers, or in anything else.

James Thurber
Fables for Our Time
(Harper & Row, 1939)

TOPICS

4.1 THE IDEA OF A RANDOM VARIABLE

We have now been through the rules and tricks used to figure probabilities. You have learned how to calculate the probability of drawing four straight aces from a deck of cards, the probability of rolling at least one 6 with four dice, and the probabilities of even more complex outcomes. In many of these cases, numerical values are associated with the outcomes. Examples are the *number* of aces selected in four draws and the *number* of sixes obtained in four rolls.

In games of chance, a monetary payoff also may hinge on the draw of the cards or the roll of the dice. In business and economics, too, there are often monetary returns that depend on uncertain events. The returns from buying stocks, drilling for oil, expanding a business, cutting prices, and introducing a new product all have monetary values and all are uncertain. Sometimes the numerical values are not monetary. Examples are the number of boys in a family of four, the life expectancy of a 25-year-old woman, the temperature in Dallas on January 1, and the proximity of a missile to its target. If, as in these many cases, there are numbers associated with the uncertain outcomes, we can label the values a random variable.

> A **random variable** is a variable whose numerical value is determined by the outcome of an uncertain situation.

For example, how many heads will come up in the tossing of two coins? There are three possibilities: 0, 1, or 2. We can label the number of heads a random variable X. This X is a variable in that it can take on three different values: $X = 0$, $X = 1$, or $X = 2$, and X is random because we are not certain which particular value will occur.

Probability Distributions

We may be able to assign probabilities to the possible outcomes. In our coin-flipping example, if heads and tails are equally likely, then

outcome	number of heads X	probability P
TT	0	.25
HT or TH	1	.50
HH	2	.25

Such a listing of the probabilities of the different possible values of X is called a probability distribution.

> A **probability distribution** $p[x]$ gives the probabilities of each possible value x of a random variable X.

Notice that the random variable itself is capital X, while the small x denotes a particular value of X. The phrase *probability distribution* indicates that we are telling how the probabilities (which add up to 1) are distributed among the possible outcomes. Here,

$$p[0] = .25$$
$$p[1] = .50$$
$$p[2] = .25$$

Another example can be found in Chapter 3, when we looked at all of the possible sums in the rolling of two dice. These outcomes and probabilities are reproduced in Table 4.1. The dice sum is a random variable, in that X can take on eleven different values and we do not know which particular value will occur. The listing in Table 4.1 of x and $p[x]$ for the roll of two dice is one way to show a probability distribution. A probability distribution also can be displayed visually, as shown in Figure 4.1.

The concept of a probability distribution is a valuable mathematical tool that can be used in theoretical work to define various concepts rigorously and to prove some important theorems. A graph of probability distribution can be useful in showing us at a glance the range and relative likelihoods of the possible outcomes. Figure 4.1 tells us very forcefully that 7 is the most likely outcome and that the probabilities decline symmetrically as X moves away from 7 toward 2 and 12.

Household Size

Now let's do a somewhat different example. The 1980 Census found that 217,482,000 U.S. citizens live in 79,108,000 households and that 8,958,000 U.S. citizens live

Table 4.1 *Outcomes and probabilities for the roll of two dice*

Sum of dice x	Probability p[x]
2	1/36
3	2/36
4	3/36
5	4/36
6	5/36
7	6/36
8	5/36
9	4/36
10	3/36
11	2/36
12	1/36

Table 4.2   *Size of U.S. households, 1980*

Size x	Number of households	Fraction of total households p[x]
1 person	17,816,000	.225
2 persons	24,734,000	.313
3 persons	13,845,000	.175
4 persons	12,470,000	.158
5 persons	5,996,000	.076
6 persons	2,499,000	.032
7 or more	1,748,000	.022
Total	79,108,000	1.000

Source: U.S. Bureau of the Census, Current Population Survey, in Statistical Abstract of the United States. (Washington, D.C.: U.S. Government Printing Office, 1981.)

in institutions and other group quarters.* Table 4.2 shows the distribution of households of different sizes.

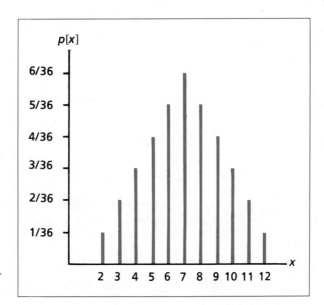

Figure 4.1   *Probability distribution for the roll of two dice.*

*The Census Bureau defines a *household* as persons who occupy a house, apartment, or other separate living quarters. One of the tests in determining a household is that the occupants do not live and eat with other persons in the same structure and that there are complete kitchen facilities for the exclusive use of the occupants. People who are not in households live in *group quarters* including rest homes, rooming houses, military barracks, jails, and college dormitories.

These data show that 22.5 percent of all U.S. households contain just one person; 31.3 percent are two-person households, and so on. Now, if we were to pick a household at random, what is the probability that we would pick a one-person household? If each household, large or small, is equally likely to be picked, then there is a .225 probability of picking a one-person household.

Objectivists advise us to be careful in making such probability statements. They would wince if I said that there is a .225 probability that I live in a one-person household. I, in fact, live in a four-person household. There is zero probability that I am a one-person household. Instead, we should say that, if a household is selected at random, then there is a .225 probability of selecting a one-person household. With our words chosen carefully, we can then interpret household size as a random variable and the relative frequencies given in Table 4.2 as probabilities. Figure 4.2 shows this probability distribution.

We can readily see in this figure that most households contain from one to four persons, and that two is the most common size. We can also see at a glance that the probabilities steadily decline as we move away from a two-person household. Figure 4.2 also illustrates a commonplace aggregation problem. The category "7 or more" aggregates data for households where $X = 7, 8, 9, \ldots$, and so it would be misleading to plot this probability at the point $X = 7$. Instead, I've put this .022 probability at $X = 7.9$, which is the average size of households with seven or more persons.

Exercises

4.1   You are about to roll a normal six-sided die. Let the random variable X be the number that will come up. Make a table like Table 4.1 showing the possible values of X and their respective probabilities.

4.2   (*continuation*) Now graph this probability distribution, making a figure comparable to Figure 4.1.

4.3   Mammoth Oil is considering an exploratory drilling in Cucamonga, California. The senior engineer in charge of this project says that the company is as likely to find significant oil and gas there as it is to draw the queen of spades out of a normal deck of cards. We can define the random variable X as follows: $X = 1$ if the drilling is successful and $X = 0$ if it isn't. What is the probability distribution of X?

4.2   EXPECTED VALUE, STANDARD DEVIATION, AND SKEWNESS

A complete probability distribution can be listed in a table or pictured in a graph. Sometimes, a few simple numbers can effectively summarize the most relevant characteristics of a probability distribution. The most popular are the expected value, standard deviation, and skewness coefficient. First, we will define these

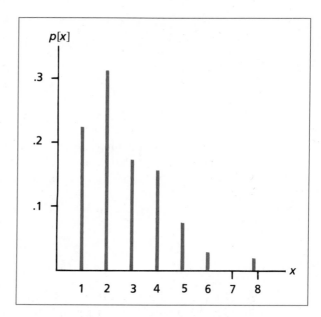

Figure 4.2   *Probability distribution of U.S. household size, 1980*

three measures and see how they describe a probability distribution. Then we'll look at several applications.

THE EXPECTED VALUE

You have seen how probabilities can be interpreted as long-run frequencies. For instance, if the probability of heads is .5, then heads should come up about half the time in a large number of flips. A similar logic applies to the example of the number of heads X obtained in two coin flips. The probabilities are $P[0] = .25$, $P[1] = .5$, and $P[2] = .25$; if we were to flip two coins many, many times, we could anticipate obtaining $X = 0$ about one-fourth of the time, $X = 1$ one-half of the time, and $X = 2$ one-fourth of the time. The average value of X would be 1. This predicted long-range average is called the *expected value*.

The **expected value** (or *mean*) of a random variable X is defined as

$$\mu = E[X] = \Sigma\, x\, p[x] \tag{4.1}$$

where the notation Σ means that we multiply each different possible value of x by its associated probability $p[x]$ and then add up these products $x\, p[x]$. The Greek symbol μ is pronounced "mu."

The expected value is a weighted average of the possible outcomes, with the probability weights reflecting how likely each outcome is. Thus, the expected value should be interpreted as what the long-run average value of X will be, if the frequency with which each outcome occurs is in accordance with its probability.

In our two-coin example, the expected value of X is

$$\mu = \Sigma \, x \, p[x]$$
$$= 0 \, p[X = 0] + 1 \, p[X = 1] + 2 \, p[X = 2]$$
$$= 0(.25) + 1(.50) + 2(.25)$$
$$= 1$$

If two fair coins are flipped n times and the outcomes are in accordance with the probabilities, then "no heads" will occur $n/4$ times, "one head" will occur $n/2$ times, and "two heads" $n/4$ times. The average value of X will be

$$\mu = \frac{0(n/4) + 1(n/2) + 2(n/4)}{n}$$
$$= 0(\tfrac{1}{4}) + 1(\tfrac{1}{2}) + 2(\tfrac{1}{4})$$
$$= 1.0$$

To reiterate, because it is very important, this expected value calculation shows us that if we were to flip a pair of coins a great many times, carefully record the results, and calculate the average number of heads, then this average would be 1.0 if heads and tails come up as often as their probabilities say they should.

To make the example more sporting, imagine that, in return for a small participation fee, your statistics instructor offers to pay you a dollar for every head obtained when two coins are flipped. Imagine that you can play as many times as you want. In the long run, what is your predicted average payoff per game? This is the question that an expected value calculation answers. If heads and tails come up in accordance with their probabilities, you will average a $1 payoff per game. If your instructor charges you $1.25 per game to play, you can anticipate going broke in the long run.

For a second example, let's return to the roll of two dice, with the probabilities shown in Table 4.1. The possible outcomes are $X = 2, 3, 4, \ldots, 12$. We want to calculate an average of these possibilities, using the respective probabilities as weights,

$$\mu = 2(1/36) + 3(2/36) + 4(3/36) + \cdots + 12(1/36)$$
$$= 252/36$$
$$= 7$$

This calculation shows that if we roll a pair of dice many, many times, the average sum will be 7 if each number comes up as often as anticipated.

Imagine a casino game in which the bettor is paid a number of dollars equal to the numbers obtained when a pair of dice are rolled. In the long run, the average payoff per roll should be very close to $7. If it costs $7.50 to play this game, the bettor can anticipate losing a considerable amount of money in the long run. On any one play, the bettor may win up to $4.50 or lose up to $5.50. But, in the long run, the losses should average 50 cents per game.

Let's do one more example. In Table 4.2, we used the random variable X to represent the size of a U.S. household selected at random. What is the expected value of X? It is a calculation of the average size of X, using the respective probabilities as weights:

$$\mu = 1(.225) + 2(.313) + 3(.175) + \cdots + 7.7(.022)$$

$$= 2.75$$

The press reports this calculation as, "The average U.S. household contains 2.75 people." The casual reader then snickers that the typical U.S. household must contain some fractured people. This weak joke is a deliberate misinterpretation of expected value. The expected value of X is not the most likely or the most typical value of X. It is the long-run average value of X, if we repeatedly select households at random. Some households have fewer than 2.75 people; some have more. The average of these different household sizes is 2.75.

This 2.75 expected value is just one summary figure for a complicated probability distribution. It may be useful in comparing household sizes for different countries or for different time periods in the United States. For instance, the U.S. Census Bureau has reported the following average household sizes:

census year	average household size μ
1950	3.37
1960	3.33
1970	3.14
1980	2.75

These figures chronicle a decline in the average size of U.S. households. To describe this decline more fully, we would want to look at the detailed probability distributions and some additional data. Are there now more single-person households? Are families now having fewer children? Are there now more older citizens, who typically live in small households? The expected value does not answer these questions, but it does suggest that there are some interesting questions that can be asked.

The Standard Deviation

The expected value is a popular summary measure that may be useful in describing a probability distribution. Another favorite is the *standard deviation* σ (pronounced "sigma").

The **variance of a random variable** X is defined as

$$\sigma^2 = E[(X - \mu)^2] = \Sigma (x - \mu)^2 p[x] \qquad (4.2)$$

The **standard deviation** σ is the square root of the variance.

The mean is the expected value of X. The variance is the expected value of $(X - \mu)^2$. Thus, the variance is the average value of the squared deviations of the possible outcomes from the expected value μ. For each possible outcome, we calculate how far x is from the expected value μ, and then we square this deviation. By squaring, we do two things. First, we eliminate the distinction between positive and negative deviations. What matters to a variance calculation is how far the outcome is from μ, not whether it is above or below μ. Second, squaring gives primary importance to large deviations. One deviation of 10 squared is as large as four deviations of 5 squared.

After calculating the squared deviations from μ for each possible outcome, we then calculate the average squared deviation using the outcome probabilities as weights. This weighted average of the squared deviations from μ is the variance, and its square root is the standard deviation. The standard deviation measures the dispersion in the possible outcomes and graphically gauges how "spread out" a probability distribution is. A distribution with a small standard deviation will be very compact, while a distribution with a large standard deviation will be dispersed.

Let's return again to the two-dice example in Table 4.1. The expected value is $\mu = 7$. Table 4.3 shows the squared deviations about this expected value. Notice that the squared deviation at $X = 7$ is zero. Notice also that the squared deviations are the same as we move in either direction away from the mean of 7, illustrating the point that the variance treats positive and negative deviations equally. Finally, notice how the squared deviations escalate as the outcomes get farther away from $X = 7$.

The variance is the probability-weighted average of these squared deviations:

$$\sigma^2 = 26(1/36) + 16(2/36) + 9(3/36) + \cdots + 25(1/36)$$
$$= 210/36$$
$$= 5.83$$

The standard deviation is the square root of the variance,

$$\sigma = 5.83^{1/2} = 2.415$$

To show how the standard deviation is related to the shape of a probability distribution, let's compare some distributions. First, imagine a pair of perfectly gimmicked dice that always come up 7. The probability distribution is shown in Figure 4.3. The expected value and variance are

$$\mu = 7(1) = 7$$
$$\sigma^2 = (7 - 7)^2(1) = 0$$

The expected value is 7 because this is the only possible outcome. The variance and standard deviation are zero because there is no uncertainty about the outcome.

Now let's imagine a single eleven-sided die, constructed so that the eleven

Table 4.3 *Squared deviations about* $\mu = 7$ *for the roll of two dice*

Outcome x	Squared deviation $(x - \mu)^2$	Probability p[x]
2	25	1/36
3	16	2/36
4	9	3/36
5	4	4/36
6	1	5/36
7	0	6/36
8	1	5/36
9	4	4/36
10	9	3/36
11	16	2/36
12	25	1/36

numbers 2, 3, 4, . . . , 12 are all equally likely. This probability distribution is also shown in Figure 4.3. The expected value, variance, and standard deviation are

$$\mu = 2(1/11) + 3(1/11) + 4(1/11) + \cdots + 12(1/11) = 7$$

$$\sigma^2 = (2 - 7)^2(1/11) + (3 - 7)^2(1/11) + \cdots + (12 - 7)^2(1/11) = 10$$

$$\sigma = 10^{1/2} = 3.16$$

This eleven-sided die has the same expected value as the sum of two standard six-sided dice, but has a larger variance and standard deviation. Figure 4.3 shows that this larger standard deviation reflects the greater dispersion in the probability distribution. There is more uncertainty with the eleven-sided die because all eleven outcomes are equally likely. As compared to the sum of two standard dice, there is a higher probability of outcomes far from 7.

For a final example, consider two six-sided dice, each with three 1s and three 6s stamped on the faces. Now there are only three possible sums: 2, 7, and 12. This probability distribution is included in Figure 4.3, too. The expected value, variance, and standard deviation are

$$\mu = 2(9/36) + 7(18/36) + 12(9/36) = 7$$

$$\sigma^2 = (2 - 7)^2(9/36) + (7 - 7)^2(18/36) + (12 - 7)^2(9/36) = 12.5$$

$$\sigma = 12.5^{1/2} = 3.54$$

Again, the mean is 7. Notice that even though there is a .5 probability of rolling a 7, still the standard deviation is the highest of any of the distributions shown in Figure 4.3. The standard deviation is high because there is a .5 probability of a 2 or a 12, and the squaring of deviations emphasizes outcomes far from the mean.

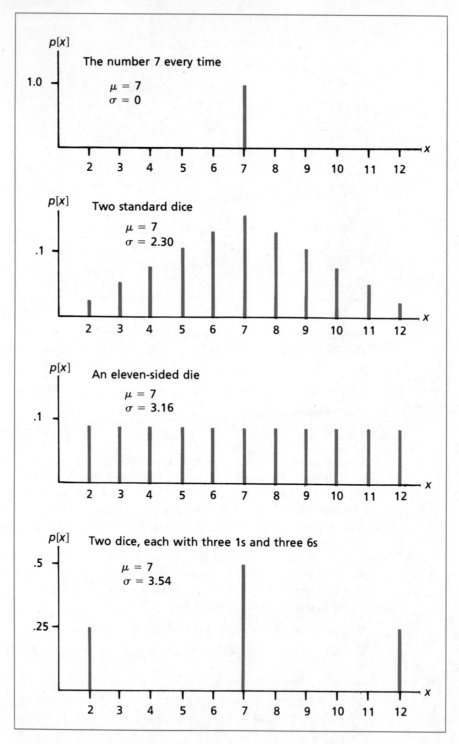

Figure 4.3 *Four probability distributions*

The Coefficient of Skewness

The mean measures the center of a distribution and the standard deviation measures its dispersion.

The **coefficient of skewness** γ (pronounced "gamma") is a measure of the symmetry of the outcomes:

$$\gamma = \frac{E[(X - \mu)^3]}{\sigma^3} \tag{4.3}$$

Here, we calculate the average value of the cubed deviations from the expected value and, to provide a uniform scale, divide this average cubed deviation by the standard deviation cubed.

The cube of a positive deviation from the mean is positive, while the cube of a negative deviation from the mean is negative. Thus, the average cubed deviation could turn out to be either positive or negative. If the outcomes are symmetrical about the mean, so that the right half of the distribution looks like a mirror image of the left half, then the positive and negative deviations are equally balanced and the average cubed deviation will be zero. If, on the other hand, the outcomes are asymmetrical, then the coefficient of skewness may be positive or negative. The cubing makes large deviations in either direction very important in this calculation. If the probability distribution looks unbalanced, then the coefficient of skewness is probably not zero.

All of the dice examples in Figures 4.1 and 4.3 are, in fact, symmetrical with a zero coefficient of skewness. But look at the distribution of household sizes in Figure 4.2. This probability distribution is clearly not symmetrical about the mean $\mu = 2.75$. Instead, household size has a high probability of being slightly less than 2.75 and a small probability of being much greater than 2.75. There is some chance of large positive deviations, and so we label this distribution *positively skewed*. The coefficient of skewness does, in fact, work out to be positive, $\gamma = 1.04.$*

Figure 4.4 contrasts positively and negatively skewed distributions. The easiest way to remember the distinction is that a positively skewed distribution diminishes or "runs off" to the right (there is some chance of outcomes much higher than the mean), while a negatively skewed distribution "runs off" to the left.

Together, these three calculations—the mean, standard deviation, and skewness coefficient—often paint an accurate mental picture of a probability distribution. The mean tells us the location of the distribution; the standard deviation tells us how dispersed the distribution is; and the skewness coefficient tells us whether or not the distribution is symmetrical.

---

*This calculation actually understates the positive skewness somewhat by lumping all values of X greater than 6 into the aggregate $X = 7.9$. The cubing of $X = 8, 9, 10$, and so on would increase the average cubed deviation.

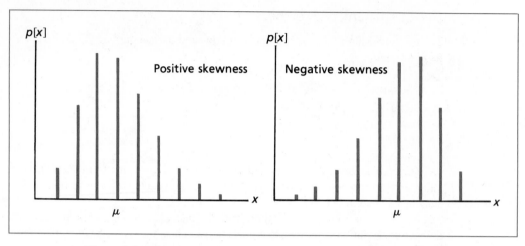

Figure 4.4 *Two skewed distributions*

Exercises

4.4 In Exercise 4.1, you found the probability distribution for the number X obtained from the roll of a single die.

a. What is the expected value of X?
b. Is this expected value also the most likely value of X?
c. What does this expected value tell us?

4.5 In the board game Careers, a player can pay $3000 to "play the stock market." The player rolls a single die and receives $1000 times the number rolled. In the long run, how much can a habitual stock market player expect to make or lose from this wager?

4.6 An investor is considering two mutual funds. Based on past performance, the following probabilities are assigned to the possible percentage rates of return:

first fund		*second fund*	
return	*probability*	*return*	*probability*
−10	.10	−15	.20
0	.10	5	.20
10	.60	15	.20
20	.10	25	.20
30	.10	45	.20

a. Graph these two probability distributions, the first on the top half of a sheet of paper and the second on the bottom half.
b. Which fund seems to have the higher expected return and which has the higher standard deviation?
c. Calculate the means and standard deviations, and see if you are right.

4.7 Use the data in Table 4.2 to calculate the mean, standard deviation, and skewness coefficient of the size of U.S. households. (Use $X = 7.9$ for the category "7 or more.")

• **4.8** The average income of 25,000 people who live in a mythical small country is nearly $50,000. There are 1,000 millionaires and then there are the 24,000 servants who earn $10,000 apiece. Given these data, the mean is an incomplete description of the income distribution. The standard deviation and skewness coefficient might help. Do you think that the standard deviation will be large or small? Do you think that the skewness coefficient will be positive, negative, or close to zero? Calculate their values and see if you are right.

4.3 USING EXPECTED VALUES

The expected value undoubtedly is the most widely used summary of a probability distribution. The variety of applications can be appreciated best through several examples.

The Numbers Game

A typical "numbers" game pays $600 on a $1 bet (for a net gain of $599) when a player correctly predicts the last three digits in the total number of dollars wagered that day at a local race track. Assuming that these three digits are completely random, what is the expected net gain from playing the numbers game? On the average, out of every dollar bet, what fraction is paid out to winners? These are some of the interesting questions that an expected value calculation answers.

The probability of winning is a multiplication problem because a winner must correctly predict the first digit, second digit, and third digit. Allowing for zeroes, there are 10 equally likely possibilities for each digit and the 3 digits are presumably independent. Therefore, the probability of winning is $(1/10)^3 = .001$. Alternatively, we can reason that the chances of winning must be $1/1000 = .001$, because there are 1000 equally likely numbers from 000 to 999.

The expected payoff from a $1 bet is

$$\$600(.001) + \$0(.999) = \$0.60$$

Thus, the expected net loss is 40 cents on a one-dollar bet. On the average, out of every dollar wagered, the winners get paid 60 cents and the organizers keep 40 cents. A 40 percent take for the house is very high; yet many people continue to play the numbers game, hoping for a $600 payoff that would make their lives a little bit nicer.

Others capitalize on these hopes by selling "dream books," which translate people's dreams into three-digit numbers that are suitable for betting. You can accurately gauge the value of these dream books by observing that the sellers spend their time peddling the books instead of peacefully dreaming up their own numbers.

State Lotteries

As another example, consider a stylized state lottery that costs 50 cents to enter and offers the chance of winning $25,000. To win, one need only correctly predict the five-digit number that the state will select. This scheme is a legal numbers game with a much larger payoff and a much smaller chance of winning. Allowing

for zeroes, there are 10 equally likely possibilities for each of the 5 digits. Therefore, the probability of winning is $(1/10)^5 = .00001$. The expected payoff from
a 50-cent ticket is

$$\$25,000(.00001) + \$0(.99999) = \$0.25$$

This is, in fact, roughly the expected payoff from most state lotteries. The habitual
player can, in the long run, anticipate getting 25 cents back for every 50 cents
spent on tickets. The state treasury will keep, on average, 25 cents out of every
50 cents taken in, a whopping 50 percent take.

Is a New Statistics Book a Good Investment?

A certain publisher is considering bringing out a new statistics book. This book
will sell for $28, with the publisher receiving $20, the bookstore $5, and the author
$3. Here are the demand and cost figures:*

number of copies sold	probability	production cost
5,000	.20	$225,000
10,000	.40	$250,000
20,000	.25	$300,000
30,000	.10	$350,000
40,000	.05	$400,000

What is the expected value of profits (receipts minus production costs)?

The random variable, profits, is equal to the number of copies sold times $20,
minus the production cost. If, for example, 5000 copies are sold, then the revenue
will be $5000(\$20) = \$100,000$; the production cost will be $225,000; and there
will be a net loss of $125,000. Here are all of the possible profit outcomes:

sales	profits x	probability p	(x)(p)
5,000	− $125,000	.20	− $25,000
10,000	− $50,000	.40	− $20,000
20,000	$100,000	.25	$25,000
30,000	$250,000	.10	$25,000
40,000	$400,000	.05	$20,000
total		1.00	$25,000

As shown, the expected value of profits is $\mu = \Sigma\, x\, p[x] = \$25,000$. The prob-
abilities are such that this sort of book will lose money 60 percent of the time, but
there is a small chance of considerable profits. The $25,000 expected value cal-
culation tells us that if the publisher keeps bringing out books with comparable
chances of success, then they can anticipate an average profit of $25,000 per book
(with the occasional big success more than offsetting the frequent small failures).

---

*For the sake of simplicity, we'll assume there are only five possible outcomes. In a more practical
sense, we can think of each outcome as a rough composite of similar, but slightly different results.

Maxwell House's Price of Coffee

Maxwell House, a division of General Foods, is the nation's largest coffee producer. It acquires coffee beans from coffee-growing nations, grinds and roasts these beans, and sells them—either as ground or as instant coffee. For many years, ground coffee came in a can that had to be opened with a key, like a sardine can. In October 1962, Folger's began marketing a coffee can that could be opened quickly without a key. A year later, Maxwell House decided that it, too, should sell coffee in a keyless can.

The keyless can was slightly more expensive to manufacture, but consumers seemed willing to pay for this extra convenience. The extra cost to Maxwell House worked out to about 0.7 cent per pound of coffee. The company considered: (a) holding the price steady and absorbing this added cost or (b) raising the price per pound by 2 cents to cover the extra cost and then some. Probabilities were assigned as to how profits would be affected by each strategy:[1]

effect of keyless can on Maxwell House profits

hold price constant			*raise price 2 cents*		
market share	*profits (millions)*	*probability*	*market share*	*profits (millions)*	*probability*
+2.8%	+$4.1	.20	+2.5%	+$11.9	.25
+1.0%	−$0.6	.50	+1.0%	+$6.5	.25
0.0%	−$0.8	.20	0.0%	+$2.9	.25
−0.6%	−$1.2	.10	−1.5%	−$1.1	.25

If the price is held constant, the expected value of the effect of the keyless can on profits is

$$\mu = (\$4.1)(.20) + (-\$0.6)(.50) + (-\$0.8)(.20) + (-\$1.2)(.10)$$

$$= \$2.4 \text{ million}$$

The anticipated enthusiastic response by consumers more than makes up for the fact that the keyless cans cost more to produce.

Maxwell House could raise its price to cover the added cost, but a higher price would dampen consumer enthusiasm somewhat. On balance, the expected value with a 2-cents-per-pound price increase works out to be

$$\mu = (\$11.9)(.25) + (\$6.5)(.25) + (\$2.9)(.25) + (-\$1.1)(.25)$$

$$= \$5.05 \text{ million}$$

Not surprisingly, Maxwell House decided to introduce the keyless can and raise the price of its coffee by 2 cents a pound.

Exercises

4.9 Chisler Corporation provides a three-year warranty on the cars it sells. They anticipate the following typical repair record:

warranteed repair	cost to Chisler	probability
none	$0	.25
minor	$200	.50
moderate	$500	.20
major	$1000	.05

What is the expected value of these warranteed repairs to Chisler? What use might they make of this expected value calculation?

4.10 A standard slot machine has three reels. The first reel has 3 walnuts, 7 cherries, 3 oranges, 5 lemons, 1 bell, and 1 jackpot bar. The second reel has 7 cherries, 6 oranges, 1 lemon, 3 bells, and 3 bars. The third reel has 4 walnuts, 7 oranges, 5 lemons, 3 bells, and 1 bar. The payoffs are:

reel 1	reel 2	reel 3	payoff in coins
bar	bar	bar	85
bell	bell	bar	18
bell	bell	bell	18
lemon	lemon	bar	14
lemon	lemon	lemon	14
orange	orange	bar	10
orange	orange	orange	10
cherry	cherry	bell	5
cherry	cherry	walnut	5
cherry	cherry	any	3

What is the expected payoff if each picture on each reel is equally likely to appear? In the long run, what fraction of every dollar bet will this one-armed bandit keep?

4.11 The *Skimmer's Digest* sweepstakes mails 20,000,000 entry forms, of which:[2]

winnings	number
$3	12,000
$10	7,900
$500	90
$5,000	4
$10,000	3
$25,000	2
$100,000	1

If you enter this sweepstakes, what is the probability that you will win something? Is your expected return more than the cost of mailing a first class letter? If only 1 out of every 20 people actually enter the sweepstakes, what is the expected cost to *Skimmer's Digest* in prize money? What does this expected cost figure mean?

• **4.12** Let's investigate the often-heard claim that if enough monkeys were given enough typewriters and enough time, they could generate every book that was ever written. If we neglect the distinction between uppercase and lowercase letters, there are 50 keys on my typewriter. What is the probability that one monkey who randomly hits 11 keys on one typewriter will correctly type the word "probability?"

Now imagine that we have a billion monkeys and a billion typewriters. Each monkey hits 11 keys every 12 seconds (a key a second and then a one-second rest before trying again). If these billion monkeys type at this rate 24 hours a day, 365 days a year for 1985 years, what is the expected number of times that "probability" will be typed correctly?

4.4 BETTING ODDS AND PROBABILITIES

If we know both the possible payoffs and their respective probabilities, then we can calculate the expected payoff. Sometimes we can work the calculation in the other direction. We may know the payoffs and have an estimate of the expected payoff. If so, these data can be used to estimate some probabilities.

For example, in 1974 London bookies were offering 3 to 1 odds on a wager that Richard Nixon would finish his four-year term as president. We can use these quoted odds to estimate the bookies' subjective probability in 1974 that Nixon would finish his term.* Odds of 3 to 1 mean that, for every £1 wagered by the bettor that Nixon would finish, the bookie wagered £3 that he wouldn't, with the winner taking all. On a £1 wager, the bettor either loses £1 or is paid £4, for a £3 gain. If the probability of Nixon finishing his term is P, then the bettor's expected gain is

$$E[X] = (+£3)(P) + (-£1)(1 - P)$$
$$= 4P - 1$$

If the bets were "fair," so that the bookie just expects to break even in the long run, then the expected gain would be zero:

$$0 = E[X]$$
$$= 4P - 1$$

implying

$$P = 1/4$$

that in 1974 the probability of Nixon finishing his second term was perceived to be about $1/4$.

Of course, bookies expect to do better than just break even. They are in business to make money. If they set the odds at 3 to 1, then they must have believed

---

*In quoting odds the bookie's stake is mentioned first. Thus odds of X to Y mean that the bettor can win X units by risking Y units.

that Nixon had less than a 25 percent chance of finishing his term. How much less? We can reason that the odds offered are intended to give the bookie a profit large enough to cover expenses, and yet small enough to attract bettors. The bookies' average profit is generally in the range of 5 percent to 20 percent of the amount wagered, implying an expected return of $-.05$ to $-.20$ for the bettor. These profit margins give a probability range:

$$5\% \text{ profit:} \quad -.05 = E[X] = 4P - 1 \text{ implies } P = .24$$
$$20\% \text{ profit:} \quad -.20 = E[X] = 4P - 1 \text{ implies } P = .20$$

Apparently the bookies felt that Nixon's chances of completing his term were in the range of .20 to .24.

Nixon's probability of survival was, of course, a very subjective probability that varied considerably from person to person. It is this subjective variation that fuels betting. If one person believes that there is a .2 probability of some event occurring and someone else believes that the probability is .3, then there is room for a bet in which each side believes its expected return is positive.* It is into this void that the bookie steps, offering bets to either or both parties. We can think of the bookies' odds as reflecting an expert or consensus opinion of the disputed probability. Those who disagree with this consensus will be tempted to back their belief with a wager.

Pari-mutuel Bets

When a bookie offers 3 to 1 odds that Nixon will complete his term, the bookie is offering to bet against people who are more optimistic about Nixon's chances. The bookie is gambling, with no guarantee of a profit either on this bet or in the long run. The bookie counts on some expertise in assessing probabilities, and then sets the odds so as to leave some margin for error and still attract customers.

Horse race odds offer an interesting contrast in that they are explicitly set to reflect a consensus probability and, at the same time, guarantee a fixed percentage return to the track. The vehicle is the *pari-mutuel system* thought up by a French chemist, Pierre Oller, in 1872. The basic pari-mutuel (''wager-among us all'') idea is to put the wagered money into a pot, take out a percentage for the track and the government, and divide up what's left among those who correctly picked the winner.

Table 4.4 gives a detailed example. A total of $117,647 is wagered on the winner of this race. Horse 1 is the favorite, and horse 6 has the fewest dollars bet on it. The track takes 15 percent of $117,647 (which comes to $17,647) out of the pool, conveniently leaving $100,000 to be paid out to the winning bettors.

---

*The mutually agreeable bet might be at 3 to 1 odds. The person with the .3 probability will put up the dollar, betting that the event will occur. The person with the .2 probability will bet £3 that the event doesn't occur. Each has a positive expected return:

$$P = .3: \quad E[X] = (£3)(.3) + (-£1)(.7) = £0.2$$
$$P = .2: \quad E[X] = (£1)(.8) + (-£3)(.2) = £0.2$$

Table 4.4 *Some horse race odds*

Horse	Dollars wagered	Odds	Probability for E[X] = 0
1	$32,468	2.0–1	.333
2	$31,915	2.1–1	.323
3	$21,052	3.7–1	.213
4	$14,022	6.1–1	.141
5	$12,366	7.0–1	.125
6	$5,824	16.1–1	.058
Total	$117,647		1.193

If horse 1 wins, then $100,000 will be returned to the people who bet $32,937 on this horse. This payoff is $3.08 for every $1 bet. The track rounds this $3.08 down to $3.00—a practice known, in an interesting choice of words, as "breakage." A payoff of $3 on a $1 bet is a net gain of $2 and represents 2 to 1 odds. Similarly, if horse 6 surprises most bettors and wins, $100,000 will be paid to the people who bet $5,824 on this longshot. This payoff is $17.17 on every $1 bet, rounded down to $17.10, and reported as odds of 16.1 to 1. The payoff odds for each of the six horses is shown in Table 4.4.

Table 4.4 also shows, from the bettor's viewpoint, how high the subjective probability of each horse winning must be to make a wager on that horse a fair bet ($E[X] = 0$). These probabilities sum to more than 1.0 because these are not fair bets; the track extracts 15 percent plus breakage. Nonetheless, each horse attracts the wagers of some optimistic bettors. As in the Nixon example, we can consider the consensus probabilities to be somewhat less than the fair-game probabilities implied by the betting odds. Optimists with subjective probabilities that are higher than the implied fair-game probabilities may be tempted to bet.

There is another way to look at this column of fair-game probabilities in Table 4.4. These are the fractions of a dollar one would have to wager on each horse to ensure a $1 payoff, no matter which horse wins. In total, one would have to bet $1.193 to be sure to get back $1. The track would make a percentage profit of .193/1.193 = .162, which is 15 percent plus breakage.

More Sports Bets

The pari-mutuel system provides the sure profit that bookies covet. Bookies do not like to gamble! They much prefer to be intermediaries, reaping a steady profit as brokers between gamblers with dissimilar subjective probabilities. However, for many bets, it is awkward to set up a formal pari-mutuel system.

For most sporting events, the bookie offers odds, often days or even weeks in advance, and then accepts bets as they trickle in. The conservative bookie would like to offer the odds that would be determined by a pari-mutuel system but is forced to guess what those odds would be. If the bookie guesses wrong, too much

The Rich Get Richer

Is there any advantage, in a fair game, to being rich or being poor? If the game is fair, then both sides have an expected gain of zero, but the player who is poor is much more likely to be the one who goes home broke. Let's say that two women, R and P, decide to play poker until one is bankrupt. These two women are equally skilled, but R has $90,000 while P has only $10,000. What is the probability that R will win?

This is a tricky problem, of a type that intrigued many of the greatest minds in the history of probability analysis. We could try to figure out all of the possible hands and bets and the various twists and turns that this poker showdown might take, but there is a much simpler route. If they are equally skilled, then this is a fair game with a zero expected gain to each woman. When it is all over, R will either have won $10,000 or lost $90,000. A zero expected gain implies that her probability of winning must be .9:

$$(\$10,000)(.9) + (-\$90,000)(.1) = 0$$

Similarly, with a .1 chance of winning, P has a zero expected gain, too:

$$(\$90,000)(.1) + (-\$10,000)(.9) = 0$$

The rich woman is much more likely to win but, of course, she will lose much more money if she doesn't win.

In general, in any fair game, a person with a certain percent of the total capital at stake has that same percent chance of winning. Here, R puts up 90 percent of the capital and has a 90 percent chance of winning. Although this precise rule only applies to a fair game, the moral can be extended to all sorts of situations, including a bettor trying to break the bank at Monte Carlo and two competitive firms trying to drive each other out of business.

money will come in on one team and the bookie will either have to gamble, pass the bets on to another bookie, or adjust the odds. Unfortunately for the bookie, the traditional rules of the game are that the adjusted odds only apply to new bets and not to wagers made at odds offered earlier.

For many sports bets, bookies offer standard odds of 10 to 11 or 5 to 6, while using a point spread to try to elicit equal dollar bets on each team. For example, in the January 1973 Super Bowl, Miami was offered as a $1\frac{1}{2}$ point favorite over Washington, meaning that $1\frac{1}{2}$ points would be added to Washington's score for betting purposes. Bettors could pick either team at, depending on the bookie, 10 to 11 or 5 to 6 odds. Those who bet on Miami would win their bets if Miami won the game by at least two points. Those who bet on Washington would win if Washington won or if Miami won by only 1 point.

Let's say that, as an academic probability exercise, it is one day before the Super Bowl and you are considering betting on one of the teams that, you believe, has a probability P of winning (taking into account the point spread). With 10 to 11 odds, your expected return,

$$(\$10)(P) + (-\$11)(1 - P) = -\$11 + \$21P$$

will be positive only if

$$P > 11/21 = .524$$

If, taking into account the point spread, you believe that one team's probability of winning is greater than .524, then you might be tempted to bet. With 5 to 6 odds, a positive expected return requires one team to have a .545 probability of winning.

In general, then, the oddsmakers want to set point spreads to equalize the number of dollars bet on each team. This generally means setting the point spread so that most people believe that the game is essentially a toss-up. There will be some people who believe that one team has more than a .524 (or .545) probability of winning. There will be other people who think that the second team has more than a .524 (or .545) probability of winning. If the point spread works as intended, an equal number of dollars will be bet on each team. With 10 to 11 odds, the happy bookie will take in $11 in bets on each team ($22 in all) and pay out $21 no matter who wins, for a safe 4.5 percent profit on every dollar wagered. With 5 to 6 odds, equally divided bets give the bookie a $1 profit on every $12 bet, an 8.3 percent take.

Exercises

4.13 In the game Hazard, the player rolls three standard dice, trying to get three of a kind. The bettor can wager on a particular three of a kind, such as three 6s, or can just bet that some three of a kind will be rolled. The payoffs are 180 to 1 for the first type of bet and 30 to 1 for the second type. What are the bettor's expected percentage returns for these two bets?

4.14 On three different occasions, the betting odds on the great racehorse Man O'War were 1 to 100. For such a bet to have a positive expected return, how high would your probability of Man O'War's winning have to be?

4.15 With 5 to 6 betting odds on a football game, what probability of winning is necessary for a bettor to have a positive expected return?

4.16 (Gambler's Ruin) Moe and Joe agree to bet a dollar on a series of coin flips until one of them is bankrupt. Moe has $1000 and Joe has $4000. What is Moe's probability of winning?

4.5 INSURANCE

Insurance is another area in which probabilities and expected values are very important. The premiums that companies charge for life, house, car, boat, business, and other insurance policies are naturally influenced by the probabilities of having to make a payoff. Companies want to charge more to insure the sickly than to insure the healthy. They want to charge more to insure a rundown wooden house than to insure a new brick house. They want to charge accident-prone drivers more than safe drivers.

Interestingly, this wasn't always so. Early life insurance policies seem to have largely ignored the life-expectancy data collected by statisticians. For example, at least as long ago as the 1500s, the British government sold life annuities, which paid a fixed annual amount over the life of the purchaser. But, up until 1789, the price of life annuities did not depend on the age of the purchaser! These life annuities were unattractive to the elderly and a bargain for the young. It is not surprising that life annuities were purchased mainly by the young and that the British government paid dearly for its neglect of life-expectancy probabilities.

Modern insurance companies pay close attention to probabilities. Within their legal constraints, they try to charge their high-risk customers more and charge everyone enough to make a generous profit.

Let's look at a specific example. In 1983, a $100,000 one-year, life insurance policy for a 25-year-old woman cost about $120. In 1980, the U.S. Census Bureau calculated that there were 2 million 25-year-old women in the country and that 1300 died that year. If we use this observed frequency as an estimate of the probability P of a 25-year-old woman dying within a year, then

$$P = \frac{1300}{2,000,000} = .00065$$

The expected value of the policy's payoff is consequently

$$(\$100,000)(.00065) = \$65$$

as compared to a cost of $120.

On any single policy, the insurance company will collect $120 and pay out either nothing or $100,000. On the average, if a fraction .00065 of the insured 25-year-old women die, the company will collect $120 and pay out $65 per policy. Roughly half of the insurance premiums collected will be paid back out to beneficiaries and half will be retained by the company to cover salaries, office buildings, and profits. This 50 percent benefit-to-premium ratio is representative of many insurance policies.

Table 4.5 shows some comparable insurance premium data for women and men of various ages. The data in this table are the typical costs in 1983, by age and sex, of a one-year $100,000 life insurance policy for someone who passes a mandatory medical exam. If we assume a 50 percent benefit-to-premium ratio, then we can calculate the implied probability P of death within a year for someone who passes such a test. Notice that men pay more than women and that the old pay much more than the young. There are actually even more detailed risk distinctions in insurance rates. For example, most companies have lower rates for nonsmokers than for smokers. Modern insurance companies do indeed use probabilities (and implicitly, expected values) to set their premiums.

Table 4.5 *The structure of life insurance premiums*

	Female		Male	
Age	*Premium*	*Implicit* P	*Premium*	*Implicit* P
25	$120	.0006	$120	.0006
35	$120	.0006	$120	.0006
45	$132	.0007	$165	.0009
55	$205	.0010	$315	.0016
65	$475	.0024	$870	.0044

Of course, insurance companies cannot sort out high-risk and low-risk people perfectly. They consequently must offer the same premiums to people of varying risks. In general, those who are above-average risks will be tempted to buy lots of insurance, while low-risk people will buy less or else buy no insurance at all. Economists call this sorting "adverse selection." Insurance companies try to protect themselves from adverse selection by considering such risk indicators as smoking habits, by requiring health examinations, and by leaving a generous profit cushion in their premium calculations.

Exercises

4.17 Under legislative and judicial pressures, life insurance companies have been moving toward "unisex" rates, in which males and females pay equal premiums. Who gains from a unisex premium structure: men or women? Why?

4.18 A standard Wheel of Fortune is a large wheel divided into 54 sections. The wheel is spun and allowed to slow gradually and then stop, with a stationary marker pointing to one of the 54 sections. Each section is apparently equally likely to be selected.

Wagers are made by putting, say, a dollar on one of six numbers 1, 2, 3, 4, 5, or 6. Each of the 54 sections of the wheel contains three numbers—either three different numbers, a pair and a different number, or three of a kind. The payoffs (including the initial dollar back) are $2 for matching a single number, $3 for matching a pair, and $4 for matching three of a kind. The wheel is arranged so that, out of 5.4 sections, each number has 4 chances for a $4 payoff, 4 chances for a $3 payoff, 7 chances for a $2 payoff, and 39 chances for no payoff. What is the expected value of the payoff? In the long run, what fraction of every dollar wagered should the bettor expect to lose?

4.19 A land developer mails out 100,000 "Urgent Insta-Grams," announcing that the recipient has won a prize that can be claimed by visiting the developer's property and listening to a sales talk about "an exciting year-round vacation idea." The 100,000 awards consist of one check for $1000, two color televisions costing $500 apiece, four black-and-white televisions costing $100 apiece, four ten-speed bicycles costing $100 apiece, and 99,989 35-millimeter cameras (cardboard, with fixed focus) costing $1 apiece. What is the expected value of claiming a prize? If 99 percent of the recipients throw these Urgent Insta-Grams into the trash and 1 percent claim their prizes, what is the developer's expected cost for the prizes?

• **4.20** In a laboratory experiment, a group of fish were offered a choice between A and B. The experiment was set up so that option A would give a reward 70 percent of the time and no reward 30 percent of the time. Option B was constructed to give a reward 30 percent of the time and no reward 70 percent of the time. The fish soon began choosing option A 70 percent of the time and option B 30 percent of the time. When a group of rats was offered the same sort of options, the rats soon began choosing option A every time.[3]

Did the fish or the rats behave more intelligently?

4.6 EXPECTED VALUE MAXIMIZATION

The costs and benefits of most of the important decisions we make are not known with complete certainty. How, then, can we rationally make decisions? The expected values of the costs and benefits seem like a good place to start. If we can assign probabilities to the possible costs and benefits, then we can calculate their expected values. If the expected value of the benefits exceeds the expected value of the costs, then we should, averaged over many decisions, come out ahead.

An expected value calculation was, in fact, the earliest proposed criterion for rational decision making under uncertainty. According to the expected value rule, you should always choose the course of action with the highest expected net gain. An expected value criterion certainly seems appropriate when the uncertain situation will be repeated over and over again. It makes good sense to look at the long-run average when there is a long run to average over. Gambling casinos, state lotteries, and insurance companies are good examples. They will try to avoid offering gambles that give them a negative expected return because these would almost certainly lose money in the long run.

It is equally clear, however, that the expected return criterion is sometimes inappropriate. State lotteries are designed to have a positive expected return for the state, and so they must therefore have a negative expected return for the people who buy the lottery tickets. Their gain is your loss. The people who buy lottery tickets are not maximizing their expected returns. Insurance is another example. Insurance rates are set to give insurance companies a positive expected return and, hence, to give insurance buyers a negative expected return. People who buy insurance must not be maximizing expected returns either. Stock selection provides yet another example. If you wanted to maximize your expected return, you would invest all of your funds in the stock that offers the highest expected return. Why, then, do investors instead buy dozens of securities?

We can also construct hypothetical situations to show that expected return maximization is not always appealing. Consider, for example, this pleasant scenario. A messenger from a rich recluse stops you after class and announces that you have been chosen to receive a gift of $1 million. He pulls out a thick wad of crisp $100 bills to show you that he is serious. As you blink and reach for them, the messenger asks if you would prefer a coin flip to make things more sporting: heads, you receive $2.1 million; tails, you get nothing but a good story. Think about it. If, like most people, you would take the sure million, then you are not maximizing expected return.

The St. Petersburg Paradox

Another counterexample is the famous *St. Petersburg Paradox* that was concocted by the Swiss mathematician Nicolas Bernoulli in the eighteenth century:

> Peter repeatedly tosses a coin until it comes up heads. He agrees to give you one dollar if he gets a head on the very first throw, two dollars if he gets the first head on the second throw, four dollars if he gets it on the third throw, eight dollars if on the fourth throw, and so on, so that the number of dollars won doubles with each additional throw.

How much would you pay for an opportunity to play this game? Think about it for a minute, before we work out the arithmetic for the expected return.

Your possible returns are $1, $2, $4, $8, . . . with respective probabilities 1/2, 1/4, 1/8, 1/16, ... Your expected return is

$$E[X] = (\$1)(1/2) + (\$2)(1/4) + (\$4)(1/8) + (\$8)(1/16) + \cdots$$

$$= 1/2 + 1/2 + 1/2 + 1/2 + \cdots$$

$$= \infty$$

Therefore, if you are a dedicated expected-return maximizer, you should be willing to pay an unlimited amount for an opportunity to play this game. As few people are willing to pay more than a few dollars to play the St. Petersburg game, most people must be thinking about something other than a simple expected return maximization.

Risk Aversion

The primary inadequacy of expected return maximization is that it neglects **risk**—how certain or uncertain a situation is. An expected-return maximizer is indifferent given the choice between $1 million, a 50 percent chance at $2 million, or a 1 percent chance at $100 million because all three options have the same expected return. In an expected return calculation, it doesn't matter that in the first case there is a 100 percent chance of receiving $1 million and in the third case there is a 99 percent chance of getting nothing. But these differences do matter to many people. Diverse individuals have different attitudes toward risk, which they reveal by the decisions they make.

> **Risk-neutral:** Indifferent toward a fair bet. Five dollars with certainty and a 50 percent chance at $10 are equally attractive. Tries to simply maximize expected return. Does not buy insurance or lottery tickets because both have negative expected returns.

Risk-averse: Turns down fair bets. Prefers $5 to a 50 percent chance at $10. Will sacrifice expected return to reduce risk. Buys insurance but not lottery tickets.

Risk-seeking: Accepts fair bets. Prefers a 50 percent chance at $10 to a sure $5. Will sacrifice expected return to increase risk. Buys lottery tickets but not insurance.

This acknowledged variety in preferences explains why some people accept gambles that others shun and why some people buy insurance that others avoid. An individual's risk preferences may depend on the particular situation. Milton Friedman, a famous economist, and Leonard Savage, a celebrated statistician, argued that the following tendencies are commonplace:[4]

1. Risk-averse toward substantial losses. Will buy insurance to protect against large reductions in living standards.
2. Risk-neutral toward small gambles.
3. Risk-averse toward moderate gains. Prefers a sure $5000 to a 50 percent chance at $10,000.
4. Risk-seeking toward large, long-shot gains that would dramatically improve living standards. Will buy lottery tickets.
5. Risk-averse toward astounding gains. Prefers $1 million to a 50 percent chance at $2 million. Prefers two tickets on a $1 million lottery to one ticket on a $2 million lottery.

Exercises

4.21 On a football betting card, the bettor picks the winners of n selected games and is paid a specified amount if all n picks win. A point spread is used to equalize the games. We'll assume here that the point spread exactly equalizes each game, so that the bettor must choose between two equally likely winners. You can spend $x on any of these three cards and be paid the indicated amount:

a. $6x for correctly picking 3 out of 3 games
b. $11x for correctly picking 4 out of 4 games
c. $16x for correctly picking 5 out of 5 games

What is the expected payoff on each of these three cards?

4.22 (*continuation*) Does this structure of payoffs on football betting cards suggest something about bettors' preferences?

4.23 Ken Harrelson, a professional baseball player, once offered the Cleveland Indians General Manager, Gabe Paul, a St. Petersburg deal. Harrelson offered to play an entire baseball season without a salary, except for 50 cents doubled for every home run he hit; his salary would be 50 cents if he only hit 1 home run, $1 if he hit 2 home runs, $2 if he hit 3 home runs, and so on. Gabe Paul turned him down and Harrelson then went out and hit 30 home runs that season. If Harrelson's offer had been accepted, how much would Cleveland have owed him?

• **4.24**   Peter has offered to let you play the St. Petersburg paradox game, but the maximum payoff is some amount 2^m. What is your expected payoff?

4.7 THE STANDARD DEVIATION AS A MEASURE OF UNCERTAINTY

Drawing on their statistical backgrounds, Harry Markowitz and James Tobin developed **mean-variance analysis** in the 1950s. Their objective was to find a useful and reasonable improvement on expected return maximization. Markowitz and Tobin proposed, as a plausible approximation, that people base their decisions under uncertainty on just two factors—the mean and the variance. The *mean* is just another word for the expected value and, as we have seen, it was long ago proposed that expected values influence decisions. The problem with an expected value criterion, as we have also seen, is that it ignores risk. Markowitz and Tobin suggested extending the expected value criterion by using the variance to measure risk.

The standard deviation measures the amount of uncertainty because it gauges the probability of outcomes far from the expected return. If widely varying outcomes are probable, then the variance will be high. If there is little difference among the possible outcomes, then the variance will be low.

Four Examples

Consider the following four alternatives:

1. $5 with certainty
2. $10 with probability .5
   $0 with probability .5
3. $5 with probability .5
   $10 with probability .25
   $0 with probability .25
4. $5 with probability .5
   $105 with probability .25
   −$95 with probability .25

In mean-variance analysis, these four alternatives are evaluated by comparing their means and variances. To illustrate the calculations, let me show you that alternative 3 has an expected return

$$\mu = \$5(.5) + \$10(.25) + \$0(.25) = \$5$$

and a variance

$$\sigma^2 = (\$5 - \$5)^2(.5) + (\$10 - \$5)^2(.25) + (\$0 - \$5)^2(.25) = 12.50$$

The standard deviation is just the square root of the variance,

$$\sigma = \$3.54$$

In a similar manner, the expected returns, variances, and standard deviations for all four of the alternatives have been calculated and are found in Table 4.6.

The four alternatives were constructed to have the same $5 expected return. On the average, they should all do equally well in the long run, but as one-shot deals, they have widely varying degrees of risk or uncertainty. This risk could be gauged by either the variance or the standard deviation; the former is just the square of the latter. The alternative with the larger standard deviation will also have the larger variance. It is just a matter of taste whether one measures risk by the standard deviation or the variance. The standard deviation easily wins this taste test. One reason is that its units are dollars, as are the units of the expected return, while the units for the variance are dollars squared. Another reason is that, as we will see in later chapters, many statistical measures and tests are based on the standard deviation. By the time this course is over, you will be thinking in terms of "two standard deviations from the mean," but we're getting ahead of ourselves. The point here is just that we could use either the standard deviation or the variance to measure risk and uncertainty, and the the standard deviation is the preferred choice. In fact, despite its name, the graphical and numerical analytics of mean-variance analysis are actually done in terms of the mean and the standard deviation!

Let's go back to Table 4.6 and look at the standard deviation to gauge the riskiness of these four alternatives. The first alternative has a standard deviation of zero, reflecting the fact that there is no uncertainty about its return. The payoff is sure to be $5. The second alternative has an uncertain return and, consequently, a nonzero standard deviation. Alternative 3 is also uncertain, but has a somewhat smaller standard deviation than alternative 2. Alternative 3 has a larger chance of returns that differ from the mean and this is what the standard deviation and variance measure. Alternative 4 has the largest standard deviation because there is a substantial chance of returns that are far from the mean.

According to mean-variance analysis, people will take both the expected return and the standard deviation into account when making decisions. The four alternatives shown in Table 4.6 have the same expected return, but quite different

Table 4.6 *Four expected returns*

Alternative	Expected return μ	Variance σ^2	Standard deviation σ
1. $P[\$5] = 1.0$	$5	0	$0
2. $P[\$0] = .5$			
$P[\$10] = .5$	$5	25	$5
3. $P[\$5] = .5$			
$P[\$0] = .25$	$5	12.50	$3.54
$P[\$10] = .25$			
4. $P[\$5] = .5$			
$P[\$105] = .25$	$5	5000	$70.71
$P[-\$95] = .25$			

Risk Has its Reward

If investors are risk-averse, then they will shun risky investments—unless the price is right, that is unless they are compensated for that risk with a relatively high anticipated return. A high return cannot, of course, be guaranteed for a risky investment because, by its definition, a risky investment has a very uncertain return. However, a return that has a high standard deviation can also be priced low enough to have a high expected value. And if investors are predominantly risk averse, high standard deviations should be associated with high expected returns.

A study of annual returns over the period 1926 through 1978 obtained these results:[5]

| | returns | |
asset	mean	standard deviation
common stocks	11.2%	22.2%
long-term corporate bonds	4.1%	5.6%
long-term government bonds	3.4%	5.7%
short-term government bonds	2.5%	2.2%

These are historical realized returns, how people did rather than how well they thought they would do. Nonetheless, the results are an intriguing confirmation of our common sense. The safest asset, short-term government bonds, has also been the least rewarding, while the riskiest, common stock, has done the best on average. Stocks went up 54% one year and down 43% another year. They have been a risky, but also a rewarding, investment.

standard deviations. A risk-averse person will choose 1; a risk-seeker will select 4; and a risk-neutral person would be happy with any of these four alternatives.

Long Shots and Skewness

People seem to be mostly risk averse. Risk aversion is consistent with the personal introspection of cowardly professors and the observed behavior of decision makers. The most important qualification is that long shots have an undeniable appeal. For example, many people buy stock in young companies, even when the expected return is very low, hoping to catch the start of another IBM or Xerox.

One inadequacy of the standard deviation or variance as a measure of risk is the symmetrical treatment of gains and losses. The variance simply squares the deviations, positive or negative, about the mean. It does not matter if these deviations are pleasant or unpleasant surprises. Of course, they can't all be one or the other. By the definition of the expected return, if there is some chance of a pleasant surprise, then there is also some chance of an unpleasant one. These surprises need not be evenly distributed, however. There might be a large probability of a slightly above-average return and a small chance of a catastrophic loss, or there might instead be a large probability of a small loss and a small chance of a bonanza. The variance and standard deviation cannot distinguish between such differences. Consider these two assets:

	probability	return	expected return	standard deviation
Asset 1	.001	$9990	$0	$316.07
	.999	−$10		
Asset 2	.001	−$9990	$0	$316.07
	.999	$10		

By mean-variance criteria, there is no difference between these assets and investors should be indifferent to a choice between them. In practice, many people prefer Asset 1 to Asset 2.

Both of these assets are very asymmetrically *skewed* gambles. Asset 1 is a long shot in that there is a small chance of a large gain. Asset 2 is a "negative" long shot with a small chance of a large loss. We can gauge this asymmetry by calculating the coefficient of skewness:

$$\gamma = [E(X - \mu)^3]/\sigma^3$$

Asset 1, with its large positive deviation, has a positive skewness coefficient:

$$\gamma = \{(\$9990 - \$0)^3(.001) + (-\$10 - \$0)^3(.999)\}/(\$316.07)^3 = 31.6$$

Asset 2, with its large negative deviation, has a negative skewness coefficient:

$$\gamma = \{(-\$9990 - \$0)^3(.001) + (\$10 - \$0)^3(.999)\}/(\$316.07)^3 = -31.6$$

The purchase of a lottery ticket is a positively skewed gamble, like Asset 1, but it has a negative expected return. A decision not to purchase fire insurance is a negatively skewed gamble, like Asset 2, but it has a positive expected return. According to mean-variance analysis, a risk-seeker might buy a lottery ticket and spurn insurance. A risk-averter might avoid lottery tickets and buy insurance. But mean-variance analysis alone cannot explain the simultaneous purchase of both lottery tickets and fire insurance without resorting to such "irrational" explanations as a zest for the suspense of gambling or a mistaken assessment of the probabilities (what Adam Smith called "absurd presumptions in their own good fortune"[6]).

Skewness may be the rational explanation. The popularity of lottery tickets and insurance suggests that positive skewness is in fact attractive, so that people like Asset 1 but not Asset 2. This preference is also suggested by the overbetting on long shots at horse races. (Long shots would yield a negative average return even if the track did not take out 15 percent of the pool.) There have also been a number of empirical studies that provide more formal evidence.[7]

These apparent preferences imply that mean-variance analysis should be used cautiously in situations with highly skewed returns such as lottery tickets and fire insurance. In other situations, such as the purchase of financial assets, the returns may be sufficiently symmetrical for mean-variance analysis to be valuable.

There is the traditional conflict here between simplicity and generality. The widespread popularity of mean-variance analysis is due to the fact that it is very simple and yet quite powerful. Most of the theoretical and empirical work on portfolio selection and the pricing of financial assets is an outgrowth of mean-variance analysis. If you take a course on security valuation and portfolio theory, you will see just how easy and useful this analysis is. These attractive features are brought out most vividly by a comparison with the alternatives. A simpler approach, such as expected return maximization, cannot handle such important questions as risk aversion. On the other hand, more general approaches are quite cumbersome and yield relatively few interesting conclusions.

Exercises

4.25 ABC stock has a .5 probability of yielding a 15 percent return and a .5 probability of yielding a 5 percent return. What are its expected return and standard deviation?

4.26 CAB stock has a .3 probability of yielding a 20 percent return, a .5 probability of yielding 10 percent, and a .2 probability of yielding 0 percent. What are its expected return and standard deviation?

4.27 (*continuation*) Which is riskier: ABC stock or CAB stock? Which stock would a risk-neutral investor buy? Which stock would a risk-seeker buy? Which would a risk-averse investor buy?

● **4.28** (*continuation*) Are the returns from ABC and CAB stock positively skewed, negatively skewed, or symmetrical?

4.8 THE MEAN, STANDARD DEVIATION, AND SKEWNESS OF LINEAR TRANSFORMATIONS

Throughout this course, we will find it useful to describe uncertain situations by referring to the mean, standard deviation, and skewness of a random variable. The mean tells us the long-run average value of the random variable. The standard deviation tells us how likely it is that the outcome will be close to its mean value. The skewness tells us whether or not the outcomes are symmetrically distributed about the mean.

It turns out, though, that our analyses will sometimes require us to look at random variables that are linear transformations of other random variables. For example, we might be interested in the temperature in Dallas on this coming January 1, at kickoff time for the Cotton Bowl. If X is the temperature in degrees

Celsius, then $32 + 1.8X$ is the temperature in degrees Fahrenheit. The Fahrenheit temperature is a linear transformation of the Celsius temperature. As another example, we might spend $5000 on advertising, trying to sell a computer game for $40 that we can manufacture for $5. If the random variable X measures the number of games that we will sell, then $-\$5000 + \$35X$ will be our profit. As a final example, we might buy 10 shares of MBI stock at $100 apiece. If the random variable X is the price that we will get when we sell this stock, then $10(X - \$100) = -\$1000 + 10X$ is our capital gain.

In each of these examples, we have a pair of random variables that are linearly related to each other. If we know the mean, standard deviation, and skewness of one member of the pair, then we can find the mean, standard deviation, and skewness of the other. Here are the formulas (the derivations are left as an exercise at the end of the chapter). If X is a random variable with mean μ, standard deviation σ, and skewness coefficient γ, then the mean, standard deviation, and skewness of a linear transformation $a + bX$ are given by

$$\text{the expected value of } a + bX = a + b\mu \qquad (4.4)$$

$$\text{the standard deviation of } a + bX = |b|\sigma \qquad (4.5)$$

$$\text{the skewness coefficient of } a + bX = \gamma \qquad (4.6)$$

MBI Stock

These formulas make good sense, as a short example will show. Let's use the 10 shares of MBI stock that were purchased for $100 apiece and assume that the selling price X has a .5 probability of being $120 and a .5 probability of being $100. The expected value of the selling price is

$$\mu = (\$120)(.5) + (\$100)(.5) = \$110$$

The variance is

$$\sigma^2 = (\$120 - \$110)^2(.5) + (\$100 - \$110)^2(.5) = 100$$

and the standard deviation is

$$\sigma = 100^{1/2} = \$10$$

The skewness coefficient is

$$\gamma = (\$120 - \$110)^3(.5) + (\$100 - \$110)^3(.5) = 0$$

If this situation were somehow to repeat itself over and over again, we would anticipate selling the stock for $120 half of the time and for $100 the remaining half. The mean $\mu = \$110$ gives the anticipated average selling price. The particular situation is, however, undoubtedly unique and will never be repeated exactly. The standard deviation $\sigma = \$10$ measures how likely it is that this unique outcome will be close to the mean of $110. A small standard deviation indicates that the outcome is almost certain to be very close to $110. A large standard deviation indicates that the price is likely to be far from $110. In this simple case here, there are only two possible outcomes, $120 and $100, and each is a 100 squared deviation from $110. Thus, the variance (the average squared deviation) is 100 and the standard deviation (the square root of the variance) is $10. The skewness coefficient $\gamma = 0$ because the possible outcomes are symmetrical about $110.

Now what about our prospective capital gain $10(X - \$100) = -\$1000 + 10X$? We could calculate the capital gain for each of the possible selling prices and then compute the mean, standard deviation, and skewness of these possible capital gains. With only two possible outcomes, these calculations would be no big deal. But, in practice, there are usually a great many possible selling prices and such capital gains calculations would be a big deal. The linear transformations, Equations 4.4–4.6, give us an easy alternative. Using $a = -\$1000$ and $b = 10$, we immediately have

the expected value of $-\$1000 + 10X = -\$1000 + 10(\$110) = \$100$

the standard deviation of $-\$1000 + 10X = 10(\$10) = \$100$

the skewness coefficient of $-\$1000 + 10X = 0$

As we have 10 shares and the $110 expected value of the selling price is $10 more than we paid, the expected capital gain is $100. This gain is not certain; the average squared deviation is 100^2 and the standard deviation is $100. There is no skewness because the symmetrical selling prices makes the possible capital gains symmetrical about $100.

Exercises

4.29 Let C be a random variable giving the Celsius temperature in Nowhere, North Dakota at noon on this coming February 8. Exhaustive National Weather Service records indicate that the mean, standard deviation, and skewness coefficient of C are $\mu = -10$, $\sigma = 10$, and $\gamma = 1$. The Fahrenheit temperature at noon on February 8 is given by $F = 32 + 1.8C$. What are the mean, standard deviation, and skewness coefficient of the random variable F?

4.30 I am going to spend $5000 on advertising, trying to sell a computer game for $40 that I can manufacture for $5. If X is the number of games that I will sell, then $-\$5000 + \$35X$ is my profit. My subjective probabilities are

x	p
0	.10
50	.40
100	.30
500	.10
1000	.10

What are the means, standard deviations, and skewness coefficients of sales and profits?

• **4.31** Show that the formulas for the mean, standard deviation, and skewness coefficient of $a + bX$ are as given in Equations 4.4, 4.5, and 4.6.

4.9 SUMMARY

A random variable X can be used to tabulate the possible outcomes and associated probabilities in an uncertain situation. These probabilities $p[x]$ comprise a probability distribution. A graph of a probability distribution can clarify a complicated collection of probabilities.

Together, three calculations—the mean, standard deviation, and skewness coefficient—often paint an accurate picture of a probability distribution. The mean gives the location of the distribution, the standard deviation gauges its dispersion, and the skewness coefficient tells us whether or not the distribution is symmetrical.

The formulas are

$$\text{mean:} \quad \mu = E[X] = \Sigma\, x\, p[x]$$

$$\text{variance:} \quad \sigma^2 = E[(X - \mu)^2] = \Sigma\, (x - \mu)^2 p[x]$$

$$\text{standard deviation:} \quad \sigma = \text{square root of variance}$$

$$\text{skewness:} \quad \gamma = \frac{E[(X - \mu)^3]}{\sigma^3}$$

The expected value is used in practice to measure the long-run average value of X; an example is the long-run payoff from a state lottery or the long-run return from a certain investment strategy. The standard deviation often is used to gauge the riskiness of a situation. A large standard deviation indicates a great deal of uncertainty, in that the outcomes are likely to be far from the expected value. The skewness coefficient tells us whether or not the possible outcomes are symmetrical about the mean. A positive skewness coefficient indicates a long-shot situation in which there is a small chance that X will be much larger than its expected value and a large chance that X will be slightly below its expected value.

Sometimes, we want to calculate the mean, standard deviation, or skewness coefficient from a linear transformation of X. If X is a random variable with mean μ, standard deviation σ, and skewness coefficient γ, then the mean, standard deviation, and skewness of $a + bX$ are given by

$$\text{the expected value of } a + bX = a + b\mu$$

$$\text{the standard deviation of } a + bX = |b|\sigma$$

$$\text{the skewness coefficient of } a + bX = \gamma$$

REVIEW EXERCISES

4.32 Massive Insurance Liability Company (MILC) is considering insuring Howard Hardsell's voice for $1,000,000. They figure that there is only a .001 probability that they will have to pay off. If they charge $2000 for this policy, will it have a positive expected value for them?

What is the expected value of this policy to Howard Hardsell? If the expected value is negative, why would he even consider buying such a policy?

4.33 In bridge, the four players are dealt 13-card hands from a standard 52-card deck. A "Yarborough" is a hand containing no honors: not a single jack, queen, king, or ace. What is the probability of being dealt a Yarborough?

4.34 The Yarborough hand is said to be named after Lord Yarborough, who offered 1000-to-1 odds against a whist opponent being dealt a 13-card hand that did not contain a single ten, jack, queen, king, or ace. What is the probability of being dealt this original Yarborough hand? What is an opponent's expected percentage return from such a wager?

4.35 I have here a special 1961 "inverted-date" Lincoln penny. I will give you $10 if you can select it, while blindfolded, either:

a. in a single draw from a box containing 10 pennies, 1 dated 1961 and 9 dated 1960,
b. in 10 draws without replacement from a box containing 100 pennies, 1 dated 1961 and 99 dated 1960, or
c. in 10 draws with replacement from a box containing 100 pennies, 1 dated 1961 and 99 dated 1960.

Do you prefer option a, b, or c?

• 4.36 Use the data in Table 4.2 to answer the following question: "If we were to select randomly one of the 217,482,000 U.S. citizens living in households, what is the probability that we would select a person who lives in a single-person household?" What is the probability that we would select a person who lives in a two-person household? Graph the complete probability distribution for this random variable (the number of people in the selected person's household).

• 4.37 Label the batting order on a baseball team 1, 2, 3, . . . , 9. If each position is equally likely to be the last batter in any given game, then over the course of a 180-game season, how many more expected times at bat will the #1 hitter have in comparison with #2? In comparison with #3? In comparison with #9?

• • 4.38 A certain weather bureau must forecast "rain" or "no rain" each day. They receive five times as many complaints when they incorrectly forecast "no rain" as they receive when they incorrectly forecast "rain." Nobody complains when their forecast is correct. Each day, they estimate a new probability P of rain. For which values of P should they forecast "rain" if they want to minimize the expected number of complaints?

4.39 A boule wheel is similar to a roulette wheel, but contains only 18 slots. Two of the slots are numbered 1, two are numbered 2, and so on through 9. Calculate the expected percentage returns from the following bets. In each case, the payoff is $1 for every $1 bet.

a. The ball lands on a low number (1, 2, 3, or 4).
b. The ball lands on a high number (6, 7, 8, or 9).
c. The ball lands on an odd number other than 5 (1, 3, 7, or 9).
d. The ball lands on an even number (2, 4, 6, or 8).

4.40 (*continuation*) At a boule wheel, one can also bet that the ball will land on a selected number: 1, 2, . . . , 8, or 9. The payoff for this bet is $7 for every $1 wagered. What is the expected percentage return?

• 4.41 The Italian national lottery, "Lotto," dates back to the 1500s. Every week, five numbers are randomly drawn from 90 tickets bearing the numbers 1, 2, . . . , 90. The bettor may make any of the following wagers.

a. Specify a number that will be among the five selected: payoff 10.5 to 1.
b. Specify a number and the order in which it will be drawn: payoff 52.5 to 1.
c. Specify two numbers that will be among the five selected: payoff 250 to 1.
d. Specify three numbers that will be among the five selected: payoff 4250 to 1.
e. Specify four numbers that will be among the five selected: payoff 80,000 to 1.
f. Specify all five selected numbers in order: payoff 1,000,000 to 1.

What are the expected percentage returns from each of these bets? What fraction, on the average, of every lira wagered will the Italian government keep?

● **4.42**   Sean Connery, the British actor who played James Bond so often, won a considerable amount of money at roulette in 1963 when he bet on the number 17 and it came up three times in a row. Joe College, an admirer of James Bond, has an extra $10 and has decided to try to duplicate this feat. He wagers $10 on the number 17. If he wins, he will have $360, which he will then bet on 17 again. If he wins again, he will leave his money on 17 for a third try. He will quit after his third win or if, unexpectedly, he loses at some point. With a 38-number wheel, what is Mr. College's chances of winning three times in a row? How much money will he have if he does win three times in a row? What is the expected value of his net gain?

●● **4.43**   In Keno, there are 80 ping pong balls, numbered 1, 2, . . . , 80. Bettors are given cards containing these 80 numbers and can select from 1 to 15 numbers. If the bettor decides to pick 10 numbers, for example, then this is called a 10-spot card. After the bettors have filled out their cards, a ''Keno goose'' picks 20 balls at random. Payoffs are based on the type of card and the number of correct picks. On a 60-cent, 8-spot card, for instance, the payoffs are $5 for 5 correct picks, $50 for 6 correct, $1100 for 7, and $12,500 for all 8. What is the expected percentage return?

● **4.44**   In August 1973, Jimmy the Greek quoted the following odds:

14 to 1 on Henry Aaron hitting a home run in his next time at bat.
4 to 1 on Henry Aaron hitting a home run in the next game he starts.

Simultaneously, Seymour Siwolff calculated that Henry Aaron, on the average, bats 3.24 times per game when he starts. Are Jimmy the Greek's odds consistent with Siwolff's calculation?

● **4.45**   At the start of the 1981 NBA playoffs, the following odds of winning the championship were offered:

Celtics	3 to 1
Lakers	4 to 1
Suns	4 to 1
Sixers	5 to 1
Bucks	5 to 1
Spurs	20 to 1
Knicks	35 to 1
Bulls	40 to 1
Blazers	40 to 1
Rockets	100 to 1
Pacers	100 to 1
Kings	100 to 1

For each team, what would the probability of winning have to have been to give a bet a zero expected net return? What is the sum of these twelve implied probabilities? Why is this probability sum not equal to 1.0? To ensure a $100 payoff no matter who wins, how much would you have to had bet on each team? What would be your net percentage gain or loss from such a blanket bet?

4.46 Jason, Jennifer, and Joshua decide to play poker until one player has won everything. Jason has $500, Jennifer has $500, and Joshua has $1000. If the three players are equally skilled so that each has a zero expected gain, what are each player's chances of winning?

• **4.47** Four quarrelsome brothers have inherited a prosperous farm. Convinced that they cannot work together, they decide to play "survival of the fittest," a vicious game that they have been playing since childhood. Each brother is given $25 at the start of the game. The two youngest brothers then flip coins, betting $1 on each flip, until one has lost his $25 stake. The winner then takes his $50 and flips coins with the next oldest brother until one is eliminated. The winner then has $75 to go up against the oldest brother. Whoever survives this final round gets the farm. Is there any advantage to being the youngest or the oldest brother in this ruthless game?

4.48 An example on page 125 discusses a Maxwell House pricing decision. Calculate the mean, standard deviation, and skewness of the change in profits for each of the two options considered. How would you characterize the choice?

• **4.49** Standardized tests, like the SAT and GMAT, convert the raw scores based on the number of right and wrong answers into scaled scores, typically with a mean of 500 and standard deviation of 100. For instance, each raw score X might be multiplied by 4.5 and then added to 180: 4.5 X + 180. In this way a raw score of 80 is converted into a scaled score of 4.5 (80) + 180 = 540. Where do you think the scaling numbers 4.5 and 180 come from?

• **4.50** On the roulette wheel used in the U.S. there are 38 numbers (00, 0, 1, 2, . . . , 36), each apparently equally likely to catch the spun ball. One bet is that one of the 12 numbers 1, 2, . . . , 12 will come up. If $1 is wagered on this bet, then the bettor will either win $2 or lose $1. Another bet is that a particular number will come up. If $1 is wagered on this bet, then the bettor will either win $35 or lose $1. What are the expected returns, standard deviations, and skewness coefficients for these two bets? Explain, in words, the different natures of the two bets.

CHAPTER 5

The Binomial Distribution

In the long run, we will all be dead.

J.M. Keynes

TOPICS

You have now learned what probabilities are, where they come from, how they are calculated, and what they can be used for. In this chapter, I will introduce you to a special probability distribution that statisticians use frequently. If we flip a fair coin, the probability of a head is .5 and the probability of a tail is .5. In the long run, we expect heads to come up about half of the time, but what about in the short run? In ten flips, what is the probability of obtaining exactly five heads? What are the chances of obtaining six heads, seven heads, or even ten straight heads? And what about that hypothetical long run? Is there any guarantee that we will get 50 percent heads in the long run? Is there any chance at all of 60 percent, 70 percent, or even 100 percent heads in the long run? These interesting questions, and many more, can be answered by the remarkable binomial distribution.

5.1 BERNOULLI TRIALS

Before explaining and using this distribution, I want to convince you of its widespread relevance. There are many uncertain situations that have the same characteristics as the classic coin-flipping example. The relevant features are:

1. There are two possible outcomes, not necessarily equally likely, that are labeled generically "success" and "failure."
2. If the uncertain situation is repeated, the probabilities of success and failure are unchanged. The probability of success is not affected by the successes or failures that already have been experienced.

An uncertain situation that satisfies these two conditions is called a **binomial trial** or a **Bernoulli trial,** after James Bernoulli (1654–1705), one of an eminent family of Swiss mathematicians.

There are many situations that qualify as Bernoulli trials. A series of coin flips satisfies the two conditions. So do the roll of dice or the spin of a roulette wheel, if we think of certain numbers as "successes" and the remaining numbers as "failures." Perhaps some fraction of the shirts, toasters, or cars produced by a certain company are defective. If each item, as it is produced or purchased, has a constant probability of being defective that does not depend on whether or not other items turn out to be defective, then the selection of these shirts, toasters, or cars qualifies as Bernoulli trials. If someone is given independent medical tests by several different doctors and the probability of a particular diagnosis is the same with each doctor, then these tests, too, are Bernoulli trials. If we conduct a political poll and, for each independent interview, have the same constant probability of selecting someone who favors a particular candidate, then these interviews are Bernoulli trials. If, each day, the percentage change in stock prices does not depend on how the market did on other days, and if the probabilities of going up or down do not vary from day to day, then the path of stock prices is also a series of Bernoulli trials.

In this book, we will encounter a multitude of situations that can be thought of as Bernoulli trials. There are several examples in this chapter and many more in the exercises at the end of the chapter. Other examples will appear in later chapters, and there will be some on your exams. By the time this course is over, you may be seeing Bernoulli trials all around you. Don't worry. That's perfectly natural and they're completely harmless.

Sampling Without Replacement

If we draw cards, one after another, from a standard deck, these would not be Bernoulli trials because the probabilities change as cards are removed from the deck. They would be Bernoulli trials, though, if the cards are replaced and the deck is reshuffled after each draw. Similarly, if we are randomly drawing households from the U.S. population, a strict Bernoulli trial would require that each selected household be put back in the deck, possibly to be drawn again.

But sometimes the "deck" is so large that we assume a Bernoulli trial even though the "cards" are not replaced after each draw. Imagine that we actually have a million decks of cards shuffled together to form one enormous deck with 52 million cards. Perhaps success is drawing a heart. As there are 13 million hearts scattered among the 52 million cards in all, the initial probability of a heart is exactly .25. If the first card drawn is a heart and it is not replaced, then the probability of a heart on the second draw falls to

$$\frac{12,999,999}{51,999,999} = .249999986$$

If the first card withdrawn is not a heart, then the probability of a heart on the second try rises to

$$\frac{13,000,000}{51,999,999} = .250000005$$

For most purposes, it would be perfectly acceptable to simply assume that the probability of a heart stays at .25, regardless of the outcome of the first draw. There is undoubtedly more error introduced by inadequately shuffling 52,000,000 cards than by neglecting to replace a few cards withdrawn from the deck.

In the same spirit, we commonly apply the Bernoulli trial model to the random selection of people, to see if they are male or female, married or unmarried, young or old, rich or poor, Republican or Democrat, or whatever. There is a slight distortion because we do not put people back into the deck, possibly to be selected again, but usually this distortion can be safely neglected. The more worrisome danger is that the deck is not adequately shuffled, and that everyone does not have the same probability of being selected and interviewed.

Exercises

5.1 Explain the Bernoulli trial assumptions in your own words.

5.2 Identify which of the following are Bernoulli trials and explain your reasoning:

a. the number of heads when a coin is flipped five times
b. the number of hits when three baseball players bat against a pitcher
c. the number of birds landing on a telephone wire in an hour's time
d. the number of Republicans elected to Congress from Oregon in the next election
e. the number of boy babies born in Cleveland tomorrow

5.2 BINOMIAL PROBABILITIES

With this introduction, let's now figure out the probability distribution for Bernoulli trials. We'll start with a specific example and then deduce the general formula. Consider some game of chance in which your probability of winning ("success") is π ("pi," a variable, not the scientific number 3.14 . . .) and your probability of losing ("failure") is $1 - \pi$. This game could involve coins, dice, a roulette wheel, or whatever. If you play the game five times, what is the probability of winning exactly three times?

The first thing to recognize is that there are several different routes to three successes and two failures. The first three games could be successes, followed by two failures: SSSFF. You could start with two failures and then finish strong with three straight successes: FFSSS. Or you could alternate SFSFS. And there are other three-success sequences. To figure the probability of three successes, we need to know how many three-success sequences are possible and how probable each sequence is.

Fortunately, because the games are independent, each three-success sequence has exactly the same probability of occurring. If the probability of a success is π, then

$$P[\text{SSSFF}] = \pi\pi\pi(1 - \pi)(1 - \pi) = \pi^3(1 - \pi)^2$$

$$P[\text{FFSSS}] = (1 - \pi)(1 - \pi)\pi\pi\pi = \pi^3(1 - \pi)^2$$

$$P[\text{SFSFS}] = \pi(1 - \pi)\pi(1 - \pi)\pi = \pi^3(1 - \pi)^2$$

Each sequence containing three successes and two failures has the probability $\pi^3(1 - \pi)^2$.

All that remains is to count the number of possible sequences carefully. What we have here is three successes and two failures, and we want to know the number of unique ways that these can be arranged. This is our old friend, the combination problem from Chapter 2!

Think of the five trials as being distinct slots, numbered 1, 2, 3, 4, and 5. We want to pick three of these numbered slots to label successes. How many different three-number combinations can be chosen? The combination formula tells us that the number of three-item combinations that can be made out of five distinct items is

$$\binom{5}{3} = \frac{5!}{3! \, 2!} = 10$$

Let's check our logic by writing out all the possible combinations:

sequence	*success slots*
SSSFF	1, 2, 3
SSFSF	1, 2, 4
SSFFS	1, 2, 5
SFSSF	1, 3, 4
SFSFS	1, 3, 5
SFFSS	1, 4, 5
FSSSF	2, 3, 4
FSSFS	2, 3, 5
FSFSS	2, 4, 5
FFSSS	3, 4, 5

There are ten possible sequences. Our logic is confirmed!

These, then, are the two parts to our answer. The probability of any particular three-success–two-failure sequence is $\pi^3(1 - \pi)^2$ and there are ten possible sequences. Therefore the probability of exactly three successes and two failures is

$$\binom{5}{3}\pi^3(1 - \pi)^2 = 10\pi^3(1 - \pi)^2$$

This logic is easily generalized:

> The **binomial distribution** states that, in n Bernoulli trials, with probability π of success on each trial, the probability of exactly x successes is
>
> $$P[x \text{ successes}] = \binom{n}{x}\pi^x(1 - \pi)^{n-x} \qquad (5.1)$$

A complete binomial distribution is found by computing the probabilities for all of the possible values of X, from 0 to n. In practice, instead of actually calculating the probabilities, we usually find it easier and more accurate to simply look them up in a convenient table, such as Table 1 in the back of this book.[1]

If you do calculate an occasional binomial probability by yourself, be aware of the special cases $x = 0$ and $x = n$. If $x = 0$, the binomial formula is

$$P[0 \text{ successes}] = \binom{n}{0}\pi^0(1 - \pi)^n = (1 - \pi)^n$$

because $\binom{n}{0} = 1$ and $\pi^0 = 1$. The answer $P[0 \text{ successes}] = (1 - \pi)^n$ is quite logical because the probability of zero successes is the probability of n straight failures, which, by the multiplication rule, is $(1 - \pi)^n$. Similarly, for $x = n$,

$$P[n \text{ successes}] = \binom{n}{n}\pi^n(1 - \pi)^0 = \pi^n$$

A Few Examples

Let's try a few examples. First, what about those five plays of a game of chance? If the probability of winning a game is $\pi = .45$, then the probability of winning exactly three games is

$$\binom{5}{3}(.45)^3(.55)^2 = .2757$$

This one is not in Table 1, so you will have to run it through a calculator if you want to confirm my arithmetic.

Here's another example. Mr. and Mrs. Steinem decide to have four children. What is the probability of two boys and two girls? In Chapter 2, we came up with .513 as the probability of a male baby. If these children's sexes are independent, then we can view Mrs. Steinem's childbirths as Bernoulli trials. The probability of exactly two boys is

$$\binom{4}{2}(.513)^2(.487)^2 = .3745$$

which is far from a sure thing.

Now, let's try a considerably more complicated example. A wildcat driller believes that there is a .5 probability of oil at a certain site. A lease is obtained and five independent tests are conducted. Each test has a .8 probability of a positive reading when there is oil and a .8 probability of a negative reading when there is no oil. It turns out that four of the tests are positive and one is negative. What is the revised probability of oil, taking this evidence into account?

This is a Bayes' rule problem. If we let S and F denote positive and negative test results, then the formula is

$$P[\text{oil} \mid 4S\&1F] = \frac{P[\text{oil}]\, P[4S\&1F \mid \text{oil}]}{P[\text{oil}]\, P[4S\&1F \mid \text{oil}] + P[\text{no oil}]\, P[4S\&1F \mid \text{no oil}]}$$

We have $P[\text{oil}] = P[\text{no oil}] = .5$. The remaining probabilities can be computed from the binomial distribution. If there is oil, then the probability of a positive reading is $\pi = .8$, so that

$$P[4S\&1F \mid \text{oil}] = \binom{5}{4}(.8)^4(.2)^1 = .4096$$

If there is no oil, then the probability of a positive reading is $\pi = .2$, so that

$$P[4S\&1F \mid \text{no oil}] = \binom{5}{4}(.2)^4(.8)^1 = .0064$$

Putting these binomial probabilities into Bayes' formula, we have

$$P[\text{oil} \mid 4S\&1F] = \frac{(.5)(.4096)}{(.5)(.4096) + (.5)(.0064)}$$

$$= .9846$$

Unrepresentative Representatives

In the 1960s, there was an increasing awareness of discrimination against women, blacks, Chicanos, and other groups. One of the arguments made was that these groups were deliberately underrepresented on juries, convention delegations, legislatures, and other bodies that are supposed to represent all segments of society. If we interpret ''representative'' as meaning randomly selected from the population as a whole, then these claims can be evaluated statistically.*

Let's say that we are randomly selecting 12 people, perhaps for a jury or as delegates to a political convention. Assume that the population is divided into two groups of equal size, say male and female. If the population is large and the selection is random, then each selection has a .5 probability of being male and a .5 probability of being female. What is the probability that all 12 selected people will be male? This is a binomial probability with $\pi = .5$, $n = 12$, and $x = 12$, so that

$$P[12 \text{ males}] = \binom{12}{12}(.5)^{12}(.5)^0$$

$$= (.5)^{12}$$

$$= 1/4096$$

$$= .00024$$

If there is reason to suspect the deliberate exclusion of females and it turns out that all 12 of the selected people are male, then the improbability of an all-male selection certainly fuels this suspicion. Similarly, the binomial distribution tells us that random selection is unlikely to result in 10 or 11 of the selected people being male:

$$P[11 \text{ males}] = \binom{12}{11}(.5)^{11}(.5)^1 = .00293$$

$$P[10 \text{ males}] = \binom{12}{10}(.5)^{10}(.5)^2 = .01611$$

If the selection of these 12 people is random with males and females equally likely to be selected, then the probability that there will be fewer than 3 females selected is $.00024 + .00293 + .01611 = .01928$. If the selected group turns out to be so disproportionately male, then there is bound to be suspicion that the selection was not really random after all.

Now we do have to be careful here in that, if we examine many twelve-person groups, we are bound to find a few that are disproportionately male or female even if the selection is truly random. On the average, with random selection, we expect to find 2 out of every 100 twelve-person groups having fewer than 3 females (and

*An alternative interpretation is that ''representative'' means a deliberate attempt to select people who represent all segments of society. In Chapter 8 we will see that such deliberate efforts may instead merely represent the biases of the person making the selections.

a like number having fewer than 3 males). It is not correct to scrutinize 100 groups, find a few that are disproportionately male or female, and then claim that these specific groups were not randomly selected. If we look at data for 100 twelve-person groups, then we should report the male-female split for all 1200 selected people, not just for some carefully chosen subsets.

A similar, but more subtle error, occurs when one set of data is examined many different ways. We might decide to carefully scrutinize a particular twelve-person group. First, we see if there is a disproportionate number of males or females. Then, we see if there is a disproportionate number of blacks or whites. Next, we turn to Chicanos, American Indians, and Jews. Then, on to the young, the poor, the rural, the blue-collar workers, the high-school dropouts, Republicans, NFL tight ends, and anything else we can think of. These categories are not independent but, still, we would be making the same kind of error in looking at many characteristics that we made in looking at many twelve-person groups.

Surprisingly, four positive readings on five imperfect tests makes oil almost a certainty. This strong conclusion follows because the chances of four positive readings when there is oil are so much greater than the chances of four positive readings when there is no oil.

Exercises

5.3 A coin is to be flipped four times to determine who pays for lunch. You can either predict that heads and tails will each come up twice or you can predict that heads and tails will not come up equally often. Which do you choose?

5.4 A certain very tired student is asleep half of the time in math class. What is the probability that this student will be caught sleeping if the math professor only looks up from the lecture notes three times? What is the probability that the student will be sleeping all three times that this professor glances up from the notes?

5.5 On your first day at college, the dean tells each student to, "Look at the student on your left and the student on your right; one of you three won't graduate from this college." Assuming that one-third of the new students do not graduate and that each student is equally likely to be one of the nongraduates, what are the probabilities that, out of three new students (you and the ones on your left and right),

a. all three will graduate?
b. one will not graduate?
c. two will not graduate?
d. all three will not graduate?

5.6 A prominent professor claims that no one can predict which stocks will do better than average ("winners") and which will do below average ("losers"). To refute this claim, a well-paid securities analyst selects six stocks to do better than average over the coming year. If the professor is right, what is the probability that all six stocks will be winners? That five will be winners? That four will be winners?

• **5.7** (*continuation*) If the professor is right and the performances of twenty securities analysts are studied, what is the probability that at least one analyst will pick six winners?

• **5.8** An organization is having a national convention of ten-person delegations from each of the fifty states. In California, 30 percent of the members of this organization are black. If the delegates are selected randomly, what is the probability that none of the ten California delegates will be black? What is the probability that fewer than two delegates will be black?

Now assume, for the sake of simplicity, that in every state 30 percent of this organization's members are black. If the delegates are selected randomly, what is the probability that at least one state will have no black delegates? What is the probability that at least one state will have fewer than two black delegates?

5.3 THE SHAPE OF A BINOMIAL DISTRIBUTION

So far, we have focused on specific binomial probabilities. Now, for a full binomial distribution, let's go back to the five plays of a game of chance. You could win anywhere from zero to five games. If the probability of winning a game is, say, $\pi = .2$, then the probabilities of winning various numbers of games are

number of wins X	probability $\binom{5}{x}(.2)^x(.8)^{n-x}$
0	.3277
1	.4096
2	.2048
3	.0512
4	.0064
5	.0003

You should check these probabilities in Table 1 to be certain that you know how to use this table.

This particular binomial distribution is graphed in Figure 5.1. If the probability of winning a game was some fraction other than .20, then the resulting binomial distribution would, of course, be different. Figure 5.1 shows two of these other distributions, one for $\pi = .5$ and another for $\pi = .8$.

Notice that the binomial distribution for $\pi = .5$ is symmetrical, while the other two distributions are asymmetrical. Notice also that, in each case, the largest probabilities seem to be near $X = \pi n$, which makes sense. If $\pi = .2$, then 1 out of 5 is the most likely result. If $\pi = .8$, then 4 out of 5 is most likely. For $\pi = .5$, we expect to win about half of the time. Half of 5 is 2.5, which of course is not feasible, but 2 or 3 wins should be very likely.

More formally, it can be shown (with some difficulty[2]) that the expected value, variance, standard deviation, and skewness coefficient for a binomial distribution are

$$E[X] = \pi n \qquad\qquad (5.2)$$

$$\text{variance of } X = \pi(1 - \pi)n \tag{5.3}$$

$$\text{standard deviation of } X = \{\pi(1 - \pi)n\}^{1/2} \tag{5.4}$$

$$\text{skewness coefficient of } X = (1 - 2\pi)/\{\pi(1 - \pi)n\}^{1/2} \tag{5.5}$$

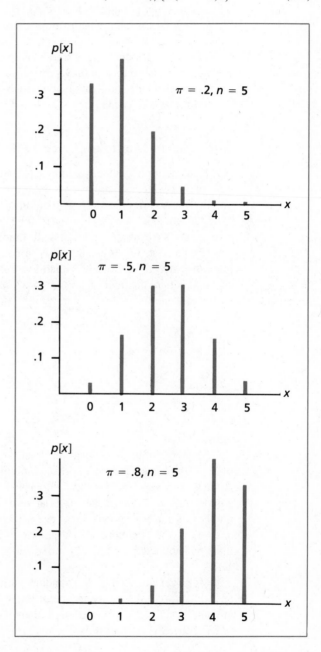

Figure 5.1 *Three binomial distributions*

The expected value is quite logical. If we conduct a sequence of n trials many times, we expect a fraction π of our trials to be successes, that is, an average of πn successes per n-trial sequence.

The equations for the variance and standard deviation show that there is always dispersion in the possible values of X unless success or failure is certain ($\pi = 1$ or 0). Beyond that, the exact formulas are difficult to explain intuitively, so we should just accept them as being correct.

The skewness coefficient shows us that, with the exception of $\pi = 1$ or 0, the binomial distribution is only symmetrical if $\pi = .5$. As Figure 5.1 illustrates, the binomial distribution is positively skewed for π less than .5 and negatively skewed for π greater than .5.

Guessing on Multiple-Choice Tests

A typical multiple-choice question has four plausible answers (A, B, C, or D), only one of which is correct. An uninformed guesser has a probability $\pi = .25$ of selecting the right answer. If there are $n = 20$ questions on the test, then the expected number of correct answers for a pure guesser is $\pi n = (.25)(20) = 5$. Over many such tests, a guesser will almost certainly average about five correct answers per test. On any single test, of course, a guesser will probably get either more than five correct or fewer than five correct. The exact probabilities are given by the binomial distribution with $\pi = .25$ and $n = 20$. Table 1 reveals that there is, in fact, only a .2024 probability of getting exactly five correct answers:

number correct	probability
<3	.0913
3	.1339
4	.1896
5	.2024
6	.1686
7	.1124
>7	.1018

Many multiple-choice tests are graded so that a guesser has an expected score of zero, the same as someone who simply doesn't bother to answer the questions. Because a guesser may get the right answer, points must be subtracted for a wrong answer to keep the expected score at zero. On a 20-question exam, the expected number of correct answers for a guesser is 5 and the expected number of wrong answers is 15. Therefore, if one point is given for a right answer, 1/3 of a point must be subtracted for a wrong answer to get a guesser's expected score down to zero.

More generally, if X is a random variable measuring the number of correct answers out of n questions; if 1 point is given for a correct answer; and if w points are subtracted for a wrong answer, then (using the fact that $E[a + bX] = a + bE[X]$), the expected score is

$$E[(X)(1) + (n - X)(-w)] = E[-wn + (1 + w)X]$$
$$= -wn + (1 + w)E[X]$$
$$= -wn + (1 + w)\pi n$$

This expected score equals zero if the penalty for a wrong answer is

$$w = \pi/(1 - \pi)$$

With four questions, $\pi = .25$ and the penalty should be $w = .25/.75 = 1/3$. With five questions, $\pi = .2$ and the penalty should be $w = .2/.8 = 1/4$. These are, in fact, the penalties used on the SAT tests, GMAT tests, and other widely used multiple-choice exams.

Is there, then, any advantage to guessing? Well, informed guessing is clearly a good strategy. If you can eliminate even one of the possible answers, guessing will give a positive expected score—which is an improvement over the zero score received when a question is left blank. For instance, let's say that there is a tough question with four possible answers (A, B, C, and D). You can eliminate one of the answers, say A, but you have no idea which of the three remaining answers is correct. If you guess, you have a 1/3 chance of being right (and getting 1 point) and a 2/3 chance of being wrong (and being penalized 1/3 of a point). Your expected score on this question is positive:

$$1(1/3) + (-1/3)(2/3) = 1/9$$

It's not much, but every little bit helps. On the average, in the long run, this sort of barely informed guessing should raise your score by 1/9 of a point per question.

What about totally uninformed guessing? If you are running out of time, is there any advantage to simply marking answers willy-nilly without regard for the questions, let alone the right answers? The test booklets say, "random guessing will most probably yield a net raw score of zero, so it is not a useful strategy." It is true that guessing has an expected net score of zero and almost certainly will not be a useful strategy, on the average, in the long run. But the test taker is interested in the single test at hand, not some hypothetical long-run average score. On a single test, guessing the answers to some questions may well raise or lower your score. We've seen that, if you guess the answers to twenty questions, there is only about a .2 probability that you will get exactly five right. There is a .8 probability that you will get either more or fewer than the expected number of correct answers. On a single test, guessing the answers to some questions will probably raise or lower your overall score. Your decision to try your luck depends on your situation.

Imagine that you somehow find yourself taking a test with no idea of the correct answers, and yet you know that a score of zero means failure. Should you leave the test blank and passively accept a zero or should you give yourself at least a slim chance by guessing? A slim chance is better than no chance, so guess away.

Fortunately, we seldom find ourselves in such a totally desperate position, but

© 1968 United Feature Syndicate, Inc.

you may well encounter situations where analogous logic applies. Perhaps you are about to graduate from college and are torn between taking a job and going to business school. You decide that you will go to business school if you are accepted by one of the very best schools; otherwise, you will work for a few years and maybe go to business school later. With your grades, you figure that you need to score at least at the 90th percentile on the Graduate Management Admission Test (GMAT) to be accepted by a top business school. The GMAT is a $3\frac{1}{2}$-hour test consisting of approximately 200 multiple-choice questions covering reading recall, verbal aptitude, mathematics, data sufficiency, and business judgment. Each question has five possible answers, with one point given for the correct answer and one-quarter point deducted for a wrong answer. The GMAT test is used by many business schools to help evaluate applicants.

You dutifully take the GMAT test and find that, with 15 seconds remaining, you still have 20 questions left to answer. Should you leave them blank or should you hurriedly guess?

In the long run, if you were to take the test over and over again, it almost certainly wouldn't make any difference to your average GMAT score, but on this particular test, guessing probably will raise or lower your score a few points. The problem, of course, is that you don't know which will happen. Your decision to take this gamble should depend on how well you think you have done on the rest of the test. If you believe that you have done well enough to hit the magic 90th percentile, then don't jeopardize a good score by guessing. However, if you think that you have done poorly and have little hope of hitting the all-important 90th percentile, then you may as well guess and take your chances.

Exercises

5.9   A fair six-sided die is rolled 30 times. What is the expected number of times that the number 1 will come up? What is the probability that the number 1 will come up its expected number of times?

5.10   In 1984, a sports columnist for the Dallas Morning News had a particularly bad week picking the winners of NFL football games—he got 1 right and 12 wrong, with 1 tie. Afterwards, he wrote that, ''Theoretically, a baboon at the Dallas Zoo can look at a schedule of 14 NFL teams, point to 1 team for each game and come out with at least 7 winners.''

a. Assuming no ties, what is the probability that a baboon will get at least 7 winners in 14 picks?
b. What is the probability that a baboon will get no more than 1 out of 13 right?

5.11   (*continuation*) The next week, Kanda the Great, a gorilla at the Dallas Zoo, made his predictions by selecting pieces of paper from his trainer. Kanda got 9 right and 4 wrong, better than all 6 Morning News sportswriters.

a. What is the probability that a baboon will pick as many as 9 out of 13 correctly?
b. What is the probability that a baboon will beat all 6 News staffers, if these staffers are no smarter than baboons when it comes to predicting NFL winners?

5.12   You have an 8:00 A.M. history class and a perfect attendance record—you've missed every class. The final exam is at 11:00, so you show up. Fortunately, the final is true-false and you've prepared by shining up your lucky coin. There are 20 questions; what is the probability that you will get at least 15 right? Your statistics final is even tougher—with 20 multiple-choice questions, each with 4 possible answers. You flip your lucky penny twice to determine the answers you choose (HH = A, HT = B, TH = C, and TT = D).

a. What is the probability that you will get 15 questions right and 5 wrong?
b. What is the probability that you will get more than 15 questions right?
c. What is the probability that you will get the first 15 questions right and the last 5 wrong?
d. What is the probability that you will get all 20 questions wrong?

• 5.13   You are taking a multiple-choice exam where each question has five possible answers: A, B, C, D, and E. This test is scored so that a pure guesser has an expected score of zero. If one point is given for a correct answer, how many points are subtracted for a wrong answer? What is your expected score on a question if you can rule out

a. one answer as definitely wrong?
b. two answers as definitely wrong?
c. three answers as definitely wrong?
d. four answers as definitely wrong?

5.14   Explain why you agree or disagree with this test-taking advice: ''Guessing is penalized on these examinations, since a percentage of the number of wrong answers is subtracted from the number of right answers. The applicant who feels that it would be a pity to leave answers blank and therefore chooses the answer that ''looks good'' will probably lower his score. The pupil who is not certain of the correct answer but has some knowledge of the question and can eliminate one or more choices as being unreasonable or contradictory, or entirely incorrect has a fairly good chance of choosing the correct answer.''[3]

5.4 THE BINOMIAL PROPORTION

Often questions are phrased, not in terms of the absolute number of successes, but rather in terms of the proportion of the outcomes that are successes. Instead of asking the probability of winning three out of five games, we could ask the probability of winning 60 percent of five games. The probability is, of course, the same. We are just using different words to say the same thing.

Our formulas for the expected value, variance, standard deviation, and skewness coefficient do change because we are speaking of the proportion x/n rather than the absolute number x. Using the linear transformation Equations 4.4, 4.5, and 4.6, we have

$$P[\text{a fraction } x/n \text{ are successful}] = \binom{n}{x} \pi^x (1 - \pi)^{n - x} \tag{5.6}$$

$$E[x/n] = \pi \tag{5.7}$$

$$\text{variance of } x/n = \pi(1 - \pi)/n \tag{5.8}$$

$$\text{standard deviation of } x/n = \{\pi(1 - \pi)/n\}^{1/2} \tag{5.9}$$

$$\text{skewness coefficient of } x/n = (1 - 2\pi)/\{\pi(1 - \pi)n\}^{1/2} \tag{5.10}$$

Acceptance Sampling

When you, a business, or the government buy things, there is always a chance that your purchases will turn out to be defective, and yet, it is often uneconomical to inspect every purchase beforehand. When you buy a dozen oranges or a dozen avocados, it doesn't make sense to cut them all open before you buy them to see if they are all sweet and ripe, for then you will be buying rapidly rotting produce. When a business purchases a million transistors, it would be prohibitively expensive to test every single transistor before accepting delivery. When the Army purchases bombs, it cannot test each bomb by exploding it, for then it would have lots of test results, but no bombs.

What people do instead is to test a small sample and infer that comprehensive tests of all of the items would probably show similar results. Statisticians call this commonsense procedure **acceptance sampling** and use the binomial distribution to make the probability inference explicit. To use the binomial distribution, we need only assume that the test samples are Bernoulli trials and that the probability of selecting a defective item is constant and independent of the other selections.

Let's use the example of the Army and its bombs. Perhaps the Army has based its military planning and weapons deployment on the assumption that at least 90 percent of its bombs will explode properly. It may decide to test each new shipment of bombs by detonating some of them and seeing how many duds turn up. It would be natural to reject a shipment if more than 10 percent of those tested are defective.

If the Army does follow this procedure, what is the probability that a shipment will slip through that is 20 percent or even 30 percent defective? With the reasonable assumption that the tests are Bernoulli trials, we can let π be the true fraction of the bombs that are defective* and let x be the number of defective bombs found in a test sample of size n. The ratio x/n is the fraction of the bombs tested that prove to be defective. Equation 5.7 tells us that the expected value of x/n is π. If 20 percent of the bombs are defective, then, in the long run, the fraction found defective in the tests should average 20 percent. The actual results will, of course, vary from test to test.

Equation 5.9 says that the

$$\text{standard deviation of } x/n = \{\pi(1 - \pi)/n\}^{1/2}$$

which is inversely related to the size of the sample. The larger the sample, the more certain it is that the fraction x/n found defective in the tests will be close to the proportion π of the entire shipment that is defective. If $\pi = .2$ and we only test five bombs, there is a high probability that x/n will not be .2, but instead will be .0, .4, or even .6, .8, or 1.0. Almost anything can happen, and so we won't be able to draw any firm conclusions from the results, whatever they turn out to be. If we instead test 1000 bombs, then the fraction x/n found defective is very likely to be close to .2. A 1000-bomb test is much more conclusive but, of course, it is also much more expensive. The whole point of testing a sample is to gauge inexpensively the quality of the product, but it must be recognized that there is a trade-off. The fewer the items tested, the less reliable the results will be.

Let's start our example by having the Army test 10 bombs, rejecting the shipment if there is more than 1 dud. The **acceptance number** is 1, in that the lot will be accepted if the number of defective bombs is less than or equal to 1. The binomial distribution tells us, for various values of π, the probabilities of accepting and rejecting shipments based on such a 10-bomb test. Table 5.1 shows some of these acceptance probabilities. If, for example, exactly 10 percent of the bombs are defective, then there is a .7361 probability that one or none of the 10 bombs

Table 5.1   *The probabilities of accepting shipments, based on a 10-bomb test*

π	x/n = 0	x/n ≤ .1	x/n ≤ .2
.05	.5987	.9139	.9885
.10	.3487	.7361	.9298
.20	.1074	.3758	.6778
.30	.0282	.1493	.3828

*For a Bayesian, π is the probability that a particular bomb is defective. An objectivist would point out that a bomb is not defective some of the time and explosive at others. It is either okay or it is a dud. For an objectivist, π is the probability that we will select a defective bomb to test.

What are the Chances of a Run on the Bank?

Bank investment decisions are naturally influenced by the chances of depositor withdrawals. No bank wants to be caught short, without enough funds near at hand to satisfy withdrawals. The fraction of deposits withdrawn on a given day is a random variable that depends on the calendar and on business cycles, credit crunches, and other economic events. For illustrative purposes, let's assume that every depositor deposits a dollar and that the bank estimates that each dollar of deposits has a .1 probability of being withdrawn. If the bank has only $1 in deposits, then caution suggests that no loans should be made because there is a 10 percent chance that the lone depositor will want to withdraw the $1.

What if there are $2 in deposits? Then $2 will be withdrawn, or only $1, or none at all. Assuming independence, the binomial probabilities are:

dollars withdrawn	probability
0	.81
1	.18
2	.01

Now, the bank may be willing to loan out $1 because the probability of $2 being claimed is only .01. With $10 in deposits, the binomial probabilities are

dollars withdrawn	probability
0	.3486784401
1	.3874204890
2	.1937102445
3	.0573956280
4	.0111602610
5	.0014880348
6	.0001377810
7	.0000087480
8	.0000003645
9	.0000000090
10	.0000000001

The odds of all deposits being withdrawn at once are now minuscule, at 1 in 10

selected will be defective, so most of the shipments that are 10 percent defective will pass this test. But notice that Table 5.1 also shows that there is an uncomfortably high .3758 probability of accepting shipments that are 20 percent defective. Even shipments that are 30 percent defective have a .1493 probability of having fewer than 2 duds in a 10-bomb test.

It appears that a 2-dud rule in a 10-bomb test does not catch unsatisfactory shipments often enough. What are the alternatives? Well, we don't want to make the test any easier by raising the rejection criterion to, say, 3 duds. Table 5.1 shows that if we did accept shipments with 2 or fewer defectives, then the probability of accepting a 20-percent-defective shipment rises to an upsetting .6778.

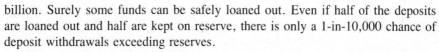

billion. Surely some funds can be safely loaned out. Even if half of the deposits are loaned out and half are kept on reserve, there is only a 1-in-10,000 chance of deposit withdrawals exceeding reserves.

The most likely outcome is that one-tenth of the deposits will be withdrawn. As the quantity of deposits increases, it becomes more and more certain that withdrawals will be extremely close to one-tenth of deposits. With $100 deposited, the odds are only 1 in 1000 that more than 20 percent of deposits will be withdrawn. With $1 million deposited, the odds are 1 in 1000 that more than 10.09 percent will be withdrawn. Almost 90 percent can now be safely lent out.

> This is an example of the general principle of *reducing risk through diversification*. In a large number of draws, independent risks will be diversified away. There will be some bad luck and good, but they will roughly balance each other out.

Notice, though, that in this numerical example I blithely assumed the independence required for applying the binomial distribution. Whether or not someone made a withdrawal had no effect on the likelihood of others making withdrawals. This is the individual risk that can be diversified away, and it concerns withdrawals made for private reasons that do not matter to others, such as the purchase of a new television, wedding expenses, or a sudden illness.

There are also public events that affect aggregate withdrawals. Some of these, like Christmas spending in December and tax payments in April, are easily anticipated. To the extent that they can be predicted, these variations are not risky. The bank simply adjusts its estimates of withdrawal probabilities and needed reserves. Other macroeconomic events may be more difficult to predict: recessions, credit crunches, and regulatory changes that allow other institutions to lure away depositors. The most dangerous and unpredictable event is a panicky run on the bank. If depositors fear that they may not be able to withdraw their deposits, they are all sure to try. Because such macroeconomic risks affect all depositors, they cannot be diversified away simply by having a large number of depositors. With macroeconomic risks, there is no safety in numbers. A bank's only protection is to keep funds near at hand that can be mobilized in an emergency.

If we want to weed out more of the unsatisfactory batches, then we must make the test tougher. We could decide to accept shipments only if all 10 bombs detonate properly. Table 5.1 shows that, as intended, the probability of accepting a 20-percent-defective batch falls to .1074, and there is now less than a 3 percent chance of accepting a shipment that is 30 percent defective. The problem is that we will also frequently reject satisfactory shipments. If a batch is 10 percent defective, there is only .3487 probability that every single bomb will explode in a 10-bomb test. Sixty-five percent of the time, these acceptable shipments will be rejected, and even if a batch is only 5 percent defective, there is a 40 percent chance that it will be rejected by a 1-dud rule.

What are we to do? If we make the test easy, then a lot of unsatisfactory shipments will slip through. If we make the test tough, then we will reject a lot of satisfactory shipments. This is, in fact, one of the basic trade-offs in acceptance sampling. The only real way to make this trade-off more appealing is to pay the additional costs of testing more bombs.

Table 5.2 shows some acceptance probabilities for a 100-bomb test. Look first at the column for the 10 percent rule, $x/n \leq .10$. A shipment that has only 5 percent defectives will pass this test almost every time. A shipment with 10 percent duds has a .58 probability of passing. Shipments that are 20 percent or 30 percent defective almost never pass this test. Increasing the size of the test from 10 bombs to 100 bombs has certainly increased the test's effectiveness in discriminating between satisfactory and unsatisfactory shipments. The price is the additional expense in testing (and destroying) 90 more bombs. If we're talking about sophisticated missiles costing millions of dollars apiece, then maybe the improved test isn't worth the additional expense, but if we're talking about inexpensive bullets, then a large test is certainly attractive. The final decision must hinge on a weighing of the need for a reliable test and the cost of a large test.

For any given test size, we still have to decide if we should use an acceptance rule that is easy or tough. The 10 percent rule shown in Table 5.2 seems a bit too tough because there is nearly a 40 percent chance of rejecting shipments that actually have only 10 percent duds. Table 5.2 shows that, as we make the test easier, we are less likely to reject satisfactory shipments, but are more likely to accept unsatisfactory shipments. A reasonable compromise might be $x/n \leq .13$.

Notice that we started out with a "natural" rule of allowing 10 percent duds in a 10-bomb test. Our binomial probability calculations suggested that a 10-bomb test wasn't large enough and that, in a larger test, a 10-percent-duds rule was too tough. The test that we finally select, perhaps a 13-percent-duds rule in a 100-bomb test, should not be chosen on the basis of its "naturalness." Instead, we should base our choice on the binomial probabilities and on a comparison of the various costs—of conducting the tests, of accepting unsatisfactory shipments, and of rejecting satisfactory shipments.

Exercises

5.15   Tweedle Dee and Tweedle Dum are running for President of the United States. Half of the voters prefer Dee and half prefer Dum. If Newstime magazine randomly polls 10 voters, what is the probability that at least 60 percent of those polled will prefer Mr. Dee? What if they poll 20 voters? What if they poll 100 voters? If they poll 100 voters, what is the probability that more than 60 percent will prefer one of the candidates, either Dee or Dum?

• **5.16**   A certain textbook has 500 pages with approximately 1000 printed characters per page. The publisher claims that there will typically be only 50 misprinted characters randomly scattered through a book of this size. To check this claim, we are going to pick a page at random and carefully count the typographical errors. Answer the following questions, assuming that the selected page has 1000 characters and the publisher's claim is correct.

Table 5.2 *The probabilities of accepting shipments, based on a 100-bomb test*

π	x/n ≤ .10	x/n ≤ .13	x/n ≤ .15
.05	.9885	.9995	1.000
.10	.5832	.8761	.9601
.20	.0057	.0469	.1285
.30	.0000	.0001	.0004

a. What is the expected number of misprinted characters? What, exactly, does this "expected number" calculation mean?

b. What is the probability of no error?

c. What is the probability of one error?

d. What is the probability of two errors?

e. What is the probability of more than two errors?

f. If you find more than two errors on this selected page, will you be skeptical of the publisher's claim? Why?

5.17 Sunspot Packing Company is inspecting the grapefruit at Littleman's farm in Porterville, California. The inspector cuts open 10 grapefruit selected at random. Sunspot will accept all of Littleman's crop if 9 of these 10 grapefruit are of satisfactory quality. If, in fact, 90 percent of all of Littleman's grapefruit are of satisfactory quality, what is the probability that his crop will be accepted?

• 5.18 (*continuation*) If 95 percent of all of Littleman's grapefruit are of satisfactory quality, what is the probability that his crop will nonetheless be rejected? What is the probability that his crop will be accepted if only 80 percent of his grapefruit are satisfactory? If only 50 percent are satisfactory? What would be some of the costs and benefits of the inspector testing more than 10 grapefruit?

• 5.19 The Quiet Night Motel has 35 rooms. Its experience has been that 20 percent of the people who make reservations never show up. How many no-shows can be expected if this motel accepts reservations for 35 rooms? For 40 rooms? For 50 rooms? What is the probability that there will not be enough rooms for those who do show up if this motel accepts reservations for 35 rooms? For 40 rooms? For 50 rooms?

•• 5.20 (*continuation*) A room at the Quiet Night Motel rents for $50 a night. If there isn't a room for someone with a reservation, their policy is to spend $100 to give this disappointed customer a free room at a much nicer motel. If they want to maximize expected profits, what is the maximum number of reservations that they should accept?

5.5 THE LAW OF AVERAGES

The binomial distribution actually was developed by early mathematicians to clarify the very meaning of probabilities. This early interest is why the *Bernoulli trial* label is affixed to the binomial scheme. Similarly, the binomial coefficients $\binom{n}{x}$

are often called *Pascal's Triangle*. These early probability mathematicians used the binomial distribution to argue that, in the long run, the proportion of successes x/n will converge to the probability of success π. Unfortunately, far too many have misinterpreted their argument as implying a fallacious "law of averages." Let's run through the mathematical logic and then see where intuition has so often been led astray.

The Law of Large Numbers

Consider some event that has a probability π of occurring. Let's label its occurrence a "success" and its nonoccurrence a "failure." Now, in n independent situations, how frequently will the event occur? This scenario qualifies as a sequence of Bernoulli trials and, therefore, the probabilities of various frequencies of occurrences x/n are given by the binomial probability distribution. The exact distribution depends, of course, on π and n.

Figure 5.2 shows four distributions, for $\pi = .5$ and $n = 10, 20, 50,$ and 100. Notice how each distribution is centered at $x/n = .5$ and how the distributions collapse on $x/n = .5$ as n increases. We can confirm this collapse more formally by looking back at Equations 5.8 and 5.9, which give the

$$\text{variance of } x/n = \pi(1 - \pi)/n$$

$$\text{standard deviation of } x/n = \{\pi(1 - \pi)/n\}^{1/2}$$

As the number of trials n increases, the variance and standard deviation of x/n decrease. These declines mean that the dispersion in the possible outcomes decreases. In the long run, as n becomes infinitely large, the variance and standard deviation go to zero, meaning that there is very little uncertainty about what the value of x/n will be. As n approaches infinity, we are virtually certain that x/n will be extremely close to π. This is **Bernoulli's law of large numbers.***

> For large values of n, the probability is very close to 1 that x/n will be very close to π, its expected value.

Equivalently, for large n the probability is small that x/n will be far from π. Consider a fair coin, with a $\pi = .5$ probability of heads. For $n = 1$, there is a .5 probability that x/n will equal 0 (no heads) and a .5 probability that x/n will equal 1 (all heads). For a large n, the chances of no heads or all heads drop precipitously. The probability of no heads in 20 flips is .000000954. The probability of no heads in 100 flips is 7.89×10^{-31}. For 100 flips, in fact, there is only a .0176 probability that there will be fewer than 40 heads ($x/n \le .4$). If n is very large, there is little chance that x/n will be far from π and, therefore, a high probability that x/n will be close to π.

*After its discoverer, James Bernoulli. His proof was published in his posthumous book *Ars Conjectandi* (1713).

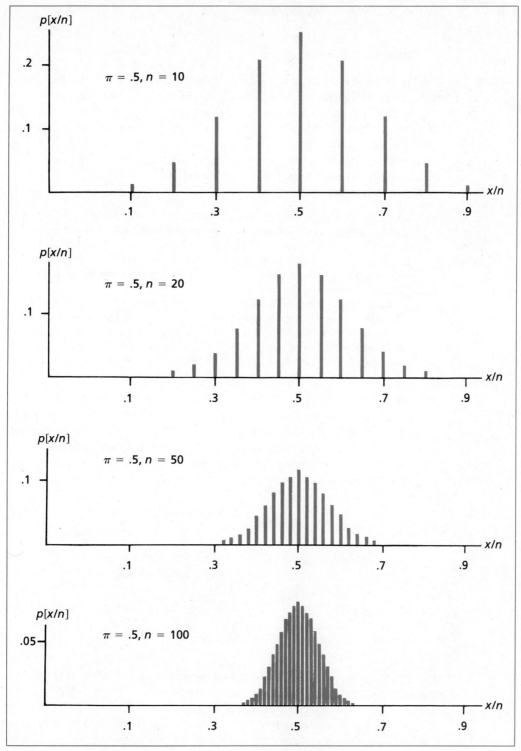

Figure 5.2 *The binomial distribution collapses as* n *increases*

A Common Fallacy

The law of large numbers is mathematically correct and intuitively obvious, but it is frequently misinterpreted as a "law of averages," which says that, in the long run, x/n must be exactly equal to π. For example, some people think that in 1000 coin flips the number of heads must be exactly 500. It follows from this logic that if tails happen to come up more than heads in the first 10, 50, or 100 flips, then heads will have to start coming up more frequently than tails to "average" things out. This argument is wrong, but it is all around us.

For example, one gambler said

> Flip a coin 1000 times and it'll come up heads 500 times, or mighty close to it. However, during that 1000 flips of the coin there will be frequent periods when heads will fail to show and other periods when you'll flip nothing but heads. Mathematical probability is going to give you roughly 500 heads in 1000 flips, so that if you get ten tails in a row, there's going to be a heavy preponderance of heads somewhere along the line.
>
> Regardless of mathematics and the theory of probability, if I'm in a crap game and the shooter makes ten consecutive passes [wins], I'm going to bet against him on his eleventh throw. And if he wins, I'll bet against him again on the twelfth. Maybe it's true that the mathematical odds on every throw of the dice remain the same, regardless of what's gone before—but how often do you see a crapshooter make 13 or 14 straight passes?[4]

We don't see 13 or 14 straight wins very often, but we don't see 12 straight wins very often either. We see 13 straight wins about half as often as we see 12 straight wins. The probability of 12 heads in a row is $(1/2)^{12}$. The probability of 13 heads in a row is $(1/2)^{13}$, a rare event indeed. But it is a very different question to ask the probability of 13 straight heads, *given that you have already tossed 12 heads in a row*. This conditional probability is

$$P[\text{13 straight heads}|\text{12 heads already}] = \frac{P[\text{13 straight heads and 12 heads already}]}{P[\text{12 straight heads}]}$$

$$= \frac{P[\text{13 straight heads}]}{P[\text{12 straight heads}]}$$

$$= \frac{(1/2)^{13}}{(1/2)^{12}}$$

$$= 1/2$$

The coin doesn't remember what happened on the last 12 flips. It is not interested in whether you win or lose, and it does not care about upholding some mythical law of averages. It is simply an inanimate object that gets repeatedly tossed into the air and examined by curious humans. If the coin is straight and fairly tossed, then heads and tails are equally likely to come up, no matter what happened on the last flip or the last 999 flips.

The Mathematical Error

The basis of the fallacious law of averages is the mistaken belief that heads and tails must come up equally often; a run of tails must consequently be balanced out by a run of heads. The law of large numbers does not say that the number of heads must equal the number of tails. Instead it says that, if we now begin to make a large number of throws, the probability is close to 1 that the fraction of these forthcoming throws that are heads will be very close to .5.

First, notice that the law of large numbers says nothing about the last 12 throws or the last 12 million throws. It is directed at the next *n* throws. The last 12 throws may have been all heads, all tails, or somewhere in between. The law of large numbers doesn't care. It says, looking ahead to predict the outcomes of the next 1000 flips, that the probability is very high that heads will come up close to half the time.

Second, a relative frequency that is close to .5 is not inconsistent with there being many more heads than tails or vice versa. In fact, while we are almost certain that, in the long run, the heads proportion will be very close to .5, we are also equally certain that the number of heads will not equal the number of tails!

Table 5.3 shows that, as the number of trials increases, the relative frequency of heads can converge to .5 even while the absolute difference between the number of heads and tails grows larger. There are 57 heads in the first 100 flips, 7 more than an exact 50 percent, yet we don't need 7 extra tails to average things out. Seven excess heads will be unimportant in a long run of 1 million or 1 trillion flips. In fact, as shown in Table 5.3, heads can continue to come up more often than tails even while the relative frequency of heads converges to .5.

We can make an even stronger statement. Not only do we not need the number of heads to equal the number of tails in the long run, but we can, in fact, be almost certain that they will not be equal. Look at Table 1 in the back of this book. With 2 flips, the probability of 1 head and 1 tail is .5. With 4 flips, the probability of 2 heads and 2 tails drops to .375. The probability that the numbers of heads and tails will be equal keeps falling as *n* increases: to .3125 for $n = 6$, to .2734 for $n = 8$, and to .2461 for $n = 10$. This trend continues. Every increase in *n* makes it less likely that the number of heads will be exactly equal to the number of tails. For $n = 100$, there is only a .08 chance of exactly 50 heads.

Table 5.3 *The numbers of heads and tails need not be equal*

Number of tosses n	Number of heads x	Relative frequency x/n	Heads minus tails x − (n − x)
100	57	.5700	14
1,000	520	.5200	40
10,000	5,040	.5040	80
100,000	50,060	.5006	120
1,000,000	500,100	.5001	200
1,000,000,000	500,001,000	.500001	2000

Table 5.4   *We are almost sure that, for a large* n, x/n *will be very close to .5 and that there will be a large difference between the numbers of heads and tails*

Number of tosses n	Probability that $.499 \leq x/n \leq .501$	Probability that $[x - (n - x)] \geq 100$
100	.08	1.6×10^{-30}
1,000	.08	.0015
10,000	.17	.32
100,000	.48	.75
1,000,000	.95	.92
1,000,000,000	≈ 1.00	.997

More confirmation comes from a comparison of Equations 5.9 and 5.4. Equation 5.9 says that the standard deviation of the relative frequency *x/n* goes to zero as *n* becomes infinite. This fact is the valid law of large numbers. But Equation 5.4 says that the standard deviation of the absolute number of successes *x* increases as *n* increases. This fact denies the fallacious law of averages. In the long run, we are very confident that heads will come up close to 50 percent of the time, but we are very uncertain about exactly how many heads will come up.

Here are two final bits of evidence against the popular interpretation of the law of averages. We have already used the binomial distribution to calculate the probability that the number of heads will exactly equal the number of tails. We can also use the binomial distribution to calculate the probability that *x/n* will differ from .5 by less than some amount, such as .001, and to calculate the probability that the number of heads differs from the number of tails by some amount, such as 100. Table 5.4 shows the results of such calculations.

With 100 flips, a heads-tails difference of 100 is very unlikely; we would need all heads or all tails for it to occur. But, as *n* increases, we become more and more confident that there will be at least 100 more heads than tails or at least 100 more tails than heads. With 1 billion flips, we are almost certain that the numbers of heads and tails will differ by 100. At the same time, we are almost certain that the relative frequency of heads will be very close to .5. The law of large numbers does not require the numbers of heads and tails to be equal!

Some More Examples

The fallacious law of averages is all around us. It is commonly appealed to by gamblers, hoping somehow to find a profitable pattern in the chaos created by random chance. When the roulette wheel turns up a red number several times in a row, there are always people eager to bet on black, counting on the law of averages. Of course, there are other people who will rush to bet red, trying to catch the "hot streak." The casino cheerfully accepts wagers from bettors of both faiths, confident that red and black numbers are still equally likely to come up.

One of the most dramatic roulette runs ever occurred at Monte Carlo on August

18, 1913. At one of the tables, black suddenly started coming up again and again. After about 10 blacks in a row, the table was surrounded by excited people, betting heavily on red and counting on the law of averages to reward them. But black came up again and again and again. After 15 straight blacks, there was a near panic as people tried to reach the table and place even heavier bets on red, and still black came up. By the 20th black, desperate bettors were wagering every chip they had left on red, hoping to recover a fraction of their losses. When this memorable run ended, black had come up 26 times in a row and the casino had won millions of francs.*

In honest games, at Monte Carlo and elsewhere, "balancing systems" based on the law of averages don't work, except by luck. In fact, the few gambling systems that have worked have been based on the opposite principle—that physical defects in a roulette wheel, for example, cause some events to occur more often than others. If the number 6 comes up an abnormally large number of times (not twice in a row, but maybe 35 times in 1000 spins), then perhaps some irregularity is responsible. Instead of betting against 6, expecting Nature to even things out, you might bet on 6, hoping that there is some physical imperfection that will cause 6 to continue to come up 35 times in every 1000 spins.†

A similar run occurred at a Chicago hospital in November 1949. Eighteen babies in a row turned out to be boys. The November 10, 1949 *Chicago Daily News* reported that the doctors and nurses expected a run of girl babies next. Yet 18 of the next 24 babies turned out to be boys. A few years later, the *Chicago Tribune* (February 3, 1953) reported that Mrs. Henry Drabik had given birth to 6 girls in a row, named Marybeth, Marykay, Marysue, Marylynn, Maryjan, and Marypat. When she became pregnant for the seventh time, "The odds against it were almost astronomical. Practically all Chicago was betting against the chance that [she] would have a seventh daughter. . . . Relatives offered to bet the Drabiks 10 to 1 the next child would be a boy," but it turned out to be another girl, named Maryrose.

The sports pages are another fertile source of law-of-averages fallacies. After the West Virginia football team lost to Penn State 13 years in a row, newspapers cheerfully reported that West Virginia at least had the law of averages on its side. Now, admittedly, sports do differ from games of chance in at least two ways. First we don't know the true probabilities. We don't really know how good a player or a team is until we gather some evidence. If Penn State and West Virginia had never played each other or common opponents, we might be very unsure of the outcome, but when Penn State beats West Virginia year after year, we became convinced that Penn State has the stronger football program. As the victories pile up, it does not become more probable that Penn State will lose the next game. If anything, we would revise Penn State's chances upward.†

---

*In 1931, 28 consecutive even numbers came up. Someone estimated that this should happen about once every 100 years, and it happened in Monte Carlo's 68th year.

†In 1983, Penn State beat West Virginia 41–23, making it 27 of the last 28. (There was a tie in 1955.) One of these years, West Virginia will win, but it won't be because of the law of averages.

The second difference between sports and games of chance is that players do have memories and emotions. They do care about wins and losses and they do remember the last game. Sometimes a team will be beaten badly and play harder the next time, seeking revenge. But often, teams that lose a lot of games also seem to lose their self-confidence and grow accustomed to losing.

Many sports events require an almost mindless repetition of perfected physical motions. The successful baseball pitcher, golfer, bowler, tennis player, and so many others all seem to settle into ''grooves'' in which they perform well, without really consciously thinking about what they are doing. When a professional basketball player gets ''hot,'' he can effortlessly hit shot after shot. Every basket he sinks makes him more confident and relaxed, allowing his body to do what it has been trained to do.

When the basketball player misses six shots in a row, the self-doubts start to build. He starts to worry about what he is doing wrong, and the more he worries, the harder it is for his body to perform well. These destructive self-doubts are seen in almost all sports. This is one reason why successful athletes so often have big egos and small minds. The less thinking and worrying, the better. Other athletes have turned to sports psychologists and even hypnotists to help them relax and forget past failures.

If West Virginia loses to Penn State year after year, West Virginia may get fired up and Penn State may get overconfident, but it is also possible that Penn State will play with confidence while West Virginia is plagued by self-doubts. Similarly, when Steve Garvey goes hitless in 12 at-bats, some sports commentator usually announces that, ''Garvey has the law of averages on his side'' or that ''he is due for a hit.'' But the probability of getting a hit doesn't go up just because he hasn't had one in awhile. It may be that his 12 outs in a row were just bad-luck line drives hit right at fielders. If so, his bad luck hasn't made him any more likely to get a hit in his next time at bat. If he is a .300 hitter, then his chances of a hit are still around 30 percent.

If it's not just bad luck, then 12 outs in a row suggests that a physical or mental problem may be causing him to play poorly. If I were the manager of a baseball player who was 0 for 12, I would usually be pessimistic. By the same reasoning, if someone has had 12 hits in his last 24 at bats, I would not bench him because he is ''due for an out.'' I'd prefer batting someone who was 12 for 24 to someone who was 0 for 12.

On another occasion, I watched a Penn State placekicker miss three field goals and an extra point in an early season game against Air Force. The television commentator said that Joe Paterno, the Penn State coach, should be happy about those misses as he looks forward to some tough games in coming weeks. This commentator explained that every kicker is going to miss some over the course of a season and it is good to get the misses ''out of the way'' early in the year. This optimism is the law-of-averages fallacy again. Those misses don't have to be balanced by successes. If I had been coaching Penn State, I would have been very worried by this poor performance. It suggests that this placekicker really isn't very

Baseball Law of Averages Taking Toll on Seaver

NEW YORK (UPI)—Let's discuss Tom Seaver and baseball's law of averages.

As everyone this side of a Tibetan monastery knows, the New York Mets' two-time Cy Young Award winner and so-called All-American boy has come upon hard times this season. He has lost five of his seven decisions, has yielded 12 homers and is a badly shaken athlete.

A perfectionist who sometimes criticizes himself after pitching a four-hit shutout, the usually personable Seaver has been talking more like a psychiatrist than a splendid 29-year-old pitcher. He wonders one day whether his fast ball has lost its velocity and the next day whether he is prematurely over the hill.

Met management and players have been wondering along with him to a degree that goes far beyond the normal concern for a star in a slump. It doesn't matter to Seaver-Watchers that American League Cy Young Award winner Jim Palmer of the Baltimore Orioles has a 2-6 record. To them Seaver is "Tom Terrific"—the best in the business—and the image has been shattered.

Well, this is to say that 75 years of baseball history must mean something and that baseball's law of averages is taking its inevitable toll on Seaver just as it has done on the greatest pitchers of this or any other era. Also that Seaver may finish the 1974 season with a won-lost record under .500 and yet go on to be a super star for many more years.

First, let's concede that Seaver and most other modern athletes deny the existence of the law of averages. Then, let's listen to Ralph Kiner, seven-time NL home run king.

"The law of averages is what baseball is all about," says Kiner. "It is the levelling influence of the long season. A .250-hitter may hit .200 or .300 for a given period. But he will eventually level off at .250. The same is true of pitchers. Illnesses, sore arms, good and bad clubs are all part of it. But the law is inflexible. A player will average out to his true ability."

What this means in Seaver's case is that he is now "paying" in the percentages for his 1969 season in which he had a 25-7 record for a .781 percentage.

That performance is .141 percentage points above the .640 lifetime percentage (135 victories and 76 losses) with which Seaver started the 1974 season. It sounds incredible—even juvenile—to insist that the 1969 performance must eventually be "levelled off." And yet it has been that way with the greatest pitchers dating back to the turn of the century.

©*New Haven Register,* June 2, 1974. Reprinted by permission of United Press International.

good, and even if the kicker does have some talent, he is certainly going to be very nervous on his next attempts.

Exercises

5.21   The Steinems are planning their family and both want an equal number of boys and girls. Mrs. Steinem says that their chances are best if they plan on having two children. Mr. Steinem says that they have a better chance of having an equal number of boys and girls if they plan on having four children. Who is right? (Assume that boy and girl babies are equally likely.)

5.22   Explain why you think that this logic is sound or unsound:

A famous baseball pitcher, Ted Lyons, was once removed for a pinch hitter on his fifth time at bat after having made a base hit on each of first four times at bat. The reason given was that it was virtually impossible for a pitcher to get five hits in a row![5]

5.23   One wartime strategy popular with soldiers is to sit in shell holes, their reasoning being that it is very improbable that any chosen spot will be hit by a second shell. Is this probability logic valid?

5.24   Exercise 2.1 involved the professor who reads only 1 of the 10 essays that each student writes on the final exam. Let's assume now that 3 of your essays would be graded A, 4 would be graded B, and 3 would be graded C. Would you prefer that this professor read all of your essays or just one of them? Explain your reasoning.

• **5.25**   Two baseball teams, the Stags and the Sagehens, will play each other for the league championship. The Stags are, in fact, the better team. (But the Sagehens have the better yell, "That's all right, that's okay. You'll be working for us someday.") If these two teams were to play each other many, many times, the Stags would win 60 percent of the time. Assuming baseball games are Bernoulli trials, what is the probability that the Stags will win the championship if these two teams play just 1 game? If they play a 3-game series? If they play a 5-game series? If they play a 7-game series? What is the moral?

Can you think of any reason why a series of baseball games is not, strictly speaking, a sequence of Bernoulli trials?

• **5.26**   Which of the following data is more convincing evidence that male and female babies are not equally likely: (a) of 3 babies, 2 are male; (b) of 100 babies, 52 are male; or (c) of 1000 babies, 520 are male?

5.6   SUMMARY

A series of n uncertain outcomes, in which the probabilities of "success" and "failure" are constant, irrespective of the other outcomes, is called a sequence of Bernoulli trials. This model is applied to a wide variety of situations, including games of chance, sampling tests of defective items, and public opinion polls.

If the constant success probability is π, then the probability of exactly x successes is given by the binomial distribution,

$$P[x \text{ successes}] = \binom{n}{x} \pi^x (1 - \pi)^{n-x}$$

Many of these binomial probabilities are in Table 1 at the end of this book.

The expected value, variance, standard deviation, and skewness coefficient for a binomial distribution are

$$E[X] = \pi n$$

$$\text{variance of } X = \pi(1 - \pi)n$$

$$\text{standard deviation of } X = \{\pi(1 - \pi)n\}^{1/2}$$

skewness coefficient of $X = (1 - 2\pi)/\{\pi(1 - \pi)n\}^{1/2}$

Sometimes we are interested in the fraction x/n of the trials that are successes:

$$P[\text{a fraction } x|n \text{ are successful}] = \binom{n}{x}\pi^x(1 - \pi)^{n-x}$$

$$E[x/n] = \pi$$

$$\text{variance of } x/n = \pi(1 - \pi)/n$$

$$\text{standard deviation of } x/n = \{\pi(1 - \pi)/n\}^{1/2}$$

$$\text{skewness coefficient of } x/n = (1 - 2\pi)/\{\pi(1 - \pi)n\}^{1/2}$$

The law of large numbers says that if n is very large, then the probability is very high that the proportion of successes x/n will be very close to π. The fallacious law of averages says that an unusual run of successes must be "balanced out" by a run of failures, so that x/n will equal π exactly.

REVIEW EXERCISES

5.27 Ten college students are asked to choose between two different brands of beer, X and Y. These beers are, in fact, so similar that each student is equally likely to choose either brand. What are the probabilities that

a. 5 students choose each brand?
b. 6 students choose brand X?
c. 7 students choose brand Y?
d. more than 5 students choose brand X?
e. at least 7 students choose brand X or at least 7 choose brand Y?

5.28 Mr. Wrists has a .3 probability of getting a hit each time he bats for the Sagehens. If the outcomes of each time at bat are independent, what are Mr. Wrist's probabilities of

a. getting 4 hits in 4 times at bat?
b. getting 3 hits in 4 times at bat?
c. getting 2 hits in 4 times at bat?
d. getting 1 hit in 4 times at bat?
e. getting no hit in 4 times at bat?
f. getting no hit in 12 times at bat?
g. What would you predict Mr. Wrist's lifetime batting average to be? Does the confidence with which you make this prediction depend on how many times he bats during his career?

5.29 Each player on the Sagehens baseball team has a .300 on-base average; that is, each gets on base, on the average, 30 times per 100 times at bat. If we assume that a baseball game is a sequence of Bernoulli trials, what is the probability that the Sagehens will be the victims of a perfect game (27 straight outs) the next time they play? Can you think of any plausible objections to the assumption that a baseball game is a sequence of Bernoulli trials?

There are about 2150 games (each involving two teams, of course) in a major league baseball season. At this rate, on average, how often should we expect to see a perfect game if your earlier probability calculation is reasonably accurate?

5.30   On a Monte Carlo roulette wheel, there are 37 slots: 18 red, 18 black, and 1 green. If you were to sit down and spin such a wheel 26 times, what would be the probability of duplicating the 26 straight blacks that occurred on August 18, 1913 at Monte Carlo?

5.31   A basketball article in the January 16, 1983 *Los Angeles Times* was titled "Wright Defies the Percentages, and USC Holds Off Oregon, 62–54." The article explained that, "Oregon's strategy was obvious in the closing minutes—foul Gerry Wright, a 37.5 percent free throw shooter. But Wright, a reserve center, didn't fold under the pressure. He made 3 of his 6 foul shots in the final two minutes."

Assuming the binomial distribution to be appropriate, what is the probability of Wright making so many free throws (at least 3 of 6)? Is the fact that he was so successful an unlikely defiance of the percentages? What assumptions are needed for the binomial distribution to be appropriate?

5.32   A week before the final exam, Professor Sailors gives his students 10 questions. At the beginning of the final examination, a student will reach into a wastebasket and blindly select 3 of these 10 questions. The final exam will then consist of these 3 selected questions. You are well prepared to answer 6 of the 10 questions and poorly prepared to answer the other 4. What are the probabilities that the 3 selected questions

a. will all be ones that you are well prepared to answer?
b. will include 2 that you are well prepared for and 1 that you are poorly prepared for?
c. will include 1 that you are well prepared for and 2 that you are poorly prepared for?
d. will all be ones that you are poorly prepared to answer?

• **5.33**   (*continuation*) Unbeknownst to his students, Professor Sailors sometimes discards 6 of the questions beforehand and only puts 4 questions into the wastebasket. In what ways, if any, does this sneaky trick affect the probabilities calculated in Exercise 5.32?

•• **5.34**   (*continuation*) Once, a long time ago, Professor Sailors dropped 10 questions into the wastebasket with a flourish, just as he had promised, but secretly he had arranged for these 10 questions to consist of 3 copies of question 2, 3 copies of question 5, and 4 copies of question 10, because he wanted to guarantee that the three selected questions would be 2, 5, and 10. He never pulled this stunt again. Can you guess why? What is the probability that Professor Sailors's devious trick would misfire?

• **5.35**   Long ago, the astragali (heel bones) of animals were used as dice. An astragalus of a hooved animal has four sides. Experiments have shown that the probabilities of each of these four sides appearing are .39, .37, .12, and .12. In ancient Greece, one of the games was to roll four astragali simultaneously, with the best outcome being "Venus," in which four different sides appear. What is the probability of throwing a Venus?

• **5.36**   This problem is intended to examine how the size and voting rules of a jury affect the chances of conviction. Let's say that a fraction π of the population would find a certain defendant guilty, while a fraction $1 - \pi$ would find this defendant innocent. Assume that a jury is randomly selected from this population. What is the probability that this defendant will be found guilty by

a. the unanimous vote of a 12-person jury?
b. the unanimous vote of an 8-person jury?
c. the unanimous vote of a 6-person jury?
d. a three-fourths vote of a 12-person jury?
e. a two-thirds vote of a 12-person jury?
f. majority vote of a 12-person jury?

For illustrative purposes, make a table showing the values of your answers to these six questions for four different values of π: .9, .75, .5, and .25.

● **5.37**   A state lottery ticket has five randomly selected numbers lined up with five concealed numbers. The buyer wins if some of the concealed numbers match the corresponding open numbers. What is the probability that the number of matched digits on a ticket will be zero? One? Two? Three? Four? Five?

   The ticket costs \$1 and pays \$1000 for five matched numbers, \$10 for four matches, \$3 for three, \$2 for two, and \$1 for one. What is the expected payoff? What fraction of every dollar collected, on the average, does the state expect to pay out in prizes?

● **5.38**   The Jolly Roger computer quiz invites contestants to complete 10 sentences by selecting the more appropriate of 2 words. For example, in the February 6, 1973 quiz, the contestant could complete sentence number 5, "Teachers sometimes have to _____ their emotions," with either "suppress" or "control." There is a \$2 entry fee, but the contestant wins \$1000 if all 10 sentences are completed correctly. If we assume that each of the 2 answers is equally likely to be right, what is a contestant's expected percentage return?

● **5.39**   You play a certain game of chance 10 times. If, for each game, the probability of losing is .7, what is the probability of losing exactly 6 games? If the probability of winning is .3, what is the probability of winning exactly 4 games? Use the symbols π, $1 - \pi$, x, and $n - x$ to show how a binomial probability-of-failure problem can always be restated as a probability-of-success problem.

● **5.40**   In the binomial distribution, the variance of x is $\pi(1 - \pi)n$. For what value of π is this variance the largest?

● **5.41**   Professor Lay Z. Mann requires a 20-page paper in his course. The paper is graded pass-fail. The rumor is that Professor Mann grades each paper by reading a few pages selected at random. Each year, a few risk-seeking students hand in papers with some pages containing acceptable material and other pages containing nonsense straight out of *Alice in Wonderland*.

   If half of the pages in a 20-page paper are nonsense, what are the chances of being caught if Professor Mann reads just 1 page? Two different pages? If Professor Mann is known to read just 1 page and a student wants at least a 90 percent chance of passing, what is the maximum number of nonsense pages to sneak into a 20-page paper?

● ● **5.42**   In major league baseball, the World Series is won by the first team to win 4 games. If the games are independent and the teams are evenly matched (each with a .5 probability of winning any game), what is the probability that the Series will end after 4 games? After 5 games? After 6 games? After 7 games?

•• **5.43**   There are four players in bridge and each is dealt 13 cards. You have 5 spades, your partner has 4 spades, and your two opponents have a total of 4 spades between them. What is the probability that these 4 spades are evenly divided, 2 to each opponent? Is it more likely that these 4 spades divide 2–2 or 3–1? (*Hint:* The probability of a 2–2 split is not $6(.5)^4$.)

5.44   Professor Smith decides to give a short and sweet multiple-choice exam consisting of 10 questions, each with three possible answers: A, B, or C. If she gives 1 point for each right answer, how much should she subtract for a wrong answer to give a pure guesser an expected score of zero?

5.45   During the January 1984 NFC championship game between Washington and San Francisco, it looked as if the game might be decided by a field goal at the end. One of the CBS radio commentators, Jack Buck, pointed out ominously that Mark Mosely has already "missed four field goals today." Hank Stram responded, "The percentages are in his favor." Do you agree?

5.46   Critically evaluate the following:

This man has kept records of play on Blackjack, craps, and Roulette, and the house percentage on all three games works out inexorably, within a fraction of a percentage point—but there are times shown by his records when there are lengthy streaks of steady house wins along with other streaks of house losses.

His records show that such streaks exist. But no matter how long he studies his figures, he hasn't been able to arrive at any pattern in them. He can see that the streaks are there, but he hasn't anything even resembling an explanation of why they occur when they do or why they last for a certain period.

"Nevertheless," he insists, "if I'm scoring red and black on a Roulette game and red has come up 500 times in 900 spins of the wheel, I'm going to put my money on black on the next 100 spins. What's more, I'll bet you that I come out ahead of the game."[6]

5.47   Explain why you either agree or disagree with Edgar Allan Poe:

Nothing . . . is more difficult than to convince the merely general reader that the fact of sixes having been thrown twice in succession by a player at dice, is sufficient cause for betting the largest odds that sixes will not be thrown in the third attempt. . . . It does not appear that the two throws which have been completed, and which now lie absolutely in the Past, can have influence upon the throw which exists only in the Future. . . . this is a reflection which appears so exceedingly obvious that attempts to controvert it are received more frequently with a derisive smile than with anything like respectful attention. The error here involved—a gross error redolent of mischief—I cannot pretend to expose within the limits assigned me at present.[7]

•• **5.48**   What is (a) the probability of x heads in $n = 2x$ flips of a fair coin, and (b) the probability of $x + 1$ heads in $n = 2x + 2$ flips of a fair coin? Is the ratio of (a) to (b) greater than, equal to, or less than 1? What is the moral?

•• **5.49**   This problem is intended to illustrate the detection of an imperfect roulette wheel. Imagine a box that is supposed to contain 18 red balls, 18 black balls, and 2 green balls—

the probability is, in fact, .999 that it will contain these numbers of balls. But, occasionally (with .001 probability), someone makes an error and puts in 20 red balls, 16 black balls, and 2 green balls. What is the probability that this error has been committed if you observe the following drawings (with replacement):

a. 1 red ball?
b. 10 red balls?
c. 20 red balls out of 38 drawn?
d. 200 red balls out of 380 drawn?
e. 2000 red balls out of 3800 drawn?

•• **5.50** You have 20 multiple-choice questions, each with 4 possible answers. Unfortunately, you have no idea of what the right answers are. One point is awarded for a correct answer and one-third of a point is subtracted for a wrong answer. If you get a net score of 4 points, you pass the test; if you get less than 4 points, you fail. If you want to maximize your chances of passing the test, how many questions should you answer? What is your probability of passing?

CHAPTER **6**

The Normal Distribution

I know of scarcely anything so apt to impress the imagination as the wonderful form of cosmic order expressed by the "Law of Frequency of Error." The Law would have been personified by the Greeks and deified, if they had known of it. . . . Whenever a large sample of chaotic elements are taken in hand and marshaled in the order of their magnitude, an unsuspected and most beautiful form of regularity proves to have been latent all along. The tops of the marshaled row form a flowing curve of invariable proportions; and each element, as it is sorted into place, finds, as it were, a preordained niche accurately adapted to it. . . .

Sir Francis Galton

TOPICS

We examined the binomial distribution in great detail because of its wide applicability and its important role in the intellectual history of probability analysis. In this chapter we will study another distribution, which was even more important in the development of probability and statistics and has wider applications. This second distribution is so pervasive that it is called the *normal distribution*. It is, by far, the most widely used probability distribution. It is so popular that, when a statistician is unsure of the appropriate probabilities, a normal distribution will be usually assumed. In this chapter, you will learn what the normal distribution is and why it is so alluring. But, first, I will explain the difference between discrete and continuous probability distributions, because we have so far only used the former, and the normal distribution is an example of the latter.

6.1 CONTINUOUS PROBABILITY DISTRIBUTIONS

All of the examples analyzed in earlier chapters involved *discrete* random variables, in which there were a countable number of possible outcomes. The coin could land heads or tails, the die could come up 1 through 6, and the student could answer 0 to 20 questions right.

A Spinner

In theory, however, some random variables can take on a continuum of values. Figure 6.1 shows one example. I've drawn a circle similar to the face of a clock, but instead of clock hands, there is a spinner that will randomly select some point on the circle. We can imagine that this is a clean, well-balanced device in which each point is equally likely to be picked, but how many points are there on this circle? In theory, there are an infinite number.

Let's say that the perimeter of the circle measures 12 inches. If our markings were so crude that we could only divide the circle into 12 equal one-inch intervals, then the probability of stopping in any particular interval would be 1/12. If we used finer markings to divide the circle into 120 intervals of length 0.1 inch, then the probability of stopping in any particular interval would be 1/120. If we could

Figure 6.1 *Pick a number, any number*

accurately measure intervals to five places, there would be 1,200,000 intervals of length 0.00001 inch; the probability for each interval would be 1/1,200,000. As we measure the stopping place more precisely, we get a larger number of possible outcomes and a smaller probability of observing any particular outcome. With infinite precision, we could identify an infinite number of points, and the probability of hitting any one point would be zero.

This argument suggests how mathematicians handle the vexing situation of an uncountable number of possible outcomes. There is a nonzero probability for a measurable interval of outcomes, but the probability of any specific outcome must be zero. The probability that the spinner will stop at some point between 1.0 and 2.0 is 1/12. The probability that the spinner will precisely hit the point 1.33. . . is zero.

We can display these probabilities by using the continuous probability distribution shown in Figure 6.2. This distribution is constructed in such a way that the probability that the outcome is within a particular interval is shown by the corresponding area under the probability distribution. The shaded area, for example, shows the probability that the spinner will stop between 1 and 2. This area is (base)(height) = (1)(1/12) = 1/12. Similarly, what is the probability that the spinner will stop between 0 and 12? This probability is the entire area under the probability distribution. We have (base)(height) = (12)(1/12) = 1, as it should be.

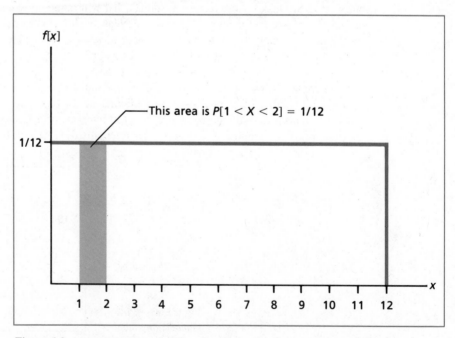

Figure 6.2 *A continuous probability distribution for the spinner shown in Figure 6.1*

The Formal Distinction

The formal distinction between the discrete and continuous probability distributions can be summarized as follows:

> In a **discrete probability distribution,** the possible outcomes are countable. We use a discrete random variable X and a discrete probability distribution $p[x]$. Each of the possible outcomes has a nonzero probability.

A graph of a discrete probability distribution will (as in Figure 4.1) consist of probability spikes showing the probability of each outcome.

> In a **continuous probability distribution,** the possible outcomes are not countable. We use a continuous random variable X and a continuous probability distribution $f[x]$. Each possible outcome has zero probability, while an interval of possible outcomes has a nonzero probability.

A graph of a continuous probability distribution will (as in Figure 6.2) show the probability of an interval of outcomes as the area under the distribution.

A Few Details

Notice that we use the different symbols $p[x]$ and $f[x]$ to distinguish discrete and continuous probability distributions. The special symbol $f[x]$ is intended to remind us that $f[x] = 1/12$ is a continuous probability distribution, not a probability. The function $f[x]$ gives the height of the probability distribution over the point x. At $X = 1.33\ldots$, $f[x] = 1/12$, while $p[x] = 0$. For a continuous random variable, nonzero probabilities only apply to intervals of outcomes, such as $P[1.0 < X < 2.0] = 1/12$.

Another fine detail is that, for continuous random variables, it doesn't really matter whether the endpoints are included in an interval. All of the following probabilities are the same:

$$P[1.0 < X < 2.0] = 1/12$$
$$P[1.0 \leq X < 2.0] = 1/12$$
$$P[1.0 < X \leq 2.0] = 1/12$$
$$P[1.0 \leq X \leq 2.0] = 1/12$$

because $P[X = 1.0] = P[X = 2.0] = 0$.

A final point is that, in practice, our data are never really continuous. We cannot measure anything to an infinite number of places. Our measurement limitations force us to aggregate all points within a certain interval. Perhaps, in our spinner example, we can make accurate measurements to three decimal places. The point 1.333 can be distinguished from 1.334, but we cannot separate 1.3331 from 1.3332 (so, we call them both 1.333). Our measurement limitations then force us to divide the circle into 12,000 intervals of length 0.001. The probability of hitting any one of these intervals is 1/12,000, not zero.

We can theoretically think of the circle as an infinite number of points, even while acknowledging our inability to identify precisely which point is hit. The advantage of a theoretical image of a continuum of points is that it allows us to readily deduce the probability of landing in an interval of any size, and it is certainly easier to draw a continuous probability distribution than to draw 12,000 probability spikes.

Exercises

6.1 Are the following variables discrete or continuous?

a. male births
b. height
c. weight
d. rainfall
e. income
f. number of cars sold
g. votes received by a candidate
h. time

6.2 Figure 6.1 shows a spinner on a numbered circle. What is the probability that the spinner stops

a. between 6 and 12?
b. between 9 and 12?
c. between 3 and 9?
d. between 1 and 2?

6.3 My computer has a random-number generator that will select a digit from 0 to 9. Each of these ten digits is equally likely to be picked. I am going to use this generator to randomly select a number between 0 and 1.

a. I let the random-number generator pick a single digit, which I put to the right of a decimal point. If, for example, the selected digit is 3, then my answer is 0.3. Graph the probability distribution for my answer.
b. I let the random-number generator pick a digit, which I put to the right of a decimal point. Then, I let the random number generator pick a second digit, which I put to the right of the first. If, for example, the computer selects a 3 and then a 7, then my answer is 0.37. I then let the computer pick a third digit, which I put to the right of the first two. I can continue this process indefinitely, to obtain as precise a fraction as I want. Graph the probability distribution for my final answer.

6.4 A certain random variable X has this continuous probability distribution:

$$f[x] = 1, \quad 0 < x < 1$$
$$f[x] = 0, \quad \text{otherwise}$$

Graph this probability distribution and determine the following probabilities:

a. $P[0 \leq X \leq 0.5]$ .5
b. $P[0.25 \leq X \leq 0.75]$ .5
c. $P[X \leq 0]$ 0
d. $P[X \geq 0.5]$ .5
e. $P[X = 0.5]$ .0

6.5 A certain random variable X has this continuous probability distribution:

$$f[x] = 2 - 2X, \quad 0 \leq x \leq 1$$
$$f[x] = 0, \qquad \text{otherwise}$$

Graph this probability distribution and determine the following probabilities:

a. $P[0 \leq X \leq 1]$
b. $P[X = 0]$
c. $P[0.5 \leq X]$
d. $P[X \leq 0.5]$
e. $P[X \leq 0.25]$

6.2 STANDARDIZING VARIABLES

Random variables can take on a wide variety of units: dollars, inches, pounds, percentages, or whatever. Usually it is easiest to interpret our models and results if we measure variables in these natural units. But, in the eighteenth and nineteenth centuries, scientists discovered that when variables are *standardized,* in a way that I'll soon show you, the probability distributions often look remarkably similar.

Many random variables are the *cumulative* result of a sequence of random events. For instance, a random variable giving the *sum* of the numbers when eight dice are rolled can be viewed as the cumulative result of eight separate random events. A second example is the percentage change in stock prices over the next six months. We can view this six-month change as the *cumulative* result of a great many daily, hourly, or even more frequent random price changes. A third example is the heights of 11-year-old males. At birth, each person's future height is unknown and, therefore, is a random variable. Again, we can think of the eventual height as the *cumulative* result of a great many events, some hereditary and some having to do with diet, exercise, and so on.

These three examples involve very different units of measurement. In addition, the values of each random variable depend on our horizon—whether we are looking at the roll of 8 dice or 800 dice, stock prices six months hence or six years hence, the heights of 11-year-olds or 21-year-olds. In each case, as we lengthen the horizon we might anticipate that both the expected value and the standard deviation of the variable will change. If we were to graph the probability distributions for varying horizons of these quite different variables, they would look very dissimilar, but researchers have found that, when the variables are standardized, the probability distributions are strikingly similar! This remarkable similarity is the most important discovery in the long history of probability and statistics.

A Mean of Zero and a Standard Deviation of One

We have seen that two of the most important tools for describing differences among probability distributions are the expected value and the standard deviation. A natural standardization would be to transform the units of our random variables somehow, so that they would all have the same expected value and the same standard deviation. This reshaping is easily done in the statistical beauty parlor.

To standardize a random variable X, we subtract its expected value μ and then divide by its standard deviation σ:

$$Z = \frac{X - \mu}{\sigma} \tag{6.1}$$

If we recall the linear transformation Equations 4.4 and 4.5, we can easily see that, no matter what the initial units of X are, the **standardized random variable** Z has an expected value of zero and a standard deviation of 1:*

$$E\left[\frac{X - \mu}{\sigma}\right] = \frac{1}{\sigma}(E[X] - \mu) = \frac{1}{\sigma}(\mu - \mu) = 0$$

$$\text{std. dev. of } \frac{(X - \mu)}{\sigma} = \frac{1}{\sigma}(\text{std. dev. of } X) = \frac{\sigma}{\sigma} = 1$$

The standardized variable Z measures how many standard deviations X is above or below its mean. If X is equal to its mean, then Z is equal to zero. If X is one standard deviation above its mean, then Z is equal to 1. If X is two standard deviations below its mean, then Z is equal to -2. Suppose for instance, that X has a mean of 20 and a standard deviation of 10. Then, here are some corresponding values of X and Z:

X	Z
0	-2
10	-1
20	0
30	$+1$
40	$+2$

Some Standardized Distributions

Let's look at some examples. Any random variable can be standardized to have a zero mean and a standard deviation of 1. Here we are especially interested in random variables that can be viewed as the *cumulative* result of a sequence of random events. First, consider the roll of a single six-sided die. Let the random

*The standardized variable $(X - \mu)/\sigma$ can be rearranged as $(-\mu/\sigma) + (1/\sigma)X$, which has a standard deviation $(1/\sigma)\sigma = 1$ because Equation 4.5 says that the standard deviation of $a + bX$ is $b\sigma$.

Table 6.1 *Standardizing the roll of a die*

P	X	Z = (X − 3.5)/1.7
1/6	1	−1.464
1/6	2	−0.878
1/6	3	−0.293
1/6	4	0.293
1/6	5	0.878
1/6	6	1.464

variable X be the number that appears. We can readily calculate the expected value and standard deviation to be $\mu = 3.5$ and $\sigma = 1.708$.* Table 6.1 shows how these numbers can be used to construct the standardized variable Z. A bit of arithmetic confirms that, as intended, Z does have an expected value of zero and a standard deviation of 1.

In the same fashion, I have constructed standardized variables for the *sum* of the numbers when $n = 2$, 4, or 8 dice are rolled. These probability distributions are shown in Figure 6.3. Notice how each distribution is centered about zero. Notice also, that as n increases, the probability distribution loses its "block" shape and becomes increasingly "bell" shaped.

For a second example, let X be the number of heads that come up when n coins are tossed. This is a binomial distribution with $\pi = .5$. The random variable X is the *sum* of the successes in n flips. Figure 6.4 shows the standardized probability distributions for $n = 1$, 2, 10, 20, and 50. Again, a distribution that is very unextraordinary for $n = 1$ turns into a pleasing bell shape as n increases.

Our first two examples involve simple symmetrical distributions. Now let's do a strongly skewed distribution. Imagine a sharply bent coin with a .9 probability of landing heads. This bent coin is a proxy for any sequence of events, each with a .9 probability of "success." Again, the random variable X is the *sum* of the successes. Figure 6.4 shows that, as n increases, even a very skewed distribution is gradually transformed into the now-familiar bell shape.

Look again at Figures 6.3 and 6.4. We began with three very different probability distributions. But as we *cumulated* a sequence of these varied uncertain events, the same bell-shaped probability distribution kept emerging. You can imagine the excitement that scientists must have felt when they first discovered this regularity. Here they were modeling uncertainty and, amidst the chaos, a regular

---

*Here are the details:

$$\sigma = 1(1/6) + 2(1/6) + 3(1/6) + 4(1/6) + 5(1/6) + 6(1/6) = 21/6 = 3.5$$
$$\sigma^2 = (1 - 3.5)^2(1/6) + (2 - 3.5)^2(1/6) + (3 - 3.5)^2(1/6) + (4 - 3.5)^2(1/6)$$
$$+ (5 - 3.5)^2(1/6) + (6 - 3.5)^2(1/6) = 17.5/6 = 2.917$$
$$\sigma = 2.917^{1/2} = 1.708$$

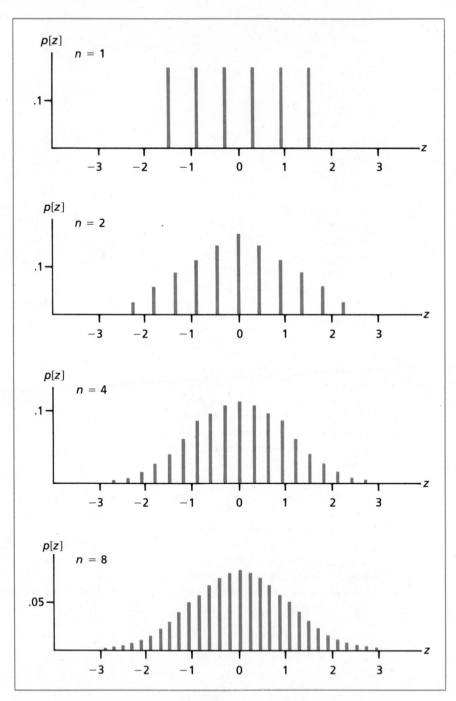

Figure 6.3 *Standardized probability distributions for* n *dice rolls*

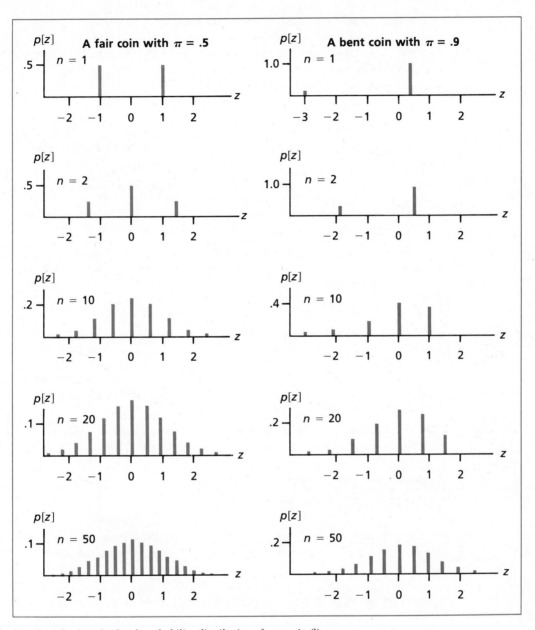

Figure 6.4 *Standardized probability distributions for* n *coin flips*

pattern kept reappearing. Even more unexpectedly, they were eventually able to prove that this same bell-shaped distribution almost always appears when the outcomes are cumulated, no matter what the shape of the initial probability distribution! No wonder Sir Francis Galton called it a "wonderful form of cosmic order" deserving deification.

Exercises

6.6   Use the data in Table 6.1 on the roll of a single die to calculate the mean and standard deviation of Z.

6.7   Let the random variable X be the number 1, 2, 3, or 4 that comes up when a four-sided die is rolled. Graph the probability distribution of X. Calculate the expected value μ and standard deviation σ of X. Now compute the possible values of the standardized variable $Z = (X - \mu)/\sigma$. What are the expected value and standard deviation of Z?

6.8   Elizabeth is just starting her career, teaching English as a Second Language (ESL). In one of her textbooks she read about grading by the curve, so she decides to give an F for $Z < -1.5$, a D for $-1.5 \leq Z < -0.5$, a C for $-0.5 \leq Z < 0.5$, a B for $0.5 \leq Z < 1.5$, and an A for $Z \geq 1.5$. On her first test, everyone gets 100. What grades should she give her students?

6.9   (*continuation*) On her second test, Elizabeth decides to use a standardized test that has been given nationally with a mean score of 75 and a standard deviation of 10. Elizabeth's ten students receive scores of 94, 89, 83, 81, 78, 76, 74, 71, 67, and 67. If she uses the national mean and standard deviation, what will her ten students' standardized scores be? If she then uses the same grading scale given in the preceding question, how many As, Bs, Cs, Ds, and Fs will she give on this test?

6.10   (*continuation*) If she uses the national mean and standard deviation, what unstandardized scores would a student need to receive an A, B, C, D, and F on this test?

6.3   THE NORMAL CURVE AND THE CENTRAL LIMIT THEOREM

An English mathematician, Abraham De Moivre (1667–1754), was the first to deduce the equation for the bell-shaped curve that emerged in our Figures 6.3 and 6.4.

The **normal distribution** of a standardized random variable Z is

$$f[z] = \left(\frac{1}{2\pi}\right)^{1/2} e^{-z^2/2} \tag{6.2}$$

This π in the equation for the normal distribution is the celebrated number 3.14159. . . , and must not be confused with the use of the symbol π in Bernoulli trials to designate the success probability. The symbol e in the normal distribution is the base of natural logarithms, $e = 2.71828. . . .$

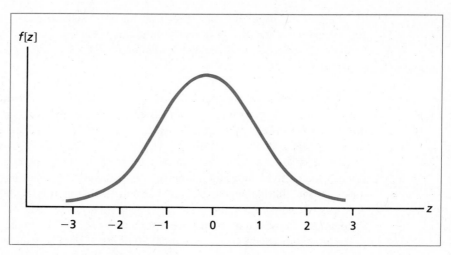

Figure 6.5 *The normal distribution*

The graph of Equation 6.2 is shown in Figure 6.5. Notice that the normal distribution is continuous. The probabilities are not shown by discrete spikes, but are instead given by areas under the curve. The normal curve is a continuous approximation to the spikes shown in Figures 6.3 and 6.4. In 1733, De Moivre concluded that, for a binomial distribution with a .5 probability of success, this approximation becomes virtually perfect as *n* increases.

The Central Limit Theorem

Nearly a century later, a French mathematician, Pierre Laplace (1749–1827), proved that this convergence is true for all success probabilities (except 0 and 1, of course). Laplace believed that his remarkable theorem could be used to explain most of the uncertainties that fill our lives, and he consequently applied the normal distribution to a wide variety of phenomena in both the natural and social sciences. Karl Gauss (1777–1855), the German "prince of mathematicians," applied the normal distribution to measurements of the shape of the earth and the movements of planets. His work was so extensive and influential that the normal distribution is now often called the *Gaussian distribution*—except in France, where it is called *Laplacean*.

Others, following in the footsteps of Laplace and Gauss, applied the normal distribution to all sorts of physical and social data. They found that these data often conform to a normal distribution, and they proved that many specific theoretical probability distributions converge to a normal distribution when they are cumulated. In the 1930s, mathematicians proved that this convergence is true of virtually all probability distributions.* This theorem, which is the culmination of 200 years of investigation, is one of the most famous mathematical theorems.

*The important restriction is that the standard deviation exists and is not equal to zero.[1]

The **central limit theorem** states that if Z is a standardized sum of any n independent, identically distributed (discrete or continuous) random variables, then the probability distribution of Z tends to a normal distribution as n increases.

The requirements are the same as for a sequence of Bernoulli trials. The probability distributions must not vary from one trial to the next and must not be affected by other outcomes in the sequence. If these assumptions are satisfied, then the sum of the outcomes will tend to the normal distribution.

As remarkable as it is, the central limit theorem would be of little practical value if the normal curve did not emerge until n was very, very large. The most important and intriguing thing about the normal distribution is that it so often appears even when n is quite small. Figures 6.3 and 6.4 showed three examples. A common rule of thumb is that the distribution of Z is usually acceptably close to the normal distribution as n gets up to 20 or 30. If the distribution for $n = 1$ is reasonably smooth and symmetrical (as with the dice roll or coin flip), then the approach to normality is very rapid. If, as with the $\pi = .9$ bent coin, the distribution is quite skewed or otherwise exotic, then the path to normality may take a bit longer.

Similarly, the central limit theorem would be just a mathematical curiosity if the Bernoulli-trial assumptions had to be strictly satisfied. The Bernoulli-trial assumptions do apply to games of chance, but in practical affairs, they are seldom if ever exactly true. Probabilities may vary slightly from one trial to the next as conditions change, and in many cases, the probabilities are affected by the outcomes of earlier trials. But, as you will see in the next section, the central limit theorem is pretty robust, in that even if the assumptions aren't quite true, the normal distribution is still a pretty good approximation. This is why the normal distribution is so popular and the central limit theorem is so celebrated.

Exercises

6.11 Explain the central limit theorem in your own words. Use some examples to show when the underlying assumptions are and are not satisfied.

6.12 Professor I.B. Gessen has a .5 probability of picking a stock whose price goes up and a .5 probability of picking a stock whose price goes down. If he picks 2 stocks, what is the probability that both will go up? That both will go down? That 1 will go up and the other down? If he picks 10 stocks, give the probabilities that all 10 will go up, that 9 will go up and 1 down, and so on.

6.13 (*continuation*) Let the number of stocks that Professor Gessen selects be n and let the number that go up be X. For $n = 1, 2,$ and 10:

a. Calculate the expected value μ of X.
b. Calculate the standard deviation σ of X.
c. Calculate the values of the standardized variable $Z = (X - \mu)/\sigma$.
d. Graph the probability distribution of Z.

What do you think will happen to the probability distribution of Z as n becomes infinitely large?

6.14   There are 25 workers on an assembly line. Each has a .2 chance of making a mistake, irrespective of whether or not the other workers have made mistakes. The total number of mistakes X in assembling the product can range from 0 to 25. What are the expected value and standard deviation of X? Calculate the possible values of the standardized variable $Z = (X - \mu)/\sigma$ and graph its probability distribution. What would happen to the probability distribution of Z as the number of workers is increased indefinitely?

● **6.15**   Find a computer program with a random-number generator that allows you to simulate the roll of a four-sided die. Let n be the number of dice rolled and let X be total number obtained (the sum of the numbers on the n dice). Conduct the following experiments for $n = 1, 2$, and 8:

a. Make the n rolls 1000 times.
b. Calculate the relative frequencies with which each total X appears.
c. Graph this observed frequency distribution.

6.4   CLOSE ENOUGH?

In practice, researchers commonly appeal to the central limit theorem when n is large even if the Bernoulli-trial assumptions are not strictly met. We may have a random variable, like the height of an 11-year-old boy, which logic tells us will be the cumulative result of a large number of uncertain events. We imagine that a boy's height depends on such factors as heredity, diet, health, and exercise, but we really have little, if any, information about the underlying probability distributions and their independence. Nonetheless, we might hope tentatively that the number of specific events that influence height is so very large that an approximately normal distribution may still emerge.

The boxed example on page 196 shows how an early study of heights did, in fact, find a striking correspondence to the normal distribution. The normal distribution also appears when we examine weights, IQ scores, the number of kernels on ears of corn, the number of ridges on scallop shells, the number of hairs on dogs, the heights of trees, and even the number of leaves on trees. If some phenomenon appears to be the cumulative result of a great many separate influences, then the normal distribution is quite often a very useful approximation.

Varying Probabilities

To demonstrate the robustness of the central limit theorem more formally, let's consider first a sequence of independent events that have varying probability distributions. Each event can be a success or a failure, but the probability of success is not constant. For example, a baseball player's chances of a base hit depend on the opposing pitcher, the ballpark, the month, and whether it is a day game or a night game. What would a probability distribution for the *total* base hits by this player over the coming season look like? We cannot formally invoke the central limit theorem because we are violating the assumption of constant probabilities. Yet, maybe the theorem is robust enough to tolerate some deviations.

This scenario of varying probabilities also applies to a student's *total* test score if the questions vary in difficulty and, similarly, to the *total* number of defective products made by workers of varying skills. It would also apply to the *total* amount of dollars withdrawn from a bank because withdrawal probabilities vary from ac-

The Heights of 11-Year-Old Boys

In the late 1800s, H.P. Bowditch measured the heights of several thousand Massachusetts schoolchildren.[2] His data for 1293 11-year-old boys are shown in Figure 1. These 1293 boys had an average height of 52.9 inches, with a 6.2-inch standard deviation. We can standardize his height data by subtracting the mean and dividing by the standard deviation. The spikes in Figure 1 show the distribution of these standardized heights among the 1293 boys he measured. We can think of each spike as the probability that a boy who is randomly selected from these 1293 children will be a certain height. Alternatively, we can view these 1293 heights as relative frequencies that can be used to estimate the distribution of heights for all 11-year-old boys at the time that this study was conducted. In either case, the normal distribution appears to be a good approximation.

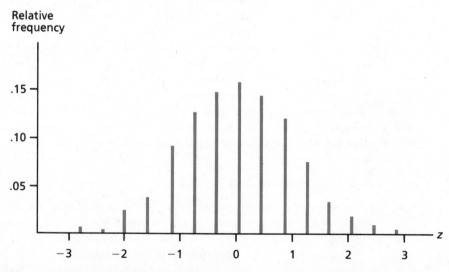

Figure 1 *The heights of 11-year-old boys*

count to account and from day to day. Clearly, there are many situations where varying probabilities are more realistic than constant probabilities. Will normality still emerge if we have a large number of trials?

Here's one experiment that offers some hope. Let's consider 19 independent events with success probabilities .05, .10, .15, . . . , .95. That is, on one occasion, the probability of success is .05; another time, the probability of success is .10; and yet another time, it is .15. It does not matter whether these probabilities appear in any particular order, only that the 19 events have these 19 different (in fact, very different) probabilities. Now, as per the central limit theorem, let's look at the total number of successes, a random variable that can be as low as zero or as high as 19. With considerable effort, I computed the standardized probability distribution and graphed it in Figure 6.6. As you probably anticipated, it has that familiar bell shape again.

There is a rough, intuitive explanation. First, the extremes are almost certainly going to be very improbable. There is only one way to get $X = 19$: to have 19 successes in a row, a most improbable event. Nineteen failures in a row ($X = 0$) is also quite unlikely. The results $X = 18$ and $X = 1$ are more likely, because there are more ways in which they could occur. For $X = 18$, we could have 18 successes and then a failure, 17 successes followed by a failure and then a success, and so on—19 different sequences in all, as compared to only 1 possible sequence for $X = 19$. There are similarly 19 different ways to get $X = 1$, as compared to

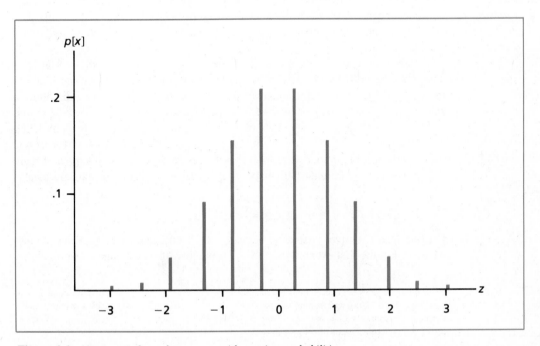

Figure 6.6 *Nineteen independent events with varying probabilities*

only 1 way to get $X = 0$. There are $\binom{19}{2} = 171$ possible sequences for $X = 17$ and for $X = 2$, and $\binom{19}{3}$ possible sequences for $X = 16$ and $X = 3$. This escalation of possible sequences peaks in the middle at $\binom{19}{10} = \binom{19}{9} = 92,378$ for $X = 10$ and $X = 9$. There are many, many ways to get a middling number of successes and very few ways to get an extreme result. This strong sequence-counting pattern overwhelms the varying probabilities and produces a bell-shaped probability distribution.*

Events That are Not Always Independent

For a second example, let's consider a hypothetical sequence of n nonindependent events. The probability of success is .5 on the odd-numbered trials. On the even-numbered trials, the probability of success is .7 if the preceding trial was a success and .3 if it was a failure. This scheme is a stylized model of a situation in which some of the events are dependent and some are independent. One illustration would be an athlete who has periodic hot and cold spells as physical and mental conditions fluctuate. Another illustration is deposit withdrawals or stock prices that are dependent during the course of a particular day but independent between days. A final illustration is heights. Some influences, such as lifetime dietary habits, are not independent. A person with an advantageous diet at age 13 will probably also have an advantageous diet at age 14. Other influences, such as genetics, are largely independent of diet.

Well, it turns out that some independence is enough to satisfy the central limit theorem. The probability distribution for the number of successes on the first and the (dependent) second trial is shown in Figure 6.7. This very same distribution applies to any odd-even pair of trials: 1 and 2, 3 and 4, and so on. As these paired trials are independent of each other, we can think of, say, 16 trials as really being 8 independent paired trials, each with the same probability distribution for $n = 2$ that is shown in Figure 6.7. It follows that the central limit theorem applies. Figure 6.7 shows that the familiar bell shape is, indeed, apparent by the sixteenth trial.

Events That Are Never Independent

For one final example, consider a scenario in which events are never really independent. For the first event, there is a .5 probability of success and a .5 probability

---

*This argument does not depend on the probabilities varying evenly from .05 to .95. They could instead vary from .2 to .4 (as with batting averages) or even from .01 to .05 (as with bank withdrawals or defective products). We saw in the bent-coin example how the cumulation of n outcomes makes skewed distributions become symmetrical as n increases.

of failure. Thereafter, whenever a success occurs, the probability is .7 that the next outcome will be a success and a .3 that it will be a failure. Whenever a failure occurs, the probability that the next event will also be a failure is .7, while the probability of a success is .3.

This is a stylized representation of a situation in which events tend to repeat themselves. The persistence might be due to psychological factors, such as the confident athlete doing well and the discouraged athlete doing poorly, or, in a Bayesian fashion, we might be repeatedly revising our probabilities in light of recent experience. Suppose we are making a string of preliminary tests for oil, water, or some mineral. After each test, we move to another nearby location and make another test. At each location, our subjective probability of a positive test result is undoubtedly influenced by the outcome of the preceding test. We will be optimistic if the last test was positive and pessimistic if the last test was negative. Similarly, when a business introduces a new product, there is uncertainty about how well it will sell. If the product starts selling well, then the firm becomes more optimistic. If sales slump, then the firm reduces its sales projections.

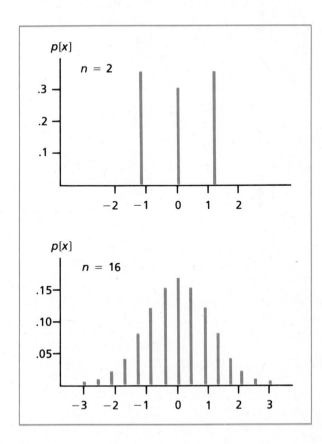

Figure 6.7 *A mixture of dependent and independent events*

Baseball Batting Averages

Baseball is a wonderful game for figuring probabilities and a great source of statistical data—the most common being batting averages. A player with a .300 batting average gets a base hit, on the average, 3 out of every 10 times at bat. (Walks don't count as official times at bat.) Each player's chances of a base hit depend on the player's mental and physical condition, the opposing pitcher, the shape of the ballpark, and even whether the game is played during the day or at night. Dedicated students of the game will collect all sorts of data on a player's performance under these varying conditions; for example, how well Robin Yount bats in August, against a certain lefthanded pitcher in night games.

Although batting is not a strict Bernoulli trial, if we look at the cumulative result of a large number of times at bat, we may find a normal distribution. To see if this is so, I looked at the annual batting averages of nine players with lifetime batting averages of about .300: Hank Aaron, Lou Brock, Al Kaline, Micky Mantle, Willy Mays, Minnie Minosa, Joe Morgan, Duke Snider, and Carl Yastrzemski. I only looked at years in which the players had 400 times at bat. In each of these years, the season's batting average is the cumulative result of at least 400 times at bat, although admittedly not with constant and independent probabilities. Table 1 shows the data I found, and Figure 2 shows the approximate bell shape.

Table 1 *The annual batting averages of nine lifetime .300 hitters*

Batting average	Number of years
.225–.234	1
.235–.244	3
.245–.254	2
.255–.264	7
.265–.274	11
.275–.284	14
.285–.294	20
.295–.304	23
.305–.314	21
.315–.324	13
.325–.334	12
.335–.344	3
.345–.354	3
.355–.364	2
Total	135

Apparently, a player's performance each season does conform roughly to the normal distribution. A .300-lifetime hitter averages above .300 some years and averages below .300 other years. Most years, the player's average is near .300, but there are some years in which the player's batting average is much higher or far lower than .300. The popular press attributes these "good" years and "bad" years to fluctuating skills. A statistician might find them consistent with a chance model in which the player comes to the plate over and over again, each time with about a .3 probability of getting a hit. The difference between a .320 year and a .280 year may be due to changes in the player's fortunes, rather than skills.

Figure 2 *The distribution of annual batting averages for nine lifetime .300 hitters*

This persistence model also applies to situations in which momentum is apparent. A nation's economy has considerable momentum because people's spending depends on their incomes, which in turn depend on the spending of others. The chances of an increase in GNP are greater if GNP went up last month than if GNP declined. Birth rates tend to follow cycles, too. The probability that a nation will have a high birth rate this year is larger if this nation had a high birth rate last year. There is also momentum in the life of cities. A city that is improving is more likely to improve again next year. A decaying city is likely to continue to decay. You can undoubtedly think of many more examples.

This model doesn't conform strictly to the assumptions of the central limit theorem, but let's see what happens to the probability distribution for the number of successes in n trials. For $n = 2$, the probability distribution is the same as in the top half of Figure 6.7. The built-in momentum makes two straight successes

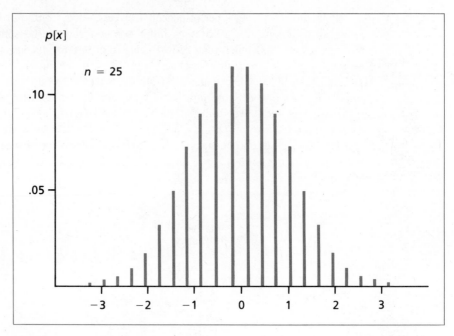

Figure 6.8   *A sequence of dependent events*

or two straight failures more likely than one success and one failure. This distribution contrasts sharply with two independent coin flips, where the most likely outcome is one success and one failure.

As *n* increases, however, the probability of an extreme outcome inexorably declines. Even with momentum, the chances of 19 or 20 successes in 20 trials is very slight. With a large number of trials, it becomes more and more certain that the results will be a mixture of successes and failures. Figure 6.8 shows the standardized probability distribution for the number of successes in 25 trials. You guessed it, the bell shape again!

A Robust Theorem

The central limit theorem tells us that the standardized sum of *n* independent, identically distributed random variables converges to the normal distribution. In practice, though, there are many interesting situations in which the central limit theorem's assumption of independent, identical distributions is not strictly valid. Fortunately, mathematicians have proven several other limit theorems that show that the normal distribution still emerges even if these assumptions are relaxed somewhat.[3] Unfortunately, the exact conditions that are sufficient to ensure normality are too complex to be very useful to us here.

Instead, I've used several examples to illustrate the robustness of the central limit theorem. It can tolerate some dependence and some variation in each trial's distribution and still yield an approximate normal distribution for the sum of the outcomes. This is why the normal distribution is so very important. However, don't be lulled into thinking that probabilities always follow the normal curve; this is only true if the outcomes are the cumulative result of a large number of Bernoulli trials, or some facsimile thereof. It is also not true that the sum of the outcomes must conform perfectly to a normal distribution; the bell shapes that have appeared in our examples are approximately, but not perfectly, normal.

Exercises

6.16 Bowditch also recorded the heights of 1253 12-year-old boys:

height (inches)	number	relative frequency
46	1	.0008
47	3	.0023
48	7	.0055
49	13	.0103
50	31	.0247
51	73	.0582
52	111	.0886
53	176	.1404
54	189	.1508
55	198	.1580
56	162	.1293
57	106	.0846
58	77	.0615
59	49	.0391
60	31	.0247
61	10	.0080
62	9	.0072
63	4	.0032
64	1	.0008
65	1	.0008
66	1	.0008
Total	1253	1.0

a. What are the mean and the standard deviation of these heights? How do these values compare with the mean and standard deviation for 11-year-old boys that are given in the text?

b. Use your computed mean and standard deviation to calculate the 21 standardized heights.

c. Plot the relative frequencies for these standardized heights.

6.17 I asked a local Boy Scout troop to measure the length of a school soccer field. Each of the 20 boys made five measurements:

	measurement (meters)				
boy	*1*	*2*	*3*	*4*	*5*
1	70.50	70.30	70.10	69.85	69.90
2	68.70	69.80	68.60	69.50	69.80
3	69.15	69.00	69.20	69.25	69.80
4	70.15	70.00	70.50	71.00	70.05
5	70.05	70.65	69.80	69.95	69.65
6	69.70	69.40	69.75	70.40	70.30
7	70.40	70.10	69.85	69.80	70.60
8	69.95	69.15	69.50	70.00	70.10
9	70.80	70.50	70.15	70.45	69.85
10	69.75	70.10	69.90	70.55	69.60
11	70.55	70.80	70.20	70.50	70.55
12	70.10	70.45	70.60	70.85	69.95
13	70.00	69.95	69.95	70.25	70.00
14	70.05	70.25	70.05	70.20	69.75
15	70.50	69.95	69.30	71.45	69.40
16	70.90	70.75	69.75	69.45	70.65
17	69.40	69.50	70.20	69.70	69.90
18	70.60	70.10	70.35	70.40	70.15
19	70.35	70.70	70.25	70.20	70.05
20	70.60	69.80	70.65	70.25	69.85

Calculate the number of observations that fall in each of the intervals 68.50–68.99, 69.00–69.49, . . . , 71.00–71.49 and then graph a histogram of these data.

6.18   A one-acre wheat field was divided into 500 plots, each measuring 0.002 of an acre, and the grain yields from each of these 500 plots were recorded. Why might the yields vary from one plot to the next? Is there any hope that the yields might be approximately normally distributed? Here is the actual yield distribution:[4]

yield (pounds)	*number of plots*
2.7–2.9	4
2.9–3.1	15
3.1–3.3	20
3.3–3.5	47
3.5–3.7	63
3.7–3.9	78
3.9–4.1	88
4.1–4.3	69
4.3–4.5	59
4.5–4.7	35
4.7–4.9	10
4.9–5.1	8
5.1–5.3	4
total	500

Calculate and graph the relative frequencies.

• **6.19** The seasonal batting averages shown in Table 1 and in Figure 2 on pages 200–201 seem to have somewhat more extreme observations than a bell-shaped curve; for instance, examine the three years in the .235–.245 range. Can you think of any reason for this?

• **6.20** A multiple-choice test has 20 questions, each with 4 possible answers. An uninformed guesser answers these 20 questions randomly. To penalize guessers, the teacher gives 1 point for a right answer and subtracts 1/3 of a point for a wrong answer. Construct a table showing the probability distribution for the guesser's score on this test. Now calculate the mean and standard deviation of this score and use these to calculate the possible standardized scores. List these standardized scores in your table and graph the standardized probability distribution. Does this distribution look bell-shaped? Carefully explain why you might or might not expect the distribution to be bell-shaped.

6.5 THE LAW OF DISORDER

Modern physics uses the normal distribution to describe the movements of molecules. The motion of each individual molecule is quite disordered, and yet their overall behavior is very predictable. This disordered movement is known as a *random walk*. The idea of a random walk was actually used by Laplace and others to analyze a gambler's chances of wandering into bankruptcy. Today, the random walk model is applied to many phenomena, including the stock market.

The Movement of Molecules

At the temperature $-273°$ Centigrade ($-459°$ Fahrenheit), molecules are motionless. This completely frozen state is known as the *absolute zero* temperature. Near absolute zero, molecules have so little energy that they are locked together into a rigid solid. At higher temperatures, molecules have more energy and begin bouncing against each other. At a sufficiently high temperature, this bouncing about is violent enough to allow molecules to break their locked pattern and move around, changing the solid into a fluid. The temperature at which this melting occurs varies from substance to substance, depending on the strength of each substance's cohesive forces. Frozen hydrogen melts at -259 °C; water (ice) melts at 0 °C; and iron melts at 1535 °C. At still higher temperatures, the molecules become so agitated that they break completely free of each other and disperse. At this point, the liquid boils and turns into a gas. Liquid hydrogen vaporizes at -253 °C, water boils at 100 °C, and liquid iron turns into a gas at 3000 °C. At even higher temperatures (on our sun, for instance), the thermal agitation is so violent that the molecules break up into atoms and then into bare nuclei and free electrons.

A Drunkard's Walk

At absolute zero, molecules are frozen into a rigid pattern, but at higher temperatures, the molecules move about, randomly bouncing off each other. As the temperature increases, this random movement becomes more agitated and the molecules become more disordered. It becomes increasingly difficult to predict where a particular molecule will be after a few seconds of chance collisions, but we can give a probabilistic prediction, which is known as the **law of disorder.**

In the early 1800s, Robert Brown, an English botanist, watched tiny plant spores through his microscope and noticed how these spores were being randomly pushed about by the surrounding molecules. The movement of each spore was the random consequence of chance collisions with molecules that were themselves randomly bouncing off of each other. This haphazard movement is now known as *Brownian motion.* The popular analogy is a drunkard leaving a lamp post in the middle of an empty city square. Each wobbly step could be in any direction. Can we say anything about the result of this drunkard's walk?

We can. Let's pick a direction, say west-east, in which to measure the drunkard's progress. A west-east line is shown in Figure 6.9. Perhaps home is to the west and a favorite bar is to the east. After an hour, the drunkard is equally likely to be 20 feet to the west or 20 feet to the east. The expected value of the west-east position is 0. There is even more to be said; we can think of each step to the west or east as a Bernoulli trial with $\pi = .5$. If there are many such steps, then the central limit theorem implies that the sum of these steps, measuring the west-east distance from the starting point, will follow a normal distribution! The drunk-

Figure 6.9   *A drunkard's walk*

ard is most likely to end up slightly west or east of the lamp post. The chances of being farther west or east are given by the normal distribution.

Galton's Apparatus

The same conclusion applies to the spores that Brown watched and, indeed, to any object moving randomly. In a classroom or science exhibit (or even on the television show, *The Price is Right*), you may have seen the apparatus (originally devised by Galton) that is depicted in Figure 6.10. Many identical balls are dropped, one at a time, onto a symmetrical array of posts. Each ball hits the first post,

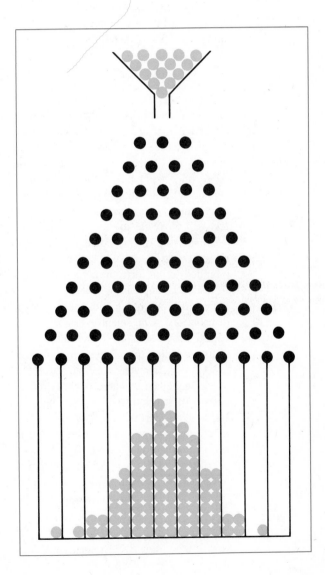

Figure 6.10   *An apparatus for demonstrating Brownian motion*

bounces to the left or right, and then bounces left or right again off a post in the next row. After randomly working its way through these posts, each ball drops into a bin that measures its horizontal distance from the starting point. As with the drunkard's walk, this horizontal distance is the summation of many independent left-right bounces, and as shown, the horizontal dispersion of the balls follows the normal distribution.

This apparatus is an ingenious depiction of the Brownian movement of plant spores or small particles suspended in a liquid. Einstein showed that the probability distribution for the distance that a particle will move from its initial position during a time period t is normally distributed with a mean zero and a variance $2D^2t$ where D is the liquid's *diffusion constant*. The same logic holds for molecules of gas colliding with other molecules and for small stars that are buffeted by the gravitational fields of other stars.

Some Improbable Events

We have seen how the movement of a molecule is random and yet can be probabilistically described by the normal distribution. A substance contains billions of molecules that are repeatedly involved in billions of collisions. The average outcome of these collisions is also governed by the central limit theorem. Think of the individual air molecules in the room that you are now in. Where will they be 60 seconds from now? Each air molecule will be involved in about 60 million collisions during the next minute. Some molecules will end up a bit to the right of where they are now; some will end up a bit to the left of their current position. A few will move far to the right, while others move far to the left. On the average, the dispersion of the molecules should be about the same as it is now, and that's a good thing! You would be very uncomfortable if all of the air molecules suddenly migrated to the far right corner of the room.

Such an unpleasant event is not impossible, but it is very improbable. It would require billions of air molecules to experience the far-right tails of their normal distributions. One scientist has estimated that we should expect to observe a room with the molecules all in one-half about once every $10^{299,999,999,999,999,999,999,999,991}$ years,[5] which is not very often.

Other scientists have figured out the probabilities of other improbable molecular arrangements. There is an extremely small chance that many more air molecules will strike this book from below than above, causing the book to leap upwards. This startling event is more likely to occur than all of the air molecules in this room bouncing to one side, but it is still not very probable. It should happen less often than once every 10^{100} years.[6]

There is also a small chance that most of the molecules in a substance will have velocities much higher or lower than the expected velocity for a given temperature.* There is a very slight probability that a teakettle of water on a hot stove

---

*The relevant probabilities come from Maxwell's law of velocities: the velocity in any fixed direction of a molecule with mass M in a gas at absolute temperature T is normally distributed with mean 0 and variance M/kT where k is Boltzmann's constant.

will freeze. In fact, there is even a chance for the proverbial snowball in hell. One scientist estimated that the probability that a piece of celluloid placed in a temperature 2.8×10^{12} absolute (the assumed temperature of hell) would survive unburned for a week.[7] This slim probability is $1/10^{10^{50}}$, which he estimated is as likely as reproducing the manuscript of Hamlet 10^{30} times in a row without error by randomly spattering ink on paper.

Exercises

6.21 Two evenly matched people play backgammon for $1 a game. If they play 100 games, what is each player's expected gain? What else can you say about the possible outcomes? Explain your reasoning carefully.

6.22 A gambler bets $1 on red over and over again at a Las Vegas roulette wheel. On each bet, she has a 18/38 probability of winning $1 and a 20/38 probability of losing $1. If she plays 1000 times, what is her expected gain? What else can you say about her possible gains and losses after 1000 plays?

6.23 A certain drunkard is trying to get from here to there. Every 10 seconds, this drunk takes a step, which is equally likely to be one foot to the left or right. After an hour, this drunk may be 360 feet to the left, 360 feet to the right, or somewhere in between. What is the exact probability distribution? Why would the normal distribution be a good approximation?

•• **6.24** Figure 6.9 shows an apparatus in which dropped balls form a normal distribution. This is, of course, not an exact normal distribution because the balls and the bins are discrete instead of continuous. Try to figure out the discrete probability that gives the probabilities of a ball falling into the various bins. Assume that there are 10 rows of pegs and 11 bins, and that at each post the ball is equally likely to fall to the left or the right.

6.6   STOCK RETURNS

In his 1900 doctoral dissertation, Louis Bachelier assumed that the prices of stocks, bonds, and other securities follow a random walk and that future price changes cannot be predicted from past price changes. Bachelier worked out several interesting implications of his model and he found a striking correspondence between his theories and the actual behavior of French security prices.

Bachelier's work went largely unnoticed and unappreciated until the late 1950s, when there began a flurry of research on the predictability of stock market prices. Here, too, researchers concluded that prices follow a random walk and that past movements of stock prices are of no value in predicting future price movements.[8] As with Brownian motion, there is no way to tell in advance in which direction prices will be pushed. The stock market is apparently very much like a large casino, where a playful god rolls dice to decide whether prices are going up or down.

The Efficient Market Hypothesis

What is the source of this randomness? Is it really a god rolling dice? Or is it, as Keynes suggested, the vagaries of unpredictable mass psychology? In the 1960s, a Nobel-prize-winning economist, Paul Samuelson, offered another possibility in a short mathematical paper entitled "Proof that Properly Anticipated Prices Fluctuate Randomly."[9] Samuelson's idea is now called the **efficient market hypothesis** and is used by many economists to explain the apparent randomness in stock prices.

In an efficient market, all traders have access to the same information, and therefore current prices take into account all available information. It is new information that causes price changes, with positive information pushing prices up and negative information pulling prices down. But, because new information is, by definition, unpredictable, we cannot predict in advance whether prices will go up or down.[10]

As you can imagine, this is a very provocative argument because it implies that security analysis is a waste of time. There is no need to pay lavish fees to experts who pick securities for you. You can do just as well by throwing darts at the financial pages. In later chapters, we will test this interesting theory in a variety of ways. For now, the important point is simply that, if the returns are independent, then the normal distribution may be appropriate.

A Normal Distribution Again

If stock prices do follow a random walk, then we again have a *law of disorder*, based on the application of the central limit theorem to Brownian motion. The cumulative price change over any period of time is the sum of all of the price changes during the period. Suppose, for instance, that the price is initially $20 a share and then follows this path:

price change	*new price*
$+\frac{1}{8}$	$20\frac{1}{8}$
$+\frac{1}{4}$	$20\frac{3}{8}$
$-\frac{3}{8}$	20
$+\frac{1}{4}$	$20\frac{1}{4}$
$-\frac{1}{8}$	$20\frac{1}{8}$
$-\frac{1}{4}$	$19\frac{7}{8}$
$+\frac{1}{8}$	20
$-\frac{1}{4}$	$19\frac{3}{4}$
$+\frac{1}{4}$	20
$-\frac{1}{8}$	$19\frac{7}{8}$
$-\frac{3}{8}$	$19\frac{1}{2}$
$-\frac{1}{4}$	$19\frac{1}{4}$
$+\frac{1}{8}$	$19\frac{3}{8}$
$+\frac{1}{8}$	$19\frac{1}{2}$
$+\frac{1}{4}$	$19\frac{3}{4}$
total $-\frac{1}{4}$	

The net price change, from $20 a share to $19¾, is the sum of the 15 price changes during this period of time. Now, and here's the punchline, if these price changes follow a random walk (in which they are independent and identically distributed), then the central limit theorem implies that their sum, the net price change over the period, is a random variable whose probability distribution converges to the normal distribution!

This argument applies to any period of time sufficient for the net price change to be the cumulation of many price changes. We could look at annual, monthly, weekly, or daily returns. As long as there are many independent and identically distributed price changes during the interval, the net price change over some longer interval becomes normally distributed.

There is, in fact, pretty convincing evidence that stock price changes are independent. But it strains credulity to assert that probability distributions are fixed forevermore. Expected returns change with financial markets and with the anticipated returns on other assets. Standard deviations vary, too, as the future of the economy is sometimes more and sometimes less certain. Nonetheless, the robustness of the central limit theorem suggests that stock return may still be described approximately by a normal distribution.

One Year with IBM

I collected data on the daily returns on IBM stock during 1983. We can think of each daily return as the sum of several price changes during the day as the price of IBM stock fluctuated. If these individual price changes are independent and identically distributed, then the central limit theorem implies that the daily returns will come from a normal distribution. My data are a fairly small sample of observed returns during one particular year. Yet, Figure 6.11 shows the frequency distri-

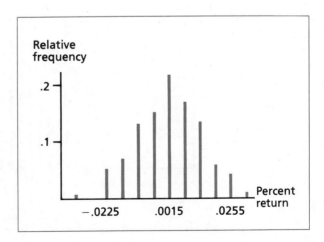

Figure 6.11 *Daily changes in the price of IBM stock, 1983*

bution of these daily returns and they, apparently, may have come from a normal distribution.

Sixty Five Years with the Market

Roger Ibbotson and Rex Sinquefield[11] have assembled data on the overall monthly returns since January 1926 for the 500 stocks included in the Standard and Poor's Composite Index. If each month's return is the cumulative result of independent and identically distributed returns over shorter intervals, then the monthly returns should come from a normal distribution. Figure 6.12 supports this hypothesis.

Exercises

6.25 Empirical investigations of the distribution of price changes have generally focused on speculative prices, such as the prices of stock and pork-belly futures. What assumptions are needed to justify the hypothesis that these price changes come from a normal distribution?

• **6.26** (*continuation*) Why might the daily change in the price of automobiles or the annual births in a country not come from a normal distribution?

6.27 I have sometimes used the following experiment to generate stock price patterns, which I then give to my technical-analyst friends to analyze, without explaining that the

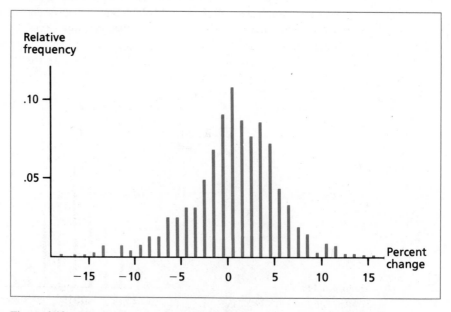

Figure 6.12 *The distribution of monthly changes in stock prices, 1926–1980*

data are fictitious. (The moral is that they can't tell the difference between real and fictitious data.) The stock's initial price is set at $20. A silver dollar is flipped, with heads signifying a 25-cent increase in the stock's price and tails signifying a 25-cent decline. The net result of 10 flips gives the change in the stock's price that day; for example, 6 heads and 4 tails implies that this imaginary stock went up 50 cents. One thousand flips gives a price chart over a 100-day period. What is the (exact) probability distribution for the daily dollar change in this stock's price?

• **6.28** (*continuation*) What is the probability distribution for the dollar change in the stock's price after 10 days? After 20 days? Explain why the distribution of the dollar change in this stock's price does or does not converge to a normal distribution as the horizon lengthens.

•• **6.29** Pick a stock and compute the daily percentage changes in its price over a one-year period. These data can be computed from the financial pages of newspapers at your college library. Separate these returns into ten equal intervals and make a relative frequency graph. Does it look bell-shaped?

•• **6.30** Use the financial pages of newspapers at your college library to compute the percentage change in the Dow-Jones industrial average each day the stock market was open in 1984. These percentage changes are an estimate of the daily stock market returns. (They are only estimates because they neglect dividends and because the Dow-Jones average only includes 30 stocks.) Separate these returns into 10 equal intervals and make a relative frequency graph. Does it look bell-shaped?

6.7   SUMMARY

In earlier chapters, we looked at discrete random variables such as the number of successes in a sequence of Bernoulli trials. This chapter introduced the bell-shaped normal distribution, which is continuous. With a continuous random variable X, the probability that X falls in the interval $a < X < b$ is shown by the area under the probability distribution between the points a and b.

A random variable X is standardized by subtracting its expected value μ and then dividing by the standard deviation σ:

$$Z = \frac{X - \mu}{\sigma}$$

The standardized random variable Z has an expected value of zero and a standard deviation of 1.

The central limit theorem says that if Z is the standardized sum of any n independent, identically distributed random variables, then the probability distribution of Z tends to the normal distribution. Many things are approximately normally distributed, even if: n is not very large; there is not complete independence; and the probabilities are not constant from one trial to the next. As a consequence, the normal distribution is widely used by virtually all of the physical and social sciences.

REVIEW EXERCISES

6.31 A certain random variable X has this continuous probability distribution:

$$f[x] = 1 + x, \quad -1 \leq x \leq 0$$
$$f[x] = 1 - x, \quad 0 \leq x \leq 1$$
$$f[x] = 0, \quad \text{otherwise}$$

Graph this probability distribution and determine the following probabilities:

a. $P[-1 \leq X \leq 1]$
b. $P[-1 \leq X \leq 0]$
c. $P[0 \leq X]$
d. $P[0 \leq X \leq .5]$
e. $P[-.5 \leq X \leq .5]$

6.32 Use the data in Table 4.1 on the roll of two dice to calculate the mean and standard deviation of X. Then calculate the 11 standardized values of Z. Check your work by calculating the mean and standard deviation of Z. Graph the probability distribution of Z.

6.33 Find a book of baseball statistics at the library and choose 20 baseball players with lifetime batting averages of about .280 (calculated over a period of at least 10 years). This will give you annual batting averages for at least 200 seasons. (Ignore seasons with fewer than 400 times at bat.) Divide these season averages into the intervals shown in Table 1 on page 200, calculate the relative frequencies for each interval, and make a relative frequency graph such as Figure 2 on page 201. Is an approximate bell shape apparent? If not, what differences do you detect?

• **6.34** Repeat exercise 6.15, this time using 100 rather than 1000 rolls. Which results look more bell shaped? Do you think this is a fluke, or should we expect systematic differences in the results of 100 and 1000 rolls?

•• **6.35** (*continuation*) Does the central limit theorem relate to the number of dice (1, 2, or 8) or the number of rolls (100 or 1000)? Why do both seem to matter here?

CHAPTER 7

Using the Normal Curve

When you can measure what you are speaking about and express it in numbers you know something about it; but when you cannot measure it, when you cannot express it in numbers, your knowledge is of a meager and unsatisfactory kind.

Lord Kelvin

TOPICS

215

By now, you should be semi-convinced that the normal distribution is worth knowing. So, let's look at the details of this pervasive bell shape. The actual equation for the normal distribution,

$$f[z] = \left(\frac{1}{2\pi}\right)^{1/2} e^{-z^2/2} \tag{7.1}$$

is pretty complicated. We could, if we had to, try to calculate probabilities by using this equation and some calculus to estimate areas under the normal curve. But fortunately, others have already calculated a great many of these probabilities for us and I've put these probabilities in Table 2 at the end of this book. It is far easier to glance at this table than to do an area computation yourself.

7.1   THE NORMAL PROBABILITY TABLE

Table 2 has been set up so that it shows the area in the right-hand tail of the normal distribution, as demonstrated in Figure 7.1. The left-hand column of Table 2 shows values of Z in 0.1 intervals, such as 1.1, 1.2, and 1.3. For finer gradations, the top row shows 0.01 intervals for Z. By matching the row and column, we can, for instance, find the probability that Z is greater than 1.25. The logic of this calculation is shown in Figure 7.1. For even finer gradations, we can interpolate the probabilities shown in Table 2.

For probabilities other than the right-hand tails, we use a bit of logic plus the fact that the normal distribution is symmetrical about the point $Z = 0$. One immediate

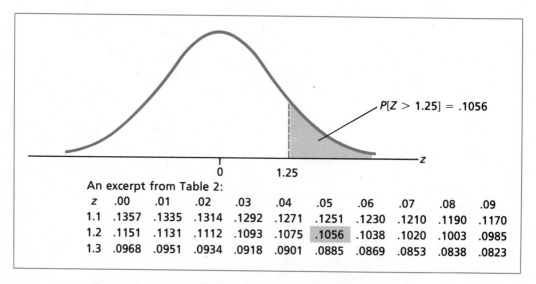

An excerpt from Table 2:

z	.00	.01	.02	.03	.04	.05	.06	.07	.08	.09
1.1	.1357	.1335	.1314	.1292	.1271	.1251	.1230	.1210	.1190	.1170
1.2	.1151	.1131	.1112	.1093	.1075	.1056	.1038	.1020	.1003	.0985
1.3	.0968	.0951	.0934	.0918	.0901	.0885	.0869	.0853	.0838	.0823

Figure 7.1   *Appendix Table 2 gives the right-hand tail probabilities*

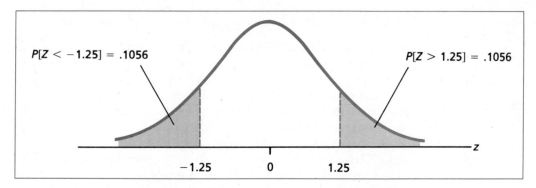

Figure 7.2 *The probabilities in the right-hand and left-hand tails are equal*

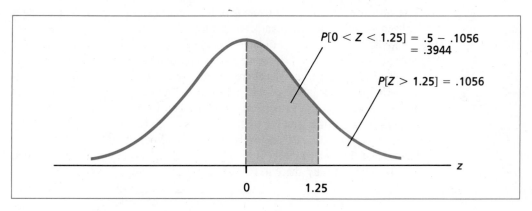

Figure 7.3 *The probability that Z is between 0 and 1.25*

Figure 7.4 *The probability that Z is between 0.75 and 1.25*

Grading by the Curve

There are two general approaches to grading student exams. One approach is to set absolute standards before grading the tests. For example, the professor might decide that 90 percent correct is an A score, 80 percent a B, 70 percent a C, 60 percent a D, and below 60 percent is an F. On essay questions, the professor can decide beforehand what sorts of answers merit an A grade, which warrant a B, and so on. With absolute grading standards such as these, it is possible for every student in the class to get an A or for every student to get an F.

A very different approach is to judge each student's performance relative to the other students in the class. For example, a professor might "grade by the normal curve." Each student is given a numerical test score, perhaps the number of questions right or the number right minus a fraction of the number wrong. The professor then uses the mean and standard deviation of these scores to calculate a standardized score, Z, for each student. A value $Z = 0$ will be an average score. Those who did above average will have positive Zs, while those who scored below average will have negative Zs. If the scores are approximately normally distributed, then they will be symmetrically scattered about $Z = 0$, in the bell shape shown in Figure 1. The particular grading scale indicated in Figure 1 gives 7 percent As, 24 percent Bs, 38 percent Cs, 24 percent Ds, and 7 percent Fs.

Proponents argue that grading by the curve is an objective way of determining how difficult a test really is. If the average score is 40 out of 100, then the teacher will realize that the test was very difficult and grade accordingly. Many students, though, abhor grading by the curve. They want to be judged by whether or not

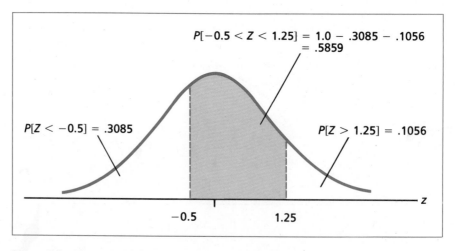

Figure 7.5   *The probability that Z is between −0.5 and 1.25*

they have mastered the material, and not by what others have done. Why, they ask, if everyone does well, do some have to be given Ds and Fs? Is it fair that the grade distribution should be the same in a class full of good students and in a class with many weak students? (And of course, they are always in the class with all the good students.) They rightly point out, that grading by the curve discourages student cooperation and camaraderie. When others do well, it makes your own performance look that much worse. Grading by the curve also encourages such unseemly practices as bribing weak students to show up for tests.

Most professors agree and use some combination of absolute and relative grading standards. They have some gut feeling about what a good score is and what a bad score is; and they will adjust their beliefs if the class does unexpectedly well or surprisingly poorly.

Figure 1   *Grading by the curve*

implication, for instance, is that the area in a left-hand tail is the same as the area in the corresponding right-hand tail. The probability that Z is less than -1.25 is equal to the probability that Z is greater than $+1.25$. Figure 7.2 shows this equivalence.

The symmetry about $Z = 0$ also implies that there is a .50 probability that Z is greater than zero and a .5 probability that Z is less than zero. This 50-50 split allows us to find the probability that Z is between zero and some number. For instance,

$$P[0 < Z < 1.25] = .5 - P[Z \geq 1.25]$$

$$= .5 - .1056$$

$$= .3944$$

Figure 7.3 shows the logic of such a calculation.

Yet another case is the probability that Z lies between two positive numbers; for example, 0.75 and 1.25 as shown in Figure 7.4. Table 2 tells us that the probability of Z exceeding 0.75 is .2266, and we already know that the probability of Z exceeding 1.25 is .1056. Therefore, the probability that Z will be between 0.75 and 1.25 must equal the difference between these two probabilities, .2266 − .1056 = .1210.

For a final illustration, consider the probability that Z is between −0.5 and 1.25. Figure 7.5 shows this situation. The desired probability can be found by subtracting the excluded tail probabilities from 1.0. The probability that Z is greater than 1.25 is still .1056. Table 2 tells us that the probability that Z is less than −0.5 is .3085. Therefore, the probability that Z will be between −0.5 and 1.25 is 1.0 − .1056 − .3085 = .5859.

With a bit of thought, Table 2 gives us the information we need to figure out all sorts of probabilities for the normal distribution. It is usually safest to make a quick sketch, as I have done in Figures 7.1–7.5. It is then readily apparent what numbers we have to add or subtract to arrive at the final answer. We will do several examples in this chapter—and there are, of course, exercises for you to practice on.

Exercises

7.1   Use Table 2 to find these five probabilities; in each case sketch the probability distribution of Z and shade in the area showing the appropriate probability:

a. $P[Z > 0.0]$
b. $P[Z \geq 1.0]$
c. $P[Z > 2.0]$
d. $P[Z \geq 3.0]$
e. $P[Z < -1.0]$

7.2   Determine each of these five probabilities; sketch the probability distribution of Z and shade in the area showing the appropriate probability:

a. $P[-1.0 < Z < 1.0]$
b. $P[-2.0 < Z < 2.0]$
c. $P[Z > 2.0 \text{ or } Z < -2.0]$
d. $P[Z \geq 1.65]$
e. $P[0.0 < Z < 1.65]$

7.3   In each of these three cases, determine the value of z:

a. $P[Z > z] = .500$
b. $P[Z > z] = .025$
c. $P[Z < z] = .025$

7.4   A certain statistics instructor gave a class a standardized test that had been administered throughout the United States. Nationwide, scores on this test are normally distributed with a mean of 0 and a standard deviation of 1. What fraction of the students nationwide

a. got negative scores?
b. got scores between 0 and 1?
c. got scores above 3.0?

7.5   (*continuation*) This instructor wants to convert her students' scores into percentiles.

That is, a score "in the 70th percentile" would be one that was better than 70 percent of the students taking the test nationwide. Find the percentiles for the following scores:

a. Ralph, 0.0
b. Mike, −1.0
c. Connie, 2.0

7.2 NONSTANDARDIZED VARIABLES

So far, to emphasize the pervasive bell shape, we have only dealt with variables that have been standardized by subtracting the mean and dividing by the standard deviation. But what about the probability distributions of the underlying, nonstandardized variables? We can determine these probabilities via an important mathematical theorem:

> If a random variable X is normally distributed, then any linear function $a + bX$ is also normally distributed.

We can use this theorem to go from a nonstandardized variable to a standardized variable, or vice versa. Let's say that X is some nonstandardized, normally distributed variable with a mean μ and standard deviation σ. We can summarize these facts with the shorthand notation

$$X \sim N[\mu, \sigma]$$

The symbol $\sim$ stands for "is distributed." The letter N signifies a normal distribution, with the first number inside the brackets giving the mean and the second giving the standard deviation. If X is normally distributed with a mean of 100 and a standard deviation of 15, we write $X \sim N[100, 15]$. For a standardized variable, we write $Z \sim N[0, 1]$. The theorem implies that there is a close relationship between standardized and nonstandardized variables.

$$X \sim N[\mu, \sigma] \text{ implies } Z = \frac{X - \mu}{\sigma} \sim N[0, 1] \qquad (7.2)$$

$$Z \sim N[0, 1] \text{ implies } X = \mu + \sigma Z \sim N[\mu, \sigma] \qquad (7.3)$$

In practice, we typically begin with a variable X in its natural units—dollars, feet, pounds, or whatever. Then we standardize this variable by subtracting its mean μ and dividing this difference by its standard deviation σ,

$$Z = \frac{X - \mu}{\sigma}$$

If this standardized variable Z has the $N[0, 1]$ distribution that is shown in Figures 7.1–7.5 and spelled out in Table 2, then X must have a normal distribution, too. The only differences are that the mean of X is μ instead of 0 and the standard deviation of X is σ instead of 1. But these are mere cosmetic differences. No matter what the values of μ and σ, all normal distributions are closely related in that they all have the very same probability of being a certain number of standard deviations away from their respective means. Stated somewhat differently, the only thing that distinguishes one normal distribution from another is that they have different means and standard deviations. Or, as the son of the great language mangler, Yogi Berra, explained, "Our similarities are different."

Other Means, Other Standard Deviations

The mean and standard deviation of a normal probability distribution tell us two things: location and dispersion. The mean tells us where the center of the distribution is, while the standard deviation tells us how spread out the distribution is. Together, the mean and standard deviation describe a normal distribution.

Figure 7.6 shows two normal distributions with the same standard deviation, but with different means. Perhaps these random variables are the percentage returns on two different investments. One investment has a 10 percent expected return and the other has a 20 percent expected return. In the long run, it is almost certain that the second investment will have the higher average return. In the short run, the equal standard deviations suggest that these two investments are equally risky, in that their returns are equally uncertain. For instance, the probability that the return will turn out to be 5 to 10 percentage points less than the expected return is the same for both investments. It is natural to describe these two investments by saying that they have expected returns of 10 percent and 20 percent and that we are equally confident of how close the returns will be to their respective expected values. If offered such a choice, most investors would choose the second investment.

Figure 7.7 shows a different situation. Here, the expected values are the same, but the standard deviations differ. If these are percentage returns, then all three investments should have nearly equal average returns in the long run. But, for the short run of a single outcome, the unequal standard deviations imply that these alternative investments are not equally risky. Look again at Figure 7.7. For the investment with a standard deviation of 2.5 percent, we are almost certain that the return will turn out to be between 5 and 15 percent. With $\sigma = 5$ percent, however,

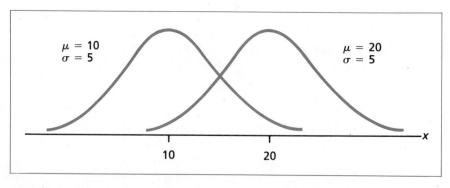

Figure 7.6   *The mean locates the center of a normal distribution*

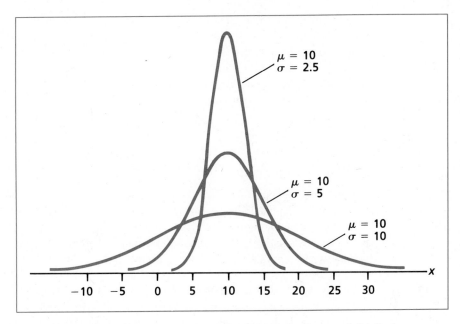

Figure 7.7 *The standard deviation describes the spread of a normal distribution*

there is a good chance that the return will be outside this 5–15 percent range. For the investment with $\sigma = 10$ percent, it is even more likely that the actual return will be far from its expected value. Risk-averse investors will prefer the investment with the low standard deviation, because it is expected to do as well, on average, as the others and its return is more certain.

Figure 7.8 shows two normal distributions with different means and standard

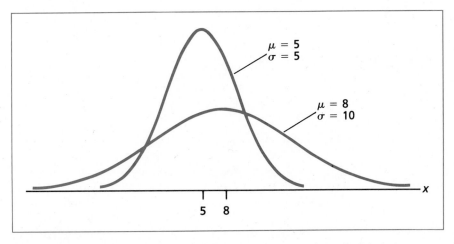

Figure 7.8 *Two normal distributions with different means and standard deviations*

deviations. The distribution with $\mu = 8$ percent is centered to the right of the one with $\mu = 5$ percent. The first distribution is also more spread out because it has a higher standard deviation. If these are investment returns, then the first investment has the higher long-run average return; however, in the short run, its return is more uncertain. Riverboat gamblers might go for $\mu = 8$ percent and $\sigma = 10$ percent, while widows and orphans might be more comfortable with $\mu = 5$ percent and $\sigma = 5$ percent.

Standardizing to Find Probabilities

We have used Figures 7.6–7.8 to help us visualize how the mean and the standard deviation describe the location and spread of a nonstandardized normal distribution. Now, let's see how the mean and standard deviation can be used to make specific probability calculations. How, then, do we find probabilities for a nonstandardized variable X? It's easy. We simply standardize the variable and look up the probability in Table 2.

Let's say, for instance, that X, the percentage return on an investment, is normally distributed with a mean of 10 percent and a standard deviation of 10 percent. What is the probability that the return will be greater than 20 percent, that is $X > 20$? The condition $X > 20$ implies $X - \mu > 20 - \mu$ which, in turn, implies $(X - \mu)/\sigma > (20 - \mu)/\sigma$. Therefore,

$$P[X > 20] = P\left[\frac{X - \mu}{\sigma} > \frac{20 - \mu}{\sigma}\right]$$

The term $(X - \mu)/\sigma$ is our standardized variable Z. For $\mu = 10$ and $\sigma = 10$, we have

$$P[X > 20] = P\left[\frac{X - \mu}{\sigma} > \frac{20 - \mu}{\sigma}\right]$$

$$= P\left[Z > \frac{20 - 10}{10}\right]$$

$$= P[Z > 1]$$

$$= .1587$$

from Table 2.

Let's run through the logic again. If the nonstandardized variable X is greater than 20, then the standardized variable $Z = (X - \mu)/\sigma$ is greater than $(20 - 10)/10 = 1$. That is, if X is greater than 20 percent, then it is more than one standard deviation above its mean. Therefore the probability that $X > 20$ equals the probability that $Z > 1$, which Table 2 tells us is .1587.

Let's do another example. If X still has a mean of 10 percent and a standard deviation of 10 percent, what are the chances of losing money, i.e., of $X < 0$? Here are the logical steps to finding the answer in Table 2:

$$P[X < 0] = P\left[\frac{X - \mu}{\sigma} < \frac{0 - \mu}{\sigma}\right]$$

$$= P\left[Z < \frac{0 - 10}{10}\right]$$

$$= P[Z < -1]$$

$$= .1587$$

If X is less than zero, then it is one standard deviation below its mean, which again has a .1587 chance of occurring.

Try one more. What is the probability that this return X will be between 5 percent and 15 percent? It is

$$P[5 < X < 15] = P\left[\frac{5 - \mu}{\sigma} < \frac{X - \mu}{\sigma} < \frac{15 - \mu}{\sigma}\right]$$

$$= P\left[\frac{5 - 10}{10} < Z < \frac{15 - 10}{10}\right]$$

$$= P[-0.5 < Z < +0.5]$$

$$= 1 - (2)(.3085)$$

$$= .383$$

Could you do one on your own, without my help? Try this one. If X has a mean of 10 percent and a standard deviation of 5 percent, what is the probability of $X < 0$ percent? If you can derive the answer .0228, then you have learned how to find probabilities for nonstandardized normal variables.

One, Two, and Three Standard Deviations

In practice, it is often convenient to use some simple rules of thumb for normal probabilities, particularly if you don't carry Table 2 around with you. Three good benchmarks are the probabilities that a normally distributed variable will be within one, two, and three standard deviations of its mean. For one standard deviation, we have

$$P[\mu - 1\sigma < X < \mu + 1\sigma] = P\left[\frac{\mu - 1\sigma - \mu}{\sigma} < \frac{X - \mu}{\sigma} < \frac{\mu + 1\sigma - \mu}{\sigma}\right]$$

$$= P[-1 < Z < 1]$$

$$= .6826$$

The other two benchmarks are

$$P[\mu - 2\sigma < X < \mu + 2\sigma] = P[-2 < Z < 2] = .9544$$

$$P[\mu - 3\sigma < X < \mu + 3\sigma] = P[-3 < Z < 3] = .9973$$

These useful rules are displayed in Figure 7.9. A normally distributed random variable has

a 68 percent (roughly about a 2/3) chance of being within 1 standard deviation of
  its mean,
a 95 percent chance of being within 2 standard deviations of its mean, and
a better than 99 percent chance of being within 3 standard deviations of its mean.

Equivalently, there is less than a 1 percent chance that a normally distributed variable will be more than three standard deviations away from its mean. There is a 5 percent chance of being more than two standard deviations from the mean and a 32 percent chance of being more than one standard deviation away.

Let's say, for instance, that we are trying to explain, as I tried earlier, why

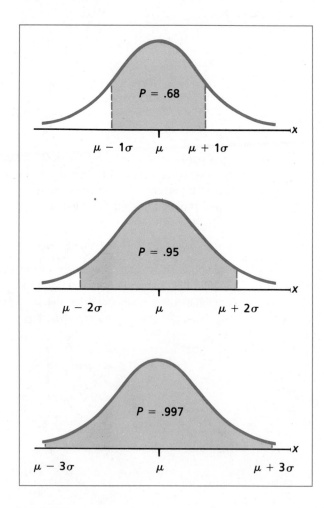

Figure 7.9   *Three normal benchmarks*

an investment with a mean return of 10 percent and a standard deviation of 5 percent is safer than an investment with a mean of 10 percent and a standard deviation of 10 percent. Our benchmarks tell us immediately that there is only a .05 probability that the first investment will have a return outside the range 0–20 percent (10 percent, plus or minus two 5 percent standard deviations). With the second investment, there is a .32 probability of being outside this 0–20 percent range (10 percent, plus or minus one 10 percent standard deviation). Clearly, the return on the first investment is the more certain.

Mathematical and Other Skills

An individual's skills in playing baseball, singing songs, and solving math problems depend on the cumulation of a great many hereditary and environmental factors. The central limit theorem suggests that measures of such skills may follow a normal distribution. And, in fact, many skill tests do yield normally distributed scores.

For example, the Scholastic Aptitude Test (SAT), Graduate Record Examination (GRE), and Graduate Management Aptitude Test (GMAT) all measure verbal, mathematical, and analytical abilities, and the scores on each of these various tests are approximately normally distributed. The raw scores (number right minus a fraction of the number wrong) are translated into scaled scores with a mean of about 500 and a standard deviation of approximately 100 for some reference group of test takers. For instance, the GMAT tests are scaled so that those who took the original test in 1955 had an average score of 500 and a standard deviation of 100. The precise means and standard deviations vary from year to year with the students taking the tests, but a rough normal distribution persists. Figure 7.10 shows the

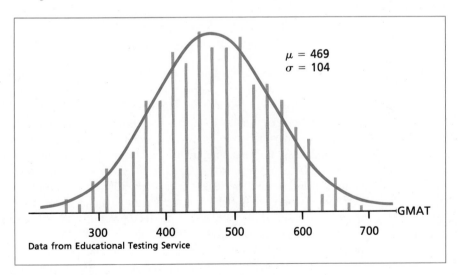

Figure 7.10 *The distribution of GMAT scores, 1980–1983*

distribution of a half million GMAT scores during the years 1980–1983. The overall mean works out to be 469 and the standard deviation 104. The figure shows a reasonably close correspondence between a theoretical normal distribution and the actual distribution of these test scores.

The shape of a normal distribution can be used as a rough gauge of a student's performance. If, for instance, the scores on one of these standardized tests are normally distributed with a mean of 500 and standard deviation of 100, then how good is a score of 700? A 700 score is two standard deviations above the mean of 500, and our rule of thumb tells us that about 5 percent of the scores should be two standard deviations away from the mean, in either direction. Because the normal distribution is symmetrical, approximately 2.5 percent of the scores will be above 700 and 2.5 percent below 300. The exact normal percentage works out to be

$$P[X > 700] = P\left[\frac{X - \mu}{\sigma} > \frac{700 - 500}{100}\right]$$

$$= P[Z > 2]$$

$$= .0228$$

from Table 2.

Let's do one more. How good is a score of 638? This is almost 1.5 standard deviations above the mean; not as good as 700, of course, but still very respectable. The fraction of the test-takers who do this well is given by

$$P[X > 638] = P\left[\frac{X - \mu}{\sigma} > \frac{638 - 500}{100}\right]$$

$$= P[Z > 1.38]$$

$$= .0838$$

Only about 8 percent of the people who take the test will score higher than 638.

Scores on most of the general aptitude tests that you have taken or will take follow a rough normal distribution. On the other hand, we could expect a nonnormal distribution, especially for adults, whenever there has been a focused, nonrandom, nonindependent cultivation of certain skills by some of the people who take a skill test. For example, Figure 7.11 shows a hypothetical distribution of athletic skills for 10-year-old boys. At this age, most of the differences in athletic ability are due to random hereditary and environmental influences, and a normal distribution emerges. But the sweaty pursuit of fame and fortune will persuade many of the more skilled athletes to devote a great deal of time to perfecting their athletic skills. Other, less athletically skilled males will work equally hard at earning their livelihoods in other ways. If we measure the athletic skills of 35-year-old men, it would not be too surprising to find the sort of twin-peaked distribution that is shown in the bottom half of Figure 7.11. The bulk of the population is relatively

Figure 7.11 *Athletic skills*

unskilled, while a small cadre is highly skilled. The overall, twin-peaked distribution might reflect two separate normal distributions: one for highly trained, dedicated athletes and one for the rest of the population.

Similar, twin-peaked distributions could be expected if we measured people's fluency in reading Spanish, skill in playing the piano, or any other trait where the population separates into those who practice a skill and those who don't. If we gave a test to either separate group, however, we could expect an approximately normal distribution. For example, the Educational Testing Service prepares a Graduate Record Exam (GRE) Advanced Economics Test that is used for admissions and fellowships for graduate study in economics. If everyone took this test, we might expect the scores to split into two groups: those who have studied economics and those who haven't. But, in practice, only the former take the GRE economics test and their scores are fairly close to a normal distribution (see Exercise 7.11).

Exercises

7.6 The monthly returns in the stock market over the years 1904–1974 have averaged 0.68 percent with a standard deviation of 6.85 percent.[1] If the monthly returns are, in fact, normally distributed with a mean of 0.68 percent and a standard deviation of 6.85 percent, then how frequently is the monthly return

a. greater than 10 percent?
b. negative?

IQ Tests

There are a number of tests designed to measure a person's IQ (Intelligence Quotient). These tests are descended from 54 mental "stunts" that two psychologists (Alfred Binet and Theodore Simon) conducted in 1904 to weed dull students out of the Paris school system. The intention is to test a person's general intelligence, including an accurate memory and the ability to reason clearly and logically.

Scores on IQ tests are approximately normally distributed for people of the same age. The standard scaling gives a mean IQ of 100 with a standard deviation of 15. Thus, a score of 100 indicates that a person's intelligence is average for people of that age. About half of the people tested will score above 100, while half will score below 100. Our two-standard-deviation rule implies that about 5 percent of the population will score more than 30 points away from 100: about 2.5 percent will score above 130, while another 2.5 percent will score below 70. Our three-standard-deviation rule similarly implies that less than one-half of one percent of the population have IQs above 145. Figure 2 shows the complete distribution of IQ scores.

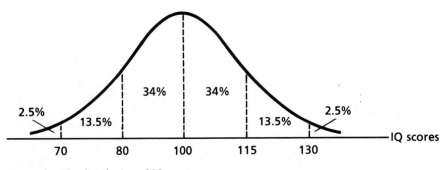

Figure 2 *The distribution of IQ scores*

c. less than − 10 percent?

d. greater than 20 percent?

7.7 (*continuation*) A security analyst predicts that the market will go up next month. How unusual is such a month? How impressed would you be if this prediction is right?

7.8 (*continuation*) Another analyst predicts that the market will go up at least 30 percent next month. How often does that happen? Would you be impressed if this prediction turns out to be correct?

7.9 Scores on an IQ test are normally distributed with a mean of 100 and a standard deviation of 15. What is the probability that a randomly selected person has an IQ above 120? Above 130? Above 140? Above 150? One psychologist has estimated that Galileo had an IQ of 185 and that Goethe had an IQ of 210. How often can we expect to find people with such high IQs?

7.10 The Scholastic Aptitude Test (SAT) scores were originally intended to be normally distributed with a mean of 500 and a standard deviation of 100. If this is the actual distribution, then what fraction of the students taking this test will be eligible for admission to a college that does not accept students who score

a. below 400 on the English SAT test?
b. below 500 on the English SAT test?
c. below 600 on the English SAT test?
d. below 700 on the Math SAT test?

7.11 The following scores were recorded on 10,720 GRE Advanced Economics Tests given between October 1978 and September 1981:

scaled score	percent of tests
>860	1
820–860	2
780–820	4
740–780	5
700–740	9
660–700	10
620–660	14
580–620	13
540–580	14
500–540	11
460–500	9
420–460	6
<420	3

The mean and standard deviation of these 10,720 scores are 606 and 108, respectively. If the scores were normally distributed, with this mean and standard deviation, what fraction of the scores would you expect to be above 860; to be between 820 and 860; and so on? Construct a table comparing these 13 theoretical percentages with the actual distribution of test scores.

7.12 Joanna is a new professor who wants to grade strictly by the curve. But, to keep up with grade inflation, she doesn't want to give as many Fs as As and as many Ds as Bs. Instead, she wants to give, on average, 20 percent As, 30 percent Bs, 35 percent Cs, 10 percent Ds, and 5 percent Fs. If her numerical scores are normally distributed, which standardized values should be graded A, B, C, D, and F? Draw a rough sketch of the normal curve, as in Figure 1 on page 219, showing Joanna's grade distribution.

7.13 At Big State University (BSU), the weights of the 20,000 male students are normally distributed with a mean of 160 and a standard deviation of 25. How many of these 20,000 males weigh more than 200 pounds? How many weigh between 150 and 170? How many weigh less than 100 pounds?

7.14 The heights of the 20,000 men at BSU are normally distributed with a mean of 70 inches and a standard deviation of 2.5 inches. How many of these men are at least 6 feet, 5 inches tall? How many are shorter than 5 feet, 6 inches? How many are between 5 and 6 feet tall?

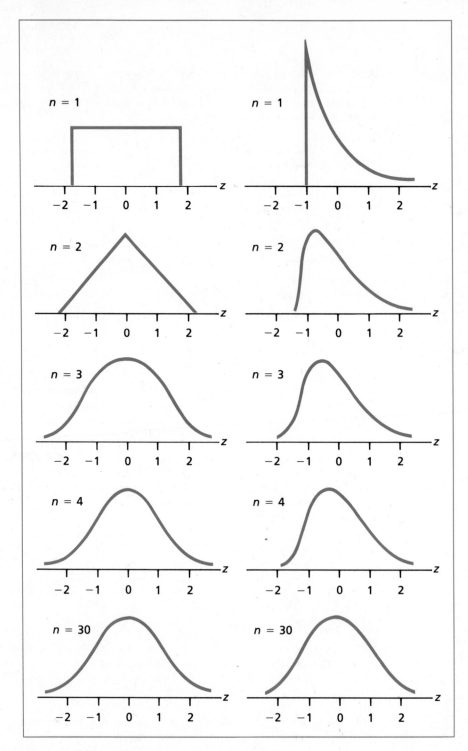

Figure 7.12 *The central limit theorem*

7.3   A CONTINUITY CORRECTION

The central limit theorem says that the sum of independent, identically distributed (discrete or continuous) random variables converges to a normal distribution. So far, we have focused on discrete variables because these are the easiest to visualize. But the central limit theorem holds for continuous variables, too. Figure 7.12 shows two examples.

The convergence is, in some sense, cleaner with a continuous variable in that the distribution is visibly transformed into a normal distribution. With a discrete variable, in contrast, a normal distribution is a continuous approximation of a discrete distribution. We saw with the spinner in Chapter 6 how a continuous distribution is, in fact, the theoretical limit of a discrete distribution as the size of the interval goes to zero. But we have also seen that, in practice, a bell shape often emerges very quickly. In Figure 6.3, for instance, the probability distribution for two dice rolls is already starting to look bell-shaped. Yet, eleven possible sums are a very far cry from the infinite number of possible outcomes allowed by a continuous normal distribution.

It turns out that, if we make a *continuity correction,* then the normal distribution may be a remarkably accurate approximation even if the number of discrete outcomes is quite small. The logic behind this continuity correction is as follows. Suppose we want to use a normal distribution to approximate the probability of obtaining a 7 when two dice are rolled. We could hardly use the probability that a normally distributed variable is exactly equal to 7, because there is zero probability that a continuous variable is precisely equal to a specific number. Let's instead imagine that the outcomes are somehow continuous and that we can group them into discrete intervals such as 6, 7, or 8. We put everything from 6.5 to 7.4999. . . into the interval labeled ''7.'' We put the outcomes from 5.5 to 6.4999. . . into the interval labeled ''6'' and we put the outcomes from 7.5 to 8.4999. . . into the interval ''8.'' Figure 7.13 illustrates the logic. This argument suggests that the

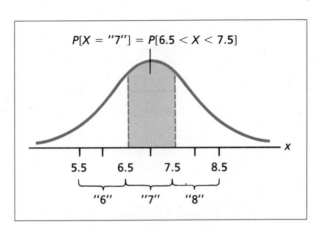

Figure 7.13 *The discrete grouping of a continuous random variable*

continuous interval 6.5 to 7.4999. . . . corresponds to the discrete outcome 7. And this is, in fact, the recommended continuity correction.

> The **continuity correction** for a given discrete interval consists of a continuous interval that is a half-unit wider at each end than the corresponding discrete interval.

For the discrete number 7, the corresponding continuous interval is 6.5 to 7.5.* For the discrete interval 6 to 8, the corresponding continuous interval is 5.5 to 8.5.

It Works!

Does it work? Well, the exact probability of rolling a 7 with two dice is $6/36 = .167$. For a normal approximation, we can use the mean $\mu = 7$ and standard deviation $\sigma = 2.415$ calculated in Chapter 4 to obtain

$$P[6.5 < X < 7.5] = P\left[\frac{6.5 - 7}{2.415} < \frac{X - \mu}{\sigma} < \frac{7.5 - 7}{2.415}\right]$$

$$= P[-0.207 < Z < +0.207]$$

$$= .164$$

which, for most purposes, is close enough.

Let's try another. With two dice rolls, what is the probability of a number from 8 to 10? Table 4.1 reminds us that the correct answer is $5/36 + 4/36 + 3/36 = .333$. The normal approximation is

$$P[7.5 < X < 10.5] = P\left[\frac{7.5 - 7}{2.415} < \frac{X - \mu}{\sigma} < \frac{10.5 - 7}{2.415}\right]$$

$$= P[0.207 < Z < 1.449]$$

$$= .344$$

which is close, but certainly not perfect.

Remember, though, that we are looking at the case $n = 2$, which is a long way from the theoretical $n = \infty$ assumed by the central limit theorem. As n increases, the normal approximation becomes even more accurate. For example, with just 8 dice here are the chances of rolling numbers that sum to 28 and of rolling either a sum of 25, 26, 27, or 28:

	X = 28	X = 25, 26, 27, or 28
exact probability	.081	.307
normal approximation	.082	.303

*I've conveniently replaced 7.4999. . . with 7.5 because the probability that a continuous variable X is less than 7.5 is the same as the probability that X is less than or equal to 7.5.

The normal approximation won't always be this close for small values of n. It depends on how quickly the probability distribution becomes bell-shaped. In Figure 6.3, we saw that the bell shape emerges very quickly for dice rolls. In some of the other examples shown in Chapter 6, it takes a while longer. The usual rule of thumb is that a normal approximation will be satisfactory if the number of trials, n, is greater than 20 or 30. If you look back at the figures in Chapter 6, you will see that a bell shape is usually pretty apparent by $n = 20$ or $n = 30$. You might use a more conservative rule, such as $n > 50$, if you demand a very accurate probability or if you're not quite sure that the central limit theorem's assumptions are satisfied. Conversely, if you have 100 trials, you can be pretty confident in using a normal approximation; with 15 trials, you might be a bit cautious.

One final point is that the continuity correction becomes less important as the number of trials increases. With a large number of trials, there will be a very large number of possible outcomes. There is, consequently, little chance that the outcome will be in an interval that is only a unit wide, and thus it doesn't matter whether or not we add a half-unit on either side to make up an interval.*

For a normal approximation of the probability that X is less than some number a, we would (with a continuity correction) use

$$P[X < a + 0.5] = P\left[\frac{X - \mu}{\sigma} < \frac{a + 0.5 - \mu}{\sigma}\right]$$

$$= P\left[Z < \frac{a - \mu}{\sigma} + \frac{0.5}{\sigma}\right]$$

If we ignored the continuity correction, we would instead use

$$P[X < a] = P\left[Z < \frac{a - \mu}{\sigma}\right]$$

The $0.5/\sigma$ difference between these two numbers becomes less important as σ increases with n.

I'll use the dice example to illustrate this point. With one die, the standard deviation of X is 1.708. With n dice, it can be shown that the standard deviation is $1.708n^{1/2}$. As n increases, σ increases, too, and the continuity correction $0.5/\sigma$ declines. The first column of Table 7.1 gives some specific numbers. Using this column, I've calculated some probability differences that would occur if we didn't make a continuity correction. The maximum difference is always right at the center of the normal distribution, where $X = \mu$ and $Z = 0$. As one moves away from this center, the continuity correction is even smaller. You can see in Table 7.1 that a continuity correction can be very important for small values of n, but it becomes less important as n increases. Perhaps $n = 100$ is a reasonable place to stop bothering with continuity corrections.

---

*To obtain a nonzero probability of obtaining a single number, such as $X = 28$, we still must add 0.5 to each side.

Table 7.1   *A continuity correction becomes less important as* n *increases*

n	0.5/σ	Probability difference without correction	
		at Z = 0	*at Z = 1*
2	.207	.082	.045
8	.104	.041	.024
20	.065	.026	.015
50	.041	.016	.010
100	.029	.012	.007
500	.013	.005	.003
1000	.009	.004	.002

For Example, Approximating the Binomial

The various rules of thumb for using normal approximations must necessarily be very rough because they are intended to apply to a great many different probability distributions. We can be more concrete when we restrict our attention to a particular distribution, such as dice rolls. In this section, I want to focus on normal approximations to the binomial distribution.

The Bernoulli scheme involves n independent trials, each with probability of success π. If we let $X = 1$ when there is a success and $X = 0$ when there is a failure, then the sum of the outcomes is the number of successes. The binomial distribution gives the corresponding probabilities. Because Bernoulli trials satisfy the conditions for the central limit theorem, it follows that the binomial distribution turns into a normal distribution as the number of trials increases. Indeed, it was De Moivre and Laplace's discovery of this metamorphosis that led to the more general central limit theorem.

Look back at Figure 6.4, where I have graphed some binomial distributions for $\pi = .5$ and $\pi = .9$. With $\pi = .5$, the binomial distribution starts out symmetrical at $n = 1$ and quickly becomes bell-shaped. With $\pi = .9$, on the other hand, the distribution is very skewed for low values of n and a bell shape takes longer to emerge.

In Chapter 5, we saw that the mean and standard deviation of the number of binomial successes are

$$\mu = \pi n$$

$$\sigma = \{\pi(1 - \pi)n\}^{1/2}$$

A normal approximation will run into trouble if the mean $\mu = \pi n$ is close to the extreme values of X, either 0 or n. Figure 7.14 shows the example of $\pi = .9$ and $n = 10$. In this figure, I've put the unstandardized values of X on the axis so that

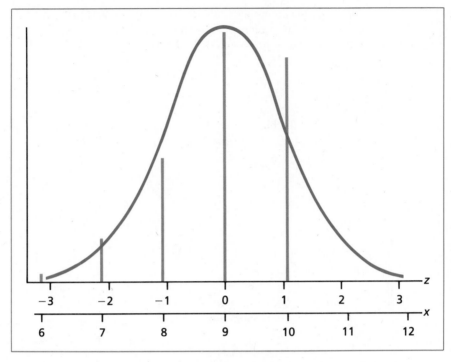

Figure 7.14   *Normal approximation to the binomial for* n = *10,* π = *.9*

you can see the endpoint problem clearly. The number of successes cannot be greater than 10, but with a mean of 9, the normal distribution has some substantial probability all the way out to $X = 12$. With this erroneous probability of X being greater than 10, the normal approximation is bound to be off in its probability estimates for when X is less than 10, too.

The other problem is that when, as here, the mean is close to an extreme boundary, the binomial distribution has no room for a symmetrical bell shape. Look again in Figure 7.14 at the mean $\mu = 9$. There is only one possible outcome, $X = 10$, to the right of the mean. One outcome can hardly show a bell pattern, and sure enough, if we look at the probabilities for $X = 9$ and $X = 10$, there is no hint of a bell.

A satisfactory normal approximation requires a large enough n to get the mean πn safely away from the extremities $X = 0$ and $X = n$. If there is a comfortable distance between the mean and the extremes, then there will be room for the binomial distribution to show a bell shape and the normal distribution won't go slopping over the boundaries into values of X that are impossible. How large an n is required? It depends on π. For $\pi = .5$, an $n = 10$ gives a mean of 5 that is safely distant from 0 and 10. For $\pi = .01$, even $n = 100$ gives a mean of only

1, which is uncomfortably close to 0. A reasonable rule of thumb is that a normal approximation to a binomial distribution will be satisfactory if the mean πn is at least 5 units away from both 0 and n, or if

$$\pi n - 5 \geq 0 \qquad \text{and} \qquad \pi n + 5 \leq n$$

Let's do a few quick computations to see if it really works. First, let's try $\pi = .5$ and $n = 10$. The mean $\pi n = 5$ is barely 5 away from 0 and n. Table 1 gives .451 as the binomial probability that X is equal to 5 or 6. Using the standard deviation $\sigma = \{\pi(1 - \pi)n\}^{1/2} = 1.58$, the normal approximation (with a continuity correction) is

$$P[4.5 < X < 6.5] = P\left[\frac{4.5 - 5}{1.58} < \frac{X - \mu}{\sigma} < \frac{6.5 - 5}{1.58} \right]$$

$$= P[-0.316 < Z < 0.949]$$

$$= .452$$

which is pretty accurate.

Second, let's try $\pi = .9$ and $n = 50$, so that the mean $\pi n = 45$ is barely 5 away from n. The probability that $X = 45$ is .185. Using $\sigma = \{\pi(1 - \pi)n\}^{1/2} = 2.12$, the normal approximation is

$$P[44.5 < X < 45.5] = P\left[\frac{44.5 - 45}{2.12} < \frac{X - \mu}{\sigma} < \frac{45.5 - 45}{2.12} \right]$$

$$= P[-0.236 < Z < +0.236]$$

$$= .186$$

which, again, is strikingly accurate.

So, the normal distribution seems to be a useful approximation to the binomial distribution, as long as the mean πn is at least 5 away from the extremes 0 and n.

The Statistical Reason for Long Multiple-Choice Tests

Here's a very practical example. A statistics professor gives a test consisting of 48 multiple-choice questions. Each question has four possible answers, so that a pure guesser has a .25 probability of picking the correct answer. What is the probability that a guesser will get 16 or more correct answers?

This is a binomial probability with $\pi = .25$ and $n = 48$ that isn't included in Table 1. But, because the mean $\mu = \pi n = 12$ is more than 5 units away from 0 and n, we can use a normal approximation. The standard deviation is $\sigma = \{(.25)(.75)(48)\}^{1/2} = 3$. With a continuity correction we have

$$P[X > 15.5] = P\left[\frac{X - \mu}{\sigma} > \frac{15.5 - \mu}{\sigma} \right]$$

$$= P\left[Z > \frac{15.5 - 12}{3}\right]$$

$$= P[Z > 1.167]$$

$$= .122$$

A guesser has about a 12 percent chance of getting at least 16 out of 48 questions right.

If the professor wants a guesser to have only a .001 chance of passing, how many correct answers should be required? In the first calculation, we had a score $X = 16$ and needed to determine a probability. Now, we have a probability and need to determine the corresponding score. Table 2 states that $.001 = P[Z > 3.08]$. This fact can be manipulated as follows:

$$.001 = P[Z > 3.08]$$

$$= P\left[\frac{X - \mu}{\sigma} > 3.08\right]$$

$$= P[X > \mu + 3.08\sigma]$$

Notice this characteristic format. There is a .001 probability that Z will be greater than 3.08, which translates into a .001 probability that X will be more than 3.08 standard deviations above its mean. Because, here, the mean is 12 and the standard deviation is 3, we have

$$.001 = P[X > 12 + 3.08(3)]$$

$$= P[X > 19.24]$$

If the professor fails those who get fewer than 20 questions right, then a guesser will have less than a .001 chance of passing.

Now let's consider the plight of a reasonably good student who can correctly answer half of all of the multiple-choice questions that this professor might conceivably ask. If the professor randomly selects 48 questions to put on the test, what is the probability that this reasonable student will get fewer than 20 of these 48 questions right? Now, the mean is $\mu = \pi n = .5(48) = 24$ and the standard deviation is $\sigma = \{\pi(1 - \pi)n\}^{1/2} = \{(.5)(.5)(48)\}^{1/2} = 3.364$. With a continuity correction,

$$P[X < 19.5] = P\left[\frac{X - \mu}{\sigma} < \frac{19.5 - 24}{3.464}\right]$$

$$= P[Z < -1.3]$$

$$= .097$$

By using a minimum of 20 correct for a passing grade, the professor will make it very difficult for guessers to pass, but will also fail quite a few reasonable students, too.

Is there any way that the professor can increase the reasonable student's probability of passing, while still giving the guesser only a .001 chance? The answer, I'm sorry to relate, is that a more reliable separation of the good student from the guesser requires a longer exam. Just as in the case of acceptance sampling of bombs, more data improves the identification of the duds. With 96 questions, for example, the guesser has less than a .001 chance of getting 38 correct answers, while our reasonable student has better than a .98 probability of getting at least 38 correct. (The details are left as Exercise 7.15.) So, remember, when a professor gives a long exam, it is really for the student's sake!

Election Polls

A very similar analysis applies to opinion polls on such matters as the better-tasting cola and an upcoming election. Let's do the election example. Suppose that 40 percent of the voters prefer candidate A. If we pick 10 voters at random, what is the probability that at least half will be supporters of A? This is a binomial probability with $\pi = .4$ and $n = 10$. Because the mean $\mu = \pi n = 4$ is not 5 units from 0, we should resist the temptation to use a normal approximation. Table 1 gives the binomial probability as .3669 that at least half of the 10 people polled prefer A.

To make the poll more reliable, we need to make it larger. Consider a poll of 100 people. Now $\mu = \pi n = .4(100) = 40$, $\sigma = \{\pi(1 - \pi)n\}^{1/2} = \{(.4)(.6)(100)\}^{1/2} = 4.9$, and a normal approximation should be satisfactory. With a continuity correction, the probability that at least half of the 100 voters polled prefer A is given by

$$P[X > 49.5] = P\left[\frac{X - \mu}{\sigma} > \frac{49.5 - \mu}{\sigma}\right]$$

$$= P\left[Z > \frac{49.5 - 40}{4.9}\right]$$

$$= P[Z > 1.94]$$

$$= .026$$

As the sample gets larger, it becomes increasingly certain that the fraction of those polled who prefer A will be very close to .4 and increasingly improbable that the poll will erroneously predict that A will win the election.

Exercises

7.15 The multiple-choice example in this chapter involved two students: a reasonable student with a .5 probability of correctly answering a selected question and a guesser with only a .25 chance. If this professor asks 96 questions and requires 38 correct answers for a passing grade, what are these two students' chances of passing?

7.16   (*continuation*) If the professor asks 60 questions and requires 20 correct answers for a passing grade, what are these two students' chances of passing? What if the professor asks 90 questions and requires 30 correct answers? Compare these probabilities.

7.17   A manufacturer uses an acceptance sampling rule that a batch of products is rejected if 10 percent of a sample is found to be defective. What is the probability that a batch that is 25 percent defective will be rejected if the size of the sample is 10? 20? 200?

● **7.18**   Mendel postulated that the self-fertilization of hybrid yellow-seeded sweet peas would yield offspring that were three-quarters yellow seeded and one-quarter green seeded. In 1865 he reported that 8023 such experiments yielded $6021/8023 = .7505$ yellow-seeded plants and $2002/8023 = .2495$ green-seeded plants. It has been suggested that these results are too good to be true, and that Mendel must have reported what he wanted rather than what he found. What is the probability of this close a correspondence between the theory and the data? Use a normal approximation.

● **7.19**   Karl Pearson reported flipping a coin 24,000 times and obtaining 12,012 heads and 11,988 tails. If heads and tails are, in fact, equally likely, what is the probability that the numbers of heads and tails would come out this close to 12,000? Use a normal approximation.

7.20   In the election poll example in this section, I stated that a normal approximation is risky for $\pi = .4$ and $n = 10$. Compare a normal approximation with the true .3669 binomial probability that X is greater than or equal to 5.

I did use a normal approximation for $\pi = .4$ and $n = 100$ to obtain .026 as an estimate of the probability that X is greater than or equal to 50. Compare this approximate calculation with the true binomial probability.

7.21   Mr. Noxin is running for dogcatcher, but only 45 percent of the voters favor him. What is the probability that more than half of the voters polled will favor Noxin if 100 voters are surveyed? If 1000 voters are surveyed?

● **7.22**   (*continuation*) There are 1,000,000 voters eligible to vote in this special election to replace the old, badly mauled dogcatcher. Only 45 percent of these eligible voters favor Noxin. But, because the weather is terrible and the race is boring, only 100 people bother to vote. If these 100 voters are a random selection from all eligible voters, what are Noxin's chances of winning? What if 1000 people vote?

From a purely statistical point of view, does a large turnout favor the underdog or the favorite? What reasons can you think of why voter turnout is not entirely random?

● **7.23**   Assume that each of the annual batting averages shown in Table 1 on page 200 is the random result of 500 times at bat, each with a .3 chance of hitting safely. If so, how many of these 135 batting averages would we expect to be in the range .295 to .304? In the range .225 to .234?

7.4   SUMMARY

Table 2 at the end of this book shows the probabilities in the right-hand tail of the standardized normal distribution. This table can be used to find the probability that the standardized variable Z is greater than some number, less than some number, between two numbers, and so on.

In practice, we usually work with nonstandardized variables X, but Table 2 also can be used to find these probabilities. If a normally distributed variable X has a mean μ and standard deviation σ, then $(X - \mu)/\sigma$ is normally distributed with a mean of 0 and a standard deviation of 1. That is

$$X \sim N[\mu, \sigma] \text{ implies } Z = \frac{(X - \mu)}{\sigma} \sim N[0, 1]$$

For instance, let's say that X is a normally distributed random variable with mean $\mu = 20$ and standard deviation $\sigma = 10$. To find the probability that X is greater than 40, we would use the manipulation

$$P[X > 40] = P\left[\frac{X - \mu}{\sigma} > \frac{40 - \mu}{\sigma}\right]$$

$$= P\left[Z > \frac{40 - 20}{10}\right]$$

$$= P[Z > 2]$$

$$= .0228$$

from Table 2.

A rough rule of thumb is that a normally distributed variable has a 68 percent (or about 2/3) chance of being within one standard deviation of its mean, a 95 percent chance of being within two standard deviations, and a better than 99 percent chance of being within three standard deviations.

The central limit theorem says that the sum of n independent, identically distributed random variables becomes normally distributed as n increases. In many cases, this convergence is quite rapid, in that the sum is approximately normally distributed for very small values of n. In general, the approximation is quite good for when n is approximately equal to 20 or 30. For the binomial distribution, we have the more specific rule of thumb: A normal approximation to the binomial distribution with success probability π is satisfactory if the mean πn is at least 5 units away from both 0 and n.

With the binomial and other discrete distributions, the approximation can be made more accurate by a continuity correction: For a given discrete interval, the corresponding continuous interval encompasses the discrete interval plus an additional half-unit at each end. For instance, to find the probability that the sum of 10 dice will be either 35 or 36, we would look at the probability that the normally distributed variable X is between 34.5 and 36.5.

REVIEW EXERCISES

7.24 The text says, "Together, the mean and standard deviation describe a normal distribution." Why didn't we also look at the skewness coefficient?

7.25 The heights of 2 million 17-year-old U.S. males are approximately normally distributed with a mean of 175 centimeters and a standard deviation of 6 centimeters. About how many of these young men are

a. more than 176 centimeters tall?
b. more than 182 centimeters tall?
c. more than 188 centimeters tall?
d. more than 194 centimeters tall?
e. more than 200 centimeters tall?

7.26 (*continuation*) A centimeter is equal to 0.3937 inch. If we looked at the heights of 17-year-old U.S. males, measured in inches, would these be normally distributed? What would be the mean and standard deviation? About how many of these young men would be

a. shorter than 5 feet, 5 inches?
b. taller than 6 feet?
c. taller than 6 feet, 2 inches?

7.27 An 1883 study estimated the heights of adult males born in the British Isles to have a mean of 67.46 inches and a standard deviation of 2.57 inches.[2] If the heights were normally distributed with this mean and standard deviation, then what fraction of the adult males were

a. shorter than 5 feet, 5 inches?
b. taller than 6 feet?
c. taller than 6 feet, 2 inches?

7.28 (*continuation*) Using the data given in Exercises 7.25–7.27, give a brief comparison of the heights of English adults in 1883 and modern U.S. 17-year-old males.

7.29 Assume that the age at death of 20-year-old females is normally distributed with a mean of 76.4 years and a standard deviation of 8.1 years. If so, what fraction of these females will live past 80? What fraction will live past 90? What fraction will live past 100?

7.30 A woman wrote to Dear Abby, saying that she had been pregnant for 310 days before giving birth. Completed pregnancies are normally distributed with a mean of 266 days and a standard deviation of 16 days.[3] What are the probabilities that a pregnancy lasts

a. longer than 270 days?
b. longer than 300 days?
c. longer than 310 days?

7.31 The Scholastic Aptitude Test (SAT) scores were designed to have a mean of about 500 and a standard deviation of about 100. After 1963, though, the average scores steadily declined throughout the 1960s and 1970s. In 1980, the average scores were 470 on the Math SAT and 430 on the verbal SAT. The scores are approximately normally distributed and the standard deviations have stayed at about 100. What fraction of the students score above 500 if the mean is

a. 500?

b. 470?

c. 430?

7.32 (*continuation*) What fraction of the students score above 600 if the mean is

a. 500?

b. 470?

c. 430?

7.33 Males and females do about equally well on the verbal SAT test, but on the average, males do better than females on the math SAT test. In 1980, for instance, the mean male score on the Math SAT test was 490, while the mean female score was 450. Both male and female scores are approximately normally distributed, with standard deviations of about 100. On the 1980 math SAT test, what fractions of the males and females scored

a. above 500?

b. above 600?

c. above 700?

7.34 (*continuation*) What score did a male need on the math SAT test in 1980 to be in the male 90th percentile (to do better than 90 percent of the males taking the test)? What score did a female need on the math SAT test in 1980 to be in the female 90th percentile?

7.35 The weights of the grapefruit grown on Harvey's farm in Porterville, California are normally distributed with a mean of 15 ounces and a standard deviation of 1.5 ounces. On David's farm, the grapefruit weights are also normally distributed, but with a mean of 14 ounces and a standard deviation of 1 ounce. What fractions of Harvey's and David's grapefruit can be classified as "Jumbo," i.e., greater than 16 ounces?

7.36 (*continuation*) The Mammoth packing plant will only accept grapefruit that weigh at least 12 ounces. What fraction of Harvey's grapefruit and David's grapefruit are unacceptable?

7.37 Whirlaway claims that the useful lifetime of its dishwashers is normally distributed with a mean of 3 years and a standard deviation of 1 year. If they guarantee their machines for 1 year, what fraction will break down within the warranty period? What fraction will break down within 2 years? What fraction will last more than 5 years?

If it costs Whirlaway $250 to replace a guaranteed dishwasher, how much do they have to add to the price to cover these costs?

• 7.38 (*continuation*) Consumer Rejects magazine tested two of Whirlaway's machines for 2 years and found that both broke down. If Whirlaway's claims are correct, what is the probability that two tested machines will both break down in less than 2 years? Does this probability calculation cast some doubt on Whirlaway's claims?

7.39 In Exercise 5.15 in Chapter 5, the binomial distribution was used to find the probable results of a Newstime magazine poll of voters' preferences for Tweedle Dee or Tweedle Dum. If the voters are evenly divided between these two candidates, what is the probability that a poll of 100 voters will find that more than 60 percent prefer one of the candidates, either Dee or Dum? Use a normal approximation and then compare your answer with the binomial probability obtained in Exercise 5.15. If 400 voters were polled, what is the probability that 60 percent would prefer one of the candidates?

● **7.40** (*continuation*) If Newstime wants there to be less than a .005 chance that more than 60 percent of those polled will prefer one of the candidates when the voters are, in fact, evenly divided, then how many people must they poll? What if they want less than a .001 chance of such a misleading poll result?

7.41 Gamma Airlines has found that 20 percent of the people who make reservations cancel at the last minute. If a plane holds 200 passengers, how many cancellations can they expect if they accept 200 reservations? If they accept 220 reservations? If they accept 240 reservations? How many reservations should they accept if they want the expected number of people who show up to equal 200?

7.42 (*continuation*) What is the probability that more than 200 people will show up if Gamma Airlines accepts 200 reservations? 220 reservations? 240 reservations? 250 reservations? Use a normal approximation.

● **7.43** (*continuation*) How many reservations should Gamma Airlines accept if they want the probability of more than 200 passengers showing up to be less than .50? Less than .05?

●● **7.44** (*continuation*) If more than 200 people show up, Gamma's policy is to give these overbooked passengers twice the value of their tickets. Gamma executives have consequently decided to accept reservations from a number of passengers n, such that the probability of empty seats is twice as high as the probability of insufficient seats. What is this value of n? With this booking policy, how frequently can they anticipate having empty seats on Gamma flights? How frequently can they anticipate having insufficient seats on Gamma flights?

7.45 A certain selective college has found that half of the students they accept for admission decide to go elsewhere. How many students should they admit if they want the expected size of their freshman class to be 400? If they follow this admission policy, what is the (approximate) probability that the entering freshman class will be larger than 400? What is the probability that it will be smaller than 400?

● **7.46** (*continuation*) By doubling up in some rooms and putting some students in a limited amount of off-campus housing, the college can accommodate a maximum of 450 new students. How many students should they accept if they want the probability of more than 450 new students coming to be less than .10? Less than .01?

● **7.47** (*continuation*) If too few students show up, then a severe financial strain is put on the college. How many students should they accept if they want the probability of fewer than 350 students coming to be less than .10? Less than .01?

●● **7.48** (*continuation*) The board of trustees has decided that, all things considered, inconvenient housing for the students is not as serious as a tuition shortfall. They have consequently instructed the admissions office that the number of students admitted should be such that the probability of fewer than 400 students coming is only 1/4 the probability of more than 400 students coming. To implement this guideline, how many students should they admit?

●● **7.49** Figure 6.9 pictured a drunkard's walk. Assume that this drunkard is equally likely to step 12 inches to the north, south, east, or west. Let X_i be the distance (in feet) that this drunkard moves eastward on step i. This distance X_i can be $+1$, -1, or 0. What are the expected value and standard deviation of X_i? Now, let $X = X_1 + X_2 + \cdots + X_n$ be the total eastward distance covered by this drunkard after n steps. What are the possible values of X? What are the mean and standard deviation of X? (*Hint:* Because the X_i are independent, the variance of X is the sum of the n variances of the X_i.) If $n = 50$, what is the probability that the drunkard will be east of the lamp post? More than 5 feet eastward? More than 10 feet eastward? More than 10 feet westward?

● ● **7.50**   (*continuation*) Now let's apply the drunkard's walk analogy to stock prices. Consider some stock that is selling for $20 a share. Let X_i be the dollar change in the price of this stock during week i and let X be the total price change after $n = 50$ weeks. We can apply the drunkard's walk by assuming that a step east is a $1 increase in the stock's price, a step west is a $1 decline, and a step north or south is no change. What is the probability that, at the end of 50 weeks, the price of this stock will be above $20? Above $25? Above $30? Below $15?

PART **2**

Statistics

Tubing in electronics factory.
Laimute E. Druskis/Taurus Photos, Inc.

CHAPTER 8

Sampling

"Data! data! data!" he cried impatiently. *"I can't make bricks without clay!"*

Sherlock Holmes
"The Adventure of the Copper Beeches"

TOPICS

8.1   INTRODUCTION

This chapter begins the statistics part of the course. You have learned now to think about the world as being uncertain and to use probabilities to quantify these uncertainties. You have also learned how to manipulate probabilities and when to use the binomial and normal probability distributions. Probability analysis is like most mathematical reasoning: We make certain assumptions and then deduce the logical implications. If 5 cards are fairly dealt from a standard, well-shuffled 52-card deck, then what is the probability of obtaining 4 aces? If 30 percent of the bombs in a large shipment are duds, then what is the probability that none of 10 tested bombs will be duds? If an asset return is normally distributed with a mean of 10 percent and a standard deviation of 10 percent, then what is the probability that the return will be negative? These are all well-defined probability questions that you have learned how to answer. Few, if any, of you knew how to answer these probability questions when you began this course, but now you do, and that's a substantial accomplishment.

Probability is, however, only half of probability and statistics. The reason is that, except in games of chance, we seldom know the correct assumptions needed to figure probabilities. In an apparently honest game of poker, we can reasonably assume that there are 52 cards in the deck, of which 4 are aces. But how many duds should we assume are in a particular bomb shipment? And how do we know that a certain asset return has a mean of 10 percent and a standard deviation of 10 percent? This is where statistics come in. Probability tells us, under certain assumptions, how often we can anticipate observing certain data—an ace, a dud, or a negative return. Statistical analysis is concerned with the reverse question. Having observed certain data, what can we infer about the number of aces in the deck, the number of duds in the shipment, or the mean and standard deviation of an asset return?

Another way of seeing the difference between probability and statistics is to distinguish between a population and a sample.

> A **population** consists of all the data that we might observe. A **sample** is the data that we actually do observe. **Probability analysis** is used to deduce the samples that are likely to come from an assumed population. **Statistical analysis** is used to infer the characteristics of the population that generated the sample at hand.

In the poker example, the population is the deck from which the cards will be dealt. A sample is the particular cards that are dealt. Probabilities tell us how likely various poker hands are, assuming the game is fair. A statistical analysis could involve using the hands that you are dealt to infer that the game is, in fact, either fair or unfair. In the bomb example, the population is the entire shipment, while a sample is the bombs selected for testing. Probability analysis can be used to figure the likelihood of finding a certain number of duds in a sample, assuming that a certain percentage of all of the bombs are duds. Statistical analysis can be used to make inferences, based on the sample results, about the number of duds in the entire shipment. In the asset return example, the population is the returns that might occur, while a sample is the returns that do occur. Probability analysis tells us how likely various returns are, assuming a normal distribution with a particular mean and standard deviation. Statistical analysis can be applied to the returns we actually observe to help us estimate the population mean and standard deviation for the asset return.

Statisticians use samples to draw inferences about the population because it is often impractical to scrutinize the entire population. If we detonate every bomb to see how many are duds, we will have none left to use. If we cut open every grapefruit to check for quality, we will have none left to sell. If we burn every lightbulb to see how long it lasts, we will have only burnt-out bulbs left. Many tests are not this destructive, but are simply too expensive to apply to the entire population. Companies simply cannot afford to test every single item they manufacture. Instead, they test a sample. Editors sample a few pages of unsolicited manuscripts, because they haven't the time or patience to read every page of every draft that crosses their desk promising to be the Great American Novel. Opinion polls are given to a sample of people, because it is too expensive to ask everyone. Even the national census is done only once every 10 years. And even then, only relatively few people are given the long questionnaire that is the basis for most of the census data.

Social scientists are often compelled to use small samples, simply because usable data are scarce. In chemistry and physics, great amounts of data can be collected in laboratories with carefully controlled, repetitive experiments. In the social sciences, however, most data come from "natural experiments" that are conducted in a haphazard fashion by the world we live in. Economists would like to know the effects of income fluctuations on consumer spending, but thankfully, they don't have the power to raise and lower the national income to test their theories. Instead, they stand back and record income and consumption data as the economy is tossed and turned by a variety of factors. They gather only a small amount of data because they cannot use the economy as a laboratory and because time is limited. They don't use data from the distant past, because the economy was very different then. And they don't wait until the distant future, because the economy will be different then, too. Also, they don't have the patience to wait for lots of data to accumulate. They want to test their theories soon, to make useful recommendations (and to publish, rather than perish). The same is true of many interesting social issues, ranging from school busing to capital punishment. Samples are small simply because nature's experiments provide few useful data.

Exercises

8.1   Pollsters interview samples of registered voters to predict the outcomes of presidential elections. What is their intended population? What are the costs and benefits of interviewing only a sample, rather than the entire population?

8.2   Congressional committees often have pollsters testify about the public's views on policy questions. If you were a member of Congress, why might you do the same thing? Can you think of any reasons why your vote might not hinge on the results of a national poll, even if you believed the survey was completely accurate?

8.3   When a new product is designed, businesses test several prototypes to see if they do what they are designed to do. What is the intended population? Why do they test a sample, rather than the population?

8.4   Businesses also make marketing tests of new products, to gauge consumer enthusiasm. What are the benefits of sampling consumer reaction? Why do businesses use only a sample, rather than the entire population?

8.5   Manufacturing processes inevitably fluctuate as there is wear and tear on people and machines. To keep the products tolerably close to specifications, companies routinely test production samples. If the output begins violating specifications, then adjustments are made in the manufacturing process. What are the costs and benefits of this monitoring?

8.6   Some managers occasionally drop in unexpectedly on their subordinates to see whether they are working or playing. These surprise visits are intended to be a sample from what population? What are the costs and benefits of using a sample rather than the entire population?

8.2   RANDOM SAMPLING

We are liable to draw invalid inferences from a sample if it isn't representative of the population. For instance, we might be interested in the physical strength of the students at the University of Nebraska. The relevant population is the entire student body, while a sample is the students who we actually test. If we use test results for the varsity football team, perhaps because these data are readily available, this would not be a representative sample. The average Nebraska football player may be able to benchpress 400 pounds, but the average student at Nebraska cannot. For measuring physical strength, the football team is a **biased sample,** in that it is clearly atypical. A biased sample such as this will give a distorted picture of the population.

We could try to put together a representative sample by wandering around the Nebraska campus and carefully selecting students who appear to be "typical," but if we did, we would surely assemble a sample that understates the diversity of students at Nebraska. We would pick what seem to be "average" students and largely ignore the gorilla athletes and the frail computer jocks. We might even forget to include women, because their strength seems "below average." We would end up with a sample that has far less variance than the population. It would probably also be biased, because those we exclude for being "above average" and those we exclude for being "below average" are unlikely to just balance each other out. Worst of all, the biases would depend, in unknowable ways, on the researcher's mistaken perception of the "typical" Nebraska student.

These subjective biases are reminiscent of the story of the Chinese researcher who was trying to estimate the height of the emperor. The researcher was not allowed to look at the emperor. Instead, he estimated the emperor's height by asking the opinions of many people, none of whom had ever seen the emperor. Each person had his or her own, uninformed opinion of how tall the emperor was. It's the same here. None of us knows how strong the typical Nebraska student is. There may not even be a typical Nebraska student, just as there's no average U.S. household with 2.75 people in it. If we try to deliberately pick a sample that is representative, all we will get is a sample that shows how strong we think Nebraska students are!

To avoid the subjective biases of the researcher, statisticians advise that, paradoxically, the "fairest" sample is one in which the researcher exercises no control over who is selected! Similarly, a "fair" hand in a card game is not one in which the dealer turns the deck face up and carefully selects representative cards. Instead, a fair hand is whatever results from a blind deal from a well-shuffled deck. What card players call a fair deal, statisticians call a random sample.

> In a **random sample,** each member of the population is equally likely to be selected for the sample, and the chances of being selected do not depend on the previous selections.

There is, admittedly, a possibility that a sample chosen by chance methods will, by the luck of the draw, end up with only football players or computer jocks. But that slight risk is needed to avoid samples that tell us little more than the researcher's subjective opinions of what's typical.

One of the subtle advantages of a random sample is that probabilities can be calculated and used to make statistical inferences about the population; we will be able to make statements such as, "We are 95 percent confident that Candidate A will receive 54 percent of the vote, plus or minus 2 percent." With a subjectively picked sample, we are helpless. We may be able to say something about the person who made the selections, but there is no basis for drawing inferences about the population that the sample is intended to represent.

When analyzing the theoretical properties of a random sample, it is assumed that the drawing is with replacement, so that the probability of being picked remains constant. Otherwise, the mathematics are overly complicated. In practice, however, most sampling is done without replacement, because it seems silly to pick the same item twice. This divergence between theory and practice is justified by the fact that samples are usually taken only when the population is so large that the probabilities are barely affected by sampling without replacement.

Notice also that the word *random* is used differently in the probability phrase *random variable* and in the statistical phrase *random sample*. A random variable is just a variable whose value is uncertain. In this sense, random simply means uncertain. A random sample means much more, in that it is a series of outcomes conforming to the strict Bernoulli-trial assumptions of constant probabilities and independent outcomes. The strengths of Nebraska football players are random variables, but they do not constitute a random sample from the student population.

What if we were to test the physical strength of every entering freshman at Nebraska? This is a large sample, but it is not a random sample from the Nebraska student body—most students would have no chance of being included in this sample. This exclusion causes an obvious bias because there are systematic physical differences between freshmen and more mature students. Similarly, graduating seniors, the students in an advanced math class, or the females in a P.E. class are not a random sample. In each case, there are easily identifiable reasons why the group is not representative of the student body as a whole.

We would ideally like to put each student's name into a box and pick names out randomly. Each student, whether weak, strong, or somewhere in between, would then have an equal chance of inclusion in our sample. In practice, somewhat different methods are often used, but these are satisfactory as long as there is no systematic relationship between the method and what we are measuring. For example, we may have access to Nebraska student identification numbers. If so, then we can construct a random sample by picking each student whose identification number ends with, say, the number 3. Our sample will then include about 10 percent of the student body, selected in a manner that is apparently unrelated to their physical strength. If a smaller sample is desired, then we could pick those students whose last two digits are, say, 24. Or we might reasonably assume that a physical test of every student whose last name is Smith would be a random sample. In each case, we want to use a selection method that seems unrelated to what we are measuring; in this case it is physical strength.

The 1954 Nationwide Tests of a Polio Vaccine

Poliomyelitis (''Polio'') is an acute viral disease that causes paralysis, muscular atrophy, permanent deformities, and even death. It is an especially cruel disease in that most of its victims are children. The United States had its first polio epidemic in 1916 and, over the next 40 years, hundreds of thousands of Americans were afflicted. In the early 1950s, more than 30,000 cases of acute poliomyelitis were reported each year.

At the same time, researchers discovered that most adults had experienced a polio infection during their lives. In most cases, this infection had been mild and had caused the person's body, in trying to ward off the infection, to produce antibodies that made them immune to another attack. Similarly, they found that polio is rarest in societies with the poorest hygiene. The explanation is that all of the children in these societies are exposed to this contagious virus while still young enough to be protected by their mother's antibodies, and so they develop their own antibodies without ever suffering from the disease.

Scientists hoped to find a safe vaccine that would provoke the body to develop antibodies, without causing paralysis or worse. A few vaccines had been tried in the 1930s and then abandoned after apparently causing the disease that they had been designed to prevent. By the 1950s, extensive laboratory work had turned up

Statistics in World War II

Many United States and British statisticians used statistical analyses to help their countries during World War II. In the process, they refined their techniques and proved the value of statistical analysis. There are many examples, but I'll only mention a few here.

With war rationing, the U.S. Office of Price Administration (OPA) needed estimates of the inventories held by tire dealers. They first tried to make a complete tabulation by mailing questionnaires to every single dealer in the country, but many dealers didn't mail the questionnaires back. The OPA suspected that the inventories of the dealers who didn't respond were quite different from those who did, so they put together a small sample of dealers and used follow-up phone calls and visits to ensure responses from almost every dealer in the sample. The small but reliable sample proved to be less expensive and more accurate than the large tabulation.

A similar thing happened with estimates of German output. The Germans tried to make a complete tabulation of how much they were producing, but the reports from individual factories were often late and not always reliable. The British and U.S. statisticians were keenly interested in estimating German war production too, but they could hardly ask the German factories to send them reports. Instead, they were forced to base their estimates on the manufacturing serial numbers on captured equipment. These serial numbers provided a very small sample, but it was random. Special studies made after the war discovered that the British and U.S. estimates of German production were more accurate and timely than Germany's own estimates!

---

several promising vaccines that seemed to safely produce antibodies against polio.

In 1954, the Public Health Service organized a nationwide test of Jonas Salk's polio vaccine, involving 2 million schoolchildren.[1] Polio epidemics varied greatly from place to place and from year to year throughout the 1940s and early 1950s. For this reason, the Public Health Service decided not to offer the vaccine to all children, either nationwide or in a particular city. Otherwise, they would not have been able to tell if variations in polio incidence were due to the vaccine or to the vagaries of epidemics. Instead, it was proposed that the vaccination be offered to all of the second graders at selected schools. The experience of these children (the *treatment group*) could then be compared to first and third graders (the *control group*) at these schools, who were not offered the vaccine. Ideally, they would have liked the treatment group and the control group to be alike in all respects, but for the fact that the treatment group received the vaccine and the control didn't.

There were two major problems with this proposed test of the Salk vaccine. First, participation was voluntary and those who agreed to be vaccinated tended to have higher incomes and better hygiene and, as explained earlier, to be more susceptible to polio. Thus, there was selection bias in the sample. Second, school doctors were instructed to look for both acute and mild cases of polio, and the mild cases were not easily diagnosed. If the doctor knew that some second graders were vaccinated, while first and third graders were not, this knowledge might influence the diagnosis. A doctor that hoped the vaccine would be successful would subconsciously be more apt to see polio symptoms in the unvaccinated than in the vaccinated.

A second proposal was to run a *double-blind* test, in which only half of the volunteer children would be given the Salk vaccine, and neither the children nor the doctors would know whether a child received the vaccine or a placebo solution of salt and water. Each child's injection fluid would be chosen randomly from a box and the serial number recorded. Only after the incidence of polio had been diagnosed, would it be revealed whether the child received vaccine or placebo. The primary objection to this second proposal was the awkwardness of asking parents to support a program in which there was only a 50 percent chance that their child would be vaccinated.

As it turned out, about half of the schools decided to inoculate all second-grade volunteers and use the first and third graders as a control group. The remaining half insisted on a double-blind test using the placebo children as a control group. The results are shown in Table 8.1. In both approaches, the Salk vaccine reduced the incidence of polio, but the gains are more dramatic in the double-blind experiment. The number of diagnosed polio cases fell by about 54 percent in the first approach and by 61 percent with the placebo control group. The effectiveness of the Salk vaccine is partially masked in the first experiment because selection bias makes the second-grade volunteers different from the first and third graders. If the double-blind experiment had not been conducted, the case for the Salk vaccine would have been less convincing because the observed differences were smaller and a skeptic could have attributed these differences to a subconscious desire by doctors to have the vaccine work.

The Salk vaccine was eventually replaced by the even safer and more effective Sabin preparation, but the 1954 tests stand as a landmark national public health experiment that provided convincing evidence of the value of a polio vaccine. Nowadays, 90 percent of all U.S. children have received three or more oral doses of polio immunization, and the nationwide incidence of polio has been reduced to about a dozen cases a year.

Table 8.1   *The results of a nationwide test of a polio vaccine*

	First and third graders as control group		Double-blind test with placebo control group	
	Number of children	*Polio incidence per 100,000*	*Number of children*	*Polio incidence per 100,000*
Treatment group	221,998	25	200,745	28
Control group	725,173	54	201,229	71
No consent	123,605	44	338,778	46

Source: Holden-Day, Inc., Oakland, CA 94609.

The Nielsen Ratings

The A.C. Nielsen Company makes most of its money from its Retail Index, which keeps track of store sales of food and drug products.[2] Companies may know how much they are producing, but they don't have up-to-the-minute data on whether their products are selling or gathering dust on store shelves, so they pay the Nielsen Company to monitor a sample of stores for them.

Nielsen is best known, through, for monitoring our television viewing habits. Their primary tool is an electronic gadget, called an audimeter, that can keep track of which channels are being watched on a television set. Nielsen pays 1200 households throughout the country a small fee for allowing them to attach audimeters to their TV sets and phone lines. Every 30 seconds, the audimeter checks the television to see if it is on and, if so, which channel is being watched. Twice a day, a Nielsen computer telephones the audimeter and automatically processes the viewing habits that have been recorded.

Nielsen then computes a "rating" and an "audience share." The Nielsen rating is an estimate of what fraction of all of the homes in the nation watched a particular program. On a typical evening in "prime time," about 2/3 of the nation's homes are watching television. If they all watch the same show, that lucky show will get a Nielsen rating of 66.7 percent and the other networks will get big fat zeros. In practice, the three major networks divide up the 67 percent pretty evenly, with local stations, UHF stations, and cable television taking what's left over. Nielsen also reports audience-share figures, which estimate what fraction of the televisions that are turned on are tuned to that show. A network show is usually in trouble if it gets a rating of less than 20 percent and a share of less than 30 percent.

Because this sample of 1200 households is used to estimate the behavior of 70 million homes, each represents 60,000 households—an awesome responsibility! If 12 of these chosen households switch channels, that will cost a show a rating point and perhaps its life. With all of this power, each of Nielsen's 1200 households must sign an agreement promising not to let anyone connected with the communications industry know that they are among the chosen few.

The nice thing about Nielsen's audimeters is that they really do show what channels the television is turned to. With personal interviews or viewing diaries, there is a great temptation to vote for shows you like, even if you didn't find time to watch them that week. Of course, the audimeter only shows what channel was on, not how many people watched. A *Los Angeles Times* reporter broke through Nielsen's code of secrecy and located one of the 1200, dubbed "Deep Eyes." Deep Eyes claimed that he had his television on at least 50 hours a week, winning points for favored shows, even though he didn't really spend nearly that much time watching television. After the story was printed in the *Times,* other Nielsen households contacted the reporter to say that they were honest watchers and to express outrage at Deep Eyes's abuse of the system.

The Nielsen audimeters don't tell advertisers whether the viewer is young or old, rich or poor. In addition, the 1200 are too thinly spread across the country to give reliable ratings of local stations or local viewing of the network stations. For these data, Nielsen uses viewer diaries. There are also three ''sweep weeks'' each year, when Nielsen mails out a few hundred thousand viewer diaries to gather detailed data on local viewing habits and the demographic and economic characteristics of viewers. Advertisers want to know not only how many sets are on, but how many big spenders are watching. They also want to avoid advertising shaving cream on shows watched only by women and children. The television stations respond to sweep weeks in a predictable fashion, showing their blockbuster movies and other specials during these three important rating weeks. The next time you notice that all three networks are showing great movies at the same time, you can reasonably conclude that it is sweep week again.

Random-Number Generators

Instead of putting names into a box, random sampling is often done through some sort of numerical identification combined with the random selection of numbers. First, a numbering is decided upon that encompasses every member of the target population. If we're sampling people, we might use Social Security numbers, telephone numbers, or street addresses. If we're conducting a scientific experiment, then we could number each batch, beaker, or bunny as it is received. Sometimes, events can be labeled by a time of day or by the day of the week, month, or year.

The second step is to randomly select numbers that determine the items to be included in the sample. You or I could easily design a brief experiment for randomly picking these numbers. For instance, we could play a scientific numbers game by using the digits in the attendance figures at a local race track. Or we could be a little more formal and set up a small game of chance. To pick a digit from 0 to 9, we could shuffle 10 cards, ace through ten, and select 1 card. For a two-digit number, we could do this twice.

To illustrate some other approaches, let's say that we have 64 patients that we want to divide into two groups, one group to receive a new medication and the other group to receive a placebo. For each patient, we could simply flip a coin, with heads being the new medication and tails the placebo; we could separate the patients alphabetically, according to their last names; we could number the patients 1 to 64, and pick 32 numbers out of a hat; or we could use ten cards numbered 0–9 to randomly pick 32 two-digit numbers between 1 and 64, the number 0 and numbers greater than 64 being simply ignored.

A statistician who doesn't want to go to the trouble of flipping coins or drawing cards can use a table of *random numbers* constructed by someone else. Random numbers are generated by some physical process in which each digit from 0 to 9 has a 1/10 chance of being selected. The most famous of these tables contains a million random digits obtained by the RAND Corporation from an electronic roulette wheel using random frequency pulses.[5] I have put some of these digits, which I picked at random, in Table 3 at the back of this textbook. These random numbers are arranged in 25 columns of 50 two-digit numbers, and are separated by a space after every fifth column and row for ease of reading.

I'll illustrate the use of this table by the selection of 32 out of 64 numbered patients. First, we see that we're interested in two-digit numbers, ranging from 01 to 64. Next, we have to find a place to begin in Table 3. We could begin at the beginning, with the very first number 10. But statisticians don't like to always begin at the beginning. There is a slight danger that the researcher will eventually memorize the numbers at the beginning of the table and thereby destroy their randomness. If I know that 10 is always the first number picked, then, when I am numbering patients, I may (consciously or subconsciously) give the number 10 to someone who I want to receive the medication. Or, later, when I am evaluating the patient's condition, I may remember that 10 always gets the medication and consequently I will be more inclined to see an improvement in patient 10's condition.

Statisticians advise randomly picking a place to begin in a table of random numbers. You could simply close your eyes and point, or you could make up some more formal procedure. I closed by eyes and pointed, but missed the table completely. On my second try, I hit the 11th number in the 6th column, which happens to be 14. So my first random number is 14. Now I can quickly move up, down, sideways, or even diagonally to find the rest of my numbers. I decided to move down the 6th column: 39, 06, and so on. The next numbers, 86 and 87, are ignored since there are only 64 patients. Then comes 17 and yet another 17, which is ignored. Thus the patients 14, 39, 06, 17, . . . would receive the medication.

Random numbers can also be plucked out of computers. Most computers, large or small, have built-in procedures for randomly generating numbers. Sometimes, two large numbers are multiplied and then divided by a third large number. Other programs take a large number and raise it to a power. In either case, some of the digits in the answer are used as the random number. Modern computers can make many such calculations extremely quickly. Many years ago, Karl Pearson spent weeks flipping a coin 24,000 times. Now, with a computer program for generating random numbers, 24,000 coin flips can be simulated in a few minutes.

Some theorists object that the digits appearing in a table or programmed into a computer are not strictly random. They call these digits ''pseudo-random numbers.'' This is a variant of the argument that, once a coin has been flipped, the outcome is no longer a random variable, even if no one yet knows what that outcome was. By the same logic, the numbers in a table cannot be random because those numbers have already been determined. (Indeed, the RAND table was constructed in 1947.) For the objectivist, randomness comes from picking a random path through the table. Call them what you will, random-number tables can be used to construct random samples successfully, as long as they give each member of the population an equal chance of being selected.

Sampling a Railroad's Bills

An accurate tabulation of a company's inventories would seem to require a mindless enumeration of each and every item on the premises. Similarly, an accurate assessment of a company's income and expenses apparently requires an exhaustive (and exhausting) accounting of each dollar that flows in or out of the business. Accountants have found that partial tabulations often suffice, if these incomplete records are a random sample from a complete enumeration.

Even more surprisingly, they have found that a statistical sample can be more accurate than a full tabulation! A complete count allows lots of chances to make errors, and it is easy to err if the counters are inadequately trained or benumbed by their repetitive task. A partial enumeration by fresh, well-trained personnel may be more successful.

The Chesapeake and Ohio Railroad Company conducted a study to see how much difference there would be between a sample of their "waybills" and a comprehensive tabulation.[4] A waybill is a document accompanying each railroad car, recording its weight and the route traveled. When a shipment goes over several railroad lines, each railroad is entitled to part of the total shipping charge; however, the necessary clerical deciphering of the waybill and the arithmetic computations are tedious and time consuming.

The Chesapeake and Ohio studied 23,000 waybills accumulated over a six-month period. These were divided into five strata, according to the size of the total shipping charge:

stratum	waybill charge	fraction sampled
1	$5.00 or less	1%
2	$5.01 to $10.00	10%
3	$10.01 to $20.00	20%
4	$20.01 to $40.00	50%
5	more than $40.00	100%

Their statisticians advised them to take relatively larger samples from the population of expensive waybills, where there was a greater chance of making an expensive mistake.

For the actual sampling, they used the last two digits on the waybill's serial number. These last two digits could be any of 100 numbers from 00 to 99. To attain their desired sampling percentages, they needed 1 of these 100 numbers for the first stratum, 10 numbers for the second stratum, and so on. A table of random numbers yielded the following specifications:

stratum	intended fraction sampled	serial numbers ending in
1	1%	02
2	10%	2
3	20%	2 or 4
4	50%	00 to 49
5	100%	00 to 99

Batch Sampling

Sometimes the most economical way to do sampling is in batches. For example, the military takes a blood sample from each new soldier to test for syphilis. Instead of testing each individual's blood sample separately, it is less expensive to mix several blood samples and then test this mixture. If there turns out to be no evidence of syphilis in the batch, then one test did the work of several separate tests. If there is evidence of syphilis in the batch, then each person in that group is tested separately. This retesting results in one extra test, the batch test, that could have been avoided by testing everyone separately in the first place. Batch tests save time and money when the disease is sufficiently rare and the batches sufficiently small so that, often, no disease shows up in the batch test.

Let's make π the probability of disease and consider $100/n$ batches of size n. If there is no disease in a batch, then one test suffices. If there is some disease in the batch, then $n + 1$ tests are conducted. The probability of no disease in a batch is $(1 - \pi)^n$ and the probability of some disease is one minus that. Therefore, the expected number of tests per batch is

$$\{(1)(1 - \pi)^n + (n + 1)(1 - (1 - \pi)^n)\}$$

and the expected number of tests per 100 soldiers is

$$E[T] = \text{(number of batches)(expected number of tests per batch)}$$
$$= (100/n)\{(1)(1 - \pi)^n + (n + 1)(1 - (1 - \pi)^n)\}$$
$$= 100\{1 + (1/n) - (1 - \pi)^n\}$$

During World War II, the Selective Service Administration reported that a fraction $\pi = .0453$ of the men aged 21–35 had syphilis. Using this value, we can calculate the expected number of tests $E[T]$ for various batch sizes n:

n	$E[T]$
1	100.00
2	59.75
3	47.60
4	43.55
5	42.62
6	43.16
7	44.45

There are many batch sizes that reduce the expected number of tests by more than 50 percent. The expected number of tests is minimized by using a batch size $n = 5$. During World War II, the military used similar reasoning and tested for syphilis in batches of size 5. This intelligent use of statistical reasoning reduced their testing costs by almost 60 percent.

Apparently, they plucked two numbers out of a table of random numbers: a 2 and then a 4. The 2 gave them their rule for the first two strata, and the 4 added the second number needed for the third strata. For the fourth strata, 00 to 49 was probably based on the fact that 2 is in the lower half of the digits 0 to 9. No random number is needed for the fifth strata, because all of these waybills are examined.

Overall, it turned out that 9 percent of the waybills were sampled, yielding an estimate of $64,568 as the amount due the Chesapeake and Ohio Railroad. To test the validity of the sampling procedure, the railroad also made a complete tabulation of all 23,000 waybills and came up with a figure of $64,651. There was only an $83 difference between the results of a sample and a complete tabulation! They figured that it cost less than $1000 for a sample and about $5000 for a complete tabulation, and so they were persuaded that sampling made good economic sense.

In another study, the Chesapeake and Ohio Railroad looked at the allocation of ticket revenue for passengers who traveled on more than one rail line. They found that a 5 percent sample gave an inexpensive estimate that was within one-half a percentage point of the result of a complete tabulation. A similar study by three airlines found that a sample of about 12 percent of the interline tickets gave a division of the ticket revenue that was within a tenth of a percent of the result of a full tabulation. They estimated that this sort of sampling saved the airline industry about one-half million dollars annually in clerical expenses.

Exercises

8.7 Answer this student's question:

First, statisticians tell us that a sample should be representative of the population. Then, they tell us to pick the sample completely randomly, with no guarantee that it will be representative. Why, if a representative sample is so important, don't we make some effort to ensure that the sample is representative?

8.8 A vaccine called BCG was tested to see if it could reduce deaths from tuberculosis.[5] A group of doctors gave the vaccine to children from some tubercular families and not to others, apparently depending on whether or not parental consent could be obtained easily. The results over the subsequent six-year period (1927–1932) were

	number	TB deaths	percent
vaccinated	445	3	0.67
not vaccinated	545	18	3.30

A second study was then conducted in which doctors vaccinated only half of the children with parental consent. The results over an eleven-year period were

	number	TB deaths	percent
vaccinated	556	8	1.42
not vaccinated	528	8	1.52

Is there any logical explanation for these contradictory findings?

8.9 One week, 240 of Nielsen's 1200 households watched a certain television show on CBS, 216 watched NBC, 264 watched ABC, 80 watched other stations, and 400 had their sets off. What are Nielsen's ratings and audience shares for the three networks?

8.10 Three ambiguities for the Nielsen computations are that most households have more than one person in them, many have more than one television set, and some may watch only part of a show. The Nielsen ratings assume that everyone in a household watches every set that is on and watches all of any program if they watch at least six minutes of it. How do these assumptions bias Nielsen's estimate that 2/3 of us will watch television at 9:00 tonight? Explain your reasoning carefully, with numerical examples if you wish.

8.11 The Chesapeake and Ohio Railroad Company once studied the economic advantages of allocating interline passenger revenue on the basis of a sample of tickets, rather than by an exhaustive tabulation. A complete tabulation determined that their share of the revenue over a four-month period come to $212,164 from Railroad A and $79,710 from Railroad B. A 5 percent sample yielded the respective estimates $212,063 and $80,057.

a. How much revenue would the Chesapeake and Ohio have lost if it had used these samples?

b. If sampling cost $1000 while a complete tabulation cost $5000, what would have been the net gain to the Chesapeake and Ohio of using this sample instead of a complete tabulation?

c. If the samples are randomly chosen, how much can the Chesapeake and Ohio anticipate saving, on average, each four-month period by sampling these tickets?

8.12 Pepsi-Cola had a "blind taste test" in which people tasted Pepsi from a glass marked M and Coca-Cola from a glass marked Q.[6] More than half of the people preferred Pepsi. Coca-Cola then ran its own test, letting people drink Coke from a glass marked M and Coke from a glass marked Q. They found that most people preferred Coke from the glass labeled M! This prompted their advertising headline: "The day Coca-Cola beat Coca-Cola." Is there any rational explanation for these strange results?

Pepsi then ran another test, serving Pepsi in glasses marked L and serving Coke in glasses marked S. Again, most people preferred Pepsi. As a statistician, how would you have designed a "blind taste test"?

8.13 Critically evaluate the following passage:

> . . . it is the farmer, not the importuning salesman, who leads in the consumption of alcohol. Results of a survey of drinkers classed by occupation, which was published last week by the Keeley Institute of Dwight, Illinois . . . show that of 13,471 patients treated in this well-known rehabilitation center from 1930 through 1948, a total of 1,553 (11.5%) were farmers. Next in line came salesmen, merchants, mechanics, clerks, lawyers, foremen and managers, railroad men, doctors and manufacturers.
>
> Since Keeley is located in the heart of the farm belt, it might be expected that its proportion of farmer patients would be unusually large. This is not the case, according to James H. Oughton, institute director. The patients in the survey were drawn from all over the world.[7]

8.14   A researcher wants to estimate the average weight of students at Pomona College. A convenient sample is obtained by asking the first 10 students in line when the dining hall opens for lunch at noon. What systematic biases might be introduced by this researcher's procedure?

8.15   Estimate the proportion of students at your college who are left-handed by asking 25 students. Tell how you selected these students and explain why you think they are a good sample.

8.16   Estimate the proportion of students at your college who come from out-of-state by asking 25 students. Tell how you selected these 25 students and explain why you think they are a good sample. Can you think of any reason why more care should be exercised in selecting this sample than in selecting a sample to estimate the number of left-handed people?

8.17   The Educational Testing Service wanted a representative sample of college students[8] so they first divided all schools into groups, such as large public universities, small private colleges, and so on. Then they chose a "representative" school from each group. Finally, they wrote to the administrations of these selected schools and asked them to choose some students for the study. In what ways might their sample not be representative of the college student population?

8.3   OPINION POLLS

Public opinion polls are undoubtedly the most difficult random sample to construct, but they can also be among the most interesting. In an election, for instance, the statistical population consists of every person who votes. The winner will not be known for certain until the votes are actually cast and counted, but statisticians can use a sample of a few thousand voters to predict the election outcome ahead of time. That is, they will use the expressed preferences of a few voters to estimate the preferences of all voters. For these estimates to be accurate, statisticians need a sample that is fairly chosen and representative of the population as a whole. Sometimes samples are not representative and the results are very misleading. The 1936 *Literary Digest* fiasco is a favorite example of an embarrassingly inaccurate poll.

The 1936 *Literary Digest* Poll

In 1932, the Great Depression drove Herbert Hoover out of the White House and brought in Franklin Roosevelt. Roosevelt's efforts to end the Depression were largely unsuccessful, but he retained the public's faith that he was trying at least and that he was doing as well as any president could. In 1936, he ran for reelection against Alf Landon, the rather unexciting governor of Kansas. Most veteran political observers thought that Roosevelt would be reelected easily. But the *Literary Digest* attracted considerable attention with its prediction of a landslide victory for Landon, 57 percent to 43 percent. The *Digest* polled 2.4 million people, the largest political poll ever conducted, and claimed that its prediction would be "within a fraction of 1 percent'' of the actual vote. The *Digest* had, in fact, successfully forecast the five previous presidential elections. But this time they were woefully wrong. It was Roosevelt who won in a landslide, 62 percent to 38 percent, and the *Literary Digest* soon folded, with its reputation permanently tarnished.

The *Digest* poll was incredibly ambitious. They mailed questionnaires to 10 million people, a full quarter of the voting population. But, in sampling, quality is much more important than quantity. Two thousand randomly sampled voters is much better than 2 million unrepresentative voters. The *Literary Digest* got the bulk of its 10 million names from an examination of every single telephone book in the United States. Nowadays, this sort of examination would encompass virtually every household—except those with unlisted numbers, new numbers, or those few households without phones. Indeed, one present-day pollster, Albert Sindlinger, conducts success polls by having interviewers dial randomly selected telephone numbers.

In 1936, however, telephones were far from universal. Phone service was still relatively new and the Depression had made the telephone a luxury for many households. There were only 11 million residential phones in 1936 and these homes were disproportionately well-to-do and in favor of Republican candidate Landon. Those people without phones were relatively poor and overwhelmingly for the Democrat, Roosevelt. The telephone books in 1936 yielded a biased sample that was unrepresentative of the voter population. The *Literary Digest* also used some names and addresses collected from car registrations, club memberships, and its own subscriber lists, but these sources were even more biased than the telephone directories.

To get a random sample, the *Literary Digest* should have focused on lists of registered voters. They were, in fact, one of the first to use voter registration lists at all, but they only used a few lists and these were swamped by the names from telephone directories and other atypical sources. Thus, the 1936 *Literary Digest* poll had a great deal of selection bias.

> **Selection bias** is a systematic exclusion of certain groups from consideration for the sample.

Mail Polls

The *Literary Digest* poll had another problem that is common to polls conducted by mail. Most people do not waste time carefully reading and responding to their junk mail. Only those who care a great deal about an issue or an election are going to bother to read a poll's instructions, fill out the form, and mail it in. Those who do take the time and trouble may be atypical of the population as a whole. This sampling problem is called nonresponse bias.

> **Nonresponse bias** is systematic refusal of some groups to respond to a poll.

For example, the *Literary Digest* mailed voting questionnaires to one-third of the registered voters in Chicago. Only 20 percent of these registered voters bothered to fill out the questionnaires and mail them back to the *Digest*. Landon was favored by more than half of the people who responded to this mail poll, but, in the election, two-thirds of all Chicago voters voted for Roosevelt. The *Literary Digest* poll apparently had nonresponse bias as well as selection bias.

Statisticians have discovered that one pattern in nonresponses is that mail questionnaires tend to be discarded by lower-income and upper-income households. Perhaps the lower-income groups don't trust polls and the upper-income groups have more valuable things to do with their time, or maybe these two income groups don't bother reading any junk mail. In any case, those who do respond to mail polls tend to be disproportionately middle-income households. So, if a statistician wants all income groups to be fairly represented, then a mailed questionnaire is not a good approach.

The main distinguishing feature between respondents and nonrespondents is, of course, that the respondents feel strongly enough about the questions asked to take the time to complete the poll. Who is going to bother to mail in an answer "I don't know," "no opinion," or "I haven't made up my mind"? It follows that those who do respond will be more sharply divided than the population as a whole. Let's say, for example, that questionnaires are mailed to 1000 people, of whom 200 strongly favor a certain policy, 200 strongly oppose the policy, and 600 are largely indifferent. The responses might come from 100 of those in favor and 100 of those opposed, indicating that half the people are in favor and half opposed. This survey result correctly shows that opinion is evenly divided, but it completely misses the important fact that most people haven't made up their mind on the issue.

Now let's change the numbers slightly. It's eighteen months before a presidential election and four candidates are beginning their long run for the Democratic nomination. One thousand questionnaires are mailed out: to 200 people who favor candidate A, 100 people who favor B, 50 people who favor C, 50 people who favor D, and 600 people who don't really know any of these candidates, let alone which one they favor. Responses might be received from 100 people who favor A, 50 who favor B, 25 C, and 25 D. This mail poll shows that A is favored by a 2-to-1 margin over B and that C and D have almost no support. The fragility of these numbers is completely hidden. The mail poll doesn't tell us that 60 percent of the people polled haven't made up their minds yet. When the undecided do make up their minds, any of these candidates could turn out to be the people's choice.

Let's change the numbers one more time. Some time has passed and now there are just two candidates, A and B, left in the race for the Democratic nomination. One thousand questionnaires are mailed out: to 200 people who strongly favor A; to 400 people who would vote for B, but don't feel very strongly about it; and to 400 people who still haven't made up their minds. It turns out that 150 of the A supporters promptly mail in their choice, while only 50 of the B supporters bother to respond. Even though B is favored 2-to-1 by those who have made up their minds, the mail poll shows a 3-to-1 lead for A. Again, the mail poll is distorted by nonresponse bias.

In each case, we can't tell how many people haven't made up their minds, because the undecided don't bother to express this indecision. In addition, those with strong opinions are more apt to respond than those with more balanced opinions. Unfortunately, the nature of U.S. politics is that candidates who do not do well in the early polls do not get the financial support they need to run a competitive campaign. Thus, special-interest candidates who are strongly favored by a small number of voters have a big advantage over candidates whose appeal is more broadly based, but not as fervent. Mail polls exaggerate this distortion and this is one reason why impartial political pollsters no longer use mail questionnaires.

A mail poll is naturally more suspect, the fewer the people who bother to respond. In the 1940s, the makers of Ipana Tooth Paste boasted that a national survey had found that "Twice as many dentists personally use Ipana Tooth Paste as any other dentifrice preparation. In a recent nationwide survey, more dentists said they recommended Ipana for their patients' daily use than the next two dentifrices combined." The Federal Trade Commission banned this ad after it learned that less than 1 percent of the dentists surveyed had named the brand of toothpaste they used and that even fewer had named a brand recommended to their patients.[9]

Quota Sampling

Let's go a bit farther with the example of a presidential election poll. In theory, we would like to put every voter's name into a large box, mix the pieces of paper thoroughly, and then pull out some names for our sample. But, in practice, we don't really know the names of all voters. It would be a major effort to collect accurate, up-to-date voter registration lists from every precinct in the nation. Also, many registered voters will not actually vote on election day. The correct population is those who will vote, not those who could vote, and there is no way to identify these voters ahead of time. Even if we could somehow get the right names in the box, it would be very difficult to track down every person whose name is drawn. Some will be in very out-of-the-way places. Does it make sense to spend two days of a pollster's time finding a recluse in Nowhere, North Dakota? Some people will have moved. Many will not be home when the pollster calls. We may get a badly biased sample if we ignore people in isolated places, people who have moved, and people who aren't home at convenient times for the pollster.

Because of these problems, pollsters don't follow the theoretical random sampling model of collecting every name and then drawing a sample. One alternative is quota sampling.

In **quota sampling,** a sample is constructed by filling quotas of certain characteristics that are thought to be true of the population as a whole.

Based on surveys of past elections, pollsters can estimate the fractions of voters who are in various age, sex, geographic, and economic categories. Interviewers can then poll people who are in these same categories. For example, in the 1948 presidential election, one interviewer for the Gallup poll was told to interview fifteen people in St. Louis, of whom seven were to be male and eight female.[10] In addition, the interviewer was told that nine of the people polled should live downtown while six should live in the suburbs. Six of the men were to be white and one black. Three of the men were to be under 40 years of age and four were to be over 40. Two of the white men should pay less than $18 a month for rent, three should pay between $18 and $44, and one should pay more than $44. There were analogous quotas for the eight women. Beyond these quotas and the requisite mental gymnastics, the interviewer was free to select the persons to be polled.

Quota sampling avoids the painstaking drudgery of mechanical random sampling, but the danger is that it leaves too much discretion in the hands of the interviewer. One simple mechanical problem is to verify the categories. Where do you draw the dividing line between city and suburb? Also, people may well misstate (or not reveal) their ages or rents. To "play it safe," the interviewer may decide to avoid people near the dividing points. If you only poll 20-year-olds and 60-year-olds, then the subjects definitely will be under or over 40, as required. But playing it safe means that people near 40 years of age will get slighted in the survey, and 40-year-olds may well have different opinions from those who are 20 or 60 years old.

In addition, most interviewers meet their quotas in the easist possible ways— which means that people in risky, unfamiliar, or inconvenient places will be ignored. Interviewers do not want to waste their time or risk their lives. If it's easiest to interview people during the day, then those with 9-to-5 jobs will be slighted. If door-to-door interviews in the evening are easier for the interviewer, then those who go out at night will be missed.

If you take a part-time polling job to help pay your way through college, you will probably interview a lot of your fellow students. You may even misstate their ages, addresses, and so on, because that's a lot easier than finding people who do fit the categories. Interviewers have even been known to fill out the questionnaires themselves to avoid venturing into unfamiliar parts of town. Even if a conscientious interviewer does try to locate people to fill every category, there will still be a subconscious tendency to avoid those who look disreputable or possibly dangerous. In theory, quotas ensure a more balanced sample than mailing lists, but in practice, quota sampling tends to be "convenience" sampling rather than genuine random sampling. In his provocative book, *How to Lie With Statistics,* Darrell Huff put it this way,

> You have pretty fair evidence to go on if you suspect that polls in general are biased in one specific direction, the direction of the *Literary Digest* error.
>
> This bias is toward the person with more money, more education, more information and alertness, better appearance, more conventional behavior, and more settled habits than the average of the population he is chosen to represent.[11]

After the 1936 *Literary Digest* fiasco, political pollsters turned from mail questionnaires to quota sampling as an inexpensive way of assuring a representative sample. But, for the reasons just discussed, quota sampling is biased, too. The bias may be less severe than with mail surveys, but it is still uncomfortably large. Given the freedom to select their poll subjects, interviewers tend to choose people who dress well, live in nice neighborhoods, and are also disproportionately Republican.

The Gallup poll, for example, was just starting at the time of the 1936 presidential election. Using quota sampling, the Gallup poll did better than the *Literary Digest*. Still, the Gallup poll overestimated the vote the Republican candidate would receive in each of the first three elections it covered:

year	*Gallup prediction of Republican %*	*actual Republican %*	*prediction minus actual*
1936	44%	38%	+6%
1940	48%	45%	+3%
1944	48%	46%	+2%

The selection bias in quota sampling caused Gallup to overestimate the vote for the Republican candidate, but luckily, in each case the bias was not large enough to cause an embarrassing, erroneous prediction of Republican victory. In the next election, though, the vote was close and Gallup was one of several pollsters who incorrectly predicted that the Republican candidate would be elected.

Franklin Roosevelt died in 1945 and the presidency passed to his vice-president, Harry Truman, a scrappy, but largely unknown, small-time politician from Kansas City. In 1948, Truman had to seek election on his own against Thomas Dewey, who achieved national fame as a crime-fighting New York City district attorney and then gained political prominence as the Governor of New York. Gallup predicted that Dewey would get 50 percent of the vote and Truman only 44 percent, with 6 percent going to two minor party candidates. The other major pollsters, using quota sampling too, agreed that Dewey would win easily. The October issue of *Fortune* stated that

> Barring a major political miracle, Governor Thomas E. Dewey will be elected the thirty-fourth president of the United States in November. So decisive are the figures given here this month that *Fortune,* and Mr. Roper, plan no further detailed reports. . . . Dewey will pile up a popular majority only slightly less than that accorded Mr. Roosevelt in 1936 when he swept by the boards against Alf Landon.[12]

The editors of the *Chicago Tribune* were so certain of the outcome that they printed up the Dewey victory headlines even before the votes were counted. Again there was a Republican bias in the polls' quota sampling: Truman got 50 percent of the vote and Dewey only 45 percent. Truman went to bed thinking he would lose and woke up to find that he had won. He triumphantly posed for photos, waving a newspaper that had prematurely announced Dewey's victory. Truman went on to become a successful president, while the pollsters went looking for ways to improve their samples.

Cluster Sampling

The mistaken pollsters were an easy target. One oft-repeated quip was that, "Everyone believes in public opinion polls—from the man in the street right on up to President Dewey." Even the former editor of the *Literary Digest* managed a few digs: "Nothing malicious, mind you, but I get a very good chuckle out of this."[13] The embarrassed political pollsters concluded that they had made two big mistakes. The first was that they had stopped polling too early because a lot of people didn't decide to vote for Truman until the last two weeks before the election. The second was that their samples had not been really representative of the voter population.

They wanted to find a way to make their samples more random, without incurring the staggering expenses associated with a complete random sample. What they settled on is a sequential sampling procedure that is called **cluster sampling.** The nation is divided into geographic regions and then into states, counties, and cities of different sizes. A random-number generator is used to pick specific cities, with each city's chance of being selected made proportionate to its size. Then, in each of these selected cities, a random-number generator is used to choose some voting precincts. Voter registration lists are obtained for the selected precincts and a random-number generator is used again, this time to choose households. Interviewers (who, incidentally, are overwhelmingly female) are then sent to the selected households to conduct the survey. To maintain randomness, interviewers are told to interview a specific person, not necessarily the person who answers the door. Otherwise, a systematic bias may be introduced by the fact that age, sex, and work habits may influence both who opens the door and their political preferences.

The sequential nature of the sampling process makes it unnecessary to list every single household in the country. Yet the random selection at each stage means that, in theory, every household has an equal chance of being included in the sample, no matter what its physical appearance or the condition of the neighborhood. Inconvenient, out-of-the-way precincts may well be chosen. This possibility is needed for a true random sample. Yet clustering also makes it more economical to sample out-of-the-way places because several households are interviewed within each precinct. Remember, one of the problems with a one-stage random sample is that the selected names will probably be scattered all over the map. Interviewers would spend more time traveling than interviewing. Cluster sampling is more convenient for interviewers, without giving them the discretion of choosing their own sample.

In practice, the pollsters' procedures are not quite this pure. Most don't consider excessively out-of-the-way sampling places, such as Alaska. Many allow their interviewers to choose the particular houses to visit and people to interview within a given sampling area. Many scrutinize the age, sex, race, and income of the respondents and will either adjust the results or throw out the poll if the sample seems unrepresentative.

Thus, pollsters' practices are a commonsense blend of random and quota sampling. But their hybrid has most of the economic advantages of quota sampling and few of the disadvantages. It is a logical and economically feasible approximation of a simple one-stage random sample from the entire population. And it works! Here is Gallup's presidential forecasting record since 1948:

year	Gallup prediction of Republican %	actual Republican %	prediction minus actual
1952	51%	55.4%	−4.4%
1956	59.5%	57.8%	+1.7%
1960	49%	49.9%	−0.9%
1964	36%	38.7%	−2.7%
1968	43%	43.5%	−0.5%
1972	62%	61.8%	+0.2%
1976	50.5%	48.9%	+1.6%
1980*	47%	51%	−4%

The Republican bias has been eliminated by cluster sampling in that the Republican vote is now underestimated as often as it is overestimated. In addition, the size of the prediction error has dropped dramatically. With quota sampling, Gallup's average prediction error in the 1936 through 1948 elections was 4 percent. Using cluster sampling, the average prediction error has been less than 2 percent. What is most impressive is that Gallup and the other political pollsters have become more accurate even while sharply reducing the size of their samples. Gallup's embarrassing 1948 prediction was based on a poll of 50,000 registered voters. Nowadays, using cluster sampling, Gallup obtains much more accurate predictions from interviews with less than 4000 people! To be reliable, a sample needs to be random much more than it needs to be large.

More Polling Pitfalls

There are, of course, still some pitfalls in opinion polling that cannot be avoided just by sampling procedure. Many registered voters do not vote, and the pollsters' objective is to predict the preferences of those who do vote, not the preferences of those who could vote. Good pollsters try to identify nonvoters by asking such questions as "Did you vote in the last election?" and "Do you feel strongly about the upcoming election?"

*The 1980 election included an independent candidate who received, as predicted, 7 percent of the vote. The Democrat, Jimmy Carter, was predicted to get 44 percent, but only got 41 percent. A *New York Times*/CBS post-election poll found that 20 percent of the voters changed their minds on who to vote for or whether to vote at all during the last four days of the campaign, and 60 percent of this group decided not to vote for Carter. (*The New York Times*, November 16, 1980, p. 1)

Another response problem is that some people in the sample may not be home at the right time, even if the interviewer tries again and again. And even if someone is home, they may have things to do which seem more important than answering some nosy questions. Pollsters usually "piggyback" their polls, having their interviewers ask hundreds of questions for many different clients. After an hour or two of this grilling, many bored or irritated subjects will understandably become more careless in their answers.

Another problem is that interviewers are human and some may be a bit lazy or even dishonest. It is always easier to give a questionnaire to your friends or fill it out yourself than to track down the people that are supposed to be interviewed, particularly if they live in an unfamiliar or seemingly dangerous neighborhood. Good pollsters discourage such dishonesty by making random followup calls to see if the people who were supposed to be interviewed really did get interviewed.

Appearances can work the other way, too. The answers people give may be influenced by the demeanor of the interviewer. We have a natural tendency to suppress feelings that might be provocative or embarrassing and, instead, say what we think people want us to say. With the occasional exception of a Barry Goldwater or George McGovern, our presidential candidates are usually so bland that this is not a problem for political polls. It doesn't take much courage to admit who you are going to vote for. In addition, the interviewers sometimes give each person a ballot that can be marked secretly and dropped unsigned into a box that the interviewer carries. (Of course, there is then no guarantee that the person answers the questions at all!)

An interesting postelection phenomenon is that, often, more people claim they voted for the winner than actually did. An extreme example is John F. Kennedy, who got barely half of the votes cast in 1960. After his assassination and elevation to hero status, pollsters found it almost impossible to find anyone who would say they voted against Kennedy in 1960. This particular halo effect is undoubtedly exaggerated by the fact that Kennedy's 1960 opponent was Richard Nixon, who has fallen from grace. Nowadays, most people say they didn't vote for Nixon in 1972 either, even though he won that election by a landslide over George McGovern.

In other, even more controversial opinion polls, some people either are evasive or misstate their position. Darrell Huff[14] tells the example of the National Opinion Research Center, which used two teams of interviewers, one white and one black, to poll 500 southern blacks during World War II. One question asked was, "Would Negroes be treated better or worse here if the Japanese conquered the United States?" The black interviewers reported that 9 percent of those polled thought the Japanese would treat blacks better and 25 percent thought blacks would be treated worse. The white interviewers, however, found that only 3 percent of the blacks said that blacks would be treated better while 45 percent said they would be treated worse. The most reasonable explanation for this disparity is that blacks were less candid with white interviewers. Another possibility is that the white interviewers were more reluctant to poll surly-looking blacks.

Sometimes, it's the question itself, rather than the questioner, that biases the answers. A 1964 issue of *Fact* magazine had the attention-grabbing headline,

1,189 Psychiatrists say Goldwater Psychologically Unfit to be President

The story was based on a mail poll of 12,000 doctors, asking such loaded questions as

"Does he seem prone to aggressive behavior and destructiveness?"
"Can you offer any explanation for his public temper tantrums?"
"Do you believe that Goldwater is psychologically fit? No or yes?"

About 20 percent of the doctors responded, with the provocative headline based on the fact that about half of these answered "no" to the vague question of Goldwater's psychological fitness. Goldwater sued for libel and was eventually awarded $50,000 in damages.

For a less extreme example, consider this question that the Gallup poll once asked:

The U.S. Supreme Court has ruled that a woman may go to a doctor to end pregnancy at any time during the first three months of pregnancy. Do you favor or oppose this ruling?

Gallup found that 47 percent were in favor, while 44 percent were opposed. These answers were undoubtedly influenced by the careful avoidance of the word "abortion" and by the inclusion of the Supreme Court decision. A pro-abortion group substituted the phrase "for an abortion" for "to end pregnancy" and found that only 41 percent approved while 48 percent were opposed. They then omitted the Supreme Court reference by asking this question: "as far as you yourself are concerned would you say that you are for or against abortion, or what do you think?" Then they found only 36 percent in favor and 59 percent opposed.[15]

There is no best way to ask a controversial question. The point is just that the phrasing sometimes has a big effect on the answers. One pollster, Peter Hart, claims that by deliberately wording the questions to favor your position, "you can come up with any result you want." Of course, most pollsters don't have favored positions. They are honest professionals, trying to obtain an accurate gauge of public opinion. But many controversial issues are not as cut and dried as "who are you going to vote for?" They are complex questions that are difficult to word fairly in a way that will still yield simple "yes" or "no" answers. Here, the art of polling is not in choosing a random sample, but in asking the right questions. And, as in all fields, there are some unscrupulous pollsters whose primary objective is getting the answers that the client wants to hear. The founder of the Roper poll put it this way,

While we are probably the newest profession in existence, we have managed in a few short years to take on many of the characteristics of the world's oldest profession.[16]

Some polls are biased by the fact that they are mailed out with material arguing one side of a particular issue. For example, I used to get letters from one congressman boasting how hard he was fighting to control wasteful government spending. Included with these letters were questionnaires that asked whether we thought government spending should be reduced or increased.

Randomizing Answers to Sensitive Questions

The problem with mail interviews is nonresponse bias, that the people who take the time and effort to respond will not be a random sample. For an unbiased sample, it is better to track down randomly selected people. However, personal interviews may elicit biased answers from an unbiased sample. For instance, we've seen cases where black respondents told white interviewers one thing and then told black interviewers something quite different. Many interesting questions are pretty personal and perhaps embarrassing:

''What is your annual income?''
''Do you frequently steal from your employer?''
''Are you having an affair?''
''Have you ever had an abortion?''
''Do you smoke pot?''
''Are you a homosexual?''

The most honest answers would be given anonymously, but we don't want to use mail polls to provide this anonymity.

One solution is to select a random sample, track down the selected people, and then hand each person a questionnaire. The questionnaire can be filled in while the interviewer's back is turned and then sealed in a plain envelope. The Gallup presidential poll, for example, uses a secret ballot.

However, some respondents' answers may be influenced by a suspicion that the curious pollster will promptly rip open the envelope and snoop at the answers. An ingenious alternative is to use randomized questioning.[18] The respondent can be given two alternative questions, with the pollster not knowing which is being answered. For example, the person can be handed a questionnaire that says

To protect your privacy, we are asking two alternative questions here, and no one will know which you are answering.
Is your birthdate an even number or an odd number?
If it is an even number, please answer question (a); if it is odd, please answer question (b):
    a. Is your birthdate before the 15th of a month?
    b. Have you ever cheated on an exam?

Another construction could be

Darrell Huff provides another example.[17] The *New York Times* once ran a story "DOCTORS REPORTED FOR SECURITY PLAN" that began, "A recent poll in New Jersey indicates that most of the country's doctors would like to come under the Social Security old age and survivors insurance program, according to Representative Robert W. Kean, Republican of New Jersey." It turns out that this

We have designed this question to protect your privacy. You have been given a bag containing three balls: one red, one white, and one blue. Please close your eyes and draw one ball out of this bag. If the ball is red write "yes" below. If the ball is white, write "no" below. If the ball is blue, answer the question "Have you ever cheated on an exam?" Your "yes" or "no" answer is completely confidential since no one knows which color ball you drew.

Let's say that the second construction is used and that 40 percent of the answers are "yes" and 60 percent are "no." What is our estimate of the fraction π of the population who cheat on exams? On average, we would expect that

1/3 draw a red ball and answer yes
1/3 draw a white ball and answer no
$(1/3)\pi$ draw a blue ball and answer yes
$(1/3)(1 - \pi)$ draw a blue ball and answer no.

Overall,

$$\text{yes answers:} \quad (1/3) + (1/3)\pi$$

$$\text{no answers:} \quad \underline{(1/3) + (1/3)(1 - \pi)}$$

$$\text{total:} \qquad\qquad 1$$

If, in fact, there are 40 percent yes answers, then we can estimate π by

$$(1/3) + (1/3)\pi = .40$$

implies that

$$1 + \pi = 1.2$$

so that

$$\pi = .2$$

Say, for instance, that 300 people are polled. We expect 100 yes answers from people who draw red balls and, if $\pi = .2$, 20 yes answers from the 100 people who draw blue balls. Altogether, there would be $120/300 = .4$ yes answers.

Randomized responses increase sampling error because fewer people actually answer the question of interest, and it is uncertain exactly how many people did answer this question. But giving anonymity to those who answer the sensitive questions, encourages truthful answers. And, again, a small, unbiased sample is much better than a large, biased one.

story was based on a postcard questionnaire that was included in an issue of the Bulletin of the Essex County Medical Society that contained an article by Representative Kean explaining why he thought doctors should be included in the Social Security program. Can you spot the major reasons for giving little credence to this poll?

First, there is a potential sampling bias, because Essex County doctors may not be representative of "most of the country's doctors." Second, there is the nonresponse bias inherent in a postcard questionnaire (which 80 percent of the readers did not answer). Third, those who did respond may have been temporarily biased by having just finished reading arguments on one side of the issue. After their emotional momentum subsided and after they heard the other side, they might well have felt differently.

Exercises

8.18 A Los Angeles television station includes a poll as part of its nightly local news show. A provocative "question of the day" flashes on the screen and viewers are asked to call in their "yes" or "no" votes. Can you think of any reason why these poll results might not be representative of community opinion?

8.19 Congresswoman Louise Day Hicks mailed 200,000 questionnaires to the people in her district, asking whether or not they favored using mandatory busing to integrate the public schools. The *Boston Globe* reported that 80 percent of the 23,000 people who responded were opposed to busing, which "proved decisively that the 'silent majority' does care about the country and its problems and, given the opportunity, will speak out on the issues."[19]

Is there any reason to use caution in interpreting these poll results? Who was the real "silent majority" here?

8.20 In July 1983, Congressmen Gerry E. Studds (a Massachussetts Democrat) and Daniel Crane (an Illinois Republican) were censured by the House of Representatives for having had sex with teenage pages. A questionnaire in the Sunday (July 17) *Cape Cod Times* asked readers whether Studds should "resign immediately," "serve out his present term, but not run for re-election," or "serve out his present term, and run for re-election." Out of a paid Sunday circulation of 51,000 people, 2770 returned this questionnaire. Of these, 45.5 percent (1259) wanted Studds to resign immediately, while 46 percent (1273) wanted him to serve out his term and run for re-election. Another 7.5 percent (211) wanted him to serve out his term but not seek re-election and 1 percent (27) were undecided. Why might these survey results be misleading?

8.21 Estimate the average Grade Point Average (GPA) of students at your college by asking 10 students to tell you their GPAs. Tell how you selected these 10 students and explain why you think they are a good sample. Did any students refuse to tell you their GPAs? What sort of nonresponse bias might arise in a GPA survey? Are there any other reasons why your estimate might be used cautiously?

8.22   Almost all of the interviewers employed by pollsters are women. Why do you think this is?

8.23   A poll taken by the National Opinion Research Center asked blacks if the Army is unfair to blacks. Only 11 percent said yes to white interviewers, while 35 percent said yes to black interviewers.[20] What could account for this disparity?

8.24   A variety of data were collected on the boys at a summer Boy Scout camp. One scout leader noticed an interesting relationship between foot size and speed:

foot length	average time for 50-yard dash
< 9 inches	9.5 seconds
≤ 9 inches	8.6 seconds

Do big feet help people run faster? Why do you suppose that the boys with big feet were faster than the boys with small feet?

This scout leader also discovered that the boys with big feet had more merit badges than the boys with small feet. Do big feet make people smarter, too?

8.25   A newspaper selected 100 names at random out of the city telephone book and sent a reporter out to ask these 100 people whether they felt Social Security benefits are "too high," "too low," or "about right." Only 60 of these people were home when the reporter tried to interview them. Rather than use a sample with such a small response rate, the newspaper selected another 100 names at random and sent the reporter out again to try names in this second batch until 40 more people were interviewed successfully. Does the newspaper's procedure eliminate the small response rate? Is their poll a random sample or could it be biased in some way?

8.26   In 1952, the Chicago Police Department banned the public showing of the Italian film, "The Miracle." The American Civil Liberties Union (ACLU) subsequently showed this film at several of its private meetings and reported that,

> Of those filling out questionnaires after seeing the film, less than 1 percent felt it should be banned. "It thus seems," said Sanford I. Wolff, Chairman of the Chicago Division's Censorship Committee and Edward H. Meyerding, the Chicago ACLU's Executive Director, "that the five members of the [police] Censorship Board do not represent the thinking of the majority of Chicago citizens."[21]

Why is the ACLU's poll not convincing statistical evidence?

8.27   A randomized response poll was given to 30 students in a Tuesday statistics class:

> Is your birthdate an even or odd number? If it is even, please answer question (a); if it is odd, please answer question (b).
> a. Is today Tuesday?
> b. Have you ever handed in a course paper that was substantially written by someone else?

Eighteen "yes" answers were handed in along with 12 "no" answers. If we assume that even and odd birthdates are equally likely, what is your estimate of the fraction of the class that has handed in papers that were written by others?

8.4 SUMMARY

Samples are used in a variety of situations because a complete enumeration is too expensive or difficult. We sample food when we take a taste: "You don't have to eat the whole thing to know its rotten." Many of the courses you take at college are a sample of a discipline, to help you make career decisions. Your dates can be a sample of married life. Soon, an employer will take a sample of your intelligence, training, and personality by using a job interview to learn something about you. Government agencies sample products to see if they are safe. The military samples weapons to see if they will work. In business, samples are used to help design new products, test product reliability, gauge the quality of raw materials, monitor production methods, measure worker productivity, and conduct advertising campaigns.

Samples are intended to be representative of an entire population. If they are, then they can provide accurate estimates of population characteristics. Deliberate attempts to construct representative samples are unwise, though, because "representative" is in the eye of the beholder. If a researcher carefully assembles what is thought to be a representative sample, then we will learn something about this researcher's opinion, but little more. Instead, statisticians recommend that a random sample be used, in which each member of the population is equally likely to be selected. This is analogous to a fair deal from a deck of cards. In practice, a random sample can be constructed by enumerating the members of the population and then using a table of random numbers to select the sample.

Polls are used to gauge public opinion on all sorts of things, including the President's performance, political candidates, controversial legislation, economic conditions, new products, the effectiveness of advertising campaigns, and even the appeal of prospective movie plots. These can be very interesting and even useful, but require considerable care in construction and interpretation. A selection bias may inadvertently exclude some members of the population from consideration for the poll. Nonresponse bias involves the refusal by some groups to participate in an opinion poll. In addition, it is difficult to phrase questions in a balanced way which, nonetheless, invites simple answers. Slight changes in the working of an opinion poll may well affect many people's answers. Also, many questions are too complex to be answered easily with a simple "yes" or "no." The statistics of opinion polling is to design a random sample; the art is to ask good questions.

REVIEW EXERCISES

8.28 Estimate the average parental income of students at your college by asking 10 students to tell you their heights. Tell how you selected these 10 students and explain why you think that they are a good sample.

8.29 (*continuation*) Do you have any reason to be cautious about interpreting these income declarations? If you suspect a bias, explain your reasoning. Do you think that the average declared income is more likely to be too high or too low?

8.30   A Chinese census for famine relief showed a population of 105 million people. Yet a census taken a few years earlier for military and tax purposes had shown a population of only 28 million. Why do you suppose these census figures were so far apart?

8.31   *Consumer Report*'s annual automobile issue includes frequency-of-repair records, based on letters received from their readers. Is this a random sample? If not, what biases might appear?

8.32   The Harris Poll doesn't include people in Alaska or Hawaii, because it is too expensive to send interviewers to these two states. How might this economization bias the poll results?

8.33   In 1964, pollsters found that presidential candidate Barry Goldwater did better in their polls when interviewers used secret ballots. What could explain this curious phenomenon?

• **8.34**   A certain advertising agency is looking for magazines in which to advertise inexpensive imitations of designer clothing. Their target audience is households earning less than $15,000 a year. A survey finds that the readers of one magazine have an average household income of $17,500. Is the agency correct in concluding that the people in their target audience do not read this magazine?

8.35   The Census Bureau has estimated the lifetime earnings of people by age, sex, and education. The *Cape Code Times* (July 7, 1983) reported that

> 18-year-old men who receive graduate education will be 'worth' more than twice as much as peers who don't complete high school. On the average, that first 18-year-old can expect to earn just over $1.3 million while the average high-school dropout can expect to earn about $601,000 between the ages of 18 and 64.

Mike O'Donnell was getting poor grades in high school and was thinking of dropping out and going to work for his dad's construction firm. But his father, an avid reader of the *Cape Cod Times*, saw this article and told Mike that dropping out would be a $700,000 mistake. Is Mike's dad right?

8.36   A newspaper columnist wrote that women's goal of

> an equal chance at a good job . . . has happened. . . . Consider the changes from census to census—from 1970 to 1980. Briefly, there were only 13,000 female "lawyers and judges" back then. Today there are 74,000. Stop the presses: There were 61,000 "editors and reporters" then—and 103,000 now. Another X-ray scan: There were 45,000 "physicians and dentists" then—and 76,000 now.[22]

Do these statistics prove that women now have an equal chance at a good job? What other data might be of interest?

8.37   During World War II, 408,000 U.S. citizens were killed in military duty and 375,000 U.S. citizens were killed by accidents in the United States. Does this show that it was almost as dangerous to stay home as to fight in the war?

8.38   In 1984, a congressman asked his constituents "Which statement is closest to your view with respect to the federal budget deficit?" Of three options, 69 percent of those who responded chose the statement "We should reduce the deficit by raising taxes and by reducing spending in many areas of the federal budget, including the military."[23]

Explain any reservations you might have about this congressman's conclusion that "69 percent . . . oppose the current buildup in military spending . . . confirm[ing] my belief that the people of Southeastern Massachusetts are appalled to see defense spending soar while the rest of the federal budget is suffering severe cutbacks."

● **8.39** "Seventy percent of all the cars we've produced are still on the road." Does this statistic prove that this company's cars are durable? Why might it be misleading?

● **8.40** The useful life of a certain car is normally distributed with an expected value of 70,000 miles and a standard deviation of 10,000 miles. What is the probability that one of these cars will last longer than 100,000 miles? The advertising agency has suggested an ad featuring an owner whose car has lasted 100,000 miles. The agency telephones 100 people who have owned this car sufficiently long so that the car either has 100,000 miles or has died. What is the probability that at least one of these 100 cars will have lived to see 100,000 miles? Why are the owners cited in this ad a biased sample?

8.41 Males who have never smoked average 14.8 days of restricted activity per year, while present smokers average 22.5 days and former smokers average 23.5 days.[24] Do these data show that it is healthiest to never smoke, but once you start, it's better not to stop?

8.42 A polio vaccine was tested in a town with 1000 children. Half of the children were vaccinated and half weren't. The study found that none of the children who were vaccinated got polio. Does this prove that the vaccine worked? What other data would you like to see?

8.43 (*continuation*) None of the children who were not vaccinated got polio either. What was wrong with this sample?

8.44 During the 1976 presidential primaries, Lou Harris asked Democrats and Independents to choose from a variety of candidates. When a full list of 25 possibilities was offered, Edward Kennedy got the most votes and George Wallace finished second with 17 percent of the votes. When Kennedy's name was removed, Hubert Humphrey finished first and Wallace second, this time with 19 percent. Jimmy Carter, the eventual nominee, got only 2 percent. Yet when Harris asked this sample to choose between Carter and Wallace, Carter got 43 percent and Wallace 38 percent, with 19 percent undecided.[25]

If you were Wallace's campaign manager, how would you interpret these poll results?

8.45 A *Newsday* (July 13, 1983) story was titled "Poll shows strong U.S. work ethic." The story told how a poll had counted workers as having a strong work ethic if they agreed with the statement, "I have an inner need to do the best I can regardless of pay." The poll found that the percentage of U.S. workers expressing a strong work ethic was higher than in West Germany or Japan. Yet, U.S. worker productivity has been lagging behind these other countries. The report accompanying the poll results concluded that, "Studies of work behavior show that slackening effort may be making a significant impact on the U.S. economy. . . . The challenge, therefore, is to find means to harness the latent but untapped power of the U.S. work ethic." One of the researchers associated with the poll offered the following theory:

> From an economy dominated by assembly line jobs, we have moved to a situation where white-collar and service workers have a great deal more control over their work. The decision to work harder is more than ever in the hands of the individual

worker. Many managers don't yet realize how you go about motivating a worker who has a lot of freedom in his job.[26]

This seems to be a farfetched explanation of the disparity between the poll's finding of a strong work ethic and the evidence of slackening worker effort. If workers have a strong work ethic and more freedom to work as hard as they want, then I would expect them to work harder. If, as the report concludes, people are not working harder, then perhaps the strength of their work ethic is exaggerated. Is there any reason to suspect that the results of this sort of poll might be biased?

8.46 *Dial* magazine published a long article on how different people are using home computers, based on a survey of its readers. One of their conclusions was that "the huge majority (82 percent) feel 'very favorable' about the computers in their homes. Another 12 percent feel 'somewhat favorable,' and not one of the 1,000 in the random sample tabulated for the survey indicated feeling 'very unfavorable.' " Comment on the following description of their random sample:

> *Dial* asked its readers who use home computers or who have experience with computers at work to respond to a two-page questionnaire in the magazine. We received nearly 5,200 responses; more than 600 of them included letters of up to 15 pages in length. Most of these letters were written on computers.
>
> A random sample of 1,000 responses was pulled from the group. The statistics in the article are based on a tabulation of that sample. . . .[27]

● **8.47** Critically evaluate:

> The more children you have, the less likelihood there is that you will ever be divorced.
>
> This is an idea that many have suspected to be true. But it remained for the Metropolitan Life Insurance Company to prove it with the statistics printed below. The possibility that a childless couple will be divorced is about twice as great as it would be if they had two or more dependent children. . . .[28]

number of children	divorces per 1000 marriages
0	15.3
1	11.6
2	7.6
3	6.5
4 or more	4.6

8.48 A randomized response poll included this question:

> Please flip a coin. If it is heads write down "yes." If it is tails, please answer this question truthfully, "Have you ever shoplifted?" The answers turned out to be 62 "yes" and 38 "no."

Estimate the fraction that have shoplifted.

8.49 (*continuation*) The researcher who administered this poll suspects that some people who were proud of never having shoplifted may have answered "no" even though their coin flip turned out to be a head. If so, is the estimate you made in the preceding question too high or too low?

• **8.50**   A randomized response poll of 300 people included this question:

Please flip this coin and then answer question (a) if it lands heads and (b) if it lands tails.
  (a) Please roll this die and write down the number that comes up.
  (b) Please write down the number (from 1 to 6) that is closest to your monthly income (in 1000s of dollars).

The answers turned out to be

number	1	2	3	4	5	6
responses	85	61	52	40	34	28

Use these data to estimate the income distribution.

CHAPTER 9

Estimation

In solving a problem of this sort, the grand thing is to be able to reason backward. That is a very useful accomplishment, and a very easy one, but people do not practice it much. . . . Most people, if you describe a train of events to them, will tell you what the result would be. . . . There are few people, however, who, if you told them a result, would be able to evolve from their own inner consciousness what the steps were which led up to that result. This power is what I mean when I talk of reasoning backward.

Sherlock Holmes
A Study in Scarlet

TOPICS

Sampling is an economical attempt to estimate characteristics of the underlying population. Election polls estimate the fraction of the population who favor a candidate; opinion polls estimate the fraction of the population who favor certain positions; bomb tests estimate the fraction of a shipment that are duds; and product tests estimate the fraction of manufactured items that are defective. In each of these four examples, a fraction is estimated. Absolute numbers and averages can be estimated, too. The Nielsen ratings can be used to estimate the number of people who watched a particular television program. Marketing samples are used to estimate the demand for a new product. The Federal Reserve uses samples to estimate the nation's money supply. Samples are used to estimate the amount of cholesterol in a person's body, the number of unmarried senior citizens in Florida, and the number of fish in a lake. Weather stations use samples at different locations to estimate the average temperature, rainfall, and so on. Samples are used to estimate the average breaking strength of fishing lines, the average acidity of a pond, and the average rate of increase of prices.

In each case, sample data are used to estimate a population value. But exactly how should the data be used to make these estimates? And how much confidence can we have in estimates that are based on just a small sample? I will answer these questions by focusing on one particular example, then we will apply these procedures to other examples.

9.1 USING A SAMPLE MEAN TO ESTIMATE A POPULATION MEAN

Consider a certain brand of crackers sold in a box that says "net weight 16 ounces." The producer may intend to put 16 ounces of crackers in each box, but slight imperfections in the manufacturing and packaging process cause variations in the actual weight. Because the imperfections are many and varied, the central limit theorem suggests that the net weight may be normally distributed. For the sake of argument, let's say that the net weight is, in fact, normally distributed with a mean of $\mu = 16$ ounces and a standard deviation of $\sigma = .1$ ounce. Thus, a person buying a box of these crackers is drawing from a population with this normal distribution. There is a 50 percent chance that the chosen box will turn out to have a net weight greater than 16 ounces and a 50 percent chance that the net weight will be less than 16 ounces. Ninety-five percent of the time, the net weight will be within two standard deviations of the mean—between 15.8 and 16.2 ounces.

These probability computations are based on the assumed population distribution. Now, of course, no one can really know how the cracker weights are distributed unless they open every single box and weigh the contents. This is where statistics comes in. The company, the government, or some other interested party can use a sample to estimate the actual distribution. A sample of 10 boxes yields the following net weight measurements (in ounces):

16.10   16.01   15.82   15.93   16.05

16.05	15.86	15.90	16.05	16.13

How could we use these data to estimate the mean net weight of all of the boxes of crackers sold by this company? Remember, we are interested in the mean of a population, from which we have a small sample of 10 boxes. It is natural to use the sample mean $\overline{X}$ to estimate the population mean μ. The sample mean works out to be

$$\overline{X} = \frac{16.13 + 16.01 + \cdots + 16.10}{10} = 15.99$$

The sample mean $\overline{X} = 15.99$ ounces is, for this particular sample, very close to the population mean $\mu = 16$ ounces. Another sample would almost surely yield a somewhat different result. Someone else conducting such a test would select 10 different boxes and might obtain these net weights:

16.08	16.01	16.06	15.93	16.02
16.00	15.97	16.06	16.23	15.94

The mean of this sample is 16.03. One sample mean was too low, while another was too high, which is just what we should expect to happen.

Let's retrace our steps and, this time, affix statistical labels as we go. The net weights of cracker boxes follow a normal distribution with a population mean and standard deviation that are, in practice, unknown. A sample of 10 boxes can be used to estimate the population mean (and the standard deviation, too).

> The population mean is a **parameter** that is unknown, but can be estimated. The sample statistic that is used to estimate a parameter is called an **estimator.** The specific value of the estimator obtained in a particular sample is an **estimate.**

Sampling Error

The sample mean is the most natural estimator of the population mean. In our cracker example, one sample yielded an estimate of 15.99, while another sample gave an estimate of 16.03. Estimates vary from sample to sample because of the luck of the draw. By chance alone, a particular sample may contain many boxes with below-average weights or many boxes with above-average weights. The researcher, of course, will not know whether the sample weights happen to be above average or below average, because the population mean is unknown.

> The variation of estimates from sample to sample is called **sampling error.**

Sampling error is not due to mistakes or sloppy procedures. It is the inevitable result of the fact that we are looking at a small sample whose members are determined by chance.

In practice, we take just a single sample and use this sample mean to estimate the population mean. What we must recognize is that our particular sample is just one of many samples that might have been obtained. The mean of our random sample is, by definition, determined by the luck of the draw. If we select 10 cracker boxes, open them, weigh the contents, and calculate the average weight to be 15.99 ounces, there is a temptation to treat this result as definitive. This temptation should be resisted. A sample mean of 15.99 ounces is just one of many sample means that could have been obtained. Another sample might yield a mean of 16.03 ounces. A third sample would yield yet another mean.

The **sample mean is a random variable** that is determined by the particular items picked for the sample.

We cannot say whether a particular estimate, such as 15.99, is good or bad, because we don't know the true value of the parameter that we are estimating. We could get a 15.99 sample mean from a population with a mean of 16.0, 15.99, or 43.7, and we don't know for sure which is the case. However, we can use probability theory to deduce how likely it is that a sample will be picked whose mean happens to be far from the population mean.

The Distribution of the Sample Mean

The net weight of a cracker box is a random variable X, which, we assumed, is normally distributed with a mean of 16 ounces and a standard deviation of 0.1 ounce.

$$X \sim N[16, 0.1]$$

Our random sample consists of 10 independent draws from this population.* Let's label the net weight of the first selected box X_1. This net weight X_1 is a random variable with

$$X_1 \sim N[16, 0.1]$$

The net weight of the second selected box, X_2, is another random variable from the same normal distribution.

$$X_2 \sim N[16, 0.1]$$

The same is true of the net weights of the other boxes $X_3, X_4 \ldots, X_{10}$. Each of the 10 net weights is a random variable that is normally distributed with a mean of 16 and a standard deviation of 0.1 ounce.

The sample mean is the sum of these 10 random variables, divided by 10.

$$\overline{X} = \frac{X_1 + X_2 + \cdots + X_{10}}{10}$$

---

*Here, as in most sampling situations, the probabilities are not quite constant because the sampling is done without replacement. However, the population is so large relative to the sample that no harm is done by assuming constant probabilities.

In general, if n items are sampled, then the sample mean is the sum of n random variables, divided by n:

$$\overline{X} = \frac{X_1 + X_2 + \cdots + X_n}{n}$$

Least Squares Estimation

The German scientist Karl Gauss analyzed a great deal of data that had been collected in the fields of astronomy and geodesy (measurements of the shape of the earth and the location of places on it). Several observers had made many measurements at varying locations and times. These measurements inevitably had errors, due to imperfections in their methods and the imprecision of their equipment. Gauss wanted to combine these different measurements somehow so that "the accidental errors might as far as possible mutually destroy each other,"[1] thereby yielding a single, "best" estimate.

Gauss's basic model is as follows. In attempting to measure some distance μ, the measurements $X_1, X_2, \ldots, X_n$ are obtained. The difference between each measurement X_i and the true distance μ is measurement error ϵ_i:

$$X = \mu + \epsilon_i \qquad (9.1)$$

Now, let's say that we want to use some estimator $\hat{\mu}$ (pronounced "mu hat") of μ to predict the measurements X_i that people obtain. Our prediction errors will be $X_i - \hat{\mu}$. Gauss argued that we should use the estimator $\hat{\mu}$ that minimizes the sum of squared prediction errors.*

$$(X_1 - \hat{\mu})^2 + (X_2 - \hat{\mu})^2 + \cdots + (X_n - \hat{\mu})^2 \qquad (9.2)$$

Gauss showed that this **least squares** estimator turns out to be the sample mean of the measurements.

$$\overline{X} = \frac{X_1 + X_2 + \cdots + X_n}{n}$$

This is Gauss's novel justification for using the sample mean to estimate the population mean. He then went on to develop least squares estimators for more complicated models. This work laid the basis for what we now call *regression analysis,* which is one of the most useful and powerful statistical techniques. We will look at regression analysis in later chapters.

Gauss also showed that when measurement errors are independent and identically distributed, then the sample mean tends to be normally distributed with an expected value equal to the population mean. This important finding, *Gauss's Law of Errors,* is the primary subject of this chapter.

*The least squares idea apparently was introduced around 1805 by a French mathematician, Adrien M. Legendre (1752–1833).

The sum of independent, normally distributed random variables is normally distributed, too, with a mean equal to the sum of the individual means and a variance equal to the sum of the individual variances. Therefore,* the sample mean is normally distributed with an expected value μ and a standard deviation $\sigma/\sqrt{n}$:

$$\overline{X} \sim N[\mu, \, \sigma/\sqrt{n}] \tag{9.3}$$

Now, in practice, we will seldom know whether or not we are sampling from a normal distribution. Here, I just blithely assumed that the errors in the manufacturing and packaging process are such that the net weights turn out to be normally distributed. What if we are a little more cautious in our assumptions? Or, even more drastically, what if we know that what we are measuring is not normally distributed? It doesn't matter!

> The central limit theorem implies that, no matter what the underlying distribution, the sample mean will tend to a normal distribution.

A random sample is a set of independent and identically distributed measurements; these are the very assumptions that are used in the central limit theorem. This theorem states that the sum of n independent, identically distributed random variables approaches a normal distribution as n increases. Therefore, the sample mean, which is just the sum of n independent, identically distributed random variables divided by n, must approach a normal distribution as n increases.

Thus, the central limit theorem is not only a very important part of probability, it is also an absolutely crucial part of statistics. In probability analysis, the central limit theorem tells us that many of the uncertainties about us, ranging from IQ scores to the movements of molecules, conform to a normal distribution. In statistical analysis, the central limit theorem tells us that the mean of a random sample conforms to a normal distribution. The only cautions we need to exercise are to ensure that it really is a random sample and that it is large enough to justify an appeal to the central limit theorem. With something like cracker weights, which are themselves approximately normally distributed, a sample of size 10 is large enough. With an unknown distribution, the usual rule of thumb is that a sample of size 20 or 30 will be satisfactory. If the underlying distribution is known to be highly skewed, then 50, 100, or more observations may be needed. Figure 9.1 shows four examples.

If a random sample is drawn from a normal distribution, then Equation 9.3 always holds. Even if the underlying distribution is not normal, a sufficiently large sample will ensure that Equation 9.3 still holds:

$$\overline{X} \sim N[\mu, \, \sigma/\sqrt{n}]$$

This is undoubtedly the most important formula in statistics. It is absolutely crucial that you remember it and understand it.

---

*The sum of the Xs has an expected value $n\mu$ and a variance $n\sigma^2$. Equation 9.3 then follows from the linear transformation Equations 4.4 and 4.5.

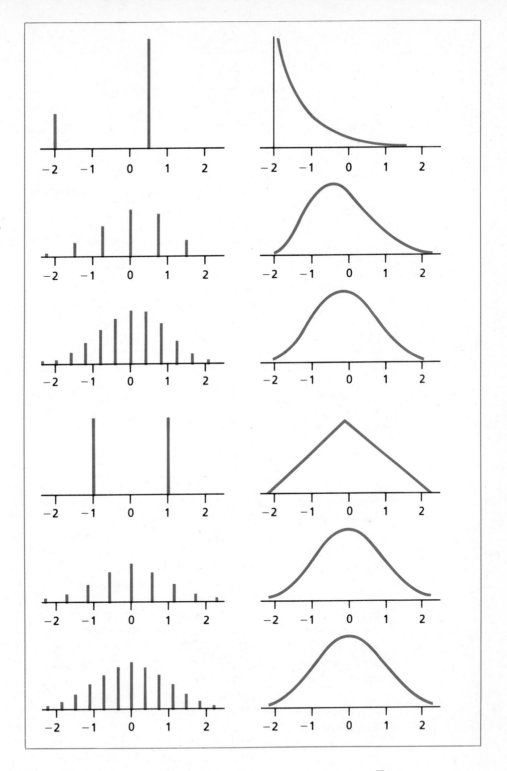

Figure 9.1 *The distributions of some standardized sample means,* $Z = \dfrac{\overline{X} - \mu}{\sigma/\sqrt{n}}$

The Expected Value of the Sample Mean

The sample mean is a random variable that is determined by the luck of the draw in selecting the sample. Equation 9.3 states that the probability distribution for the sample mean is symmetrical about the population mean, μ. There is a .5 probability that the sample mean will be above the population mean and a .5 probability that it will be below it. The expected value of the sample mean is equal to the population mean. The sample mean is consequently said to be an **unbiased estimator** of the population mean.

> An estimator is **unbiased** if its expected value is equal to the parameter being estimated.

Unbiased estimators have a considerable appeal. It would be discomforting to use estimates that one knows are systematically too high or too low. A statistician who uses unbiased estimators can anticipate estimates with errors that, over a lifetime, average very close to zero. But, of course, average performance is not the only thing that counts. There was the lawyer who summarized a career by saying that, "When I was young, I lost many cases that I should have won. And when I was old, I won many cases that I should have lost. So, on average, justice was done." The conscientious statistician should be concerned with not only how good the estimates are on average but also how accurate they are in particular cases.

The Standard Deviation of the Sample Mean

Equation 9.3 states that the standard deviation of the sample mean is $\sigma/\sqrt{n}$. If the sample has only one observation in it ($n = 1$), then its standard deviation will be σ. As n increases, the standard deviation of the sample mean declines. To understand this, remember that the standard deviation is a measure of the uncertainty of the outcome. With a small sample, we are not at all sure what the sample mean will turn out to be. With a large sample, on the other hand, it is extremely unlikely that all of the observations will be way above μ and equally unlikely that all of the observations will be far below μ. Instead, we are almost certain to have a sample whose mean is very close to μ. As the sample size n becomes infinitely large, the standard deviation of the sample mean goes to zero, reflecting our commonsense judgment that, as the sample encompasses the population, the sample mean is certain to be the population mean.

Now let's apply Equation 9.3 to the cracker example. We'll assume that the manufacturing and packaging process yields boxes with net weights that are normally distributed with a mean $\mu = 16$ ounces and a standard deviation $\sigma = 0.1$ ounce. If we weigh a random sample of 10 boxes, the mean of this sample is a random variable, which is normally distributed with a mean of 16 ounces and a standard deviation of $0.1/\sqrt{10} = 0.032$ ounce. Figure 9.2 shows this probability distribution. Using our two-standard-deviation rule, there is a .95 probability that the average weight of 10 boxes will turn out to be in the range $16 \pm 2(0.032)$ ounce, i.e., between 15.936 and 16.064 ounces.

These calculations tell us that there is only a 5 percent chance that the sample mean will be more than 0.064 ounce away from the population mean. If we use the sample mean to estimate the population mean, then there is only a 5 percent chance that our estimate of the population mean will be off by more than 0.064 ounce. If we use a larger sample, we can be even more confident that our estimate will be very close to μ. Figure 9.2 shows how the probability distribution for the sample mean collapses as the size of the sample increases. We can use the two-standard-deviation rule to quantify this convergence. If we base our estimate of the population mean on the average weight of 25 boxes, there is only a 5 percent chance that our estimate will be more than $2(0.1/\sqrt{25}) = 0.04$ ounce away from μ. With a sample of 100 boxes, there is only a 5 percent chance that our estimate will be more than $2(0.1/\sqrt{100}) = 0.02$ ounce away from μ.

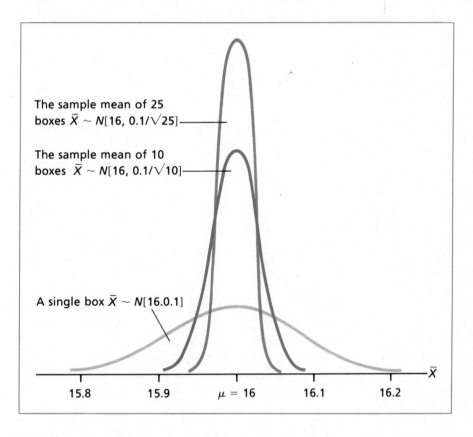

The sample mean of 25 boxes $\bar{X} \sim N[16, 0.1/\sqrt{25}]$

The sample mean of 10 boxes $\bar{X} \sim N[16, 0.1/\sqrt{10}]$

A single box $\bar{X} \sim N[16.0.1]$

15.8   15.9 $\mu = 16$ 16.1   16.2 $\bar{X}$

Figure 9.2   *The distribution of net weights*

Confidence Intervals

We can rephrase these probability computations to show the confidence we have in using the sample mean $\overline{X}$ as an estimate of the population mean μ. If there is a .95 probability that the sample mean will be within 0.064 of μ, then there is a .95 probability that μ is within 0.064 of our estimate. Figure 9.3 depicts this argument. Ninety-five percent of the time, the sample mean (our estimate of μ) will be between 15.936 and 16.064 ounces. In each of these cases, our estimate is within 0.064 ounce of μ. Five percent of the time, the sample mean will be either less than 15.936 or greater than 16.064. In each of these cases, the estimate is more than 0.064 ounce away from μ.

In practice, we won't know what the true value of μ is, but it will still be true that there is a .95 probability that the difference between μ and our estimate will be less than 0.064 ounce and a .05 probability that our error will be greater than 0.064 ounce. This probability computation is called a **confidence interval.** If the sample mean turns out to be 15.99 ounces, then we report that our estimate of μ is 15.99 ounces and that we are 95 percent confident that the range 15.99 $\pm$ 0.064 (i.e., 15.926 to 16.054) encompasses μ. The standard, shorthand reporting form is

$$\mu = 15.99 \pm 0.064 \text{ ounce}$$

or

$$.95 = P[15.926 < \mu < 16.054]$$

These are just quick-and-dirty computations using the two-standard-deviation

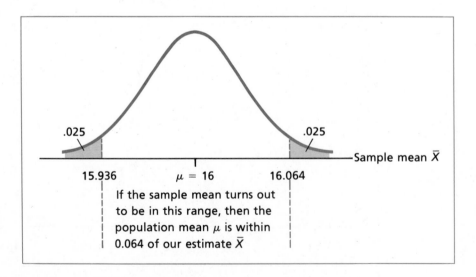

Figure 9.3 *Confidence interval logic*

rule of thumb. A more formal calculation would proceed as follows. First, decide how much confidence you want to attach to your interval. If you want to be 99 percent certain that the interval contains μ, then you will have to make the interval wide. If you are satisfied with saying, "I'm 50 percent sure that this interval contains μ," then a small interval will do. Ninety-five percent intervals are standard, but there is no reason why you can't use others.

I'll work out the standard 95 percent confidence interval here and leave the others for you to do as exercises. We've taken the first step, which is to decide how much confidence to attach to the interval. The second step is to consult the normal distribution in Table 2 to see how many standard deviations are appropriate. Our rule of thumb is that about 95 percent of the observations should be within two standard deviations of the mean. But let's look in Table 2 to get a more precise number. Table 2 shows that, in fact, there is a .95 probability that a standardized normal variable Z will be between -1.96 and $+1.96$. The last step is to translate this probability statement about Z into a probability statement about the sample mean. To standardize the sample mean, we subtract its expected value μ and divide by its standard deviation $\sigma/\sqrt{n}$:

$$Z = \frac{\overline{X} - \mu}{\sigma/\sqrt{n}}$$

Therefore,

$$.95 = P[-1.96 < Z < +1.96]$$

$$= P[-1.96 < \frac{\overline{X} - \mu}{\sigma/\sqrt{n}} < +1.96]$$

which can be rearranged to show that

$$.95 = P[\overline{X} - 1.96(\sigma/\sqrt{n}) < \mu < \overline{X} + 1.96(\sigma/\sqrt{n})] \qquad (9.4)$$

This is the general equation for a 95 percent confidence interval. The logic is apparent: Because there is a .95 probability that Z will be between -1.96 and $+1.96$, it follows that there is a .95 probability that the sample mean will be within 1.96 standard deviations $(\sigma/\sqrt{n})$ of its expected value (μ). The shorthand formula is

$$\mu = \overline{X} \pm 1.96 \, \sigma/\sqrt{n}$$

In the cracker example, with $\overline{X} = 15.99$, $n = 10$, and $\sigma = 0.1$, a 95 percent confidence interval works out to be

$$.95 = P[15.99 - 1.96(0.1)/\sqrt{10} < \mu < 15.99 + 1.96/\sqrt{n}]$$

$$= P[15.99 - 1.96(0.032) < \mu < 15.99 + 1.96(0.032)]$$

$$= P[15.99 - 0.062 < \mu < 15.99 + 0.062]$$

$$= P[15.928 < \mu < 16.052]$$

The exact answer, 15.99 ± 0.062, differs slightly from our two-standard-deviations rule of thumb answer, 15.99 ± 0.064.

The logic of this computation is straightforward and parallels my explanation using the two-standard-deviations rule of thumb. The only slip that students sometimes make is to forget that we are concerned with the standard deviation of the sample mean. They don't divide σ by the square root of the sample size, and consequently, they get the wrong answer. What must be remembered is that we are using the sample mean to estimate μ and that the accuracy of this estimate depends critically upon the sample size. With a large sample, there is little chance that the sample mean will be far from its expected value μ and, therefore, we can be more confident that the sample mean is an accurate estimate of μ. This intuition shows up in the arithmetic when we calculate the standard deviation of the sample mean $\sigma/\sqrt{n}$ and see that it declines as n increases.

Notice, also, that sampling error is the reason for the uncertainty concerning our estimate. We are assuming that the boxes are randomly selected and that the weighing scales are unbiased. There is uncertainty only because the net weights vary from box to box and the sample mean depends on the luck of the draw. Our estimate may be too high or too low, and we gauge this sampling error by computing a confidence interval. With a sample of 10 boxes, we are 95 percent confident that the sample mean will not be more than 0.062 ounce away from μ. This 0.062-ounce leeway is a margin for sampling error.

> The spread in a confidence interval is a **margin for sampling error.** For a 95 percent confidence interval, the margin for sampling error is $\pm 1.96(\sigma/\sqrt{n})$, or about ± 2 standard deviations of the sample mean.

Notice that it is the sample mean and the confidence interval that vary, and not the population mean. The equation

$$.95 = P[15.928 < \mu < 16.052]$$

is interpreted as meaning, "There is a .95 probability that the sample mean will turn out to be sufficiently close to μ that the confidence interval I calculate includes the true value of μ. There is a .05 probability that the sample mean will turn out to be so far from μ that my confidence interval does not include μ." The probabilities refer to the confidence intervals that result from repeated sampling; they do not refer to μ. In the long run, it can be anticipated that 95 percent of these confidence intervals will include μ and 5 percent won't. A clever analogy is to a game of horseshoes,

> A ringer occurs when the shoe rings or encloses the peg. What is the interpretation of the statement that the probability is .95 that a ringer will be thrown? Does it mean that 95% of the shoes thrown will ring the peg? Or does it mean that 95% of the time the peg will come up through the horseshoe? The correct statement is fairly obvious. It is a particularly good example, because the wider the spread of the shoe, the more chance there is of making a ringer, other things being equal.[2]

There is a subtle distinction, though, between Bayesian and objectivist interpretations of confidence intervals. A Bayesian is willing to put probabilities on different possible values for μ, but an objectivist isn't. Thus, a Bayesian will say that there is a .95 probability that a particular confidence interval includes μ. The interpretation is that the Bayesian is indifferent between a bet that μ is somewhere in this particular interval and a bet that a red card will be selected from a box containing 19 red cards and 1 black card.

An objectivist resists putting probabilities on μ, because μ is a fixed parameter. The population mean μ either is 16 ounces or it isn't 16 ounces. It is not sometimes 16 ounces and sometimes 15 ounces. There is no relative frequency interpretation of a .95 probability for μ. Similarly, a strict objectivist will not say that there is a .95 probability that a particular interval, such as 15.99 ± 0.062 includes μ, because that would place a probability on something that has already occurred. What the strict objectivist will say is that, ''There is a .95 probability that the interval I am about to calculate contains μ'' or ''My interval is 15.99 ± 0.062; you should know that I chose my procedure anticipating that 95 percent of such intervals will include μ.''

Choosing a Sample Size

We took a sample of 10 boxes and calculated the average net weight to be 15.99 ounces. Recognizing that this is just a sample, we allow for sampling error by calculating a 95 percent confidence interval, based on the fact that 95 percent of the time, a normally distributed variable will be within two (actually, 1.96) standard deviations of its expected value. For a sample mean, the expected value is μ and the standard deviation is $\sigma/\sqrt{n}$. With $\sigma = 0.1$ and $n = 10$, the standard deviation of the sample mean works out to be 0.032 ounce. Thus, the 1.96 standard deviation margin for sampling error is 0.062 ounce, and we report our estimate as 15.99 ± 0.062 ounces.

How could we obtain a more precise estimate, that is, one with a smaller margin for sampling error? Well, the margin for sampling error is computed from

$$1.96(\sigma/\sqrt{n})$$

The 1.96 Z value comes from the normal table and there's nothing that can be done about that. The underlying standard deviation, $\sigma = 0.1$ ounce, comes from the manufacturing and packaging process, which the statistician has no control over. The only lever the statistician has is the sample size n. A larger sample will give a smaller margin for sampling error, as shown by the following illustrative calculations:

sample size n	margin for sampling error $1.96(\sigma/\sqrt{n})$
10	0.062
25	0.039

sample size	*margin for sampling error*
n	$1.96(\sigma/\sqrt{n})$
100	0.020
400	0.010
1,000	0.006
10,000	0.002

If we sample 100 boxes, our 95 percent confidence interval will be $\overline{X} \pm 0.02$ ounces, whatever the sample mean $\overline{X}$ turns out to be. With 10,000 boxes, the confidence interval will be $\overline{X} \pm 0.002$ ounces, again using whatever $\overline{X}$ turns out to be.

We can use these sorts of calculations to decide in advance how many boxes we want to sample. If we will settle for an estimate with a 0.062-ounce margin for sampling error, then 10 boxes is enough. If we need an estimate with only a 0.02-ounce margin for error, then 100 boxes are needed. If we need an extremely precise estimate, one that we are 95 percent sure will be within 0.002 ounce of μ, then we will have to open and weigh 10,000 boxes. The tradeoff, of course, is the time and energy spent on a larger sample plus the larger number of boxes that will be tested instead of sold.

In making this kind of choice, it is usually best to lay out a table of the alternatives, as I have done. You can then see at a glance exactly how the margin for sampling error varies with the size of the sample. Such a table isn't needed, of course, if you happen to know in advance exactly what margin of error you want. Perhaps you've decided that your estimate of net weights should be accurate to within 0.05 ounce. If so, then you can directly calculate the requisite sample size by setting the margin for sampling error, $1.96(\sigma/\sqrt{n})$, equal to 0.05. This equality,

$$1.96(\sigma/\sqrt{n}) = 0.05$$

implies

$$n = (1.96(\sigma)/0.05)^2$$

$$= (1.96(0.1)/0.05)^2$$

$$= 15.4$$

or 16 boxes, to be on the safe side. (If you are going to weigh 4/10 of a box, you may as well weigh the whole thing!)

Notice that one very interesting characteristic of this requisite sample size is that it does not depend on the size of the population. Regardless of whether the population consists of 100,000 boxes or 100,000,000 boxes, a 0.05 margin for sampling error requires a sample of 16 boxes. At first glance, this conclusion may seem surprising. If we're trying to estimate a characteristic of a large population, then there is a natural tendency to believe that a large sample is needed. If there are only 100 boxes in the population, then a sample of 16 uses 1 out of every 6 boxes. But, if there are 100,000 boxes in the population, then a sample of size 16 only looks at 1 out of every 6,000 boxes. And if there are 100 million in the population, then a sample of 16 uses only 1 out of every 6 million! If there are 100 million in the population, then how can we possibly obtain a reliable estimate with a sample of size 16, looking at just 1 out of every 6 million boxes?

A moment's reflection shows why the size of the population doesn't matter. Sampling error is present because the luck of the draw yields samples whose means differ from the population mean. What matters to these chances is the distribution of the population, and not its absolute size. In particular, sampling error depends on the number of boxes that are far from the population mean *relative* to the number near the mean, and not how many boxes there are altogether. Thus, the requisite sample size depends on the standard deviation of the population distribution, but not the size of the population.

In fact, our calculations implicitly assume that the population is infinite, because we don't adjust the probabilities even though we are sampling without replacement. The exact formula for the standard deviation of the sample mean when the sampling is without replacement from a finite population of size N is

$$\frac{\sigma}{\sqrt{n}} \sqrt{\frac{N - n}{N - 1}} \qquad\qquad (9.5)$$

The new term

$$\sqrt{\frac{n - 1}{N - 1}}$$

is known as the **finite population correction.** It scarcely matters whether a sample of 16 is drawn from a population of 100,000 or 100,000,000. The sample size n has to be pretty close to the population size N for our probability calculations to change significantly. The effect would be to shrink the confidence intervals and reduce the requisite sample sizes. If the population had only 16 boxes, for an extreme example, then a sample (without replacement) of 16 boxes would have no sampling error, because the sample mean is sure to be the population mean. In practice, the finite population correction is usually ignored unless the sample includes more than 20 percent of the population, i.e., $n > .2N$.

Once More

We have just been through the essential features of most statistical analyses, so let's recall the highlights. We want to estimate a population mean, here the average net weight of all of the boxes produced by a certain company. A random sample is selected and measurements are taken; in this case they are the net weights of the boxes. The average of these weights (the sample mean) is an estimate of the population mean. This estimate is subject to sampling error, because the particular sample selected depends on the luck of the draw. The sample mean may turn out to be above or below the population mean. This risk can be gauged by calculating a confidence interval, which is equal to the sample mean, plus or minus the margin for sampling error. With a 95 percent confidence interval, the margin for sampling error is $1.96(\sigma/\sqrt{n})$, or about two standard deviations of the sample mean. The larger the sample, the smaller the sampling error will be. The choice of a desired margin for sampling error determines the requisite size of the sample.

Exercises

9.1   The life of a Rolling Rock tire is normally distributed with a mean of 30,000 miles and a standard deviation of 5,000 miles. What are the probabilities that

a. a tire will last more than 30,000 miles?
b. a tire will last more than 40,000 miles?
c. the average life of four tires will be more than 30,000 miles?
d. The average life of four tires will be more than 40,000 miles?

9.2   The 50,000 students at Enormous University have an average age of 18.8 years, with a standard deviation of 1.7 years. The 25 students on an entertainment committee are selected at random from the student body. What is the probability that the average age of these 25 students will be under 18 years? To answer this question, do you have to assume that student ages are normally distributed?

9.3   A certain grade of oranges has a weight that is normally distributed with a mean of 9 ounces and a standard deviation of 1 ounce. What percent of these oranges weighs less than 8 ounces? These oranges are sold by the bag, with 25 oranges in each bag. What percent of these bags has a net weight of less than 200 ounces?

9.4   A package of Cow Country butter says "net weight = 16 ounces." The net weight is, in fact, normally distributed with a mean of 16.05 ounces and a standard deviation of 0.05 ounce. What proportion of the packages weigh less than 16 ounces? How high would the company have to raise the mean weight so that only 1 percent of the packages will weigh less than 16 ounces?

A government agency has decided to weigh a sample of Cow Country butter packages to see if the mean net weight really is at least 16 ounces. What is the probability that the average weight of n packages will be less than 16 ounces if $n = 1$? If $n = 4$? If $n = 16$? Why does this probability change as n increases?

9.5   The net weights of cracker boxes are normally distributed with the mean of 16 ounces and a standard deviation of 0.1 ounce. Assume that the standard deviation is known to be 0.1 ounce but that the mean is unknown. A sample of 10 boxes yields a sample mean of 15.99 ounces.

a. Construct a 90 percent confidence interval for the mean.
b. Construct a 95 percent confidence interval for the mean.
c. Construct a 99 percent confidence interval for the mean.
d. Is a 99 percent confidence interval wider or narrower than a 90 percent confidence interval? Carefully explain your answer.

9.6   Assume that Scholastic Aptitude Test (SAT) scores are normally distributed with a mean of 500 and a standard deviation of 100. If student SAT scores are picked at random:

a. What is the probability of picking a student whose math SAT score is above 650?

b. What is the probability of picking 100 students whose average math SAT score is above 650?

A certain college has an entering freshman class of 100 students whose average math SAT score is 650. Do you think that these freshmen are a random sample of the students who take the SAT test?

9.7 Explain why you agree or disagree with this reasoning:

. . . the household [unemployment] survey is hardly flawless. Its 60,000 families constitute less than 0.1 percent of the work force.[3]

9.8 What is the probability that a statistician who estimates 20 independent 95 percent confidence intervals will mistakenly miss a population mean at least once? Only once? Not at all?

9.2 A FEW EXAMPLES

Fishing Line Strength

The strength of a fishing line depends on its composition and thickness. However, even lines of the same material and thickness are not identical, because inevitably there are imperfections in the raw materials and in the manufacturing process. Because there are many such imperfections, let's assume that their effects on breaking strength are normally distributed. A certain company may make 30-weight nylon Proline fishing line with a breaking strength that is normally distributed, with a mean $\mu = 30$ pounds and a standard deviation $\sigma = 3$ pounds. A person who buys 30-weight nylon Proline is drawing fishing line from this normal population. Half the time, the line will turn out to have a breaking strength greater than 30 pounds, and half the time, the line purchased will have a smaller breaking strength. Ninety-five percent of the time, the line will have a breaking strength within two standard deviations of the mean, or between 24 and 36 pounds.

Now, let's say that a consumer research group wants to estimate the mean breaking strength of this fishing line. They take a sample of 25 lines and find that the average breaking strength of these lines is 30.5 pounds. To take into account sampling error, they note that when 25 items are drawn from a population with a standard deviation of 3 pounds, the mean of such a sample has a standard deviation of $\sigma/\sqrt{n} = 3/\sqrt{25} = 0.60$ pound. For a 95 percent confidence interval, a two-standard-deviation margin for sampling error is ± 1.2 pounds. Thus, the consumer group's conclusion is "The average breaking strength of 30-weight nylon Proline fishing line is 30.5 pounds ± 1.2 pounds."

Does the Enzyme Work or Doesn't It?

A pharmaceutical company tested a new enzyme that they hoped would increase the yield from a certain manufacturing process.[4] The data were calculated as the ratio of the actual yield with the enzyme to an assumed yield with the old process (based on a lot of past experience). A value of 110.2 meant that, in this particular test, the yield was 10.2 percent higher with the enzyme than with the old process. If the enzyme had no effect on the expected yield, then the measured yields should average about 100. A sample of 41 batches found an average yield of 125.2 with a standard deviation of 20.1. A member of the company's research department argued that

> There is no good theoretical reason for believing that the mean yield should be higher than 100 with the enzyme. Moreover, in the 41 batches studied, the standard deviation of individual yields was 20.1. In my opinion, 20 points represents a large fraction of the difference between 125 and 100. There is no real evidence that the enzyme increases yield.

This logic is wrong! It is the standard deviation of $\overline{X}$, and not the standard deviation of X, that is of interest. If the standard deviation of X is 20.1, then the standard deviation of $\overline{X}$ is only

$$\sigma/\sqrt{n} = 20.1/\sqrt{41} = 3.14$$

If the expected value is 100 and the standard deviation 20.1, then there is, indeed, a good chance that a single observation might be as high as 125, but there is not much chance that the average of 41 observations would be so high. A 95 percent confidence interval for the expected value of the yield with the enzyme is

$$\mu = \overline{X} \pm 2(\sigma/\sqrt{n})$$
$$= 125.2 \pm 2(3.13)$$
$$= 125.2 \pm 6.26$$

which is far from 100.

Insurance Risks

Insurance companies take advantage of the statistical fact that there is less uncertainty about an average outcome than about an individual outcome. Automobile accidents, fires, and serious illnesses are events that are very unlikely, but financially crippling if they do occur. There is a great risk for the individual, because we cannot predict who will be hit by catastrophe. However, there is little risk for a large group, to the extent that we can predict the number of automobile accidents, fires, and serious illnesses that will occur.

I'll use life insurance as an example. Assume that the age of death of men who are now 20 years old has a mean of 65 years and a standard deviation of 10 years. The individual does not know how long he will live, and the early death of a breadwinner can be financially crippling to a family. Consider an insurance company that writes life insurance policies for 10,000 20-year-old men. If we can assume that the deaths are independent (which insurance companies try to ensure by writing their policies to exclude war and other national catastrophes), then we can invoke the central limit theorem. The average age at death of these 10,000 men is normally distributed with a mean of 65 years and a standard deviation of $10/\sqrt{10,000} = 0.1$ year. There is only a .01 probability that a standardized normal variable Z will be less than -2.33. Thus, there is only a 1 percent chance that the average age at death of these 10,000 men will be 0.233 year (about 3 months) less than 65 years. The insurance company can confidently write insurance policies priced on the assumption that the average 20-year-old lives to be 65. There is little chance that the insurance company will be financially crippled.

Exercises

9.9   Whirltag claims that the useful lifetime of its dishwashers is normally distributed with a mean of 3 years and a standard deviation of 1 year. Consumer Rejects magazine tested 25 of these dishwashers and found that the average useful life was only 2.5 years. If Whirltag's claims are correct, what is the probability that the average life of 25 machines will turn out to be no greater than 2.5 years? Using Whirltag's reported 1-year standard deviation, what is Consumer Reject's 95 percent confidence interval for the average lifetime of Whirltag dishwashers?

9.10   The manufacturer of a television guarantees the picture tube for 2 years. The lifetimes of these picture tubes are normally distributed with a mean of 4 years and a standard deviation of 2 years.

a. What is the probability that one of these picture tubes will need to be replaced before the guarantee expires?
b. If it costs the manufacturer $200 to replace a picture tube, how much must be added to the price to cover the cost of the guarantee?
c. A consumer research group tested four of these televisions and found that none of the tubes failed within 2 years. What is the probability of this occurring?
d. The average lifetime of these four picture tubes turned out to be 5.1 years. Using a standard deviation of 2 years, what is a 95 percent confidence interval for the life of this manufacturer's picture tubes?

9.11   Over the period 1929–1933, scientists measured the speed of light 2,500 times and obtained an average value of 186,270 miles per second, with a standard deviation of 8.7 miles per second. Assuming that these are independent, unbiased measurements, find a 99 percent confidence interval for the speed of light.

9.12   A company wants to estimate the average Friday lunch break taken by its salaried executives. One Friday, 25 executives are monitored and it is found that their average lunch break is 94.6 minutes. If the standard deviation is assumed to be 25 minutes, calculate a 95 percent confidence interval for the average Friday lunch break for all this company's executives.

• **9.13**   (*continuation*) Sometimes statisticians report 50 percent confidence intervals, with the sampling error described as the *probable error*. The estimate of the mean lunch break, 94.6 minutes, is said to have a probable error of E minutes if there is a .5 probability that the interval 94.6 ± E includes the population mean. What would the value of E be in this example?

•• **9.14**   An elevator is designed to carry a maximum of 2000 pounds. The weights of the people who will use this elevator are normally distributed with a mean of 175 pounds and a standard deviation of 25 pounds. Government regulations specify that a sign must be posted saying, "Maximum capacity is *n* people" where *n* is chosen so that if *n* randomly chosen people are on the elevator, there is less than a 1 percent chance that their weight will exceed the maximum weight that the elevator can carry. What is the appropriate *n* for this elevator?

9.3   ESTIMATES OF THE STANDARD DEVIATION

So far, to simplify matters, I have assumed that the underlying standard deviation of cracker weights is known to be $\sigma = 0.1$ ounce. However, the standard deviation will seldom, if ever, be known by the statistician. It, too, is a parameter that must be estimated. The most natural course is to use the sample standard deviation as an estimate of the population standard deviation. The sample standard deviation *s* is the square root of the sample variance, which in turn is the average squared deviation of the data about the sample mean:

$$s^2 = \frac{(X_1 - \overline{X})^2 + (X_2 - \overline{X})^2 + \cdots + (X_n - \overline{X})^2}{n} \tag{9.6}$$

The relationship between the population variance and the sample variance is analogous to the relationship between the population mean and the sample mean. The *population mean* μ is the expected value of the random variable *X*, and is determined by the probabilities of observing the various values of *X*. The *sample mean* is an average of the observed values of *X*, and is determined by the how frequently each value of *X* happens to occur. The population mean and sample mean will be essentially equal in a very large sample in which the relative frequencies are very close to the probabilities. In the same way, the *population variance* σ^2 is the expected value of the squared deviation of *X* about the population mean μ. This expected value of the squared deviations is determined by the probabilities of observing the various values of *X*. The *sample variance* s^2 is an average of the observed squared deviations of *X* about its observed sample mean. This average value is determined by how frequently various values of *X* happen to occur. The population variance and sample variance will be essentially equal in a very large sample in which the relative frequencies are quite close to the probabilities.

There is one little hitch in this analogy, however. The sample variance is calculated from the squared deviations about the sample mean, instead of the true population mean. A brief appendix at the end of this chapter shows that, if the sample mean doesn't equal the population mean, then the squared deviations about the sample mean are always less than the squared deviations about the population mean. Thus, the sample variance is a biased estimator of the population variance. To correct this bias, we can use the adjusted sample variance.

The **adjusted sample variance**

$$s_a^2 = \frac{(X_1 - \overline{X})^2 + (X_2 - \overline{X})^2 + \cdots + (X_n - \overline{X})^2}{n - 1} \tag{9.7}$$

divides the sum of the sample squared deviations by $n - 1$ rather than n, to correct the bias introduced by the use of the calculated sample mean rather than the unknown population mean.

One inadequacy of this adjustment is that it relates to the bias of variance estimates, whereas it is usually the standard deviation that we are interested in. Our calculations of sampling error, confidence intervals, and the requisite sample sizes all use the standard deviation, and not the variance. It can be shown that s_a is, in fact, a biased estimator of the standard deviation! Unfortunately, statisticians don't know how to ensure an unbiased estimate of the standard deviation. The expected value of a square root is very complicated and depends on the particular probability distribution being analyzed, so some statisticians use s and others use s_a to estimate σ. In large samples, it doesn't make much difference which is used. If $n = 100$, for instance, then division by 100 or 99 will give almost the same answer.

Student's t Distribution

The need to estimate the standard deviation creates another source of uncertainty in gauging the reliability of the estimated mean. The sample mean is still a good estimator of the population mean, but the calculation of a 95 percent confidence interval, using Equation 9.4,

$$.95 = P[\overline{X} - 1.96(\sigma/\sqrt{n}) < \mu < \overline{X} + 1.96(\sigma/\sqrt{n})]$$

requires a value for the standard deviation σ. If we must estimate σ, then we cannot be quite so confident that our estimated interval will encompass μ. Sometimes, the confidence interval will miss μ, not because the sample mean is off, but rather because our estimate of the width of the confidence interval is off. This added uncertainty implies that we have to make the calculated confidence interval a little bit wider to allow a little more margin for error.

In 1908, W.S. Gosset figured out the exact widening that is needed. He was a statistician for the Irish brewery, Guinness, which encouraged statistical research but not publication. Gosset persuaded Guinness to allow his work to be published under the pseudonym "Student." His calculations became known as **Student's distribution.**

To standardize the sample mean, we subtract its expected value and divide by its standard deviation:

$$Z = \frac{\overline{X} - \mu}{\sigma/\sqrt{n}}$$

This variable has a standard $N[0, 1]$ distribution. Gosset wanted to find the distribution when the sample mean is standardized, using an estimate of the standard deviation:*

$$t = \frac{\overline{X} - \mu}{s_a/\sqrt{n}}$$

The distribution of t depends on the sample size n, because the reliability of the standard deviation estimate is greater when the sample size is larger. For an infinite sample, s_a should equal σ and the distributions of t and Z should coincide. With a small sample, s_a may be either much larger or smaller than σ and the distribution of t is consequently more dispersed than Z.

This dispersion depends not only on the size of the sample, but also on how many parameters must be estimated with the sample. The more data we have, the more confidence we can have in our results; the more parameters we have to estimate, the less confidence we have. Statisticians keep track of these two factors by calculating the **degrees of freedom:**

$$\begin{matrix} \text{degrees of} \\ \text{freedom} \end{matrix} = \begin{matrix} \text{number of} \\ \text{observations} \end{matrix} - \begin{matrix} \text{number of parameters that} \\ \text{must be estimated beforehand} \end{matrix}$$

Here, to construct a confidence interval, we calculated s_a by using n observations and estimating one parameter (the mean). Thus there are $n - 1$ degrees of freedom here.†

The distribution of t depends on the degrees of freedom, ranging from a normal distribution when $n - 1 = \infty$ to much more dispersed distributions for small $n - 1$. Figure 9.4 compares the distributions of Z and t for $n = 10$ (9 degrees of freedom); they are very similar, with the t distribution slightly more spread out. One way of gauging the greater dispersion of the t distribution is to see how wide an interval will encompass 95 percent of the observations. The probability is .95 that Z will be between -1.96 and $+1.96$. With $n = 10$, there is a .95 probability that t will be between -2.26 and $+2.26$. This implies that if we must estimate σ on the basis of 10 observations, then our 95 percent confidence interval should be

$$.95 = P[\overline{X} - 2.26(s_a/\sqrt{n}) < \mu < \overline{X} + 2.26(s_a/\sqrt{n})] \tag{9.8}$$

---

*Gosset used the adjusted sample standard deviation, but we could easily redo his calculations using the unadjusted sample standard deviation. Exercise 9.20 works out the details.

†There is another way to think of degrees of freedom that is more closely related to the name itself. We calculate s_a from n squared deviations about a mean, but this mean is calculated so that the sum of these n deviations is zero. Thus if we know $n - 1$ deviations, then we know the last deviation, too. Only $n - 1$ deviations are freely determined by the sample.

The confidence interval would be even wider for a smaller sample size. As the sample size increases, we are more confident of our estimate of σ and the margin for sampling error approaches ± 1.96 standard deviations, as when σ is known with certainty. The following table shows this pattern:

sample size n	degrees of freedom n − 1	95 percent confidence interval for μ
2	1	$\overline{X} \pm 12.71(s_a/\sqrt{n})$
5	4	$\overline{X} \pm 2.78(s_a/\sqrt{n})$
10	9	$\overline{X} \pm 2.26(s_a/\sqrt{n})$
15	14	$\overline{X} \pm 2.15(s_a/\sqrt{n})$
20	19	$\overline{X} \pm 2.09(s_a/\sqrt{n})$
25	24	$\overline{X} \pm 2.06(s_a/\sqrt{n})$
30	29	$\overline{X} \pm 2.05(s_a/\sqrt{n})$
∞	∞	$\overline{X} \pm 1.96(s_a/\sqrt{n})$

Frankly, the difference is usually pretty slight. If you have the 20 or 30 observations recommended for invoking the central limit theorem, then you also have a large enough sample to ignore the distinction between the normal distribution and Student's t distribution. A two-standard-deviations rule of thumb is close enough. It is more important to ensure the randomness of the sample than to worry about whether the margin for sampling error is precisely 2.05 or 1.96 standard deviations. But for those occasional very small samples, I've put several t distributions in Table 4 at the end of the book.

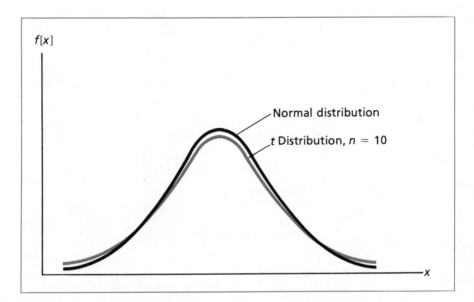

Figure 9.4   *A* t *distribution, in comparison with the normal distribution*

Exercises

9.15   *The Official Preppy Handbook*[5] claims that the students at Hamilton College are unusually short. Let's assume that the heights of male college students are normally distributed with a mean of 70 inches and a standard deviation of 3 inches. What is the probability that 900 male students, who are selected randomly with regard to height, will have an average height of less than 69.5 inches?

Now assume that 16 students at Hamilton College are selected at random and their heights measured. It turns out that the sample average is 66 inches and the adjusted sample standard deviation is 4 inches. Construct a 95 percent confidence interval for the average height of the students at Hamilton College.

9.16   An economist wants to estimate the average annual income of widows living in a certain city. A random sample of 25 widows gives a sample mean of $11,700 with an adjusted sample standard deviation of $2,400. Calculate a 90 percent confidence interval for the average income of the population.

9.17   A farmer wants to estimate the average wheat yield of some land that has been used to grow corn. Ten plots are set aside and planted with wheat. The yields (in bushels per acre) are

14.8	12.0	6.8	16.8	15.6
16.4	17.2	12.0	14.2	16.0

Use these data to construct a 95 percent confidence interval for the mean wheat yield of this farmland.

9.18   An investment counselor wants to estimate the average return from a certain investment, based on past experience. During the past 10 years, the percent returns have been

12	9	24	26	9
29	10	8	0	7

Use these data to construct a 95 percent confidence interval for the mean return from this investment.

9.19   A sample of 10 cracker boxes yielded the following net weights (in ounces):

16.10	16.01	15.82	15.93	16.05
16.05	15.86	15.90	16.05	16.13

a. What is the sample mean?
b. What are the sample standard deviation s and adjusted standard deviation s_a?
c. Use the adjusted standard deviation and the t distribution to construct a 95 percent confidence interval for the population mean μ.

•• **9.20**   (*continuation*) Use the unadjusted sample standard deviation and the t distribution to construct a 95 percent confidence interval for the population mean μ.

9.4 ESTIMATES OF A POPULATION PROPORTION OR SUCCESS PROBABILITY

In many sampling situations, we want to estimate a *population proportion* or *success probability*. Political polls, for instance, are used to estimate the fraction of the population who will vote for a candidate. Similarly, opinion polls estimate the proportion of the population who behave in certain ways or have certain opinions. Television polls estimate the proportions of the population who watch various television shows. Samples of manufactured products are used to estimate the fraction that are defective.

In probability analysis, our logic runs from assumed probabilities to predicted outcomes. We use the binomial distribution to tell us how likely we are to observe x successes in n trials, when the probability of success is assumed to be π. In statistical analysis, our logic runs in the other direction, from outcomes to probabilities; we observe x successes in n tests and want to use these data to estimate the probability of success π.

The statistical analysis of such tests follows exactly the same lines as when estimating a population mean. It is easy to see why this should be so. Think of each item sampled as being either a "success" or a "failure." These designations could correspond to "yes" or "no," "candidate A" or "not candidate A," or whatever is appropriate. Now let X be a random variable such that X equals 1 if the ith sampled item is a success and X equals 0 if it is a failure. The sample mean $\overline{X}$ is then the number of successes divided by the number of items tested, i.e., the fraction that are successes. Thus, the fraction that are successes is really just the sum of the observed values of X divided by n—a sample mean that can be analyzed by the very same procedures that you have already learned.

The Mean and Standard Deviation

The only quirk is in the relationship between the mean and the standard deviation. When X is normally distributed, the mean and standard deviation are specified separately, but when X can only equal 1 or 0, then there is an intimate relationship between the mean and standard deviation. If we take a sample of size n from a population in which the probability of a success is π, then the probability of x successes is given by the binomial distribution:

$$P[x \text{ successes in } n \text{ trials}] = \binom{n}{x} \pi^x (1 - \pi)^{n-x}$$

In Chapter 5, Equations 5.7 and 5.9 gave the expected value and standard deviation of the success proportion $p = x/n$ as

$$\mu = \pi \tag{9.9}$$

$$\sigma = \{\pi(1 - \pi)/n\}^{1/2} \tag{9.10}$$

The mean and standard deviation are both determined by the success probability π. Therefore, instead of separately specifying the mean and standard deviation, we specify π, and this jointly determines the mean and standard deviation.

A Political Poll

A political poll will illustrate the details of the statistical analysis. Two candidates, Mary Jones and John Martin, are running for governor. It so happens that 55 percent of the voting population favor Mary and 45 percent favor John. These population proportions are, of course, not known to anyone until after the votes are counted, but we can use a sample of voters to estimate them. If the poll is a genuine random sample, then each voter has an equal chance of being interviewed. As each participant is chosen, there is a $\pi = .55$ chance of picking a Mary supporter and a $1 - \pi = .45$ chance of picking a John partisan. A sample of 100 voters is taken and the results turn out to be

54 favor Mary

46 favor John

We want to use these data to estimate π and $1 - \pi$. The most natural estimator of the population proportion π is the sample proportion p:

$$p = 54/100 = .54$$

Indeed, as explained earlier, this corresponds precisely to using a sample mean to estimate the population mean.

Based on the outcome of this poll of 100 voters, we would estimate that 54 percent of the voters favor Mary and 46 percent favor John. We must realize though that samples are subject to sampling error. We only interviewed 100 voters and, even in a well-designed poll, the luck of the draw may turn up 54 people who favor an unpopular candidate. We can gauge the reliability of our poll result by estimating a margin for sampling error and a corresponding confidence interval for our estimate.

The central limit theorem tells us that the sample proportion p is normally distributed because it is a sample mean. It immediately follows that there is a .95 probability that the sample proportion p will be within two (actually 1.96) standard deviations of its expected value π. Equation 9.10 gives the standard deviation of p.

For a 95 percent confidence interval for a population proportion π, the margin for sampling error is

$$\pm 1.96\{\pi(1 - \pi)/n\}^{1/2} \tag{9.11}$$

or about ± 2 standard deviations of the population proportion p. The confidence interval is

$$.95 = P\left[p - 1.96\left\{\frac{\pi(1-\pi)}{n}\right\}^{1/2} < \pi < p + 1.96\left\{\frac{\pi(1-\pi)}{n}\right\}^{1/2}\right]$$

$$(9.12)$$

The shorthand formula is

$$\pi = p \pm 1.96\left(\frac{\pi(1-\pi)}{n}\right)^{1/2}$$

Notice, though, that the calculation of a confidence interval requires a value for π, which is the very thing we are trying to estimate. One logical solution is to use our estimate p.* A more conservative approach is to use $\pi = .5$, which gives the theoretical maximum value for the standard deviation of p. (You can quickly convince yourself of this mathematical fact by trying a few different values of π.) In practice, if p is close to .5, then it won't make much difference whether we use p or .5. But if p is close to 0 or 1, then the conservative confidence interval will be the much wider of the two. The following chart provides some illustrative calculations for $n = 100$:

π	$\pm 2\{\pi(1-\pi)/n\}^{1/2}$
.5	.100
.4 or .6	.098
.3 or .7	.092
.2 or .8	.080
.1 or .9	.060
.01 or .99	.020

In our political poll example, we have $p = .54$. If we use this estimate of π to calculate the standard deviation of p, we get

$$2\{\pi(1-\pi)/n\}^{1/2} = .0997$$

which is very close to the .10 margin for sampling error obtained when the conservative value $\pi = .5$ is used, so let's just use this latter value.

A margin of $\pm.10$ for sampling error implies that the 95 percent confidence interval that goes with our estimate of Mary's vote is

$$p = .54 \pm .10$$

or

$$.95 = P[.44 < p < .64]$$

---

*Just as s^2 is a biased estimator of σ^2, so $p(1-p)/n$ is a biased estimator of $\pi(1-\pi)/n$. This bias can be verified by again thinking of each outcome as a random variable that equals either 0 or 1. It then can be shown that $\pi(1-\pi)/n = \sigma^2$ and $p(1-p)/n = s^2$, and we already know that s^2 is a biased estimator of σ^2.

Based on our poll, we estimate that Mary will receive 54 percent of the votes, but because our sample only encompasses 100 voters, there is considerable uncertainty attached to that prediction. Our ±10 percent margin for sampling error is too large to rule out the possibility that John is actually the people's choice.

Choosing a Sample Size

Elections are almost always sufficiently close so that a ±10 percent margin for sampling error renders a poll inconclusive. The sampling error Equation 9.11 confirms our intuition that a more useful poll requires a larger sample. The following chart shows some illustrative calculations using $\pi = .5$:

sample size n	margin for sampling error $\pm\ 2\{\pi(1 - \pi)/n\}^{1/2}$
10	±.316
100	±.100
400	±.050
1,000	±.032
1,600	±.025
2,500	±.020
4,000	±.016
10,000	±.010

In general, if you know that the desired margin for sampling error is, say, .07, then you can solve for *n*:

$$2\{\pi(1 - \pi)/n\}^{1/2} = .07$$

implies

$$n = \frac{\pi(1 - \pi)}{(.07/2)^2}$$

$$= 204.1$$

for $\pi = .5$.

In practice, it is usually best to base one's choice on the previous table of options and a consideration of the costs of conducting different size samples. Sampling error falls very rapidly at first as the sample size increases. However, beyond $n = 1000$, significant reductions of sampling error require substantial increases in sample size. The choice of a sample size hinges on a comparison of the need for reliability with the costs of interviewing people. Modern political pollsters base their predictions on a sample of 1500 to 4000 people, giving a sampling error of around ±3 to ±1.5 percent.

Table 9.1 shows some data for the Gallup presidential polls. Several of the questions asked are used to predict whether or not the person will actually vote in the election. Only about 60 percent of those polled are identified as likely voters

Table 9.1 *The Gallup presidential poll's theoretical sampling errors and actual forecast errors**

Year	Number polled	Number of likely voters	Standard deviation	Sampling error assuming a simple random sample	Actual error
1952	5,385	3,350	0.9%	±1.9%	4.4%
1956	8,144	4,950	0.7%	±1.4%	1.7%
1960	8,015	5,100	0.7%	±1.4%	0.9%
1964	6,625	4,100	0.8%	±1.6%	2.7%
1968	4,414	2,700	1.0%	±2.0%	0.5%
1972	3,689	2,100	1.1%	±2.2%	0.2%
1976	3,439	2,000	1.1%	±2.2%	1.6%
1980	3,500	1,950	1.1%	±2.2%	4%

Source: The Gallup Poll (American Institute of Public Opinion).

*Gallup's estimates of the sampling error are somewhat larger since it is not a simple random sample.

and used to predict the outcome. If we assume that this 60 percent is a true random sample from the population of actual voters, then we can calculate the standard deviation and sampling errors as I have done. In theory, there is a .95 probability that the prediction will be within about two standard deviations of the actual election outcome. In practice, Gallup has missed by more than two standard deviations in four of these eight elections (1952, 1956, 1964, and 1980). However, two of these large misses were back in the 1950s shortly after Gallup had switched from quota sampling to cluster sampling, for the reasons explained in Chapter 8. It is tempting to believe that the polls have become more accurate over the years as pollsters have refined and improved their sampling procedures.

It must be remembered, too, that the Gallup poll is not a simple random sample. First, it is an approximation obtained from a sequence of selecting cities, precincts, and then people. Second, some of those selected may refuse to be interviewed, give misleading answers, or change their minds before the actual election. Third, there is inevitably a substantial chance for error in predicting which of the interviewees will actually vote. Public opinion polls present a most difficult sampling problem. There are very good reasons why the theoretical sampling error, which assumes a pure random sample, may substantially understate the margin for error in opinion polls. And yet, in the last several presidential elections, the pollsters' accuracy has been impressive.

Exercises

9.21 A sample of 100 voters finds that 54 prefer Mary while 46 prefer John. What is the probability of finding this strong a sample preference for Mary if, in fact,

a. 50 percent of all voters prefer John?
b. 55 percent of all voters prefer John?
c. 60 percent of all voters prefer John?

9.22   A poll will be conducted to predict the winner of the upcoming gubernatorial election. The pollsters want to be 95 percent certain that their prediction will be within 2 percentage points of the actual result. How large a sample do they need to reduce their sampling error to this level?

9.23   Charlie Hustle is a professional baseball player. Each time at bat, he has a .3 probability of getting a hit and a .7 probability of making an out. Batting averages are calculated by dividing the number of hits by the number of times at bat. A person who gets 50 hits in 200 times at bat is batting .250 and is said to be hitting "two-fifty." Assume that Charlie Hustle has 500 times at bat each baseball season. What are the probabilities that he will have a batting average of

a. at least .300 next season?
b. at least .325 next season?
c. at least .350 next season?
d. at least .400 next season?
e. at least .325 over the next five seasons?

9.24   It's two weeks before the election and an underdog politician is favored by only 45 percent of the voters. Badly needing some last-minute financial support, this desperate politician commissions three private pollsters to each poll 100 people. What is the probability that at least one of these pollsters will predict that this politician will win the election? If the politician releases only the most favorable of the three poll results, why will this be a biased sample?

9.25   A pollster asked people if they thought a poll of only 2000 people could be trusted. The answers were 47 percent "yes," 45 percent "no," and 8 percent "undecided." How would you answer? Explain your reasoning.

• 9.26   In political polls, the margin for sampling error depends on the standard deviation of the sample proportion p: $\{\pi(1 - \pi)/n\}^{1/2}$. Use calculus to show that this standard deviation is maximized by $\pi = .5$.

• 9.27   Probability theory claims that if the probability of some event is $1/2$, then in a very large number of trials the relative frequency with which this event occurs is "almost certain" to be "very close" to $1/2$. To make this claim more precise, consider the flip of a fair coin with the probability of obtaining heads apparently equal to $1/2$. Let p be the fraction of n flips in which heads appear. Calculate $P[.5 - .001 < p < .5 + .001]$ for

a. $n = 10{,}000$
b. $n = 1{,}000{,}000$
c. $n = 100{,}000{,}000$

9.5   SUMMARY

Samples are used to estimate characteristics of a population; for instance, a sample mean is used to estimate a population mean and a sample proportion is used to estimate a success probability. Such estimates are subject to sampling error, in that the luck of the draw determines the particular sample that will be obtained.

If a random variable X is normally distributed with mean μ and standard deviation σ, then the mean $\overline{X}$ of a sample of size n will also be normally distributed,

$$\overline{X} \sim N[\mu, \sigma/\sqrt{n}]$$

Notice that the expected value of the sample mean is equal to the expected value of X. Thus, $\overline{X}$ is said to be an unbiased estimator of X. The standard deviation of the sample mean gauges the variation to be expected in $\overline{X}$ from one sample to the next. The larger the sample size n, the smaller the standard deviation.

Even if X itself is not normally distributed, the central limit theorem tells us that the mean of a random sample will tend to be normally distributed as n increases. In practice, the usual rule of thumb is that a normal approximation is satisfactory for a sample size of around 20 or 30.

Confidence intervals are a standard way of measuring the degree of sampling error. There is a .95 probability that a sample mean will be within approximately two of its standard deviations of the expected value μ. Thus estimates are commonly written as

$$\mu = \overline{X} \pm 2(\sigma/\sqrt{n})$$

The interpretation is that 95 percent of the intervals so constructed should encompass the true population mean μ.

The confidence interval formula is usually used to compute a margin for sampling error to accompany our estimates. If we know our desired margin for sampling error in advance, then we can use the confidence interval formula to determine the requisite sample size.

If X is normally distributed and, as is usually the case, the standard deviation σ is not known but must be estimated, then Student's t distribution can be used in place of the normal distribution for figuring confidence intervals. The effect is to make the confidence interval more than two estimated standard deviations wide, and thus take into account our possible error in estimating the standard deviation. In practice, if the sample is large enough to invoke the central limit theorem, then there is not much difference between a normal distribution and Student's t distribution.

A very similar logic applies when a success probability π is estimated by the sample proportion p, giving the fraction of the observed outcomes that are successes. If we now think of the random variable X as equaling 1 if the outcome is a success and 0 if a failure, then the sample proportion p is just a sample mean and can be analyzed like any other sample mean. The only new wrinkle is that both the expected value of p and its standard deviation are determined by π:

$$\mu = \pi$$

$$\sigma = \{\pi(1 - \pi)/n\}^{1/2}$$

APPENDIX: SOME STANDARD DEVIATION ARITHMETIC

The sum of the squared deviations about the sample mean can be rewritten as

$$(X_1 - \bar{X})^2 + \cdots + (X_n - \bar{X})^2$$

$$= (X_1 - \mu + \mu - \bar{X})^2 + \cdots + (X_n - \mu + \mu - \bar{X})^2$$

$$= (X_1 - \mu)^2 + \cdots + (X_n - \mu)^2$$

$$+ (\bar{X} - \mu)^2 + \cdots + (\bar{X} - \mu)^2$$

$$- 2(\bar{X} - \mu)\{(X_1 - \mu) + \cdots + (X_n - \mu)\}$$

$$= (X_1 - \mu)^2 + \cdots + (X_n - \mu)^2 - n(\bar{X} - \mu)^2$$

$$- 2(\bar{X} - \mu)\{(X_1 - \bar{X} + \bar{X} - \mu) + \cdots + (X_n - \bar{X} + \bar{X} - \mu)\}$$

$$= (X_1 - \mu)^2 + \cdots + (X_n - \mu)^2 - n(\bar{X} - \mu)^2$$

because the sum of the deviations about the sample mean is zero. Thus, the sum of the squared deviations about the sample mean is less than the sum of the squared deviations about the population mean by an amount equal to $n(\bar{X} - \mu)^2$.

Now, if we take the expected values of both sides of this equation (and use the fact that the variance of the sample mean is σ^2/n), we get

$$E[(X_1 - \bar{X})^2 + \cdots + (X_n - \bar{X})^2] = n\sigma^2 - \sigma^2$$

$$= (n - 1)\sigma^2$$

It follows that dividing the sum of squared deviations about the sample mean by n gives a biased estimator of σ^2, while dividing by $n - 1$ gives an unbiased estimator.

REVIEW EXERCISES

9.28   Estimate the number of words in this book. Explain how you made your estimate.

9.29   Use a random sample to estimate the fraction of the students at your school who are female. Explain how you constructed your sample.

9.30   The gasoline mileage for A cars is normally distributed with a mean of 26 miles per gallon (mpg) and a standard deviation of 4 mpg. If an impartial group computes the average mpg for a sample of these cars, what is the probability that their average will be greater than 30 mpg if only 1 car is tested? If 25 cars are tested?

9.31   (*continuation*) Why does gasoline mileage have a probability distribution in the first place? If the average mpg of 25 cars turns out to be 30, then doesn't that show that the mean is, in fact, 30 and not 26? Finally, why is there a probability that the average mpg of 25 cards will be greater than 30, less than 20, or some other value?

9.32 (*continuation*) Was the assumption that mileage is normally distributed crucial to your calculation? Explain your reasoning.

9.33 A consumer research group believes that the lives of television picture tubes are normally distributed with a standard deviation of 2 years. How many sets must they test if they want to be 95 percent sure that their estimate of the mean lifetime will not be off by more than

a. 2 years?
b. 1 year?
c. 1 month?

● **9.34** If we want to halve the size of the confidence interval, then must we double the size of the sample?

●● **9.35** In a boxed example on page 289, I asserted that the sample mean of the measured distances is the least squares estimate of the true distance. Use calculus to show that this assertion is true.

9.36 The Gallup poll interviews fewer than 4000 people to predict who almost 100,000,000 voters will elect President of the United States. How can they make accurate predictions when they only interview 1 out of every 25,000 voters?

9.37 Chisler Corporation is considering issuing a three-year warranty for major repairs on its cars. It would like to be 95 percent sure that its estimate of the probability of a major repair is within .01 of the actual probability. How many cars must it test to obtain this accurate an estimate?

9.38 There are 10,000 people and one hospital in Smalltown. On any given day, there is a .001 probability that a person will require a hospital bed. How many beds must the hospital have to be 99.9 percent sure that, on any given day, there will be enough beds for everyone who requires one?

9.39 A random sample of 1000 homes finds that 999 have television sets. Find a 95 percent confidence interval for the percentage of all homes that have television sets.

9.40 The Nielson television ratings are based on a sample of 1200 homes out of a population of 80,000,000 homes. If they estimate that 30 percent of these homes were watching a football game, what is their margin for sampling error?

9.41 A critic of a 1952 government survey wrote

> Only 25,000 families were interviewed. . . . The main fault of the report is the limited scope of its available figures. 25,000 families are not a sound representation for the 46,000,000 families in the U.S.[6]

Is this logic sound?

9.42 A friend claims that she has a special coin-flipping technique that causes heads to come up more often than tails. Hearing of your statistical training, she asks you to estimate accurately the probability of obtaining a heads with this special technique. How many times must she flip a coin for you to be 99 percent sure that your estimate is within .01 of the true probability of heads?

•• **9.43** (*continuation*) Your friend says that she cannot sustain her special technique through a long series of trials, so you will have to estimate her probability of heads based on just a small sample. What is your 99 percent confidence interval for her probability of heads if she gets

a. 3 heads in 4 flips?
b. 7 heads in 10 flips?
c. 13 heads in 20 flips?

• **9.44** (*continuation*) Which of the preceding three sample results would you consider more convincing evidence that your friend really can flip heads more than half the time?

• **9.45** A government agency wants to estimate the number of fish in a lake. They catch 100 fish, tag them, and put them back in the lake. A short while later, they catch another 100 fish and find that 10 have been tagged. Think of this second batch as a random sample of all of the fish in the lake. Based on this sample, what is your estimate of the fraction of the fish in the lake that are tagged? Because you know that 100 fish are tagged, what is your estimate of the total number of fish in the lake?

• **9.46** Engineers are trying to estimate the probability π that a certain system will work. So far, it has been successful in 8 out of 10 trials. The chances of succeeding 8 times in 10 trials depends of course on the probability of success π. What is the exact formula for the probability of 8 successes in 10 trials? For what value of π is this probability highest?

• **9.47** A circle has a radius ρ and an area $\pi\rho^2$. It is difficult to measure the radius of a circle accurately. We can view a measurement as a random variable X that has an expected value equal to the true radius ρ. Two statisticians have measured the radius of a circle and obtained measurements X_1 and X_2.

a. Is the average of their measurements, $r = (X_1 + X_2)/2$, an unbiased estimator of the radius ρ?
b. Is πr^2 an unbiased estimator of the area $\pi\rho^2$?
c. If they each estimate the area and then average, $(\pi X_1^2 + \pi X_2^2)/2$, will they have an unbiased estimator of the area?

(*Hint:* the variance of X can be written as $\sigma^2 = E[X^2] - \mu^2$.)

•• **9.48** Statistical theory assumes, for convenience, that sampling is done with replacement, while the usual statistical practice is to sample without replacement. This exercise is intended to explore the implications of this divergence between theory and practice. Consider a population of 10 machines, of which 5 are acceptable and 5 are defective. A prospective buyer does not know that half of these machines are defective, but has decided to test 4 of them. Let p be the fraction of these sampled machines that turns out to be defective.

a. What are the possible values of p?
b. What are the probabilities of these different values of p if the sampling is done with replacement?
c. What are the probabilities if the sampling is done without replacement?
d. Is sampling with replacement or without replacement more likely to give a value of p that is close to the population value .5?
e. Why?
f. Does this conclusion suggest that the true margin for sampling error is larger or smaller than the margin that we calculate by assuming sampling with replacement?

•• **9.49** Two statisticians are trying to estimate the mean shelf-life of a new drug. The first statistician has tested a sample of 25 packages and obtained an average shelf-life of $\overline{X}_1 = 48$ months. The second statistician has tested 100 packages and found an average shelf-life of $\overline{X}_2 = 40$ months. The government wants to combine these two independent samples into a single estimate. Show that the standard deviation of $\overline{X}_1$ is twice as large as the standard deviation of $\overline{X}_2$. The following formulas have been suggested for obtaining a combined estimate:

a. $(1/2)\overline{X}_1 + (1/2)\overline{X}_2$
b. $(1/3)\overline{X}_1 + (2/3)\overline{X}_2$
c. $(1/4)\overline{X}_1 + (3/4)\overline{X}_2$
d. $(1/5)\overline{X}_1 + (4/5)\overline{X}_2$
e. $\overline{X}_2$

Which, if any, of these estimates are unbiased? Which has the smallest standard deviation? (*Note:* The variance of $a\overline{X}_1 + b\overline{X}_2$ is a^2(variance of $\overline{X}_1$) + b^2(variance of $\overline{X}_2$).)

•• **9.50** A random sample $X_1, X_2, \ldots, X_n$ can be used in many different ways to estimate μ, the expected value of X. Some possible estimators are X_1, $(X_1 + X_2)/2$, and $(3X_1 + 2X_2 + X_3)/4$. Each of these estimators is an example of a linear combination of the data:

$$\hat{\mu} = \alpha_1 X_1 + \alpha_2 X_2 + \cdots + \alpha_n X_n$$

a. What constraint must be placed on the α_1 to ensure that the estimator is unbiased?
b. Which unbiased linear estimator has the smallest variance? (Use calculus.)

CHAPTER 10

Hypothesis Tests

It is a capital mistake to theorize before you have all the evidence. It biases the judgements.

Sherlock Holmes

TOPICS

10.1   INTRODUCTION

One of the most commonly encountered statistical inferences is the use of data to confirm or refute theories. Chapter 8 related how nearly two million school children participated in a nationwide test of the effectiveness of the Salk polio vaccine. Data have been used to test the theories that vitamin C wards off colds, that cigarette smoking is dangerous to your health, and that rich people are smarter than poor people. Data have also been used to support the contention that minorities have been systematically excluded from certain schools, occupations, and juries. National income data were used to test Keynes's theory that consumer spending depends on income.

It would be nice if data such as these could prove conclusively that a theory is either true or false, but in this uncertain world, few things are 100 percent certain. The data are almost always a sample and therefore subject to sampling error. A new sample might turn out to be sufficiently different from the first to discredit a previously confirmed theory. For example, one theory might be that a certain presidential candidate is favored by a majority of the voters. Data related to this theory are provided by a random sample of 400 voters. If 52 percent of those surveyed prefer this candidate, then these data support the theory that the candidate is the people's choice. But a second survey of another 400 voters may find that 53 percent favor the other candidate. We cannot be certain who will win until all of the votes have been counted.

Most theories are in a permanent state of uncertainty because there is no final counting of the votes; more data are always coming in. There are always new experiments and fresh observations of the world around us. Social scientists have so few data that old results can easily be undone by a few more observations of people's behavior. Keynes's consumption function was confirmed in the 1940s and found inadequate in the 1950s. Even in the physical sciences, where innumerable laboratory experiments can generate mountains of data, theories remain fragile. Edward Leamer, a very talented UCLA statistician, wrote that,

> All knowledge is human belief, more accurately human opinion. What often happens in the physical sciences is that there is a high degree of conformity of opinion. When this occurs, the opinion held by most is asserted to be an objective fact, and those who doubt it are labeled "nuts." But history is replete with examples of opinions losing majority status, with once objective "truths" shrinking into the dark corners of social intercourse.[1]

Scientists are always thinking of new ways to test old theories or fresh ways to interpret old data, and thus the weaknesses of old theories may become exposed.

If we can never be sure that a theory is true, then the next best thing would be to make probability statements such as, "Based on the available data, we are 90 percent certain that this theory is true." A Bayesian wouldn't hesitate to say this, but the classical, objectivist interpretation of probabilities precludes such statements because objectivists believe that a theory is either true or it isn't. A theory can't be true 90 percent of the time and false 10 percent of the time, with its truth or falsity determined each day by a playful god's random-number generator.

Statistics has followed another route. Instead of this forbidden conditional probability,

$$P[\text{theory is true} \mid \text{observed data}]$$

statisticians calculate the reverse conditional probability,

$$P[\text{observed data} \mid \text{theory is true}]$$

The first statement says, given the available data, this is the probability that the theory is true. The second statement says, if this theory were true, this is the probability that the data would look like they do.

These are two very different statements, and a recognition of the difference is crucial to an understanding of the meaning and limitations of classical hypothesis tests. Hypothesis tests are really an attempted proof by *statistical contradiction*. For any particular theory, statisticians can deduce that, if the theory is true, then a sample of data is likely to look like this and unlikely to look like that; then they go out and gather some data. If these sample data are the likely kind, then the data are consistent with the theory and, so, the theory is confirmed. If, on the other hand, the data are the unlikely kind, then the data are not consistent with the theory, and the theory is refuted.

A theory is rejected if it can be shown statistically that the data we observe would be very unlikely to occur if the theory were in fact true. In this sense, it is a proof by statistical contradiction. Because the data are unlikely if the theory were true, we conclude that the theory is not true. Of course, we are never 100 percent certain, because the unlikely may well have happened. Notice, too, that for a theory to be accepted, it need only not be rejected by the data. This is a relatively weak conclusion, because there are invariably many other theories that are consistent with the data, too. In the next section we'll look at a specific example to make these ideas more concrete.

Exercises

10.1   There are two candidates for governor, Wiseman and Fullhead, and on the eve of the election each predicts that he will get 53 percent of the vote. A random sample of 100 voters finds 49 percent for Wiseman and 51 percent for Fullhead. Whose claim is supported by these data? Why would an objectivist resist giving a probability that Wiseman is the people's choice?

10.2   (*continuation*) Explain what each of these probability statements means:

a. $P[51 \text{ percent of those polled favor Fullhead} \mid 53 \text{ percent of the voters favor Fullhead}]$
b. $P[53 \text{ percent of the voters favor Fullhead} \mid 51 \text{ percent of those polled favor Fullhead}]$

Which probability statement would an objectivist feel most comfortable with?

10.3   (*continuation*) Which of these probabilities do you think is larger:

P[51 percent of those polled favor Fullhead | 53 percent of the voters favor Wiseman] or P[51 percent of those polled favor Fullhead | 53 percent of the voters favor Fullhead]? Check your reasoning by computing these probabilities.

● **10.4**   (*continuation*) If we were to use Bayes' formula to compute P[53 percent of the voters favor Fullhead | 51 percent of those polled favor Fullhead], what information would we need? How could we interpret a Bayesian probability that Wiseman is the people's choice?

● **10.5**   (*continuation*) Assuming that, prior to the poll, we believe that each candidate's claim is equally likely to be correct, P[Wiseman will get 53 percent of the vote] = P[Fullhead will get 53 percent of the vote] = .5. (For simplicity, assume that no other outcomes are possible!) Compute the revised probabilities, taking the poll into account: P[53 percent of the voters favor Wiseman | 51 percent of those polled favor Fullhead] and P[53 percent of the voters favor Fullhead | 51 percent of those polled favor Fullhead].

10.2   CRAMMING FOR THE MATH SAT TEST

Let's consider a firm's claim that its two-week cram course can raise student scores on the math Scholastic Achievement Test (SAT) by 50 points. Average SAT scores for the nation do vary slightly from year to year, but here we'll assume that math SAT scores are normally distributed with a mean of 500 and a standard deviation of 100.

Let's imagine that we work for a consumer advisory group who wants to test this firm's claim. A natural procedure would be to enroll a random sample of say 25 students in this course and then see how well they do on the math SAT test.* If these students' average score is 550, then the firm's claim would seem to be supported. If their average score is only 500, then the firm's claim would seem to be refuted. But matters are not that simple, because we only have data for a small random sample. The students' average score will probably not turn out to be either exactly 500 or exactly 550. There is inevitably going to be some sampling error, because the 25 students selected by chance may be either above average or below average. Their average score may be 452, 521, 554 or some other number.

There are two implications. First, we can anticipate an average score other than the convenient numbers 500 or 550. Second, whatever the score and whatever the conclusion we draw, sampling error may lead us astray. Even if the course is worthless, we may happen, by the luck of the draw, to pick 25 above-average students who score 550 on their own. Seeing their 550 scores after having taken the course, we may erroneously conclude that the course added 50 points to their scores.

---

*Another possible design is to have 25 students take the math SAT, take the cram course, and then take the SAT again to see if there is any improvement in their scores. The problem with this procedure is that their scores may improve simply from the experience gained by taking the test.

Taking sampling error into account, how well do the 25 students have to score to convince us that the course is worthwhile? An average score of 500 is certainly unconvincing, and an average of 505 or 510 is not very impressive either. But what about 520? Or 530? Or 548? Where do we draw the line and say, "Now, those are sufficiently high scores to persuade me that this course is worthwhile"?

The Chances of Incorrectly Accepting a Useless Course

Let's think a bit more about the likely size of the sampling error. If the course is worthless, then our sample of 25 students will be drawn from a population whose scores X are normally distributed with a mean $\mu = 500$ and a standard deviation $\sigma = 100$,

$$X \sim N[500, 100]$$

The average score $\overline{X}$ of a sample of size 25 is normally distributed, too, with a mean $\mu = 500$ and a standard deviation $\sigma/\sqrt{n} = 100/\sqrt{25} = 20$:

$$\overline{X} \sim N[500, 20]$$

This distribution of the sample mean is shown in Figure 10.1.

An average score of 510 is unimpressive because, even if the course is worthless, there is a .31 probability that we will select 25 students who do at least this well. If we allow ourselves to be convinced by an average score of 510, then there is a .31 probability that we will be persuaded that a worthless course is worthwhile.

The .31 probability shown in Figure 10.1 was calculated by standardizing $\overline{X}$ to be a $Z \sim N[0,1]$ variable that can be looked up in Table 2:

$$P[\overline{X} > 510] = P\left[\frac{\overline{X} - \mu}{\sigma/\sqrt{n}} > \frac{510 - 500}{100/\sqrt{25}}\right]$$

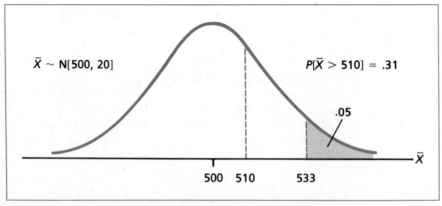

Figure 10.1   *The distribution of the sample mean $\overline{X}$ of 25 math SAT scores when a preparation course is worthless*

$$= P[Z > 0.5]$$

$$= .31$$

An average score of 510 is too easy a hurdle, in that there is too high a probability that a worthless course will clear this hurdle. We want a criterion that is sufficiently difficult that there is only a small chance that a worthless course will appear effective. We are trying to distinguish between merit and luck here and, to do so, we need to set a cutoff point that is unlikely to be achieved by luck alone.

A standard rule is to set a cutoff point so that there is only a 5 percent chance that a worthless test will appear worthwhile. In the next chapter, we'll scrutinize the logic behind this rule; for now, let's just work out the details of its application. How much higher do we have to raise the hurdle to reduce that probability from .31 to .05? Table 2 tells us that there is a .05 probability that Z will exceed 1.65. Our standardized variable is $Z = (\overline{X} - \mu)/(\sigma/\sqrt{n})$. We can combine these two facts to obtain the answer:

$$.05 = P[Z > 1.65]$$

$$= P\left[\frac{\overline{X} - \mu}{\sigma/\sqrt{n}} > 1.65\right]$$

$$= P[\overline{X} > \mu + 1.65(\sigma/\sqrt{n})]$$

$$= P[\overline{X} > 500 + 1.65\,(100/\sqrt{25})]$$

$$= P[\overline{X} > 533]$$

Notice the characteristic form. There is a .05 probability that Z will exceed 1.65. Therefore, there is a .05 probability that the sample mean will be 1.65 standard deviations above its expected value. Because the standard deviation of the sample mean is 20 and the expected value is assumed to be 500, there is a .05 probability that the sample mean will exceed $500 + 1.65(20) = 533$.

Let's run through the statistical logic again, because we will use it over and over again. The population consists of students whose math SAT scores are normally distributed with a mean of 500 and a standard deviation of 100. We pick 25 students from this population, enroll them in this course, and then see how well they do on the math SAT. If these 25 students obtain an average score of 533 or higher, then we will be persuaded that the course has some value. If the course is, in fact, worthless, there is a 5 percent chance that we will pick 25 students who average 533 or higher all by themselves. But that substantial a sampling error is sufficiently unlikely, so that an average score of 533 persuades us that something more than the luck of the draw is involved.

The Chances of Incorrectly Rejecting a Useful Course

Sampling error can, of course, work in the other direction, too. We may happen to pick 25 below-average students who would score only 450 on their own. Even if the course does, as advertised, raise their scores by 50 points, these below-

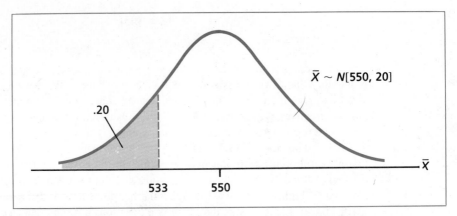

Figure 10.2   *The distribution of the sample mean $\overline{X}$ of 25 math SAT scores when a preparation course raises scores by 50 points*

average students will still only score 500. Seeing their 500 scores, we will erroneously conclude that the course is worthless. Or we might pick 25 students who would average 480 on their own and 530 with the course. Because 530 is below 533, we would again mistakenly conclude that the course didn't work as advertised.

Figure 10.2 shows how to figure the probability of making this kind of mistake. If the course does raise math SAT scores by 50 points, then our sample is drawn from a population that, after taking the course, would average $\mu = 550$ with a standard deviation $\sigma = 100$. The average score $\overline{X}$, for the 25 students we happen to pick, comes from a normal distribution with an expected value $\mu = 550$ and a standard deviation $\sigma/\sqrt{n} = 100/\sqrt{25} = 20$. The probability that the sample mean will fall below the 533 cutoff point is

$$P[\overline{X} < 533] = P\left[\frac{\overline{X} - \mu}{\sigma/\sqrt{n}} < \frac{533 - 550}{100/\sqrt{25}}\right]$$

$$= P[Z < -0.85]$$

$$= .1977$$

or, roughly 20 percent.*

Sampling error inevitably implies that there are two kinds of erroneous statistical conclusions that can be drawn. We may conclude that a worthless course is useful or we may conclude that a useful course is worthless. With a 533 cutoff point, there is a 5 percent chance that a bad course will appear to be successful and a 20 percent chance that a good course will appear to be a failure.

Notice that we did not try to calculate the probability that the course is useful.

---

*Equivalently, we could find the probability of picking 25 students who would score less than 483 on their own and, hence, less than 533 after taking a course that raises their scores by 50 points. As Exercise 10.8 shows, this probability also is 20 percent.

We resisted putting a probability on the value of the course, because objectivists insist that it isn't a fit subject for a probability: either the course works or it doesn't. Instead, we calculated the probability of an average score above 533 if the course is, in fact, useless and the probability of an average score below 533 if the course is, in fact, useful.

This logic, plus the inevitable sampling error, is why we never "prove" theories to be true or false. Instead, we say that the data "reject" a theory in the sense that, were the theory true, such data would be very unlikely. A theory that is "accepted" by the data is one that is consistent with the data in the sense that the deviation between theory and experience can plausibly be explained by sampling error. An average score of 520 by 25 students doesn't prove that the course is worthless. It is just that a 520 average could well be due to the luck of the draw (sampling error) and, so, is not sufficiently improbable to rule out an expected value of 500.

Exercises

10.6 *The Los Angeles Times* reported the following story.

> They all laughed when Texas A&M Coach Jackie Sherrill came up with his version of the 12th Man, a kick-off return team made up entirely of students.
>
> It's no longer a joke. Going into today's game against Texas, the 12th-man unit has allowed an average of only 13.6 yards per return.
>
> "These guys cover kickoffs better than anybody who plays against us," Sherrill said.
>
> And A&M's road kickoff-return unit, made up of regular players since the 12th-Man team doesn't travel, is allowing more than 18 yards per return.
>
> Even the White House has been impressed. After a presidential press aide attended an Aggies game, President Reagan sent each 12th Man member an autographed picture along with a personal message.[2]

What other information would you like to see before concluding that the students cover kickoffs better than the football players?

10.7 The text uses the example of gauging the effects of a cram course on math SAT scores. In this example, 25 students are selected at random, enrolled in the course, and then given the math SAT. Why do you suppose the students were picked at random and then enrolled in the course, rather than picked at random from those already enrolled in the course?

10.8 In the SAT example, math scores were assumed to be normally distributed with a mean of 500 and a standard deviation of 100. What is the probability that a random sample of 25 students will have an average score of less than 483 on their own and, hence, less than 533 after taking a course that raises their scores by 50 points?

10.9 A professor claims that the college's education majors have an average IQ of 80, as compared to a mean of 100 for the population as a whole. We'll assume that the standard deviation is 15 in either case. If 25 education majors are selected at random, what is the probability that their average IQ will be below 90

a. if this professor is right?

b. if the college's education majors have an average IQ of 100?

c. if the college's education majors have an average IQ of 120?

10.10   (*continuation*) The Dean of the School of Education claims that the average IQ of the college's education majors is 110. To test the competing claims of the dean and the professor, a random sample of 25 education majors will be selected and their IQs determined. What cutoff should be used for accepting the professor and rejecting the dean if we want only a 5 percent chance that the dean's claim will be rejected if it is, in fact, true? If we use this cutoff, what is the probability that we will accept the dean's claim if, in fact, the average IQ of education majors is 80?

10.3   A GENERAL FRAMEWORK

The SAT example illustrates the logic that underlies statistical tests of all sorts of hypotheses. This logic has been codified into a standard framework, with the appropriate jargon. I'll describe this framework here and then we'll apply it to several situations.

The Null and Alternative Hypotheses

This statistical analysis is designed to choose between two competing theories. One theory is labeled the **null hypothesis, H_0** while the other is labeled the **alternative hypothesis, H_1**. This terminology comes from the fact that the null hypothesis is often that there is no, or *null*, effect. This is true in our example, where the competing theories are two different expected values μ for the math SAT scores of students who take a cram course:

$$H_0: \mu = 500$$

$$H_1: \mu = 550$$

The null hypothesis is that the course has no effect, while the alternative hypothesis is that it raises scores by 50 points. Data are used to choose between these two competing hypotheses, accepting one and rejecting the other.

Typically, we gather data that we hope represents a random sample and then, based on these data, choose between the two hypotheses. In the example, we picked 25 students, had them take the cram course, and then we calculated their average SAT score. Our *decision rule* (cutoff point) was to accept H_0 if the sample mean turns out to be less than 533 and to reject H_0 if it is greater than 533.

Type I and Type II Errors

Whichever hypothesis is correct, there is a chance that sampling error will cause us to reject that hypothesis. We may reject a null hypothesis that is true or we may accept a null hypothesis that is false. These two types of mistakes are imaginatively called Type I and Type II errors.

A **Type I error** rejects a null hypothesis that is true. A **Type II error** accepts a null hypothesis that is false.

The probabilities of committing these errors are labeled α and β:

$$\alpha = P[\text{Type I error}] = P[\text{reject } H_0 \mid H_0 \text{ is true}]$$

$$\beta = P[\text{Type II error}] = P[\text{accept } H_0 \mid H_0 \text{ is false}]$$

The actual probabilities depend, of course, on where the cutoff point is drawn for choosing between the two hypotheses. In the example, the 533 cutoff gives an α of .05 and a β of .20. A comparison of Figures 10.1 and 10.2 shows that raising the cutoff above 533 would reduce α, but raise β. Lowering the cutoff below 533 would reduce β, but raise α. This is the fundamental trade-off in hypothesis testing. In practice, researchers traditionally choose the cutoff so that α equals .05 and then let β be whatever it turns out to be.

If the observed data reject the null hypothesis, then the results are said to be **statistically significant.** What this cryptic phrase means is that the observed difference between the sample mean and its expected value under the null hypothesis is large enough to lead to the rejection of that hypothesis. Statistically, the observed difference is too large to be plausibly attributed to chance alone, and so it is statistically significant in the sense that its statistical improbability persuades us to reject the null hypothesis.

An Appropriate Sample Size

In the previous example, we had a given sample of size 25, chose a cutoff point to set α at .05, and then computed β to be .20. Often the researcher has some freedom in choosing the sample size and can exercise that freedom to set α and β at prescribed levels.

Perhaps a Type II error probability of .20 is considered excessive. For a fixed sample size, the only way to reduce β is to increase α. By increasing the sample size, however, the researcher can reduce α, β, or both. The exact formula is shown in the footnote below,* but the idea is more important than the specific formula

---

*The values of α and β are determined by

$$\bar{X}_c = \mu_0 + Z_\alpha \sigma / \sqrt{n}$$
$$\bar{X}_c = \mu_1 - Z_\beta \sigma / \sqrt{n}$$

where $\bar{X}_c$ is the cutoff point, μ_0 and μ_1 are the values of μ under the null and alternative hypotheses, and Z_α and Z_β are the Z values corresponding to the selected values of α and β. The subtraction of the second equation from the first gives

$$0 = (\mu_0 - \mu_1) + (Z_\alpha + Z_\beta)\sigma / \sqrt{n}$$

Solving for the sample size,

$$n = \left\{ \frac{(Z_\alpha + Z_\beta)\,\sigma}{(\mu_1 - \mu_0)} \right\}^2 \tag{10.1}$$

for its implementation. A larger sample gives more information about the population and thus provides a more reliable identification of correct and incorrect hypotheses. With only a few observations, we cannot make a very informed judgment; if we observe the entire population, then we'll be certain of the answer. Because a large sample can be expensive, a reasonable strategy is to lay out the options of the values of α and β for different sample sizes, and then make a choice.

In the math SAT example, with α fixed at .05, the sample sizes needed for a variety of values of β are

desired β	needed n
.20	25
.10	34
.05	43
.01	63
.001	89

Exercises

10.11   In general, what do the probabilities of Type I and Type II error measure? Specifically, what do these two error probabilities mean for the example of the math SAT cram course?

10.12   Let's modify the math SAT example so that, because of budget limitations, only 9 students are tested. The null and alternative hypotheses are still

$$H_0: \mu = 500$$

$$H_1: \mu = 550$$

and the standard deviation is still assumed to be 100. What cutoff sets the probability of Type I error at $\alpha = .05$? What is the probability of Type II error?

10.13   In the math SAT example, a cutoff of 533 for the average score of a random sample of 25 students implied a .05 probability of Type I error and a .20 probability of Type II error. For a given sample size, how can the probability of Type II error be diminished to .10? Is there any reason why a researcher might choose not to so reduce β? Alternatively, how might the sample be altered to reduce β to .10, while keeping α at .05?

10.14   A large corporation's secretaries have typing speeds that are normally distributed with a mean of 70 words per minute and a standard deviation of 15 words per minute. A manufacturer of word processors claims that its revolutionary keyboard can increase average typing speeds by 10 percent, with no change in the standard deviation. The corporation agrees to let 25 randomly selected secretaries try these machines to test this claim. Set up a test of the competing hypotheses

$$H_0: \mu = 70$$

$$H_1: \mu = 77$$

based on the average typing speed $\overline{X}$ of these 25 secretaries. Find the cutoff point so that there is only a 5 percent chance of believing that there has been a 10 percent increase in typing speed when there has, in fact, been none at all. If the word processing firm's claim is correct, what is the probability that your test will incorrectly reject their claim?

10.15 (*continuation*) If 100 secretaries are tested, where should the cutoff be set to keep the probability of Type I error at 5 percent? Now what is the probability of Type II error?

10.4 COMPOSITE HYPOTHESES

We are seldom confronted with just two possible values for a population parameter; instead, there is usually a continuum. In our math SAT example, we constructed a test for choosing between two possibilities for the expected value: 500 or 550. But there is no good reason for ruling out 549, 573, 484, or many other numbers, and consequently, we need to restructure our test to allow for these many possibilities. The details depend on the precise nature of the hypotheses, but the principles are the same as in the simple case that we began with.

A One-Sided Alternative Hypothesis

The firm may claim that its cram course significantly raises math SAT scores, without putting a precise number on the magnitude of the improvement. To test this claim, the null and alternative hypotheses would be

$$H_0: \mu = 500$$
$$H_1: \mu > 500$$

The null hypothesis is that the course has no effect, and the alternative hypothesis is that it raises scores by an unspecified amount. A natural test of these competing hypotheses would be to see if the average score of 25 students who take this course is much above 500. The exact cutoff for choosing between the two hypotheses is defined by specifying the probability of Type I error. If we set $\alpha = .05$, then 533 is again the cutoff. If the null hypothesis is true, and the course has no effect on student scores, then there is only a 5 percent chance that we will pick 25 students whose average score is above 533. Thus, with a 533 cutoff, there is only a 5 percent chance that we will be persuaded that a useless course is useful.

The one change in our analytics is that, with many possible alternative values for μ, there are now many possible values for β (the probability of Type II error), depending on how much the course actually does raise scores. Figure 10.3 shows the β values for $\mu = 525$, 550, and 575. The Type II errors for all values of μ between 500 and 575 are shown in Figure 10.4. If the course has only a small effect on student scores (raising them by just 25 points, for example), then we are very likely to conclude erroneously that it has no effect at all. If the course has a very large effect on scores (raising them by 75 points, for example), then there is almost no chance that sampling error will hide this positive effect.

A Bayesian could calculate an overall probability of committing a Type II error as an average of these βs, weighted by the probabilities that the course raises scores by 25 points, 50 points, and so on. If the Bayesian thinks that the course probably has only a small effect on student performance, then the probability of Type II

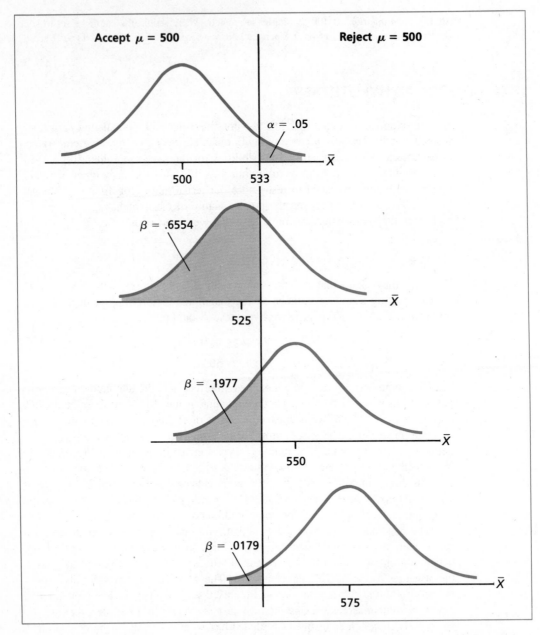

Figure 10.3   *A composite alternative hypothesis implies a variety of possible Type II errors*

Figure 10.4   *A graph of Type II errors for* μ *between 500 and 575*

error will be high. If this Bayesian thinks that the course is likely to have a large effect, then the probability of Type II error is small. An objectivist avoids such calculations, because they require that subjective probabilities be placed on the population parameter μ.

Composite Null and Alternative Hypotheses

So far, we have ruled out the possibility that the firm's course worsens math SAT scores. To allow for a negative effect, we can let our competing hypotheses be

$$H_0: \mu \leq 500$$

$$H_1: \mu > 500$$

The null hypothesis is now that the course does not have a positive effect on math SAT scores: it either worsens them or leaves them unchanged. The alternative hypothesis is that the effect is positive. Again, it is natural to choose between these two hypotheses based on the scores of a random sample of students who take the course. If these students do well, then we will be persuaded to reject the null hypothesis of "no benefits." Exactly how well these students have to do to persuade us to reject the null hypothesis is determined by the probability of Type I error that we are willing to tolerate.

The added complication here is that, because the null hypothesis includes many different values of μ, there are many different probabilities of Type I error. Let's say that we keep 533 as the cutoff point. Figure 10.5 shows that there are now different values of both α and β. Again, a Bayesian could obtain an overall probability of Type I error by assigning subjective probabilities to the different possible values of $\mu \leq 500$. Objectivists will not make such a weighting, so instead they look at a single α, to be conservative, the maximum value of α. This maximum α occurs at the borderline value of the mean, $\alpha = 500$. In Figure 10.5, you can

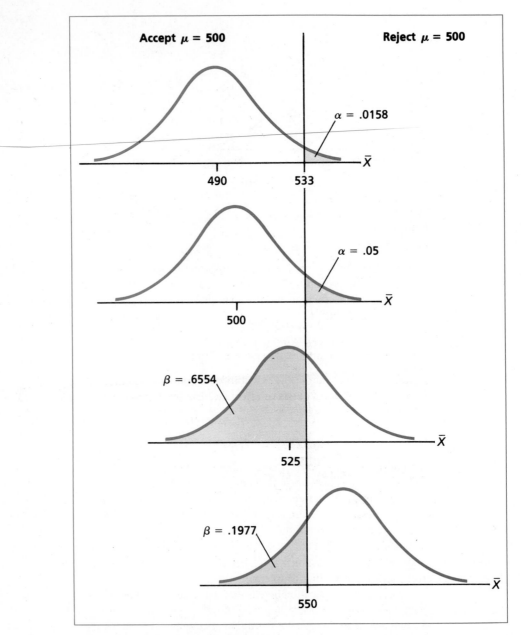

Figure 10.5   *There are many probabilities of Type I and Type II errors when there are composite null and alternative hypotheses*

see that, if μ is less than 500, then the probability distribution is shifted to the left and the probability of Type I error declines. Thus, 533 is still the appropriate cutoff point, but now it is because it gives a maximum value of α equal to 5 percent.

We have now looked at three hypothesis-testing situations and all three have given the same decision rule: An average score of 533 or higher indicates that the course does improve student scores. The only differences are in the implications of using this decision rule. If there are only two possible values of μ, then there is one probability of Type I error (α) and one probability of Type II error (β). If the alternative hypothesis allows a variety of values of μ, then there are a variety of βs. If the null hypothesis allows a variety of values of μ, then there are a variety of αs. In each case, the standard procedure for choosing the cutoff point is to set α (or the maximum value of α) equal to .05.

Two-Sided Composite Alternative Hypotheses

So far, we have looked at *one-sided* tests, in that the alternative hypothesis has been on just one side of the null hypothesis (above it). There has consequently been a single cutoff for choosing between the competing hypotheses. We reject the null hypothesis if the sample mean is above 533 and we accept the null hypothesis if the mean is below 533. It is also possible to construct *two-sided* tests in which the alternative hypothesis is on both sides of the null hypothesis. The null hypothesis may be that a certain action has no effect on the population mean, while the alternative hypothesis is that the action has some effect, either positive or negative, but we don't know which.

In the cram course example, the competing hypotheses would be

$$H_0: \mu = 500$$

$$H_1: \mu \neq 500$$

The null hypothesis is that a two-week cram course has no effect on math SAT scores. These scores are determined by a student's intelligence and education, and two weeks of studying isn't going to make any difference one way or the other. The alternative hypothesis is that the course does have some effect, either positive or negative. The course may stuff in a few useful facts and may give students some useful test-taking strategy, or the crash course may leave students so exhausted and irritable that they do poorly. We don't know which effect will dominate, so we leave them both open as alternatives.

Now what sort of scores would be decisive evidence against the null hypothesis of no effect? If the students score either much above 500 or much below 500, then we will be persuaded that the course does indeed affect their performance; a two-sided alternative hypothesis leads to a two-sided test.

The exact cutoff points are set by fixing the probabilities of Type I error. Remember that a Type I error occurs when we incorrectly reject the null hypothesis. Here, the luck of the draw might give us either 25 above-average students or 25 below-average students. In the former case, the above-average students do so well that we are persuaded that the course has positive effects. In the latter case, the below-average students do so poorly that we conclude the course has negative effects. We want to set our cutoff points sufficiently far from 500 to keep these error probabilities low. The standard practice is to allow for a 2.5 percent chance of incorrectly concluding that there are positive effects and a 2.5 percent chance of incorrectly concluding that there are negative effects, giving an overall 5 percent chance of committing a Type I error.

Figure 10.6 illustrates this logic. When you are first constructing hypothesis tests, it is a good idea to draw such a sketch to crystalize your own logic. Because the normal distribution is symmetrical, the cutoff points will be equidistant from 500. How far? Our two-standard-deviations rule of thumb tells us that there is about a 5 percent chance that a normally distributed variable will be more than two standard deviations away from its mean. Here, if the null hypothesis is correct, individual scores are normally distributed with a mean of 500 and a standard deviation of 100. The sample mean of 25 scores is then normally distributed with a mean of 500 and a standard deviation of $100/\sqrt{25} = 20$. Thus, there is approximately a 5 percent chance that the sample mean will be more than 40 points above or below 500, and our cutoff points are consequently 540 and 460.*

Figure 10.6 shows that the probabilities of Type II error are also two-sided. These probabilities are displayed in Figure 10.7. Again, we are most likely to err by concluding that the course has no effect if the effect is small. If the course has a large effect, either positive or negative, on student scores, then we are almost certain to see that effect reflected in their scores.

Let's briefly review the logic and implications of one-sided and two-sided tests. With a one-sided test, we see whether the observed sample mean is 1.65 standard deviations away from its expected value under the null hypothesis. The cutoff point in our example works out to be 533. With a two-sided test, we can see whether the observed sample mean is two standard deviations above or below its expected value under the null hypothesis. This works out to be 40 points in either direction, and the scores would be either above 540 or below 460.

Notice that with a two-sided test, the cutoff scores have to be even higher than those of a one-sided test to convince us that the course has a positive effect. This means that a two-sided test has the greater chance of making a Type II error by concluding that a beneficial course has no effect. You can see these higher βs by

---

*A more formal derivation would proceed as follows. Table 2 says that there is a .025 probability that a standardized normal variable Z is greater than 1.96. The sample mean is standardized by subtracting its mean $\mu = 500$ and dividing by its standard deviation $\sigma/\sqrt{n} = 20$. Therefore,

$$.025 = P[Z > 1.96]$$
$$= P[(\bar{X} - \mu)/(\sigma/\sqrt{n}) > 1.96]$$
$$= P[\bar{X} > \mu + 1.96(\sigma/\sqrt{n})]$$
$$= P[\bar{X} > 500 + 1.96(20)]$$
$$= P[\bar{X} > 539.2]$$

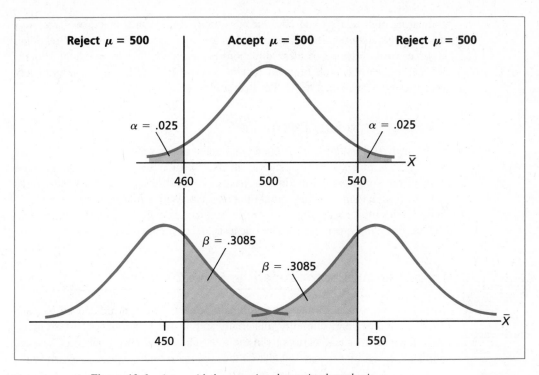

Figure 10.6 A two-sided composite alternative hypothesis

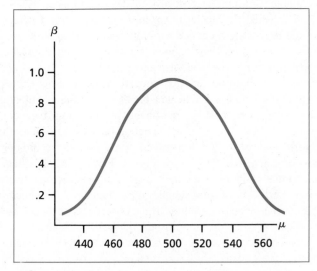

Figure 10.7 *Type II errors for a two-sided composite alternative hypothesis*

comparing Figures 10.4 and 10.7 for $\mu = 550$. The reason is that a two-sided test has to be more conservative, because it has to worry about erring in two directions. If we can rule out one of these directions ahead of time, then we should do so. We can reduce the probability of making a Type II error if we can legitimately justify using a one-sided test rather than a two-sided test.

Two Quick and Easy Extensions

In the math SAT example, I assumed that student scores were known to be normally distributed with a standard deviation of 100. What if the random sample is not drawn from a normal distribution? It makes little difference, as long as the sample is large enough to invoke the central limit theorem. With a sufficiently large sample, the central limit theorem implies that the sample mean will be normally distributed and we can consequently construct our test just as we have done before.

Process Control at the American Stove Company

Manufacturing processes are not unfailingly perfect. They are influenced by variations in temperature, humidity, materials, and human performance. These inevitable fluctuations cause variations in the size, shape, and performance of finished products. In addition, wear and tear on the equipment and operators may cause the process to deteriorate. Manufacturers would like to separate process deterioration from the inevitable variation, because process deterioration can usually be corrected but, if left uncorrected, it can result in unacceptable product defects. Naturally, they would like to catch a process deterioration as soon as possible, but there are at least two constraints on their actions. First, it is often impractical to inspect every single item closely. Second, it doesn't make sense to stop the process for repairs every time a slight deviation is noticed. Most such deviations are normal, inevitable variations and do not indicate a breakdown in the manufacturing process.

Statistical **process control** is a reasonable procedure for balancing these competing concerns. A mean and standard deviation for some attribute of interest (size, weight, or performance) can be determined from historical records or by the company's target objectives (its "specifications"). This mean and standard deviation measure the normal variation that can be expected when the manufacturing process is operating properly. A periodic sample of manufactured items can then be compared to this normal range of variation. If the observed deviation between a sample and the historical mean is too large to be explained by chance variation, then the process is apparently deteriorating and requires some corrective action.

To illustrate these ideas, we'll look at a process control procedure used by the American Stove Company.[3] This firm produced a certain metal piece whose height, under normal manufacturing conditions, was approximately normally distributed with a mean of 0.8312 inch and a standard deviation of 0.006169 inch. If the manufacturing process deteriorated, these items might become so much longer or shorter than usual that they would be unusable.

What if we don't know the standard deviation? Then we'll just have to estimate it. With a large sample, we can assume that our estimate of the standard deviation is correct and proceed as shown earlier. With a small sample, though, the estimate may be off by a bit. If the underlying distribution is approximately normal, then the extra uncertainty can be taken into account by using the t distribution rather than the normal distribution to calculate the cutoff points. The effect will be to make the cutoff points a bit farther from the expected value under the null hypothesis. To keep the probability of incorrectly rejecting the null hypothesis at 5 percent while acknowledging that we may be off in our estimate of the standard deviation, we must require the sample mean to be even farther removed from what would be expected if the null hypothesis were true.

For instance, the American Stove Company based its process control test on a daily sample of just five items. If they had estimated the standard deviation from each day's sample, instead of using the historical value of 0.006169, then this

To guard against this, the American Stove Company carefully measured a random sample of five items from each day's production to see whether or not the mean height of this sample was within three standard deviations of its expected value, assuming no deterioration in the process. If the observed disparity was greater than three standard deviations, then they concluded that something more than chance variation was at work—production was stopped and corrective action taken.

Implicitly, they were making a two-tailed test of the null hypothesis that the expected height is 0.8312 inch,

$$H_0: \mu = 0.8312$$

$$H_1: \mu \neq 0.8312$$

If the standard deviation of an individual item is 0.006169, then the standard deviation of the mean of a random sample of 5 items is $0.006169/\sqrt{5}$. Their decision rule was to accept H_0 as long as the sample mean was within three standard deviations of its expected value under the null hypothesis

accept H_0 if $0.8312 - 3(0.006169/\sqrt{n}) < \overline{X} < 0.8312 + 3(0.006169/\sqrt{n})$

that is, if

$$0.8229 < \overline{X} < 0.8395$$

The probability of Type I error is the chance that a sample mean will be outside this range even though the null hypothesis is correct. Table 2 at the end of this book tells us that there is a .0013 chance that a normally distributed variable will be three standard deviations above its expected value and a similar chance of being three standard deviations below its expected value. Thus, the probability of Type I error is .0013 + .0013 = .0026.

would have provided an extra reason for error, and hence, for caution. Table 4 shows the t values for $n - 1 = 4$ degrees of freedom to be 2.776 for $\alpha = .05$ and 4.604 for $\alpha = .01$. Thus, a three-standard-deviations rule has about a .05 (rather than .0026) chance of Type I error if the standard deviation must be estimated each day. A 1 percent α would require almost a five-standard-deviations rule.

Exercises

10.16   Proline fishing line has a breaking strength that is normally distributed with a mean $\mu = 30$ pounds and a standard deviation $\sigma = 3$ pounds. The engineers have developed a new, less expensive manufacturing process, but are worried that the mean breaking strength may be adversely affected. The competing hypotheses are

$$H_0: \mu = 30$$

$$H_1: \mu < 30$$

They assume that the breaking strength is unchanged, unless there is convincing evidence to the contrary. A sample of 100 of these new lines will be tested and their average breaking strength calculated. Assuming that the standard deviation is unchanged, find the cutoff point for the sample mean that gives a 5 percent probability of incorrectly rejecting the null hypothesis. The sample mean turns out to be 28.4 pounds. Can this be explained by sampling error or is it compelling evidence that the new lines are weaker?

10.17   IQ scores are normally distributed with a standard deviation of 15. Using a 5 percent chance of Type I error, find the cutoff points for using a random sample of 100 people to test the hypotheses

$$H_0: \mu = 100$$

$$H_1: \mu \neq 100$$

A random sample of 100 children who regularly watch "Seesaw Street" had an average IQ score of 102.2. Is this value sufficient to show that the average IQs of children who watch "Seesaw Street" is not 100?

10.18   A tobacco company claims that its new brand of cigarette, Life, contains less than $\frac{1}{2}$ mg of nicotone. Tests of 16 Life cigarettes yield an average nicotine content of 0.3 mg, with an estimated standard deviation of 0.3 mg. Do these data support the tobacco company's claim? (Use a t test.)

● **10.19**   In the text, I argued that a two-sided test has a greater probability of incorrectly concluding that a useful cram course is useless than a one-sided test does. With a one-sided test, the course is considered useless unless the average score of the 25 students is above 533. With a two-sided test, the course is considered useless unless the average score is above 540 or below 460. If the expected value of the student scores is, in fact, 550, then what is the probability of incorrectly concluding that the course is worthless if the test is one-sided? If it is two-sided?

● **10.20**   When there are several possible values for μ, there are several βs. A Bayesian could calculate an overall probability of Type II error by putting subjective probabilities on the possible values for μ. Consider the math SAT cram course and assume, for the sake of simplicity, that, if the null hypothesis is false, then there are only three possible values for μ:

$$P[\mu = 525 \mid \mu \neq 500] = .50,$$
$$P[\mu = 550 \mid \mu \neq 500] = .30, \text{ and}$$
$$P[\mu = 575 \mid \mu \neq 500] = .20$$

The overall probability of Type II error is then

$$\begin{aligned}
\beta &= P[\text{accept } \mu = 500 \mid \mu \neq 500] \\
&= P[\text{accept } \mu = 500 \mid \mu = 525] \, P[\mu = 525 \mid \mu \neq 500] \\
&\quad + P[\text{accept } \mu = 500 \mid \mu = 550] \, P[\mu = 550 \mid \mu \neq 500] \\
&\quad + P[\text{accept } \mu = 500 \mid \mu = 575] \, P[\mu = 575 \mid \mu \neq 500]
\end{aligned}$$

If a sample of 25 is used with a cutoff of 533, find the probabilities of accepting $\mu = 500$ if, in fact, $\mu = 525$, 550, and 575, and then find the overall probability of Type II error.

10.5 BINOMIAL TESTS

Our tests can also be easily extended to the binomial distribution. R.A. Fisher, who was one of the pioneers in developing hypothesis tests, used the example of an English lady who claims that, when having tea with milk, she can usually tell whether the tea or the milk was poured into her cup first. To test this remarkable claim, 8 cups of tea are prepared. For each cup, a coin is flipped to determine whether to pour in the tea or the milk first. These cups are brought to the woman, who takes a sip from each and correctly identifies 6 of the 8 cups!

Is that performance good enough to satisfy the statistician in the crowd? Or might the statistician reason that, by chance alone, a person will frequently get 6 out of 8 correct? This is an hypothesis-testing situation, in which the binomial distribution is appropriate rather than the normal. We can let π be the probability that this woman will correctly identify whether the tea or the milk was poured first. The null and alternative hypotheses can be

$$H_0: \pi = .5$$
$$H_1: \pi > .5$$

The null hypothesis is that this woman has only a 50 percent chance of being correct, the same as if she simply guesses without tasting. The alternative hypothesis is her claim that she is right more often than wrong.

How good does her performance have to be to be considered statistically significant? The relevant binomial probabilities are given in Table 1, using the null hypothesis assumption that $\pi = .5$. If she were merely guessing, there would be a .0039 probability of correctly identifying 8 out of 8 cups, a .0312 probability for 7 out of 8, a .1094 probability for 6 out of 8, and so on. We want to set our cutoff point so that there is less than a 5 percent chance of making a Type I error by incorrectly rejecting the null hypothesis that she is just guessing. The appropriate cutoff is thus 7 out of 8, because there is only a .0039 + .0312 = .0351 probability that a guesser will get at least 7 out of 8 right.* Because this lady only got 6 out of 8 right, we do not reject the null hypothesis that she is an uninformed guesser. Another way of looking at her record is that a pure guesser has a .0039 + .312 + .1094 = .1445 probability of getting at least 6 out of 8 right. Therefore, her performance is not remarkable enough to rule out lucky guesses as the explanation.

Acceptance Sampling at Dow Chemical

Chapter 5 included a discussion of *acceptance sampling,* which is the use of a sample to determine whether or not to accept a box of oranges, a batch of batteries, or a shipment of bombs. This kind of decision can be recast as an hypothesis test. The null hypothesis is that the population meets some minimal standards. The quality of a random sample is then tested and the null hypothesis is either accepted or rejected. The cutoff between acceptance and rejection can be determined by setting the probability of Type I error at, say, 5 percent.

An example is provided by Dow Chemical's auditing of invoices for bulk mailing and duplicating items.[4] Their null hypothesis was that no more than one-fourth of one percent of the weekly entries on these invoices contained clerical errors:

$$H_0: \pi \leq .0025$$

$$H_1: \pi > .0025$$

where π is the fraction of the week's entries that are incorrect.

They decided to examine a random sample of 225 entries each week. This sample is not really large enough to use a normal approximation to the binomial distribution, because the expected number of errors, $\pi n = (.0025)225 = .5625$, is not larger than 5, the rule of thumb given in Chapter 5. If the null hypothesis is true, then the binomial probabilities are

$$P[\text{no errors}] = (.9975)^{225} = .569$$

$$P[\text{one error}] = 225 \, (.0025)(.9975)^{224} = .321$$

$$P[\text{two errors}] = \left(\frac{(225)(224)}{2}\right)(.0025)^2(.9975)^{223} = .090$$

$$P[\text{more than two errors}] =$$

$$1 - P[\text{no errors}] - P[\text{one error}] - P[\text{two errors}] = .02$$

*For an exact 5 percent probability of making a Type I error, we can use a randomized hypothesis test in which a random-number generator is used to determine whether 6 out of 8 will be accepted as statistically significant. The details are left as Exercise 10.48. Frankly, such a procedure has an unscientific aura and is usually more trouble than it's worth.

If Dow rejected the week's invoices based on the discovery of more than two errors in their sample, there would have been a .02 probability of Type I error. If, instead, they refused to accept invoices if more than one error were found, then their probability of Type I error would have been .02 + .09 = .11. The two-error cutoff is closer to $\alpha = .05$, and that is just what Dow did.

Racial Awareness in Children

The binomial test of the exceptional tea taster used a very small sample of just eight observations. If the sample were larger, we could use a normal approximation to the binomial distribution. As an illustration, consider a 1958 study of the racial awareness of black children.[6] The sample consisted of 253 black children, 134 from Arkansas and 119 from Massachusetts. The children's ages ranged from 3 to 7 years. Each child was offered four dolls, two white and two black, and told to,

Does the Dropped Bread Fall Jelly Side Down?

Murphy's law states that, "If anything can go wrong, it will." Most people can remember lots of personal examples of Murphy's law in action. One researcher was apparently so impressed (or devastated) by the law that he set out to conduct a controlled laboratory experiment.[5] His vehicle was the familiar lament, "If I'm putting jelly on a slice of bread and drop it, why does it usually land jelly side down?" One of this researcher's experiments involved 1712 slices of bread smeared with peanut butter and a variety of jellies. Each was dropped and the results dutifully recorded:

$$\text{jelly-side-up:} \quad 206$$
$$\text{jelly-side-down:} \quad 1506$$

The null hypothesis is that the bread has an equal chance of landing jelly side up or down. Murphy's law suggests a preponderance of jelly-sides-down:

$$H_0: \pi = .5$$
$$H_1: \pi > .5$$

where π is the probability of landing jelly side down. The outcomes can be described by a binomial distribution. To use a normal approximation, we need only remember that the sample proportion p has an expected value π and a standard deviation $\{\pi(1 - \pi)/n\}^{1/2}$. Under the null hypothesis, the expected value is .5 and the standard deviation is $\{.5(.5)/1712\}^{1/2} = .000146$. The observed proportion, 1506/1712, = .88 is several thousand standard deviations away from .5, showing decisively that dropped bread is not equally likely to land jelly side up or down. This researcher concluded that Murphy's law is 88 percent correct. An improved formulation is, "If something can go wrong, it probably will."

"Give me the doll that you would like to play with." It turned out that 83 children chose a black doll and 169 chose a white doll. (One child was apparently not interested in playing with dolls and refused to choose one.)

Overall, about two-thirds of these black children (169/252 = .671) preferred to play with a white doll. Can this result reasonably be explained by chance, either in the random selection of the children or in their haphazard choice of a doll? Or does it suggest that young black children are well aware of race and, indeed, have a negative image of their race and of themselves? Let π be the probability that a randomly selected black child will choose a white doll. The competing hypotheses are

$$H_0: \pi = .5$$

$$H_1: \pi \neq .5$$

Are Mendel's Data Too Good to be True?

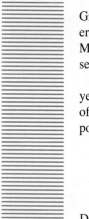

Gregor Mendel's probabilitistic model of how genes pass traits on from one generation to the next is one of the most important and elegant scientific theories. Mendel reported many experimental results confirming his theory, and many subsequent supporting experiments have been conducted by others.

One of Mendel's original experiments involved the self-fertilization of hybrid yellow-seeded sweet peas. His theory said that the offspring have a .75 probability of being yellow-seeded and a .25 probability of being green-seeded. Mendel reported the following results:

offspring	number
yellow-seeded	6021
green-seeded	2002
total	8023

Do these numbers support or reject Mendel's theory?

We can use the binomial model with π the probability of a yellow-seeded offspring. The competing hypotheses are

$$H_0: \pi = .75$$

$$H_1: \pi \neq .75$$

The null hypothesis is that Mendel's theory is correct. The two-sided alternative hypothesis is that Mendel is wrong. The sample, $n = 8023$, is sufficiently large so that the sample proportion p should be normally distributed. Under the null hypothesis,

$$p \sim N[\pi, \{\pi(1 - \pi)/n\}^{1/2}]$$
$$\sim N[.75, \{(.75)(.25)/8023\}^{1/2}]$$
$$\sim N[.75, .005]$$

The null hypothesis is that the color of the doll's skin is unimportant to black children as a whole; for every black child who would pick a white doll, there's another who would pick a black doll. The alternative, two-sided hypothesis is that the color of a doll's skin does matter to black children. (The test must be two-sided, because we cannot rule out *a priori* the possibility that black children prefer black dolls.)

The binomial distribution can be applied here, and the sample is large enough to allow a normal approximation to the binomial distribution. Under the null hypothesis, the sample proportion p preferring a white doll has a normal distribution with a .5 expected value and 0.0315 standard deviation:

$$p \sim N[\pi, \{\pi(1 - \pi)/n\}^{1/2}]$$
$$\sim N[.5, \{(.5)(.5)/252\}^{1/2}]$$
$$\sim N[.5, 0.0315]$$

There is about a .95 probability that a normally distributed variable will be within two standard deviations of its expected value, here $.75 \pm 2(.005) = .75 \pm .01$. Thus, allowing the usual 5 percent chance of Type I error, the cutoffs for rejecting Mendel's theory are an observed value of p below .74 or above .76.

What do his data show? Mendel's reported value of p is $6021/8023 = .7505$, which is almost exactly as predicted. Or, put somewhat differently, 75 percent of 8023 is 6017.25. Mendel's reported number, 6021, is off by less than 4 plants in an experiment involving over 8000 plants! Mendel's data support his theory strikingly, perhaps too strikingly. Some 70 years later, the eminent statistician, R.A. Fisher, argued that Mendel's data are literally too good to be true.

Fisher asked the reverse question: Assuming Mendel's theory is true, what is the probability of observing a value of p so close to .75? Mendel's reported .7505 is $1/10$ of a standard deviation away from its expected value. Table 2 tells us that there is only about an 8 percent chance that a normally distributed variable will be within 0.1 standard deviation (in either direction) of its mean. Such a close correspondence between theory and data takes a bit of luck or something less innocent.

In fact, Mendel studied seven inherited characteristics of pea plants and, in every single case, there was this close a correspondence between his results and his predictions. The probability such a phenomenal run of experimental luck is about .000004. It is very hard to believe that Mendel was that lucky. Even worse, in one of his studies, he miscalculated the theoretical probability and then reported data that fit this erroneous probability almost exactly and reject the correct probability. It is hard to disagree with Fisher's conclusion that Mendel's data are too good to be true. Fisher was, however, so impressed by Mendel's scientific contributions and by the fact that Mendel was a monk that he placed the blame elsewhere.

I have no doubt that Mendel was deceived by a gardening assistant, who knew only too well what his principal expected from each trial made.[7]

The probability is about .95 that a normally distributed variable will be within two standard deviations of its mean. Therefore, a two-sided test with a 5 percent chance of Type I error would put the cutoff points $2(0.0315) = 0.0630$ on either side of .5. That is, we reject the null hypothesis if the sample proportion turns out to be less than .437 or greater than .563. The observed $p = .671$ in this study decisively rejected the null hypothesis that black children are color-blind.

Exercises

10.21   A small firm claims that its patent medicine can cure half of the people suffering from a certain disease. The Food and Drug Administration administers this medicine to 10 people suffering from this disease and finds that 2 are cured. Do these data support the firm's claim?

10.22   Karl Pearson reported that when he flipped a coin 24,000 times, he obtained 12,012 heads and 11,988 tails. Are these data consistent with the null hypothesis that the probability of a head is .5?

10.23   (*continuation*) Are Pearson's data too good to be true?

10.24   A home scientist claims that people are weakened when they wear watches. To test his claim, 10 volunteers have their strength measured with and without watches. If the variations in these measurements are due just to inadequacies in measuring strength (and not at all to the wearing of watches), then what is the probability that 7 of the 10 volunteers will show a decrease in strength when they wear a watch? If we decide to accept this person's watch-weakness theory if at least 7 volunteers do show a decrease in strength, then what is the probability of Type I error? (Be sure to reveal your null and alternative hypotheses.)

10.25   In the 1960s, only males who were 21 years old and older were eligible for jury duty in Alabama. About 26 percent of the 21-year-old males in Talladega County, Alabama at that time were black. The murder conviction of a black man in Talladega County was appealed to the Supreme Court on the grounds that there were no blacks on the jury, and indeed no black men had served on juries in Talladega County "within the memory of persons now living." The U.S. Supreme Court (*Swain* vs. *Alabama*, 1965) denied the appeal, noting that there had been 8 blacks on the 100-person panel from which the final jury was selected. (The prosecution had ruled out these 8 blacks with constitutionally protected peremptory challenges.) What is the probability that a randomly selected panel of 100 citizens will have as few as 8 blacks? Do these data support or refute the hypothesis that the panel selection is color-blind?

10.6   TWO DIFFERENT WAYS OF TESTING HYPOTHESES

I have shown you the most common way of testing hypotheses. There are also two alternative methods, which are actually equivalent to the original method you learned. These two alternatives are just different ways of saying the same thing, but because the logic of hypothesis tests is a bit complicated, it is worthwhile to look at other ways of explaining what it is we're doing.

P-Values

Our hypothesis-testing logic runs as follows. First, specify the null and alternative hypotheses. Second, figure out what values of the sample statistic would have less than a 5 percent chance of occurring if the null hypothesis were true. Finally, see if the observed value of sample statistic falls in this unlikely region. The order of the second and third steps can be reversed without affecting the conclusions. We can look at the sample statistic and then calculate the probability of observing such an extreme value. If this probability is less than 5 percent, then the null hypothesis can be rejected.

Let's go back to the SAT scores and use the example of a single null hypothesis and a composite alternative hypothesis:

$$H_0: \mu = 500$$

$$H_1: \mu > 500$$

As explained before, allowing a 5 percent chance of Type I error implies a 533 cutoff point for the average score of 25 students. Now let's say that the sample mean turns out to be 542, which leads us to reject the null hypothesis. Another route to this rejection would be to calculate the probability of observing a sample mean as high as 542 if the null hypothesis were true. This probability is

$$P[\bar{X} > 542] = P\left[\frac{\bar{X} - \mu}{\sigma/\sqrt{n}} > \frac{542 - \mu}{\sigma/\sqrt{n}}\right]$$

$$= P\left[Z > \frac{542 - 500}{100/\sqrt{25}}\right]$$

$$= P[Z > 2.1]$$

$$= .0179$$

from Table 2. Thus, if the null hypothesis were true, there would be less than 2 percent chance that 25 students selected at random would average as high as 542 after taking the course. Because this probability is less than 5 percent, we conclude that the difference is statistically significant and the null hypothesis (that the course is worthless) should be rejected. Even more simply, we could reason that a score of 542 is 2.1 standard deviations above the expected score, if the null hypothesis is correct. Because a difference of 1.65 standard deviations is good enough for a one-sided test, 2.1 standard deviations calls for the rejection of the null hypothesis. This is just too big a difference to be explained by chance alone.

Let's generalize the argument by retracing our steps. First, we look at the sample mean, whatever it turns out to be. Then we standardize it by subtracting the expected value of the sample mean and dividing by the standard deviation of the sample mean, assuming the null hypothesis is to be true:

$$\textbf{Z-statistic} = \frac{\text{observed sample mean} - \text{expected value under null hypothesis}}{\text{standard deviation of the sample mean}}$$

Next, we use Table 2 to find the probability of observing such an extreme value. This probability is called a **P-value.** If the P-value is less than 5 percent (or 2.5 percent for a two-tailed test), then the null hypothesis is rejected. A glance at Figure 10.1 confirms that this procedure is fully equivalent to our first method. If the null hypothesis is true, there is less than a 5 percent chance of observing sample mean higher than 533. If the sample mean does turn out to be greater than 533, then the value of the Z-statistic will be greater than 1.65, the P-value will be less than 5 percent, and the null hypothesis will be rejected.

To reinforce the concept, let's run through it once more, this time using a two-tailed test. There is only a 5 percent chance that a normally distributed variable will be more than two standard deviations from its mean. Therefore, we reject a null hypothesis if the sample mean is more than two standard deviations from its expected value under the null hypothesis. Perhaps the average score of 25 students who take the cram course is 520. Is this difference statistically significant, or is it easily explainable by the luck of the draw in picking these students? Well, the standard deviation of the average score of 25 students is $100/\sqrt{25} = 20$. An average score of 520 is therefore only one standard deviation above the expected value of 500 under the null hypothesis. The Z-value is $(520 - 500)/20 = 1.0$ and the P-value is $P[Z > 1.0] = .16$, far greater than .025. There is a 32 percent chance that a sample mean will be at least one standard deviation either above or below its expected value. A one-standard-deviation difference is not sufficiently unlikely to reject the null hypothesis that the expected value is 500. It is not statistically significant, because it could well be explained by sampling error.

Confidence Intervals

There is yet another approach that helps to further clarify hypothesis testing. Let's say that we had set out to estimate the expected value μ of the math SAT scores of students who take this cram course. We would use the sample mean as our estimate and use a two-standard-deviations rule of thumb to compute a 95 percent confidence interval. If the sample mean is, as shown earlier, 520, then our 95 percent confidence interval is

$$\mu = 520 \pm 2(20)$$
$$= 520 \pm 40$$

Because 500 is well within this confidence interval, we cannot rule out the possibility that the course has no effect on student performance.

There is, in fact, a logical equivalence between hypothesis tests and confidence intervals, in that a hypothesis will be rejected only if it lies outside a corresponding confidence interval! This equivalence is easily seen. A two-sided hypothesis test asks if the sample mean is within two standard deviations of the null hypothesis.*

---

*A slight adjustment is needed with a one-sided test. Because a one-sided test asks whether the sample mean is within 1.65 standard deviations of the null hypothesis, the corresponding confidence interval should be ± 1.65 standard deviations, i.e., a 90 percent confidence interval. You will, of course, only look at the appropriate side of the confidence interval.

A confidence interval includes all values for μ within two standard deviations of the sample mean. If the sample mean is more than two standard deviations from the value specified by the null hypothesis, then the null hypothesis is outside the confidence interval. Therefore, hypothesis tests can be conducted simply by using the sample to construct a confidence interval.

Even more fundamentally, we can think of hypothesis tests as being just a reinterpretation of estimation. When we say that we are 95 percent certain that a confidence interval includes the true value of μ, we are also saying that, if μ were equal to one of the excluded values, there would be no more than a 5 percent chance that the sample mean would be so far from this value. The improbability of this disparity rules out these excluded values.

Do Some NFL Teams Consistently Beat the Pointspread?

In football wagers, points are commonly added to the underdog team's score. If, for instance, the Dallas Cowboys are favored by $2\frac{1}{2}$ points over the Washington Redskins, then $2\frac{1}{2}$ points are added to Washington's score. Those who pick Dallas win their bets if the Cowboys beat the Redskins by more than 2 points. Those who bet on Washington win if the Redskins either win or else lose by less than 2 points. The bookmaker makes a profit by only putting up $10 against every $11 wagered by the bettor.

A natural null hypothesis is that the bookmaker's point spreads are set so that each team has an equal chance of winning. There are, of course, a variety of systems that are designed to bankrupt the bookies, and two researchers tested some of these theories statistically over the period 1969–1974.[8]

One theory is that some teams consistently beat the point spread while others repeatedly fall short. Thus, the bettor need only find teams that would have paid off and then begin putting wagers on these teams. These researchers applied this theory by following teams that had winning records against the point spread in the preceding year. The competing hypotheses are

$$H_0: \pi = .5$$

$$H_1: \pi > .5$$

where π is the probability that one of these selected teams will beat the point spread. They found that this strategy led to 616 bets, of which 312 were won and 304 lost. The observed proportion $312/616 = .506$ is not significantly different from .5. Under the null hypothesis, the expected proportion is .5 with a standard deviation of $\{.5(.5)/616\}^{1/2} = .020$, giving a Z-value of $(.506 - .500)/.020 = .3$. That is, the observed .506 is only a third of a standard deviation away from .5, and not nearly far enough to persuasively reject the null hypothesis. They also looked at a similar stategy of betting against teams that had losing records against the point spread the previous year. This led to 693 bets, of which 343 were won and 350 lost—not statistically significant and the wrong direction to boot! We can only hope that this research interest was purely academic.

Exercises

10.26   At some colleges, students write senior essays that are graded twice, once by an advisor and once by an anonymous reader. It is conceivable that the advisor, who knows the student and may have helped with the essay, will grade more leniently than the reader: "Anonymity encourages objectivity, or meanness at least." A sample of 26 senior essays in economics written at Yale in 1976 yielded the following data:

reader's grade	number
higher than advisor's	5
equal to advisor's	7
lower than advisor's	14

Let π be the probability that a grade that is different from the advisor's will be greater than the advisor's grade. Use these data to find the Z- and P-values and to test the null hypothesis that $\pi = .5$ against the alternative $\pi \neq .5$.

10.27   The chemists at a major soft-drink company have developed a new, less expensive formula for their cola. These chemists claim that the new cola tastes better, too. However, the company's executives fear that their customers won't like this new concoction. A random sample of 400 people are given unlabeled glasses of the old and new colas: 170 prefer the new cola, while 230 prefer the old cola. Can this difference be explained by sampling error, or do the data indicate that people prefer the old cola? Be precise in stating your statistical conclusion. What are the sources of sampling error in this problem?

10.28   A carnival wheel of fortune is divided into 10 sections, numbered 1, 2, . . . , 10. A prominent local citizen has complained to the sheriff that this wheel is rigged somehow. The sheriff suggests that the citizen may have been unlucky, but the citizen protests that too much money was lost for it to be luck alone. The sheriff enlists the help of a statistician from a nearby college. This statistician has several students take turns observing the operations of this wheel, and they report the following data:

number of bets placed	number of bets won
1542	91

What are the Z-value and P-value? Do the data support the citizen's theory or the sheriff's theory?

10.29   In 1973, a federal judge ruled that statistics proved a *prima facie* case of discrimination in the Montgomery County, Alabama jury rolls. The Montgomery Jury Commission was ordered to reconstitute the jury rolls to include a cross-section of the community. The judge noted that blacks made up 30 percent of the jury-age population, but only 12 percent of the jury rolls, and that women made up 54 percent of the jury-age population, but only 16 percent of the jury rolls. If there are 100 people on a jury roll, what are the probabilities that random selection would yield

a. no more than 12 percent blacks?
b. no more than 16 percent females?

Do these data support or reject the null hypotheses that jury rolls are chosen without regard to race or sex?

10.30   Courts have held that there is *prima facie* evidence of discrimination (under Title

VII) if there is a statistically significant difference between the percentage of a firm's employees who are black and the percentage of people in the area who are black. Assume that 20 percent of the people in the area are black and that every firm has exactly 100 employees. What would be the cutoff for showing a statistically significant shortfall in the number of black employees? (Use a one-tailed test.) If a firm's hiring decisions are, in fact, color-blind, what are its chances of being found guilty of race discrimination by this criteria? If all firms are color-blind, what fraction of them can expect to be found guilty of race discrimination?

10.7 SUMMARY

An hypothesis test asks the question, "If the null hypothesis is true, what is the probability that a random sample will yield a statistic whose value is so far from its expected value?" If this probability is very small, then we reject the null hypothesis by concluding that the discrepancy is too large to be explained by chance alone. The observed difference is then said to be statistically significant. If, on the other hand, the probability is not small, then we accept the null hypothesis by concluding that the observed discrepancy may well be due to chance, i.e., sampling error. In this case, the observed data are said to be statistically consistent with the null hypothesis.

There are a variety of ways to conduct statistical tests about the population mean μ for a random variable X. Each approach uses the fact that the mean of a random sample is normally distributed if X is normally distributed or (according to the central limit theorem) if the sample is large. The expected value of the sample mean is μ and the standard deviation is $\sigma/\sqrt{n}$, where σ is the standard deviation of X and n is the size of the random sample. The standard deviation of the sample mean reflects sampling error—the fact that chance affects the mean of a randomly selected sample. This sampling error is why we cannot be 100 percent confident about the implications of statistical tests. Naturally, the smaller the random sample, the larger the margin for sampling error must be.

The usual testing procedure is to begin by specifying the null and alternative hypotheses. Second, figure out which values of the sample mean would have a small chance of occurring if the null hypothesis were true. For a two-tailed test at the 5 percent level, these are values that are two standard deviations of the sample mean, i.e., $2(\sigma/\sqrt{n})$, away from the expected value under the null hypothesis. For a one-tailed test at the 5 percent level, 1.645 standard deviations are used. Then, see whether or not the sample mean falls in the unlikely region.

P-values, Z-values, and confidence intervals also can be vehicles for hypothesis testing. The Z-statistic measures how many standard deviations the sample mean is from its expected value under the null hypothesis,

$$Z\text{-statistic} = \frac{\text{observed sample mean} - \text{expected value under null hypothesis}}{\text{standard deviation of the sample mean}}$$

For a two-tailed test, there is about a 5 percent chance of being two standard deviations away from the expected value, and thus of having a Z-value greater than 2. For a one-tailed test, there is about a 5 percent chance of being 1.645 standard deviations to one side of the expected value. Z-values greater than these numbers cast doubt on the null hypothesis. For any particular observed Z-value, the normal table shows the probability of being so far from the expected value. This probability is called a *P*-value.

Yet another approach is to use the sample mean and standard deviation to construct a confidence interval. A null hypothesis will be rejected at the 5 percent level if and only if it lies outside a corresponding 95 percent confidence interval. The reasoning is simple: If the sample mean is more than two standard deviations from its expected value under the null hypothesis, then it has a Z-value greater than 2, a *P*-value less than .05, and a 95 percent confidence interval that excludes the null hypothesis.

The very same logic is used for binomial tests of the success probability π. For small samples, the table of binomial probabilities is used, but for large samples, we can use the normal distribution and the fact that the sample proportion p has an expected value π and standard deviation $\{\pi(1 - \pi)/n\}^{1/2}$.

REVIEW EXERCISES

10.31   In a large high school in New York City, 60 randomly selected students tried a new math textbook, while the rest of the students used the old text. On an achievement test given at the end of the year, the students using the old book averaged 74, with a standard deviation of 9, while the students using the new book averaged 79, with a standard deviation of 9. Assuming scores to be normally distributed with a mean of 74 and a standard deviation of 9, can the observed performance of the students using the new book be plausibly attributed to sampling error? Why might there be sampling error here? Is the normal distribution assumption important?

10.32   Critically evaluate this statistical argument:
"Left-handers and right-handers continue to debate about who hits a baseball better, but the answer may lie in the eye of the beholder.

"A University of North Carolina researcher gives the edge to left-handers. In a New England Journal of Medicine article, Arthur Padilla explains that the right eye is dominant in most right-handers. But most natural right-handers who bat from the right side are forced to watch the ball coming toward the plate with their left eye.

"But the pattern does not hold as frequently with left-handers, Padilla said, because many who hit from the left side also have a dominant right eye, the one closest to the pitcher. He said only a small percentage of right-handers have a dominant left eye.

"However, the ultimate authority—statistics—do not support Padilla's theory. Among the 10 leading hitters in the major leagues as of Wednesday, five bat right-handed, two left-handed, and three are switch hitters."

"Morning Briefing" *Los Angeles Times,* April 26, 1984.

10.33 Consumer Inspects magazine has decided to test the net-weight claims of several makers of peanut butter. Each company claims that its jars contain 18 ounces of peanut butter. From previous tests, it is known that the standard deviation of peanut butter weights is 0.2 ounce. Consumer Inspects will weigh the contents of 100 jars of each brand of peanut butter. What should they use for a cutoff for the average net weight of 100 jars if they want there to be no more than a .01 probability of falsely accusing a company of selling jars with an average net weight of less than 18 ounces (and thus risking a law suit)?

10.34 The stopping distance (at 55 mph) for a company's premium tire is 54 meters with a standard deviation of 10 meters. Two consultants conduct independent tests of a new tread design. The first consultant tests 25 tires and gets an average stopping distance of 48 meters. The second consultant tests 100 tires and gets an average stopping distance of 50 meters. Which test result provides the more convincing statistical evidence that the new tread design does reduce the average stopping distance? Explain your reasoning.

10.35 The average weight of a certain breed of cattle is 1800 pounds, with a standard deviation of 125 pounds. A new feed is tried on 25 cattle and it gives an average weight of 1750. Is this difference statistically significant at the 5 percent level? Use a two-sided test and give the Z- and P-values. Give a 95 percent confidence interval for the expected weight of cattle using this new feed.

10.36 Ralph is an avid bowler. He has an expected score of 180 with a standard deviation of 40. Assume that his scores are normally distributed and independent. What are the probabilities that

a. his score will be above 200?
b. his score will be below 100?
c. his average score for three games will be above 200?
d. his average score for five games will be above 200?

10.37 (*continuation*) Ralph moves to a new city and wants to join a first-place bowling team, the Boomers, that happens to have an opening. Ralph tells the Boomers that he averages 195, and they ask him to bowl five games to verify this claim. The statistician on the Boomers views the situation as follows:

$$H_0: \mu = 195$$
$$H_1: \mu < 195$$

What cutoff five-game average should the Boomers' statistician set so that there will be only a 5 percent chance of incorrectly rejecting Ralph's claim? (Assume that the standard deviation for bowlers of this caliber is known to be 40.) What are Ralph's chances of successfully passing himself off as a 195-average bowler?

10.38 Gusto beer claims that its cans contain 12 ounces of beer. However, a chemistry fraternity carefully weighed the contents of 144 Gusto beer cans and found an average net weight of only 11.9 ounces, with a standard deviation of 0.9 ounce. Construct a 95 percent confidence interval for the net weight of Gusto beer cans. Does this fraternity's study refute Gusto's claim? (Use a two-sided test with a 5 percent significance level.)

10.39 Researchers separately asked 153 married men and their wives to state the highest school grade completed by the wives.[9] The difference, X = husband's answer − wife's answer, is a measure of the extent to which men exaggerate or belittle their wife's educational accomplishments. Whelpton and Kiser found that the average value of X was 0.32 with a standard deviation of 1.1. Use these data to make a two-sided test of the null hypothesis that the population mean of X is zero. Can the positive sample mean plausibly be explained by sampling error?

• **10.40**   An Ace delivery truck has a maximum capacity of one ton, in that if the net weight exceeds this amount, there is likely to be severe engine damage. This truck is to deliver cartons whose weights average 40 pounds, with a standard deviation of 4 pounds. What is the maximum number of cartons that can be loaded if the probability of exceeding one ton is to be kept below 1 percent?

•• **10.41** X is a normally distributed random variable with known standard deviation $\sigma = 100$ and unknown mean μ. The competing hypotheses are

$$H_0: \mu = 500$$

$$H_1: \mu = 550$$

The choice between these two hypotheses is to be based on a random sample of size 25. For a test with .05 probability of Type I error, the text uses a 533 cutoff for the sample mean:

$$\text{reject } H_0 \text{ if } \overline{X} > 533$$

$$\text{accept } H_0 \text{ if } \overline{X} \leq 533$$

Why is a one-tailed test such as this all in the tail? In particular, compare this test to these tests:

$$\text{reject } H_0 \text{ if } 516 < \overline{X} < 519$$

$$\text{accept } H_0 \text{ otherwise}$$

or

$$\text{reject } H_0 \text{ if } 516 < \overline{X} < 518 \text{ or } \overline{X} > 540$$

$$\text{accept } H_0 \text{ otherwise}$$

10.42   During 1975–1979, there were 16,466,000 recorded births in the United States, of which 8,444,000 were males. Use these data to test the hypothesis that male and female babies are equally likely.

10.43   An upcoming election was considered to be a tossup until one of the candidates admitted that she didn't like apple pie. A new poll of 100 randomly selected voters found 46 percent favoring this candidate and 54 percent favoring the opponent. Are these data sufficient to reject the null hypothesis that the voters are evenly divided between the two candidates, or can it reasonably be attributed to sampling error? What is the nature of the sampling error here?

10.44   Consumer Retorts magazine tested the reliability of a new electronic table wiper. Three of these machines were used for three months. Consumer Retorts certifies an appliance as trouble-free if there are no problems with any of the three machines. What is the probability that these electronic table wipers will be certified as trouble-free if a machine's probability of breaking down within three months is

a. .10?

b. .20?

c. .50?

10.45 A certain professor gives true-false exams because they are so easy to grade. During his long career, this professor has accumulated nearly 8000 true-false questions, which are conveniently stored on index cards. For each exam, the professor shuffles the cards and selects the exam questions. (The students have also accumulated a set of these questions over the years and pass them on from one class to the next.) The professor's intention is to pass students who have learned enough to answer 70 percent of these 8000 questions correctly. If an exam consists of 100 questions, how many correct answers should this professor require for a passing grade in order to be 99 percent sure that a student who knows the answers to 70 percent of these 8000 questions passes the course? What, then, is the probability of passing for a student who only knows the correct answers to 60 percent of these 8000 questions? To 50 percent?

10.46 Two researchers looked at the performance of NFL teams that were big underdogs (given more than 15 points by bookmakers) over the period 1969–1974.[10] Including their point spreads, these underdogs won 32 of 50 games. Is this winning proportion statistically significantly different from .50?

10.47 Willard H. Longcor conducted some tests of inexpensive and precision-made dice.[11] Two million rolls were made with the precision-made dice, recording on each roll whether an even or odd number appeared. A new die was used after every 20,000 tosses, to guard against imperfections from the wear and tear of being rolled over and over. The same experiment was conducted with inexpensive dice, but Longcor stopped after 1,160,000 rolls:

dice	rolls	fraction even
precision-made	2,000,000	.50045
inexpensive	1,160,000	.50725

For each type of dice, test the null hypothesis that even and odd numbers are equally likely to be rolled.

• **10.48** The text discusses R.A. Fisher's example of a lady who claims that she can usually tell whether milk or tea is poured into her cup first. The probability of a Type I error is .035 when we decide to accept her claim only if she correctly identifies at least 7 out of 8 randomly prepared cups. We can make this probability of Type I error exactly 5 percent by using a randomized binomial test: If she identifies 6 out of 8 cups, there is a probability P that we will accept her claim and a probability $1 - P$ that we will reject her claim. (We will still always accept her claim if she gets 7 or 8 right.) How high should we set P to make the probability of Type I error 5 percent? How could we implement this randomized binomial test?

•• **10.49** Eight cups are used to test a lady's claim that she can usually tell whether the tea or milk was poured first. If she correctly identifies 7 of the 8 cups, is this performance more convincing if she knows that

a. with each cup, a coin is flipped to determine whether the tea or milk is poured first, or

b. it is decided in advance to pour the tea first in 4 cups and the milk first in the other 4 cups?

••**10.50**   A chartist claims an ability to find patterns in stock prices that help tell whether a stock's price is going to go up or down. To test this claim, the chartist is shown graphs of stock prices for 10 unidentified companies over unidentified periods of time. For 5 of these companies, the stock's price rose sharply shortly after the end of the period shown in the chart. For the other 5 companies, the stock's price dropped sharply shortly after the period charted. The chartist is asked to identify which 5 stocks went up in price and which 5 went down. As it turns out, 3 of the 5 stocks identified as "winners" did go up in price, while 3 of the 5 put in the "losers" pile did go down. If the selections had been made randomly, what would be the chances of doing this well?

   If we demand a performance that would have no more than a 5 percent chance of occurring by luck alone, how many must the chartist identify correctly to convince us?

CHAPTER **11**

The Use and Abuse of Statistical Tests

If you torture the data long enough, Nature will confess.

Ronald H. Coase

TOPICS

Hypothesis tests are undoubtedly one of the most commonplace applications of statistics. The professional journals are full of statistical tests of all sorts of interesting, if somewhat esoteric theories. Indeed, it is almost impossible to publish empirical work now without doing the requisite statistical tests.

The more useful or outrageous theories find their ways into the popular press. Newspapers, magazines, and television news shows frequently report theories that have been "proven" statistically. For instance, I have before me newspaper clippings reporting that

> Vitamin C does help ward off colds. . . . there were statistically significant differences between treatment groups in the duration of morbidity.
>
> Statistics proved a "prima facie" case of discrimination against blacks and women [in Alabama jury rolls]
>
> Irrefutable Proof the History of United States is Shaped and Controlled by an Eternal, Non Human Mind and Hand!

In order to be intelligent consumers and/or producers of such tests, we must think a bit more carefully about just what it is that hypothesis tests do and don't do. First we'll reexamine the structure of the tests and then we'll look at their application.

11.1 SETTING UP TESTS

There are two troublesome, yet very practical questions in classical hypothesis testing. The first is choosing which theory to label the null hypothesis and which to label the alternative hypothesis. The second is why α, the probability of Type I error, should be set precisely equal to .05, with little or no attention paid to β, the probability of Type II error. These issues are closely related. Think back to Chapter 10 and the two hypotheses describing the effectiveness of a cram course intended to improve SAT scores:

$$H_0: \mu = 500$$

$$H_1: \mu = 550$$

With $\alpha = .05$, the cutoff for rejecting $\mu = 500$ is $\overline{X} > 533$. If we reverse the labels, so that

$$H_0: \mu = 550$$

$$H_1: \mu = 500$$

then $\alpha = .05$ implies that the cutoff is 33 points below the new null hypothesis 550, at 517. Similarly, the cutoff is 517 if we use the original labels, but set $\beta = .05$ rather than $\alpha = .05$. Figure 11.1 shows this logic.

Thus, it is really a dual question: On what basis do we choose a null hypothesis, with an accompanying 5 percent probability of Type I error? A formal rationale is complicated and not completely satisfying because it requires the placement of subjective probabilities on the competing hypotheses. A brief exposition of this rationale is in an appendix at the end of this chapter, but the general idea can be explained intuitively.

Choosing a Null Hypothesis

In most situations, there are a variety of competing possible values for the parameter of interest, say μ, and a multiplicity of αs and βs. The usual testing procedure is to set the cutoff point so as to fix $\alpha = .05$ for one particular value of μ. That is, we choose one particular hypothesis and set the test so that there is only a small probability that we will reject this hypothesis if it is, in fact, correct. Little or no attention is paid to the other possible values of μ, with their various αs and βs. This concentration of interest implies that the incorrect rejection of this null hypothesis is our paramount concern. What reasons, then, could justify focusing on the probability of incorrectly rejecting one particular hypothesis? Several ideas come to mind.

Figure 11.1 *The cutoff depends on which error probability is set at .05*

1. One of the hypotheses represents the conventional wisdom, based on theoretical logic and earlier studies. The weight of this wisdom argues that we should not hastily reject this hypothesis, based on our meager study, and so we make this favored hypothesis the null hypothesis to ensure a small probability of incorrectly abandoning it.

2. We don't have strong feelings favoring any of the competing hypotheses, but we do know that there will be serious consequences if we erroneously reject a particular hypothesis. So, we make this hypothesis the null hypothesis to ensure that there is only a small probability of incorrectly rejecting it.

3. The statistical rejection of a hypothesis is a stronger statement than is statistical acceptance. All of the values inside a confidence interval are acceptable hypotheses. Accepting a hypothesis just puts it on a list with other unrejected hypotheses. The rejection of a hypothesis, on the other hand, is a definitive conclusion. Thus, researchers may choose as the null hypothesis a *straw hypothesis* that they hope to reject. In fact, the terminology *null* hypothesis comes from this approach. To prove that there is an effect, we attempt to reject the hypothesis that there is no (*null*) effect.

Let's run through a few examples, starting with the cram course. The conventional wisdom is that such courses have little or no effect, arguing for "no effect" as the null hypothesis. It is not clear whether it is more dangerous to recommend a worthless course or to spurn a useful course. Those who want to show that the course is effective would almost be compelled to make "no effect" the null hypothesis, hoping to show its effectiveness by rejecting this straw hypothesis. So, there are at least two reasons for making "no effect" the null hypothesis.

Now consider the example of a new additive that gives food a more appetizing color, but may cause cancer. The consequences of mistakenly approving a carcinogenic additive are far worse than the consequences of incorrectly withholding a safe additive. Unless it is a substance that scientific knowledge tells us is almost surely safe, the null hypothesis should be that the additive is a carcinogen. The additive should be presumed dangerous until proven otherwise. The same logic applies to our justice system, although trials aren't usually decided by statistical analysis. The consequences of sending an innocent person to prison are thought to be far worse than the consequences of letting a guilty person go free. So, the appropriate null hypothesis is that a person is innocent until proven guilty.

What about a medicine that may be either beneficial or worthless? There may be some scientific knowledge about whether or not a particular substance may be of any value. An independent researcher's feelings also may be influenced by the fact that there are always plenty of unscrupulous charlatans around who are eager to sell anything that people can be persuaded to buy. On the other hand, the consequences of withholding a miraculous drug may be more serious than the consequences of allowing the peddling of a worthless drug. This argument suggests letting the null hypothesis be that the drug is effective. Finally, the straw hypothesis approach argues for proving a drug's value by making "no effect" the null hypothesis. Here, we have a split decision that could go either way.

The Right Level of α

We can continue this line of reasoning by thinking more carefully about the appropriate α. The selected probability of Type I error, α, is called the **significance level** of the test. With the usual $\alpha = .05$, the researcher will report that the results either were or were not "significant at the 5 percent level." The 5 percent α is so ingrained that some researchers simply say that their results "are statistically significant," with the reader understanding that the test was constructed to allow a 5 percent chance of Type I error. But why use 5 percent? Why not 1 percent or 0.0001 percent? Frankly, there is not much more than acquired habit behind the 5 percent rule. There is no single right level for α! It's like asking "How far is far?" If you tell me the cutoff should be precisely at $\alpha = 5$ percent, I'll ask why not 4 percent or 6 percent? And neither you nor anyone else has a convincing answer.

The logic of our tests is that we choose as the null hypothesis some hypothesis that we want to be cautious about incorrectly abandoning. If deviations between this hypothesis and the data can be plausibly explained by sampling error, then we'll explain them that way. If it strains credulity to appeal to sampling error, then we will reluctantly abandon the null hypothesis. So the α question is really, "How improbable does the sampling error explanation have to be before we abandon it?" Five percent seems like a reasonable, ballpark answer. It's pretty improbable, but it's not so incredible that we never let go of a null hypothesis.

In some situations, a little more caution may be called for. If we're testing a potentially dangerous drug, then we may well demand very strong evidence before approving it. A tough standard can be imposed by having the null hypothesis be that the drug is dangerous and setting α at 1 percent, 0.1 percent, or even lower. Or, in cases where the conventional wisdom is very strong, convincing evidence will have to be even stronger. If the null hypothesis is a widely accepted conventional wisdom, then α should be set very low, so as to rule out firmly the possibility of sampling error. An interesting example of this logic is the *Journal of Experimental Psychology*, which publishes research on extrasensory perception (ESP) and other controversial matters. The editor of this journal explained that

> In editing the *Journal* there has been a strong reluctance to accept and publish results . . . when those results were significant [only] at the .05 level, whether by one- or two-tailed test. This has not implied a slavish worship of the .01 levels, as some critics may have implied. Rather, it reflects a belief that it is the responsibility of the investigator in a science to reveal his effect in such a way that no reasonable man would be in a position to discredit the results by saying they were the product of the way the ball bounces.[1]

The best that can be said for using a standard α is that it provides a common vocabulary and benchmark, but there is no reason to pay slavish homage to $\alpha = .05, .01$, or to any other particular number, and few researchers do. Everyone realizes that a P-value of 4.9 percent is "barely significant," that 5.1 percent is "almost significant," that 1 percent is "highly significant," and so on. As long as the *P*-value or *Z*-value is reported, readers can judge for themselves whether the sampling error explanation is sufficiently implausible to discredit the null hypothesis.

Exercises

11.1 A police department requires that dealers supply tires with an expected tire life of at least 30,000 miles. To ensure that a dealer meets this requirement, the police department tests a random sample of 16 tires and obtains a sample mean of 25,800 miles with a standard deviation of 8,000 miles. Allowing a .05 probability of Type I error, use these data to test the null hypothesis

$$H_0: \mu \geq 30,000$$

If a dealer supplies tires that have an actual expected life of 27,500 miles with a standard deviation of 8,000 miles, what is the probability that a sample of 16 tires will pass the police department's test?

11.2 (*continuation*) Does this test give the benefit of the doubt to the tire dealer? Compare it with a decision to buy from a dealer only if a test of 16 tires leads to the rejection of the null hypothesis that $\mu < 30,000$.

11.3 The text has used the example of testing whether or not a cram course raises SAT scores by 50 points. Two competing hypotheses are that the average test scores of students taking this course are $\mu = 500$ and $\mu = 550$. If we conduct a standard statistical test at the 5 percent level, does it make any difference which value of μ we use as the null hypothesis and which we use as the alternative hypothesis?

11.4 (*continuation*) Why do you think $\mu = 500$ was used as the null hypothesis in the text?

11.5 Some chemists have invented a cola sweetener that is slightly less expensive to produce than the sweetener that a company now uses. Fearful of bad publicity and expensive lawsuits, the company's president orders some tests to determine whether or not this new sweetener is a carcinogen. Should the null hypothesis be that it does or does not cause cancer?

11.6 A computer software company has stumbled on a bizarre computer game concept unlike any other now on the market. The company's president thinks that it is equally likely that this new game will be a sensation or a flop. If it does flop, there will be substantial losses, but if it is a sensation, the gains will be enormous. The president orders a very small marketing survey to test consumer interest without letting the new concept fall into the hands of their competitors. Should the null hypothesis be that the game will be a sensation or that it will be a flop? What value of α would you recommend?

11.7 A doctor suspects that a patient may have a rare disease. This disease is seldom serious, but the treatment is less expensive the earlier the disease is discovered. In testing for the disease, should the null hypothesis be that the patient does or does not have the disease? What value of α would you recommend?

11.8 A renowned political forecaster conducts an election-day opinion poll, hoping to make an early prediction of a presidential race that has been considered too close to call.

There will be considerable glory if the prediction is correct, but even larger embarrassment if the prediction is wrong. If poll's results are not decisive, the forecaster will just say, ''It is too close to call.'' Should the null hypothesis be that the incumbent will get more than 50 percent of the votes, less than 50 percent, or exactly 50 percent? What value of α do you recommend?

11.2   BUT IS IT IMPORTANT?

In testing hypotheses, it is easy to be confused by the distinction between statistical significance and practical importance. A statistically significant result may be of little or no consequence. Conversely, a researcher may find a potentially very important result that does not happen to be statistically significant. To illustrate what may appear paradoxical, let's return again to the math SAT cram course.

A random sample of n students takes the cram course and then the SAT test. Their average score $\overline{X}$ is normally distributed,

$$\overline{X} \sim N[\mu,\ 100/\sqrt{n}]$$

The standard deviation is assumed to stay at 100, but it is not known whether their expected score will go up, go down, or be unchanged. The null hypothesis is that the average score of students who take the course is 500, the same as for students who don't take the course,

$$H_0\colon \mu = 500$$

One way of using the sample to test this null hypothesis is to compute a 95 percent confidence interval and see whether or not 500 is inside this interval. Using our two-standard-deviations rule of thumb, we have

$$.95 = P[\overline{X} - 2(100/\sqrt{n}) < \mu < \overline{X} + 2(100/\sqrt{n})]$$

To exaggerate our impending conclusion, let's pretend that this SAT cram course garners as much national attention as the polio vaccine tests in the 1950s. A sample of 1,000,000 students take the cram course and obtain an average score of 500.3. Our confidence interval is

$$.95 = P[500.3 - 2(0.1) < \mu < 500.3 + 2(0.1)]$$

$$= P[500.1 < \mu < 500.5]$$

These data are sufficient to reject the null hypothesis. The average score of 500.3 is three standard deviations above 500, and so we conclude that cramming does have a statistically significant effect on math SAT scores. But this statistically significant effect is of little or no practical importance; no rational person would spend time and money to raise his or her score by less than half a point! The course should be abandoned, even though it has a statistically significant effect on math SAT scores.

Now let's look at the reverse case. Our underfunded researcher can only afford to enroll and test four students. Their average score after taking the course turns out to be 598, which is better than 84 percent of the students taking the test. Our confidence interval is very wide, though, because we have so few data:

$$.95 = P[598 - 2(100/\sqrt{4}) < \mu < 598 + 2(100/\sqrt{4})]$$
$$= P[498 < \mu < 698]$$

The confidence interval is so large that we cannot rule out the possibility that the course has no effect. By the luck of the draw, we may have picked four 84th-percentile students and not raised their scores at all. On the other hand, we may have picked four 16th percentile students and raised their scores 200 points. Our best guess is a 98-point improvement, but the small sample size gives a 100-point margin for error, ranging from a 2-point decrease to a 198-point increase. The result is not statistically significant, but it may be of great importance. A course that, at worst, lowers scores 2 points and, at best, raises scores 198 points would appeal to many students. This researcher has found a potential bonanza; the course will thrive and additional research will be done.

These two examples are deliberate caricatures that are designed to make a point. As the sample size increases, our confidence interval shrinks to zero. If our sample is the entire population, the sample mean will exactly equal the population mean and there will be no sampling error at all. Any null hypothesis would be rejected, except for the one that has exactly the right number for the population mean. And, yet, without knowing the whole population, there is no chance of picking the precise value of this number. It follows that, whatever null hypothesis we use, we are sure to reject it if we just gather enough data! Thus, a cynical way of looking at hypothesis tests is that accepted hypotheses are those that we don't yet have enough data to reject.

Remember, hypothesis tests only evaluate statistical significance, and not practical importance. Think of the expected value of math SAT scores after a cram course. If scads of data give a confidence interval 500.0003 ± 0.0002, then 500 is indeed rejected by the data. We were sure that it eventually would be, as soon as we gathered enough data. But, as a practical matter, the distinction between 500 and 500.0003 is of no importance whatsoever. The meaningful conclusion is that the course has little or no effect, and that conclusion should be drawn whether the confidence interval is 501 ± 2 (with 500 "accepted" by the data) or 500.0003 ± 0.0002 (with 500 "rejected" by the data).

Hypothesis tests can be a contrived and misleading exercise. When we select a specific hypothesis and then conclude that it is either accepted or rejected by the data, we are only giving a partial glimpse at the implications of the data. A confidence interval often paints a clearer picture of the data than does a hypothesis test. With a confidence interval we can see the estimate and use our common sense to judge whether, as a practical matter, this estimate is a large or small number. A confidence interval also shows the margin for sampling error, whose practical importance can also be judged. Finally, a confidence interval shows which numbers are rejected by the data and, again, we can judge whether particularly interesting numbers differ from the estimate in a practical as well as a statistical sense.

Unfortunately, hypothesis tests are the usual reporting style, perhaps because they sound so decisive. But they may be misleading. Consider, for example, the question of whether men and women are equally likely to be right-handed. A sample of 6,672 people found that 90 percent of the men and 92 percent of the women were right-handed. The rest were left-handed or ambidextrous. This difference is statistically significant, but of no real importance.

Darrell Huff gives the example of a *Reader's Digest* study in the 1950s that was designed to see if there were any real differences in the amounts of nicotine, tar, and so on in different brands of cigarettes. The conclusion was that the brands they studied were virtually identical. But, as Huff explains,

> In the lists of almost identical amounts of poisons, one cigarette had to be at the bottom, and that one was Old Gold. Out went the telegrams, and big advertisements appeared in newspapers at once in the biggest type at hand. The headlines and the copy simply said that of all the cigarettes tested by this great national magazine Old Gold had the least of these undesirable things in its smoke. Excluded were all the figures and any hint that the difference was negligible.[2]

For an example going the other way, consider the conclusion of two economists studying the effect of inflation on election outcomes. They estimated that, in the 1976 election, the inflation issue added 7 percentage points to the Republican vote. A standard deviation of 5 percentage points gave them a 95 percent confidence interval of 7 percent $\pm$ 10 percent. They concluded that "in fact, and contrary to widely held views, inflation has no impact on voting behavior."[3] That is, of course, not at all what their data say. The fact that they cannot definitively rule out 0 percent does not show that 0 percent is the true value. The confidence interval does include 0 percent, but it also includes everything from -3 percent to $+17$ percent. Their best estimate is 7 percent $\pm$ 10 percent, and 7 percent is more than enough to swing most elections one way or the other.

Sometimes, it is a comparison of apples and oranges that leads to an erroneous conclusion. For instance, during the Spanish-American War, the death rate was 9 per 1000 in the U.S. Navy and 16 per 1000 in New York City. Navy recruiters claimed that it was safer to be fighting in the Navy than to be living in New York. A meaningful conclusion, however, would require a comparison of the death rates of the same group, here healthy young men.

Exercises

11.9 A junior high school student made a wooden die in wood shop. The instructor suggested that this die looked a bit lopsided, so that the number 6 might not come up exactly one-sixth of the time. In 18,000 careful rolls of this die, the number 6 came up 3126 times. Is this difference from 3000

a. of statistical significance?
b. of practical importance?

11.10   The president of a large state university boasts that the entering freshman class has significantly better English skills than the average high school student who is considering a college education. Nationwide scores on a standardized English test are normally distributed with a mean of 500 and a standard deviation of 100. Is this president's boast justified by the fact that the average score of this college's 10,000 freshmen is 503?

11.11   (*continuation*) The owner of a small bookstore boasts that four new employees have significantly better-than-average English skills. Is this owner's boast justified by the fact that the average score of these four new employees is 580?

11.12   A "new, improved" toothpaste claims that it significantly reduces cavities for children in their cavity-prone years. Cavities per year for this age group are normally distributed with a mean of 3 and a standard deviation of 1. A study of 2500 children who used this toothpaste found an average of 2.95 cavities per child. Explain why you are or are not persuaded of this toothpaste's cavity-reducing ability.

11.13   Mercury and Venus are "inner" planets, in that they are closer to the sun than the earth. The other six planets in our solar systems are "outer" planets. Relative to the earth, the two inner planets have an average mass of 0.43, while the six outer planets average 74. A statistics text proposes to test whether this difference is statistically significant.[4] Why is such a test nonsensical?

11.14   *The New York Times* reported that

> Trying to discern any sort of seasonality in stock market movements may be a futile exercise. Perhaps the most ingenious "analysis" was done by the Rothschild firm, which noted that February begins the Year of the Dragon in the Chinese calendar. . . . during the 20th century . . . there were twice as many up Dragon years [4] as down Dragon years [2].[5]

Are you convinced by this evidence?

•• **11.15**   Critically evaluate:

> Is it ever possible to have too large a sample? Some statisticians feel that it is. Suppose we are looking at two groups of students, each of which has been taught to read by a different system. We want to know if one system works better than the other. If the groups are small, then the amount of error to be expected will be large, so only a very large difference between the performance of the two groups will count as evidence for the superiority of one method over the other. Now as we increase the size of the groups, the amount of error will decrease. Perhaps there is a point at which a really insignificant difference in performance will count as evidence because small as it is, it is still larger than the expected amount of error. Although this situation is theoretically possible, it is hardly a common problem, since the time and money needed to do any research make it relatively unlikely that too large a sample will be studied.[6]

11.3   DATA MINING

A selective reporting of results is potentially the most serious abuse of hypothesis tests. To illustrate the pitfalls, I'll pretend that I'm a psychic and you pretend that you're a statistician. I come into your office, claiming that I have a psychic ability to predict the outcomes of coin flips. I don't claim to be perfect, but I do get more than 50 percent right. My "secret" is that I have discovered a pattern in coins flips: After a head occurs, the next flip is likely to be a tail, and vice versa. You pull out a pencil, paper, and coin and dutifully test my wild theory.

Because the conventional wisdom is that there are no patterns in coin flips, you let the null hypothesis be that my probability of a correct prediction is $\pi = .5$. The alternative hypothesis is my claim that $\pi > .5$. Pressed for time and scornful of my claim, you have the test consist of just 20 flips of a coin. How many do I have to get right to convince you that I am not just a guesser? Ten correct is unimpressive, while 20 out of 20 is astonishing. Where do we draw the line? If the null hypothesis is true, so that $\pi = .5$, then the binomial distribution (in Table 1) tells us that there is a .058 probability of getting 14 or more right. So, let's make that the cutoff.

Well, the truth of the matter is that I am not a psychic and my theory is worthless. I make my 20 guesses and perhaps I only get 8 right. You rightly throw me out of your office and go back to work. As I go out the door, another alleged psychic walks in, with her theory that coin flips have momentum: a head is likely to be followed by another head and a tail is likely to be followed by another tail. In the interest of science, you flip your coin 20 more times and test her theory. She's a fraud, too, and only gets 12 out of 20 right. Not bad, but not good enough. Out she goes and in comes another, with yet another theory: a head tends to be followed by a head, but two or more heads in a row tend to be followed by a tail—another test and another fraud exposed.

Somewhere along the line, however, one of these frauds is going to get lucky and get 14 or more right. A 5 percent chance of Type I error implies that about 1 out of 20 worthless theories will be statistically significant. This reasoning is not limited to fraudulent psychics; it applies to all statistical tests of all theories. Even if you never test anything but fraudulent theories, you are sure to give your statistical seal of approval to some, if only you test enough of them.

In practice, with powerful computers, mountains of data, and incredible pressures to produce statistically significant results, untold numbers of worthless theories get tested. The harried researcher will try 20 theories, write up the result that is most statistically significant (lowest P-value, for instance) and throw the rest in the trash. Twenty struggling graduate students may each try one theory; one will get a statistically significant result, a thesis, and a research grant, and the other 19 will transfer to law schools. The problem for science and society is that we only see the tip of the statistical iceberg. We see the result that is statistically significant, but not the other 19 that didn't work out. If we knew that this one was 1 out of 20 tries, we would surely be less impressed by its statistical significance.

This testing of many theories is known as **data mining** (also "data grubbing" or "fishing expeditions"). The eager researcher takes a body of data, tests countless theories, and reports the one that is the most statistically significant. The end result, which is that a statistically significant result has been obtained, shows little more than the energetic efforts of the researcher. We know beforehand that, even if only worthless theories are examined, the researcher will eventually stumble on a worth-

Cartoon by Rob Pudim, courtesy *The Skeptical Inquirer*

less theory that seems confirmed by the data, due to the inevitable sampling error. It is not surprising, then, when a data miner finds a statistically significant result, and it should not convince us that the researcher has found anything more than sampling error. We cannot tell whether the end product of a data mining expedition shows the veracity of a useful theory or the perseverence of a determined researcher.

The Sherlock Holmes Inference

Many theories get rejected out of hand without a formal statistical test. Think of the 20 coin flips again. In these tests, each quack walked into the office with a harebrained scheme for predicting coin flips, and a coin was flipped 20 times. In practice, researchers often have the data in hand before they concoct the theories to be tested. A practiced observer can look at the data and quickly see which theories are promising and which aren't going to work; maybe 5 tests are run through the computer and 50 are run through the mind.

For example, I just flipped a coin 20 times. The results were

T H H T H T T T T T H H T H T T H H T T

In less than 30 seconds, I found a pattern, a "theory," to explain these coin flips. My theory is that a flipped coin tends to give a tail followed by two heads, over and over again. If we test my theory using these data, we find that it correctly predicts 15 out of 20 outcomes, a statistically significant result! These data reject your suspicion that I am just a hopeless guesser.

Yet, would you bet that my system will continue to hit 15 out of 20? Of course not, because I told you how I came up with my "theory," and my method is not convincing. I looked at the data, tried many possible theories in my mind, and found one that would have been right 15 out of 20 times, if only I had known the theory before the coin was flipped—but I didn't.

This is pure and simple data mining. When you see how it is done and then see it applied to something like coin flips, the results are not persuasive; your intuition resists such theories. But professional data mining is usually applied to situations where we don't have much intuition. And you don't get to see the data mining in action; you only see the final results.

If I came to you and said that, as a professional economist, I have been studying the stock market and have come up with a theory that works, you might pay attention. If I told you that in 15 of the last 20 years, this theory has correctly predicted whether the stock market will go up or down, you might get very interested. Yet, I may have found my stock market system in the very same way that I found my system for predicting coin flips. If H stands for an up year and T for a down year, then the 20 coins flips recorded earlier might well be a history of the stock market over some 20-year period. I could look at this history of ups and downs and, in less than 30 seconds, find a pattern that seems to explain the stock market: The market goes backward one step and then up two steps. And sure enough, this theory is right 15 out of 20 years. Subjected to statistical tests, we would find that this 75 percent accuracy decisively rejects the null hypothesis that I have only a 50 percent chance of guessing which way the market is going. The statistical evidence sounds pretty impressive, unless you know how I did it.

The theoretical logic behind hypothesis tests is quite straightforward. The researcher has some competing theories, gathers some data to test these theories, and reports the results. But, in a hurried effort to get publishable (or salable) results, some researchers work in the other direction; they study the data until they find theories that will be shown to be statistically significant. This is the Sherlock Holmes method of reasoning, as indicated by the quotations prefacing the last three chapters: examine the data to find theories that explain these data. It can be a very useful method of operation. Many important scientific theories, including Mendel's genetic theory, were discovered by attempts to find theories that explain the data. But Sherlock Holmes research has also been the source of thousands of quack theories.

How do we tell the difference? How can we separate the genius from the quack? There are two good antidotes to unrestrained data mining: common sense and fresh data. Unfortunately, there are short supplies of both. The first thing we should think about when confronted with statistical evidence in support of some hypothesis, is "Does it make sense?" If it is a ridiculous theory, then you shouldn't be persuaded by anything less than mountains of evidence. One of the reasons you laughed off my claims of predicting coin flips is that your common sense tells you that coin flips are unpredictable. Even if I walked in with data showing that I had successfully predicted 99 out of 100 flips, you would still be unconvinced. Instead of accepting my coin-calling prowess, you would suspect that somehow I had cheated or massaged the data. As Thomas Paine once wrote, ''is it more probable that nature should go out of her course, or that a man should tell a lie?''

Most situations are not as clear cut as these coin predictions, but nonetheless, you should still exercise common sense in evaluating statistical evidence. Unfortunately, common sense is an uncommon commodity, and many silly theories have been seriously tested by honest researchers. I'll give you some examples shortly.

The second antidote is fresh data. I've explained before why it is not a fair test of a theory to use the very data that were used to choose the theory. For an impartial test, we should specify the theory before we see the data that will be used to test the theory. If certain data have been used to concoct the theory, then look for fresh data that have not been contaminated by data mining. Think of the coin-flipping example again. When I announce that I have a system that was right 15 out of 20 times, your likely response is, ''Oh, yeah. Let me get out a coin and we'll see how well you do.'' This will be fresh data that will most likely expose my fraudulent system. Researchers should do the same with any theory that is dug up by data mining.

In chemistry, physics, and the other natural sciences, this is standard procedure. Whenever someone announces an important new theory, a dozen people will rush to their laboratories to see if they can duplicate the results. Unfortunately, most social scientists don't have laboratories where they can conduct experiments and generate fresh data. Instead, they have to wait for the world to turn and then patiently record data as they occur. If they have a theory about the economy, presidential elections, or peace, they may have to wait several years or even decades to accumulate enough fresh data to test their theories.

When economists have done this further testing with fresh data, the results are usually disappointing. They often find that their theory doesn't explain fresh data nearly as well as it did the original data. Their usual explanation is that there have been ''structural changes'' in the economy that necessitate modifications of their original models. They then mine the fresh data for a new theory. In this way, a provocative first paper turns into a career. An alternative explanation of the disappointing results with fresh data is the data mining itself.

Exercises

11.16   An eager graduate student has found several worthless theories to test. This student hopes that for at least one of these theories, the data will reject (at the 5 percent significance level) the null hypothesis that the theory is worthless. If so, the student will have provocative conclusions and perhaps a thesis topic. Assuming that the tests are independent, what is the probability that this student will be successful if the number of theories tested is

a. one?

b. two?

c. ten?

d. twenty?

e. ∞?

11.17 A psychic claims an ability to predict the outcome of coin flips. To test this claim, a coin is flipped 100 times, with the psychic predicting each flip in advance. It is decided to accept the psychic's claim if at least 60 outcomes are forecast correctly. What is the probability that this psychic's claim will be accepted if, in fact, the psychic is a fraud? What is the probability that the psychic's claim will be rejected if, in fact, the psychic's probability of making a correct prediction is 51 percent? 60 percent? 75 percent? 90 percent?

11.18 A professor conducts a coin-calling experiment with a class of 32 students. Half of the students predict heads for the first flip and half predict tails. The coin is flipped: it's a head and the first half is right. These 16 students then predict a second flip, with half saying heads and the other half tails. It comes up tails. The 8 students who have been right twice in a row now try for a third time. Half predict heads and half tails, and it comes up tails. The 4 students who were right divide again on whether the next flip will be heads or tails. It's tails and now we're down to 2 students. One calls heads and the other tails. It's heads and we have our winner—the student who correctly predicted five in a row.

a. What is the probability of correctly calling five coin flips in a row?

b. Does five in a row satisfy the usual statistical test of the null hypothesis that a claimed psychic is just a guesser?

c. Would you bet $2 against my $1 that the winner of this contest will call the next flip correctly?

11.19 An unscrupulous investment adviser mails sample investment advice to 3200 wealthy investors. Half of the letters predict that the stock market will go up this month and half predict that it will go down. At the end of the month, it turns out that the market went down. This adviser crosses out the 1600 investors who were given bad advice and mails another sample prediction to the 1600 who were given correct advice. Half of these 1600 people are told that the market will go up in the second month and half are told that it will go down. At the end of this month, 400 investors have been given two correct predictions in a row. These people are given a third month's predictions; again, half are told that the market will go up and half are told that it will go down. By the end of five months, there are 100 investors who have received five correct predictions in a row and they should be eager to subscribe to the adviser's expensive investment service.

a. If the stock market is equally likely to go up or down, what is the probability of five correct predictions in a row?

b. As an investor who received five sample predictions, all of which were correct, would you be impressed?

c. As someone who saw how it was done, would you be impressed by five correct predictions?

d. What is the statistical fallacy here?

11.20 While playing bridge recently, Ira Rate picked up his 13-card hand and found that it contained no spades (and very few honors, either). He promptly threw his cards down and declared that the deal had not been random. He read in a book on probability and statistics that (a) the probability of being dealt a hand with no spades is less than 5 percent and (b) this low a probability is sufficient evidence to reject the null hypothesis of a fair deal. Point out a fault or two in his reasoning.

11.21   A researcher wants to show that a subject has a statistically significant ability to predict the outcomes of coin flips. The conventional null hypothesis is that the probability of a correct prediction is $\pi = .5$. If a test consists of 10 coin flips, then how many must this subject predict correctly for the probability of Type I error to be about 5 percent?

This researcher has decided that if the subject does not make enough correct predictions to pass the first test, then these results will be discarded and a second 10-coin test will be given. What is the probability that a guesser

a. will pass the first test?
b. will fail the first test, but pass the second?
c. will fail two tests, but pass a third?
d. will eventually pass a test?

• **11.22**   (*continuation*) This researcher has been criticized for discarding data and, in response, decides on a modified procedure. If the subject does not get enough correct answers to pass the first test, then 10 more flips will be predicted and the data combined to give a 20-flip test. How many correct predictions are required in a 20-flip test for about a .05 probability of Type I error?

If the subject does not pass this 20-flip test, then 10 more flips will be predicted and the researcher will use a 30-flip test. What is the probability that the subject will eventually pass one of these expanded tests?

•• **11.23**   (*continuation*) What is the probability that the subject will fail the 10-flip test, but pass the 20-flip test?

11.4   SOME FLIMSY THEORIES

Let's now look at several examples of theories that are statistically significant, but dubious at best.

How Not to Win at Craps

A book was written (and sold, of course) explaining a system for winning at craps. The author had recorded the outcomes of 50,000 dice rolls at a Las Vegas casino. The numbers came up just about as often as would be expected with fair dice, but a careful scrutiny of the sequence in which the numbers appeared revealed some unusual patterns. For example, the sequence 4–4–11 could be expected about 20 times in 50,000 roles, but it happened 31 times! If you had bet $100 on 11 whenever 4 came up twice in a row, you would have made a $13,700 profit. Similarly, the author found that the sequence 7–12–7 occurred 38 times and that on 10 of these 38 occasions, the next number was either a 2, 3, or 12. If you had bet $100 on craps (2, 3, or 12) whenever the sequence 7–12–7 appeared, you would have won $4,200.

Are you convinced by this evidence? This is exactly analogous to my finding a pattern in 20 coin flips. Your common sense should reject this system strongly. I hope that common sense is enough and that you don't go to Las Vegas to gather fresh evidence.

Tall Presidents

A month before the 1972 presidential election pitting Richard Nixon against George McGovern, *Parade* magazine reported that sociologist Saul Feldman of Case Western Reserve University,

> . . . whose research interest is height, took a reading of Presidential candidates for the past 40 years. He reports that with only one exception (Wendell Wilkie in 1940), the taller of the two candidates has always won the electoral victory. In 1968, he points out, Nixon just barely defeated Humphrey who at 5′11″ stands a half-inch shorter than the president. . . . "Heightism" is a prejudice just like sexism and racism, Feldman believes.[7]

Do Feldman's data show a statistically significant relationship between height and electoral success? If height is unimportant, then the winner is equally likely to be the shorter or taller candidate. Under this null hypothesis, the probability that the winner is the taller of the two candidates is $\pi = .50$. The binomial distribution tells us that if $\pi = .50$, then there is only a .01 probability of as many as 9 successes in 10 trials. Thus, the evidence seems to decisively reject the null hypothesis that height is unimportant and to confirm Feldman's "heightism" theory.

But let's think about this evidence a little more carefully. Presidential elections are not the Bernoulli trials assumed by a binomial distribution. Presidential candidates often run again and again, so that the outcomes are not independent. Dwight D. Eisenhower beat Adlai Stevenson in 1952 and he beat him again in 1956. The 1956 election did not provide fresh evidence about candidates of different heights; it just told us once again that Eisenhower was more popular than Stevenson. In fact, four of Feldman's ten elections involved Franklin Roosevelt winning again and again and again. So, the data are not quite as conclusive as they seem.

In addition, we can't help but wonder why Feldman started with the 1932 election. Why did he look back 40 years, instead of 20 years, 60 years, or some other number? Perhaps this 40-year period yielded the data that was most favorable to his theory, but it is not appropriate to discard data simply because it does not support one's theory. Whenever someone uses only part of the available data, we should wonder why the rest wasn't used.

What about common sense, our first antidote to data mining? My mind is not entirely made up, but my common sense rejects Feldman's simplistic theory. I cannot believe that a half-inch difference in height is responsible for Nixon's victory over Humphrey. Nor can I believe that height explains the four victories by Roosevelt, whose legs were paralyzed. If someone who is 6′4″ runs against someone who is 5′4″, then this height difference may well influence some voters. However, hardly anyone will notice an inch or two of difference, especially because the candidates hardly ever stand next to each other. Did anyone other than Feldman really know that Humphrey was a half-inch shorter than Nixon, let alone care?

What about the second antidote, fresh data? Well, one reason Feldman's theory was reported in *Parade* magazine was that he was virtually alone in predicting a McGovern victory in 1972. Because McGovern was $1\frac{1}{2}$ inches taller than Nixon, Feldman predicted that McGovern "should inch out Nixon this November." McGovern lost every state but Massachusetts. In 1976, Jimmy Carter beat Jerry Ford despite a $2\frac{1}{2}$-inch height disadvantage. In 1980, the taller man, Ronald Reagan, did win. So, using fresh data, Feldman's tall-president theory has been wrong two out of three times.

Presidential Names

If we scrutinize the characteristics of successful presidential candidates, it is easy to find patterns that make even less sense than "heightism." One is that the major party candidate with the longest last name wins. From 1900 through 1960, this theory was right an astounding 14 out of 15 times. It missed 3 of the next 4 times, but after the 1980 election it was still 15 out of 19 correct. What about the first letter of the last name being later in the alphabet than the opponent's? This one was right 10 out of 13 times from 1900 through 1948. It has only been right 4 out of 8 times since then, but that's still a credible 14 out of 21.

The statistical success of both of these theories is enhanced by the fact that many candidates win or lose more than once. For instance, five of these twentieth century winners were Roosevelts, which happens to be a long name that begins with a letter late in the alphabet. Once we've noticed all the Roosevelt victories, it is easy to find theories that work. Nominate a candidate named Roosevelt, for instance. Or if you want to be more adventurous, nominate a candidate whose last name has an S in the middle, but not on either end. There have been 10 such candidates and every single one won. If you believe this theory, that "S-ism" leads voters to favor candidates with an S in the middle of their name, then you don't yet understand the pitfalls of data mining.

Baseball and the President

The President of the United States has often thrown out the first pitch to start a new baseball season. What many people do not realize is that during presidential election years, the league that wins the World Series determines which party wins the White House. *The New York Times* carried an article in October 1976 explaining that the Democrats win the White House if the National League wins the World Series and the Republicans win if the American League does. As of 1976, there had been 18 presidential elections since the first World Series in 1903, and this theory worked 12 out of 18 times. In the modern baseball era, since 1940, the theory has been right 8 out of 9 times—the exception being 1948, when Truman surprised everybody in winning. So, with the Cincinnati Reds winning the 1976 World Series, this article concluded, "I am pleased to announce that the winner of the 1976 Presidential election will be Jimmy Carter." And what do you know, it worked again! (In 1980, though, the National League's Phillies beat Kansas City, while the Democrat Carter lost to Reagan.)

Football and the Stock Market

On Super Bowl Sunday in January 1983, both the business and sports sections of the *Los Angeles Times* carried articles on the "Super Bowl Stock Market Predictor." The theory is that the stock market takes off every time the National Football Conference (or a former NFL team now in the American Football Conference) wins the Super Bowl. The market goes down every year the AFC wins. This theory has proven to be correct for 15 out of the 16 Super Bowls. The one exception was

---

If NFC Wins, Buy Stocks

If you are a 49er football fan and a stock market investor as well—assuming you can afford both sports—you'll do well in 1984 if the Niners win Super Bowl XVIII.

Even if the 49ers don't make it to the Super Bowl but the Detroit Lions or Washington Redskins do and win, the stock market, based on the Standard & Poor's index of 500 stocks, will be up next year.

But if the Miami Dolphins, Los Angeles Raiders, Pittsburgh Steelers or Seattle Seahawks win the Super Bowl gonfalon next month, run for cover. The market will go down in the next 12 months.

Don't laugh. The Super Bowl Stock Market Predictor, as concocted by a distinguished market analyst, has been on the money since the professional football gala started in 1967.

When Robert Stovall, senior vice president and director of investment policy for Dean Witter Reynolds, started tracking the correlation between Super Bowl winners and the stock in the late 1960s and early 1970s, his work was viewed as just another analytical aberration. No longer.

Stovall's theory is simple as pumpkin pie. If an American Football Conference team wins the Super Bowl, the market will go down. If a Na-

tional Football Conference team wins, the market goes up.

"In January 1983, Super Bowl XVI was won by an old NFL team, the Washington Redskins by 27 to 17 over the Miami Dolphins," Stovall says. "Consequently, followers of the Super Bowl Omen were not too concerned when the stock market had a series of rolling corrections during 1983. They had faith . . . subsequently rewarded. As of December 15, the S&P 500 was up 13.2 percent for the year."

The best possible match-up in the up-coming extravaganza would pit the AFL's (formerly NFL) Pittsburgh Steelers against the NFL team entry.

"A stock market winner under this theory would thus be assured," says Stovall. The market analyst agrees that the Super Bowl-market correlation being proven correct in 16 of the last 17 years ain't bad. But he is a little defensive about the one miss, in 1970.

"The sole exception for the S&P 500 was in 1970 when Kansas City (an original AFL team) won and the S&P went up 0.1 percent," Stovall says. "According to the predictor theory the S&P should have declined that year. Would that all forecasters' flubs were by such a small margin!"

© Donald K. White, *San Francisco Chronicle*, December 28, 1983. Reprinted by permission.

1970, when Kansas City beat Minnesota and the market went up 0.1 percent. Thus *The Times* quoted a broker for Dean Witter Reynolds as saying, "Market observers will be glued to their TV screens . . . today it will be hard to ignore an S&P [market index] indicator with an accuracy quotient that's greater than 94 percent." And indeed, it was. I, too, watched Super Bowl XVII and rooted for the Washington Redskins. (As it turned out, Washington won, the market went up, and the Super Bowl system was back in the newspapers the next year, stronger than ever.)

Patterns in the Stock Market

In 1982, *Fortune* magazine told of a company selling a computer program for forecasting the stock market 80 days ahead. The company selling this program claimed to have found a complex pattern in stock prices that would have enabled a user to realize a 72.1 percent profit over the preceding three years, while the stock market as a whole went down 6.1 percent. Just like my 20 coin flips and the 50,000 dice rolls, it should be easy to find such apparent patterns even if the stock market, like coin flips and dice rolls, is completely random.

A *Fortune* editor ordered one of these programs and used it for 80 days, from August 13 through December 6, 1982. The August 13th forecast was that the market would drop 7.5 percent over the next 80 days. Indeed, every single day during this 80 day period, it advised selling stocks. Well, it turned out that these three months were the heart of the great 1982 stock market rally. The Dow Jones Industrial Average went up 11 points on August 13, and 300 more points over the next few weeks. This was one of the strongest advances in stock market history and the computer program missed it completely. Back to the charts.

Extrasensory Perception

Professor J. B. Rhine and his associates at Duke University have produced an enormous amount of evidence concerning extrasensory perception (ESP). For example, they have conducted several million trials involving persons attempting to identify cards that they cannot see. For a stylized illustration, consider an experiment with five cards numbered 1, 2, 3, 4, and 5. (In practice, they usually use five pictures instead of five numbers, but this distinction is of no statistical importance.) The five cards are shuffled and a card is selected at random. The subject states which of the five cards he or she believes to have been selected and the results are recorded. The experiment is repeated 25 times.

How many cards must the subject identify correctly to reject the null hypothesis of no ESP? Under the null hypothesis that mere chance is involved, the probability of a correct selection is $1/5 = .2$. Because these are Bernoulli trials, with independent outcomes and constant probabilities, we can use the binomial distribution. The most likely result for a pure guesser is to be right $1/5$ of the time: 5 right and 20 wrong. Some of the exact binomial probabilities are

number of successes ($\pi = .2$, n = 25)		probability
0		.0038
1		.0236
2		.0708
3		.1358
4		.1867
5		.1960
6		.1633
7		.1108
8		.0623
——	cutoff	——
9		.0294
10		.0118
11		.0040
12		.0012
13		.0003

For a 5 percent probability of Type I error, we can draw the cutoff line between 8 and 9 correct. A pure guesser has only a .047 chance of getting more than 8 out of 25 correct. Therefore, 9 or more correct is sufficiently improbable to enable us to reject the null hypothesis of no ESP.

A messy complication is that many people are tested. Even if only guessers are tested, about 1 out of every 20 guessers will get at least 9 correct. If 400 guessers are tested, we expect about 20 of them to do sufficiently well to lead to the conclusion that they have ESP. If millions of tests are conducted, some astoundingly remarkable performances should be found, even if nothing more than lucky guesses are involved.

This, then, can be seen as another form of data mining—run a large number of tests and report only the most remarkable results. A score with a one-in-a-thousand chance of occurring is not really so remarkable, if you take into account the fact that this is just one of out of a thousand tests that were conducted.

Our first antidote to data mining is common sense. Here, common sense is divided. Many people do not believe in ESP, but others do. Perhaps the safest thing to say is that if there is such a thing as ESP, the evidence is not yet strong enough to convince the skeptics. Even if ESP is of statistical significance, it has yet to be shown to have practical importance. It is of little or no importance to find three people whose probability of identifying a chosen card is .2001 instead of .2000. There is certainly no public evidence that people have such strong mind powers that they can knock planes out of the sky, have long distance conversations without a telephone, or even win at Las Vegas.

The second antidote to data mining is fresh data. Those people who score well should be retested to see whether it is ESP or data mining. Of course, with many, many subjects, some will doubtless compile high scores through several rounds. When Rhine retested his high scorers, he reported that they almost always show a marked decline in ability after their initial success. He wrote that, ''This fatigue is understandable . . . in view of the loss of original curiosity and initial enthusi-asm.'' An alternative explanation is that the high scores on the early rounds were just lucky guesses.

The large number of subjects tested isn't the only difficulty in assessing the statistical significance of Rhine's results. He also looked for test periods where the subjects did well: at the start of a test, in the middle, or at the end. This is very similar to the statistical pitfall of testing several people and reporting only the highest scores. A remarkable performance by 1 of 20 subjects or by 1 of 5 subjects on one-fourth of a test, isn't really that remarkable.

Rhine also looked for either ''forward displacement'' or ''backward displace-ment,'' where the subjects' choices didn't match the contemporaneous cards, but did match the next card, the previous card, two cards hence, or two cards previous. In this way, one test can be multiplied into several tests, increasing the chances of finding ''remarkable'' coincidences. Rhine also considered it remarkable when there was ''avoidance of target'' or ''negative ESP,'' in which the subject got an unusually low score. Rhine explained how a subject

> . . . may begin his run on one side of the mean and swing to the other side just as far by the time he ends the run; or he may go below in the middle of the run and above at both ends. The two trends of deviations may cancel each other and the series as a whole average close to ''chance''.

He described the results of one test as follows:

> . . . the displacement was both forward and backward when one of the senders was looking at the card, and only in the forward direction with another individual as sender; and whether the displacement shifted to the first or the second card away from the target depended upon the speed of the test.[8]

With so many subjects and so many possibilities, it should be easy to find patterns, even in guesses.

ESP research is very interesting and even provocative. But, unfortunately, the enthusiasm of the researchers has often led to a variety of forms of data mining. They would be less controversial and more convincing—one way or the other—if there were more uses and fewer abuses of statistical tests.

Exercises

11.24 The following letter to the editor was printed in *Sports Illustrated*:

> In regard to the observation made by *Sports Illustrated* correspondent Ted O'Leary concerning this year's bowl games (Scorecard, January 16), I believe I can offer an even greater constant. On Jan. 2 the team that won in all five games started the game going right-to-left on the television screen. I should know, I lost a total of 10 bets to my parents because I had left-to-right in our family wagers this year.
>
> John Doe
> Anytown, U.S.A.

Under the null hypothesis that the eventual winner is equally likely to have started the game from the left or right side of the television screen, what is the probability that all five winners would start on the right side? Are you convinced by this statistical proof that the right-to-left team has an advantage? Is there any logical explanation for this apparent advantage?

11.25 Scott Ostler, a *Los Angeles Times* reporter, noticed that in 1983 the San Francisco 49ers were 11–0 in games in which they flew in DC10s. Does this astounding fact persuade you that the 49ers would benefit from only flying DC10s? What hesitations, if any, might you have about jumping to this conclusion?

11.26 Critically evaluate the following statistical argument that a god must have shaped the history of the United States:

> **Q**—What are the odds against accident that the 2nd and 3rd presidents should both die on the 50th anniversary of 7/4/1776, on the 50th Jubilee Day July 4, 1826?
>
> **A**—The odds against a person taking any action on any particular day of the calendar is 365/1. So it is that any two persons dieing on the same day of the year is 365/1 × 365/1. That *two presidents* of the United States, should both die on the *day of independence of that nation* is then 365/1 × 365/1 × 365/1.
>
> The odds that two individuals present at an event should both die on the 50th Jubilee Day of that event are then increased by 50/1 for each person, (the odds then are . . . 365 × 365 × 365 × 50 × 50 = odds against accident are 121,568,812,500/1 . . .
>
> Reason says—This can never be an accident. Some cause must be sought that can do this thing.[9]

11.27 Choose a subject and conduct an ESP test. Carefully record how you conducted your test and what your results were.

11.28 An ESP test has been set up with five different cards. These five cards will be shuffled, a prediction made, and one card selected. If this procedure is repeated 25 times, how many correct predictions are needed to reject the no-ESP hypothesis

a. at the 5 percent level?
b. at the 1 percent level?

● **11.29** (*continuation*) If everyone in your class conducts an ESP test, what is the probability that, by chance alone, at least one person will obtain scores that are statistically significant at the 5% level? at the 1% level?

● **11.30** (*continuation*) An ESP test has been calibrated so that there is a 5 percent chance that a pure guesser will make enough correct predictions to pass. If it turns out that there are not enough correct predictions, then the researcher will look for "negative ESP," a statistically significant (at the 5 percent level) small number of correct predictions. If this doesn't work, then the researcher looks for forward displacement by one card, forward displacement by two cards, backward displacement by one card, and finally backward displacement by two cards (in each case, at the 5 percent level). If we assume, for simplicity, that the results of each of these six tests are independent, then what is the approximate probability that a pure guesser will demonstrate a statistically significant amount of ESP on at least one of these tests?

11.5 SUMMARY

Hypothesis tests focus on the probability of incorrectly rejecting a particular hypothesis, the null hypothesis. By setting up the test to give a low probability of Type I error, the researcher ensures that sampling error is unlikely to lead to the incorrect rejection of this particular hypothesis. Which specific hypothesis should be chosen for this special attention? At least three considerations may influence the choice of the null hypothesis and the probability of Type I error.

1. Theoretical logic or previous empirical studies may indicate that one hypothesis is likely to be true. If so, we can guard against a hasty rejection based solely on these data, by making this "conventional wisdom" the null hypothesis.

2. If there are serious consequences of incorrectly rejecting a particular hypothesis, then we can keep the chances of making that error slight by making this hypothesis the null hypothesis.

3. A researcher may want to reject a particular hypothesis convincingly to demonstrate the correctness of the alternative. Often, the null hypothesis is a "no effect" hypothesis that the researcher hopes will be rejected decisively.

A 5 percent probability of Type I error is commonplace, but there is little more than acquired habit behind this particular number. The objectives just enumerated may argue for a lower or higher number. For instance, a very low α defuses the argument that the results may well be due to chance. One attractive approach is simply to report the P-value and let the reader decide whether or not it is convincingly low. Still, the question most readers will instinctively ask is whether or not the reported P-value is less than 5 percent.

Statistical significance is not at all the same as practical importance. A statistically significant result is one that cannot be reasonably explained by sampling error. Such a result may well be of little or no practical importance. Conversely, research may indicate a very important phenomenon, even though there are too few data to rule out sampling error. A confidence interval is an informative reporting format that allows readers to judge for themselves whether the result is both important and statistically significant.

Hypothesis tests reject a selected hypothesis by showing that, were the hypothesis true, the observed data would be very improbable. However, the testing of many hypotheses makes it very likely that the determined researcher will find at least one case in which the data, considered in isolation, seem improbable. It is not at all improbable that an examination of 20 situations will yield 1 situation with only a 5 percent chance of occurring. Because data mining will inevitably lead to statistically significant results, we cannot tell whether the results of such an expedition reflect the discovery of a useful theory or just perseverance. The only way to tell is by using common sense and fresh data.

APPENDIX: A BAYESIAN RATIONALE

If we adopt a Bayesian perspective for a few moments, an intuitive rationale can be provided for the structure of hypothesis tests. To keep the analytics simple, consider the choice between the two hypotheses

$$H_0: \mu = 500$$
$$H_1: \mu = 550$$

The probabilities of Type I and Type II errors are

$$\alpha = P[\text{reject } H_0 \mid H_0 \text{ true}]$$
$$\beta = P[\text{accept } H_0 \mid H_1 \text{ true}]$$

For a Bayesian, it is more natural to inquire of the reverse error probabilities,

$$P[H_0 \text{ true}|\text{reject } H_0]$$
$$P[H_1 \text{ true}|\text{accept } H_0]$$

The conversion from the first set of probabilities to the second is made via Bayes' theorem, using subjective, *a priori* probabilities for the two hypotheses, $P[H_0 \text{ true}]$ and $P[H_1 \text{ true}]$. For example,

$P[H_0 \text{ true}|\text{reject } H_0]$

$$= \frac{P[H_0 \text{ true}]P[\text{reject } H_0 \mid H_0 \text{ true}]}{P[H_0]P[\text{reject } H_0 \mid H_0 \text{ true}] + P[H_1]P[\text{reject } H_0 \mid H_1 \text{ true}]}$$

$$= \frac{P[H_0 \text{ true}]\alpha}{P[H_0 \text{ true}]\alpha + P[H_1 \text{ true}](1 - \beta)}$$

Similarly,

$$P[H_1 \text{ true}|\text{accept } H_0] = \frac{P[H_1 \text{ true}]\beta}{P[H_1 \text{ true}]\beta + P[H_0 \text{ true}](1 - \alpha)}$$

If the two hypotheses are, *a priori*, judged to be equally likely,

$$P[H_0 \text{ true}] = P[H_1 \text{ true}]$$

then the Bayesian conditional error probabilities become

$$P[H_0 \text{ true}|\text{reject } H_0] = \frac{\alpha}{\alpha + 1 - \beta}$$

$$P[H_1 \text{ true}|\text{accept } H_0] = \frac{\beta}{\beta + 1 - \alpha}$$

The 533 cutoff analyzed at the beginning of the chapter gives $\alpha = .05$ and $\beta = .1977$, so that

$$P[H_0 \text{ true}|\text{reject } H_0] = .059$$

$$P[H_1 \text{ true}|\text{accept } H_0] = .172$$

Here it turns out that the reverse probabilities are not far from α and β, but this isn't necessarily so. For example, if the (equally likely) alternative hypothesis is $\mu = 525$, then $\beta = .6554$ and

$$P[H_0 \text{ true}|\text{reject } H_0] = .13$$

$$P[H_1 \text{ true}|\text{accept } H_0] = .41$$

If the null and alternative hypotheses are not perceived to be equally likely, then there is even more room for disparities.

A Bayesian would report these revised probabilities and let the user decide how to use them. A yes-no decision, such as accepting or rejecting hypotheses, requires more than probabilities. We have to know what the consequences of such decisions will be. We'll use the symbols

$$G_0 = \text{gain if accept } H_0 \text{ when } H_0 \text{ is true}$$

$$G_1 = \text{gain if accept } H_1 \text{ when } H_1 \text{ is true}$$

$$L_0 = \text{loss if reject } H_0 \text{ when } H_0 \text{ is true}$$

$$L_1 = \text{loss if reject } H_1 \text{ when } H_1 \text{ is true}$$

These gains and losses should be measured in dollars, utiles, or whatever, so as to express the relative seriousness of the consequences. The net expected gain is then

$$E[\text{gain}] = P[H_0 \text{ true and accept } H_0](G_0) + P[H_0 \text{ true and reject } H_0](-L_0)$$

$$+ P[H_1 \text{ true and accept } H_1](G_1) + P[H_1 \text{ true and reject } H_1](-L_1) \qquad (10.1)$$

$$= P[H_0 \text{ true}]\{(1 - \alpha)G_0 - \alpha L_0\} + P[H_1 \text{ true}]\{(1 - \beta)G_1 - \beta L_1\}$$

Let's take as a starting point the case where the competing hypotheses are equally likely and the costs are symmetrical,

$$P[H_0 \text{ true}] = P[H_1 \text{ true}], \ G_0 = G_1, \text{ and } L_0 = L_1$$

In this central case, the expected gain is

$$E[\text{gain}] = .5\{G_0 - (\alpha - \beta)(G_0 + L_0)\}$$

The expected gain is maximized if $(\alpha + \beta)$ is minimized, and this occurs when the cutoff is put halfway between the two hypotheses, at $\overline{X} = 525$. You can see from the shapes of the curves (or from some quick calculations) that α rises more than β falls if the cutoff is reduced below this midway point, and β rises more than α falls if the cutoff is increased. So, the first conclusion (and it makes good sense) is:

If the two hypotheses are equally likely and the potential gains and losses are symmetrical, then the cutoff should be midway between the hypotheses, at the point where $\alpha = \beta$.

Conversely, intuition or the application of a little arithmetic to Equation 10.1 shows that, if the hypotheses are not judged to be equally likely or if the gains or losses are not symmetrical, then the cutoff should be set so that α and β are not equal. In particular, because

$$\text{lower } \alpha => \text{ less likely to reject } H_0 \text{ if } H_0 \text{ is true}$$

$$\text{higher } \beta => \text{ more likely to accept } H_0 \text{ if } H_1 \text{ is true}$$

it follows that α should be set lower than β if

1. $P[H_0 \text{ true}] > P[H_1 \text{ true}]$. Because H_0 is the more likely hypothesis, we want to reduce the chances of making an error if H_0 is true.

2. $L_0 > L_1$. If the losses from incorrectly rejecting H_0 are greater than the losses from incorrectly rejecting H_1, then we want to reduce the chances of incorrectly rejecting H_0.

3. $G_0 > G_1$. If the gains from correctly accepting H_0 are greater than the gains from correctly accepting H_1, then we want to reduce the chances of incorrectly rejecting H_0.

With more than two hypotheses, the analysis and the conclusions are considerably more complex, but the flavor lingers.

REVIEW EXERCISES

11.31 The 1980 census recorded the sizes of 79,108,000 U.S. households. The distribution (shown in Table 4.2) has a mean of 2.75 persons and a standard deviation of 1.56 persons. Can you use these data to test the null hypothesis that the average size of U.S. households is 3.0?

11.32 Explain what is wrong with these conclusions:

a. The data show that this person has a statistically significant ability to forecast whether the stock market is going up or down. Therefore, we are 95 percent sure that this person can predict which way the market is going.

b. The data do not show a statistically significant ability to forecast in which direction the market is going. Therefore, we are 95 percent certain that this person cannot predict which way the market is headed.

c. This person's forecasting record has a P-value of 8 percent. Because it is significant at the 10 percent level, but not the 5 percent level, the data show that this person has a weak forecasting ability.

11.33 It has been said that the null hypothesis is the "favored" hypothesis. Is it always true that the probability of accepting the null hypothesis when it is, in fact, correct is greater than the probability

a. of rejecting the null hypothesis when it is false?

b. of accepting the alternative hypothesis when it is true?

11.34   It has been claimed that pickles cause cancer, war, communism, and travel accidents:[10] 99.9 percent of all cancer victims have eaten pickles during their lifetimes, as have 100 percent of all soldiers, 96.8 percent of all communists, and 99.7 percent of those involved in auto and plane accidents. Do you agree that this evidence is persuasive?

11.35   Oswald Jacoby, a backgammon, bridge, and poker expert, has estimated that four or five times a year someone playing bridge in the United States should be dealt a hand in which all thirteen cards are the same suit. Yet two dozen or so such hands get reported each year, and the suit is usually spades. How would you explain this phenomenon?

11.36   (*continuation*) What is the probability of being dealt a hand containing all spades? All cards of the same suit, but not necessarily spades?

11.37   A certain tire has an estimated life of 45,000 miles with a standard deviation of 8,000 miles. A competitor tests 1,000 tires made of a new "space-age" material and finds that 20 of these tires last more than 60,000 miles. Why is it statistically misleading for this company to launch an advertising campaign showing these 20 tires and announcing that, "In actual road tests, these tires lasted more than 60,000 miles!"

11.38   Table 3 at the end of this book is supposed to contain random numbers. But look at the 22nd through 24th numbers in the 25th row (20, 73, 17) and the 5th through 8th numbers in the 30th row—they are the same! The chances that three randomly selected numbers will match three other randomly selected numbers is 1/1000. Does this discovered match show that these are not random numbers after all?

11.39   It has been argued that a football bettor should bet on the team that had the most lopsided win in the previous week. As evidence, it was reported that during the 1970 season, this strategy would have produced 11 winning bets and only 2 losses, taking the bookmaker's point spread into account. An investigation of the strategy over the six-year period 1969–1974 yielded these results:[11]

season	wins	losses
1969	5	8
1970	11	2
1971	6	7
1972	2	11
1973	8	5
1974	4	9
total	36	42

The researchers concluded that the 1970 season was "distorted evidence," reflecting a chance aberration. Why is it a distortion to focus on the 1970 season and ignore the data from other years? Do the results from these six years as a whole, 36 wins and 42 losses, show a statistically significant deviation from the null hypothesis that the probability of a winning bet is $\pi = .5$?

11.40   Critically evaluate this news article:

BRIDGEPORT, Conn.—Christina and Timothy Heald beat "incredible" odds yesterday by having their third Independence Day baby.

Mrs. Heald, 31, of Milford delivered a healthy 8-pound 3-ounce boy at 11:09 a.m. in Park City Hospital, where her first two children, Jennifer and Brian, were born on Independence Day in 1978 and 1980, respectively.

Mrs. Heald's mother, Eva Cassidy of Trumbull, said a neighbor who is an accountant figured the odds are 1-in-484 million against one couple's having three children born on the same date in three different years.[12]

11.41 X is a normally distributed random variable with a known standard deviation of 100. We want to choose between the following two, equally likely, hypotheses about the expected value of X:

$$H_0: \mu = 100$$

$$H_1: \mu = 150$$

The mean of a random sample of size 25 is found to be 136. At the 5 percent level of significance, do we accept $\mu = 100$ or 150?

If we had set the hypotheses up as

$$H_0: \mu = 150$$

$$H_1: \mu = 100$$

which hypothesis would have been accepted? For which values of the sample mean does it make a difference whether the null hypothesis is $\mu = 100$ or $\mu = 150$?

• 11.42 (*continuation*) Now assume that the costs of incorrectly concluding that $\mu = 100$ are greater than the costs of incorrectly concluding that $\mu = 150$ (and that there are no costs associated with being correct). Will a test at the 5 percent level have lower expected costs if the null hypothesis is $\mu = 100$ or $\mu = 150$?

•• 11.43 (*continuation*) It is decided to let the null hypothesis be $\mu = 100$ and let the alternative hypothesis be $\mu = 150$. The cutoff point is set so that the probability of Type I error is 5 percent. If the two hypotheses are initially regarded as being equally likely to be correct, what is the probability that H_0 is true if we reject H_0? What is the probability that H_0 is false if we accept H_0?

•• 11.44 It is known that the random variable X has this continuous density function

$$f[x] = 1/\theta \quad \text{for } 0 \le x \le \theta$$

$$f[x] = 0 \quad \text{otherwise}$$

but it is not known whether the value of θ is 1 or 2. You will have just a single observation of X upon which to base your choice between

$$H_0: \theta = 1$$

$$H_1: \theta = 2$$

a. What are the probabilities of Type I and Type II errors if you decide to accept $\theta = 1$ if $X \le 0.9$ and to accept $\theta = 2$ if $X > 0.9$?

b. What are the probabilities of Type I and Type II errors if you decide to accept $\theta = 1$ if $X \le .5$ and to accept $\theta = 2$ if $X > .5$?

c. Which of these two rules is more appropriate if the consequences of a Type II error are more serious than the consequences of a Type I error?

d. Which of these two rules is more appropriate if, *a priori*, you think that $\theta = 1$ is the more likely value?

• **11.45** "As January goes, so goes the year" is an old stock market adage. The idea is that if the market goes up in January, then it will also go up for the entire year; if the market drops in January, then it will be a bad year. *Newsweek* cited this theory in its February 4, 1974 issue, and reported that "this rule of thumb has proved correct in twenty of the past 24 years."[13]

Let's assume that the probability that the stock market will go up in any given month is .5 and that the probability that the market will go up in any given year is .5. If the market's performance in January and for the entire year are independent, then what is the probability that the market will go the same direction in January and during the entire year? Use the given data to test the null hypothesis that how the market does in January is independent of how it does during the entire year.

• **11.46** (*continuation*) Check data on the Dow Jones Industrial Average for the years 1974 to the present to see how well this theory has done since the *Newsweek* article. Use these data to test the null hypothesis that how the market does in January is independent of how it does during the entire year.

• • **11.47** (*continuation*) Still assume that how the market does each month and how it does for the entire year are completely independent. Also assume that the probabilities that the market will go up in any given month and for the entire year are both .5. If we examine 24 years of data, what is the probability that we will find some month (January, February, or some other month) for which, in at least 20 out of 24 cases, the market has gone the same direction in that month and for the entire year?

• • **11.48** (*continuation*) There are at least two problems with the calculations so far. First, January and the entire year are not really independent because January is part of the year. What we should be looking at (both as statisticians and as investors) is January and the remainder of the year (after January). Second, we shouldn't be using the same probabilities for a month and for a year (unless P really is .5, which it isn't).

To remedy these deficiencies, go to the library and collect some actual data for the years 1950 to the present. For each year, see whether the stock market (as measured by the Dow Jones Industrial Average) went up or down in January and during the remainder of the year. Use these data to test the null hypothesis that the market's performance in January is unrelated to its performance during the remainder of the year.

• **11.49** The Usual Foods Company claims that there are, on average, 100 raisins in a box of its cereal. To test this claim,

$$H_0: \mu \geq 100$$

a consumer group considers the following possible test designs:

1. $n = 25$, $\alpha = .05$
2. $n = 25$, $\alpha = .01$
3. $n = 100$, $\alpha = .05$

a. Which design has the smallest probability of falsely rejecting the company's claim?
b. Does design 1 or 2 have the smaller probability of incorrectly accepting the company's claim? Why?
c. Does design 1 or 3 have the smaller probability of incorrectly accepting the company's claim? Why?

•• **11.50** A bag contains 4 balls, of which n are black and $4 - n$ are white. The null hypothesis is that there are an equal number of black and white balls. The alternative hypothesis is that the numbers are unequal:

$$H_0: n = 2$$

$$H_1: n \neq 2$$

We will draw 2 balls from the bag and accept the null hypothesis if 1 ball is black and the other white. We will reject the null hypothesis if the 2 balls are the same color. Find the probabilities of Type I and Type II errors if

a. the sampling is without replacement
b. the sampling is with replacement

Which sampling procedure is superior?

CHAPTER 12

A Few More Tests

A friend of mine once remarked to me that if some people asserted that the earth rotated from east to west and others that it rotated from west to east, there would always be a few well-meaning citizens to suggest that perhaps there was something to be said for both sides, and that maybe it did a little of one and a little of the other; or that the truth probably lay between the extremes and perhaps it did not rotate at all.

Maurice G. Kendall
''On the Reconciliation of Theories of Probability''

TOPICS

Often, we are interested in a comparison of two populations: whether cigarette smokers have a shorter life expectancy than nonsmokers; whether children who watch television frequently are more violent than children who seldom watch television; whether people who take large doses of vitamin C have fewer colds than other people. Educators compare the performance of students who have been taught in different ways; engineers compare the reliability of different missile designs; and economists compare the rates of return on different assets. We will begin this chapter by extending the tests that you've already learned so that they encompass these sorts of comparative situations. Then we'll look at a new kind of test, which can be used for comparisons and much more.

12.1   THE DIFFERENCE BETWEEN TWO MEANS

In the math SAT example, we had a benchmark mean score of 500 against which to measure the performance of students who take the cram course. Sometimes, however, there is no such benchmark. We may want to compare two groups and we may not know the population mean for either group. Students may take two different crash courses, and we may want to test to see if there is a significant difference in their performance. We may want to test to see if there is a significant difference in the life expectancies of two groups who have different lifestyles. Or we may want to test to see if there is a significant difference in the number of miles per gallon for two different types of cars. There are many interesting questions of this sort, and we have to modify our procedures slightly to handle them.

As an illustration, consider the question of whether there is a significant difference in the stock market forecasts of economists and stockbrokers. The objective is to forecast the Dow Jones Industrial Average for one year from now. The economists' forecasts have an unknown mean μ_e and standard deviation σ_e, while the brokers' forecasts have an unknown mean μ_b and standard deviation σ_b. A random sample of 25 economists and 36 stockbrokers yields the following information:

	number	average forecast	standard deviation
economists	25	1324	75
stockbrokers	36	1408	150

The stockbrokers are more optimistic than the economists who were interviewed. Is this difference statistically significant, indicating that economists and stockbrokers as a whole have different views about the market, or can the reported difference be attributed to sampling error?

A statistical answer can be provided by a test of these competing hypotheses:

$$H_0: \mu_b = \mu_e$$
$$H_1: \mu_b \neq \mu_e$$

The null hypothesis is that the mean forecast of the stockbroker population and the mean forecast of the economist population are equal. Any difference that is observed in a sampling of these two groups is due to sampling error. The alternative hypothesis is that the two populations have different means. It is a two-sided hypothesis because we have no *a priori* reason for believing that economists as a whole are more optimistic than stockbrokers, or vice versa.

These hypotheses pose the right question, but you are not quite prepared to answer it. You have learned to test the null hypothesis that a parameter is equal to a specified number. Now, we have a null hypothesis that two parameters are equal to each other. Fortunately, a simple trick transforms the new hypothesis into the familiar format:

$$H_0: \mu_b - \mu_e = 0$$
$$H_1: \mu_b - \mu_e \neq 0$$

The question of whether or not μ_b is equal to μ_e can be rephrased as a question of whether or not the parameter $\mu_b - \mu_e$ is equal to zero.

The difference in the population means can be tested by looking at the difference in the sample means. If the samples are reasonably sized, then the central limit theorem tells us that each sample mean is normally distributed.

$$\overline{X}_b \sim N[\mu_b, \sigma_b/\sqrt{n_b}]$$
$$\overline{X}_e \sim N[\mu_e, \sigma_e/\sqrt{n_e}]$$

where n_b and n_e are the respective sample sizes. If the samples are independent, then the difference in the sample means is also normally distributed, with an expected value equal to the difference in the separate expected values and a variance equal to the *sum* of the separate variances:

$$\overline{X}_b - \overline{X}_e \sim N\left[\mu_b - \mu_e, \left(\frac{\sigma_b^2}{n_b} + \frac{\sigma_e^2}{n_e}\right)^{1/2}\right] \tag{12.1}$$

The individual variances are summed because squaring converts the negative sign into a positive sign.

Now let's apply this distribution. Under the null hypothesis, the difference in the population means is zero. We don't know the population standard deviations but we can estimate them from the sample standard deviations, 150 and 75. The sample sizes are 36 and 25. Thus, if the null hypothesis is true, an observed difference in the sample means comes from this distribution:*

$$\overline{X}_b - \overline{X}_e \sim N\left[0, \left(\frac{150^2}{36} + \frac{75^2}{25}\right)^{1/2}\right]$$
$$\sim N[0, 29.15]$$

---

*Because the standard deviations are estimated, a *t* distribution may be more appropriate. With this many observations, however, the difference between the *t* and normal distributions is slight enough to be ignored.

The difference in the sample means is normally distributed with an expected value of zero (according to the null hypothesis) and a standard deviation of 29.15. If the null hypothesis is true, then our observed difference should almost certainly (.95 probability) be within two standard deviations of zero: between -58.3 and $+58.3$. The actual difference is $1408 - 1324 = 84$, which is far outside this range. Because this 84-point difference is too large to be plausibly explained by sampling error, we conclude that the null hypothesis is incorrect.

A second way of looking at these data is to say that 84 points is $84/29.15 = 2.88$ standard deviations away from zero. This 2.88 Z-value implies a P-value of .002. There is only a .002 chance that a normally distributed variable will be this far from its expected value. The improbability of this occurrence leads us to conclude that zero is not, in fact, the correct expected value.

A third way to examine the data is to estimate the true difference in the population means. A 95 percent confidence interval is

$$\mu_b - \mu_e = 84 \pm 2(29.15)$$

$$= 84 \pm 58.3$$

or

$$.95 = P[25.7 < \mu_b - \mu_e < 142.3]$$

Since zero is outside this confidence interval, we rule out the hypothesis that the stock market forecasts of stockbrokers and economists have the same mean.

Assistance for Handicapped Children

We can also test the difference between two binomial probabilities. As an illustration, consider the implementation of federal laws concerning special education for handicapped children. In California, a student can qualify for government aid or for special schooling if there is a statistically significant discrepancy between the student's scores on an intelligence test and on an achievement test. The idea is that special assistance may be needed when performance is far below capability.[1]

For a stylized example, consider an intelligence test with n_1 questions and a reading test with n_2 questions. We can think of the test questions as random samples from the populations of all the questions that might be asked on these sorts of tests. If this student can correctly answer a fraction π of all such questions, then the probability of correctly answering a randomly selected question is also π. Let π_1 be the probability of correctly answering an intelligence question and π_2 be the probability of correctly answering a reading question. We can see whether or not there is a statistically significant difference in the student's intelligence and reading achievement by testing the hypotheses

$$H_0: \pi_1 - \pi_2 = 0$$

$$H_1: \pi_1 - \pi_2 > 0$$

The null hypothesis is that the student's intelligence and achievement are equal. The alternative, one-sided hypothesis is that the student has not learned as much as he or she could.

It is natural to choose between these two hypotheses based on the student's scores on the two tests. Let

$$x_1 = \text{number of correct answers on intelligence test}$$

$$x_2 = \text{number of correct answers on achievement test}$$

$$p_1 = x_1/n_1, \text{ fraction correct on intelligence test}$$

$$p_2 = x_2/n_2, \text{ fraction correct on achievement test}$$

With a reasonable number of questions, the student's score will be normally distributed,* measured either in terms of absolute numbers

$$x_1 \sim N[\pi_1 n_1, (\pi_1(1 - \pi_1)n_1)^{1/2}]$$

$$x_2 \sim N[\pi_2 n_2, (\pi_2(1 - \pi_2)n_2)^{1/2}]$$

or, equivalently, in fractions

$$p_1 \sim N[\pi_1, (\pi_1(1 - \pi_1)/n_1)^{1/2}]$$

$$p_2 \sim N[\pi_2, (\pi_2(1 - \pi_2)/n_2)^{1/2}]$$

The difference in the two scores, whether absolute or fractional, will also come from a normal distribution, with an expected value that is equal to the difference in the expected values and a variance equal to the sum of the variances:

$$x_1 - x_2 \sim N[\pi_1 n_1 - \pi_2 n_2, \{\pi_1(1 - \pi_1)n_1 + \pi_2(1 - \pi_2)n_2\}^{1/2}] \quad (12.2)$$

$$p_1 - p_2 \sim N[\pi_1 - \pi_2, \{\pi_1(1 - \pi_1)/n_1 + \pi_2(1 - \pi_2)/n_2\}^{1/2}] \quad (12.3)$$

These formulas are very general and can be applied to any problem of this type.

The absolute and fractional scores are just two different ways of looking at the same thing. In some situations, such as political polls, it is most natural to look at fractions or percentages. Here, it is more natural to work with the absolute scores and we will do so. Let's say that there are 50 questions on each test. To obtain the all-important standard deviations, we also need to put in some values for π_1 and π_2. We could estimate these from the student's performance, but to be conservative (and to derive a test that can be readily applied to every student), let's use .5 for these probabilities. Under the null hypothesis that $\pi_1 = \pi_2$, Equation 12.2 implies that

---

*Do not confuse these distributions with the distribution of scores across students. Each student's score has a probability distribution because there is sampling error in measuring intelligence or achievement. If you take several IQ tests, your scores will vary slightly from one test to the next. There is also a distribution of scores across people, in that abilities vary from person to person. Because there are many inherited and environmental factors that influence ability, this variation across individuals is approximately normally distributed, too. The standard deviation of an individual's score is much smaller than the standard deviation of scores across individuals.

$$x_1 - x_2 \sim N[(.5)50 - (.5)50, \{(.5)(.5)50 + (.5)(.5)50\}^{1/2}]$$

$$\sim N[0, 5]$$

If a student's intelligence and achievement are comparable, then the difference in scores on two 50-question tests should follow a normal distribution with an expected value of 0 and a standard deviation of 5.

How large a difference in the two scores can be explained as sampling error, the inevitable variation in scores from one test to the next? We have a one-tailed test here, because we are only interested in the case where the achievement score is lower than the intelligence score. Thus, we use 1.65 standard deviations, which work out to be 1.65(5) = 8.25 points. Because questions cannot be partially right, we can continue being conservative by using 9 as our decision rule.

> If a student gets 9 more questions correct on a 50-question intelligence test than on a 50-question achievement test, then this disparity is statistically sufficient to reject the hypothesis that the student's achievements and intelligence are equal.

Matched-Pair Samples

Many factors influence the outcome of any sampling experiment. For instance, a company may want to test consumer reaction to two cola formulas. One sampling design is to select two random samples of size 10. The people in the first sample test and rate one cola, while the second sample tests and rates the other cola. The mean ratings can then be compared in the manner you have learned so far in this chapter.

Perhaps the ratings have the results shown in Table 12.1. The first cola seems

Table 12.1   *Cola ratings for two independent samples*

	First sample's ratings of first cola X_1	Second sample's ratings of second cola X_2
	5.9	6.0
	8.0	7.1
	6.4	9.2
	6.9	6.0
	8.3	5.9
	6.5	5.2
	6.7	7.9
	6.7	6.4
	6.5	5.6
	6.1	6.7
mean	6.80	6.60
standard deviation	0.77	1.20

Do Men or Women Think They are Smarter?

A provocative, if not very useful, question is whether men or women are smarter. The Gallup Organization asked 523 college students this question in September 1983 and obtained these results[2]:

	people interviewed	
	260 males	263 females
"men are smarter"	16%	6%
"women are smarter"	10%	24%
"no difference"	73%	70%

Slightly more than two-thirds of both sexes answered "no difference," but there was an interesting male-female divergence for those who saw a difference. Most of the males who said there was a difference thought that males were the smarter sex, while most of the females who saw a difference thought that females were smarter:

	people interviewed who said there is a difference	
	69 males	79 females
"men are smarter"	61%	20%
"women are smarter"	39%	80%

Is this chauvinistic divergence statistically significant, or can it reasonably be attributed to sampling error? The competing hypotheses are

$$H_0: \mu_m = \mu_f$$

$$H_1: \mu_m \neq \mu_f$$

where μ_m and μ_f are the respective fractions of all males and females seeing a difference who think that males are smarter. Under the null hypothesis, the difference in the corresponding sample proportions, $p_m - p_f$ has a zero expected value and a standard deviation $\{\pi_m(1 - \pi_m)/69 + \pi_f(1 - \pi_f)/79\}^{1/2} = 0.082$, using the conservative .5 for the population proportions.

Our two-standard-deviations rule tells us that if the null hypothesis is true, there is .95 probability that the observed difference in the sample proportions will be within 2(0.082) of zero: between -0.164 and $+0.164$. The observed difference, $0.61 - 0.20 = 0.41$, is much farther from zero, and thus decisively rejects the null hypothesis that those males and females who perceive a difference in male-female intelligence agree on which is the smarter sex.

to be the more popular of the two, but a statistical comparison must take into account sampling error, which arises because of the inevitable variation in people's tastes. Some people like cola and some don't and, in addition, each cola has its own partisans. The second cola may have received the lower ratings simply because, by the luck of the draw, its sample consisted primarily of cola haters. To take this possible sampling error into account, our statistical test looks at the standard deviation of the ratings and the size of the samples, to gauge the chance of drawing a sample that is disproportionately full of cola haters. With a small standard deviation and/or a large sample, there is little chance that an imbalance of cola haters will sway the results.

In accordance with Equation 12.1 the standard deviation of the difference in the sample means is

$$(\sigma_1^2/n_1 + \sigma_2^2/n_2)^{1/2}$$

Using the data shown in Table 12.1, the estimated value of this standard deviation is

$$(0.77^2/10 + 1.20^2/10)^{1/2} = 0.45$$

which is sufficiently large so that the observed 0.2 difference in the mean ratings is not statistically significant—it's less than half a standard deviation away from zero. The samples are so small and the sample standard deviations so large that we cannot rule out sampling error as the explanation; the second cola may have been victimized by bad luck.

Another way to control this possible source of sampling error, that some people like cola while others don't, is to do the Pepsi Challenge—have the same people, a single sample, rate both colas. Perhaps a sample of 10 tasters yields the results shown in Table 12.2. Each observed difference in the ratings can be treated as a

Table 12.2 *A single sample's ratings of both colas*

First cola	Second cola	Difference x
7.4	5.4	2.0
7.6	7.2	0.4
6.0	6.7	−0.7
5.9	4.9	1.0
5.9	4.7	1.2
8.4	7.7	0.7
8.2	7.7	0.5
5.1	5.6	−0.5
7.8	7.4	0.4
6.0	4.4	1.6
	Mean	0.66
	Standard deviation	0.85

single observation x in a random sample. If the underlying individual ratings are normally distributed or if the sample is sufficiently large, then the sample mean comes from a normal distribution and a standard test can be made of the null hypothesis that its expected value is zero, i.e., that there is no difference in the average population ratings of the two colas.

Here, the estimated standard deviation of the sample mean is $0.85/\sqrt{10} = 0.27$, which implies that the observed sample mean of 0.66 is statistically significantly different from zero.*

Notice that the 0.27 standard deviation for the single comparison sample is much smaller than the 0.45 standard deviation for two independent samples. The reason is that the comparison sample controls for one source of sampling error—that one cola may draw mostly cola haters while the other gets cola lovers. (There are, of course, still reasons for possible sampling error. In particular, each cola has its own partisans, and a sample may draw disproportionately from either group.)

A comparison sample can be used in all sorts of taste tests and in many other situations, too; for instance, two machines can be compared by giving identical tasks to each one. Sometimes, however, a comparison test is unfair or impractical. In taste tests, the first item may leave a lingering taste that distorts the rating of the second item. In comparing the opinions of Republicans and Democrats or any other two groups, two samples are required by the very nature of the poll. In testing bombs dropped from different altitudes, the same bomb cannot be tested twice. In medical experiments, two drugs cannot be compared by giving both to the same patient. Instead, the medical researcher can try to construct two samples containing **matched pairs.** If truly identical twins could be found, then it would be as if a single person had made a comparison and, hence, the two matched samples could be used as a single sample of differences.

To illustrate the procedure, consider researchers who are interested in seeing if a certain cholesterol-reducing drug reduces the risk of a heart attack. Other factors figure in, too—including age, gender, smoking habits, and blood pressure—and so if two independent samples are taken, the observations will have a substantial standard deviation. Statistically conclusive results will consequently require a large sample. There is a chance, for example, that the drug might be given mostly to young women, while the control group consists mostly of old men. In this way, a lower incidence of heart problems might be attributed to the drug when it is, in fact, at least partly due to age and gender differences between the two samples. A large sample is needed to reduce the chance of this sort of this sampling error.

A single-sample comparison would eliminate some of the sources of sampling error, but we can hardly give the drug to a person and simultaneously use the same person as the control group. Instead, matched pairs can be assembled and this is, in fact, just what researchers at the National Heart, Lung, and Blood Institute did. They took a sample of 3806 middle-aged males who had high cholesterol levels

---

*Because the sample is so small, the t distribution should be used. With $n - 1 = 9$ degrees of freedom, the critical t-value for a 5 percent test is 2.262; the observed mean must be 2.262 standard deviations away from the null hypothesis to reject that hypothesis. Here, it is 2.44 standard deviations away from zero.

but no history of heart disease. These were divided into two samples, with each person in the treatment group matched with someone in the control group according to age, cholesterol level, smoking habits, blood pressure, and other factors that were thought to affect one's chances of a heart attack. These matched pairs served as twins, as if a single person were simultaneously in the treatment and control groups.

The patients were selected by doctors at 12 medical centers throughout the United States. Those in the treatment group were given a cholesterol-reducing drug over a ten-year period, while those in the control group were given a placebo. Neither the patients nor their doctors knew if they were taking the drug or the placebo. The results over this ten-year period were that those in the treatment group had 19 percent fewer heart attacks, 20 percent fewer chest pain attacks, and 21 percent fewer coronary-bypass operations.[3]

As in this medical study, there are often several advantages of matched-pair sampling. Most importantly, it allows for a smaller sample, because controlling for some factors means that the researcher doesn't have to rely solely on sample size to reduce sampling error. In addition, as a practical matter, it defuses the criticism that the samples may have slanted the results. Critics cannot make the easy claim that one cola may have been tasted by cola haters or that one medication may have been given only to people with low blood pressure, if, in fact, the same people tasted both colas and similar people took both medications.

On the other hand, matching pairs is a time-consuming process if done properly. It requires a considerable knowledge of the important factors that need to be controlled and a careful attention to the matching process. Even though it allows for testing a smaller sample, a large initial sample may be needed to find close matches. The matching process itself is subjective and prone to error. Some factors may have been held constant at unrepresentative levels; for example, a sloppy researcher might test a cholesterol-reducing drug on young women—who are not the target patients. Other factors might be inadvertently negelected, so that the matched pairs aren't really that similar after all; for example, the sloppy researcher might not take smoking habits or blood pressure into account. Sometimes matching simply isn't practical because the researchers don't have the necessary information. For instance, if the "lingering taste" issue argued against having people taste both colas, we would hardly know where to begin finding "twins." However, when it is feasible and done carefully, matched-pair samples offer an attractive sample design.

Exercises

12.1 The Federal Tobacco Commission has estimated the average nicotine content of two brands of cigarettes, Life and Death:

brand	number tested	average nicotine	standard deviation
Life	16	0.3 mg	0.3
Death	16	0.5 mg	0.4

Is the difference in their average nicotine content statistically significant (at the 5 percent level)? Be sure to state your null hypothesis explicitly.

12.2 U.S. soldiers in World War II were taller, heavier, and stronger than those in World War I. To see if the same was true of U.S. women in those periods, a statistics class at Mount Holyoke College collected the following data:[4]

	1918 (250 freshmen) mean	std. dev.	1943 (308 freshmen) mean	std. dev.
height (cm)	161.7	6.3	164.8	5.9
weight (lb)	118.4	16.6	128.0	17.2
grip (kg)	30.9	4.6	32.3	5.4

Do these data show statistically significant differences in the heights, weights, and grips of 1918 and 1943 students? (Test each physical characteristic separately.)

12.3 A study found that derelicts are less often balding than are college professors:[5]

	number studied	median age	percent balding
derelicts	141	47.5	36
professors	49	47.5	71

Assuming these to be scientific random samples, test the null hypothesis that balding is equally likely for derelicts and professors.

12.4 A *Los Angeles Times* baseball story ("The Honeymoon Might be Over for Steve Garvey," September 18, 1983) quoted the manager of the San Diego Padres as saying, "I'm not taking anything away from Steve [Garvey], but we've played better won-lost percentage ball without him." At the time, the Padres had won 50 and lost 52 with Garvey and won 24 and lost 22 without him. Is this difference statistically significant?

12.5 A Gallup poll in September 1983 asked 260 male students and 263 female students

Considering differences which may exist between men and women overall, would you say there are significant differences between the ways in which men and women think?[6]

The responses were

	260 males	263 females
"yes"	57%	65%
"no"	43%	35%

Is the eight-percentage-point difference in the male and female responses statistically significant?

12.6 Gallup Polls periodically ask, "Do you approve of the way . . . is handling his job as President?" Richard Nixon's approval rating jumped from 27 percent to 31 percent after Gerald Ford was confirmed as Vice President, replacing Spiro Agnew. If 1000 people were included in each poll, was this change statistically significant?

12.7 In 1973, the U.S. Public Health Service studied the effects of vitamin C on the incidence of colds at a Navajo boarding school in Arizona.[7] The study covered a 14-week period, from February to May. Half of the children were given daily doses of from 1 to 2 grams of vitamin C, while the other half were given placebos, which were identical in taste and appearance to the vitamin C tablets. The researchers concluded that the children who took vitamin C daily had significantly fewer colds and sick days than those who didn't. For example, in the six-to-ten age group, 150 children were given one gram of vitamin C daily and 150 were given placebos. Thirty-two percent of those who took vitamin C and 16 percent of those on placebos had no sick days during this 14-week period. Is this difference, in fact, statistically significant?

12.8 In 1973, two Columbia University social scientists studied the effects of prejudicial news coverage on jury verdicts. They selected people from actual jury pools and used real lawyers to reenact a murder trial. Before the mock trial, some jurors read prejudicial news stories concerning the case, while others read objective reports. In one case, 47 of 60 jurors who read the prejudicial stories voted guilty, while 33 of 60 jurors who read objective reports voted guilty. Is this difference statistically significant?

12.9 A study was made of 10,590 pairs of men, who were matched statistically so that the only apparent difference between them was that one had a vasectomy and the other didn't. Over the 5 to 14 years that the study covered, 212 of the vasectomized men and 326 of the non-vasectomized men died. Is this difference statistically significant? Assume the samples are independent and then explain why the matched pairs make a difference.

12.10 If the cola ratings in Table 12.2 had represented two independent random samples, would they have rejected decisively the null hypothesis that the two colas are rated equally by the population as a whole? Why does the test described in the text not come to an identical conclusion? (Explain the reason in simple English, that a corporate vice president could understand.)

12.2 CHI-SQUARE TESTS

So far, our hypothesis tests have been concerned with averages. We looked at the average performance of a sample of students to gauge the average performance of all students. We looked at the average weight of a sample of cracker boxes to gauge the average weight of the population. And so on. But often, we are interested in the fine detail that an average misses—we don't want to suffer the fate of the statistician who drowned crossing a river that had an average depth of 3 feet.

For instance, we may suspect that a certain gambling casino is using loaded dice to affect the frequencies with which various numbers appear. It's not much consolation to the bettor if a pair of loaded dice have an average sum of 7; instead, bettors are interested in how frequently specific numbers appear. The long-run average sum will be 7 if we roll two fair dice, dice that always sum to 7, or dice that sum to 7 half the time and sum to 2 or 12 the other half. These three sets of dice have the same expected value, but very different implications for dice games.

No casino would dare use dice that were so obviously rigged, but a crooked casino might use dice that were loaded to have more subtle effects. Let's say that we carefully record 720 rolls of a suspicious casino's dice. Table 12.3 shows the theoretical expected frequencies for the various possible numbers, along with the

Table 12.3 *Actual and expected outcomes for 720 rolls of a pair of dice*

Number	Expected frequency E_i	Observed frequency O_i	$O_i - E_i$	$(O_i - E_i)^2$	$\dfrac{(O_i - E_i)^2}{E_i}$
2	20	26	+6	36	1.80
3	40	38	−2	4	0.10
4	60	57	−3	9	0.15
5	80	74	−6	36	0.45
6	100	113	+13	169	1.69
7	120	106	−14	196	1.63
8	100	101	+1	1	0.01
9	80	77	−3	9	0.11
10	60	65	+5	25	0.42
11	40	41	+1	1	0.03
12	20	22	+2	4	0.20
Total	720	720	0		6.59

actual observed frequencies. These expected frequencies show how often, on average, we can expect each number to appear if we repeat this 720-roll experiment many times. For example, because the probability of a 2 with fair dice is 1/36, the number of 2s we should average in every 720 rolls is (1/36)720 = 20. In any particular 720 rolls, the number of 2s will most likely be somewhat higher or lower than 20. The statistical question is how many more or fewer 2s are needed to fuel our suspicion that the dice are rigged. In particular, does the fact that the number of 2s in these 720 rolls was 26 show that these dice are crooked, or is that the sort of chance deviation that we should anticipate?

Our earlier test procedures suggest calculating the standard deviation to gauge the difference between observed and expected values. If the probability of a 2 is $\pi = 1/36$, then the number of 2s obtained in 720 rolls has an expected value and standard deviation,

$$\mu = \pi n = (1/36)(720) = 20$$
$$\sigma = \{\pi(1 - \pi)n\}^{1/2} = (1/36)(35/36)(720) = 4.41$$

Because there is about a .95 probability of being within two standard deviations of the expected value, there is a .95 probability that the number of 2s obtained in 720 rolls of fair dice will be between 11 and 29 (rounding off to whole numbers). Thus, the occurrence of twenty-six 2s is not sufficient to reject the null hypothesis that the probability of a 2 is 1/36.

This analysis is fine as far as it goes, but we want to go farther. We want to look at all 11 possible numbers, 2 through 12, and yet there are several reasons for not examining them one-by-one. First, the outcomes are interdependent because they must add up to 720. If we have six more 2s than expected, then we must have six fewer of some other numbers. We are, in a sense, repeating ourselves in that every number we test tells us a little more about the outcomes that we haven't yet tested. At the end, after we've tested all but one number, we'll know how many times that last number appeared even before we look.

Second, if we make several tests, each with a .05 probability of Type I error, then the overall probability of committing a Type I error will be considerably greater than 5 percent. The more tests we make, the more likely it is that we will draw at least one wrong conclusion. We would like to adjust our tests somehow, while also taking into account their interdependence, so as to put the overall probability of Type I error at 5 percent.

Third, there is a strong temptation to look at the data and pick out anomalies to be tested. The casual statistician might look at Table 12.3, notice that there were fourteen fewer 7s than expected, thirteen extra 6s, and six extra 2s, and then see if one of these disparities is statistically significant. But this is plain and simple data mining; in choosing to write down a test of the number of 7s, 6s, or 2s, this statistician mentally tested each of the other numbers and concluded that their differences were less statistically significant. As with the statistician who meticulously tests each number, the probability of Type I error is much larger than 5 percent.

The Chi-Square Statistic

In 1900, Karl Pearson developed a test that avoids these problems. It is a single test that simultaneously compares the observed and expected values for each of the possible outcomes. It can be motivated as follows. In testing a single outcome, such as the number 2, we looked at the Z-statistic

$$Z = \frac{(X - \pi n)}{\{\pi(1 - \pi)n\}^{1/2}}$$

which tells us how many standard deviations the number of observations X is away from its expected value πn. The square of this statistic can be rearranged to give

$$Z^2 = \frac{(X - \pi n)^2}{\pi(1 - \pi)n}$$

$$= (X - \pi n)^2 \left\{ \frac{1}{\pi n} + \frac{1}{(1 - \pi)n} \right\}$$

$$= \frac{(X - \pi n)^2}{\pi n} + \frac{\{(n - X) - (1 - \pi)n\}^2}{(1 - \pi)n}$$

$$= \frac{(O_1 - E_1)^2}{E_1} + \frac{(O_2 - E_2)^2}{E_2}$$

The O_i are the observed values of the two possible outcomes: 2s or non-2s. The E_i are the corresponding expected values. What the algebra shows is that a squared Z-statistic can be rearranged to give another, quite logical way of looking at the discrepancies between the observed and expected values: take the observed number of 2s, subtract the expected number, and square this difference. Then scale this squared deviation by dividing by the expected number of 2s. Do the same thing for non-2s and then add the two scaled squared-deviations together. This is a logical way of measuring the extent to which the observed data differ from their expected values. Because it is a Z-statistic squared, we can calculate just how likely various values are.

Karl Pearson carried this logic one step further by suggesting that statisticians can make the same scaled squared-deviation calculation when there are more than two possible outcomes. Table 12.3 shows the arithmetic:

1. *For each possible outcome, 2 through 12, calculate the deviation* $O_i - E_i$ *between the observed and expected occurrences.* It would do no good to calculate the average such disparity, because the deviations sum to zero.

2. *Square each deviation, instead.* Now, positive and negative deviations count equally and they don't cancel each other out. In addition, large disparities are more important than small disparities. This weighting makes sense, because the improbability of large deviations makes their presence convincing evidence that more than chance is involved.

3. *After squaring the deviations, divide by the expected number of occurrences,* E_i. This scaling is needed to put the squared deviations into perspective and to make different studies comparable. The fact that there were thirteen extra 6s in this study is actually less surprising than the fact that there were six extra 2s, because 6s are five times as likely as 2s. There were only 13 percent more 6s than expected, but 30 percent more 2s than expected. Dividing by E_i scales each squared deviation relative to the expected number of occurrences. In addition, scaling is absolutely essential to calibrate studies using different units, such as millions versus billions.

4. *Add up the scaled squared-deviations.* This is like calculating the average scaled squared-deviation. We just neglect to divide by 11, the number of possible outcomes.

Pearson called the end result a **chi-square statistic**

$$\chi^2 = \frac{(O_1 - E_1)^2}{E_1} + \frac{(O_2 - E_2)^2}{E_2} + \cdots + \frac{(O_m - E_m)^2}{E_m} \qquad (12.4)$$

where O_i and E_i are the observed and expected occurrences for m (exhaustive and mutually exclusive) possible outcomes.

Table 12.3 shows that the chi-square statistic for these dice data is 6.59. Now, the question is whether this 6.59 is sufficiently large to persuade us that it is unreasonable to attribute the deviations to chance alone. Are deviations this large sufficiently improbable to make rigged dice the more plausible explanation? To answer this question, we need to know the probability distribution for the chi-square statistic.

The Chi-Square Distribution

It takes a high-powered computer to determine the exact probability distribution for the chi-square statistic. Pearson didn't have such a computer, so he figured out an approximation. I've shown you how the square of a single standardized binomial leads to a chi-square statistic with $m = 2$. Because the standardized binomial can be approximated by the standardized normal distribution if the sample is large, it follows that the general chi-square statistic, Equation 12.4, can be approximated by the sum of $m - 1$ squared, standardized normal distributions. This is what Pearson did.*

> The **chi-square distribution,** with $m - 1$ degrees of freedom, is the distribution of the sum of $m - 1$ independent, squared standardized normal variables $Z_1^2 + Z_2^2 + \cdots + Z_{m-1}^2$.

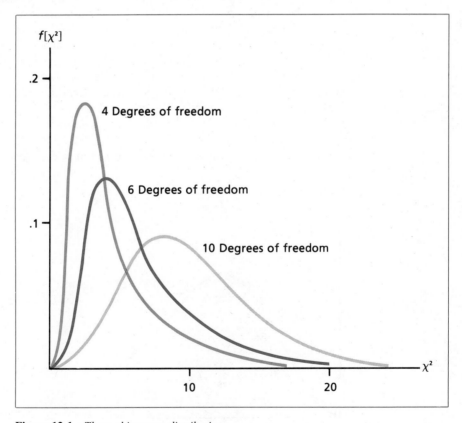

Figure 12.1   *Three chi-square distributions*

*The chi-square distribution was first discovered in 1876 by F.R. Helmert (1843–1917), a German physicist, and then rediscovered and popularized by Pearson.

When there are m possible outcomes, there are only $m - 1$ degrees of freedom because we know the number of occurrences of the last outcome if we know the occurrences of the other $m - 1$ outcomes.

The chi-square distribution can be calculated readily and is shown in Table 5 at the end of the book. Figure 12.1 shows three chi-square distributions, for $m - 1 = 4$, 6, and 10 degrees of freedom. Notice that negative values are not possible, because χ^2 is a sum of squares. Notice also that the chi-square distribution is positively skewed. As $m - 1$ increases, though, the chi-square distribution becomes increasingly symmetrical and approaches a normal distribution.

Pearson used the (continuous) chi-square distribution to approximate the (discrete) distribution of the chi-square statistic. The generally accepted rule of thumb is that this approximation is satisfactory as long as there are at least 10 (some say 5) expected occurrences of every possible outcome; i.e., none of the E_i are less than 10. (If any E_i are less than 10, they can be boosted by combining categories.)

In our dice example, the smallest value of E_i is 20, so the chi-square distribution should be satisfactory. Because there are $m = 11$ possible outcomes, there are $m - 1 = 10$ degrees of freedom. Figure 12.2 shows the chi-square distribution for 10 degrees of freedom. If the value of the chi-square statistic were zero, the observed and expected frequencies would all coincide, providing no evidence whatsoever against the null hypothesis that the dice are fair. Doubt is cast on this hypothesis when the value of the chi-square statistic is large; this indicates that the deviations are too large to be attributed to chance alone.

Figure 12.2 shows that, with 10 degrees of freedom, there is only a 5 percent chance that the chi-square statistic will exceed 18.31. Therefore, in order to set the probability of Type I error at 5 percent, we require a chi-square statistic of

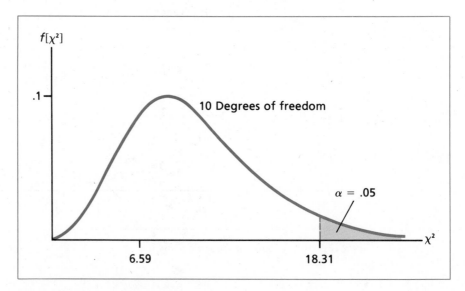

Figure 12.2 *Testing for fair dice*

18.31 before we reject the null hypothesis that the die are fair. Table 12.3 shows that the actual value of the chi-square statistic turns out to be 6.59, which is far below the 18.31 needed to reject the null hypothesis. With 10 degrees of freedom, a chi-square statistic of 6.59 is not at all surprising; indeed, there is about a .75 probability that the chi-square statistic will be that high or higher. Thus, these deviations between the observed and expected frequencies can be explained by chance and do not provide statistical evidence that the dice are rigged.

Can the Famous Postpone Death?

In 1972, David Phillips published a provocative statistical investigation.[8] He began his paper by observing that

> In the movies and in certain kinds of romantic literature, we sometimes come across a deathbed scene in which a dying person holds onto life until some special event has occurred. For example, a mother might stave off death until her long-absent son returns from the wars. Do such feats of will occur in real life as well as in fiction?

Phillips went out and collected readily available data—the birth and death dates of famous people—his idea being that people may postpone death until after the celebration of their birthday. Famous people were used because their birth and death dates were easily obtained. For his first sample, he chose 348 deceased people from the book *Four Hundred Notable Americans*. Then, he compared their death and birth dates to see how many months separated the two. Table 12.4 shows his data.

Table 12.4 *Phillips's data on deaths before, during, and after the birth month*

Number of months before ($-$) or after ($+$) birth month	Expected number of deaths E_i	Actual number of deaths O_i	$O_i - E_i$	$(O_i - E_i)^2$	$(O_i - E_i)^2/E_i$
-6	29	24	-5	25	0.86
-5	29	31	$+2$	4	0.14
-4	29	20	-9	81	2.79
-3	29	23	-6	36	1.24
-2	29	34	$+5$	25	0.86
-1	29	16	-13	169	5.83
0	29	26	-3	9	0.31
$+1$	29	36	$+7$	49	1.69
$+2$	29	37	$+8$	64	2.21
$+3$	29	41	$+12$	144	4.97
$+4$	29	26	-3	9	0.31
$+5$	29	34	$+5$	25	0.86
Total	348	348	0		22.07

Are Heights Really Normally Distributed?

Exercise 7.27 discussed an early study of the distribution of the heights of adult males born in the British Isles. These data are shown in Table 1. Now, the chi-square test allows us to investigate statistically the claim made in Chapters 6 and 7 that heights often tend to be normally distributed. First, though, notice that some of the intervals have fewer than 10 observations and, it turns out, fewer than 10 expected observations, too. To get all of the expected number of observations above 10, some of the extreme intervals need to be combined, as shown in Table 1.

The mean and standard deviation of these data are 67.46 inches and 2.57 inches. Under the null hypothesis that the population of heights follows a normal distribution with this mean and standard deviation, we can calculate the standardized intervals, and then the interval probabilities from Table 2. Multiplication by the total number of observations, 8585, then gives the expected number of men in each interval. A comparison with the actual observations yields the value of the chi-square statistic. With 16 degrees of freedom, there is a 5 percent chance of a chi-square statistic greater than 26.3. Although there are some noticeable deviations, particularly the excessive number of men out in the tails, the chi-square value of 23.53 is not large enough to reject the null hypothesis that these data come from a normal distribution.

Table 1 *The 1883 heights of 8585 adult males born in the British Isles*

Height (inches)	Observed number of men O_i	Standardized interval	Probability	Expected number of men, E_i	$\left(\dfrac{O_i - E_i}{E_i}\right)^2$
57–58	2 ⎫				
58–59	4 ⎬	< -2.927	.0017	14.59	2.00
59–60	14 ⎭				
60–61	41	-2.927 to -2.538	.0038	32.62	2.15
61–62	83	-2.538 to -2.149	.0103	88.77	0.38
62–63	169	-2.149 to -1.760	.0234	200.55	4.96
63–64	394	-1.760 to -1.371	.0460	394.48	0.00
64–65	669	-1.371 to -0.981	.0781	670.57	0.00
65–66	990	-0.981 to -0.592	.1137	975.94	0.20
66–67	122	-0.592 to -0.203	.1426	1224.14	0.00
67–68	139	-0.203 to 0.186	.1542	1323.89	0.02
68–69	1230	0.186 to 0.575	.1436	1232.89	0.01
69–70	1063	0.575 to 0.964	.1152	988.56	5.61
70–71	646	0.964 to 1.352	.0793	680.96	1.79
71–72	392	1.352 to 1.742	.0474	407.27	0.57
72–73	202	1.742 to 2.131	.0242	207.59	0.15
73–74	79	2.131 to 2.520	.0107	91.52	1.71
74–75	32	2.520 to 2.910	.0041	35.20	0.29
75–76	16 ⎫				
76–77	5 ⎬	> 2.910	.0018	15.45	3.69
77–78	2 ⎭				
Total	8585		1.0	8585	23.53

The data come from reference 2 in Chapter 7. (The actual intervals are 56 15/16 − 57 15/16, and so on.) The expected numbers are based on the null hypothesis that heights at the time were normally distributed with a mean of 67.46 inches and a standard deviation of 2.57 inches. The standardized intervals are calculated as follows. The interval 67 15/16 to 68 15/16 is standardized by subtracting the mean and dividing by the standard deviation:

$$\frac{67\ 15/16 - 67.46}{2.57} \text{ to } \frac{68\ 15/16 - 67.46}{2.57} = 0.186 \text{ to } 0.575$$

Appendix Table 2 shows the corresponding probability to be .1436, implying that the expected number of men in this interval is .1436(8585) = 1232.89.

The null hypothesis that birth and death dates are unrelated implies that a person's death is equally likely to occur one month before a birthday, one month after a birthday, or in any other month. (This is not quite right, because some months have slightly more days than others, but it is close enough.) If 348 deaths were equally divided over twelve months (measured relative to birthdays), there would be $348/12 = 29$ deaths in each month. Table 12.4 shows that, in fact, there were only 16 deaths in the month immediately preceding a birthday, but 36 deaths in the month after. There are also fewer-than-expected deaths during the birth month itself and 3 to 4 months before a birthday, and more-than-expected deaths 2 and 3 months after a birthday. Is this "death dip" before a birthday large enough to be statistically significant, or is it explainable by chance fluctuations?

Table 12.4 shows that the chi-square statistic works out to be 22.1. With 29 expected occurrences in each month, the chi-square distribution is usable. The twelve monthly divisions give $m = 12$, so that there are $m - 1 = 11$ degrees of freedom. Table 5 shows that, with 11 degrees of freedom, there is a .05 probability that a chi-square statistic will exceed 19.7 and a .01 probability that it will exceed 24.7. There is about a 2.5 percent chance that a chi-square statistic will exceed 22.1. Thus, the observed relation is significant at the 5 percent level, but it is not "highly significant" in that it is not significant at the 1 percent level.

Phillips's own description of his results is "an unexpected connection," and most people are surprised by his evidence. Phillips's explanation is that some people can successfully postpone death until after the celebration of a birthday. An alternative explanation is that the excessive food, drink, and excitement on a birthday are bad for one's health. Another possibility is that it is just a fluke in the data, one of those one-out-of-twenty occasions when the null hypothesis is incorrectly rejected. We should be wary of "unexpected connections," because statistical relationships without a convincing explanation are often due just to chance.

This latter possibility is supported by the fact that Phillips gathered some other data that were not so kind to his theory. He took three more samples that were drawn from people listed in *Who Was Who in America,* who also had their surnames listed as among "The Foremost Families of the U.S.A." There is a slight death dip in each of these other three samples, but the deviations are not statistically significant. If we put the four samples together, the chi-square statistic falls to 17.03, which is not statistically significant either. Phillips naturally prefers to emphasize his first sample, because it gives a surprising, publishable result. His stated rationale is that these people are more famous and that famous people have more reason to postpone death until after a birthday, because they receive larger gifts and more public attention. However, choosing the sample that gives the most favorable result is a statistically treacherous practice. Those who are intrigued by Phillips's theory should go out and gather some fresh data.

Exercises

12.11   Three-fourths of an animal population have a certain trait A, while the remaining one-fourth have trait a. Similarly, three-fourths of this animal population have trait B, while one-fourth have trait b. If these traits are inherited independently (in accordance with Mendel's law), then the probabilities of various combinations of these traits are $P[A \text{ and } B] = 9/16$, $P[A \text{ and } b] = 3/16$, $P[a \text{ and } B] = 3/16$, and $P[a \text{ and } b] = 1/16$. A breeding experiment yielded the following data:

	A and B	A and b	a and B	a and b
number of observations	216	83	68	33

Use a chi-square test to see if these data are consistent with Mendel's law.

12.12   Karl Pearson reported dealing 3400 thirteen-card hands from an ordinary deck of playing cards.[9] He kept track of whether each hand had few trumps (0–2), a moderate number of trumps (3–4), or a large number of trumps (5–13). His results were

number of trumps	expected number of hands	actual number of hands
0–2	1015.67	1021
3–4	1784.79	1788
5–13	599.54	591
total	3400	3400

Are these results consistent with the null hypothesis that the cards are fairly dealt? Are his results too good to be true?

12.13   An economist claims that each day the stock market has a .5 probability of going up and a .5 probability of going down, regardless of what has happened on previous days. If this economist is right, what is the probability that, in any given week, the market will go up exactly 5 days? 4 days? 3 days? 2 days? 1 day? 0 days?

A study of 500 five-day weeks yielded the following data:

number of days market went up during week	number of occurrences
5	32
4	76
3	136
2	142
1	88
0	26
total	500

Use a chi-square test to see if these data are consistent with the economist's claim.

12.14   A random number generator on my computer simulated 60 rolls of a single 6-sided die:

number	observed frequency
1	9
2	9
3	5
4	13
5	14
6	10
	60

Make a chi-square test of the null hypothesis that each of these six numbers is equally likely to appear. Were this hypothesis rejected, what course of action would you recommend?

12.15 A study of the relationship between auto weight and accident frequency used the following data:[10]

auto weight (pounds)	registration frequency	accident frequency
<3,000	21.04%	162
3,000–4,000	46.13%	318
4,000–5,000	31.13%	689
>5,000	1.70%	35
total	100.00%	1204

Test the hypothesis that auto weight and accident frequency are statistically independent.

12.16 W.F.R. Weldon carefully recorded the number of dice showing a 5 or 6 when 12 dice were rolled 26,306 times:[11]

number of dice showing a 5 or 6	expected frequency	observed frequency
0	203	185
1	1,217	1,149
2	3,345	3,265
3	5,576	5,475
4	6,273	6,114
5	5,018	5,194
6	2,927	3,067
7	1,254	1,331
8	392	403
9	87	105
10 or more	14	18
total	26,306	26,306

Make a chi-square test of the null hypothesis that these dice were fair.

12.17 Chapter 10 included a discussion of the American Stove Company's process control procedure for the height of a metal piece they manufactured. This procedure assumed that when the production process was operating properly, the heights would come from a normal distribution with a mean of 0.8312 inch and a standard deviation of 0.006169 inch. Measurements of a random sample of 145 pieces yielded the following sample distribution:[12]

height (inches)	number of pieces
<0.8245	14
0.8245–0.8274	14
0.8275–0.8304	21
0.8305–0.8334	55
0.8335–0.8364	23
0.8365–0.8394	7
>0.8394	11

Make a chi-square test of the null hypothesis that these data came from the assumed population.

12.18   Exercise 6.16 shows Bowditch's data on the heights of 1253 12-year-old boys. Use a chi-square test to see if these data are consistent with the null hypothesis that the population of heights is normally distributed.

12.19   Exercise 7.11 shows the distribution of 10,720 GRE Advanced Economics Test scores. Make a chi-square test of the null hypothesis that these data are normally distributed with a mean of 606 and a standard deviation of 108.

12.20   If two dice are rolled, what is the probability distribution for the sum of the two numbers obtained? Roll two dice 100 times and record the sums. Use a chi-square test to compare your expected and observed frequencies.

12.3   CONTINGENCY TABLES

The nice thing about Pearson's chi-square test is that it can be applied to a wide variety of situations. All we need are a set of mutually exclusive possible outcomes and a null hypothesis giving the probabilities that these outcomes will occur. We can then calculate how often each outcome would be expected to occur if the null hypothesis were true and compare these expected frequencies to the actual frequencies with which the outcomes occur. Pearson's chi-square test gauges whether the deviations between the observed and expected frequencies can reasonably be attributed to chance, or whether they are so large that the null hypothesis should be rejected.

The framework is so general that it is often given the informative label, **goodness-of-fit tests.** Pearson's chi-square test is a way of statistically gauging how closely the data agree with the detailed implications of a null hypothesis. One application is, as we have seen, where there is a single list of possible outcomes, such as dice rolls, heights, or death months relative to birth months. Another application, which I will now explain, is where the data are labeled in more than one way.

For example, the number 7 can be either a winning roll or a losing roll in craps, depending on the outcomes of previous rolls. In looking for a crooked dice game, we might ask not only how often 7 comes up but, more specifically, how often 7 comes up when it is a winning roll and when it is a losing roll. We are then labeling the outcomes in two ways: by the numbers rolled and by when they are rolled. A natural null hypothesis is that these two facets of the data are unrelated and that the odds of rolling a 7 do not depend on whether 7 is a winning or losing roll. If the data are not consistent with this null hypothesis, then they provide statistical evidence that the game is crooked, in that the casino may switch dice as needed to increase its edge. This line of thought leads to a very useful application of chi-square tests.

> If we want to test whether or not two factors are independent, we can label the data by these two factors, let the null hypothesis be that they are independent, and then use a chi-square test to see how closely the data agree with this independence hypothesis.

Income and Political Opinions

Consider a hypothetical poll that rates a Republican president's performance:

President's rating	number of people
excellent	200
good	250
fair	300
poor	250
total	1000

This poll shows a pretty evenly balanced evaluation of the President's performance, but we may suspect that the President's support is not uniform throughout society. Beneath the surface, there may be significant differences in the evaluations made by different segments of society: rich vs. poor, young vs. old, or along other lines. Perhaps we believe that the high-income and low-income people have very different views of the President's performance. If so, then the poll results can be labeled in a second direction, according to the income of the respondent. In Table 12.5, the sample is labeled in two ways, by income class and by performance evaluation. Statisticians call such a table a **two-way contingency table.**

Table 12.5 *Poll responses classified by rating and income*

Rating	Respondent's income class			
	Low-income	Middle-income	High-income	Total
Excellent	32	102	66	200
Good	55	118	77	250
Fair	114	148	38	300
Poor	99	132	19	250
Total	300	500	200	1000

It is easy to think of reasons why a person's income and political opinions may be related. People who are down and out tend to blame the government for their misfortune. Those who are well off are more likely to be satisfied with the present administration and reluctant to make changes. In addition, presidents often pursue policies that have uneven effects on the different income classes. Franklin Roosevelt was perceived to favor the poor and the unemployed, and these low-income groups were big Roosevelt supporters. Ronald Reagan, on the other hand, is believed to favor the well-to-do, and they respond by favoring him. Other presidents have been perceived as being more even-handed.

A brief study of Table 12.5 reveals that low-income people tend to judge this President more harshly, while high-income people are more favorably impressed. The statistical question is whether this disparity can reasonably be explained by the luck of the draw in selecting this particular sample. If not, then we conclude that the poll shows a population relationship between income-class and evaluation of the President. This statistical question can be answered by Pearson's chi-square test. The competing hypotheses are

H_0: income and opinion are unrelated

H_1: income and opinion are related

The null hypothesis implies certain expected values for the entries in Table 12.5. Once these are calculated, they can be compared to the actual entries and a chi-square statistic computed.

First take the totals from 12.5:

	low-income	middle-income	high-income	total
excellent				200
good				250
fair				300
poor				250
total	300	500	200	1000

If income-class and rating were independent, how would we expect these totals to be allocated across the table? Well, 20 percent of all 1000 respondents gave the President an "excellent" rating. If income class and rating were unrelated, we would expect 20 percent of the 300 low-income people, 20 percent of the 500 middle-income people, and 20 percent of the 200 high-income people to give the President an excellent rating:

	low-income	middle-income	high-income	total
excellent	.2(300) = 60	.2(500) = 100	.2(200) = 40	200
good				250
fair				300
poor				250
total	300	500	200	1000

Now, let's fill in the row of "good" ratings. Twenty-five percent of all 1000 respondents rated the President's performance "good." If income class and rating were unrelated, then 25 percent of the low- , middle- , and high-income groups could be expected to give a "good" rating:

	low-income	middle-income	high-income	total
excellent	60	100	40	200
good	.25(300) = 75	.25(500) = 125	.25(200) = 50	250
fair				300
poor				250
total	300	500	200	1000

Continuing with this reasoning, we can complete the entire Table 12.6*

Now we can make an informed scrutiny of the disparities between the actual responses and the responses that we would expect if income and rating were independent. A comparison of Tables 12.5 and 12.6 reveals that there are some large deviations. Instead of 60 low-income people giving the President an excellent rating, only 32 did. In sharp contrast, 66 high-income people rated the President's performance excellent, instead of the expected 40. Are these and the other disparities statistically significant, or can they be explained as chance variation in the random selection of a sample? We can answer this question by calculating Pearson's chi-square statistic, Equation 12.4, using the data in Table 12.5 as the observed frequencies O_i and the data in Table 12.6 as the expected frequencies E_i:

$$\chi^2 = \frac{(32-60)^2}{60} + \frac{(102-100)^2}{100} + \frac{(66-40)^2}{40} + \frac{(55-75)^2}{75} + \cdots + \frac{(19-50)^2}{50}$$

$$= 92.10$$

To see if this chi-square statistic is statistically significant, we need to know which degrees of freedom to use in Table 5. We've seen that when the data are labeled in one direction, with m possible outcomes, there are $m - 1$ degrees of

Table 12.6 *The expected frequencies if ratings and income class are unrelated*

	Low-income	Middle-income	High-income	Total
Excellent	60	100	40	200
Good	75	125	50	250
Fair	90	150	60	300
Poor	75	125	50	250
Total	300	500	200	1000

*We filled the table row-by-row. What if we instead work column by column? We get exactly the same answers. For example, 30 percent of the 1000 respondents are low-income. If income and rating were independent, then we would expect 30 percent of the 200 excellent ratings to come from low-income people: .3(200) = 60, the same answer as when we reasoned row by row.

freedom because there is one constraint on the data. Here, the data are labeled in two directions, with three possibilities one way and four possibilities the other way. Our chi-square statistic is the sum of (3)(4) = 12 squared deviations. But there are also constraints in both directions. Only two of the three entries in any row of Table 12.5 or 12.6 can be independently specified; given those two, the third entry is known immediately. And only three of the four entries in any column of Table 12.5 or 12.6 are independent. Overall, there are only (3 − 1)(4 − 1) = 6 independent entries in these tables and, thus, only 6 degrees of freedom.*

The degrees of freedom for a contingency table is

(number of rows − 1) (number of columns − 1).

Table 5 at the end of this book tells us that, with a 5 percent significance level, the cutoff point for a chi-square statistic with 6 degrees of freedom is 12.59. Our computed chi-square value 92.10 has a P-value far below .005, the smallest probability given in Table 5. There is virtually no chance that the luck of the draw would give a sample with such large deviations between the observed and expected frequencies, so we reject the null hypothesis that rating and income class are independent and conclude that, among the population as a whole, different income classes rate this President differently.

Do John McEnroe's Grunts Help?

An article entitled ''Should John McEnroe Grunt?'' began

> A third of a million people munched something like 11 tonnes of fresh strawberries and drank 17,000 bottles of champagne as John McEnroe sweated and grunted his way to the men's singles title at Wimbledon. . . . His winning way with officials and loud service grunt make him one of the most audible players in the modern game. But does the McEnroe grunt affect his game?[13]

Dr. Dennis Lendrum, an animal-behavior analyst at Nottingham University in England kept careful records of McEnroe's grunts during the 1983 Wimbledon matches and drew some interesting conclusions.

If McEnroe's grunts were a sign of extra effort, then we might expect more grunting on the first serve than on the second, when the primary objective is to hit the ball accurately. Lendrum's data were:

---

*Another explanation is that the sum of 12 squared deviations has 11 degrees of freedom, because it represents the sum of 11 independent squared normal variables. But this chi-square statistic requires the estimation of five parameters: the fractions of the population that are low-income and middle-income, and the fractions that rate the President as excellent, good, and fair. (The other two fractions, high-income and poor rating, can be computed from these five.) Because we lose 1 degree of freedom for every parameter that must be estimated from the data, the degrees of freedom fall by 5, from 11 to 6.

	grunts	silent	total
first serves	171	69	240
second serves	62	26	88
total	233	95	328

The proportions of the first and second serves accompanied by grunts were remarkably similar:

$$\text{grunts on first serve: } 171/240 = 0.71$$

$$\text{grunts on second serve: } 62/88 = 0.70$$

For a formal chi-square test, we can compare the observations to the expected values, if the grunting is unrelated to whether it is a first or second serve:

	grunts	silent	total
first serves	170.5	69.5	240
second serves	62.5	25.5	88
total	233	95	328

The value of the chi-square statistic is virtually zero, 0.01. Thus, there is no evidence that McEnroe grunts significantly more on his first serves. His grunting may be psychological, rather than a reflection of extra effort.

   Dr. Lendrem inquired whether the grunt serves were more effective than the silent ones:*

	grunts	silent	total
aces	61	35	96
errors	32	8	40
other	144	53	197
total	237	96	333

A calculation of the proportions,

	grunts	silent
aces	25.7%	36.5%
errors	13.5%	8.3%
other	60.8%	55.2%
total	100.0%	100.0%

shows that grunt serves were less often aces and more often errors. For a formal chi-square test, the expected values if grunts didn't matter are

	grunts	silent	total
aces	68.3	27.7	96
errors	28.5	11.5	40
other	140.2	56.8	197
total	237	96	333

*There are slightly more serves here, because of the inclusion of five third serves.

The value of the chi-square statistic works out to be 4.56, which (with $(2 - 1)$ $(2 - 1) = 1$ degree of freedom) is statistically significant. Dr. Lendrem concludes that McEnroe should ''shut up when serving.''

The Unshuffled Draft Lottery

For another example, consider the national lottery that was held in 1969 to determine the order in which men born in 1950 would be drafted to fight in the Viet Nam War. The Selective Service System prepared 366 capsules, each containing a birthdate, January 1, January 2, and so on. Each month's capsules were carried to the drawing in a separate box. At the appropriate time, the boxes were emptied into a large drum, one after another—first January, then February, and on through the months with December poured in last. The drum was rotated a few times and then the capsules were drawn out, one by one. Those capsules drawn first would be drafted first, those drawn last would most likely not be drafted at all. The results are summarized in Table 12.7.

A casual inspection suggests that the late months, August through December, got more than their share of the low, ''first-drafted'' numbers. The early months, January through May, got more than their share of the late, ''not-drafted-at-all'' numbers. A plausible explanation is that a few rotations of the drum did not do a very good job of mixing up the capsules. The early months stayed at the bottom of the heap, while the late months stayed on top, ready to be picked out first. Is this suspicion an unwarranted criticism from a desperate statistician with a December birthday? After all, someone has to go first and, by the luck of the draw, the

Table 12.7   *The 1969 draft lottery*

	Priority numbers			
Month	*1–122* *(First-drafted)*	*123–244* *(Middle)*	*245–366* *(Last-drafted)*	*Total*
January	9	12	10	31
February	7	12	10	29
March	5	10	16	31
April	8	8	14	30
May	9	7	15	31
June	11	7	12	30
July	12	7	12	31
August	13	7	11	31
September	10	15	5	30
October	9	15	7	31
November	12	12	6	30
December	17	10	4	31
Total	122	122	122	366

Does Smoking Cause Sex?

Contingency tables are a useful way of organizing data and looking for dependencies, but the discovery of a statistical dependency does not tell us its cause. Two variables may be related because the first influences the second, because the second influences the first, because some other factor influences both, or because of sampling error. Only additional data or common sense can sort out the reason for a statistical dependency. Additional data may reveal that it was an accidental relation, a mere sampling error. Or, in an experimental context, if we suspect that some third influence is responsible, we may be able to hold that factor constant and see what happens. In many cases, common sense suffices.

A good example is provided by the following deliberate misinterpretation, which was intended to show the need for common sense (and to provoke a chuckle, too).[15] A survey asked 508 girls aged 14–17 whether or not they smoked and whether or not they used oral contraceptives. Oral contraceptive use was interpreted to indicate sexual activity, because "the pills have some side effects and make your skin blotchy and you have to have a real good reason to take them." The results of this survey can be arranged in a contingency table as follows:

	sexually active	not sexually active	total
smokers	24	122	146
nonsmokers	11	351	362
total	35	473	508

Sixteen percent of the smokers are sexually active, while only 3 percent of the nonsmokers are. There is a very high "risk of sex for smokers." For a chi-square test, we compare these observed data with the expected values if sex were independent of smoking:

	sexually active	not sexually active	total
smokers	10.1	135.9	146
nonsmokers	24.9	337.2	362
total	35	473	508

The value of the chi-square statistic is

$$\frac{(24 - 10.1)^2}{10.1} + \frac{(11 - 24.9)^2}{24.9} + \frac{(122 - 135.9)^2}{135.9} + \frac{(351 - 337.2)^2}{337.2} = 28.88$$

which is highly significant. Thus, the author concludes that smoking not only causes cancer and cardiovascular disease, but sexual activity as well.

The data, of course, show only association and not causation. It may be that smoking encourages sexual activity, that sexual activity encourages smoking, or that girls who smoke also happen to be sexually active, without either activity causing the other. Common sense is needed to sort through these competing explanations of the data. I'll put my money on the third explanation.

first few choices may well turn out to be November and December days. Are the deviations seen in Table 12.7 so large that they cannot be explained by chance alone?

This is a fitting question for a chi-square test to answer. The null hypothesis is that the capsules were well-shuffled, so that each date was equally likely to be chosen. If this null hypothesis were true, we would expect each month to have its days equally divided among the three categories 1–122, 123–244, and 245–366. For November and other months with 30 days, the expected number of days in each of these three categories is 10. Months with 31 days would average $31/3 = 10.33$ days per category. February, with 29 days, would average $29/3 = 9.67$ days per category in the long run, over many such drawings. To gauge how severely the 36 actual frequencies shown in Table 12.7 depart from these expected frequencies, we calculate the chi-square statistic

$$\chi^2 = \frac{(9 - 10.33)^2}{10.33} + \frac{(12 - 10.33)^2}{10.33} + \cdots + \frac{(4 - 10.33)^2}{10.33}$$

$$= 37.2$$

Because Table 12.7 has 12 rows and 3 columns, there are $(12 - 1)(3 - 1) = 22$ degrees of freedom. A chi-square statistic with 22 degrees of freedom has a 5 percent chance of exceeding 33.9 and a 1 percent chance of exceeding 40.3. There is only about a 2 percent chance of a chi-square value being as large as the observed 37.2. Thus, at the 5 percent level at least, these data reject the hypothesis that the capsules were well shuffled in the 1969 draft lottery. In response to such criticism, the Selective Service was more careful the following year, when they conducted a draft lottery for men born in 1951. In the 1970 lottery, two drums were used—one with dates and another with numbers—and each drum was loaded in a random order.[14]

Exercises

12.21 Yale University admitted its first women undergraduates in 1969. For the first few years, male and female students were admitted separately, in an effort to preserve Yale's tradition of "graduating 1000 fine young men each year." However, a separate admission policy can cause disparities between the caliber of the male and female students. A University Committee on Coeducation compared the academic performance of Yale male and female undergraduates, using data such as these:

	course grades, spring 1972	
	males	*females*
honors	6591	1593
high pass	7573	1655
pass	3108	539
other	590	117

Are grades and gender unrelated?

12.22 Four toothpastes were tested by randomly dividing 400 children into four groups of 100. Each group used a different brand of toothpaste for one year, and then the following results were observed:

brand of toothpaste	*number of new cavities*		
	0–1	*2–3*	*4 or more*
A	50	28	22
B	41	30	29
C	39	23	38
D	36	27	37

Use a chi-square test to see if these data are consistent with the null hypothesis that there are no significant differences in the effectiveness of these toothpastes in preventing cavities.

12.23 After attempting to imitate a popular television character, a young man concluded that whether one is right-handed or left-handed affects how far apart the two middle fingers on each hand can be spread. If a wider "V" is made with the right hand, then the person is probably left-handed. If a wider V is made with the left hand or there is no difference, then the person is probably right-handed. After an article explaining this theory appeared in the February 20, 1974 issue of *Current Science,* 3225 readers reported the following results:

	test correct	*test wrong*
right-handed readers	2097	783
left-handed readers	289	56

Find the probabilities that a person picked from this group will be:

a. right-handed
b. left-handed
c. right-handed if the test predicts right-handed
d. left-handed if the test predicts left-handed
e. correctly identified by this test

Use a chi-square test to see if there is a statistically significant relationship between handedness and the test predictions.

12.24 A Gallup poll asked 260 males and 263 females whether male or female students are more assertive in class:[16]

	males	*females*
"men are"	80	61
"women are"	104	112
"no difference"	76	90
total	260	263

Make a chi-square test of the null hypothesis that the answer given does not depend on whether the student is a male or female.

12.25 (*continuation*) This same Gallup poll divided the answers to this question by class, too:

	freshman	sophomore	junior	senior
"men are"	26	29	44	48
"women are"	72	60	38	39
"no difference"	37	44	43	43
total	135	133	125	130

Make a chi-square test of the null hypothesis that the answers do not depend on a student's class.

12.26   Roll two dice 50 times, each time rolling first one die with the left hand and then the other die with the right hand. For each turn, record whether the left-hand die is

a. greater than 3, or
b. less than or equal to 3,

and record whether the sum is

c. greater than 7, or
d. less than or equal to 7.

Make a chi-square test of the null hypothesis that the sum is independent of the outcome of the first roll.

12.27   Here are data on the hair and eye color of 6800 Germans:[17]

	eye color		
hair color	blue	brown	grey or green
fair	1768	115	946
brown	807	438	1387
black	189	288	746
red	47	16	53

Do these data show a statistically significant relationship between hair color and eye color?

12.28   There were 88,273 births in Sweden in 1935. These births were not evenly distributed throughout the year. For example, 26.5 percent of the births were in the spring, although the spring contains only 25 percent of the days of the year. A statistics text applies a chi-square test to the seasonal data and concludes that they reject the hypothesis that births in Sweden in 1935 occurred equally often throughout the year.[18] What is the population from which these data are a sample? Does this test make sense?

12.29   Data were collected from 247 professional geographers on their proficiency in meeting their graduate foreign language requirements and their later professional use of the foreign language:[19]

	use after doctoral work	
graduate proficiency	yes	no
extremely high	27	1
better than average	37	12
average	64	51
minimal	23	32

What proportion of these geographers used their foreign language after graduate work? Is there a statistically significant relationship between graduate proficiency and later use of a foreign language?

12.30 Five hundred students were asked to evaluate a statistics course on a scale from 1 to 5, with 5 being best:

	5	*4*	*3*	*2*	*1*
freshmen	4	16	16	10	4
sophomores	54	124	87	28	7
juniors	10	44	29	13	4
seniors	2	16	18	9	5

Is there a statistically significant relationship between the students' class and evaluation?

12.4 SUMMARY

We often want to test to see if the difference between two means μ_1 and μ_2 is statistically significant. We can do so by testing the null hypothesis that the difference between the means is equal to zero,

$$H_0: \mu_1 - \mu_2 = 0$$

$$H_1: \mu_1 - \mu_2 \neq 0$$

The test is based on the statistical fact that the means $\overline{X}_1$ and $\overline{X}_2$ of two independent random samples of size n_1 and n_2 tend to be normally distributed, as does their difference,

$$\overline{X}_1 - \overline{X}_2 \sim N[\mu_1 - \mu_2, (\sigma_1^2/n_1 + \sigma_2^2/n_2)^{1/2}]$$

Normality is assured if X_1 and X_2 are normally distributed and approximated in accordance with the central limit theorem, if the samples are reasonably sized.

The test itself can be conducted by setting a cutoff point for $\overline{X}_1 - \overline{X}_2$, by calculating a Z-value and corresponding P-value for the observed $\overline{X}_1 - \overline{X}_2$, or by constructing a confidence interval.

A similar logic applies to the difference in two success probabilities π_1 and π_2, because the observed success proportions p_1 and p_2 can be interpreted as sample means. The only added wrinkle is that the expected value and standard deviation of the p_i are π_i and $\{\pi_i(1 - \pi_i)/n_i\}^{1/2}$. Thus

$$p_1 - p_2 \sim N[\pi_1 - \pi_2, \{\pi_1(1 - \pi_1)/n_1 + \pi_2(1 - \pi_2)/n_2\}^{1/2}]$$

A paired-sample test looks at differences for individual observations within a single sample, or for "twins"—matched pairs in the sample. Individuals might compare two colas, or two medicines might be compared by administering them to similar individuals. The observed differences are then the random variable X, and we can use the sample mean to test in the usual way whether or not the expected value of X is zero.

Chi-square tests provide a handy procedure for testing a wide variety of hypotheses. The basic idea is to identify m mutually exclusive categories, compute the expected number of observations E_i in each category under the null hypothesis, and then make a comparison with the actual number of observations O_i by computing the value of the chi-square statistic,

$$\chi^2 = \Sigma(O_i - E_i)^2/E_i$$

If all of the $E_i \geq 10$, then the distribution of this statistic can be approximated by the chi-square distribution with $m - 1$ degrees of freedom shown in Table 5. These are called *goodness-of-fit* tests because they gauge how closely the sample distribution agrees with the population distribution under the null hypothesis.

A special application of chi-square tests is two-way contingency tables. The data are labeled by two factors—for instance, opinion poll responses that are classified by both the rating given a president's performance and the income of a respondent. A chi-square statistic can be used to test the null hypothesis that these two factors are independent, by comparing the observed data with the expected values if the factors are independent.

REVIEW EXERCISES

12.31 A study of changes over a 100-year period in the lead content of people's hair, measured in micrograms (millionths of a gram) of lead per gram of hair, used these data:[20]

	sample size	sample mean	standard deviation
children, 1871–1923	36	164.2	124.0
adults, 1871–1923	20	93.4	72.9
children, 1924–1971	119	16.2	10.6
adults, 1924–1971	28	6.6	6.2

Are there statistically significant differences in average lead content between

a. children 1871–1923 and adults 1871–1923?
b. children 1924–1971 and adults 1924–1971?
c. children 1871–1923 and children 1924–1971?
d. adults 1871–1923 and adults 1924–1971?

12.32 Between October 1, 1978 and September 30, 1981, 4845 English majors and 1792 math majors took the GRE test:[21]

	4845 English majors		1792 math majors	
	mean	std. dev.	mean	std. dev.
verbal score	576	111	514	132
quantitative score	515	113	669	107

Interpreting these as random samples of the abilities of all math and English majors, do these results show a statistically significant difference between English and math majors in

a. verbal abilities?
b. quantitative abilities?

12.33 Jack and Jill each take a 200-question IQ test. The number of correct answers is the test's estimate of a person's IQ. As it turns out, Jack's IQ score is 110 and Jill's is 132. Is this difference statistically significant at the 5 percent level?

• **12.34** Jack and Jill each take a 100-question IQ test. This test estimates IQs by multiplying the number of correct answers by 2; for example, a person who gets 50 correct answers is estimated to have an IQ of 100. This test estimates Jack's IQ to be 108 and Jill's to be 133. Is this difference statistically significant at the 5 percent level? Compare your conclusion with the preceding question and explain any noticeable differences.

•• **12.35** (*continuation*) Why, in Exercise 12.33, would it have been of no help to know that IQ scores on this test are normally distributed with a mean of 100 and a standard deviation of 16?

• **12.36** A school psychologist administers tests to see if there is a statistically significant difference (at the 5 percent level) in a student's intelligence and achievement scores. What is the probability of incorrectly concluding that there is a statistically significant difference if

a. just one pair of tests (intelligence and reading) is administered?
b. five pairs of tests (intelligence and reading, intelligence and writing, intelligence and math, and so on) are administered? (Assume independence.)

•• **12.37** (*continuation*) If five pairs of independent tests are administered, how can we reduce the overall probability of making a Type I error to 5 percent? Do you think that independence is a reasonable assumption here?

• **12.38** The bowlers on two teams have the following expected scores and standard deviations:

team	bowler	expected score	standard deviation
	Bob	200	30
Boomers	Ralph	180	30
	Gary	190	30
	Arv	170	20
Bouncers	Mike	190	30
•	Walt	180	30

The teams add their players' scores together to determine which team wins. What is the probability of the Boomers winning a game between these two teams? If they play three games, what is the probability that the Boomers will win all three games? Two games? One game? No games? State your assumptions.

• **12.39** (*continuation*) The Boomers and the Bouncers agree to a showdown to determine which is the better team. Each team member will bowl n games, and the team with the highest average over these n games is the winner. What is the probability that the Bouncers will win if $n = 1$? If $n = 3$? If $n = 5$? If $n = 25$? How high does n have to be for it to be 99 percent certain that the better team, the Boomers, will win?

12.40 A 1954 study of the effects of the original Salk vaccine on the incidence of paralytic polio yielded the following data (from Table 8.1):

children inoculated	number inoculated	number of polio cases
with Salk vaccine	200,745	28
with placebo	201,229	71

Is there a statistically significant difference in polio incidence between the two groups of children?

12.41 Kate claims that she is a better baseball batter than her sister Julie. This season Kate got 46 hits in 59 times at bat, while Julie got 36 hits in 56 times at bat. What are their batting averages? Is this difference sufficient to show that Kate has a higher probability of getting a hit than Julie does?

12.42 To gauge the effects of writing deficiencies on college performance, Pomona College examined the freshman records of those 45 students in the 1983 freshman class of 409 with the lowest verbal SAT scores. Of the 66 students who received low grade notices in the fall term, 23 had low verbal SATs. Of the 14 students placed on academic probation, 8 had low verbal SATs. By each measure, are the differences between the low-verbal-score students and the remaining freshmen too large to be explained by sampling error? From what population are these students a sample?

12.43 A psychic claims an ability to "destabilize" coins so that heads and tails do not come up equally often. A "destabilized" coin is flipped 200 times and comes up heads 93 times. Construct a 95 percent confidence interval for the probability π of obtaining a head with this coin. Now test these hypotheses (at the 5 percent level)

$$H_0: \pi = .5$$

$$H_1: \pi \neq .5$$

First, use a normal approximation to the binomial and, second, use a chi-square test. Do both tests give the same conclusion?

12.44 David Phillips collected the following data on the relationship between death and birth dates:

number of months before(−) or after(+) birth month	observed number of deaths		
	sample 2	sample 3	sample 4
−6	17	10	39
−5	23	14	32
−4	26	12	29
−3	27	11	35
−2	28	8	31
−1	28	12	30
0	42	15	36
+1	32	15	35
+2	31	15	38
+3	34	13	26
+4	36	20	31
+5	30	13	29
total	354	158	391

For each of these three samples, test the hypothesis that the death month is unrelated to the birth month.

12.45 Make a chi-square test of the null hypothesis that the batting averages shown in Table 1 on page 200 come from a normal distribution.

12.46 Four hundred people were asked to evaluate the President's performance:

	excellent	good	poor
males	56	111	33
females	30	121	49

Is there a statistically significant difference in the responses of males and females?

12.47 To study social mobility in Great Britain, a 1954 sample of 3497 male workers determined the occupations of the workers and of their fathers. These occupations were then divided into upper, middle, and lower class:[22]

		worker's status		
		u	m	l
father's	u	588	395	159
status	m	349	714	447
	l	114	320	441

If there was no social mobility whatsoever, what would the data look like? If there was completely free social mobility, what would you expect the data to look like? Make a chi-square test of the null hypothesis that worker and father status are independent.

12.48 At Metro University, statistics is taught in 10 sections, and each section has 50 students. The students are randomly assigned to a section. Each section has a different instructor, but uses the same textbook and gives the same tests. The final scores in the course are

section	500–400	400–300	300–200	200–100
1	6	24	13	7
2	3	13	21	13
3	10	28	11	1
4	9	24	15	2
5	0	25	20	5
6	7	23	20	0
7	7	17	20	6
8	1	14	24	11
9	10	20	17	3
10	7	32	9	2

Do these data support or reject the hypothesis that student performance is independent of the instructor?

12.49 As part of the investigation of the inheritance of various traits, the athletic skills of brothers were evaluated:[23]

second brother	first brother			
	athletic	betwixt	non-athletic	total
athletic	906	20	140	1066
betwixt	20	76	9	105
non-athletic	140	9	370	519
total	1066	105	519	1690

Make a chi-square test of the null hypothesis that the athletic skills of brothers are independent.

•• **12.50**   Do you think that baseball batting averages during the first half of the season (before the All-Star break) and for the entire season are independent? Use data for the last baseball season to test the null hypothesis that they are independent.

CHAPTER 13

The Idea of Regression Analysis

Econometricians, like artists, tend to fall in love with their models.

Edward Leamer

TOPICS

Scientists use models to explain various phenomena. For example, Newton said that the force applied by a body in motion depends on its mass and acceleration. Agronomists say that crop yields depend upon weather, soil conditions, and nutrients. Economists say that the demand for a product depends on its price. In each case, there is a simple model that purports to explain a complex reality. Statistics can be used to quantify such theories and to give them practical application. For a detailed example, let's look at one of the most famous economic theories.

13.1   KEYNES'S CONSUMPTION FUNCTION

John Maynard Keynes, a great British economist, wanted to explain fluctuations in consumer spending. He believed that consumer spending was one of the keys to understanding economic booms and busts, and so he naturally wondered what it was that caused consumer spending to go up or down. Keynes hypothesized that household income was the primary determinant of household spending. When income goes up, people spend more; when their income drops, they spend less. He wrote that this is a ". . . fundamental psychological law, upon which we are entitled to depend both *a priori* from our knowledge of human nature and from the detailed facts of experience."[1]

A Model

A simple algebraic representation of Keynes's theory is

$$Y = \alpha + \beta X \tag{13.1}$$

where Y is consumer spending and X is income. In regression models, α and β are not the probabilities of Type I and Type II errors. Instead, α and β are two unknown parameters that describe the relationship between income and consumption. Income is the **explanatory variable,** because changes in income *explain* changes in spending. Spending is the **dependent variable,** because spending *depends* on income.

> Models usually embody an assumed **causal relationship;** the researcher believes that changes in the explanatory variable *cause* changes in the dependent variable.

The sign of the parameter β tells us whether there is a positive or negative relationship between the explanatory and dependent variables. Figure 13.1 shows three possibilities: a positive relationship, a negative relationship, and no relationship at all. In the consumption model, the parameter β, which Keynes called "the marginal propensity to consume," tells us the effect of income changes on spending. Keynes argued that β is surely positive, but undoubtedly less than 1.0. If β is .8, then $1 of additional income increases spending by 80 cents and, similarly, a $1 decline in income reduces spending by 80 cents.

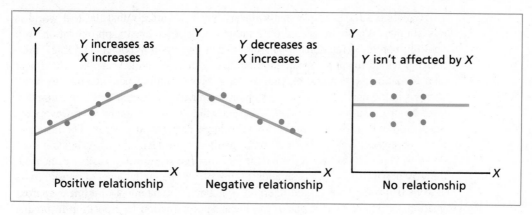

Figure 13.1 *Three possible relationships between* X *and* Y

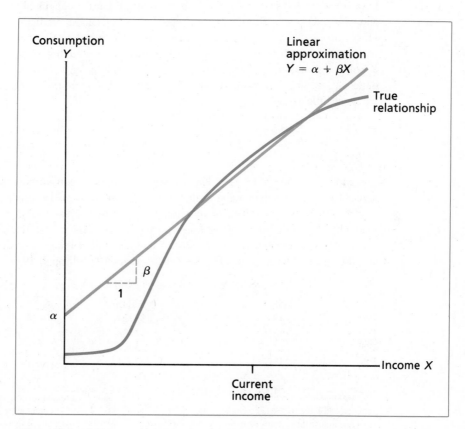

Figure 13.2 *A linear approximation to a nonlinear relationship*

Equation 13.1 is conveniently linear, but it is unlikely that the real world is this simple. We should think of Equation 13.1 as a linear approximation to a possibly nonlinear relationship. Figure 13.2 compares a hypothetical "true" relationship with a linear approximation that has a slope β and intercept α. This linear approximation is accurate enough as long as we confine our attention to small changes in income. As income goes up or down from its current level, consumption goes up or down by approximately β times the change in income. However, the linear approximation goes awry for very large changes in income. For instance, the intercept α gives a very inaccurate prediction of spending when income goes down to zero. Unless we're confident that the true relationship really is linear all the way down to $X = 0$, we shouldn't think of α as being the level of consumption at $X = 0$. Instead, we should interpret α as being the intercept of a linear approximation, an intercept that places the linear approximation in a position to predict consumption accurately for values of income near the current level.

In truth, economists are rightfully wary of predicting what consumption would be if a nation's income were zero. Presumably, such an economic disaster would have drastic effects on people's behavior that are hardly imaginable to our stable and well-fed society. Similarly, we should be cautious about predicting what grade-school dropouts would earn if they had gone on to earn Ph.D.s, what the productivity of labor will be 200 years from now, or what my batting average would be if I played professional baseball. Linear approximations are very useful and usually quite satisfactory as long as we don't try to extrapolate them to situations for which we have little knowledge or evidence.

Some Data

The model, Equation 13.1, is Keynes's explanation of consumption. If we had values for the parameters α and β, then the model could be used to predict consumer spending for various values of income. It is natural to test and implement this model by collecting some data and seeing what, if any, relationship there is between consumption and income. Here are some data on real per capita household spending and disposable income (net of taxes) for the years 1977 through 1981:*

year	disposable income X	household spending Y
1977	$3319	$3042
1978	$3421	$3124
1979	$3404	$3108
1980	$3276	$2994
1981	$3271	$2971

*The economic term *real* means that an adjustment has been made for inflation. These data are all in terms of 1967 dollars—what a dollar would have bought in 1967. In 1981, commodities cost, on the average, almost three times as much as they did in 1967. Thus 9000 1981-dollars are about the same as 3000 1967-dollars.

Figure 13.3 plots these data in what is called a **scatter diagram.** If, as is illustrated in Figure 13.4, there is too much scatter in the data, then there isn't a convincing empirical relationship between X and Y. In Figure 13.3, there seems to be a fairly close positive relationship between income and spending. If we fit a line to these data, we can obtain values for the parameters α and β and thereby quantify Keynes's consumption function, Equation 13.1. I've used a transparent ruler and some squinting to draw the line shown in Figure 13.3. The slope seems to be about .98, while the intercept appears to be -227.*

Economic forecasters used models like Figure 13.3 to predict consumer spending in 1982. Let's imagine that it is the beginning of 1982 and we want to make a forecast too. We specify our model, gather some data, and come up with an

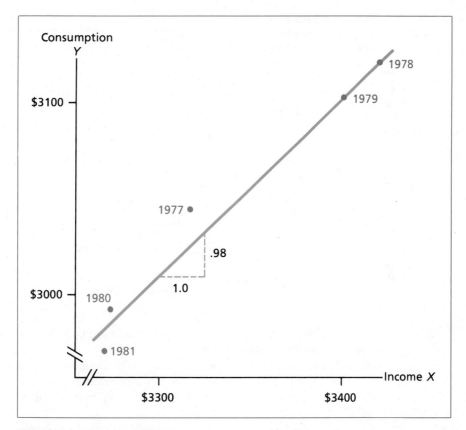

Figure 13.3 *Some data on household spending and income*

*To show the variation in these data, Figure 13.3 focuses on a small range of income and spending. Using the "guesstimated" slope .98 and the fact that the fitted line seems to run through the point $X = 3300$, $Y = 3007$, we can determine the intercept: $3007 = a + .98(3300)$ implies $a = -227$.

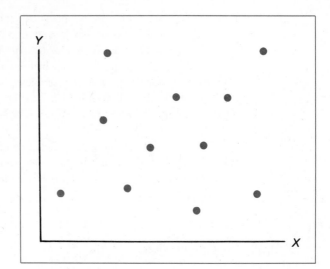

Figure 13.4 *If there is too much scatter in a scatter diagram, then there is no apparent relationship between* X *and* Y

intercept of -227 and a slope of .98. Our predicted value for spending $\hat{Y}$ is given by the fitted equation

$$\hat{Y} = -227 + .98X \qquad (13.2)$$

If we believe household income will be \$3300 in 1982, then our model predicts that household spending will be

$$\hat{Y} = -227 + .98(3300)$$
$$= 3007$$

Were per capita income \$100 higher in 1982, spending would then be .98(\$100) = \$98 higher, or

$$\hat{Y} = -227 + .98(3400)$$
$$= \$3105$$

These sorts of calculations can create a variety of possible scenarios, ranging from pessimistic to optimistic forecasts, or they can be used to determine the effects of government policy decisions. If, for instance, Congress is debating a tax cut, an economic model like this can predict the consequences for consumer spending. According to our model, a tax cut that raises per capita disposable income by \$100 will raise consumer spending by \$98.

The model can also answer hypothetical historical questions. In 1980, per capita income was \$3276 and spending was \$2994. If Congress had enacted a tax increase in 1980 that reduced per capita disposable income by \$100, what effect would that tax hike have had on consumer spending? Our model predicts that spending would have been reduced by \$98 per person.

Economists do, in fact, build models to answer just these sorts of questions. In practice, of course, empirical economic models include many equations, which predict not only consumer spending, but also prices, interest rates, unemployment, and income itself.

Exercises

13.1 Here is a plot of the midterm and final exam scores for Alice, Bill, Carrie, David, and Elaine.

a. Which student earned the highest score on the midterm?
b. Which student earned the highest score on the final?
c. Which student's score increased the most between the midterm and the final?
d. Which student's score fell the most between the midterm and the final?
e. Was the average score higher on the midterm or on the final?
f. Was there a greater dispersion of scores on the midterm or on the final?
g. Select one of the following statements:

"Midterm and final scores are positively related";
"Midterm and final scores are negatively related"; or
"Midterm and final scores are unrelated."

13.2 Professor Smith claims that a student's score on the final exam can be predicted from his or her score on the midterm. Here are some midterm and final exam scores:

students	midterm X	final Y
Fred	92	87
Gail	65	71
Hannah	75	75
Irene	83	84
Joshua	95	93

a. What are the average midterm and final scores?

b. Plot these data with midterm scores on the horizontal axis and final scores on the vertical axis.

c. Does there seem to be any evidence of a relationship between final and midterm scores?

d. Using only your judgment, draw a line that appears to fit these data, and then calculate the (approximate) intercept and slope.

13.3 Explain why you think that each of the following pairs of data are positively related, negatively related, or essentially unrelated. If you think that there is a relationship, which is the dependent variable?

a. the height of a father and his eldest son

b. the age of a mother and her oldest child

c. the income and age of male lawyers aged 21 to 54

d. the height and weight of 21-year-old males

e. a woman's age and the cost of her life insurance

13.4 Explain why you believe that each of the following pairs of data are positively related, negatively related, or essentially unrelated. If there is some relationship, which is the dependent variable?

a. a child's Little League batting average and the number of hours spent practicing

b. the temperature in Houston and attendance at the city's Fourth of July parade

c. the number of automobiles on a freeway and their average speed

d. the weight of a car and the miles per gallon

e. the mileage on a five-year-old Chevrolet and its current market price

13.5 Explain why you believe that each of the following pairs are positively related, negatively related, or not related at all. If there is a relationship, which is the dependent variable?

a. advertising expenditures and sales

b. the current price of corn and the number of acres planted by Iowa farmers

c. the price of steak and the amount purchased by your college dining hall

d. the price of oil and the demand for cars

e. the number of wins by the New York Yankees and the price of tea in China

13.2 LEAST SQUARES ESTIMATION

Fitting a line by hand to scattered data points is a hopelessly crude method for coming up with values for the intercept and slope. It's hard to know where to draw the line and it is hard to read the intercept and slope from a smudged piece of graph paper. It would be much better to have some standard formula, one analogous to estimating a population mean by calculating the sample mean. But here we are trying to simultaneously estimate two parameters, α and β, and a natural formula is not apparent.

Least Squares Estimates of a Population Mean

In Chapter 9, you were introduced to Gauss's justification for using the sample mean to estimate a population mean. Gauss extended this justification to obtain a method for estimating two parameters, like α and β. Gauss's initial concern was with using physical measurements Y to estimate a distance μ. The individual measurements can be distinguished by using an i subscript:

observation i	*measurement* Y_i
1	115.1
2	114.4
3	112.5
4	116.2
5	114.8

The difference between each measurement Y_i and the true distance μ is the (unobserved) measurement error ϵ_i. That is,

measured value = true value + measurement error

In symbols,

$$Y_i = \mu + \epsilon_i \tag{13.3}$$

Let's try to interpret Gauss's equation as a model similar to our model of household spending. Equation 13.3 says that measurements depend on the true value and on the measurement error. We can view μ as an unknown parameter, like α and β, that we want to estimate. Our estimate $\hat{\mu}$ of this parameter is a prediction $\hat{Y} = \hat{\mu}$ of the measurements that people will obtain. The error term ϵ_i allows for the fact that the measurements inevitably diverge from the true value in ways that can't be predicted ahead of time.

Gauss argued that we should use the estimate that minimizes the sum of the squared prediction errors for the data we have:*

$$(Y_1 - \hat{Y})^2 + (Y_2 - \hat{Y})^2 + \cdots + (Y_n - \hat{Y})^2$$

$$= (Y_1 - \hat{\mu})^2 + (Y_2 - \hat{\mu})^2 + \cdots + (Y_n - \hat{\mu})^2$$

$$= (115.1 - \hat{\mu})^2 + (114.4 - \hat{\mu})^2 + \cdots + (114.8 - \hat{\mu})^2$$

Gauss showed that the sample mean, or the average of our measurements, is in fact the estimator $\hat{\mu}$ that minimizes the sum of these squared prediction errors. The mean of these particular five measurements is

$$\overline{Y} = \frac{115.1 + 114.4 + 112.5 + 116.2 + 114.8}{5}$$

$$= 114.6$$

*Notice that Gauss did not try to minimize the difference between the true value and the estimate, $(\mu - \hat{\mu})^2$, because the true value μ is unknown.

The sample mean, $\overline{Y} = 114.6$, is an estimate of the true distance μ. We know that, inevitably, measurements will sometimes be above and other times be below the true distance, but there is no way to predict the size of these measurement errors in advance. For the five observations we have, the sample mean $\overline{Y} = 114.6$ is the measurement predictor that has the smallest sum of squared prediction errors. Thus, the sample mean is called the **least squares estimator.**

The Least Squares Logic

Let's think a bit more about this logic. Figure 13.5 shows the measurement data, together with the sample mean. The horizontal axis lists the observations and the vertical axis gives their distance measurements; our prediction line is horizontal with an intercept equal to the sample mean, $\overline{Y} = 114.6$. (There is no slope, because we assume that the order in which the observations are numbered is unimportant.) Our prediction errors e_i are the vertical distances between the actual measurements Y_i and our prediction $\hat{Y}_i = \overline{Y}$:

$$e_i = Y_i - \hat{Y} \qquad (13.4)$$

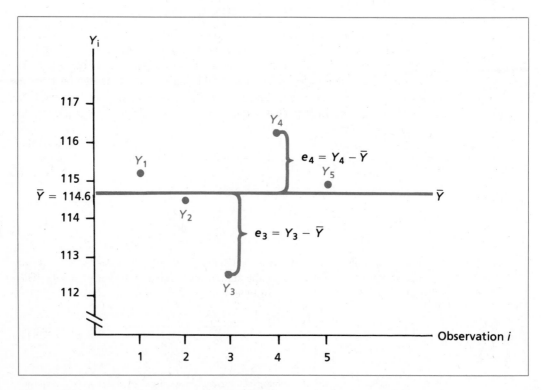

Figure 13.5 *Data, an estimate, and prediction errors*

Gauss's least squares criterion is to minimize the sum of the squared prediction errors, that is, the sum of the vertical discrepancies between the data and our fitted line in Figure 13.5.

Squaring the prediction errors means that positive and negative errors count equally. We don't care if our prediction is too high or too low, only how far off we are. Squaring the errors also means that large errors are more worrisome than small errors. We prefer an estimate that has 99 one-inch errors to an estimate that has 1 ten-inch error. This logic has considerable appeal. In addition, as Gauss discovered, least-squares mathematics are very tractable and the recommended estimators (like the sample mean) are quite sensible.

One final note is that these are not true forecasts in the sense that we make them before we see the data. We can postulate a model beforehand, but we cannot estimate the model's parameters without looking at the data. The least squares logic begins with a certain model that is to be used for predictions. For the data we have, we can determine the parameter estimates that give the smallest sum of squared prediction errors. The real test of the model will, of course, come when we use it to predict data that we have not yet seen.

Least Squares Estimates of a Linear Equation

Once the logic is clear, it can be extended to a variety of situations. One example is a linear equation, such as Keynes's consumption function,

$$Y = \alpha + \beta X \qquad (13.5)$$

We want to predict consumer spending Y for various levels of income X, but we recognize that our model is not perfect. There are other factors besides income that influence household spending decisions, and we can put these other influences into the catch-all error category—differences between observed spending and spending as determined by income:

$$\epsilon = Y - (\alpha + \beta X)$$

That is,

$$Y = \alpha + \beta X + \epsilon \qquad (13.6)$$

These errors are, in part, measurement errors in tabulating household spending, but they also involve other considerations. It is mathematically convenient to treat the error term ϵ as if it were the chance result of rolling dice. However, consumer spending is determined not by dice rolls, but by households purposefully acting on the basis of all sorts of real and fanciful information. The error term ϵ includes the effects of these neglected influences. We invariably omit some factors—such as credit availability, inflation expectations, and consumer confidence—because we don't think that they are all that important, because we don't have reliable data on them, or because we simply haven't thought of them. Some influences are so poorly understood—what Keynes called "animal spirits"—that we can consider them essentially random variation. In addition, our data are based on *some* rather than *all* households and are therefore subject to sampling error.

> We do not observe all of the factors that influence household spending; nor do we observe all households or measure spending perfectly. Because of these errors and omissions, our predictions won't be perfect and we have to introduce an **error term ε** to allow for this imperfection.

Figure 13.6 shows the least squares logic. The data points are the observed levels of income X_i and spending Y_i, while the fitted line gives our spending predictions $\hat{Y}_i$. The difference is our prediction error,

$$e_i = Y_i - \hat{Y}_i$$

Gauss's least squares procedure says that we should choose the prediction line that

Figure 13.6 *Fitting a line to spending and income data*

minimizes the sum of these squared prediction errors; that is, we should estimate the intercept α and the slope β by minimizing the sum of the squared errors in predicting spending. This is a most logical procedure, but how do we do it?

The Least Squares Estimates of α and β

We want to determine the estimates a and b of the parameters α and β that minimize the sum of squared prediction errors for the data we have. The easiest procedure is to use some calculus, but because calculus is not a prerequisite for reading this book, I will just show you the answers and deposit a derivation in an appendix at the end of the chapter.

The formula for the least squares slope estimate

$$b = \frac{\Sigma(X_i - \overline{X})(Y_i - \overline{Y})}{\Sigma(X_i - \overline{X})^2} \tag{13.7}$$

is a complex reckoning of the interrelationship between X and Y.* Once b has been calculated, it is easy to compute the intercept estimate, because one property of least squares estimates is that the fitted line goes through the average values of the data: $\overline{Y} = a + b\overline{X}$. Thus,

$$a = \overline{Y} - b\overline{X} \tag{13.8}$$

Table 13.1 illustrates a detailed application of these least squares formulas to our consumption data. The first thing to do is to write down the paired values of

Table 13.1 *A least squares computation of income and consumption data*

Year	X	Y	X − X̄	Y − Ȳ	(X − X̄)(X − X̄)	(X − X̄)(Y − Ȳ)
1977	3319	3042	−19.2	−5.8	368.64	111.36
1978	3421	3124	82.8	76.2	6855.84	6309.36
1979	3404	3108	65.8	60.2	4329.64	3961.16
1980	3276	2994	−62.2	−53.8	3868.84	3346.36
1981	3271	2971	−67.2	−76.8	4515.84	5160.96
	$\overline{X} = 3338.2$	$\overline{Y} = 3047.8$	0.0	0.0	19,938.8	18,889.2

$$b = \frac{(X_1 - \overline{X})(Y_1 - \overline{Y}) + \cdots + (X_n - \overline{X})(Y_n - \overline{Y})}{(X_1 - \overline{X})(X_1 - \overline{X}) + \cdots + (X_n - \overline{X})(X_n - \overline{X})} = \frac{18,889.2}{19,938.8} = 0.9474$$

$$a = \overline{Y} - b\overline{X} = 3047.8 - (.9474)(3338.2) = -114.7$$

Thus, $\hat{Y} = 115 + .947X$

---

*An alternative formula for the slope, which is less logical but often easier to compute, is

$$b = \frac{\Sigma X_i Y_i - n\overline{X}\overline{Y}}{\Sigma X_i^2 - n(\overline{X})^2}$$

Okun's Law

In the early 1960s, President John F. Kennedy's Council of Economic Advisers tried to convince a reluctant Congress of the benefits of a tax cut to "get the country moving again." The Council argued that the prevailing unemployment rate of 6 to 7 percent was unnecessarily high, and that, in addition to the individual hardship suffered by unemployed workers and the owners of idle factories, the nation lost a considerable amount of potential output. Arthur Okun tried to quantify this output loss by estimating an empirical relationship between changes in unemployment rate (Y) and changes in gross national product (X),

$$Y = \alpha + \beta X + \epsilon$$

(The equation is estimated with unemployment as the dependent variable because business decisions to hire and fire workers depend on sales.)

A scatter diagram of annual data for the period studied by Okun is shown in Figure 1. As anticipated, there appears to be a *negative* relationship—increases in output are associated with declines in the unemployment rate. The least squares fitted line is

$$\hat{Y} = 1.18 - 0.33X$$

indicating that a 1 percent increase in output is associated with about a 0.33 percent decline in the unemployment rate. Thus, each percentage point of excessive unemployment signals that the nation's output is about 3 percent below its potential. This three-for-one rule became known as *Okun's Law* and, as time passed, proved to be a remarkably accurate rule of thumb.[2]

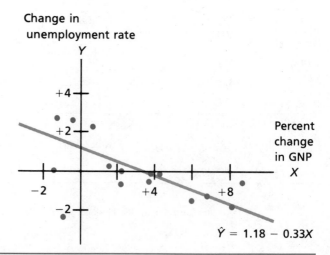

Figure 1 *Okun's law, 1947–1960*

X and Y. Second, compute their average values $\overline{X}$ and $\overline{Y}$. Third, calculate the deviations about these averages, $X - \overline{X}$ and $Y - \overline{Y}$. Fourth, find the products $(X - \overline{X})(X - \overline{X})$ and $(X - \overline{X})(Y - \overline{Y})$. Fifth, add these two products up and take their ratio to determine the least squares estimate of β, in accordance with Equation 13.7. Finally, use this estimate, along with the average values of X and Y, to determine the least squares estimate of α, in accordance with Equation 13.8.

Here, as shown in Table 13.1, the least squares estimates turn out to be

$$a = -114.7$$
$$b = 0.947$$

so that the least squares fitted line is

$$\hat{Y} = -114.7 + 0.947X$$

This is certainly close to the line I drew with a clear ruler, but the differences are not negligible. A precise calculation reveals that the sum of squared errors is 440 with my hand-drawn line and only 362 with the least squares line.*

Exercises

13.6   There are two competing academic theories regarding the relationship between student course evaluations and the number of years that a professor has been teaching. One theory holds that the most experienced professors will get the highest ratings. The second theory says that the young and energetic, although inexperienced, professors will score highest. What would a scatter diagram of evaluations (Y) and experience (X) look like if the first theory is correct? (Make a rough sketch.) What would the scatter diagram look like if the second theory is right? In either case, why might we anticipate that the data will not lie exactly on a line $Y = \alpha + \beta X$?

A college dean believes that there is no relationship at all between course evaluations and teaching experience. If this dean is right, what would a scatter diagram of evaluations and years look like?

13.7   In Exercise 13.2, you plotted a scatter diagram of midterm (X) and final exam (Y) scores, and used your judgment to fit a line to these data. Now calculate the least squares estimates of the parameters α and β for the equation

$$Y = \alpha + \beta X + \epsilon$$

Are the two fitted lines similar?

13.8   A certain armchair economist argues that there is a positive relationship between world coffee prices and sugar prices: "When people buy more coffee, they'll buy more sugar to put in their coffee, and everyone knows that a greater demand means higher prices." Here are some data to test this theory:

---

*There is another practical reason why calculated estimates are better than hand-drawn ones. Researchers often estimate equations with more than one explanatory variable, but it is difficult or impossible to draw graphs with more than two dimensions.

year	coffee price ($/lb)	sugar price ($/lb)
1975	0.68	0.245
1976	1.21	0.126
1977	1.92	0.092
1978	1.81	0.086
1979	1.55	0.101
1980	1.87	0.223
1981	1.56	0.212

Plot these data on a scatter diagram with coffee price (X) on the horizontal axis and sugar price (Y) on the vertical axis. Do these data appear to confirm the theory? Calculate the least squares estimates of the parameters of the equation $Y = \alpha + \beta X + \epsilon$. Do these estimates support the theory?

13.9 Dorothy Brady estimated Keynes's consumption function with the following cross-section budget data on family income and spending during 1935–1936:[3]

income X	spending Y
$292	$493
$730	$802
$1,176	$1,196
$1,636	$1,598
$2,292	$2,124
$3,243	$2,814
$4,207	$3,467
$6,598	$4,950
$22,259	$12,109

Calculate the least squares estimates of the parameters α and β in the equation $Y = \alpha + \beta X + \epsilon$.

13.10 Plot the following data and calculate the least squares estimates of the parameters α and β in the equation $Y = \alpha + \beta X + \epsilon$:

X	1	3	5	7	9
Y	5	5	5	5	5

13.11 Plot the following data and calculate the least squares estimate of the parameter β in the equation $Y = \alpha + \beta X + \epsilon$:

X	5	5	5	5	5
Y	1	3	5	7	9

13.12 Estimate the parameters α and β in the linear equation

$$Y = \alpha + \beta X + \epsilon$$

using the following data

X	0	3	−4	5	−3	4	−3	0	3	4	−5	−4
Y	5	4	−3	0	4	−3	−4	−5	−4	3	0	3

Now plot these data and draw in your fitted line. Do you think that the fitted line accurately describes the relationship between X and Y?

● **13.13**   The text estimates Okun's Law using annual data for 1947–1960, the years originally scrutinized by Okun. Reestimate this equation using data for 1947–1980 collected from the monthly publication *Business Conditions Digest*.

●● **13.14**   We are trying to estimate the average age μ of people who are attending a certain movie by asking a random sample of four people for their ages: X_1, X_2, X_3, and X_4. Show that the sample mean is the estimator $\hat{\mu}$ that minimizes the sum of squared errors

$$(X_1 - \hat{\mu})^2 + (X_2 - \hat{\mu})^2 + (X_3 - \hat{\mu})^2 + (X_4 - \hat{\mu})^2$$

13.3   PROBABILITY DISTRIBUTIONS FOR THE ESTIMATES

It is tempting to think that a given set of historical data cannot reflect random variation. This is another of those temptations that should be resisted. An analogous error is to ignore the effect of random variation on a sample mean. The researcher sees only one particular sample mean, but must remember that this is just one of many samples that might have been selected. The same is true of Y here. The researcher sees a particular historical value of Y that occurred, but must remember that it is but one of many that might have occurred.

In regression models, the randomness that underlies historical data comes from the error term ϵ, which reflects inaccurate measurements, omitted influences, and sampling error. Because the exact effects of these inaccuracies, omissions, and luck of the draw are uncertain, we can conceive of a probability distribution for ϵ. The simplest assumptions are:

1. The expected value of ϵ is zero.
2. The standard deviation of ϵ is σ, which does not vary from observation to observation.
3. The values of ϵ are independent of X and each other.

These are just the Bernoulli-trial assumptions (Chapter 5) that are so useful throughout probability and statistics. An irreverent caricature goes as follows. The model $\alpha + \beta X$ determines a "justified" value of Y. However, to keep things interesting, a bemused god rolls a pair of dice to push the observed Y up or down a bit. If the dice come up 7, then ϵ is zero. If an 8 is rolled, then $\epsilon = +1$; if a 6, then $\epsilon = -1$. If 9 is rolled, then $\epsilon = +2$; if 5, then $\epsilon = -2$, and so on. The value that will come up for ϵ is uncertain. It has a mean of zero and a constant standard deviation, and is independent both of X and of the values that come up on other rolls.

While the Bernoulli-trial assumptions are certainly familiar and convenient, we should think a bit about their applicability. The first assumption that was made simply reminds us that we are using the intercept to locate the model. The value of the intercept α is chosen so that the expected value of ϵ is zero. The second assumption is also very natural. We know little or nothing about what the value of ϵ will turn out to be for each observation. The standard deviation of ϵ is a measure of the degree of our uncertainty, and we assume that there is no reason to be any more or less uncertain about ϵ from one observation to the next.   ●

The third assumption is the strongest of the batch, and the one that is the most likely to get us into trouble. To simplify our computations, we assume that the error terms for different observations are independent of each other. However, these error terms involve omitted variables whose values may not be independent. For instance, the price level may be one of these omitted variables, and prices are not determined by independent dice rolls. Whether prices are high or low this year may depend on whether prices were high or low last year and, if there is such a dependence, then our computations are not quite right. Advanced courses show how such correlations between errors can be detected and how the least squares procedure can be modified to take this additional information into account. Even more serious is our assumption that the value of the error term is independent of the value of X. This may not be so. Because this possibility has very important, but complicated, implications, let's postpone the anxiety until the next chapter.

The Distribution of the Parameter Estimates

Although we don't know the values of the error term that occur, we can be certain that their inevitable presence does affect our estimates.

> The **parameter estimates** depend on the observed values of Y, which, in turn, depend on the signs and magnitudes of the error term ϵ. Thus, the parameter estimates depend on what the values of ϵ turn out to be.

For any given value of X, the expected value of Y is $\alpha + \beta X$, but the actual value of Y will diverge from this expected value to the extent that ϵ is not zero. Because the error term is the sum of many separate influences that involve measurement errors, omitted variables, and sampling error, the central limit theorem suggests that the probability distribution for ϵ may be approximately normal, as is shown in Figure 13.7. For any value of X, the expected value of ϵ is zero and the expected value of Y is $\alpha + \beta X$. If ϵ is positive, then Y will be greater than $\alpha + \beta X$. If ϵ is negative, then Y will be less than $\alpha + \beta X$.

Figure 13.8 shows one possible set of data. For the first observation X_1, the error term ϵ_1 turns out to be positive and, hence the observed value of Y_1 is above $\alpha + \beta X_1$. For the second observation X_2, the error happens to be negative, so that Y_2 is below $\alpha + \beta X_2$. Of course, we have no way of knowing this in practice, because the ϵs are not observed. All that we see are the paired observations (X_1, Y_1) and (X_2, Y_2). The line $\hat{Y} = a + bX$ that we fit to these particular data underestimates the slope and overestimates the intercept.

This is just one possible outcome, which results from a positive value for ϵ_1 and a negative value for ϵ_2. If, instead, it happens that ϵ_1 is negative while ϵ_2 is positive, then the resulting data will lead us to overestimate the slope and underestimate the intercept. If the ϵs turn out to be both positive or both negative, then our estimates may be either both too high or both too low. And the sizes of our misestimates depend on the magnitudes of the ϵs.

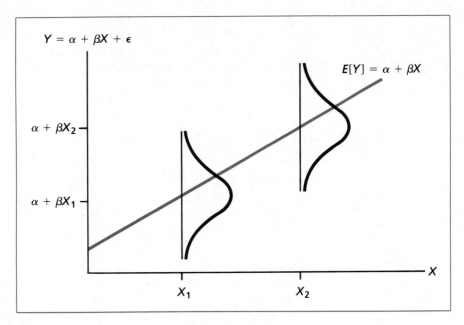

Figure 13.7 *The theoretical determination of* Y

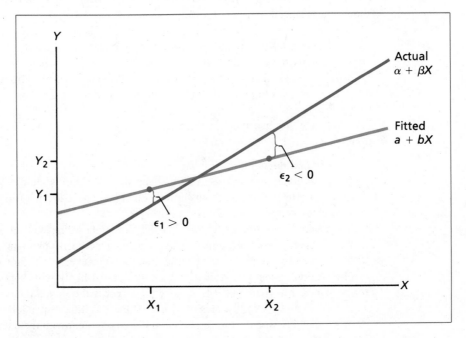

Figure 13.8 *The actual values of the error term determine the observed values of* Y *and, hence, the estimates of* α *and* β

Just as there is a probability distribution for ϵ, so are there probability distributions for our estimates of α and β. The estimation formulas, Equations 13.7 and 13.8 show that a and b are linear combinations of the observed values for Y, which, in turn, depend on ϵ. Thus it can be shown that, if $\epsilon \sim N[0, \sigma]$, then

$$b \sim N[\beta, \sigma/(n^{1/2} s_X)] \tag{13.9}$$

$$a \sim N[\alpha, \sigma(\overline{X^2})^{1/2}/(n^{1/2}s_X)] \tag{13.10}$$

where σ is the standard deviation of ϵ and n is the number of observations. The term

$$s_X = \left\{ \frac{\Sigma(X_1 - \overline{X})^2}{n} \right\}^{1/2}$$

is the standard deviation of the observations of X, and

$$\overline{X^2} = \frac{\Sigma X_i^2}{n}$$

is the average value of X^2.

Notice first that a and b are each unbiased estimators of the respective parameters α and β. A researcher's estimate of β will sometimes be too high and sometimes be too low. If the model's assumptions are satisfied, however, then it is very unlikely that researchers will continually underestimate or overestimate the parameters. On the average, over many studies using fresh data, the underestimates should be balanced out by overestimates.

However, being right on average is not all there is to it. Again, we would like something better than the lawyer who allows innocent people to be convicted but wins acquittals for the guilty. It is of little comfort to know that the statistician's estimate is just as likely to miss by a mile to one side as to miss by a mile to the other side. We would prefer the statistician who seldom, if ever, misses by a mile to either side.

To gauge the dispersion in the estimates, we can look at their standard deviations. Equation 13.9 shows that

1. the standard deviation of b is smaller the lower is the standard deviation of ϵ. If the observed ϵ are close to zero, then the fitted line is almost certain to be very close to the true relationship. If, however, the ϵ are far from zero, then wild estimates of α and β may result.
2. the standard deviation of b is smaller the more data we have. With lots of data, the observed errors are almost certain to balance each other out and yield a fitted line that is close to the true line. If, however, there are only a few observations, then almost anything can (and most likely will) happen.
3. the standard deviation of b is smaller the larger is the standard deviation of the X data. Figure 13.9 illustrates this logic. If there is little dispersion in the values of X, then almost any slope and intercept are consistent with the data, and slight variations in the ϵ can then have a considerable impact on our estimates. We can hardly hope to gauge the effects of income on spending if we have never seen income change.

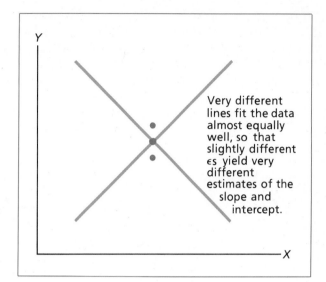

Figure 13.9 *There is considerable uncertainty about α and β when there is little dispersion in the observed values of* X

Equation 13.10 shows that the standard deviation of the intercept estimate depends on these very same factors, plus one additional consideration—the average squared value of X. The average squared value of X tells us whether the data are close to the Y-axis or far from it. If the data are far from the Y-axis, then small errors in estimating the slope will cause very large errors in estimating the Y-intercept. Thus, the larger the average squared value of X is, the bigger the standard deviation of a.

Estimating the Standard Deviation of the Error Term

In practice, we aren't likely to know the value of the standard deviation of ϵ, because we don't know precisely what comprises the error term. But there is a natural way of estimating it. The (unobserved) error term is

$$\epsilon = Y - (\alpha + \beta X)$$

while our (observed) prediction error is

$$e = Y - \hat{Y}$$
$$= Y - (a + bX)$$

If we use a and b to estimate α and β, then we can use the standard deviation of e to estimate the standard deviation of ϵ.

The adjusted standard deviation of e is called the **standard error of estimate (SEE):**

$$SEE = \{(e_1^2 + e_2^2 + \cdots + e_n^2)/(n - 2)\}^{1/2}$$

where $e_i = Y_i - \hat{Y}_i$ is the prediction error for the ith observation. Notice that the sum of the squared prediction errors is divided by $n - 2$ rather than by n or $n - 1$. This is because the estimation of two parameters (α and β) uses up two degrees of freedom.* With the division by $n - 2$, the SEE^2 is an unbiased estimator of σ^2.

In our consumption function example, the standard error of estimate works out to be SEE = 10.98. Thus, using Equation 13.9, the estimated standard deviation of b is

$$s_b = \frac{\text{SEE}}{n^{1/2}\, s_X}$$

$$= \frac{10.98}{(5)^{1/2}(140.77/5)^{1/2}}$$

$$= 0.078$$

Similarly, using Equation 13.10, the standard deviation of a works out to be

$$s_a = 260$$

We calculate a single pair of estimates of α and β, using the observed data. These estimates depend on the particular values of ϵ that happened to occur and thus have a standard deviation because there are many different values of ϵ and, correspondingly, many different estimates that might have occurred.

Confidence Intervals for the Parameters

Once we know the distributions of a and b, it is a straightforward matter to construct confidence intervals. Let's use b as an example. Our estimate b comes from a normal distribution with expected value β and standard deviation σ_b, whose formula is given in Equation 13.9. If b is normally distributed, then (as shown in Figure 13.10) there is a .95 probability that this estimate will be within (approximately) two standard deviations of the true parameter value β. We can write this statistical relationship as

$$.95 = P[\beta - 2\sigma_b < b < \beta + 2\sigma_b]$$

Rewriting this as a confidence interval, we have

$$.95 = P[b - 2\sigma_b < \beta < b + 2\sigma_b] \tag{13.11}$$

If there is a .95 probability that the estimate b will be within two standard deviations of β, then there is correspondingly a .95 probability that $b \pm$ two standard deviations will encompass β. In the consumption function example, the 0.947 estimate of b and 0.078 standard deviation imply a 95 percent confidence interval 0.947 ± 0.156.

*One interesting way to see this is to consider the case where there are only two observations. The least squares line goes right through both points and there are no prediction errors. The division by $n - 2$ correctly warns us that the standard deviation of ϵ cannot be estimated from just two observations.

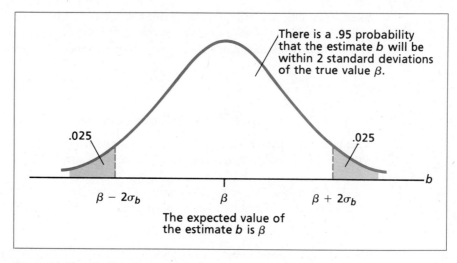

There is a .95 probability that the estimate b will be within 2 standard deviations of the true value β.

.025

.025

$\beta - 2\sigma_b$

β

$\beta + 2\sigma_b$

b

The expected value of the estimate b is β

Figure 13.10   *The distribution of the least squares estimate of* β

There is an analogous relationship between a and α, in that there is a .95 probability that a will be within two standard deviations of α. For $\alpha = -115$ with a standard deviation of 260, the 95 percent confidence interval stretches from -635 to 405.

Because the standard deviations of a and b must be estimated, the Student's t distribution with $n - 2$ degrees of freedom can be used in place of the normal distribution. However, with any sort of reasonably sized sample, the exact t-value will be close to 2 and this is why I persist in just using the two-standard-deviations rule of thumb.*

Hypothesis Tests for the Parameters

It is one short step from confidence intervals to hypothesis tests for the parameters. The most common null hypothesis is undoubtedly that β equals zero:

$$H_0: \beta = 0$$

$$H_1: \beta \neq 0$$

If β does equal zero, then the explanatory variable X has no influence on Y. Thus, $\beta = 0$ is usually a *straw hypothesis* that the researcher hopes to disprove. The researcher begins with the theory that X influences Y and wants to confirm this theory statistically by rejecting the possibility that $\beta = 0$.

The simplest testing procedure is to see whether or not zero is outside a confidence interval for β. If, in fact, zero is outside a 95 percent confidence

*To focus our attention on the logic rather than the numbers, I used very few data ($n = 5$) in the consumption example. With $n - 2 = 3$ degrees of freedom, the appropriate t-value is 3.182 rather than 2.0. In practice, we would almost always use more data.

interval, then the data reject (at the 5 percent significance level) the null hypothesis that $\beta = 0$. Zero will be outside such a confidence interval whenever the estimate is more than two standard deviations away from zero, on either side:

$$\text{if } b > 0 + 2\sigma_b, \text{ then } (b/\sigma_b) > +2$$

or

$$\text{if } b < 0 - 2\sigma_b, \text{ then } (b/\sigma_b) < -2$$

That is, the null hypothesis that β equals zero is rejected if the ratio of the absolute value of the estimate b to its standard deviation is greater than two.

> The quick-and-easy test of the commonplace hypothesis $\beta = 0$ is to see whether or not the absolute value of the ratio of the estimate to its standard deviation is greater than two.

Using the consumption function again as an example, the results might be reported as follows:

> Keynes's consumption function was estimated by ordinary least squares, using annual data for the years 1977–1981. The results are
>
> $$\hat{Y} = -115 + .947\,X$$
> $$\phantom{\hat{Y} = } (260) \quad (.078)$$
>
> The standard deviations of the parameter estimates are in parentheses under the estimates.

Most readers will automatically take the ratio of the estimated slope to its standard deviation to see whether or not this

$$t\text{-statistic} = b/s_b$$

is greater than 2. If so, then we can conclude that income has a statistically significant effect on consumption; in other words, zero is outside a 95 percent confidence interval for this estimate and, so, we can reject the null hypothesis that $\beta = 0$.

Here, the value of the t-statistic for b is a whopping $0.947/0.078 = 12.2$, giving a decisive rejection of $\beta = 0$. For α, on the other hand, the t-value is only $-115/260 = -0.442$. We cannot reject the null hypothesis that the intercept is zero.

This is such a standard operating procedure that most researchers report their t-values along with their parameter estimates, to save readers the trouble of doing the division themselves. Thus, another standard reporting format is:

> Using annual data for 1977–1981, the least-squares estimates of Keynes's consumption function turned out to be
>
> $$\hat{Y} = -115 + 0.947\,X$$
> $$\phantom{\hat{Y} = } [0.44] \quad\quad [12.2]$$

[ ]:t-values

Some researchers only report their *t*-values, for example:

> To test Keynes's theory that income influences consumption, a regression was run using annual data for 1977–1981. The *t*-value turned out to be 12.2, which decisively confirms Keynes's theory.

Still others report *Z*-values or *P*-values in parentheses under the parameter estimates.

Of course, $\beta = 0$ is not the only possible null hypothesis. Any interesting hypothesis can be tested by finding the appropriate cutoff points, the *P*-value, or a confidence interval. For instance, Keynes argued that the slope β is almost certainly less than 1.0. This hypothesis can be tested by seeing whether or not 1.0 is inside a confidence interval for β. In this case it is, and so these data do not reject the possibility that β is actually greater than 1. Notice that these data do not reject Keynes's hypothesis that β is less than 1. Indeed, the preferred estimate, $b = 0.947$, is less than 1, but (because the sample is so small) the confidence interval is sufficiently wide, stretching from 0.791 to 1.103, that we cannot rule out $\beta > 1$.

Confidence Intervals for $\alpha + \beta X$

Models are usually intended for predictions, either in actual or hypothetical situations. We may want to predict consumption spending next year or how consumption would be affected by a purely hypothetical change in income. Our estimates of α and β are the basis for such predictions and, because these estimates are of uncertain accuracy, so are our predictions. The exact estimates *a* and *b* that we obtain depend on what the error term ϵ happens to be in the sample data. Different values for ϵ give different data, parameter estimates, and predictions.

Let's say that we want to predict what *Y* will be for a value X_0 for the explanatory variable. Because *a* and *b* are unbiased estimators of α and β, our prediction $\hat{Y}_0 = a + bX_0$ is an unbiased estimator of $\alpha + \beta X_0$, with a standard deviation that can be computed, although with some difficulty. If the error ϵ is normally distributed, then so are *a*, *b*, and $\hat{Y}_0$:

$$\hat{Y}_0 \sim N\left[\alpha + \beta X_0, \left(\frac{\sigma}{\sqrt{n}}\right)\left(1 + \frac{(X_0 - \overline{X})^2}{s_X^2}\right)^{1/2}\right] \tag{13.12}$$

The exact formula for the standard deviation of $\hat{Y}_0$,

$$\sigma_{\hat{Y}_0} = \left(\frac{\sigma}{\sqrt{n}}\right)\left(1 + \frac{(X_0 - \overline{X})^2}{s_X^2}\right)^{1/2} \tag{13.13}$$

is far from obvious, but its implications are quite logical. Our predictions are less certain (and more likely to be inaccurate) if:

1. the standard deviation σ of ϵ is large, because then there is a greater chance that the data will yield misleading estimates;

The Cost of Another Dozen Stockings

In the 1930s, Joel Dean pioneered the use of regression models to analyze business production costs.[4] One of his classic studies involved a mill for knitting silk stockings. Using silk prepared by another plant, this mill knitted stockings, which were then sent on to another plant for dyeing and finishing. Professor Dean used monthly data for the period 1935–1939 to see how this knitting mill's production costs (Y) depended on its output (X). The scatter diagram of his data shown in Figure 2 reveals a positive, linear relationship. Using least squares, Dean estimated the following equation,

$$\hat{Y} = 2935.59 + 1.998\,X$$
$$(0.017)$$

( ): standard deviation

where costs Y are recorded in dollars and output X is measured in dozens of pairs of stockings. The t-value of $1.998/0.017 = 117.5$ decisively rejects the null hypothesis that the mill's costs do not depend on its output. It costs this mill about $2 to knit an extra dozen pair of stockings. A 95 percent confidence interval for this marginal cost is 1.998 ± 0.034, or $1.964 to $2.032.

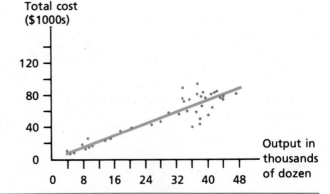

Figure 2 *Production costs and output at a hosiery mill*

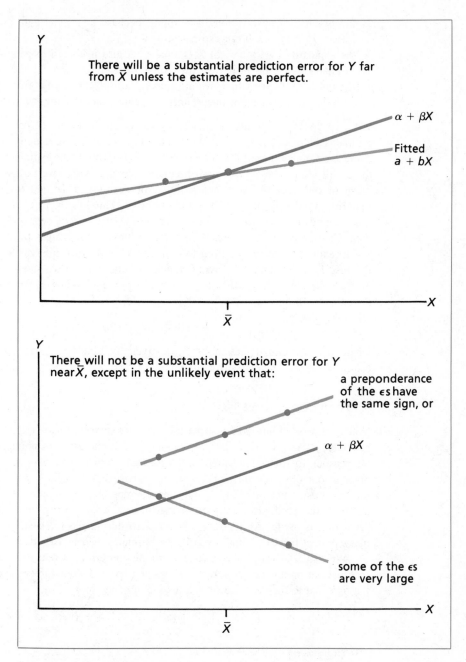

Figure 13.11 *The prediction errors are unlikely to be large near the mean of the observations*

2. the number of observations n is small, because additional data provide more information to use in our estimates;

3. the standard deviation s_X of X is small, because it is hard to gauge the effects of changes in X on Y, if we hardly observe any change in X; and

4. the value of X_0 for which we are making a prediction is far from the average value of X, because our uncertainty is greatest on the fringes of our data.

The first three points are easily understood—these are all reasons why the estimates of α and β may be inaccurate. The fourth point is new, but it makes good sense, too. Figure 13.11 illustrates this logic. Unless the estimates are perfect, there will always be a substantial prediction error as we move far away from the mean of our data. A large prediction error near the mean, on the other hand, requires an unlikely string of bad luck in the ϵs. Thus, the researcher can be much more confident about a model's implications and predictions near the center of the data. Caution is called for when you are working on the fringes of the data.

Equation 13.12 can be used to construct a confidence interval for $\alpha + \beta X_0$. Because $\hat{Y}_0$ has about a 95 percent chance of being within two standard deviations of $\alpha + \beta X_0$, it follows that there is a .95 probability that $\hat{Y}_0 \pm$ two standard deviations will encompass $\alpha + \beta X_0$:

$$\alpha + \beta X_0 = \hat{Y}_0 \pm 2\sigma_{\hat{Y}_0}$$

where the standard deviation of $\hat{Y}_0$ is given by Equation 13.13 and σ can be estimated by the standard error of estimate.

A Prediction Interval for Y

You've now seen how to construct a confidence interval for $\alpha + \beta X_0$. Normally, however, it is $Y_0 = \alpha + \beta X_0 + \epsilon_0$ that we are interested in predicting. One of the reasons for inaccurate predictions is, as I've just explained, the luck of the draw in our observed data. The specific values of ϵ that happen to occur cause imperfect estimates of α and β and, hence, imperfect predictions of $\alpha + \beta X_0$. In addition, our predictions may be off because of what ϵ turns out to be when the prediction is made. As long as ϵ is not zero during the forecast, we still won't make perfect forecasts of Y, even if our estimates of α and β are perfect.

We can take this added source of prediction error into account by using the fact that our prediction error $Y_0 - \hat{Y}_0$ has an expected value of zero and a variance that is equal to the variance of $\hat{Y}_0$ plus the variance of ϵ_0:*

$$\text{variance of } Y_0 - \hat{Y}_0 = (\text{variance of } \hat{Y}_0) + (\text{variance of } \epsilon_0) \qquad (13.14)$$

---

*The prediction error can be rearranged as

$$Y_0 - \hat{Y}_0 = (Y_0 - E[Y_0]) + (E[Y_0] - \hat{Y}_0)$$

with a variance equal to the sum of the variances of the two parenthetical terms. The first term is ϵ_0 and so, has its variance. The variance of the second term is equal to the variance of $\hat{Y}_0$.

Table 13.2   *Ninety-five percent prediction intervals for consumer spending*

Value of income X_0	Predicted spending Y_0	Standard deviation of prediction	95% prediction interval
3038.2	2763.6	26.3	2711.1 to 2816.1
3138.2	2858.3	19.7	2819.0 to 2897.7
3238.2	2953.1	14.3	2924.4 to 2981.7
3338.2	3047.8	12.0	3023.7 to 3071.9
3438.2	3142.5	14.3	3113.9 to 3171.2
3538.2	3237.3	19.7	3197.9 to 3276.6
3638.2	3332.0	26.3	3279.5 to 3384.5

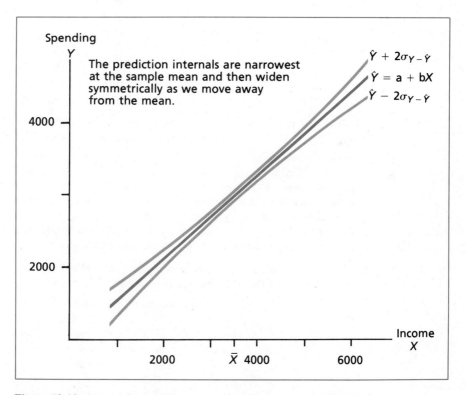

Figure 13.12   *Ninety-five percent prediction intervals for consumer spending*

The variance of $\hat{Y}_0$ is given by Equation 13.13, while the SEE provides an estimate of the variance of ϵ_0. If there is a .95 probability that $Y_0 - \hat{Y}_0$ will be within two standard deviations of zero, then there is a .95 probability that $\hat{Y}_0$ will be within two standard deviations of Y_0. Thus, a 95 percent confidence interval for Y_0 is

$$Y_0 = \hat{Y}_0 \pm 2 \text{ standard deviations of } Y_0 - \hat{Y}_0$$

This confidence interval is commonly called a **prediction interval**. Table 13.2 shows 95 percent prediction intervals for selected values of X_0, while Figure 13.12 shows a more complete picture. Notice that the confidence interval is narrowest at $\overline{X}$, and then it widens as we move away from the mean of our data.

Exercises

13.15 A marketing consultant has been hired to evaluate the effect of advertising expenditures on the sales of a certain beer. Differing advertising expenditures in eight similar cities gave these results:

advertising ($1000)	sales ($1000)
20	370
25	350
25	330
30	350
30	400
35	380
35	410
40	400

Use these data to determine the least squares estimates of the slope and intercept of the equation $Y = \alpha + \beta X + \epsilon$, where X is advertising expenditures and Y is sales.

a. What is the estimated effect of advertising on sales?
b. If this estimate is correct, does an extra $1 of advertising pay for itself? (Assume that the firm makes a 10-cent profit on every $1 of sales.)
c. Is the estimated effect of advertising on sales statistically significant?
d. What does "statistically significant" mean?
e. Calculate a 95 percent confidence interval for the effect of advertising on sales.
f. If you were this consultant, what would your recommendation be?

13.16 An ice cream store wants to investigate the relationship between its sales and the average temperature. The following data are collected:

month	temperature (°F)	sales (gal)
Jan	28.4	25
Feb	30.3	27
Mar	39.2	82
April	51.2	135
May	61.1	171

June	70.4	197
July	73.6	230
Aug	71.9	216
Sept	65.2	182
Oct	54.2	121
Nov	41.7	73
Dec	30.7	41

Use least squares to estimate the parameters of the equation $Y = \alpha + \beta X + \epsilon$, where Y is ice cream sales and X is the average temperature during the month. Is there a statistically significant relationship between temperature and sales? By how much should we expect a 10°F increase in the monthly temperature to increase ice cream sales at this store?

13.17 Exercise 13.8 examined the relationship between coffee and sugar prices. Now we can determine whether or not this relation is statistically significant. Is it?

13.18 In Exercise 13.9, you estimated a consumption function using cross-section data. Make a test at the 5 percent level of the null hypothesis that the slope of this relation is zero. In simple English, what is the implication if the hypothesis is rejected? If it is accepted?

13.19 A least squares regression, using quarterly data for the period 1952–1970, yielded the following estimated consumption function:

$$Y = -30.6 + 0.91 \ X$$
$$\quad\ (2.1) \quad\ \ (0.08)$$

where Y is consumer spending, X is disposable income, and the standard deviations of the parameter estimates are in parentheses under the estimated parameters.

a. What is the estimated effect on consumer spending of a $1 increase in disposable income?
b. Can we reject the null hypothesis that disposable income does not affect consumer spending?
c. Can we reject the null hypothesis that a $1 increase in disposable income raises consumer spending by $1?
d. Calculate a 95 percent confidence interval for the effect of disposable income on consumer spending.

13.20 (*continuation*) Use the estimated equation to answer these questions:

a. What are the t-values for this estimated equation?
b. What do these t-values tell us about the estimates?

13.21 A random sample of ten college freshmen yielded these data on their heights and weights:

height (inches)	weight (pounds)
58	110
61	118
63	130
66	132
66	162
68	156
70	146
71	162
73	170
77	190

Plot these data with height (X) on the horizontal axis and weight (Y) on the vertical axis. Does there appear to be a linear relationship between weight and height? Do taller people tend to weigh more, less, or about the same as shorter people? Find the least squares estimates of $Y = \alpha + \beta X + \epsilon$ and draw this line on your graph. Is the relationship between weight and height statistically significant?

13.22   A random sample of ten college seniors yielded these data on their heights and grade point averages (GPAs):

height (inches)	GPA (0–4.0)
64	3.65
67	2.04
68	3.30
69	2.82
69	2.36
70	3.21
71	3.15
71	2.70
73	3.81
76	3.47

Plot these data with height (X) on the horizontal axis and GPA (Y) on the vertical axis. Does there appear to be a relationship between GPA and height? Are the grades of taller people better, worse, or about the same as those of shorter people? Use these data to find the least squares estimates of $Y = \alpha + \beta X + \epsilon$ and draw this fitted line in your graph. Is the relationship between GPA and height statistically significant?

13.4 · CORRELATION COEFFICIENTS

It is natural to inquire how successful a model is, and the obvious place to begin is to see whether the prediction errors are large or small. Large prediction errors suggest that the model is of little use and may be fundamentally flawed. Small prediction errors indicate that the model is useful and may contain some important insights.

Because we estimate the parameters by minimizing the sum of squared prediction errors, Σe_i^2, this sum is a logically consistent measure of the model's success. Remember, though, that this criterion embodies two implicit assumptions about the researcher's objectives. First, positive and negative errors are treated equally; it doesn't matter whether the prediction is too high or too low, only how far off it is. Second, the squaring means that large errors are much more costly than small errors. One $100 billion error increases the Standard Error of Estimate (SEE) by more than ninety-nine $10 billion errors. These implicit judgments are sensible, but there may be occasions when a different criterion is necessary.

If you are trying to predict the money you will make by investing in pistachio nuts, then an unexpected gain may not be as discomforting as an unexpected loss. For a gambler who is trying to predict the winner of the next Super Bowl, the most important thing is whether or not the point spread is beaten, and not by how much it is beaten. If you think that success should be judged by something other than the sum of squared errors, then you should also use your criterion to estimate your model's parameters. Conversely, if you do use least squares estimates, then the sum of squared prediction errors is the logical measure of your model's success.

How do we gauge whether the prediction errors are large or small? A $1-billion error for one model is not necessarily more embarrassing than a $1 error for another model, because a $1-billion error in predicting a $1-trillion item can be better than a $1 error in predicting a $2 item. A reasonable benchmark should take the scale of our dependent variable Y into account. We should also consider whether Y fluctuates a great deal or is essentially constant, because it is not at all difficult to forecast a $1-trillion item that is always equal to $1 trillion.

One appealing benchmark is to compare the sum of the squared prediction errors with the sum of the squared deviations of Y about its mean,

$$\frac{\Sigma(Y_i - \hat{Y}_i)^2}{\Sigma(Y_i - \overline{Y}_i)^2}$$

This specific ratio can be justified as follows. If we thought that X had no influence on Y, then we would set β equal to zero, leaving our model as

$$Y = \alpha$$

Because $\overline{Y} = a + b\overline{X}$, the least squares estimate of α when $b = 0$ is the mean of Y,

$$a = \overline{Y}$$

and the sum of the squared prediction errors would be

$$\Sigma(Y_i - \overline{Y}_i)^2$$

Thus, the ratio

$$\Sigma(Y_i - \hat{Y}_i)^2/\Sigma(Y_i - \overline{Y}_i)^2$$

compares the sum of the squared prediction errors for the model with what the sum of squared prediction errors would be if b were set equal to zero. This ratio is a measure of how much prediction accuracy is improved by allowing for the possibility that Y depends on X (that β is not zero).

Because the numerator and denominator are both sums of squared errors, their ratio cannot be negative. Also, because least squares chooses the estimate of b that minimizes the prediction errors, this ratio cannot exceed 1. Thus

$$0 \le \frac{\Sigma(Y_i - \hat{Y}_i)^2}{\Sigma(Y_i - \overline{Y}_i)^2} \le 1$$

The relevant question is whether this ratio is near 1 or 0. If the ratio is close to 1, then not much is gained by allowing for the possibility that X influences Y. If the ratio is close to 0, then there is a relatively large improvement in predictive accuracy by allowing for the effect of X on Y.

In practice, statisticians subtract this ratio from 1, giving the **coefficient of determination**:

$$R^2 = 1 - \frac{\Sigma(Y_i - \hat{Y}_i)^2}{\Sigma(Y_i - \overline{Y}_i)^2} \tag{13.15}$$

Can Anyone Suggest a Good Hedge Against Inflation?

Inflation erodes the real purchasing power of money, bonds, and other assets with fixed-dollar values. Consider, for instance, $100 deposited in a bank at a fixed 5 percent interest rate, which pays $105 after a year. If prices increase by 5 percent during the year, then this $105 at the end of the year will buy no more than $100 would now. If prices increase by 10 percent, $105 at the end of a year buys 5 percent less than $100 does now.

Investors try, of course, to find investments that keep ahead of inflation. Reluctant to settle for a 5 percent return in the face of 10 percent inflation, they shop around for bonds that pay higher yields. If this fails, they buy land and other physical assets that may appreciate during inflation or they buy stock in firms that own assets that may appreciate. This last possibility is investigated in Figure 3, which is a scatter diagram of annual inflation rates and stock returns (dividends plus capital gains) over the period 1926 through 1980.[5] Stock returns have averaged more than inflation (the numbers work out to be 11.7 percent versus 3.0 percent), but they have also been much more variable and appear to bear little or no relation to the rate of inflation. Whether it is a year of deflation or double-digit inflation doesn't seem to affect the stock market's chances of collapse or boom. A least squares regression of the percent return (Y) on the rate of inflation (X) confirms that there is little relation between the two:

$$\hat{Y} = 11.72 - .009\,X, \qquad R^2 = .000004$$
$$[3.36] \quad\;\; [.02]$$

[   ]: *t*-values

The estimated coefficient of X, the *t*-value, and R-squared are all virtually zero. There is no evidence whatsoever here that stocks provide a hedge against inflation. If you've got another suggestion, drop me a line—and please do it fast, before prices go up again!

Figure 3 *Stock returns and inflation, 1926–1980*

This is commonly called **R-squared**. The square root of the coefficient of determination is called the **correlation coefficient, R**. Because a square root can be either positive or negative, the convention is to let R be positive when b is positive (indicating a positive relationship between Y and X) and to let R be negative when b is negative (indicating a negative relationship).

Yet another measure is to adjust R-squared for the degrees of freedom:

$$R_a^2 = 1 - \frac{\Sigma(Y_i - \hat{Y}_i)^2/(n - 2)}{\Sigma(Y_i - \overline{Y}_i)^2/(n - 1)}$$

The model's errors are divided by $n - 2$ because two parameters (α and β) are estimated from the n observations, while the denominator uses $n - 1$ because only one parameter (the mean of Y) is estimated.

R-squared (or one of these alternative measures) gauges what fraction of the variation in Y is explained by allowing for a nonzero value of β. Specifically, these measures tell us how successful the model is in predicting Y, relative to the benchmark of setting $b = 0$ and using the sample mean to predict Y. Figure 13.13 shows three examples. If there is little or no improvement in our predictions when we take into account the effect of X on Y, then the ratio of the prediction errors will be almost 1.0 and, thus, R-squared will be close to 0. If taking the effect of X on Y into account improves our predictions dramatically, then the ratio of prediction errors will fall almost to 0, and R-squared will be close to 1.

Our consumption model is quite successful by this standard. Table 13.3 shows the predicted and actual values of consumption. The model's sum of squared prediction errors is 361.93. If X is omitted and the mean of Y is used for predictions, then the sum of squared errors leaps to 19,048.83. The ratio is .019 and the value of R-squared is .981.

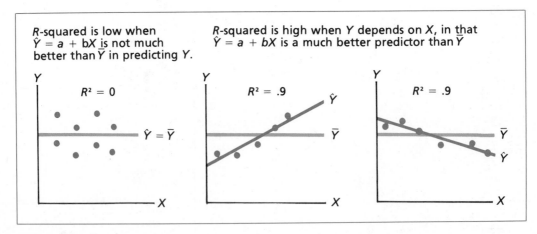

Figure 13.13   *Three correlation coefficients*

Table 13.3   *The consumption model's prediction errors*

Income X	Actual spending Y	Predicted spending Ŷ	Prediction error e = Y − Ŷ	Squared prediction error
3319	3042	3029.61	− 12.39	153.49
3421	3124	3126.24	2.24	5.02
3404	3108	3110.14	2.14	4.56
3276	2994	2988.87	− 5.13	26.28
3271	2971	2984.14	13.14	172.58
Total			0.00	361.93

Exercises

13.23   A classic study of the IQ scores of 34 identical twins who were raised apart obtained these intelligence scores:[6]

1st born	2nd born	1st born	2nd born	1st born	2nd born
22	12	13	4	38	27
36	34	32	33	33	26
13	10	30	34	16	28
30	25	27	24	27	25
32	28	32	18	4	2
26	17	27	28	19	9
20	24	22	23	41	41
30	26	15	9	40	38
29	35	24	33	12	9
26	20	6	10	13	22
28	22	23	21	29	30
21	27				

Calculate the R-squared for a regression of the intelligence score of the second born on the intelligence score of the first born. (This R-squared has been used to gauge the influence of genes on intelligence, while $1 - R$-squared measures the influence of one's environment.)

13.24   In the Heightlands, men always marry women who are exactly six inches shorter than themselves. Write down an equation predicting the height of a woman Y from the height of her husband X. What is the correlation coefficient for this equation?

13.25   The relationship between inflation (X) and the rates of return on Treasury bills (Y) was examined by estimating a regression equation using annual data for the years 1926–1980,

$$Y = 2.13 + 0.234\, X, \qquad R^2 = .20$$
$$[5.6] \qquad [3.59]$$

[ ]: *t*-values

Compare this estimated equation with that for stock returns reported in the text. Imagine that you are an investment counselor and write a paragraph summarizing your conclusions.

13.26   A businessperson is trying to estimate the relationship between price (X) and sales (Y) of a certain line of clothing. Tests in similar cities throughout the country have yielded these data:

price (X)	sales (Y)
$20	10,300
$25	9,100
$30	8,200
$35	6,500
$40	5,100
$50	2,300

Use these data to estimate the equation $Y = \alpha + \beta X + \epsilon$. What are the estimates of α and β? What is the Standard Error of Estimate (SEE)? What is the R-squared?

13.27   (*continuation*) If sales are measured in thousands (10.3, 9.1, etc.), do we get the same estimates of α and β, SEE, and R-squared? Are our conclusions affected?

13.28   (*continuation*) If the price is measured in cents instead of dollars (2,000, 2,500, etc.), do we get the same estimates of α and β, SEE, and R-squared? Are our conclusions affected? (Use the original units for sales: 10,300, 9,100, and so on.)

13.29   (*continuation*) If the price is measured in the amount above $20 ($0, $5, and so on), do we get the same estimates of α and β, SEE, and R-squared? Are our conclusions affected?

13.30   (*continuation*) Summarize the morals of the three preceding exercises.

13.5   SUMMARY

In the regression model $Y = \alpha + \beta X + \epsilon$, changes in Y (the *dependent* variable) are explained by changes in X (the *explanatory* variable). The error term ϵ reflects measurement errors, omitted influences on Y, and sampling error. Because these factors cannot be predicted in advance, ϵ is a random variable and Y is too. This random variation implies that the parameters α and β cannot be known with certainty, although they can be estimated.

The least squares estimation procedure determines the estimates a and b that minimize the sum of squared prediction errors $\Sigma(Y_i - \hat{Y}_i)^2$ for the data at hand. The formulas are

$$b = \frac{\Sigma(X_i - \overline{X})(Y_i - \overline{Y})}{\Sigma(X_i - \overline{X})^2}$$

$$a = \overline{Y} - b\overline{X}$$

Because the error term is unknown, it can be described by a probability distribution. The usual assumptions are that this probability distribution is normal with a zero expected value and constant variance, and that the values of ϵ are independent of each other and of X. With these assumptions, the least squares estimates are normally distributed, too,

$$b \sim N[\beta,\ \sigma/(n^{1/2}\ s_X)]$$

$$a \sim N[\alpha,\ \sigma(\overline{X^2})^{1/2}/(n^{1/2}s_X)]$$

where σ is the standard deviation of ϵ; n is the number of observations;

$$s_X = \left\{\frac{\Sigma(X_i - \overline{X})^2}{n}\right\}^{1/2}$$

is the standard deviation of the observations of X; and

$$\overline{X^2} = \frac{\Sigma X_i^2}{n}$$

is the average value of X^2. Because the standard deviation σ of the error term is usually unknown, it can be estimated by the standard error of estimate (SEE),

$$\text{SEE} = \frac{\Sigma(Y_i - \hat{Y}_i)^2}{n - 2}$$

The probability distributions for the estimates provide the information needed to construct confidence intervals and conduct hypothesis tests. For instance, there is a .95 probability that the estimate b will be within approximately two standard deviations of its expected value β. To test the null hypothesis that $\beta = 0$ (that X has no influence on Y), we can calculate b's t-value—the absolute value of the estimate divided by its standard deviation. If the t-value is greater than 2.0, then the estimate is more than two standard deviations away from zero and, hence, zero is outside of a 95 percent confidence interval and can be rejected as a null hypothesis at the 5 percent level.

A prediction of Y for some particular value X_0 is provided by $\hat{Y}_0 = a + bX_0$. This prediction has a 95 percent confidence interval (or *prediction interval*),

$$Y_0 = \hat{Y}_0 \pm 2 \text{ (standard deviations of } Y_0 - \hat{Y}_0)$$

where the standard deviation is a complicated formula spelled out in Equations 13.13 and 13.14.

The predictive accuracy of the model can be gauged by the

$$\text{coefficient of determination} = R^2 = 1 - \frac{\Sigma(Y_i - \hat{Y}_i)^2}{\Sigma(Y_i - \overline{Y}_i)^2}$$

R-squared compares the sum of squared prediction errors for the model and for the assumption that β is zero, that X does not influence Y. If allowance for the influence of X on Y substantially reduces the prediction errors, then R-squared will be close to 1.0. If not, then R-squared will be close to zero.

APPENDIX: THE LEAST SQUARES SOLUTION

We want to minimize the sum of squared prediction errors,

$$S = e_1^2 + \cdots + e_n^2 = (Y_1 - a - bX_1)^2 + \cdots + (Y_n - a - bX_n)^2$$

This minimum is found by setting the partial derivatives with respect to a and b both equal to zero. The derivative with respect to a yields

$$0 = \frac{\delta S}{\delta a} = -2(Y_1 - a - bX_1) - \cdots - 2(Y_n - a - bX_n)$$

This implies

$$Y_1 + \cdots + Y_n = na - b(X_1 + \cdots + X_n)$$

so that

$$a = \bar{Y} - b\bar{X}$$

where $\bar{Y}$ and $\bar{X}$ are the average values of Y and X.

The derivative with respect to b yields

$$0 = \frac{\delta S}{\delta b} = -2X_1 (Y_1 - a - bX_1) - \cdots - 2X_n (Y_n - a - bX_n)$$

This implies, using $a = \bar{Y} - b\bar{X}$,

$$0 = X_1\{(Y_1 - \bar{Y}) - b(X_1 - \bar{X})\} + \cdots + X_n\{(Y_n - \bar{Y}) - b(X_n - \bar{X})\}$$

so that

$$b = \frac{X_1(Y_1 - \bar{Y}) + \cdots + X_n(Y_n - \bar{Y})}{X_1(X_1 - \bar{X}) + \cdots + X_n(X_n - \bar{X})}$$

Finally, taking into account the computational fact that

$$X_1(Y_1 - \bar{Y}) + \cdots + X_n(Y_n - \bar{Y})$$
$$= (X_1 - \bar{X})(Y_1 - \bar{Y}) + \cdots + (X_n - \bar{X})(Y_n - \bar{Y})$$

for either Y or X, we have

$$b = \frac{(X_1 - \bar{X})(Y_1 - \bar{Y}) + \cdots + (X_n - \bar{X})(Y_n - \bar{Y})}{(X_1 - \bar{X})(X_1 - \bar{X}) + \cdots + (X_n - \bar{X})(X_n - \bar{X})}$$

REVIEW EXERCISES

13.31   Here are some data on the normal precipitation P (in inches) and average daily temperature T (in °F) in Chicago, Los Angeles, and New York during the twelve months of the year:

month	Chicago T	Chicago P	Los Angeles T	Los Angeles P	New York T	New York P
Jan	22.9	1.70	54.5	2.52	32.2	2.71
Feb	26.1	1.30	55.6	2.32	33.4	2.92
Mar	35.7	2.52	56.5	1.71	41.1	3.73
Apr	48.8	3.38	58.8	1.10	52.1	3.30
May	58.4	3.41	61.9	0.08	62.3	3.47
June	68.1	4.15	64.5	0.03	71.6	2.96
July	71.9	3.46	68.5	0.01	76.6	3.68
Aug	71.1	2.73	69.5	0.02	74.9	4.01
Sept	63.7	3.01	68.7	0.07	68.4	3.27
Oct	53.8	2.32	65.2	0.22	58.7	2.85
Nov	39.2	2.10	60.5	1.76	47.4	3.76
Dec	27.1	1.64	56.9	1.75	35.5	3.53

The equation $P = \alpha + \beta T + \epsilon$ can be used to see whether there is a relationship between temperature and precipitation over the course of a year. Estimate this equation using data for

a. Chicago
b. Los Angeles
c. New York

What conclusions do you draw from these results?

13.32 (*continuation*) Now use these data to see whether there is any relationship between these cities' monthly temperatures, by estimating the equation $Y = \alpha + \beta X + \epsilon$, where

a. X = Chicago temperature, Y = L.A. temperature
b. X = Chicago temperature, Y = N.Y. temperature
c. X = L.A. temperature, Y = N.Y. temperature

What conclusions do you draw from these results?

13.33 (*continuation*) Now examine the relationship between these cities' monthly precipitation by estimating $Y = \alpha + \beta X + \epsilon$, where

a. X = Chicago precipitation, Y = L.A. precipitation
b. X = Chicago precipitation, Y = N.Y. precipitation
c. X = L.A. precipitation, Y = N.Y. precipitation

What conclusions do you draw from these results?

13.34 The U.S. National Center for Health Statistics reported the following average weights for 18–24-year-old U.S. males:

height (inches) Y	weight (pounds) X	height (inches) Y	weight (pounds) X
62	130	69	162
63	135	70	166
64	139	71	171
65	143	72	175
66	148	73	180
67	152	74	185
68	157		

Use these data to obtain the least square estimates of the equation $Y = \alpha + \beta X + \epsilon$. Give the SEE and R-squared, too. On average, an extra five inches of height is associated with how many additional pounds?

13.35   (*continuation*) Now use these data to find the least-squares estimate of the equation $Y = \alpha + \epsilon$. What are the SEE and R-squared for this equation? Is this equation a better or worse predictor than the equation estimated in the preceding exercise? Is the relationship between height and weight statistically significant?

13.36   The U.S. National Center for Health Statistics reported the following average weights for 18–24-year-old U.S. females:

height (inches) Y	weight (pounds) X	height (inches) Y	weight (pounds) X
57	111	63	131
58	114	64	134
59	118	65	137
60	121	66	141
61	124	67	144
62	128	68	147

Use these data to obtain the least squares estimates of the equation $Y = \alpha + \beta X + \epsilon$. Give the SEE and R-squared, too.

13.37   (*continuation*) Briefly compare the empirical relationships between height and weight for males and females found in Exercises 13.34 and 13.36.

13.38   Explain why you either agree or disagree with this reasoning: "A person with zero height will have zero weight. Therefore, a regression of weight on height must go through the origin."

13.39   A researcher recently reported that her investigation of the relationship between height and weight obtained "a *t*-value much larger than 2." Why would we be interested in knowing her *t*-value?

13.40   An economics professor gives her students a final exam consisting of 100 multiple-choice questions. In her grade book, she writes down the number of questions Y that each student got right and the number X that each student got wrong. If she uses these data to estimate the equation $Y = \alpha + \beta X + \epsilon$, what will be her estimate of α, her estimate of β, and the correlation coefficient?

13.41   In the standard regression model, what happens to the standard deviation of $Y_0 - \hat{Y}_0$ as the number of observations n becomes very large? What is the explanation?

● **13.42**   A researcher has a model $Y = \alpha + \beta X + \epsilon$, where the error term ϵ has a zero expected value and is independent of X. Show that the least squares estimates of α and β are unbiased, that $E[a] = \alpha$ and $E[b] = \beta$.

● **13.43**   The least squares estimates of α and β in the equation $Y = \alpha + \beta X + \epsilon$ are not uncorrelated. If we knew that our estimate of β was too high, we would also want to revise our estimate of α. Would we want to revise it upward or downward?

●● **13.44**   (*continuation*) Find the covariance $E[(a - \alpha)(b - \beta)]$. Does its sign agree with your intuition?

●● **13.45**   Researcher A believes that egg production E depends on the number of chickens C:

$$E = \alpha + \beta C + \epsilon$$

Researcher B argues that the number of chickens C depends on the number of eggs E:

$$C = -(\alpha/\beta) - (1/\beta)E - (\epsilon/\beta)$$

If they each run a regression using the same data, will they agree on their estimate of β?

●● **13.46**   (*continuation*) If researchers A and B run their preferred regressions using the same data, will they get the same correlation coefficient?

● **13.47**   Two statisticians, who are working independently with different data, each used 10 observations to calculate least squares estimates of the equation $Y = \alpha + \beta X + \epsilon$. We'll call the first statistician's estimate of the slope b_1 and the second statistician's estimate b_2. If they were to get together and pool their data, they would obtain a least squares estimate b.

a. How is b related to b_1 and b_2?
b. Is b the same as the average of the two separate estimates, $(b_1 + b_2)/2$?

●● **13.48**   (*continuation*) Find the expected value and variance of the pooled estimate b and of the average estimate $(b_1 + b_2)/2$. Which would you use?

● **13.49**   An economist regressed Gross National Product (Y) on employment (X) and got an R-squared of .99. Another economist used the same data, but regressed the logarithm of Y on the logarithm of X and got an R-squared of only .95. Should we conclude that the first economist has the right formulation or, at least, fits the data better? If not, how would you compare these two models?

•• **13.50** There is a linear relationship between Y and X

$$Y = \alpha + \beta X + \epsilon$$

The errors ϵ are independent, with mean 0 and a constant variance σ^2. Three estimators of β have been proposed:

1. least squares
2. the average change in Y divided by the average change in X

$$\frac{\{(Y_2 - Y_1) + (Y_3 - Y_2) + \cdots + (Y_n - Y_{n-1})\}/n}{\{(X_2 - X_1) + (X_3 - X_2) + \cdots + (X_n - X_{n-1})\}/n}$$

3. the slope of a line between the first data point and the last data point

$$\frac{Y_n - Y_1}{X_n - X_1}$$

Find the expected values and variances of these three estimators.

a. Which are unbiased?
b. Which has the smallest variance?

CHAPTER 14

The Practice of Regression Analysis

"The cause of lightning," Alice said very decidedly, for she felt quite sure about this, *"is the thunder—no, no!"* she hastily corrected herself, *"I meant it the other way."*

"It's too late to correct it," said the Red Queen, *"When you've once said a thing, that fixes it, and you must take the consequences."*

Lewis Carroll
Alice in Wonderland

TOPICS

Regression analysis is one of the most powerful and useful statistical tools. This chapter will examine several detailed applications, to show the variety of questions that regression analysis can answer. You will see just how simple and yet powerful a tool it is; you will also be warned of several pitfalls that endanger an incautious user of regression analysis.

Professors generally see a consistency in student scores. Those students who do well on the midterm usually do well on the final examination, while those who do poorly on the midterm have trouble with the final exam, too. If this relationship were perfect, professors could dispense with final exams, pleasing everyone (except a few hopelessly optimistic students, who think that their low midterm scores were an accident).

Table 14.1 shows some data on midterm (X) and final (Y) scores for one

Table 14.1   *Midterm and final exam scores*

Student	Midterm	Final
AB	76	81
CC	75	84
GC	66	81
CD	61	62
HG	72	60
JG	56	69
BH	72	82
CH	85	82
FH	63	85
KK	60	53
CL	80	81
JL	25	49
SM	66	84
BM	76	56
DO	89	83
RP	59	70
SR	78	65
AS	68	91
OS	40	48
MS	82	86
CT	77	88
JV	76	83
MW	90	94
VW	76	79
LW	56	67

```
]RUN        SIMPLE REGRESSION

HOW MANY OBSERVATIONS
OF EACH VARIABLE? 25

DO YOU WANT TO SEE EACH
PREDICTION ERROR?
(Y=YES,N=NO): Y

ENTER EACH PAIR X,Y
?76,81
?75,84
?66,81
?61,62
?72,60
?56,69
?72,82
?85,82
?63,85
?60,53
?80,81
?25,49
?66,84

THE AVERAGE VALUE OF X IS 68.96
THE AVERAGE VALUE OF Y IS 74.52
THE LEAST SQUARES ESTIMATED EQUATION
IS Y = 31.3082712 + .626620197X

T    X    PREDICTED Y    ACTUAL Y    ERROR
1    76   78.931         81          -2.069
2    75   78.305         84          -5.695
3    66   72.665         81          -8.335
4    61   69.532         62           7.532
5    72   76.425         60          16.425
6    56   66.399         69          -2.601
7    72   76.425         82          -5.575
8    85   84.571         82           2.571
9    63   70.785         85         -14.215
10   60   68.905         53          15.905
11   80   81.433         81            .438
12   25   46.974         49          -2.026
13   66   72.665         84         -11.335
14   76   78.931         56          22.931
15   89   87.077         83           4.077
16   59   68.279         70          -1.721
17   78   80.185         65          15.185
18   68   73.918         91         -17.082
19   40   56.373         48           8.373
20   82   82.691         86          -3.309
21   77   79.558         88          -8.442
22   76   78.931         83          -4.069
23   90   87.704         94          -6.296
24   76   78.931         79           -.069
25   56   66.399         67           -.601

THE STANDARD ERROR OF ESTIMATE IS SEE = 10.0901132

THE COEFFICIENT OF DETERMINATION IS R-SQUARED = .465852516

THE PARAMETER ESTIMATES ARE
               INTERCEPT    SLOPE
PARAMETERS:    31.308       .627
STD. DEV.:     9.861        .14
T STATS:       3.175        4.477

DO YOU WANT TO COMPUTE SOME PREDICTED VALUES OF Y?
(Y=YES N=NO):Y

WHAT VALUE OF X?70
FOR X = 70 THE PREDICTED VALUE OF Y IS 75.198
THE STANDARD DEVIATION FOR THIS PREDICTION IS 10.2909664
SO THAT A TWO-STANDARD DEVIATIONS RULE OF THUMB GIVES
Y = 75.198 PLUS OR MINUS 20.5819328
I.E., 54.6160672 TO 95.7799328

DO YOU WANT ANOTHER PREDICTION?
(Y=YES N=NO):Y

WHAT VALUE OF X?90
FOR X = 90 THE PREDICTED VALUE OF Y IS 87.738
THE STANDARD DEVIATION FOR THIS PREDICTION IS 10.7030416
SO THAT A TWO-STANDARD DEVIATIONS RULE OF THUMB GIVES
Y = 87.738 PLUS OR MINUS 21.4060831
I.E., 66.3319169 TO 109.144083

DO YOU WANT ANOTHER PREDICTION?
(Y=YES,N=NO): N
```

Figure 14.1   *A least squares regression of final exam scores* Y *on midterm scores* X randomly selected statistics class. Figure 14.1 shows how I entered these data into a computer regression program. First, the computer asks how many observations I have. Because there are 25 students, I have 25 observations. Next, the program asks if I want to see each of the 25 prediction errors—the discrepancies between the actual values of Y and those predicted by the regression equation. I answered "yes." Then the program asks me to enter my data—first X and then Y for each of the 25 observations. The computer encourages me to enter my data by printing a question mark to show that it is asking for data.

After the twenty-fifth observation is entered, the computer will make the necessary (but tedious) calculations very quickly and then print out the regression results shown in Figure 14.1. First, it shows the average values of X and Y. Here, I can see that the students as a group did somewhat better on the final exam than on the midterm. Then the computer prints out the estimated equation

$$\hat{Y} = 31.3 + 0.627\,X$$

I have plotted this line, together with the data, in Figure 14.2. There is a positive relationship, but it is not one-for-one. A student who does 10 points better than another student on the midterm can only be expected to do about 6 points better on the final exam.

Next, the computer prints out the actual and predicted values of Y for each of the 25 observations so that we can see where the big surprises are. The biggest shock is the fourteenth student, who got a 76 on the midterm and was predicted to get a 79 on the final, but only earned a score of 56—a 23-point shortfall! On the other side is the eighteenth student, who got a 68 on the midterm and was predicted to get a 74 on the final, but actually got the second-highest grade on the final, 91, a full 17 points better than expected. We can also see that the predicted

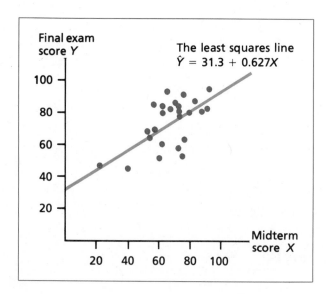

Figure 14.2   *A scatter diagram of the relationship between midterm and final exam scores*

final exam score was off by more than 5 points for 14 of these 25 students. Apparently, final exams do contain useful information, because student scores are not predicted very accurately from midterm performance.

The next data that are printed by the computer are the standard error of estimate (which is pretty large here) and the R-squared (which is far from 1.0). Then come the standard deviations and t-values for the parameter estimates. Even though final exam scores cannot be predicted perfectly from midterm scores, there is a statistically significant relationship between the two. The 4.477 t-value convincingly rejects the null hypothesis that midterm scores are of no value in predicting the final exam scores.

This computer program also asks if we want to use the estimated equation to make some specific predictions. I answered "yes." When the computer asked which values of X, I typed in 70 and then 90. You can see from the wide confidence intervals given in response that midterm scores are far from a precise predictor. For a student who scores 70 on the midterm, the regression equation predicts a score of 75 on the final, with a 95 percent confidence interval of ± 20 points. We can only say that there is .95 chance that the interval 54.6 to 95.8 will encompass the final score. The confidence interval for $X = 90$ reminds us that we have to exercise some common sense when we get away from the middle of the data. Mathematically, the confidence interval is 66.3 to 109.1, but no student is going to score more than 100 points on my final, because only 100 points are possible.

Overall, the bottom line on this statistical exercise is that there is, as expected, a statistically significant relationship between midterm scores and final scores. A student who does well on the midterm can also be expected to do well on the final exam, but this relationship is far from perfect. Many students do far better or worse than might be expected.

Exercises

14.1   A certain college wants to see if there is any relationship between math SAT scores and grades in a required freshman math course. A random sample of 10 students gave these data:

math SAT X	480	540	660	720	570	420	590	630	520	550
math course Y	82	73	79	95	85	54	71	92	61	82

Plot these data and then use them to estimate the equation

$$Y = \alpha + \beta X + \epsilon$$

Sketch this least squares fitted line on your scatter diagram.

a. What are the least squares estimates of α and β?

b. What are the standard error of estimate and R-squared?

c. Does there appear to be a positive relationship, a negative relationship, or no relationship at all between math SAT scores and course scores?

d. Are math SAT scores a good predictor of math course scores?

e. Could the college eliminate this math course and just give math grades on the basis of SAT scores?

14.2   A dean at SML college estimated the relationship between math SAT scores (X) and freshman math course scores (Y):

$$Y = 25.0 + 0.10\ X, \qquad R^2 = .21$$
$$\quad (8.1) \quad (0.06)$$

(   ): standard deviations

The average SAT score for these students was 580.

a. What is the students' average score in this course?
b. According to these least squares estimates, what is the predicted math course score for a student with a math SAT score of 500? Of 600? Of 700?
c. If there is a 100-point difference in the math SAT scores of two students at this college, what is the predicted difference in their math course scores?
d. Is this difference substantial?
e. Is it statistically significant?

14.3   (*continuation*) A dean at BIG college also estimated the relationship between math SAT scores (X) and freshman math course scores (Y):

$$Y = 70.0 + 0.02\ X, \qquad R^2 = .74$$
$$(100.0) \quad (0.005)$$

(   ): standard deviations

The average math SAT score was 500 for these students. Answer the same five questions asked in the preceding exercise.

14.4   A certain college administrator is interested in seeing whether math or verbal SAT scores are the better predictor of performance in a required freshman history course. Here are data for a random sample of 20 students:

math SAT X_1	verbal SAT X_2	history course Y
520	570	71
650	740	88
540	700	92
490	520	74
410	420	59
530	650	83
690	790	97
740	570	73
500	370	47
570	580	77
660	710	94
600	560	81
570	430	51
550	510	82
790	760	91
640	640	85
530	480	68
650	610	79
490	520	72
720	620	87

Use these data to obtain the least squares estimates of each of these equations

$$Y = \alpha_1 + \beta_1 X_1 + \epsilon_1 \quad \text{and} \quad Y = \alpha_2 + \beta_2 X_2 + \epsilon_2$$

a. Is there a statistically significant relationship between math SAT scores and history course scores? Is it a positive or negative relationship?

b. Is there a statistically significant relationship between verbal SAT scores and history course scores? Is it a positive or negative relationship?

c. Is the math or verbal SAT score a better predictor of success in this history course?

14.5 A random sample of ten male soccer players yielded these data on heights and weights:

height (inches) X	65	67	67	68	69	70	71	72	72	75
weight (pounds) Y	142	154	143	155	161	158	179	157	181	190

Use these data to estimate the equation

$$Y = \alpha + \beta X + \epsilon$$

where ϵ is assumed to be normally distributed with an expected value of zero and a variance σ^2.

a. What are the least squares estimates of α and β?

b. What are the standard error of estimate and R-squared?

c. Test (at the 5 percent level) the null hypothesis that $\beta = 0$.

d. Give a 95 percent confidence interval for β.

• **14.6** (*continuation*) Use your data and estimates for the preceding exercise to answer these questions:

a. What is the predicted weight for a 72-inch tall soccer player?

b. What is a 95 percent confidence interval for this weight?

c. What is the predicted weight for an 80-inch tall soccer player?

d. What is a 95 percent confidence interval for this weight?

14.2 THE CAPITAL ASSET PRICING MODEL

One of the primary lessons of portfolio theory is that risk-averse investors can reduce their risk by choosing diversified investment portfolios. A portfolio of several stocks can be safer than any individual stock in the portfolio. Think of each investment as a coin flip—heads you win 100 percent, tails you lose 50 percent. If you put all of your eggs in a single basket by investing in a single coin flip, then there is a .5 probability that you will lose 50 percent of your wealth. If instead you *diversify* by investing half of your wealth in one coin flip and half in a second flip, then you won't lose half of your wealth unless you lose both coin flips. Diversification reduces the probability of a 50 percent loss from .50 to .25. With 100 coin flips, the probability of losing half of your wealth drops to $(.5)^{100}$.

For a single flip, you will be either a big winner or a poor loser. But with many flips, you are almost certain to have about half heads and half tails. Bad luck with some investments will undoubtedly be offset by good luck with others. It is very unlikely that you will have bad luck with almost all of your investments.

This coin flip analogy assumes that the outcomes are independent, in that whether you have good or bad luck on one investment does not depend on how your other investments turn out. In practice though, when people buy stocks, bonds, and other assets, the investment outcomes are not independent, because most assets are affected to some extent by the overall state of the economy and by interest rates. Most stocks and bonds tend to go up and down together.

An extreme analogy is two bets on the same flip of a coin. If you bet ''heads'' with Jack and ''heads'' with Jill, too, there are no gains from diversification, because there is no chance that good luck on the second investment will offset bad luck on the first. The opposite, and equally extreme, situation is a perfect inverse relationship between the results of two investments: If you have bad luck on the first, then you are sure to have good luck on the second. For instance, you could bet ''heads'' with Jack and ''tails'' with Jill on a single flip. No matter which way the coin lands, you are sure to have a 100 percent gain on one investment and a 50 percent loss on the other—a guaranteed 25 percent return overall. This, in fact, is exactly the hedged bet that risk-averse bookies covet.

Most investments are not perfectly correlated, either positively or negatively. But the moral remains, that the advantages of diversification depend on the correlation between asset returns. There is little diversification to be gained from putting half of your wealth in one international oil company and half of your wealth in another. Investing in one oil company and one computer firm reduces risk much more effectively.

Overall, if the stock market is dominated by institutions that hold enormous portfolios, which stocks will be considered risky and which will be considered safe? The lesson of portfolio theory is that the riskiness of an asset depends on how correlated its return is with other assets in the portfolio. An asset that always does poorly when other assets are doing poorly is a risky asset, because it has no diversification potential. An asset whose return is independent of others or, even better, does well when others are doing poorly, reduces portfolio risk. Thus, the proper gauge of risk for portfolio managers is some measure of how an asset's return is related to the returns on other assets.

The *Capital Asset Pricing Model* (CAPM) formalizes these ideas. Suppose there are n assets, each with some (uncertain) percentage return r_i ($i = 1, 2, \ldots, n$). The overall ''market'' return on all n assets is r_M. Let's assume that there is a linear relationship between r_i and r_M:

$$r_i = \alpha_i + \beta_i r_M + \epsilon_i \tag{14.1}$$

The parameter β_i measures the extent to which the return on this particular asset moves with the returns on all assets. The parameter α_i is the intercept of this relationship. The error term ϵ_i is a random variable, reflecting the fact that, no matter what happens to the market, the return on this particular asset may be pushed up or down by various unexpected developments, such as technological break-throughs, the loss of a key executive, favorable tax changes, or legal setbacks. The i subscripts indicate that the parameters α_i and β_i and the error term ϵ_i vary from asset to asset.

Now consider a portfolio with n assets: $i = 1, 2, \ldots, n$. If a fraction λ_i of wealth is invested in asset i, then the overall percentage return on the portfolio will be

$$r = \lambda_1 r_1 + \lambda_2 r_2 + \cdots + \lambda_n r_n$$
$$= (\lambda_1 \alpha_1 + \cdots + \lambda_n \alpha_n) + (\lambda_1 \beta_1 + \cdots + \lambda_n \beta_n) r_M + (\epsilon_1 + \cdots + \epsilon_n)$$
$$= \alpha + \beta r_M + \epsilon$$

The portfolio intercept α and slope β are weighted averages of the intercepts and slopes of the assets in the portfolio. The portfolio error term, too, is a weighted average of the underlying error terms. However, to the extent that these individual errors are independent, their weighted sum, ϵ, will be close to zero!

Intuitively, we can think of each ϵ_i as the flip of a coin—heads is a pleasant surprise ($\epsilon_i > 0$) and tails an unpleasant one ($\epsilon_i < 0$). With a large number of flips, the average outcome should be close to zero—no surprise at all.*

Thus, the return on a diversified portfolio depends on the portfolio's α and β, and on how well the market does. The critical uncertainty for a diversified portfolio is what r_M will be. A portfolio manager can't do anything about r_M, but can do something about the portfolio's β, which is what determines how sensitive the portfolio is to market fluctuations. A portfolio with a β of 1.0 is about as risky as the overall market. If the market return turns out to be 10 percent higher than expected, then this portfolio should do about 10 percent better than expected; if the market drops 10 percent, then this portfolio will probably drop about 10 percent, too. A portfolio with a β greater than 1.0, in contrast, is aggressive in that it has above-average risk. If the market return turns out to be either 10 percent better or 10 percent worse than expected, then a portfolio with a β of 2.0 should do 20 percent better or worse than expected. Finally, a portfolio with a β less than 1.0 is a conservative portfolio. Market fluctuations, up or down, of 10 percent only cause about 5 percent fluctuations in a portfolio with a β of .5. *Thus for portfolio managers, β is the appropriate measure of risk.* High-β stocks are risky because they give risky, high-β portfolios. Low-β stocks are safer, because they give low-β portfolios. It is not surprising, then, that portfolio managers routinely calculate

---

*More formally, consider an equal amount invested in each asset, $\lambda_i = 1/n$, and let each error term have the same standard deviation σ. If the error terms are independent, then the variance of the overall ϵ is

$$\left(\frac{1}{n}\right)^2 \sigma^2 + \cdots + \left(\frac{1}{n}\right)^2 \sigma^2 = \left(\frac{1}{n}\right) \sigma^2$$

which approaches zero as n increases.

the βs for their portfolios and also look at the βs of individual stocks that they consider putting into their portfolios.

Figure 14.3 shows a scatter diagram of the annual percentage returns (dividends plus capital gains) for Merrill Lynch stock and for the market as a whole over the period 1972 through 1980. A least squares regression yielded the following results:

$$\hat{r}_{ML} = -2.35 + 1.82 \; r_M, \quad SEE = 34.3, \quad R^2 = .61$$
$$[0.18] \quad [3.28]$$

[   ]: t-values

Merrill Lynch is the nation's largest brokerage firm and its success is heavily dependent on the course of the stock market. When the market rises, lots of eager investors buy stocks and pay commissions to Merrill Lynch. When stock prices slump, investors leave the market and Merrill Lynch suffers too. The 1.82 beta

Figure 14.3 *The returns on Merrill Lynch stock and on the market as a whole*

coefficient indicates that Merrill Lynch stock tends to go up or down almost twice as fast as the market as a whole. Notice though, that while this relationship is statistically significant, it is far from perfect. The scatter diagram, Standard Error of Estimate (SEE), and R-squared all tell us that, even if we knew how well the market was going to do, we still wouldn't know how well Merrill Lynch would do; other things matter, too.

Table 14.2 shows the data behind this regression and some similar data for three other stocks. IBM and General Mills are more typical companies that tend, on the average, to go up or down about as fast as the market as a whole: they have βs near 1. Least square regressions yielded these estimates:

$$\hat{r}_{IBM} = -2.84 + 0.87 \ r_M, \quad SEE = 13.1, \quad R^2 = .70$$
$$[0.59] \quad [4.08]$$

$$r_{GMills} = -0.62 + 0.96 \ r_M, \quad SEE = 20.7, \quad R^2 = .54$$
$$[0.08] \quad [2.88]$$

[ ]: t-values

American Telephone (AT&T), on the other hand, was a heavily regulated utility over this period and the profits of utility companies depend more on regulatory commissions than the overall economy. Thus, the return on AT&T's stock is not as volatile as most companies (a lower variance) and is insulated from overall market swings (lower beta). For this particular period, the estimated beta coefficient turns out to be only 0.35:

$$\hat{r}_{AT\&T} = 5.34 + 0.35 \ r_M, \quad SEE = 12.2, \quad R^2 = .31$$
$$[1.19] \quad [1.77]$$

[ ]: t-values

Table 14.2 *Some annual stock returns, percent dividends plus capital gains*

Year	Market	Merrill Lynch	IBM	General Mills	AT&T	Portfolio
1972	18.98	−8.0	21.1	57.4	23.9	23.6
1973	−14.66	−55.0	−21.9	−13.0	0.5	−22.5
1974	−26.47	−12.8	−29.7	−24.4	−4.5	−17.9
1975	37.20	37.2	37.4	50.4	21.6	36.7
1976	23.84	79.7	28.1	17.3	32.3	39.4
1977	−7.18	−36.7	1.3	−9.3	1.9	−10.7
1978	6.56	7.5	13.6	0.7	7.6	7.4
1979	18.44	31.2	−9.1	−11.8	−5.6	4.7
1980	32.42	98.3	10.8	13.1	1.4	30.9

The market data, giving the return on Standard and Poor's 500 stocks, is from Roger G. Ibbotson and Rex A. Sinquefield, *Stocks, Bonds, Bills, and Inflation: Historical Returns (1926–1978)* (Charlottesville, Virginia: Financial Analysts Research Foundation, 1979); and from their updated data. The portfolio return is the return from an equal dollar investment in Merrill Lynch, IBM, General Mills, and AT&T.

Now, let's look at a portfolio consisting of an equal investment in each of these four stocks. A well-diversified portfolio would have at least 20 or 30 carefully selected stocks, but this simple four-stock portfolio can hint at the effects of diversification. The portfolio return r_{port} is shown in Table 14.2 and a scatter diagram is shown in Figure 14.4. A least squares regression of this return on the market return yielded these estimates:

$$\hat{r}_{port} = \underset{[0.06]}{0.19} + \underset{[6.73]}{1.01}\ r_M, \qquad SEE = 9.3, \qquad R^2 = .87$$

[   ]: t-values

The portfolio β is the average of the βs for the securities in the portfolio. Here it works out to be almost exactly 1.0. The important result, though, is that the portfolio has a lower Standard Error of Estimate (SEE) and higher R-squared than any of the four stocks in the portfolio. For any given overall performance of the stock market, how well the portfolio does is more certain than the behavior of any

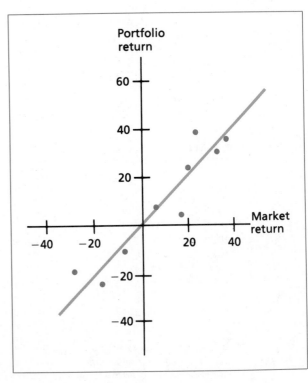

Figure 14.4 *A portfolio of Merrill Lynch, IBM, General Mills, and AT&T*

Table 14.3   *Mutual funds have βs that are generally consistent with their stated objectives*

Investment objective	Number of funds	Average β
Maximum capital gain	117	1.23
Growth	85	1.04
Long-term growth and income	13	1.01
Growth and current income	31	0.99
Growth, income, and stability	14	0.90
Income and growth	12	0.85
Income, growth, and stability	12	0.86
Income, stability, and growth	8	0.71
Income	20	0.71
Stability, income, and growth	9	0.74

of the individual stocks in the portfolio. This is why βs are so important for portfolio managers.

Table 14.3 shows that there is a correspondence between the stated objectives of mutual fund managers and the portfolio βs they choose. A researcher examined the investment objectives given by 321 mutual funds and divided these goals into ten categories ranging from most aggressive ("maximum capital gain") to most defensive ("stability, income, and growth"). This researcher then examined the portfolio βs to see if funds with more aggressive intentions do, in fact, have high-β portfolios. Table 14.3 shows that this is indeed the case.[1]

Risk-averse investors will not choose high-β securities unless the expected return is higher than for low-β securities. Therefore, if investors are risk-averse, then high-β securities must be priced to offer above-average expected returns to

Table 14.4   *Mutual funds with high-β portfolios have done better, on average, than those with low-β portfolios*

β Range	Number of funds	Assets ($ millions)	Average β	Average monthly return
0.0–0.4	3	27.3	0.23	0.43%
0.4–0.8	35	94.3	0.68	0.63
0.8–1.0	44	137.4	0.91	0.79
1.0–1.2	30	73.7	1.07	0.86
1.2+	13	90.8	1.33	1.05
Average		102.6	0.91	0.78

compensate for their greater risk. Various studies have found that high-β securities do, on the average, earn higher returns than low-β securities. Table 14.4 shows one such study that compares mutual fund performance over the same period as Table 14.3. Aggressive high-β funds took greater risks, but did better on average than more conservative funds.[2]

Exercises

14.7   Here are some data on the annual percentage returns for the market as a whole and for three selected stocks:

year	market	U.S. Home	Kloof	Consolidated Natural Gas
1970	4.01	9.6	38.5	23.0
1971	14.31	51.4	6.3	7.1
1972	18.98	−17.2	53.6	7.3
1973	−14.66	−77.3	107.9	−13.4
1974	−26.47	−48.8	1.1	−3.7
1975	37.20	128.0	−38.1	25.1
1976	23.84	56.5	−45.1	59.3
1977	−7.18	−8.8	58.2	29.0
1978	6.56	22.7	16.2	−8.3
1979	18.44	113.1	304.4	15.0

U.S. Home is the nation's largest homebuilder and its profits are very sensitive to the state of the economy. A weak economy and high interest rates are bad for the stock market and very bad for U.S. Home. What kind of results do you think we would obtain if we estimated the equation

$$r = \alpha + \beta\, r_M + \epsilon$$

where r is the return on U.S. Home stock and r_M is the overall market return? Use the data to estimate this equation and see if you are right.

14.8   (*continuation*) Kloof is a South African gold mining stock. Use the data in Exercise 14.7 to estimate the equation

$$r = \alpha + \beta\, r_M + \epsilon$$

where r is the Kloof return and r_M is the market return. Interpret your results.

14.9   (*continuation*) Consolidated Natural Gas is a regulated utility company. Use the data in Exercise 14.7 to estimate

$$r = \alpha + \beta\, r_M + \epsilon$$

where r is the return on Consolidated Natural Gas and r_M is the market return. Interpret your results.

14.10   (*continuation*) If a portfolio were constructed by investing an equal number of dollars in each of these three stocks, what would be this portfolio's β? Use the data to calculate the annual returns on such a portfolio over the ten years 1970–1979. Estimate the equation

$$r = \alpha + \beta \, r_M + \epsilon$$

where r is the portfolio return and r_M is the market return. Interpret your results.

● **14.11**   (*continuation*) How could a portfolio that has a β of zero be constructed out of these three stocks?

14.12   Explain why you either agree or disagree with this statement

A stock with a low β is safer than a high-β stock, because the lower β is, the less variation there is in a stock's return.

● **14.13**   Many investors estimate the β and R-squared of their portfolios. It has been argued that

If the market was expected to rise, an investor might increase the R-square of the portfolio. If the market was expected to decline, a portfolio with a low R-square would be appropriate.[3]

Explain why you agree or disagree with this advice.

14.3   THE POLITICAL BUSINESS CYCLE

Economic events often seem to have a decisive influence on political elections. People take into account their economic well-being when casting their votes. If they are prospering, they are apt to think that the incumbent party is doing a pretty good job and should be allowed to continue with more of the same; there's no reason to take a chance on something new. As folk wisdom says, "If it ain't broke, don't fix it." If, on the other hand, people are out of work or in fear of soon losing their jobs, they are more apt to vote for a change in policy: "Throw the bums out and give someone else a chance."

Now, of course, the state of the economy isn't the only item on the minds of the electorate. International issues of war and peace are obviously important, and so are the candidates' individual personalities—particularly in local elections. But economists and political scientists tell us that national elections are often a referendum on the incumbent party's economic policies. In particular, it seems that the incumbent party is more likely to win congressional and presidential elections if voters perceive that the economy is improving.[4]

For a simple investigation of this idea, Table 14.5 shows some relevant data for 21 presidential elections since the turn of the century. Here we will just look at the 14 elections since 1928; an analysis of all 21 elections is left as an exercise.*

---

*In the 1912 and 1924 elections, there were three major candidates and it is not obvious how the votes should be counted for and against the incumbent party in a way that would be comparable to two-party elections.

Table 14.5   *Some data on the economy and election results*

Election year	Unemployment change* X	Incumbent % of vote† Y
1900	−1.5	53.2
1904	+1.5	60.0
1908	+5.2	54.5
1912‡	−2.1	54.7
1916	−3.4	51.7
1920	+3.8	36.1
1924‡	+2.6	54.3
1928	+0.9	58.8
1932	+7.7	40.9
1936	−3.2	62.5
1940	−2.6	55.0
1944	−0.7	53.8
1948	−0.1	52.4
1952	−0.3	44.6
1956	−0.3	57.8
1960	0.0	49.9
1964	−0.5	61.3
1968	−0.2	49.6
1972	−0.3	61.8
1976	−0.8	48.9
1980	+1.3	44.7

*unemployment change = unemployment rate in election year minus unemployment rate in preceding year

†%vote = fraction of the total presidential vote for the Democratic and Republican candidates received by the party in office at the time of the election.

‡In 1912, there were three major candidates: Roosevelt, Taft, and Wilson. The Roosevelt and Taft votes were taken to be votes for the incumbent party. In 1924, the major candidates were Davis, LaFollette, and Coolidge and the Coolidge votes were counted as votes for the incumbent.

Source: Ray C. Fair, "The Effect of Economic Events on Votes for President," *The Review of Economics and Statistics* 60 (May 1978), pp. 159–173.

The direction in which the economy is moving is gauged by the change in the unemployment rate. The incumbent party's vote is calculated as a percentage of the total vote cast for the two major-party candidates.

What can we conclude from these data? First, let's divide the 14 elections from 1928–1980 into years in which the unemployment rate went up and years in which it went down:

unemployment up		unemployment down	
year	*% vote*	*year*	*% vote*
1928	58.8	1936	62.5
1932	40.9	1940	55.0
1980	44.7	1944	53.8
		1948	52.4
		1952	44.6
		1956	57.8
		1964	61.3
		1968	49.6
		1972	61.8
		1976	48.9
average	48.1		54.8
std. dev.	7.7		5.8

Notice the imbalance in these data. The unemployment rate has gone up in an election year only once since 1932 (during Jimmy Carter's ill-fated 1980 reelection bid). Overall, considering both election and nonelection years, the unemployment rate goes up about as often as it goes down. The fact that the unemployment rate nowadays almost always seems to drop in election years suggests that the politicians, at least, believe that a stronger economy wins votes. They apparently choose policies that are designed to boost the economy during election years.

Does it work? Well, the incumbent won 7 of the 10 elections when the unemployment rate went down and only 1 of 3 when the unemployment rate went up. This difference is suggestive, but not conclusive.* Similarly, the average vote for the incumbent was only 48.1 percent when the unemployment rate was increasing, but 54.8 percent when the unemployment rate was falling. This also is suggestive, but the standard deviations are too large to rule out chance variation. (The actual test is left as an exercise.)

An inadequacy of these first two comparisons is that we paid no attention to the size of the change in the unemployment rate, only its sign. It is likely that the effect (positive or negative) on the election outcome is stronger when the change in the unemployment rate is larger. Regression analysis offers a way to take this kind of quantitative consideration into account. Let's use the linear model

$$Y = \alpha + \beta X + \epsilon$$

---

*If election outcomes were Bernoulli trials with probabilities π_u when the unemployment rate goes up and π_d when it goes down, then a statistical test of the null hypothesis that $\pi_u = \pi_d = \pi$ could be based on the statistical fact that the difference in the sample proportions p_u and p_d would be distributed normally with a mean zero and variance $\pi(1 - \pi)(1/n_u + 1/n_d)$. Using 8/13 for an estimate of π, the estimated variance is $(8/13)(5/13)(1/3 + 1/10) = .103$ and the estimated standard deviation is .32. Thus, the observed .37 difference between the sample proportions .33 and .70 is not statistically significant.

where Y is the incumbent vote, X is the change in the unemployment rate, and ϵ is the error term that reflects all of the other factors that affect election outcomes.*

A least squares regression yields

$$\hat{Y} = 53.10 - 1.70\ X, \qquad R^2 = .37$$
$$[34.8] \qquad [2.67]$$

[ ]: t-values

According to these estimates, the change in the unemployment rate has a substantial (and statistically significant) effect on election outcomes. If the unemployment rate is steady ($X = 0$), then the model predicts that the incumbent will get 53.1 percent of the vote. A 2 percent increase in the unemployment rate during the election year reduces the predicted vote by 3.4 percent, down to 49.7 percent—the difference between victory and defeat!

There are some reasons for caution in interpreting these estimates, however. First, even though the slope estimate is statistically significant, the prediction intervals are pretty wide. The 53.1 percent prediction works out to be ± 11.8 percent, while the 49.7 percent prediction is ± 12.1 percent. So, even while the data say that the unemployment rate makes a difference, they also say that a lot of other things matter, too. The incumbent has the edge and a healthy economy helps, but a healthy economy is no guarantee of victory and a sick economy does not ensure defeat.

The second reason for caution can be seen from the scatter diagram shown in Figure 14.5. Cover up the 1932 result (when, in the depths of the Great Depression, Franklin Roosevelt clobbered the much maligned Herbert Hoover) and try to imagine where you would draw a line that best fit the remaining points. The answer is far from obvious. An outlier like the 1932 election can have a decisive influence on a regression line because, in least squares estimation, many small prediction errors are more tolerable than one big error. The fitted line will avoid large prediction errors by going very close to the outlier. Figure 14.6 shows an extreme example in which there is a perfect negative relationship between X and Y, except for the outlier—which causes the fitted line to have a positive slope.

In these sorts of situations, the researcher must decide whether it is reasonable to report results that are so dependent on a few observations. If, as was shown in Figure 14.6, all of the data except for this one outlier suggest a completely different slope, then there is reason for suspicion. Perhaps the outlier is wrong—the unfortunate consequence of a typographical error somewhere along the line. Or perhaps something extraordinary happened that year that caused a very misleading value

---

*This error term can be interpreted as a sample from the probability distribution describing the many possible extraneous influences on Y. In any particular election year with any given change in the unemployment rate, many things (war and peace, for instance) can happen that influence the outcome. The observed data reflect what actually happened to occur that year.

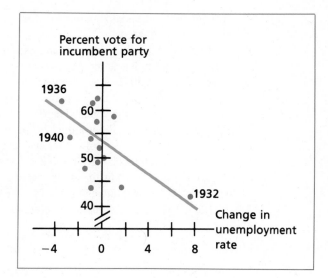

Figure 14.5 *The state of the economy and election outcomes*

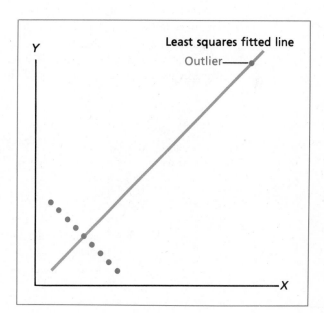

Figure 14.6 *Outliers can strongly influence least squares estimates*

for the dependent variable. If either of these things is true, then the outlier can be corrected or discarded.

These sorts of obvious errors and extraordinary circumstances do happen. But another possibility is that most of the data show so little variation in the explanatory variable that it is difficult to fit any sort of line. Perhaps the unemployment rate is usually up or down a mere 0.1 percent, and it is hard to tell whether or not this is having any effect on the voters. Then, in one particular year, there is a large change in the unemployment rate: it jumps 7.7 percent and the incumbent party is soundly defeated. Doesn't this sort of outlier answer the very question that we are posing—whether a substantial change in the unemployment rate has a substantial effect on the election outcome? In this situation, we wouldn't want to discard the outlier. Indeed, it's the most valuable piece of data we have!

Here, I reran our regression excluding 1932 and obtained these results

$$\hat{Y} = 52.8 - 2.10\ X, \qquad R^2 = .17$$
$$\quad\ [29.3] \quad\ [1.49]$$

[ ]: t-values

If we exclude the three outliers 1932, 1936, and 1940, then we get

$$\hat{Y} = 52.9 - 1.89\ X, \qquad R^2 = .03$$
$$\quad\ [27.2] \quad\ [0.60]$$

In this particular example, leaving out an outlier (or three) doesn't make much difference to the estimated slope, but it makes a great deal of difference as to whether or not the relationship is statistically significant. Without the outliers, R-squared and the t-value for the slope drop dramatically. Since 1940, politicians have apparently managed to manipulate the economy so that the unemployment rate almost always falls slightly during an election year. It is up to the reader to decide whether 1932, 1936, and 1940 are misleading outliers or the most convincing evidence of the effects of the economy on voters.

Exercises

14.14 Professor McTower has made a study of the relationship between the unemployment rate and the outcomes of presidential elections. Her results are

$$V = 55.0 - 2.00\ U$$
$$\quad [3.5] \quad [4.0]$$

where

V = percent of vote received by the incumbent party; average value = 53 percent

U = change in the unemployment rate in the year of the election, average value = 1.0

[ ] = t-values

a. What is her estimate of the effect of unemployment on presidential elections? Is her estimate substantial?

b. What would be a 95 percent confidence interval for her estimate? Is her estimate statistically significant, in that we can reject the hypothesis that there is no effect of unemployment changes on presidential elections?

c. If we were to use her equation to predict the outcome of the next presidential election, for which value of U would we be most confident about our prediction? Why?

d. According to her equation, what fraction of the vote will the incumbent party receive if the unemployment rate falls by 15 percent ($U = -15$) during the election year? Is there any special statistical reason for caution about such a forecast?

14.15 The text used presidential election data for the years 1928 through 1980 to test the idea that the state of the economy influences voters. How would the results be affected if we threw out, as outliers, the four elections in which the absolute value of the change in the unemployment rate was greater than 1.0? Does this discarding make sense?

14.16 (*continuation*) The data for 1900 through 1924 shown in Table 14.5 were not used because of some uncertainty about how to calculate the incumbency vote in a three-person race. How are the results affected if we use all 21 elections, 1900–1980? What if we use the elections from 1900 to 1980, excluding 1912 and 1924? Are the estimates of β substantial and/or statistically significant?

• 14.17 (*continuation*) Let μ_u and μ_d be the expected percentage votes for the incumbent party when the unemployment rate goes up and down, respectively. If the data in Table 14.5 are considered a random sample, construct a statistical test of the null hypothesis that $\mu_u = \mu_d$.

14.18 Here are some data on the unemployment rate and per capita spending (in 1980-dollars $) at motion picture theaters:

year	% unemployment rate (X)	motion picture spending (Y)
1975	8.5	$10.51
1976	7.7	$11.59
1977	7.1	$14.70
1978	6.1	$15.99
1979	5.8	$14.89
1980	7.1	$12.76
1981	7.6	$10.87

Do you think that there may be a relationship between these variables? Is it a positive or negative relationship? Explain your reasoning and then check your logic by estimating the equation $Y = \alpha + \beta X + \epsilon$.

14.19 Many economists believe that there is an inverse relationship between the unemployment rate (X) and the rate of inflation (Y). This is why the government sometimes "fights inflation with unemployment." Estimate the equation $Y = \alpha + \beta X + \epsilon$ using the following data:

year	% unemployment	% inflation
1960	5.5	1.6
1961	6.7	1.0
1962	5.5	1.1
1963	5.7	1.2
1964	5.2	1.3
1965	4.5	1.7
1966	3.8	2.9
1967	3.8	2.9
1968	3.6	4.2
1969	3.5	5.4

According to your estimates, how large a change in the inflation rate (give a 95 percent confidence interval) is associated with a one percentage point increase in the unemployment rate?

14.4   SOME REGRESSION PITFALLS

Although regression analysis is very simple and powerful, it can also be misused—yielding inaccurate or misleading conclusions. Let's look at several pitfalls that should be avoided.

Careless Extrapolation

Researchers are often interested in situations for which they have little or no data. One possible approach is to analyze a situation that has plentiful data and then try to extrapolate the results to cover the situation of interest. For example, some years ago, a group of scientists got together to project population and income hundreds of years from now. They used data for the present and then extrapolated their calculations into the future.

Sometimes the extrapolation is almost an afterthought. A researcher may fit a regression model in the usual way and then, to explore some of the implications of the results, he or she may calculate the predicted values of the dependent variable for various assumed values of the explanatory variable: These calculations may wander off into virgin territory, where there are no data.

Extrapolators should proceed cautiously. It is not enough to plug in a value of X and mechanically compute the predicted value of Y. The calculation of a confidence interval for the prediction is a bit of extra work, but it may well be eye-opening. The prediction interval widens as we get away from the center of the data, and provides a fair warning that predictions on the fringes of the data are less trustworthy. If we find that the prediction is "$Y = 1.235 \pm 232.6$," then we may realize that our data don't really tell us very much about Y for this particular value of X.

Even the widening confidence intervals may understate the unreliability of our extrapolations, because our model is probably not appropriate for any and all values of X. Linearity, for example, is a very convenient assumption and a satisfactory approximation as long as we confine our attention to modest changes in the explanatory variable. However, if we are extrapolating our model to large changes in X, then we should stop and think about the range over which linearity is a reasonable assumption. A linear model assumes that the effect on Y of a change in X is constant, no matter what the value of X. But for most phenomena, there comes a point where the effect of X on Y either becomes stronger or diminishes, and violates the linearity assumption.

For instance, the application of fertilizer increases crop yields, but there comes a point when the effects get smaller and smaller and then turn negative. Too much fertilizer damages crops. Similarly, plants cannot grow without water or light, and the application of either stimulates plant growth. But again, there comes a point where additional water or light doesn't help much and another point, farther along, where more water or light actually will stunt growth or even kill plants.

Keynes's consumption function is a useful approximation to the relationship between household income and spending. People tend to spend more when their income goes up and to spend less when their income goes down. There is no doubt that their behavior would change radically if the economy collapsed and their incomes fell to zero. Who would be foolish enough to believe that the intercept of a linear consumption function (perhaps zero, perhaps a negative number) accurately predicts consumer behavior in such an economic disaster? And yet, the authors of some economics textbooks say just that foolish thing.

There are other examples that are so ludicrous that everyone recognizes the error of incautious extrapolation. In 1940, there were an average of 2.2 people in each car on the highway in the United States. By 1950, this average had dropped to 1.4. At this rate, by 1990, every third car on the road will be empty! Another researcher, with tongue firmly in cheek, extrapolated the observation that automobile deaths declined after the maximum speed limit in the United States was reduced to 55 miles per hour:

> . . . To which Prof. Thirdclass of the U. of Pillsbury, stated that to reach zero death rate on the highways, which was certainly a legitimate goal, we need only set a speed limit of zero mph. His data showed that death rates increased linearly with highway speed limits, and the line passing through the data points, if extended backwards, passed through zero at zero mph. In fact, if he extrapolated even further to negative auto speeds, he got negative auto deaths, and could only conclude, from his data, that if automobiles went backwards rather than forwards, lives would be created, not lost.[5]

Other tongue-in-cheek extrapolations have found that:

1. If the number of microscope specimen slides acquired by a certain St. Louis hospital continues to increase at the current rate, then St. Louis will be buried under three feet of glass by the year 2224.
2. If *National Geographic* magazines continue to accumulate in basements and garages at the present rate, the North American continent will sink beneath the seas.

More than one hundred years ago, Mark Twain came up with this one:

> In the space of one hundred and seventy-six years the Lower Mississippi has shortened itself two hundred and forty-two miles. This is an average of a trifle over one mile and a third per year. Therefore, any calm person, who is not blind or idiotic, can see that in the Old Oolitic Silurian Period, just a million years ago next November, The Lower Mississippi River was upward of one million three hundred thousand miles long, and stuck out over the Gulf of Mexico like a fishing rod. And by the same token any person can see that seven hundred and forty-two years from now the Lower Mississippi will be only a mile and three-quarters long, and Cairo and New Orleans will have joined their streets together. . . . There is something fascinating about science. One gets such wholesale returns of conjecture out of such a trifling investment of fact.[6]

Regression Toward the Mean

Regression toward the mean is a phenomenon that was first noticed by Sir Francis Galton in a study of the relationship between the heights of fathers and their sons. And, indeed, Galton is the source of the label *regression* for the least squares estimation technique. He found that unusually tall fathers tend to have sons who are shorter than themselves, while very short fathers usually have somewhat taller sons. He concluded that the world is "regressing towards mediocrity." However, these data do not mean that soon everyone will be the same height: instead, they reflect the statistical consequences of two chance factors.

The first factor is genetic; a person's height depends on the heights of both the mother and the father. Also, very tall men generally marry women who are not so exceptionally tall—not because they prefer shorter women, but because height is not the only factor they consider in choosing a mate. A man who is two standard deviations taller than the average male may well choose a woman who is two standard deviations taller than the average female. Or, taking attributes other than height into account, he may marry a woman who is either more or less than two standard deviations taller than the average female. If so, she is much more likely to be a woman who is less than two standard deviations taller than the average female, just because there are so many more of them. For every woman whose height is more than two standard deviations above the average, there are 40 women whose height is less than two standard deviations above the average. Thus, most very tall men marry women who are not as exceptionally tall as they are and, thus, have sons who are not as exceptionally tall either. In the same way, most very small men marry women who are not so exceptionally short and consequently have somewhat taller sons.

The second chance factor is that diet, exercise, and other environmental factors influence heights. People will be either taller or shorter than the height that would be expected, based solely on their parents' genes. Some people with tall parents will be short and some people with short parents will be tall. Thus, observed height is not a perfect reflection of one's genes and, hence, not a perfect predictor of the genetically expected height of one's children. To predict the heights of children, the important question is, what can we infer about a person's genes from his or her observed height? Someone who is very tall is much more likely to be the unusually tall result of more average genes than the unusually short result of extremely tall genes, just because there are so few extremely tall genes. Thus, the observed height of a very tall person is usually an overstatement of his or her genetic height, which is what determines the expected height of the child. In the same way, a short person is much more likely to have been the unusually short child of more average parents than the unusually tall child of exceptionally short parents. A short parent's genetic height is probably somewhat taller and, so, the children will be taller too.

These explanations do not mean that we will soon all be the same height. Indeed, we could just as well turn the argument upside down by noting that most very tall people had somewhat shorter parents, while most very short people had somewhat taller parents—does this mean that heights are diverging? No, heights are neither converging nor diverging. There will always be unusually tall and unusually short people. What we must recognize is that heights are influenced by chance, so that those who are unusually tall most likely had chance influences that pulled them above their genetically expected height. The *regression-toward-the mean fallacy* is to conclude that some important trend is at work, when it is really just the complex implications of chance.

The midterm/final example that was analyzed earlier is a good illustration of the regression-toward-the-mean phenomenon at work. Our estimated equation is

$$\hat{Y} = 31.3 + .627\,X$$

where Y is the score on the final exam and X is the score on the midterm. Here are the predicted final exam scores for three different midterm grades:

midterm score	predicted final exam score
59	68.2
69	74.6
79	80.8

A student who gets the average score on the midterm (69) is predicted to receive an average score on the final (about 75). A student who scores 10 points below the class average on the midterm is predicted to score only 6 points below the average on the final. A student who is 10 points above the class average on the midterm is predicted to be only 6 points above the average score on the final.

Does this mean that students converge to a depressing mediocrity, with the weak getting stronger while the strong get weaker? Or, turning the argument on its head, does the fact that the highest scorers on the final did not do as well on their midterms show that scores are diverging from the mean? The answer to both questions is no! The most plausible explanation is that high scores involve a bit of good luck. Those students with the highest scores on any particular test are mostly above-average students who did exceptionally well because the questions that were asked happened to be ones that they were well prepared to answer. It is more probable that they are good students who did unusually well than that they are great students who had an off day. Thus, the students with the highest scores on the midterm are more likely to have somewhat lower scores on the final than to have even higher scores. Similarly, those students with the highest scores on the final probably had somewhat lower scores on the midterm. The highest scorers on any given test most likely did not do as well on their last exam and will not do as well on their next exam, but this does not mean that scores are either diverging or converging.

Regression toward the mean involves a subtle sort of data mining. If, beforehand, we select students at random from some population (perhaps those who have had special counseling), their average score will be an unbiased estimate of the population mean. But here we are picking out those students who happened to have done exceptionally well on the test. These are not unbiased estimates of some population's ability, because they are not a random sample; they were deliberately selected because they had the highest scores. In any population distribution, the highest scores are an overestimate of that population mean. If we want to estimate some expected score or see whether the dispersion in the scores is increasing or decreasing, then we need to use a random sample that is not chosen based on the scores themselves.

We also see this regression toward the mean in IQ scores:

> . . . 4 year olds with IQs of 120 typically have adult scores around 110. Similarly, 4 year olds with scores of 70 have an average adult score of 85. . . . This does not mean that there will be fewer adults than children with very high or very low IQs. While those who start out high or low will usually regress toward the mean, their places will be taken by others who started closer to the mean.[7]

An economic example occurs in the estimation of household consumption functions. Researchers find that people with relatively high incomes one year tend to have relatively less income the next year, while those with low incomes improve their relative position. This does not mean that incomes are becoming more and more alike. A person who is observed to have had a relatively high income is more likely to have had an unusually good year than an atypically bad year. A normal year would see relatively less income. Of course, their places will be taken by other people who have unusually good years and atypically high incomes. At the other end, people with relatively low incomes are more likely to have had a bad year than a good year. A normal year would be one with a somewhat higher income.

Another economic example is provided by a book published some time ago with the provocative title *The Triumph of Mediocrity in Business*. The author discovered that businesses with exceptional profits in any given year tended to have smaller profits the following year, while most firms with very low profits did somewhat better the next year. From this evidence, he concluded that strong companies were getting weaker, and the weak stronger, so that soon they would all be mediocre. The author's fallacy is now obvious. A famous statistician explained it as follows:

> . . . while [businesses] at the margins . . . often go toward the center, those in the center of the group also go towards the margins. Some go up and some down; the average of the originally center group may, therefore, display little change, since positive and negative deviations cancel in averaging; while for an extreme group, the only possible motion is toward the center.[8]

Correlation Is Not Causation

Usually the basis for a regression equation is the belief that changes in X *cause* changes in Y. For example, our estimation of a consumption function was based on Keynes's argument that income affects spending. Similarly, our investigation of the political business cycle began with the idea that the state of the economy influences the outcome of presidential elections. A strong economy wins votes for the incumbent party, while a weak economy is politically costly.

Do Champions Choke?

As of 1983, there had been 17 Super Bowls and only 4 champions were able to repeat their feat the following year. In baseball, of the last 20 World Series champions (1964–1983), only 4 have repeated. No professional basketball team has repeated as NBA champion since the Boston Celtics did in 1969. This doesn't mean that champions choke or that the teams in each of these sports are becoming increasingly equal in ability. Instead, these can be explained as regression toward the mean. There is a considerable amount of luck involved in winning a championship. Injuries, bad bounces, and questionable officiating all play a role. The team that ends up as champion is more likely to have had its share of good fortune. The next year, some other team will probably get the breaks.

There is plenty of other, more detailed evidence of this regression toward the mean in sports.[9] Of those major league baseball teams that finish a season with winning records, 2/3 win fewer games the next season. Of those teams with losing records, 2/3 do better the next season. Of those teams that win more than 100 out of 162 games in a season, 90 percent will find their record deteriorating the next season. Looking at individuals, there were 28 major league baseball players who batted above .300 in 1979, and 23 of these 28 had lower batting averages in 1980 than in 1979. This is to be expected because someone who bats .320 in any given year is more likely to be a .300 hitter having a good year than a .340 hitter having a bad year, just because there are so few (if any) .340 hitters around. The regression-toward-the-mean fallacy is to conclude that good hitters' skills deteriorate. The correct conclusion is that those with the highest batting averages in any particular year aren't really as skillful as their high batting averages suggest, in that they undoubtedly had more than their share of good luck that year.

It is sound practice to have a logically plausible model that motivates the regression equation. However, this sound practice is not always followed, in that often researchers accidentally stumble upon unexpected correlations. The art of regression analysis is then to interpret these empirical results. This is what Ed Leamer calls "Sherlock Holmes' inference" and, as I pointed out in earlier chapters, it can lead to both useful and useless models.

There are three major reasons why empirical correlations can be misleading:

> simple chance
> reverse causation
> omitted factors

The first explanation, simple chance, involves the statistical reasoning that even unrelated things may, by historical accident, be correlated. In the model $Y = \alpha + \beta X + \epsilon$, we say that X has a statistically significant effect on Y if there is less than a 5 percent chance that our estimate of β would be so far from zero, if β really were zero. What we must realize is that even if β really is zero, there is a 5 percent chance that the data will be such that we will conclude there is a statistically significant relationship. If we spend all of our lives looking at unrelated variables, we will still find statistical significance on about one out of every twenty tries. Or, turning it around, if we run twenty regressions and report the best one, we may have nothing more than chance correlation.

The second reason why correlations can be misleading is that perhaps it is Y that determines X, rather than the other way around. Let's say, for instance, that it is a Sunday afternoon and, with nothing better to do, we are rummaging through some data looking for impressive correlations. We stumble upon a regression of the change in the unemployment rate (Y) on the vote for the incumbent party (X)— the reverse of the regression run earlier.

Using the data shown in Table 14.5, the results turn out to be

$$\hat{Y} = \begin{matrix} 11.7 \\ [2.67] \end{matrix} - \begin{matrix} 0.22 \ X, \\ [2.67] \end{matrix} \qquad R^2 = .37$$

[ ]: t-values

This statistically significant relationship tempts us to find some logical explanation. Why would the reelection of an incumbent cause the unemployment rate to fall, *preceding* the reelection? Perhaps, the jubilant incumbent who foresees reelection celebrates with expansionary policies, while the bitter incumbent who foresees defeat punishes the electorate with a recession. Or perhaps businesspeople love stability and when they believe that the incumbent is going to be reelected, they happily increase employment and production. However, when businesspeople see a new administration coming, they grow fearful and cut back. Interesting theories all! But none so plausible as the possibility that it is not election prospects that determine unemployment, but rather unemployment that influences election outcomes.

There are plenty of other examples, some less obvious and some more so. For clarity, let's go with the more obvious ones. There are empirical correlations between people's ages and their insurance rates, between the nylon content of ropes and their breaking strength, and between fertilizer applications and crop yields. In each case, we have to use our powers of reasoning to decide what is affecting what. Does increasing age cause insurance companies to charge more? Or do high insurance rates cause people to age faster? Does nylon increase breaking strength or does breaking strength create nylon? Does additional fertilizer increase yields or does productive land persuade farmers to reward the soil with a fertilizer treat?

The third reason for misleading correlations is that there may be some third factor that influences both X and Y. In the regression model

$$Y = \alpha + \beta X + \epsilon$$

we assume that the omitted factors collected in the error term ϵ are uncorrelated with the explanatory variable X. If they are not, then we may misestimate the effect of X on Y, or even identify an effect when there really is none. In this unfortunate situation, Y may appear to depend on X, when in fact, Y depends on ϵ, which happens to be correlated with X.

Think of Keynes's consumption function again, with Y being consumer spending and X being income. Perhaps consumer spending depends not only on income but also on prices: high income encourages spending, while high prices discourage spending. By using income as the explanatory variable, we relegate prices to the error term. Now, what if prices tend to be high when income is high, and to be low when income is low? If so, then we will be fooled into underestimating the effect of income on spending, because whenever income goes up, the positive effects of income on spending will be partly offset by the negative effects of the higher prices. Even worse, the negative effects of higher prices may be so strong that spending actually falls whenever income goes up. We would erroneously conclude that income discourages spending, when in fact, it is higher prices that discourage spending.

Our mistakes can also go in the other direction. Perhaps spending doesn't really depend on income; instead, spending depends solely on what happens in the stock market. When the market goes up, buoyed consumers spend happily, and when the market crashes, depressed consumers cut back. Now it may so happen that in the particular data we examine, stock prices have increased in years when income has been high and have fallen in years when income has been low. If so, then when we see income and spending going up and down together, we will erroneously conclude that spending depends on income, when spending really depends on the stock market. Or, to make it sillier, perhaps the National Football Conference happens (by pure chance) to have won the Super Bowl in the same years that the stock market went up and to have lost in those years when the market went down. If so, then a regression of consumer spending on Super Bowl scores will lead us to conclude erroneously that consumer spending depends on which conference wins the Super Bowl.

A Few Examples

A blurry causation does not necessarily render a regression equation worthless. The estimated equation may still be useful in describing the nature of the data. The error is in misperceiving causation. For example, Exercise 13.31 in the previous chapter gave some monthly data on precipitation (P) and temperature (T) in Chicago, Los Angeles, and New York. A least-squares regression using the Chicago data yields

$$\text{Chicago: } \hat{P} = 0.71 + 0.04\ T, \qquad R^2 = .68$$
$$\qquad\quad [1.62] \quad [4.67]$$

[ ]: t-values

There is a (statistically significant) positive relationship between temperature and precipitation. A 10-degree increase in temperature is associated with about a half-inch of additional precipitation.

Fine enough. But if we use the Los Angeles data, we get

$$\text{Los Angeles: } \hat{P} = 11.2 - 0.17\ T, \qquad R^2 = .82$$
$$\qquad\qquad [7.43] \quad [6.81]$$

indicating that a 10-degree increase in temperature is associated with an almost 2-inch *decrease* in precipitation! The New York data gives yet different results:

$$\text{New York: } \hat{P} = 2.95 + 0.01\ T, \qquad R^2 = .10$$
$$\qquad\quad [6.79] \quad [1.05]$$

Here, precipitation is apparently unrelated to temperature.

These three conflicting results are only contradictory if we attempt to find a causal relationship between temperature and rainfall. Temperature and precipitation are complex climatological phenomena that depend critically on a city's geographic location. Chicago is so located that it happens to have a rainy season during the warm summer months. This doesn't mean that the sun causes rain. Los Angeles, in contrast, has its rainy season during the cool winter months. And New York gets almost the same amount of precipitation every month—winter, spring, summer, and fall. That is all these three regressions are telling us: that it rains a lot in Chicago during the summer; that Los Angeles gets most of its rain in the winter; and that New York rainfall is pretty evenly distributed throughout the year. These conclusions are informative and correct. We just have to avoid the incorrect conclusion that rain is caused by sunshine, or vice versa.

Because regression results are often just descriptive, cautious researchers use language such as this: "The results show that changes in Y are associated with changes in X." The readers are left to draw their own conclusions and, it is hoped that they will remember that a sound theory is needed for a causal interpretation of the results.

Our example of final and midterm scores is similar. We don't really believe that it is the score on one test that determines the score on another; it is the person taking the test who determines the scores. However, there is some noticeable consistency in performance in that a bright, conscientious student does well on most tests, while a goof-off will do poorly. Their scores vary from test to test, because there is some randomness in the specific questions asked, in how the professor grades the questions, and in each student's fitness on test day. But, logically, there is some consistency, too, and that consistency is what we tried to identify with our regression estimates—the extent to which final exam scores can be predicted from midterm scores. Our results were interesting and informative: there is some consistency in scores; there is some regression toward the mean; and there is substantial variation in scores from one test to the next. As long as we are clear about causation, we are okay.*

Unfortunately, there are lots of examples of incorrect conclusions that can be drawn by seeing causation when there is only correlation. Spurious correlations are undoubtedly the most serious hazard in building and estimating useful regression models. The only real safeguard is to use common sense in specifying models and to reexamine suspicious results with fresh data. For instance, a positive correlation has been reported between stork's nests and births in northwestern Europe. Few would conclude that storks bring babies. A more logical explanation is that storks like to build their nests on buildings. Where there are more people, there are usually more buildings and, hence, more places for storks to nest.

Another study found that a certain state had both an unusually high milk consumption and an abnormally high cancer rate. Does this show that milk causes cancer? It turns out that many elderly people live in this state and that cancer strikes the elderly more than the young. Because of this state's large elderly population, it had an unusually high cancer rate. Anything else that was unusual about this state might seem to be an explanation for the high cancer rate, but it was really just the unusual number of elderly citizens.

Similarly, Arizona has the highest death rate in the nation from bronchitis, emphysema, asthma, and other lung diseases, but this doesn't mean that Arizona's climate is hazardous to one's lungs. On the contrary, doctors recommend that patients with lung problems move to Arizona for its beneficial climate. Many do move to Arizona and benefit from the dry, clean air. Although some die of lung disease in Arizona, it is not because of the Arizona climate.

---

*The same is true of our estimated relationships between the market return and the returns on individual stocks. We don't believe that there is a living, breathing "market return" that decides how well each individual stock will do. The market return is nothing more than the average return on all stocks. However, what we do believe is that stocks exhibit varying degrees of sensitivity to the economic events that buffet the economy. We try to gauge these relative sensitivities by regressing individual returns on the calculated market return.

The Radiophobic Farmer

Darrell Huff tells the story of a farmer who claimed that his fruit trees were being damaged by radio waves from a nearby station. He put a wire fence around some of his trees to "shield" them from these radio waves and, sure enough, they quickly recovered, while the unshielded trees still suffered. About the same time, many citrus trees throughout the country were threatened by the spread of "little leaf" disease. Then some farmers in Texas found that a solution of iron sulphate cured this disease. However, it didn't always work in Texas and it almost never worked in Florida or California. Huff explains that these mysteries were solved when it was discovered that the real problem was a zinc deficiency in the soil:

> The radiophobic farmer's fence wire was galvanized; enough zinc washed off the wire to give the trees the tiny trace of zinc they needed. The iron sulphate did nothing for the other trees, but the zinc-coated buckets in which it was carried saved them. In regions where buckets other than galvanized were used, the trees went right on ailing.[10]

Data Grubbing

If we have no logically sound model to guide us, then we may well fall into one of these correlation-is-not-causation pitfalls. The usual route to a pitfall is an overly zealous researcher who gives the computer a good workout by running hundreds or even thousands of regressions, and then he or she reports those results that are most statistically significant. Because this pure and simple data grubbing is sure to turn up something that is statistically significant, we do not know whether the reported result validates an interesting model or merely demonstrates the researcher's endurance. Only common sense and fresh data can tell the difference.

Many business and economic variables present a special problem in that they grow over time with the overall economy. If we pick two such variables at random, they will usually appear correlated, simply because they have both been growing. One way of seeing this logic is to think of time itself as the omitted factor. Let's say that X and Y are two unrelated variables, each of which grows over time, plus or minus some random disturbance:

$$Y = \alpha_1 + \beta_1 t + \epsilon_1 \tag{14.2}$$

$$X = \alpha_2 + \beta_2 t + \epsilon_2 \tag{14.3}$$

The new variable t is a measure of time; for instance,

$$t = 1 \text{ in } 1971$$

$$t = 2 \text{ in } 1972$$

and so on. Each year, the passage of time increases Y by β_1 and X by β_2. In addition, the random disturbances ϵ_1 and ϵ_2 cause Y and X to diverge somewhat from their long-run growth paths. If ϵ_1 and ϵ_2 are independent, then we would say that X and Y are two unrelated variables that follow their separate courses.

Figure 14.7 shows an example of this. I set $\alpha_1 = 10$, $\beta_1 = 2$, $\alpha_2 = 5$, and $\beta_2 = 1$. Twenty observations for Y and X (for $t = 1$ to 20) were generated by flipping a coin 40 times, 20 for ϵ_1 and 20 for ϵ_2:

$$\epsilon_1 = \begin{array}{l} +2 \text{ if heads} \\ -2 \text{ if tails} \end{array} \quad \epsilon_2 = \begin{array}{l} +1 \text{ if heads} \\ -1 \text{ if tails} \end{array}$$

From the way the data are constructed, Y and X are clearly unrelated. We would not say that X determines Y, or that Y determines X. Instead, each wanders along its own path; these paths are shown in Figure 14.7.

But what happens if we estimate the regression equation $Y = \alpha + \beta X + \epsilon$? It turns out that we get

Figure 14.7 *Two unrelated variables that grow over time*

$$\hat{Y} = -1.75 + 2.07\ X, \qquad R^2 = .95$$
$$[0.98] \qquad [19.3]$$

[ ]: t-values

Although Y and X are generated independently, there turns out to be a highly statistically significant relationship between them! The reason is that both grow over time; that is, they both depend on the same third factor, the passage of time.

A second way of seeing this important point is to remember what R-squared measures—the mean squared forecasting error of the estimated model $Y = \alpha + \beta X + \epsilon$ relative to the mean squared forecasting error when the average value of Y is used to forecast Y.* If Y has been growing over time, then the average value of Y will be such a lousy forecaster of Y that any variable X that also has been growing over time will seem to be a wonderful predictor by comparison.

Edward Ames and Stanley Reiter did a very interesting data mining experiment in which they randomly selected 100 economic variables.[11] They then ran regressions, trying to predict each of these variables by selecting an explanatory variable at random. This was intended to mimic the behavior of a completely uninformed data miner. They found that it usually took only from two to six tries to find an explanatory variable that gave an R-squared of at least .5. This is *not* a recommended research strategy! It is intended to show that we should not be overly impressed by high R-squareds and t-values, because these are so easy to obtain. Rather, we must exercise common sense and, if there is doubt, gather some fresh data.

Exercises

14.20   An agronomist has collected these data on the effects of fertilizer on crop yields:

fertilizer X (pounds/acre)	yield Y (bushels/acre)
0	5
50	12
100	18

Find the least squares estimates of the parameters α and β in the equation $Y = \alpha + \beta X + \epsilon$.

14.21   (*continuation*) Encouraged by these results, the agronomist collects some more data:

fertilizer X (pounds/acre)	yield Y (bushels/acre)
100	19
150	15
200	9

*Recall that the formula for R-squared is

$$R^2 = 1 - \frac{\Sigma(Y_i - \hat{Y}_i)^2}{\Sigma(Y_i - \overline{Y}_i)^2}$$

Use just these three new observations to estimate the parameters α and β in the equation $Y = \alpha + \beta X + \epsilon$. Now use all six observations to estimate α and β. Compare your three sets of estimates. What should the agronomist conclude?

14.22 A business is interested in the effects of room temperature on worker productivity. It would like to reduce its heating bills, but not if lower temperatures substantially impair productivity. A consulting firm conducts an experiment, setting the temperature at 50°F in one of the business's office buildings, 60°F in a second building, and 70°F in a third. The observed average typing speeds (words per minute) turn out to be

temperature X	typing speed Y
50	63
60	74
70	79

Calculate the least squares estimates of the parameters α and β in the equation $Y = \alpha + \beta X + \epsilon$. Is the estimate of β substantial? What are the predicted typing speeds for $X = 30$ and for $X = 90$? Would you use these predictions in making recommendations?

14.23 A "study" was made of the average sentence lengths of British public speakers over the period 1598 to 1940:[12]

speaker	year X	words/sentence Y
Francis Bacon	1598	72.2
Oliver Cromwell	1654	48.6
John Tillotson	1694	57.2
William Pitt	1777	30.0
Benjamin Disraeli	1846	42.8
David Lloyd George	1909	22.6
Winston Churchill	1940	24.2

Find the least squares estimates of the equation

$$Y = \alpha + \beta X + \epsilon$$

What is the predicted value of Y for

a. $X = 1984$?
b. $X = 2100$?
c. $X = 2200$?

14.24 A history teacher finds that several students do poorly on his midterm. He aims his lectures "a notch lower" and is pleased to find that these weaker students do better on the final exam; this success is tainted only slightly by the fact that his best students on the midterm do not do as well on the final exam. Does his experience show that weak students can handle basic material, but that strong students have trouble with elementary concepts?

14.25 In professional baseball, a National League and American League "Rookie of the Year" is selected each year. Most Rookies of the Year do not do as well in their second year of professional baseball as they did in their first year. Sportswriters call this the "sophomore slump" and attribute it to the pressure put on a star and to the distractions that fame brings. Is there any simpler, purely statistical explanation? Explain your reasoning so carefully that even a sportswriter could understand it.

14.26   Here are some batting averages for the 1983 and 1984 seasons:

player	1983	1984
Baker	.320	.295
Fred	.240	.220
Jones	.260	.250
Marv	.220	.240
Moose	.250	.260
Slim	.295	.320

Do Baker and Marv show that batting averages are converging to the mean? Or do the batting averages of Fred and Slim show that batting averages are diverging from the mean?

14.27   At Harvey Mudd College, students are given an achievement test when they enter as freshmen and then they are given the same test again as graduating seniors. The college has found that those students who do exceptionally well as freshmen do not do as well when they are seniors. Is a college education less useful to the brightest students? Do the very intelligent unlearn at college, perhaps by exposure to the less intelligent? Or what?

14.28   A study of U.S. males ages 21–34 found a positive correlation between income and weight. Does extra weight increase one's earning power? Do high-income people overeat? Or what?

14.29   A 1978 Gallup poll found that 30.3 percent of the people with a college education smoke cigarettes, while 43.5 percent of those with only a high school education smoke. Do these data show that smoking makes it harder to finish college?

14.30   People who have a college education earn much more, on average, than those who don't. Here are some census data on the median incomes of U.S. males, 18 years and older:

years of schooling	approximate years X	median income Y
less than 8	6	$7,035
8	8	$8,960
9–11	10	$9,924
12	12	$14,583
13–15	14	$15,674
16	16	$22,173
more than 16	18	$26,927

I have put in approximate years-of-education numbers so that you can use least squares to estimate the parameters of the regression equation $Y = \alpha + \beta X + \epsilon$. Is there a statistically significant relationship between education and income? According to your estimates, a person with an extra year of education earns, on average, how much extra income? Can we infer the value of another year of education from this estimate? Explain why you either would or would not use this estimate to advise a friend who is thinking of quitting school. According to your estimated equation, what is the predicted income of a "professional student," say someone who went to school for 30 years?

14.5 SUMMARY

A regression analysis begins with an explanatory variable X and a dependent variable Y. A scatter diagram is a useful first step to seeing whether or not there is any relationship between these two variables. We may find that there is a close linear relationship, a nonlinear relationship, or no relationship at all. A scatter diagram can also help identify outliers in the data. These outliers may have been recorded incorrectly, or they may reflect very atypical circumstances. In either case, outliers warrant closer inspection. If there is a recording error, then it can be corrected and we can be thankful that we found it before it ruined our regression. If the numbers are not in error, then we must decide whether the outlier is a misleading curiosity (which can be discarded) or an important piece of information that should be retained.

The next step is to fit a line to our data by computing the least squares estimates of the equation $Y = \alpha + \beta X + \epsilon$. We will be pleased if the estimate of β is plausible—that it has the right sign and a reasonable magnitude (taking into account the width of the confidence interval). If it has the wrong sign or an implausible magnitude, then we have a puzzle to unravel: perhaps our theory is wrong, or maybe there is an important omitted factor in the error term that is distorting our estimate.

The closeness of the fit can be gauged by the R-squared. If R-squared is close to 1, then most of the variation in the dependent variable is explained by the explanatory variable. If R-squared is close to 0, then the explanatory variable is of little predictive value; the regression equation's squared forecasting errors are not much smaller than those that can be obtained by discarding X and just using the average value of Y. For a more formal measure, we can see whether or not the t-value is greater than 2. If the t-value is greater than 2, then the data reject the null hypothesis that $\beta = 0$: the improvement in predictive ability from using X as an explanatory variable is "statistically significant," which means that it is too great to be plausibly explained by chance alone. If the t-value is less than 2, then 0 is inside our confidence interval for β and cannot be rejected as a possible value for β.

That β is 0 is an interesting null hypothesis to consider, but it is not the only question to be asked. We want our estimate of β (and the associated confidence interval) to be substantial and plausible. Let's say that we are on a Business School admissions committee and that we believe GMAT scores are a useful predictor of success at our school, as measured by grade-point average (GPA). Using data for last year's class, we estimate the equation $Y = \alpha + \beta X + \epsilon$, where Y is GPA and X is GMAT score. If our estimate of β is -0.010, with a standard deviation of 0.002, then our t-value is a pleasing 5.0, but our estimate has the "wrong" sign! According to this estimate, those who do well on the GMATs do poorly in business school. We had better reexamine our data or rethink our theory, as there may be some other factor that is correlated with GMAT scores and is really affecting grades.

Another possible result is that our estimate of β turns out to be 0.00010 with a standard deviation of 0.00002. Again, the t-value is 5.0 and, this time, the estimate has the right sign. But still we would be disappointed in these results. A β of 0.00010 $\pm$ 0.00004 means that a 100-point difference in GMAT scores is associated with only a 0.006 to 0.014 difference in GPAs—hardly enough to make GMAT scores of any real value. A third possibility is that our estimate of β is 0.010 with a standard deviation of 0.006. This t-value is less than 2, but the estimate is substantial and suggestive. The 0.01 value of β means that a 100-point difference in GMAT scores is associated with a resounding 1.0 difference in GPAs. Our 95 percent confidence interval (from -0.2 to $+2.2$) is too wide to rule out no effect at all, but it is also centered at a place that encourages us to gather more data and keep watching GMAT scores. A fourth possibility, and the most satisfying of all, is a β estimate of 0.005 with a standard deviation of 0.001. Now, we've got an estimate with the right sign, a substantial and plausible magnitude, and a t-value that we can brag about.

REVIEW EXERCISES

14.31   A rope manufacturer believes that the breaking strength of its ropes depends on what fraction of the cord consists of nylon, rather than cotton. Ten ropes are constructed to study this relationship:

% nylon	breaking strength (pounds)
X	Y
0	260
10	360
20	490
20	510
30	600
30	600
40	680
50	820
60	910
70	990

Plot these data and then find the least squares estimates of the relationship $Y = \alpha + \beta X + \epsilon$. Draw this estimated line on your scatter diagram.

a. What is the predicted breaking strength of a 33 percent nylon rope?
b. What is the predicted breaking strength of a 66 percent nylon rope?

• **14.32**   (*continuation*) Answer these questions that were posed by the company's management:

a. Why are the observed breaking strengths of the two 20 percent nylon ropes not the same?

b. What is the equation's predicted breaking strength for a 0 percent nylon rope? Why isn't this prediction 260 pounds, the same as the measured breaking strength for a 0 percent nylon rope?

c. What is a 95 percent confidence interval for the breaking strength of a 0 percent nylon rope?

d. Would you discard your results if it turned out that the measured breaking strength of a . 0 percent nylon rope was outside of this 95 percent confidence interval?

•• **14.33** (*continuation*) The cost C ($/foot) of manufacturing rope depends on the nylon content (X). The price P ($/foot) that the rope can be sold for depends on its breaking strength. If the cost of manufacturing the rope is given by the equation $C = 0.02 + 0.10X$, then use your least squares estimates to find the minimum price that the firm must charge to make a profit on a rope with a predicted breaking strength of 500 pounds. What about a rope with an 800-pound predicted breaking strength?

14.34 The Ace Software Company has developed a new computer game. To determine the most profitable price to charge, the company decides to sell this game at different prices in five similar cities. The results are

city	price	sales
A	$20	1010
B	$25	813
C	$30	721
D	$35	542
E	$50	305

Plot these data with price (X) on the horizontal axis and sales (Y) on the vertical axis. Find the least squares estimates of the equation $Y = \alpha + \beta X + \epsilon$.

a. Is there a statistically significant relationship between price and sales?

b. According to the estimated equation, what will be the effect on sales of a $1 increase in price?

c. Is this estimated effect substantial?

•• **14.35** (*continuation*) Use this estimated equation to find the price that maximizes profits (revenue less costs). The revenue equals the price multiplied by sales. Assume that the cost is $2 per game, so that the total cost is $2 multiplied by sales.

14.36 You are considering two risky investments, each with a .5 probability of a 100 percent gain and a .5 probability of a 50 percent loss. If you put half of your wealth in each investment, what are the possible overall returns (and associated probabilities) if the two outcomes are

a. independent?

b. perfectly positively correlated, so that the outcome of the second investment will be the same as the first?

c. perfectly negatively correlated, so that the outcome of the second investment will be the opposite of the first?

Which of these three scenarios seems the safest? Which seems the riskiest?

14.37   You are considering *n* investments, each with a .5 probability of a 100 percent gain and a .5 probability of a 50 percent loss. The returns are independent. If you divide your wealth equally among these *n* investments, what are the possible overall returns (and associated probabilities) if *n* is

a. 1?

b. 2?

c. 10?

Which of these three strategies is safest? Which is riskiest? Explain.

• **14.38**   You are the middleman between two eager gamblers. One wants to bet that some interesting event will happen, while the other wants to bet that it won't. The first will put up $1 against your $1. The second will put up $1.30 against your $0.70. If you have $10,000 available, how should you divide your wagers between these two gamblers to assure yourself a fixed profit, regardless of whether or not the event happens?

14.39   An agronomist has used ordinary least squares to estimate the effect of fertilizer dosage *X* on crop yield *Y*:

$$Y = 50.5 + 0.05 \, X$$
$$[1.7] \quad [2.5]$$

The *t*-values are in brackets. The fertilizer dosage data had a mean value of 210 gallons, with a standard deviation of 20 gallons.

a. Does fertilizer dosage have a statistically significant effect on crop yield?

b. What would be a 95 percent confidence interval for the estimate of the effect of fertilizer dosage on crop yield?

c. If we were to use this estimated equation to predict *Y* for different values of *X*, for which value of *X* would we be most confident about our predictions?

d. What is our predicted value of *Y* for *X* = 300? For *X* = 500? Is there any reason for extra caution about our forecasts of *Y* for *X* = 500?

14.40   Is there any reason why a stock's beta coefficient and expected return should be related? Calculate the average returns and estimated beta coefficients for the four stocks in Table 14.2 to see if there is any apparent relationship.

• **14.41**   Investment advisory services routinely adjust their estimated beta coefficients. For instance, a firm with an estimated β of 1.7 might be assigned a β of 1.5, while a firm with an estimated β of 0.3 might be given a β of 0.5. Can you think of any logical reason for this peculiar practice?

14.42   Baseball players who are batting close to .400 at the halfway point in the season almost always find that their batting average declines during the second half of the season. This slump has been blamed on such factors as fatigue, pressure, and too much media attention. Is there any possible statistical explanation? In view of these data, if you were a major league manager, would you take a .400 hitter out of the lineup in order to play someone who was batting only .250 at the halfway point?

14.43   The National Football League (NFL) reported that most teams that won more than half their games in 1972 did not do as well in 1973 as they had done in 1972. Conversely, most teams that lost more than half of their games in 1972 did better in 1973 than they had done in 1972.[13] The NFL claims that these data show that teams are balanced by the college player draft, in which the teams with the poorest records choose first. What alternative interpretation is provided by statistical theory?

14.44   In the first 17 Super Bowls (through 1983), only 4 teams repeated as champs. Sid Gillman attributes this falling off to human psychology:

> In this game, you are dealing with the human mind and nothing else.
>
> You know, it's a study for psychologists, what winning Super Bowls does to people. Coaches who win it say they'll keep things the same the following season, but they never do. Players don't either. Everything becomes deaccelerated. Humans just cannot deal with prosperity.[14]

Even if people could deal with prosperity, why might we expect most Super Bowl champions not to be repeat winners?

14.45   Albert Ando and Franco Modigliani collected the following data on the income and consumption of non-self-employed homeowners:[15]

income bracket ($)	average income ($)	average consumption ($)
0–999	556	2,760
1,000–1,999	1,622	1,930
2,000–2,999	2,664	2,740
3,000–3,999	3,587	3,515
4,000–4,999	4,535	4,350
5,000–5,999	5,538	5,320
6,000–7,499	6,585	6,250
7,500–9,999	8,582	7,460
10,000–above	14,033	11,500

Use least squares to estimate the equation $Y = \alpha + \beta X + \epsilon$, where Y is consumption and X is income. What is the estimated effect on consumption of $1000 higher income?

14.46   (*continuation*) Ando and Modigliani were concerned about the regression-toward-the-mean phenomenon. People with unusually high income in these data were more likely to have had atypically good years than bad years. Their observed income is consequently an overestimate of the "typical" income on which their consumption is based. In the same way, those with very low incomes are more likely to have had a bad year than a good year. Because their observed income understates the "typical" income on which their spending is based, they will seem to be spending a very high fraction of their income (indeed, more than 100 percent!).

Ando and Modigliani regrouped these families by the values of their homes, reasoning that the homes people buy are related to their typical incomes, rather than income in any particular year.

home value ($)	average income ($)	average consumption ($)
7,500–9,999	4,649	4,600
10,000–12,499	5,191	5,140
12,500–14,999	5,729	5,610
15,000–17,499	5,948	5,949
17,500–19,999	7,547	7,170
20,000–24,999	9,607	9,500
25,000–above	11,267	11,100

Because there is no reason to expect the people in any particular home-value bracket to have had either atypically good or bad years, average income should be a good estimate of typical income, which is what influences consumption.

Use these consumption and income data to estimate $Y = \alpha + \beta X + \epsilon$. Compare these estimates with those obtained in the previous exercise. Is there evidence of regression toward the mean?

14.47   A study of U.S. males ages 21 to 54 found a positive correlation between income and blood pressure, a positive correlation between income and age, and a positive correlation between blood pressure and age. What do you think is causing what here?

14.48   A doctor notices that more than half of the young patients are male, while more than half of the older patients are female. Does this indicate that elderly females are less healthy than elderly males?

14.49   Let Y be the first 8 numbers in the second column of Table 3 at the end of the book, and let X be the 24th through 31st numbers in the seventh column. Run a regression to see if there is a statistically significant relationship between Y and X. If so, does this statistical significance convince you that the numbers in Table 3 aren't really random as advertised?

14.50   To investigate the correlation between two unrelated variables that are both growing over time, use 20 coin flips to generate 10 observations of Y and X:

$$Y = 2t + \epsilon_1 \qquad X = 2t + \epsilon_2$$

where $t = 1, 2, \ldots, 10$ and the ϵs are equal to $+1$ if heads and -1 if tails.

a. Carefully record the data you construct.
b. Plot these data with X and Y on the vertical axis and t on the horizontal axis.
c. Use least squares to estimate $Y = \alpha + \beta X + \epsilon$.
d. Is there a statistically significant relationship between Y and X?

CHAPTER 15

Multiple Regression

The mouse is an animal which, killed in sufficient numbers under carefully controlled conditions, will produce a Ph.D. thesis.

Anonymous

TOPICS

In the natural sciences, researchers can often conduct controlled laboratory experiments to isolate the effects of one variable on another. For instance, an agronomist may be interested in the effects of nitrogen on the growth of a certain plant. This agronomist believes that the plant's growth depends on how much light, water, and nutrients (such as nitrogen, phosphorus, potassium, and boron) it receives. To isolate the effects of nitrogen on plant growth, the researcher can conduct a controlled experiment involving 50 similar plants, and try to give each plant the same amounts of light, water, and important nutrients (other than nitrogen), in order to control for these effects on plant growth. The 50 plants will be given different amounts of nitrogen and their growth will be recorded. Because the other important growth factors have been held constant, the researcher can attribute the observed variations in plant growth to the differing applications of nitrogen.

There will, of course, still be some inevitable chance variation in observed plant growth, because (a) not all plants are created equal; (b) there are errors in measuring growth; (c) the applications of light, water, and non-nitrogen nutrients cannot be precisely identical for each plant; and (d) there are always other growth influences over which the researcher had no control. However, if the most important influences have been identified and the controls imposed carefully, then the experiment should yield useful data for estimating the equation

$$Y = \alpha + \beta X + \epsilon$$

where Y is a measure of plant growth, X is the amount of nitrogen applied, and ϵ allows for the slight imperfections in the experiment.

In the social sciences, researchers can seldom set up these sorts of controlled laboratory experiments. Instead, they must make do with "nature's experiments"—and try to unravel the effects of one variable on another in a world in which many variables are changing at the same time. Did X_1 cause Y to go up, or was it caused by X_2 or maybe X_3? There are always lots of other Xs.

For instance, economists think that consumer spending depends both on household income and the value of household wealth. Normally, household wealth changes very little and thus has little effect on consumer spending. Therefore, little harm is done by relegating wealth to the error term and only taking into account the effect of income on consumer spending. However, there are other occasions when wealth changes dramatically due to stock market booms and busts, and economists suspect that consumer spending may be affected substantially during these occasions. The stock market crash in the 1930s has long been given some of the blame for the Great Depression. Although not as catastrophic, there have been wild swings in the stock market in recent years, too. In 1980, for instance, the market value of stocks went up by $300 billion and this stimulus may have helped fuel consumer spending.

How can we estimate the effect of stock prices on consumer spending? When both income and stock prices collapsed in the 1930s, how much of the drop in consumer spending was due to the decline in income and how much was due to the decline in stock prices? If economists could follow the example of the agronomist's controlled experiments, they would hold the nation's income constant while varying stock prices to see how much consumer spending was affected. But economists can't use the economy as their laboratory! They can't satisfy their intellectual curiosity by freezing everybody's income and manipulating the stock market.*

Instead, they have to make do with analyzing whatever data nature provides, and what they have come up with is a multiple regression procedure.

> In **multiple regression,** an equation with several explanatory variables is estimated, in an attempt to isolate the separate effect of each on the dependent variable.

15.1   THE LOGIC AND A FEW DETAILS

In general, a multiple regression equation can be written as

$$Y = \alpha + \beta_1 X_1 + \beta_2 X_2 + \cdots + \beta_k X_k + \epsilon \qquad (15.1)$$

This model says that the dependent variable Y depends on k explanatory variables, plus an error term that encompasses various unspecified omitted factors. It doesn't matter in what order the explanatory variables are listed. What does matter is which k variables the researcher chooses to identify and which are left unspecified in the error term. Because there are, in principle, virtually an unlimited number of possible explanatory variables, the art of regression analysis is choosing those with important effects and ignoring those with negligible effects.

The parameter β_1 gauges the effect of the first explanatory variable X_1 on the dependent variable Y, *holding the other explanatory variables constant.* Similarly, β_2 gives the effect of X_2 on Y, holding the remaining explanatory variables constant. These parameters measure the same thing that controlled laboratory experiments seek, which is the effect on Y of an isolated change in one explanatory variable. But while a controlled experiment can estimate a parameter β_i by actually holding the other variables constant, a multiple regression procedure estimates β_i by taking into account how uncontrolled changes in the other variables influence Y.

The mechanics for computing multiple regression estimates are quite complicated. They are best done with matrix algebra, and a thorough understanding requires at least one entire course advertised as *regression analysis, econometrics,* or some similar label. However, the logic is actually quite simple, because multiple regression is a straightforward extension of the least-squares estimation of an equation with just one explanatory variable. Because researchers invariably use computers to calculate their estimates, I will explain the logic and show you some computer results, without getting us bogged down in computational details.

---

*And even if they did, the results would be artificial, because people's behavior would be influenced by their knowledge of this temporary economic manipulation. For instance, they would rush to sell if they knew that an increase in a stock's price was part of an experiment, and therefore unrelated to its actual value.

Equation 15.1 is our model of how Y is determined. We want to obtain parameter estimates a, b_1, b_2, . . . , b_k, in order to make accurate predictions $\hat{Y}$, for selected values of the explanatory variables:

$$\hat{Y} = a + b_1X_1 + b_2X_2 + \cdots + b_kX_k \tag{15.2}$$

The least squares criterion says that we should compute parameter estimates a, b_1, b_2, . . . , b_k so as to minimize the sum of squared prediction errors for the data we have. This can be done, although the actual calculations are usually left to a computer.

The standard error of estimate (SEE) is an estimate of the standard deviation of ϵ:

$$\text{SEE} = \frac{\Sigma(Y_i - \hat{Y}_i)^2}{n - (k + 1)}$$

Because we are using n observations to estimate $k + 1$ parameters, we divide by $n - (k + 1)$, the degrees of freedom. R-squared gauges predictive accuracy by comparing the model's errors to the errors of a benchmark model in which all of the β_i are set equal to zero and the sample mean alone is used to predict Y.

$$R^2 = 1 - \frac{\Sigma(Y_i - \hat{Y}_i)^2}{\Sigma(Y_i - \overline{Y}_i)^2}$$

The adjusted (for degrees of freedom) R-squared is

$$R^2 = 1 - \frac{\Sigma(Y_i - \hat{Y}_i)^2/(n - k - 1)}{\Sigma(Y_i - \overline{Y}_i)^2/(n - 1)}$$

We can also compute a standard deviation s_{b_i} for each estimate b_i (and for the intercept too, although this is usually the least interesting parameter). The actual formulas are complicated, and again it is best to let a computer do the work. Once a computer has done its job and revealed the estimated standard deviations, we can easily calculate a "plus or minus two standard deviations" 95 percent confidence interval for any parameter:

$$\beta_i = b_i \pm 2s_{b_i}$$

that is,

$$b_i - 2s_{b_i} < \beta_i < b_i + 2s_{b_i}$$

Hypothesis tests can be conducted directly, or they can be done implicitly by seeing whether or not the hypothesized value is inside the confidence interval. For the particular hypothesis

$$H_0: \beta_i = 0$$

we can see whether the t-statistic

$$t_{b_i} = |b_i|/s_{b_i}$$

is greater than or less than 2. (This is, of course, still just a rule of thumb; the exact cutoff, using Appendix Table 5 with $n - (k + 1)$ degrees of freedom, will be either a bit larger or smaller than 2.0.)

An Expanded Consumption Function

To illustrate the multiple regression procedure, let's include both income and wealth as explanatory variables in our consumption function. The expanded equation is

$$Y = \alpha + \beta_1 X_1 + \beta_2 X_2 + \epsilon$$

where

$$Y = \text{real per capita consumption}$$

$$X_1 = \text{real per capita disposable income}$$

$$X_2 = \text{real per capita value of corporate stocks}$$

I entered annual data for 1977 through 1981 for consumption, income, and wealth into a multiple regression computer program. The results are shown in Figure 15.1. These results could be reported either as

$$\hat{Y} = -176 + 0.935 \ X_1 + 0.047 \ X_2, \quad \text{SEE} = 7.935, \quad R^2 = .993$$
$$\quad\quad (190) \quad (0.057) \quad\quad (0.024)$$

( ): std. deviations

or as

$$\hat{Y} = -176 + 0.935 \ X_1 + 0.047 \ X_2, \quad \text{SEE} = 7.935, \quad R^2 = .993$$
$$\quad\quad [0.9] \quad [16.5] \quad\quad [1.9]$$

[ ]: t-values

Notice first that the inclusion of wealth in the consumption function does not substantially alter the estimated coefficient for income. In the simple regression reported in Table 13.1, with only income as an explanatory variable, we estimated that a \$1 rise in income raises spending by $0.947 \pm 2(0.078)$. Our multiple-regression estimate is that, holding wealth constant, a \$1 rise in income increases spending by $0.935 \pm 2(0.057)$. Our estimate is little affected by taking into account the possible effects of wealth on spending.

It might have been the case that consumption depends only on wealth, but that income and wealth tend to go up and down together. If so, then a simple regression of consumption on income would indicate that extra income increases spending when, in fact, it is the concurrent rise in wealth that increases spending. This is apparently not the case. Even when we allow for the influence of wealth on spending, we still find that \$1 of additional income raises spending by close to \$1.

The second thing to notice is that wealth, too, has a separate influence on spending. Even when we hold income constant, a \$1 increase in stock prices tends

```
                    MULTIPLE REGRESSION

          HOW MANY EXPLANATORY VARIABLES?: 2

          WHAT ARE THE NAMES OF YOUR
          VARIABLES? (8 LETTERS MAX.)

          DEPENDENT VARIABLE: CONS
          EXPLAN. VAR. 1: INCOME
          EXPLAN. VAR. 2: WEALTH

          HOW MANY OBSERVATIONS
          OF EACH VARIABLE?: 5

          ENTER YOUR DATA

          OBSERVATION 1
                         INCOME: 3319
                         WEALTH: 2481
                         CONS: 3042
          OBSERVATION 2
                         INCOME: 3421
                         WEALTH: 2229
                         CONS: 3124
          OBSERVATION 3
                         INCOME: 3404
                         WEALTH: 2125
                         CONS: 3108
          OBSERVATION 4
                         INCOME: 3276
                         WEALTH: 2133
                         CONS: 2994
          OBSERVATION 5
                         INCOME: 3271
                         WEALTH: 2064
                         CONS: 2971


          VARIABLE   ESTIMATE   STD DEV   T-STAT
          INTERCEPT  -176.086   190.288   -.925
          INCOME       .935       .057    16.521
          WEALTH       .047       .024     1.936

          STANDARD ERROR OF ESTIMATE = 7.93509308

          COEFFICIENT OF DETERMINATION
          IS R-SQUARED = .993102228
```

Figure 15.1 *A multiple regression of consumption on income and wealth*

to raise spending by about 5 cents. A \$1 drop in stock prices tends to reduce spending by about 5 cents. Five cents may not seem like much, but the stock market is so volatile that these nickels can add up. A \$100 billion swing in stock prices is not at all unusual, and at 5 cents to the dollar, a \$100 billion swing in stock prices means a \$5 billion change in consumer spending—which can be the difference between prosperity and recession. Notice, though, that our estimate of the effect of wealth on spending is not quite statistically significant. Our two-standard-deviations rule of thumb is $0.047 \pm 2(0.024)$, i.e., between -0.001 and 0.095. We cannot quite rule out zero as the true value, nor can we rule out the possibility that the effect may be almost 10 cents of additional spending for every \$1 of extra wealth.

Third, compare the standard error of estimate and R-squared for our multiple regression with those for our simple regression. The sum of squared prediction errors is always reduced by the inclusion of additional explanatory variables. Consider the equation

$$Y = \alpha + \beta_1 X_1 + \beta_2 X_2 + \epsilon$$

The least squares procedure selects those parameter estimates that minimize the sum of squared prediction errors. A simple regression with X_2 omitted assumes that β_2 is zero. A multiple regression, with X_2 included, can use a zero estimate for β_2 if that minimizes the sum of squared prediction errors and can use a nonzero estimate if that does even better. Thus, a simple regression can never have a smaller sum of squared prediction errors than a corresponding multiple regression. By the same reasoning, a simple regression can never have a higher R-squared than a corresponding multiple regression. The Standard Error of Estimate (SEE) and adjusted R-squared are a bit different because both take into account the degrees of freedom, and every extra parameter that is estimated uses up a degree of freedom. Thus, a simple regression can have a smaller SEE and a larger adjusted R-squared than a corresponding multiple regression, if the increase in the sum of the squared prediction errors is smaller than the accompanying increase in degrees of freedom.

In our consumption function example, it turns out that the multiple regression reduces the SEE (from 10.98 to 7.94) and increases the R-squared (from .980 to .993). The 30 percent reduction in the SEE does seem substantial. The R-squared increase is small, because we are already so close to 1.0. We can also ask whether these improvements are statistically significant: Is the improvement in predictive accuracy sufficiently impressive to convince us that wealth belongs in the consumption function? If we rephrase the question slightly, the answer is immediately apparent. We want to know if the improvement in predictive accuracy is sufficient to warrant the rejection of the null hypothesis that wealth has no effect on consumption,

$$H_0:\ \beta_2 = 0$$

Our t-statistic for b_2 answers this question! Here, it turns out that the t-statistic is 1.939, which is not high enough to show convincingly that wealth does indeed belong in the consumption function. The decrease in the sum of squared prediction errors and corresponding increase in R-squared are not quite large enough to rule out chance as the explanation.

Is History Math or English?

Exercise 14.4 examined the relationship between grades in a freshman history course (Y) and math (X_1) and verbal (X_2) SAT scores. Simple regression yielded these results:

$$\hat{Y} = 29.3 + 0.08\ X_1, \qquad R^2 = .34$$
$$\qquad\quad [1.8] \quad\ \ [3.1]$$

$$\hat{Y} = 14.1 + 0.11\ X_2, \qquad R^2 = .85$$
$$\qquad\quad [2.2] \quad\ [10.2]$$

[ ]: t-values

History grades seem to be positively related to math scores and verbal scores. These statistical relationships are substantial and statistically significant—a 100-point advantage on the math SAT test is worth 8 (± 5) extra points on the history test, while 100 points on the verbal SAT test is worth 11 (± 2) history points.

However, if we now run a multiple regression, using both math and verbal scores to predict history performance, we get

$$\hat{Y} = 16.5 - 0.01\ X_1 + 0.11\ X_2, \qquad R^2 = .85$$
$$\quad\ [2.1] \quad\ [0.5] \qquad [7.8]$$

Now the estimated effect of math scores on history scores is negative and not statistically significant! What's going on here?

This example illustrates the difference between simple and multiple regression, and the need for care in interpreting their parameters. The multiple regression coefficients measure the effect on Y of an increase in the associated explanatory variable, *holding the other explanatory variables constant*. Thus, the coefficient of math scores asks, if Moe and Joe both have 570 verbal SATs, but Moe has a 740 math SAT and Joe only a 520, should we expect Moe to get the higher grades in history courses? The answer, according to these data, is "No." Similarly, the coefficient of the verbal SAT scores asks, if two students have the same math score, should the one with the higher verbal score be expected to do better in history courses? This answer is "Yes."

The simple regression equations ask somewhat different questions: If all we know about two students is that one had the higher verbal SAT score, would we predict a difference in history scores? If all we know is that one had the higher math SAT score, would we predict a difference in history scores? The answer to both of these questions is "Yes," because verbal and math SAT scores are positively related and verbal scores are apparently a good predictor of success in history courses. That is, students with high math SAT scores tend to do well in history classes, not because of their math skills, but because they also tend to have high verbal SAT scores and these do matter.

The apparent relationship between math and history scores is an example of a spurious correlation, in that one variable (history scores) seems to be related to another (math scores) but is, in fact, related to a third (verbal scores), which happens to be correlated with the second. One of the great appeals of multiple regression analysis is that it can sort out these interrelationships.

Exercises

15.1 An academic economist believes that consumer spending depends not only on income (positively) but also on interest rates (negatively). Having only read Chapters 13 and 14, he regresses consumption on interest rates and forgets about income. Are there any perils to this procedure?

15.2 (*continuation*) As it turns out, he obtains a positive slope estimate—high interest rates apparently encourage spending. Is there any possible statistical explanation of this result that is consistent with his theory?

15.3 (*continuation*) His sister, who is a chemist, proposes a controlled experiment in which incomes are held constant while interest rates are varied: "In this way, you will be able to see the effects of interest rate changes alone on spending." Why might the economist resist this sisterly advice?

15.4 A government economist has estimated the following consumption function

$$\hat{Y} = -25.0 + 0.90 \ X_1 - 2.5 \ X_2, \qquad R^2 = .98$$
$$\quad [0.8] \quad [9.0] \quad\quad [1.5]$$

[ ]: *t*-values

where

$$Y = \text{consumption (\$ billions), average 2200}$$

$$X_1 = \text{income (\$ billions), average 2500}$$

$$X_2 = \text{interest rate (percent), average 10}$$

What is the predicted value of consumption if

a. income is 2500 and the interest rate is 10?
b. income is 2600 and the interest rate is 10?
c. income is 2500 and the interest rate is 11?
d. income is 2600 and the interest rate is 11?

15.5 (*continuation*) In this estimated consumption function, explain what each of these numbers measures:

a. 0.90
b. −2.5
c. −25.0
d. 9.0
e. 0.98

15.6 (*continuation*) Economists have long debated whether a higher interest rate encourages consumption, discourages consumption, or has no effect at all. Does this estimated equation settle that debate?

15.7 (*continuation*) What does *R*-squared tell us about this estimated equation? Would the *R*-squared be significantly affected if we omitted the interest rate and just regressed consumer spending on income?

15.8 Data collected by a county agricultural agency led to the following multiple regression:

$$Y = -120 + 0.10\,X_1 + 5.33\,X_2, \qquad R^2 = .50$$
$$ [13.4] \quad [5.1] \qquad [3.7]$$

[ ]: *t*-values

where

$$Y = \text{corn yield (bushels/acre), average value } 30$$

$$X_1 = \text{fertilizer (pounds/acre), average value } 100$$

$$X_2 = \text{rainfall (inches), average value } 30$$

a. What does the coefficient of X_1 measure? If the population value of this parameter really is 0.10, what is the implication (in simple English)?

b. What does the coefficient of X_2 measure? If the population value really is 5.33, what is the implication?

c. What does the estimate -120 measure? If this is the correct population value, should we conclude that Y will equal -120 if there is no rainfall or fertilizer?

15.9 (*continuation*) The *Farmer's Almanac* predicts 2 inches less rain this year than usual. If the previous estimates are the correct population values, then how much additional fertilizer must farmers apply if they want to offset this rain shortfall?

15.10 (*continuation*) Corn is expected to sell for $2 per bushel, and an extra pound of fertilizer costs $0.25. If the previous estimates are correct, should farmers apply more fertilizer?

15.11 (*continuation*) Can we be certain that the true value of the fertilizer coefficient is positive? It is so small; might it just as well be negative? And, doesn't excessive fertilizer damage crops anyway?

15.2 SEVERAL APPLICATIONS

To see multiple regression in action, we'll now look at a variety of applications. In each case, we are trying to explain some phenomena, but a simple regression model with one explanatory variable just won't do. We have good reason to suspect that there are several important influences, and relegating some to the error term leaves the model impotent. Instead, we will use a multiple regression with multiple explanatory variables.

The Effect of Auto Speeds on Fuel Consumption

Since the 1970s, we have been very concerned about energy. The enormous U.S. consumption of fuel is expensive and makes us dependent on uncertain foreign oil supplies. A primary component of this fuel consumption is our 150 million motor vehicles—cars, trucks, buses, and motorcycles. Each year, these vehicles use about 800 gallons of fuel apiece, more than 100 billion gallons of fuel in all. The amount of fuel consumed by our vehicles depends on how much we travel, how much horsepower our vehicles have, and how fast we drive.

Some data are shown in Table 15.1. The speed data are based on a government sample of several hundred thousand cars traveling on rural interstate highways during offpeak hours. You can see how travel, horsepower, and speed all declined during the 1973–1974 oil embargo. So did fuel consumption. In the late 1970s, speed and travel both crept back up, while horsepower kept falling. Fuel consumption went up, too. Then in 1979–1980, oil prices were jacked up again, and travel and speed fell once more.

It would be interesting to untangle these separate influences and see how much fuel consumption depends on travel, horsepower, and speed. For example, has the general reduction in speed had a substantial impact on our national fuel consumption? If we just looked at speed and fuel consumption, there would seem to be a direct positive relationship: fuel consumption has gone down as average speed has declined. But that conclusion is premature, because we haven't held the other important factors constant. The decline in fuel usage may actually be due to reduced travel and horsepower. A multiple regression can provide the answer by taking all three influences into account.

The U.S. government does conduct controlled laboratory experiments, running cars on treadmills and the like, but these are not the same as actual highway driving conditions—mistuned cars driven by amateurs in foul weather on imperfect roads. Thus, the government's estimates are accompanied by the disclaimer, "Actual mileage may vary and will probably be lower." The governments in Sweden and Denmark, in contrast, have conducted experiments right on their highways to see

Table 15.1 *Some data on U.S. motor vehicle fuel consumption*

Year	Fuel used per vehicle (gallons) Y	Travel per vehicle (miles) X_1	Horsepower per vehicle X_2	Average speed (MPH) X_3
1970	851.5	10,341	178.3	63.8
1971	863.4	10,496	183.5	64.7
1972	884.7	10,673	183.0	64.9
1973	879.1	10,414	183.2	65.0
1974	818.3	9,900	178.8	57.6
1975	820.2	10,008	178.7	57.6
1976	835.4	10,195	175.7	58.2
1977	839.9	10,372	175.7	58.8
1978	843.0	10,431	174.5	58.8
1979	804.3	10,072	175.3	58.3
1980	738.1	9,763	175.6	57.5

the effects of speed limits on traffic accidents. A variety of speed limits were set for extended periods of time over long stretches of road representing a variety of driving conditions. The results were mixed, indicating that lower speed limits reduced traffic accidents in Sweden, but were less effective in Denmark![1]

The U.S. government has not been as ambitious, but a multiple regression may be able to untangle what U.S. data are available. A least squares regression using the data shown in Table 15.1 gives these results:

$$\hat{Y} = -1201.1 + 0.132\ X_1 + 5.07\ X_2 - 3.57\ X_3, \qquad R^2 = .86$$
$$\quad\ [2.28] \qquad [3.83] \qquad [1.62] \qquad [0.81]$$

[ ]: t-values

The first explanatory variable, miles traveled, has a substantial and statistically significant effect on fuel usage. When, as a nation, we travel an average of one extra mile per vehicle, we use up about an extra 0.132 gallons of gasoline per vehicle. This works out to about 8 extra miles per additional gallon of gasoline. (You probably get better mileage than this, but remember that we're including trucks and buses, which get very few miles per gallon. Remember, too, that the estimate has a standard deviation of 0.035, which gives a 95 percent confidence interval 0.132 ± 0.07 and a corresponding miles per gallon range of 4.95 to 16.13.)

The second explanatory variable, horsepower, is also substantial, but not statistically significant. According to this estimate, the national reduction of average horsepower by almost 10 per vehicle during the 1970s saved about 50 gallons of fuel per vehicle. However, we must be cautious about this estimate, because it has a standard deviation of 3 (that's where the $5/3 = 1.6$ t-value comes from). Our 95 percent confidence interval is 5 ± 6, and we can't rule out the possibility that the true value is zero. Of course, it almost might be as high as 11!

The third explanatory variable, speed, gives the least satisfying result. The estimate is small, has the "wrong" sign, and is statistically insignificant. The United States reduced its speed limits in the 1970s, believing that this would reduce fuel consumption substantially, but our regression provides little empirical support for this hope. The estimated effect of a 1 MPH increase in speed is a 3.6 gallons per vehicle *decrease* in fuel consumption, with a standard deviation of 4.4 gallons. So, our 95 percent confidence interval of $-3.6 \pm 2(4.4)$ ranges from -12.4 to $+5.2$. Over the 1970s, the average vehicle speed has fallen by about 7 MPH. Our estimate implies that this has reduced fuel consumption per vehicle by, at best, 35 gallons, and at worst, has actually increased fuel consumption by as much as 87 gallons per vehicle.

Another Attempt to Predict Final Exam Scores

In Chapter 14, we saw that midterm scores are not a completely successful predictor of final exam scores. Perhaps the predictions can be improved by a multiple regression that uses other information in addition to the midterm grades. In some of my courses, students are graded on the basis of their weekly homework as well as their midterm and final exams. Table 15.2 shows these data for a randomly selected course. A regression of the final exam score Y on the midterm score X_1 yields

$$\hat{Y} = 13.4 + 0.80\ X_1, \quad \text{SEE} = 6.77, \quad R^2 = .25$$
$$\quad\quad [0.6] \quad [3.0]$$

[ ]: t-values

If we try using homework grades X_2 to predict the final exam scores, the results are

$$\hat{Y} = 39.6 + 0.49\ X_2, \quad \text{SEE} = 6.42, \quad R^2 = .33$$
$$\quad\quad [3.4] \quad [3.6]$$

[ ]: t-values

Table 15.2   *Midterm, homework, and final exam scores*

Student initials	Midterm X_1	Homework X_2	Final exam Y
LC	82	94	77
CC	94	96	90
JC	80	84	70
MC	78	94	94
DD	83	84	87
MG	86	88	69
BH	81	92	77
PH	88	84	82
LK	86	76	75
DL	81	72	72
BM	80	68	62
LM	97	86	88
PM	90	90	86
LO	88	80	88
JP	89	86	83
MR	79	78	77
NR	83	84	84
AS	90	96	83
FS	91	94	86
SS	88	92	83
AT	80	78	81
BT	86	88	90
NT	83	96	77
HV	84	82	87
JV	86	96	87
RW	80	66	73
SW	83	68	73
VW	93	88	90
WW	86	94	87

Table 15.3   *Final exam scores are not predicted perfectly from midterm and homework scores*

Name	Final score	Predicted score	Prediction error
LC	77	82.9	−5.9
CC	90	89.7	.3
JC	70	78.1	−8.1
MC	94	80.9	13.1
DD	87	79.6	7.4
MG	69	82.7	−13.7
BH	77	81.6	−4.6
PH	82	82.2	−.2
LK	75	78.1	−3.1
DL	72	74.1	−2.1
BM	62	72.1	−10.1
LM	88	87.5	.5
PM	86	85.4	.6
LO	88	80.7	7.3
JP	83	83.4	−.4
MR	77	75.3	1.7
NR	84	79.6	4.4
AS	83	87.7	−4.7
FS	86	87.5	−1.5
SS	83	85.2	−2.2
AT	81	75.8	5.2
BT	90	82.7	7.3
NT	77	84.1	−7.1
HV	87	79.4	7.6
JV	87	85.7	1.3
RW	73	71.3	1.7
SW	73	73.6	−.6
VW	90	86.2	3.8
WW	87	84.9	2.1

As measured by the standard error of estimate and *R*-squared, homework grades are somewhat more useful than midterm grades in predicting final exam scores. I was frankly surprised by this result. The midterm and final exam have very similar formats, a number of analytical questions answered under considerable time pressure, while the weekly homework, in contrast, has no time constraints and no rules against student collaboration. *A priori,* I expected the final exam scores to be more similar to the midterm scores. Apparently I was wrong. Perhaps the homework grades reflect diligent, conscientious effort, which pays off by the end of the term.

What if we use both midterm and homework scores to predict final exam grades? We can do this with a multiple regression:

$$\hat{Y} = 5.80 + 0.51\, X_1 + 0.38\, X_2, \quad SEE = 6.1, \quad R^2 = .42$$
$$[0.3] \quad [2.0] \qquad [2.7]$$

[ ]: t-values

The t-values indicate that midterm and homework scores are both useful in predicting final exam scores. The inclusion of a second explanatory variable causes a statistically significant drop in the standard error of estimate (and corresponding increase in R-squared).

The relationship is still far from perfect. Table 15.3 compares the final exam scores with those predicted by the estimated equation. In one-third of the cases, the actual score differs from the prediction by more than 5 points. The two largest surprises are MC, who did 13.1 points better than predicted, and MG, who did 13.7 points worse than predicted. Apparently the final exam is a necessary evil, in that it contains information that is not obtainable from the midterm and homework scores.

Can College Success Be Predicted from SAT Scores?

Colleges use a variety of criteria in deciding which applicants to accept for admission—including high school grades, SAT or ACT test scores, and letters of recommendation. Their primary objective is to identify those who are most likely to be successful college students. A college that routinely admits students who do poorly or drop out is not doing itself or the students any favors.

Many colleges have tried to estimate formal regression models using admissions criteria to predict college success. The first thing needed for such an endeavor is some measure of college success. College Grade Point Average (GPA) is a natural yardstick. We must be careful, though, in that courses are not all equally difficult. It may be harder to get an A in nuclear physics than in physical education, and harder to get an A in nonlinear differential equations than in introductory statistics. Because freshmen usually take very similar courses, we can reduce the differences between departments and between advanced and beginning courses by using the freshman-year GPA to gauge whether or not the admitted student is succeeding in college.

For explanatory variables, the obvious choices are those very factors that admissions committees look at. It may be a bit of work, though, to quantify some factors. For example, committee members must read carefully (and often between the lines) in deciding whether a letter of recommendation is "enthusiastic," "strong," "lukewarm," or "negative." Committee members also commonly "adjust" high school GPAs to take into account whether or not the applicant took challenging courses at a demanding high school.

Once data have been assembled on college success and admissions criteria, then a multiple regression equation can be used to see whether or not useful predictions can be made. Some colleges do this on their own. Others use the data analysis provided by the College Entrance Examination Board, which administers the SAT tests. To illustrate the procedure, I've obtained the actual regression equation estimated for 359 freshmen who enrolled at a certain very selective liberal arts college in the fall of 1977. The data are:

$$Y = \text{freshman year GPA, average 3.0}$$

$$X_1 = \text{high school GPA, average 3.7}$$

$$X_2 = \text{verbal SAT score, average 591}$$

$$X_3 = \text{math SAT score, average 629}$$

The least squares estimates are

$$\hat{Y} = 0.437 + 0.361\ X_1 + 0.0014\ X_2 + 0.0007\ X_3, \qquad R^2 = .26$$
$$\quad\ [20.3]\quad\ [6.23]\qquad\ \ [5.50]\qquad\quad [2.64]$$

[ ]: t-values

Each of the three estimated coefficients of the admissions variables is positive, substantial, and statistically significant. A student with a 3.7 high school GPA and with 600 verbal and math SAT scores is predicted to have a 3.03 freshman GPA at this college. Were the high school GPA a point lower (2.7 instead of 3.7), the predicted college GPA would fall to 2.67, all other things being equal. A 100-point decline in the verbal SAT score reduces the predicted freshman GPA by 0.14. So does a 200-point drop in the math SAT. A student with a 3.0 high school GPA and 500 SAT scores has a 2.46 predicted freshman GPA at this college.

This college has used its regression equation in a variety of ways. In some years, it calculates a predicted freshman GPA for each applicant and then admits some applicants solely on the basis of their high predicted GPAs. The remaining admissions are based not only on predicted GPA, but also on other criteria that are more difficult to quantify, such as letters of recommendation and special talents. In some years, this college does not formally calculate a predicted GPA, but it adds together the math SAT score plus twice the verbal SAT score and uses this together with other, more subjective criteria to select students. The math-plus-twice-verbal rule of thumb is based on the relative weights in the estimated regression equation.

How accurate are these predictions? One measure is provided by a 95 percent confidence-interval calculation. Here it turns out that, for the average student, the predicted freshman GPA is 3.0 ± 0.8—about what one might expect. Admissions committees have a rough idea about how well a student will do, but there are always some surprises. Figure 15.2 makes this observation a little more concrete. Of these 359 freshmen, 198 had predicted freshman GPAs in the range 3.0 to 3.33. Figure 15.2 shows that some of these students did very well and some did poorly, but most did as well as expected.

Another way to examine the accuracy of this prediction equation is to compare the performance of students with different predicted GPAs. In this freshman class, 21 students had predicted first-year GPAs in the range 3.33 to 3.67, while another

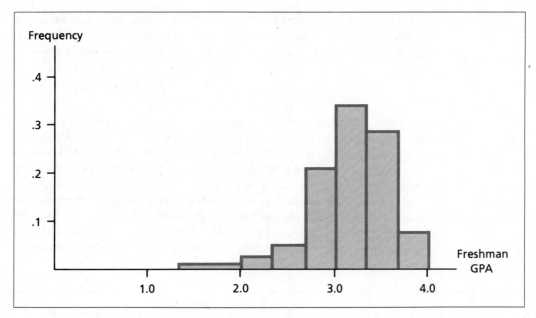

Figure 15.2   *Distribution of freshman grades for 198 students predicted to get between 3.00 and 3.33 GPA*

29 students were between 2.33 and 2.67. Table 15.4 shows that some students in the second group did better than some students in the first group, but that, again, most students in the first group did better than most in the second group. The average freshman GPA was 3.4 for those in the first group and 2.5 for those in the second group. Six students from the first group got 3.67–4.0; no one in the second group did this well. Three students from the second group got 1.33–1.67; no one in the first group did this poorly.

Table 15.4   *The college performance of two groups predicted to do differently*

Freshman grade	21 Students with predicted GPA 3.33–3.67	29 Students with predicted GPA 2.33–2.67
3.67–4.00	6	
3.33–3.67	6	1
3.00–3.67	5	2
2.67–3.00	3	6
2.33–2.67		10
2.00–2.33	1	7
1.67–2.00		
1.33–1.67		3

This GPA prediction equation is not perfect, but it does have some value, and that's why this college, like many others, uses a multiple-regression equation as part of its admissions process. So do many business schools and law schools.

Using the Stock Market to Predict Unemployment

The National Bureau of Economic Research uses the stock market as one of its leading indicators of the course of the economy. Stock prices often go down a few months before an economic recession begins, and then rise a few months before a recession ends. The stock market collapse in late 1929, shortly before the Great Depression, is the most dramatic example. But Figure 15.3 shows that this pattern also holds in recent, if less severe, times. Between 1952 and 1981, there were six recessions, which are indicated by shaded bars in the figure. Each was preceded by a slump in stock prices and, in each case, stock prices turned back up before the end of the recession. A closer inspection of Figure 15.3 reveals that the record

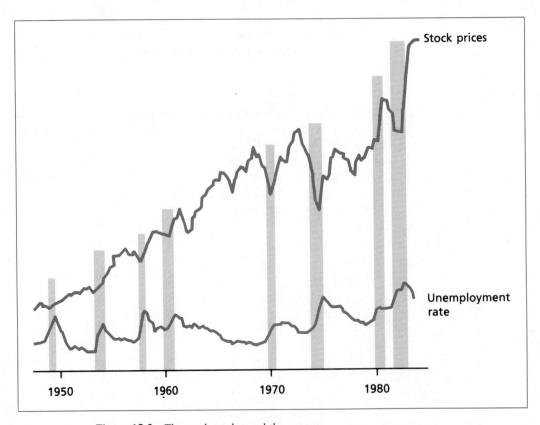

Figure 15.3   *The stock market and the economy*

is not perfect, in that stock prices sometimes go down without having a recession occur. To paraphrase Paul Samuelson, the stock market has predicted ten out of the last six recessions.

Still, there does seem to be a potentially useful empirical relationship between stock prices and the economy, and there are logical, if multiple, explanations of why this should be so. First, the stock market may influence the economy because wealth seems to affect spending. Second, the economy may influence stock prices— because profitable companies are more attractive than unprofitable ones—and stock prices may dip before a recession because farsighted security analysts can see the recession coming. Third, it may be that some other factor, such as the money supply, pushes stock prices and the economy in the same direction, but it affects stock prices more quickly than the economy.

We won't try to sort through these competing explanations here. Instead, let's just use regression analysis to see if we can find confirmation of the idea that stock prices are a useful predictor of the economy's health. Our model might be

$$Y = \alpha + \beta X + \epsilon$$

where X is the current level of stock prices and Y is the unemployment rate one quarter hence.

A least squares regression, using 120 quarterly observations for 1952 through 1981, yielded these results:

$$\hat{Y} = 4.02 + 0.018\,X, \qquad R^2 = .12$$
$$\quad [11.1] \quad\; [4.1]$$

[ ]: t-values

There does seem to be a statistically significant relationship between stock prices and the unemployment rate three months hence. But wait; it has the wrong sign! Our results say that an increase in stock prices presages an increase in the unemployment rate. Yet our intuition and a visual inspection of Figure 15.3 both say that unemployment goes up after a *slump* in stock prices. Where have we gone wrong?

When common sense and empirical results disagree, we should reexamine both to see where the error might lie. Here our common sense seems sound enough, and it is buttressed by an inspection of Figure 15.3. Yet the regression definitely says that there is a positive relationship between stock prices and the unemployment rate. The culprit here is that both sets of data have tended to increase over this 30-year period. Stock prices have risen over time as our economy has grown. The unemployment rate has also increased for a variety of reasons, including the gradual influx of more teenagers and women into the labor force—two demographic groups with relatively high unemployment rates. As I discussed at the end of Chapter 14, when two sets of data increase over time, there will often seem to be a positive relationship between them, even when there is really no relationship at all or even, as is the case here, a negative relationship.

One way to take into account this upward growth over time in both data sets is to include time itself as an explanatory variable.* We can run the multiple regression

$$Y = \alpha + \beta_1 X_1 + \beta_2 X_2 + \epsilon$$

where Y is the unemployment rate one quarter hence, X_1 is the current level of stock prices, and X_2 is a measure of the passage of time. I used the following values for X_2:

$$X_2 = 1 \text{ in the first quarter of 1952}$$
$$= 2 \text{ in the second quarter of 1952}$$
$$= 3 \text{ in the third quarter of 1952}$$
$$= 4 \text{ in the fourth quarter of 1952}$$
$$= 5 \text{ in the first quarter of 1953}$$

$$\cdot$$
$$\cdot$$
$$\cdot$$

$$= 120 \text{ in the fourth quarter of 1981}$$

This multiple regression yields the following results:

$$\hat{Y} = 5.663 - 0.052\ X_1 + 0.062\ X_2, \qquad R^2 = .46$$
$$\quad [16.3] \quad\ [5.76] \qquad\ \ [8.43]$$

[ ]: *t*-values

Now that's more like it. As anticipated, an increase in stock prices (X_1) signals a coming decline in the unemployment rate, while a decrease in stock prices presages an increase in the unemployment rate. This effect is not only very statistically significant; it is also substantial. The -0.052 estimate implies that a 10-point increase in stock prices (about 10 percent in 1980) signals a drop in the unemployment rate of about half a percentage point (from 8 percent to 7.5 percent). The estimated coefficient of X_2 (time) is positive and statistically significant. This estimate indicates that if the stock market does not change in any given quarter, then

---

*Our underlying model might be that deviations from trend values of stock prices presage deviations from trend in the unemployment rate,

$$Y - Y_T = \alpha_1 + \beta_1(X - X_T) + \epsilon$$

where the trend values are given by

$$Y_T = \alpha_2 + \gamma_2 t$$
$$X_T = \alpha_3 + \gamma_3 t$$

and t is a measure of time that increases by one each quarter. Substitution yields the equation estimated in the text.

the unemployment rate can be expected to increase by about 0.062 point. All in all, a multiple regression including time as an explanatory variable provides a worthwhile clarification of some initially puzzling results.

Another way of handling the problem of two variables that both grow over time is to run a regression using percentage rates of changes, instead of levels. Here we could regress

$$Y = \alpha + \beta X + \epsilon$$

with Y being the percentage change in the unemployment rate next quarter and X the percentage change in stock prices this quarter. The results are

$$\hat{Y} = 0.02 - 0.51\ X, \qquad R^2 = .11$$
$$[2.5] \qquad [3.7]$$

[ ]: t-values

These estimates are consistent with our multiple regression. A 10 percent increase in stock prices presages about a 5 percent decrease in the unemployment rate, say from 8 percent to 7.6 percent. This estimate is both substantial and statistically significant.

Which Statistics Matter to Investors?

The outcomes of most financial investments are uncertain. The return may turn out to be pleasingly high or painfully low, and we don't know beforehand which will be the case. We may, however, be able to quantify this uncertainty by specifying a rough probability distribution for the return. Such a specification could reflect a subjective assessment or it might be based on an historical investigation of past returns.

It is difficult to digest a complete probability distribution, but, earlier in this book, we looked at several summary measures, including the mean, variance, and skewness coefficient. The mean is the expected value of the return, a measure of the long-run average return from such an investment. The variance (or standard deviation) gauges the dispersion in the possible returns, and is thus a measure of uncertainty. The higher the variance, the less certain we are of what the return will turn out to be. If investors are risk-averse, then they will only acquire a high-variance asset if the expected return is also high.* The skewness coefficient measures whether the large deviations from the expected return are more likely to be positive or negative. A symmetrical probability distribution has a zero skewness coefficient. A positive skewness coefficient reflects a "long-shot" probability distribution that has some chance of a very high return (which is balanced by a substantial chance of a return that is slightly below the expected return). A negative skewness coef-

*For individual securities that will be part of a diversified portfolio, we've seen that the beta coefficient is a better measure of risk. But here, we are going to look at mutual funds, which are often virtually the entire portfolio for small investors.

The Determinants of Price-Earnings Ratios

The price-earnings ratio is a traditional yardstick for comparing different stocks; it shows how highly a company's shares are valued relative to its current profits. Suppose, for instance, that company XYZ earns $5 a share, while company MBI earns $10 a share. If XYZ stock sells for $50 a share and MBI for $100 a share, then they both have price-earnings ratios of 10. Their earnings are valued equally in that for a $1000 investment, we can buy 20 shares of XYZ or 10 shares of MBI, representing $100 of earnings in either case. If, instead, XYZ sells for $75 a share while MBI sells for $100, then XYZ's earnings are more highly valued because it has the higher price-earnings ratio. There are several possible explanations for differences in price-earnings ratios:

1. Reported earnings may be misleading because of unusual circumstances or creative accounting. The price-earnings ratio will be high if investors believe that reported earnings are inflated.
2. Firms with high anticipated growth rates have high price-earnings ratios, because they have higher future earnings.
3. Firms paying large dividends have high price-earnings ratios, because their future growth is not at the expense of current dividends.
4. Riskier firms have low price-earnings ratios, because risk-averse investors won't pay high prices for stock with a very uncertain return.

A classic study of the determinants of price-earnings ratios asked 17 professional security analysts for their opinions of 178 well-known stocks:[2]

P/E = price/"normal" earnings

g = anticipated growth rate

d = anticipated dividends relative to earnings

β = risk, as measured by the firm's beta coefficient (the study also used standard deviations to measure risk, and obtained similar results)

A cross-section multiple regression was then used to explain differences in price-earnings ratios among firms. The results for 1963 were

$$\hat{P/E} = 3.47 + 2.57\ g + 7.17\ d - 0.84\ \beta, \qquad R^2 = .75$$
$$[21.4] \qquad [2.9] \qquad [1.4]$$

[ ]: t-values

The signs of the estimated parameters agree with theory; high growth, high dividends, and low risk are the ingredients for a high price-earnings ratio. The first two coefficients, for growth and dividends, are substantial and statistically significant. The third coefficient, for risk, is not. This does not mean that risk is unimportant, only that these data do not show conclusively that it is important.

ficient means that there is some chance of a very low return (usually a large loss). If investors prefer positive skewness to negative skewness, then they will only make negatively skewed investments if the expected return is high.

Haim Levy and Marshall Sarnat made an intriguing empirical investigation of these ideas.[3] Using annual data covering the years 1946 through 1967, they calculated the mean, variance, and skewness coefficients for each of 58 mutual funds. They then asked whether, as anticipated, those funds with high variances also had high means and if those funds with negative skewness had higher mean returns than those with positive skewness. To separate the effects of variance and skewness on mean returns, they used a multiple regression:*

$$\hat{Y} = 7.205 + 0.019 \, X_2 - 0.000064 \, X_2, \qquad R^2 = .86$$
$$\quad [16.2] \quad\quad [9.9] \quad\quad\quad\quad [8.4]$$

[ ]: t-values

where

Y = mutual fund's average return

X_1 = variance of mutual fund's return
(average squared deviation from mean)

X_2 = mutual fund's skewness
(average cubed deviation from mean)

These empirical results corroborate the theory in that there is a statistically significant relationship between a fund's average return and both its variance and skewness. Funds with high variances tend to have high means, and so do funds with negative skewness. Unfortunately, because Levy and Sarnat did not report the average values and ranges of their explanatory variables, we cannot gauge whether these affects are substantial as well as statistically significant.

Exercises

15.12 Use the data in Table 15.1 to estimate the equation

$$Y = \alpha + \beta_3 X_3 + \epsilon$$

where Y is fuel consumption and X_3 is average speed. Is this estimate of β_3 the same as the estimate $\beta_3 = -3.57$ given in the text? Explain why they either are or are not the same.

15.13 The manager of a fleet of identical trucks wants to estimate the effect of driver speeds on fuel consumption. Monthly data are collected and the following equation estimated:

$$\hat{Y} = \quad 0.0 \quad + \quad 0.20 \, X_1 + 1000.0 \, X_2, \qquad R^2 = .86$$
$$(11.0) \quad (0.04) \quad\quad (400.0)$$

*Notice that Levy and Sarnat based their probability distributions on historical data, rather than subjective assessments. They also included 18 other summary measures of the probability distributions in their regression, but found that these did not have a statistically significant effect on mean returns.

( ): std. deviations

where

$$Y = \text{fuel consumption (gallons),}$$
$$\text{average value } 71{,}000$$

$$X_1 = \text{miles traveled, average value } 80{,}000$$

$$X_2 = \text{speed (miles per hour), average value } 55$$

Is each of these explanatory variables statistically significant? What does the estimated coefficient of X_1 measure? If the population value actually is 0.20, explain the implication (in simple English). What does the estimated coefficient of X_2 measure? If the population value is 1000.0, explain the implication (in simple English).

15.14 (*continuation*) Can we conclude from the much larger value of the second coefficient (1000 versus 0.2) that X_2 is more important than X_1 in determining fuel consumption?

15.15 (*continuation*) This firm has been offered a 1000-mile delivery that will net $200 after paying the driver and other nonfuel expenses. To complete the job on time, the truck will have to average 55 miles per hour. Does the equation in Exercise 15.13 indicate that they will make a profit or a loss on this job?

15.16 The text uses the data in Table 15.2 to analyze the relationship between midterm, homework, and final exam scores. Interpret the estimated coefficients in the simple- and multiple regression equations. In particular, how can the coefficient of midterm scores be 0.80 in the simple regression and 0.51 in the multiple regression?

15.17 (*continuation*) The data in Table 15.2 were used in this chapter to see how accurately final exam grades could be predicted from midterm and homework scores. Do you think that we would make better or worse predictions if we simply added the midterm and home-work scores together and divided by 2? Explain your reasoning.

15.18 (*continuation*) Check your logic by calculating the errors in predicting the final exam score by taking the average of the midterm and homework scores. Compute the standard error of estimate for this prediction method. Compare this to the standard error of estimate for a multiple regression.

15.19 A business wants to see how sensitive its sales are to the price it charges. Nine different prices are charged in nine different cities:

city	per capita income ($) X_1	price charged ($) X_2	sales (1000s) Y
A	6200	10	56
B	6900	20	57
C	7100	25	59
D	7700	20	68
E	6700	15	57
F	8000	30	65
G	6500	20	57
H	6100	15	52
I	7400	25	59

To control for the variations in per capita income, a multiple regression is used, with both price and income as explanatory variables:

$$Y = \alpha + \beta_1 X_1 + \beta_2 X_2 + \epsilon$$

Estimate the parameters of this equation. Do both price and income have statistically significant effects on sales? Do both seem to have important effects on sales? Give a 95 percent confidence interval for the effect on sales of a \$5 price increase.

15.20 A business is trying to estimate the contributions of labor and machines to output. Its data are

output	labor	machines
Y	X_1	X_2
34	40	20
42	60	15
33	50	10
60	60	60
37	50	15

Use these data to estimate the model

$$Y = \alpha + \beta_1 X_1 + \beta_2 X_2 + \epsilon$$

Do labor and machines both have statistically significant effects on output? Give 95 percent confidence intervals for their coefficients.

15.21 (*continuation*) It costs this firm \$25,000 to employ a person for a year and \$40,000 to rent a machine for a year. Would you recommend that they substitute labor for machines or machines for labor?

15.22 (*continuation*) Can you think of any reasons for caution in using this estimated equation to justify a complete substitution of labor for machines, or vice versa?

15.3 MULTICOLLINEARITY

In these various examples, multiple regression has handled, with varying degrees of success, the estimation of models using "nature's data" rather than experimental data. The regression model

$$Y = \alpha + \beta_1 X + \beta_2 X + \cdots + \beta_k X + \epsilon$$

asks the effects on the dependent variable Y of changes in each of the explanatory variables X_i, holding constant the other explanatory variables. This is the sort of question that could be answered by a laboratory experiment, but often it isn't because such an experiment is impractical. Instead, nature's data are sifted through a multiple regression, which provides the statistical counterpart to laboratory controls.

The statistical logic can be explained roughly as follows. Suppose we are interested in the effects of two variables, income and wealth, on spending, but cannot hold either constant while we vary the other. The available data might show the following information:

1. One year, income went up by 50, wealth fell by 100, and spending increased by 40.

2. Another year, income went up by 100, wealth went up by 100, and spending increased by 95.

What can we infer from these data? If wealth had no effect on spending, then spending, like income, should have increased by twice as much in the second year as in the first year. In fact, spending increased by more than this, indicating that the increase in wealth stimulated spending. Logically, then, an increase in wealth apparently has a positive effect on spending. For the effects of income changes, notice that wealth went down by 100 in the first year and up by 100 in the second. If income were unimportant, then spending also should have gone down in the first year and up equally in the second. In fact, spending, like income, increased in both years—indicating that increases in income have a positive effect on spending.*

It's not nearly this simple, though, because there are other factors—the trouble-making error term—that influence spending. Spending in either year may have been unusually high or low because of omitted factors, leading us to draw incorrect inferences. What we must do, statistically, to overcome this random variation is use more than two observations. With lots of data, we can hope that these annoying disturbances will average out and allow us to draw correct inferences. Multiple regression does this averaging for us by finding the parameter estimates that minimize the sum of squared prediction errors.

Our statistical reasoning can be thwarted, however, not only by too few data, but also by data that don't show the variation needed to allow inferences. If income never changes, then we obviously cannot estimate the effect of income changes on spending. A similar difficulty arises if income and wealth always change in unison, because we can't tell whether it is income or wealth that influences spending if we never see them move separately.

Suppose, for instance, that wealth is always equal to twice the income. This substitution into the regression model yields

$$Y = \alpha + \beta_1 X_1 + \beta_2 X_2 + \epsilon$$
$$= \alpha + \beta_1 X_1 + \beta_2(2X_1) + \epsilon$$
$$= \alpha + (\beta_1 + 2\beta_2) X + \epsilon$$

Whenever income goes up \$1, wealth goes up by \$2, and spending goes up by $\beta_1 + 2\beta_2$. With enough data, we can obtain a useful estimate of $\beta_1 + 2\beta_2$. But no matter how plentiful our data is, we'll never be able to obtain separate estimates of β_1 and β_2 as long as income and wealth move in unison. If we try, our computer

---

*These inferences can be quantified, as follows, by letting income be the first explanatory variable and wealth the second:

$$(+95) = \beta_1(+100) + \beta_2(+100)$$
$$(+40) = \beta_1(+50) + \beta_2(-100)$$

The addition of these two equations implies $135 = 150 \beta_1$, so that $\beta_1 = 0.9$ and, hence, $\beta_2 = 0.05$.

program will come to an abrupt stop and print a nasty error message, such as "INVALID DATA–DIVISION BY ZERO."

Fortunately, matters are seldom this extreme, because few explanatory variables move in perfect unison. But the bad news is that many variables are highly correlated, so that they move in close, although imperfect, unison. The consequence is that, while we can obtain a pretty good estimate of $\beta_1 + 2\beta_2$, we will not get accurate estimates of the separate parameters β_1 and β_2. Our regression may yield a satisfyingly high R-squared, but discomfortingly large standard deviations and low t-values for the parameters β_1 and β_2. This malaise is known as the multicollinearity problem.

> In the **multicollinearity problem,** high correlations among the explanatory variables prevent accurate estimates of the individual coefficients.

The symptoms of the problem are disappointingly low t-values. A multicollinearity problem can be diagnosed by regressing each explanatory variable on the others to see if these R-squareds reveal high intercorrelations among the explanatory variables. Unfortunately, there are no known simple cures for the multicollinearity problem. The builder can't make solid bricks without clay and the statistican can't make accurate estimates without information.

If the researcher is willing, *a priori*, to assign values to some of the parameters, then conditional estimates of the remainder can be computed. For instance, if the estimate is that

$$\beta_1 + 2\beta_2 = 1.03$$

then an *a priori* belief that $\beta_2 = 0.05$ implies a 0.93 estimate for β_1. More commonly, the desperate researcher will assign zero values to some of the parameters by dropping variables out of the equation. This practice isn't recommended unless zero is really believed to be the most plausible parameter value. Lacking such *a priori* information, the only alternative is to use additional data in which the explanatory variables are not so highly correlated.

Fortunately, multicollinearity does not undermine predictive accuracy as long as the intercorrelations persist. If wealth continues to be equal to twice the income, then we can forecast spending perfectly well without ever knowing the separate effects of income and wealth. But that's a big "if" and we do need to know the separate effects of the explanatory variables if the intercorrelations evaporate during the prediction period. The only silver lining to this dark cloud on the horizon is that, while these new data will be difficult to predict, at least they will provide the basis for better estimates next time around.

Another Look at Fuel Usage

One of the early examples in this chapter investigated the effects of vehicle travel (X_1), horsepower (X_2), and speed (X_3) on the nation's fuel consumption. The results were a bit disappointing, in that two of the three coefficients were statistically

The Coleman Report

In response to the 1964 Civil Rights Act, the U.S. government sponsored the 1966 Coleman Report, which was an ambitious effort to gauge how student scholastic performance is affected by student backgrounds and school resources. One of the more provocative findings involved the estimation of the multiple regression equation

$$Y = \alpha + \beta_1 X_1 + \beta_2 X_2 + \cdots + \beta_k X_k + \epsilon$$

The dependent variable was student performance, as measured by scores on tests of verbal ability. Some of the explanatory variables were measures of school resources (budgets, books in the library, science facilities, and so on) and others were measures of student backgrounds (family income, occupation, education, and the like).

The Coleman Report did not report the estimated coefficients. Instead, they regressed the equation first using only student background explanatory variables and, second, using both student background and school resources variables. Because R-squared only improved slightly with the inclusion of the school resources variables, they concluded that these "show very little relation to achievement." The coefficients of these school resources variables were, on the whole, apparently not statistically significant; however, not being able to reject zero as a possible value for a parameter is not at all the same thing as proving that the value is zero. Several critics pointed out the multicollinearity problem inherent in these non-experimental data. In the 1950s and early 1960s, school resources depended heavily on the local tax base and parents' interest in quality education for their children:

> The family background characteristics of a set of students determine not only the advantages with which they come to school; they are also associated closely with the amount and quality of resources which are invested in the schools. As a result, higher status children have two distinct advantages over lower status ones: First, the combination of material advantages and strong educational interests provided by their parents stimulate high achievement and educational motivation; and second, their parents' relatively high incomes and interest in education leads to stronger financial support for and greater participation in the schools that their children attend.[4]

This is not to say that the data show that resources matter, only that the high multicollinearity between resources and backgrounds made it impossible to get an accurate estimate of the effect of resources alone on student achievement.

insignificant and one had an unanticipated sign. Perhaps multicollinearity was the culprit! To check, I regressed each of the three explanatory variables on the other two:

$$\hat{X}_1 = 10{,}534.5 - 33.15\ X_2 + 93.0\ X_3, \qquad R^2 = .65$$
$$\qquad\qquad [2.7] \qquad [1.1] \qquad\quad [3.0]$$

$$\hat{X}_2 = 152.3 - 0.004\ X_1 + 1.11\ X_3, \qquad R^2 = .72$$
$$\qquad\quad [5.9] \qquad [1.1] \qquad\quad [3.7]$$

$$\hat{X}_3 = -98.3 + 0.006\ X_1 + 0.56\ X_2, \qquad R^2 = .85$$
$$\qquad\quad [4.0] \qquad\ [3.0] \qquad\quad [3.7]$$

[ ]: t-values

There are substantial intercorrelations among these explanatory variables. The third variable, speed, has a particularly high multiple correlation coefficient and this is why its coefficient in the original regression equation was not estimated very accurately. That estimate was -3.6 with a standard deviation of 4.4, giving a 95 percent confidence interval of $-3.6 \pm 2(4.4)$, from -12.4 to $+5.2$.

One of the unsatisfying aspects of our earlier fuel consumption estimates was the large standard deviations and wide confidence intervals on the individual parameter estimates, especially the estimated effect of speed on fuel usage. Now we see that the basic reason for this inadequacy is that the three explanatory variables are intercorrelated. Speed, in particular, has been highly correlated with travel and horsepower over the years covered by this study. In those years when the average speed has fallen, horsepower and travel have slumped, too. When speed has increased, horsepower and travel have also tended to increase. This multicollinearity makes it difficult to estimate how speed alone affects fuel usage. There is not much that can be done about it except to note that the data are not sufficiently uncorrelated to decisively answer all of the questions we have posed.

Exercises

15.23 It has been argued that consumer spending depends not only on current income, but also on some notion of average or "permanent" income. One way to take this possibility into account is to include income for both the current and previous year in the consumption function:

$$Y = \alpha + \beta_1 X_1 + \beta_2 X_2 + \epsilon$$

where Y is this year's consumption, X_1 is this year's income, and X_2 is the previous year's income.

Use the consumption and income data in Table 13.1 (or Figure 15.1) to estimate this equation. Interpret your estimates, including their standard deviations and t-values.

15.24 (*continuation*) Is there a multicollinearity problem here?

15.25 The data in Table 15.2 were used in the text to see how accurately final exam scores can be predicted from midterm and homework scores. What sort of multicollinearity problem might cause what sort of problems for this investigation? Is there any evidence of a multicollinearity problem here?

15.26   The preceding section included three regressions that were intended to investigate the interrelations among the data on vehicle travel, horsepower, and speed. Use these three reported regressions to describe these empirical interrelations.

15.27   An economist once attempted to estimate an asset-demand equation that included the following three explanatory variables: current wealth X_1, wealth in the previous quarter X_2, and the change in wealth $X_3 = X_1 - X_2$. Can you guess what problem he encountered?

• **15.28**   (*continuation*) Frankly, he was befuddled about how to solve his problem. (I know, because I reviewed his paper!) What would you suggest?

• **15.29**   A college admissions office wants to estimate the relationship between math SAT scores, verbal SAT scores, and freshman Grade Point Average (GPA). Larry wants to regress GPAs (Y) on math SAT scores (X) and verbal SAT scores (Z). Moe wants to regress GPA on the total SAT score ($X + Z$) and the verbal score (Z). Joe wants to regress GPA on the total SAT score ($X + Z$) and the amount by which the math score exceeds 500 ($X - 500$). They each run their preferred regressions and obtain these results:

Larry: $\hat{Y} = 0.10 + 0.003\ X + 0.002\ Z,\qquad R^2 = .74$
[3.0]   [2.0]

Moe: $\hat{Y} = 0.10 + 0.002\ (X + Z) + 0.001\ X,\qquad R^2 = .74$
[2.0]   [0.5]

Joe: $\hat{Y} = 0.60 + 0.002\ (X + Z) + 0.001\ (X - 500),\qquad R^2 = .74$
[2.0]   [0.5]

[   ]: t-values

Are their estimates consistent with each other? For example, what college GPA would each predict for a student with a 500 math score and a 600 verbal score? What can you learn from Moe's regression that is not apparent from Larry's regression?

• **15.30**   (*continuation*) Joanna thinks that GPA should be regressed on total SAT score ($X + Z$) and verbal SAT score (Z). Joshua wants to regress GPA on the amounts by which the math and verbal scores exceed 500: on ($X - 500$) and ($Z - 500$). If they do this, can you predict what their coefficient estimates will be?

15.4   SUMMARY

Multiple regression is the statistician's alternative to controlled laboratory experiments. The regression model is

$$Y = \alpha + \beta_1 X_1 + \beta_2 X_2 + \cdots + \beta_k X_k + \epsilon$$

Each coefficient β_i gauges the effects on the dependent variable Y of changes in each of the explanatory variables X_i, holding constant the other explanatory variables. This question could be investigated in a controlled experiment in which the other explanatory variables really are held constant, while X_i is varied and the effects on Y are recorded. However, many interesting questions, particularly in business and economics, do not lend themselves to laboratory experiments. Humans are reluctant to participate in such experiments and, even if they do, the artificial environment makes the results of dubious value.

Multiple regression uses "nature's data"—a recording of what transpires as people live their lives. If there happens to be sufficient variation in the explanatory variables, then accurate estimates of the parameters may be possible. The specific criterion used by multiple regression is to determine those estimates of the parameters that best explain the observed variation in Y, specifically those values that minimize the sum of squared prediction errors. Because of omitted influences, measurement error, and sampling error, there is an inevitable error term ϵ, which precludes certainty about the values of the parameters. This random variation in ϵ causes random variation in the recorded values of Y and, hence, random variation in the parameter estimates. We must remember, then, that the particular estimates we obtain come from a probability distribution. Assuming normality, this uncertainty can be quantified by computing standard deviations for the estimates. In addition, t-values (the ratio of an estimate to its standard deviation) can be used to test the null hypothesis that a parameter is equal to zero, i.e., that the associated explanatory variable doesn't really affect Y after all. The overall predictive success of the model can be measured by the standard error of estimate or, relative to the benchmark of omitting all of the explanatory variables and using only the sample mean, by R-squared.

Although multiple regression doesn't require controlled experiments, it does require some observed variation in the explanatory variables. If one variable never varies, then its effects cannot be judged. The same is true if one variable never varies independently of the others—if, for instance, one variable only goes up when either a second or a third goes down—because then we cannot tell whether it is this variable or the others that is affecting Y. The consequences are imprecise estimates, as reflected in their large standard deviations. This multicollinearity problem can be diagnosed by calculating the correlations among the explanatory variables, but can only be solved by using additional information.

REVIEW EXERCISES

15.31 Jane Daylily computes a "total" score for each of her students by adding together the midterm score, homework score, and twice the final score. Here are some sample scores:

student	midterm X_1	homework X_2	final X_3	total Y
1	74	92	83	332
2	94	87	90	361
3	82	78	88	336
4	80	78	66	290
4	89	90	97	373
5	65	73	74	286

Use these data to estimate the equation

$$Y = \alpha + \beta_1 X_1 + \beta_2 X_2 + \beta_3 X_3 + \epsilon$$

Briefly interpret your results. Do you think that homework, midterm, and final scores are a good predictor of a student's total score?

15.32   An empirical study of professors' salaries obtained the following multiple regression estimates:[5]

$$\hat{Y} = 25{,}000 + 200\ X_1 + 250\ X_2 + 50\ X_3 + 500\ X_4 + 50\ X_5$$
$$\phantom{\hat{Y} = 25{,}000} (500) \quad (20) \quad\ \ (100) \quad\ (20) \quad\ \ (50) \quad\ \ (400)$$

( ): std. deviations

where

$$Y = \text{annual salary}$$
$$X_1 = \text{years teaching}$$
$$X_2 = \text{published books}$$
$$X_3 = \text{published articles}$$
$$X_4 = \text{Ph.D.s supervised}$$
$$X_5 = \text{teacher rating } (1 = \text{above average, } 0 = \text{below average})$$

Calculate 95 percent confidence intervals and t-statistics for each of the estimated coefficients. Which of these estimates are statistically significant? Which seem substantial?

15.33   (*continuation*) According to these estimates:

a. What is the predicted salary of a professor who has been teaching for 15 years, written 3 books and 20 articles, supervised 6 Ph.D. theses, and is a below-average teacher?
b. How much higher would this professor's salary be if the teacher rating was above average?
c. How much is another published article worth, in terms of annual salary?

15.34   (*continuation*) Professors have a finite amount of time that must be allocated to these various academic activities and to a bit of leisure as well. Planning ahead over the next two years, a certain professor can either write a book, write six articles, or work on his teaching (to bring his rating up to above average). Which would you advise?

15.35   The text reports the estimation of a regression equation using travel, horsepower, and speed to explain motor vehicle fuel usage:

$$\hat{Y} = -1201.1 + 0.132\ X_1 + 5.07\ X_2 - 3.57\ X_3$$

What is the predicted fuel usage if we stop using motor vehicles ($X_1 = X_2 = X_3 = 0$)? Do you believe this prediction? If you don't believe the equation's prediction, then should the estimates be discarded?

15.36   A professional football team is trying to develop a model to predict which college players will be successful linemen in the pros. They decide that an objective measure of success is the number of games that the player starts during his professional career. The following data are collected on 16 former NFL players:

player	games started Y	height (inches) X_1	weight (pounds) X_2	speed (40 yds) X_3	IQ X_4	anger X_5
CA	22	73	240	4.8	105	91
MA	0	75	220	4.5	120	89
DB	104	79	290	5.7	84	93
FB	13	74	210	4.6	110	95
ED	97	78	260	5.3	95	92
FD	142	76	260	5.2	86	96
RG	120	78	280	5.4	92	94
TH	32	80	230	4.7	115	88
UH	9	76	245	5.2	100	92
DJ	120	75	220	4.6	105	95
EJ	172	82	250	4.9	85	94
JN	24	75	240	5.0	110	93
RN	117	71	245	5.5	82	99
MO	35	78	250	4.8	108	89
BS	45	78	300	5.7	86	86
RW	130	71	240	5.3	80	98

"Anger" is the player's score on a psychological test of aggressiveness. The higher this score, the more aggressive the person. Use these data to estimate the equation

$$Y = \alpha + \beta_1 X_1 + \beta_2 X_2 + \beta_3 X_3 + \beta_4 X_4 + \beta_5 X_5 + \epsilon$$

For each of these five explanatory variables, answer these questions:

a. What is the estimated coefficient?
b. Is the sign of this estimate plausible?
c. What is a 95 percent confidence interval for the estimate?
d. What is the value of the t-statistic?
e. Does this variable have a statistically significant effect on Y?

15.37 (*continuation*) This team is considering drafting either BG or HS. BG is 78 inches tall and weighs 280 pounds, with a 5.0 speed, a 102 IQ, and a 93 anger score. HS is 76 inches tall and weighs 260 pounds, with a 4.8 speed, a 98 IQ, and a 98 anger score. If the estimated equation is to be believed, which football player should they draft?

15.38 (*continuation*) Are there any reasons why they should not use this estimated equation alone to make their draft picks?

15.39 (*continuation*) Do you have any reason to suspect that some of the five explanatory variables might be correlated with the others? Regress each explanatory variable on the other four to see if you are right. If there were a high correlation, what disease would you have diagnosed?

● **15.40** (*continuation*) If one of these explanatory variables were highly correlated with the other four, would this invalidate the equation estimated in 15.36?

15.41 The admissions officer at a very selective law school is interested in how well law school performance can be predicted from college Grade Point Averages (GPAs) and LMAT test scores. A random sample of 20 students yields these data:

law school GPA Y	college GPA X_1	LMAT percentile X_2
3.42	3.28	.96
3.60	3.18	.97
3.28	2.89	.93
3.75	3.72	.99
3.36	3.18	.95
3.96	3.50	.98
3.31	3.04	.94
3.33	3.87	.95
3.60	3.54	.96
4.00	3.27	.99
3.28	3.30	.95
3.44	3.29	.91
3.25	3.17	.93
3.75	3.62	.97
3.30	3.34	.96
3.20	3.08	.90
3.50	3.37	.96
3.28	3.16	.94
3.17	3.20	.95
3.31	3.10	.94

Use these data to estimate the parameters of the prediction equation

$$Y = \alpha + \beta_1 X_1 + \beta_2 X_2 + \epsilon$$

What are the standard deviations of these parameter estimates? What are the *t*-values and (approximate) 95 percent confidence intervals for these parameters? Do both college GPA and LSAT scores have substantial and statistically significant predictive abilities?

15.42 (*continuation*) If you were the admissions officer at this school, is there any reason why you would not use this estimated equation alone for admitting students?

15.43 (*continuation*) An applicant scored in the 99th percentile on the LMAT test, but has only a 2.48 grade point average at Cal Tech. Is there any reason for caution in using the estimated equation to predict this student's performance in law school?

15.44 Exercise 14.4 gives some data on math and verbal SAT scores and history course scores, which were analyzed in this chapter. Is there any evidence of a multicollinearity problem here?

15.45 As an academic exercise, you want to examine the influence of interest rates X_1, and unemployment rates X_2 on stock prices Y. Lacking a suitable laboratory, you must rely on nature's experiments, using the available historical data to estimate your regression model

$$Y = \alpha + \beta_1 X_1 + \beta_2 X_2 + \epsilon$$

If these data are accurate measurements, why is there an error term ϵ? Why are there prediction errors $e = Y - \hat{Y}$? What is the difference between ϵ and e?

15.46 Is the "multicollinearity problem" a population or sample characteristic? For example, if you are trying to estimate the effect of interest rates and unemployment on stock prices, do you have a multicollinearity problem if interest rates and unemployment tend to be correlated in general or if they happen to be correlated by historical accident in the particular data you have?

• **15.47** Here are some data on the average weights (in pounds) of U.S. males, by height:

height (inches)	age 18–24	25–34	35–44	45–54	55–64	65–74
62	130	139	146	148	147	143
63	135	145	149	154	151	148
64	139	151	155	158	156	152
65	143	155	159	163	160	156
66	148	159	164	167	165	161
67	152	164	169	171	170	165
68	157	168	174	176	174	169
69	162	173	178	180	178	174
70	166	177	183	185	183	178
71	171	182	188	190	187	182
72	175	186	192	194	192	187
73	180	191	197	198	197	192
74	185	196	202	204	201	195

Can you see any reason for wariness in fitting the model

$$Y = \alpha + \beta_1 X_1 + \beta_2 X_2 + \epsilon$$

where Y is average weight, X_1 is height, and X_2 is age (the midpoint of each age interval). Use these data to estimate this equation and see if your fears are confirmed.

•• **15.48** To analyze the risk premiums on corporate bonds, the following regression equation was estimated[6]

$$Y = 0.987 + \underset{(0.032)}{0.307}\ X_1 - \underset{(0.036)}{0.253}\ X_2 - \underset{(0.031)}{0.537}\ X_3 - \underset{(0.021)}{0.275}\ X_4, \qquad R^2 = .75$$

( ): std. deviations

where

Y = corporate bond return minus return on safe U.S. Treasury bond of same maturity

X_1 = standard deviation of firm's profits, divided by the average level of profits

X_2 = length of time since firm had defaulted on any bond

X_3 = ratio of the market value of the firm's stock to maturation value of its debt

X_4 = market value of the firm's debt

The first three explanatory variables are intended to measure the riskiness of the bonds. (For instance, a large value of X_3 indicates a safe bond.) The fourth explanatory variable is intended to measure how easily the bond can be bought and sold. (It's difficult to market small issues by obscure firms.) Interpret the results. In particular, do the signs of the estimates make sense?

•• **15.49**　Arthur wants to study the effects of temperature, water, and music on plant growth. A lack of funding has forced him to study just three plants:

plant	temperature X_1	water X_2	music X_3	height Y
left	60	1.5	20	22
right	70	1.0	0	28
middle	80	0.5	10	24

The temperature is in °F, the water is in inches per day, the music is record albums per day, and the height is in inches. Use these data to estimate the equation

$$Y = \alpha + \beta_1 X + \beta_2 X + \beta_3 X + \epsilon$$

What can we conclude from this exercise? Be sure to explain your reasoning.

•• **15.50**　An economist claims that high interest rates are inflationary. To prove this, she regresses inflation on interest rates and unemployment (to gauge the state of the economy) and obtains

$$\hat{P} = 10.6 + 0.30\ I - 1.30\ U, \qquad R^2 = .985$$
$$[4.5] \quad [1.6] \qquad [6.8]$$

[ ]: t-values

where

$$P = \text{inflation rate (\%)}$$
$$I = \text{interest rate (\%)}$$
$$U = \text{unemployment rate (\%)}$$

After a colleague suggests that perhaps it is the other way around, that it is inflation that raises interest rates, this economist tries it this way and obtains

$$\hat{I} = -9.5 + 1.5\ P + 1.5\ U, \qquad R^2 = .818$$
$$[0.7] \quad [1.6] \quad [1.0]$$

[ ]: t-values

Would you conclude from the decline in R-squared that her original formulation is right?

PART **3**

Selected Topics

Self-timed sense amplifier, IBM Computer Chip.
© Phototake.

CHAPTER 16

Analysis of Variance

Nothing is good or bad but by comparison.

Thomas Fuller

TOPICS

There are many situations in which we suspect that certain equipment or procedures make a difference. Secretaries may be more productive with certain word processors; students may learn more from certain teachers; and the ill may get well sooner with certain medicines. However, observed variations in the outcomes can be caused by other factors, too. Some secretaries are more productive than others, and not all students are created equal. Some students will do better than others, regardless of the teacher. An illness may last only a short while, even without medication, or it may last a long time, even with the best treatment.

The trick is to use a variety of data to separate the other influences from the treatments of interest. If we look at only a single secretary who is working on a single machine, we will have no way of judging the machine. Even if we observe one secretary on one machine and another secretary on a second machine, we still won't know whether the observed differences in performance are caused by the secretaries or the machines. Another possible experiment is to have a single secretary do one assignment on two machines, but again, variations in performance may be caused by variations in the secretary's productivity, rather than differences between the two machines. The key is to get a handle on the variation in performances on a single machine, and for this, we need several assignments done on each machine. These could be single assignments done by many secretaries or multiple assignments completed by the same secretary. One way or another, we must get an estimate of how much variation can be expected on a single machine, and then we can compare this to the amount of variation using two machines. If the two-machine variation is about the same as the variation on a single machine, then the two machines are apparently very similar. If, on the other hand, the variation between the two machines is greater than that on a single machine, then we have identified a statistically significant difference between the machines.

It sounds plausible in theory, but how do we do it in practice? Which statistics should we calculate and what is the appropriate test? The great British statistician, Sir Ronald A. Fisher (1890–1962), wrestled with this question and came up with an **analysis-of-variance** procedure, which is an extension of the *t*-test for the differences between two means. In this chapter, you will learn how Fisher's procedure works. It turns out that Fisher's analysis-of-variance model is a special case of regression analysis, but it is most easily motivated by following Fisher's reasoning.

16.1 VARIATION BETWEEN AND WITHIN TREATMENTS

Let's use a new example to explain Fisher's logic. Several years ago, some researchers found that plants grew better when they were watered with a solution containing fluorescein.[1] In their experiment, these agronomists gave the plants on one plot of land a mixture of fluorescein and water, while the plants on a second plot, the *control group*, were just given water:

The researchers found that the plants that were given fluorescein did substantially better than those that were given plain water. However, other agronomists tried this experiment elsewhere and found that fluorescein made no difference. What went wrong? The problem with the original experiment was that the two plots of land were not identical—as they seldom are! The composition of the soil (loam, clay, or sand), the nutrients present, and the amount of shade and sunshine can all vary from one plot of land to the next. It so happened that in this experiment, plot 1 had better soil than plot 2. The plants grew more, not because of the fluorescein, but because of the richer soil.

An ideal experiment would use identical soil for both the plants given fluorescein and those given plain water. However, because growing conditions can never really be identical, the next best thing is to estimate the amount of natural variation in growing conditions. By estimating the random variation in plant growth attributable to varying plant and soil conditions, we can determine statistically whether the observed variation between the plants given fluorescein and those given plain water is of the same order of magnitude.

How do we actually decide which plants in which locations are given which treatment? The logic is very similar to public-opinion sampling. We don't want to construct the samples by trying to choose two typical plots of land, because the results will then be too dependent on our subjective assessment of what is "representative" soil. If the plots aren't identical (and they seldom will be), then our results will be biased in ways that we can't take account of. We won't know whether the observed differences in plant growth are caused by the treatments or our errors in choosing "typical" plots. This is the trap that the original fluorescein researchers fell into.

We also do not want convenience sampling. It is easiest for pollsters to interview friendly people who live nearby and it is easiest for doctors to give polio vaccines to children whose parents volunteer permission. But such easy samples are, as we have seen, also biased samples. Similarly, it is undoubtedly easiest to put all the plants that are receiving fluorescein together and all of the plants that are receiving plain water together; then all of the plants in each group can be treated at once. But again, that leads to two separate, and perhaps very different, plots of soil. Similarly, if the plants in the experiment are all new plants that arrive in several shipments, it is easiest to label all of the plants in one shipment "fluorescein" or "plain water." But the shipments may well be different, especially if they come from different nurseries or from different parts of a large nursery.

It takes some extra effort to choose random samples, but this effort is well worth it. As in opinion polling, a small random sample is much more reliable than a large biased sample. What we want to do in this experiment is spread the fluorescein and water around on randomly selected plants in randomly selected locations. If the plants are already in the ground, then this randomization will be done in one fell swoop. If the plants are new, then they can be assigned to different locations that are randomly selected to receive either fluorescein or plain water.

We do want to enforce some balance in our experiment to avoid the possibility that, by the luck of the draw, the fluorescein is used on all of the plants or on none of them. If we are using eight plants, for example, we might require that half be given fluorescein and half plain water. The randomness comes in deciding which is which. A simple procedure would be to prepare eight tags, with four marked "fluorescein" (F) and four "plain water" (W). These tags could be placed in a farmer's hat and, then, a drawing made for each of the eight plants. For a more scientific appearance, a table of random numbers could be used. I used eight playing cards to determine the following locations:

F   W   W   F
F   W   F   W

Our hope is that the other factors that influence plant growth will balance each other out, that some of the fluorescein plants will be healthy and some weak, and that some will be planted in the most fertile soil and others in less favorable locations. But, by the luck of the draw, this may not happen. By chance, fluorescein may be put only on the healthiest plants in the choicest locations. However, our statistical procedures can take this possibility into account by calculating the probability that random variation (sampling error) is responsible for the results. In the absence of random sampling, no such allowances can be made.

Perhaps the plant heights (in inches) turn out as follows:*

	treatment	
	fluorescein	*plain water*
	28	27
	33	30
	24	23
	27	24
mean	28	26
variance	14	10

First, notice that there is a difference in the means. The average height is 28 inches with fluorescein and only 26 inches with water. Second, notice that, for either treatment, the heights vary from one plant to the next. Because of this inevitable variation, we cannot be certain that the observed difference between the plants that were given fluorescein and those that were given just water is caused

---

*The variance calculations are

$$\text{fluorescein: } \{(28 - 28)^2 + (33 - 28)^2 + (24 - 28)^2 + (27 - 28)^2\}/3$$
$$= (0 + 25 + 16 + 1)/3 = 42/3 = 14$$
$$\text{plain water: } \{(27 - 26)^2 + (30 - 26)^2 + (23 - 26)^2 + (24 - 26)^2\}/3$$
$$= (1 + 16 + 9 + 4)/3 = 30/3 = 10$$

Following Fisher, both variances were calculated by dividing by the degrees of freedom $n - 1 = 3$ rather than by the sample size $n = 4$.

by the fluorescein. It may be that, by the luck of the draw, fluorescein was given to healthier plants in more productive soil.

There are two very different explanations, as shown in Figure 16.1, for the observed difference in the sample means. It may be that the expected height with fluorescein is greater than the expected height with plain water; thus, the observed means of 28 and 26 came from two different populations. Or it may be that the samples came from a single population with a large variance: if there are large height differences from one plant to the next, then it is not surprising that one mean happened to be 28 and the other only 26.

> The observed difference between two sample means can be caused by either the different means of two distributions or the large variance of a single distribution.

A formal model of plant heights, Y, would be

$$\text{plain water: } Y = \alpha_1 + \epsilon$$

$$\text{fluorescein: } Y = \alpha_2 + \epsilon$$

The population parameter α is the expected height. The error term ϵ is a random variable that encompasses all of the many reasons why, either with plain water or fluorescein, heights vary from one plant to another. If fluorescein makes no dif-

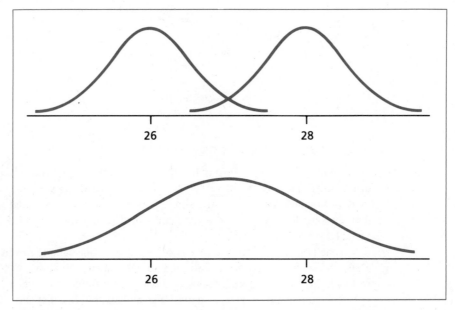

Figure 16.1 *Two different sample means may have come from two populations with different means or from a single population with a large standard deviation*

ference, then α_1 equals α_2 and the heights come from a single distribution, so that observed height variations are simply due to the random error ϵ. If fluorescein does affect plant heights, then the inequality of α_1 and α_2 is partly responsible for observed height differences.

How can we choose between these competing explanations for the observed difference in the sample means? The key to a comparison here is the difference in heights from one plant to the next. If plant heights hardly vary, then the difference between 28 and 26 inches is persuasive evidence that fluorescein makes a difference. If, on the other hand, there are large height variations from one plant to the next, then the difference between 28 and 26 inches is not convincing. So, we must compare the observed variance across plants with the observed difference in sample means.

The Mean of the Sample Variances

The variance in heights across plants is 14 with fluorescein and 10 with plain water. We can view these numbers as two estimates of the true population variance of plant heights—the variance of ϵ, which we assume is the same for both fluorescein and water. A natural estimate of this common variance across plants is the average of these two separate estimates:

$$\begin{array}{c}\text{estimated common}\\\text{variance}\\\text{across plants}\end{array} = \frac{\begin{array}{c}\text{fluorescein}\\\text{variance}\\\text{across plants}\end{array} + \begin{array}{c}\text{plain water}\\\text{variance}\\\text{across plants}\end{array}}{2}$$

$$= \frac{14 + 10}{2}$$

$$= 12$$

The Variance of the Sample Means

Now, with this estimate in our hip pocket, we can gauge whether the observed difference in the means, 28 versus 26, is large or small. If we were drawing two random samples of size 4 from a single population with mean μ and variance σ^2, then the sample means would come from a distribution with expected value μ and variance $\sigma^2/4$.

If the population variance of ϵ is $\sigma^2 = 12$, then the sample means come from a distribution with a variance $12/4 = 3$ (and a standard deviation of $\sqrt{3} = 1.73$). In this light, as Figure 16.2 shows, the observed difference between 28 and 26 is not very convincing evidence against the null hypothesis that the heights come from a single distribution. More concretely, the observed variance of the sample means is

If the standard deviation of the sample means is $\sqrt{3} = 1.73$, then the difference between the two observed sample means, 26 and 28, is not convincing evidence against the possibility that the two samples come from the same distribution.

Figure 16.2   *The fluorescein single-distribution theory*

$$\text{variance of the sample means} = \frac{(28 - 27)^2 + (26 - 27)^2}{2 - 1}$$

$$= 2$$

(Again following Fisher, we divide by $n - 1 = 2 - 1 = 1$, rather than by n.) Thus, the observed variance of 12 across plants implies a variance of 3 for sample means drawn from a single distribution. The observed variance of the sample means is, in fact, only 2. If fluorescein really did affect plant growth, the variance in sample means should be greater than 3, and not smaller.

The *F*-Statistic

Let's retrace our steps before we forget what we did. First, we estimated the variance σ^2 across plants by calculating the average value of the two sample variances. Dividing this by n gives σ^2/n, an estimate of the variance of the sample means. Second, we compared this estimate to the observed variance of the sample means. In ratio form, we have

$$F = \frac{\text{(variance of sample means)}}{\text{(mean of sample variances)}/n} \qquad (16.1)$$

or, equivalently,

$$F = \frac{n(\text{variance of sample means})}{\text{(mean of sample variances)}} \qquad (16.2)$$

This is called the **F-statistic** in honor of Fisher's pioneering work. A calculated *F*-value near 1.0 is consistent with the hypothesis that the data came from a single population with a relatively large variance. If, on the other hand, the F-statistic is much larger than 1.0, then the observed difference in the sample means is too large to be explained plausibly by sampling variation from one plant to the next.

According to the previous data, the samples are of size $n = 4$, the mean of the sample variances is 12, the variance of the sample means is 2, and the value of the F-statistic,

$$F = (4)(2)/(12) = 0.67$$

is not convincing evidence that fluorescein makes a difference.

For practice, let's run through the calculations again, using somewhat different data this time. This agricultural experiment was conducted on a different crop, using a special solution and plain water. The results (in inches) were:

	treatment	
	solution	*water*
	33	31
	32	30
	30	25
	32	27
	36	31
	29	25
	32	27
mean	32	28
variance	5	7

The sample variances of the heights are 5 for the solution and 7 for the plain water. Thus, the average variance is 6:

$$\text{mean of sample variances} = (5 + 7)/2 = 6$$

There is relatively little variation in heights with this second crop. If the heights are, in fact, from a single population with a common expected value, then the estimated variance of the sample means is $\sigma^2/n = 6/7 = 0.857$. However, the observed variance of two sample means (32 and 28) is much larger than this: .

$$\text{variance of sample means} = \frac{(32 - 30)^2 + (28 - 30)^2}{2 - 1} = 8$$

Thus, the F-value is

$$F = \frac{n(\text{variance of sample means})}{(\text{mean of sample variances})}$$

$$= (7)(8)/(6) = 9.33$$

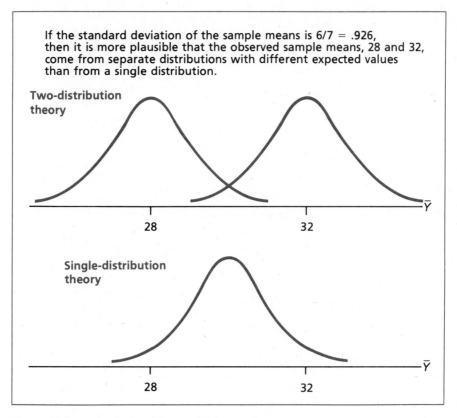

If the standard deviation of the sample means is 6/7 = .926, then it is more plausible that the observed sample means, 28 and 32, come from separate distributions with different expected values than from a single distribution.

Figure 16.3 *A convincing difference in the sample means*

Unlike the fluorescein data, this difference in the sample means is striking, as Figure 16.3 illustrates. There is relatively little variation in the heights within each sample, and so, the observed variation in the sample means is more than nine times larger than might be expected if the solution were no different than plain water. Thus, we are led to the conclusion that the solution does matter.

With the fluorescein data, we got an unimpressive F-value of 0.67. With the second batch of data, we got a striking 9.33 F-value. Where do we draw the line between unimpressive and striking? Fisher answered this question by figuring out the probability distribution for the F-statistic so that, as with any hypothesis test, we can ask whether the observed value is sufficiently unlikely to be persuasive.

The F Distribution

Fisher assumed that the variable of interest is normally distributed. Under the null hypothesis that the data come from a single distribution (that the treatments are

Figure 16.4   *An* F
distribution

unimportant), he derived the distribution of the F-statistic.* Figure 16.4 shows one
such F distribution. Remember, that an F-value that is close to 1.0 is consistent
with this hypothesis. However, as is shown in Figure 16.4, the F-value will probably be a bit larger or smaller than 1.0 because of sampling variability. The
F-value could even be as small as 0 or much larger than 1.0. As Equation 16.1
shows, a large F-value reflects large observed differences in the sample means,
which is evidence against the null hypothesis. For the usual hypothesis-testing
procedure, we choose a probability of Type I error, say 5 percent, and then find
the corresponding cutoff value of F. If it turns out that the F-value is this large,
then the improbability of this outcome persuades us that the null hypothesis is
wrong, and the treatments do matter.

The exact distribution of F depends on two considerations: the number of
treatments (k) and the number of observations (n) of each treatment. There are
essentially k samples; each is size n. The numerator of the F-statistic is the variance
of the sample means and, because there are k sample means, the numerator is said
to have $k - 1$ degrees of freedom. The denominator of the F-statistic is the mean
of the sample variances and, because each of these k variances has $n - 1$ degrees
of freedom, the denominator is said to have $k(n - 1)$ degrees of freedom.

These two degrees-of-freedom calculations

numerator: $k - 1$ = number of treatments $- 1$
denominator: $k(n - 1)$ = (number of treatments)(sample sizes $- 1$)

determine the exact distribution of the F-statistic.

Figure 16.5 shows three very different shapes for an F distribution. Notice, though,
how the F distribution becomes bell-shaped as both degrees of freedom increase.

In the fluorescein example, there were $k = 2$ treatments and $n = 4$ observa-

*Formally, if the random variables X_1 and X_2 have chi-square distributions with $k - 1$ and $n(k - 1)$
degrees of freedom, then

$$\{X_1/(k - 1)\}/\{X_2/n(k - 1)\} = nX_1/X_2$$

has an F distribuiton with $k - 1$ and $n(k - 1)$ degrees of freedom.

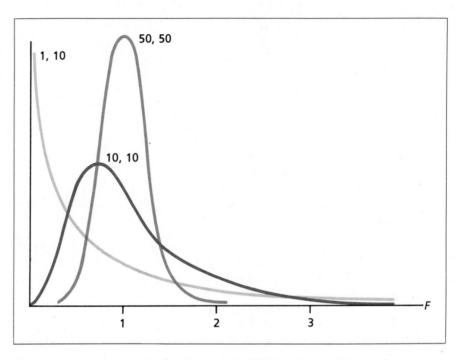

Figure 16.5 *Three varied F distributions, with differing degrees of freedom* k − 1, k(n − 1)

tions per treatment, giving the numerator $k - 1 = 1$ degree of freedom and the denominator $k(n - 1) = 2(3) = 6$ degrees of freedom. Table 6 in the back of this book shows that for these degrees of freedom there is a 5 percent chance that the value of the F-statistic will be greater than 5.99, if there really is no difference between the treatments. The complete F distribution is shown in Figure 16.6.

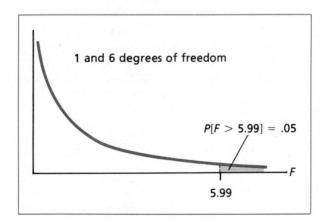

Figure 16.6 *The F distribution for the fluorescein example*

Because the observed value of 0.67 is nowhere near this large, we cannot reject the null hypothesis that the data come from a single distribution.

In the second example, there were $k = 2$ treatments and $n = 7$ observations, giving 1 degree of freedom for the numerator and 12 for the denominator. Table 6 says that there is a 5 percent chance of an F-value greater than 4.75, if the null hypothesis is true. The observed 9.33 F-value is greater than this, which leads to the rejection of the null hypothesis. If the data came from a single distribution, there would be less than a 5 percent chance of observing this large an F-value, and thus, the improbability of this outcome persuades us that the data did not come from a single distribution.

Does the Teacher Make a Difference?

Fisher's F test is actually an extension of the t test for the difference between two means. With two treatments, the F distribution has 1 and $n - 1$ degrees of freedom; a comparison of this column of Table 6 with the t distribution in Table 4 shows that F is equal to t-squared! This is no accident, because with $k = 2$, the test values of the F-statistic and the square of the t-statistic are identical (see Exercise 6.13). The major advantage of Fisher's F test is that it can be applied to more than two treatments. For an example, consider the question of whether or not student performance is affected by the teacher. At a certain large university, students who enroll in an introductory statistics course are randomly assigned to sections that are taught by different people. Each section uses the same textbook, does the same homework, and is given the same final examination. At the end of the semester, the final exam is written by all of the teachers, as a group, and is graded by all the teachers, too. To simplify the calculations, I've randomly selected four sections from the fall 1983 semester—one taught by a full professor, one by an associate professor, one by an assistant professor, and one by a graduate student. The final exam scores for these four sections are shown in Table 16.1.

We can think of these scores as being a sample from the population of prospective students that might be taught by these professors. The professors are the "treatments." We want to know if the expected student score varies from professor to professor, and so the null hypothesis is that the teacher doesn't matter. The first thing to do in testing this blasphemy is to calculate the variance in student scores within each class. These four variances are shown at the bottom of Table 16.1, and their average is about 101:

$$\begin{matrix} \text{mean of} \\ \text{sample} \\ \text{variances} \end{matrix} = \frac{103.25 + 76.41 + 136.67 + 88.81}{4}$$

$$= 101.285$$

This number gives us an idea of how much variance to expect in the sample means. If the teacher is unimportant, so that all of the scores come from a single distri-

bution, then, with 30 students per class, the variance of the sample means should
be $\sigma^2/n = 101.285/30 = 3.376$.

In fact, the observed variance of the sample means is more than five times
larger than this:

$$\text{variance of sample means} = \frac{(73.3 - 78.6)^2 + (83.7 - 78.6)^2 + (79.2 - 78.6)^2 + (77.8 - 78.6)^2}{(4 - 1)}$$

$$= 17.137$$

Table 16.1   *Final exam scores, for four different teachers*

	Graduate student	Assistant professor	Associate professor	Full professor
	71	84	79	92
	72	94	92	70
	80	77	73	74
	70	84	86	70
	85	96	82	74
	77	84	98	85
	79	86	98	70
	95	99	82	75
	63	96	91	62
	80	86	64	90
	88	93	71	87
	72	82	80	89
	63	78	65	85
	71	80	97	73
	63	98	94	81
	61	80	75	83
	64	82	59	75
	77	79	87	73
	70	85	78	59
	60	86	81	83
	87	71	70	82
	79	68	71	77
	83	69	91	87
	68	95	73	63
	54	65	92	64
	79	87	82	78
	81	82	59	76
	58	82	75	99
	88	84	71	77
	73	80	61	80
mean	73.70	83.73	79.23	77.77
variance	103.25	76.41	136.67	88.81

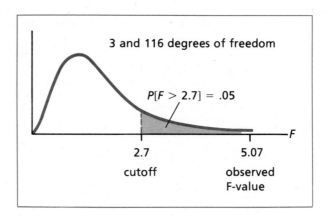

Figure 16.7 *The data reject the hypothesis that all teachers are equal*

Thus the value of the *F*-statistic is about 5:

$$F = \frac{n(\text{variance of sample means})}{(\text{mean of sample variances})}$$

$$= 30(17.137)/(101.285)$$

$$= 5.076$$

For $k = 4$ samples of size $n = 30$, the degrees of freedom are $k - 1 = 3$ for the numerator and $k(n - 1) = 4(29) = 116$ for the denominator. Table 6 tells us that if the teacher did not make a difference, there would be a 5 percent chance of observing an *F*-value of 2.7 and, thus (as is illustrated in Figure 16.7) the data in Table 16.1 are decisive evidence against the hypothesis that the teacher doesn't matter.

Are There Monthly Patterns in Stock Prices?

There is considerable Wall Street folklore about monthly patterns in stock prices; for example, it is said that prices go up with our spirits in the spring, fall in the dog days of summer, and drop again with end-of-the-year tax sales. If these tales were true, this would be valuable information. If stock prices went up in April and down in August, we could profitably buy in March and sell in July.

A contrary argument is that there are so many people looking for such patterns that the patterns could not persist. If stock prices could be counted on to go up in April, then people would stop buying stocks in April and start buying in March. Then, this March surge would persuade people to buy in February instead (or January, for people anticipating the February surge). The only situation that could persist is chaos. Any profitable pattern would self-destruct.

We can use Fisher's *F* test to see whether or not the behavior of the stock market varies with the month of the year. Stock prices go up and down because any of a large number of possible events may happen. Because it is not known in advance what will happen, stock returns are random variables whose uncertainties can be described by probability distributions. The null hypothesis here is that each month's return is drawn from a single probability distribution. The actual data are a sample of what might have happened each month.

They Call It Stormy Monday

Mondays also have a reputation on Wall Street—for being wild and often downright nasty. An empirical study of daily percentage stock returns over the period July 3, 1963 to December 18, 1978 (4132 days in all) obtained the following data:[2]

	Monday	Tuesday	Wednesday	Thursday	Friday
mean	−0.134	0.002	0.096	0.028	0.084
variance	0.670	0.551	0.644	0.483	0.479

Over this period, the average daily return was 0.0152. Only Monday had a negative average return, and it works out to be a staggering −33.5 percent on an annual basis. To see if the differences in the daily returns are statistically significant, Fisher's F-statistic can be calculated from*

$$\frac{\text{average}}{\text{variance}} = (0.670 + 0.551 + 0.644 + 0.483 + 0.479)/5 = 0.5654$$

$$\frac{\text{variance}}{\text{of means}} = \{(-0.134 - 0.0152)^2 + \cdots$$

$$+ (0.084 - 0.0152)^2\}/(5 - 1) = 0.008465$$

so that

$$F = \frac{n(\text{variance of sample means})}{(\text{mean of sample variances})} = \frac{(4132/5)(0.008465)}{(0.5654)} = 12.4$$

The numerator has 4 degrees of freedom, while the denominator has so many that we may as well use the ∞ in Table 6, giving a 2.37 cutoff for a test at the 5 percent level. The observed 12.4 F-value shatters this cutoff, indicating decisively that the days of the week do matter. More complete tables of the F distribution show that, if the day of the week were unimportant, the probability of such a high F-value is less than .0001.

Why is Monday so stormy? The researchers who compiled these data tried to find a reasonable explanation and came up empty, concluding that it is "an obvious and challenging empirical anomaly." Until proven otherwise, my advice is, "Be cautious on Monday."

*These calculations aren't quite right, because holidays left an unequal number of observations for each day of the week. The exact way to handle such data will be discussed in the next section.

Table 16.2 *Eleven years of monthly stock returns, percent*

	Jan	Feb	Mar	Apr	May	June	July	Aug	Sept	Oct	Nov	Dec
1970	-7.43	5.85	0.30	-8.89	-5.47	-4.82	7.52	5.09	3.47	-0.97	5.35	5.84
1971	4.19	1.41	3.82	3.77	-3.67	0.21	-3.99	4.12	-0.56	-4.04	0.27	8.77
1972	1.94	2.99	0.72	0.57	2.19	-2.05	0.36	3.91	-0.36	1.07	5.05	1.31
1973	-1.59	-3.32	-0.02	-3.95	-1.39	-0.51	3.94	-3.18	4.15	0.03	-10.82	1.83
1974	-0.85	0.19	-2.17	-3.73	-2.72	-1.29	-7.59	-8.28	-11.70	16.57	-4.48	-1.77
1975	12.51	6.74	2.37	4.93	5.09	4.62	-6.59	-1.44	-3.28	6.37	3.13	-0.96
1976	11.99	-0.58	3.26	-0.99	-0.73	4.27	-0.68	0.14	2.47	-2.06	-0.09	5.40
1977	-4.89	-1.51	-1.19	0.14	-1.50	4.75	-1.51	-1.33	0.00	-4.15	3.70	0.48
1978	-5.96	-1.61	2.76	8.70	1.36	-1.52	5.60	3.40	-0.48	-8.91	2.60	1.72
1979	4.21	-2.84	5.75	0.36	-1.68	4.10	1.10	6.11	0.25	-6.56	5.14	1.92
1980	6.10	0.31	-9.87	4.29	5.62	2.96	6.76	1.31	2.81	1.87	10.95	-3.15
mean	1.84	0.73	0.52	0.47	-0.26	0.98	0.45	0.90	-0.29	-0.07	1.89	1.95
var.	45.72	10.83	17.27	24.02	12.17	10.90	26.80	18.25	19.07	48.09	32.86	12.45

Source: Roger G. Ibbotson and Rex A. Sinquefield, *Stocks, Bonds, Bills, and Inflation*, Charlottesville, Virginia: Financial Analysts Research Federation, 1979 (and updates).

Table 16.2 shows the actual monthly percentage returns (dividends plus capital gains) for the Standard & Poor's 500 stocks over the eleven-year period 1970–1980. There are some differences in the average monthly returns, although not those suggested by the folklore cited earlier. April was no better than August over these eleven years, and December was the best month of all—no sign of a tax selloff!

The statistical question is whether these observed differences from one month to the next are large enough to impress us. Or, are they just the sort of averages we would expect if we just picked eleven returns at random, without paying attention to the month in which they occurred? To answer this question, we turn to the variance of the returns and find that the average variance is 23.20. If we use this as an estimate of σ, then we expect the variance of the sample means to be $23.20/n = 23.20/11 = 2.11$ if the months are unimportant. If, instead, the months are important, then the observed variance of the sample means should be larger than this. As it turns out, the observed variance of the sample means is a miniscule 0.634, giving an F-value of

$$F = \frac{n(\text{variance of sample means})}{(\text{mean of sample variances})}$$

$$= \frac{(11)(0.634)}{23.20}$$

$$= 0.30$$

Because the observed F-value is less than 1, we do not need to look at the F-table to know that these data do not show a statistically significant variation in monthly stock returns.

Exercises

16.1 You have been hired to design a sampling procedure for testing a purported "miracle" fertilizer. One hundred plants will be used; half will be given this new fertilizer and half will be given a standard fertilizer. Tell how you would decide which plants get which fertilizer. Be specific!

16.2 An agricultural researcher tests the effects of two different fertilizers on soybean yields from four different plots of land:

	treatment
fertilizer 1	*fertilizer 2*
44	48
37	32
41	40
34	48

Determine the following:

a. the mean yields for each fertilizer
b. the variances of the yields for each fertilizer

c. the mean of the variances

d. the variance of the means

e. the value of Fisher's F-statistic

f. whether or not there is a statistically significant difference in the yields with these two fertilizers

16.3   A firm that tries to find customers by phone has two alternative approaches: the "soft sell" and the "hard sell." The spirit of the soft sell is a low-key friendly manner that wins the customer's confidence. The hard sell attacks by making wild claims, promising excessive benefits, and exaggerating the dangers of not buying. A consultant is hired to decide which approach is the more effective. Half of the calls use one approach, and half the other; a shuffled deck of cards is used to determine which potential customer gets which sales approach. (A black card means soft sell, a red card hard sell.) The results can be summarized as follows:

sales/day

	soft sell	*hard sell*
mean	80	96
variance	100	120
number of days tested: $n = 20$		

a. Why does each approach have a variance in its sales?

b. What is the mean of the sample variances?

c. If the two approaches were equally effective, what would be your estimate of the variance of the sample means, based on the mean of the sample variances?

d. What is the actual variance of the sample means?

e. What is the value of Fisher's F-statistic?

f. Do these data confirm or reject the null hypothesis that each approach is equally effective?

16.4   In the monthly stock returns example discussed in the text, I didn't bother to look up the value of F for which we would reject the null hypothesis that the expected stock return does not depend on the month. Why? What is the appropriate value of F for a 5 percent probability of Type I error?

16.5   Can the value of the F-statistic ever be negative? When?

16.6   Can the value of the F-statistic ever be zero? When?

• **16.7**   Fisher's F test uses the ratio of the variance of the sample means to the mean of the sample variances. Why is this ratio multiplied by n, the sample size?

16.8   A chemical firm tested the durability of four kinds of rubber-covered fabric. The following data show the weight loss after some rubbing tests on four samples of each fabric:[3]

fabric

1	2	3	4
268	218	235	236
251	241	229	227
274	226	273	234
270	195	230	225

Use Fisher's F test to see if the observed differences in durability are statistically significant.

16.9   Professor Smith claims that stock prices are no more likely to go up in even-numbered years than in odd-numbered years. To test this theory, he gathers some data on percentage stock returns over the period 1960–1979:

even years	odd years
0.47	26.89
−8.73	22.80
16.48	12.45
−10.06	23.98
11.06	−8.50
4.01	14.31
18.98	−14.66
−26.47	37.20
23.84	−7.18
6.56	18.44

The null hypothesis is that the expected return in an even year is the same as in an odd year. If Smith's null hypothesis is right, then why aren't the sample means equal? Use these data to conduct an F test of Smith's theory.

16.10   Before selecting an investment advisory service, I compiled a record of the recommendations of three firms over a ten-year period. These ten annual returns for each firm's recommendations can be summarized as follows:

	firm 1	firm 2	firm 3
mean	2.0	10.8	14.4
variance	515.4	381.1	303.5

Do these data show a statistically significant difference in the firms' performance?

16.11   A highway department conducted an experiment with three different brands of paints for traffic lanes. Each paint was used on parts of five different streets and then measured for brightness twelve months later. The results were:

	paint	
Everbright	Neverfade	Longlast
72	80	65
67	71	59
58	65	58
72	71	63
65	66	58

a. Why do the results for any single paint vary from one street to the next?
b. What are the mean and variance for each brand of paint?
c. What is the average variance?
d. If these results come from a single distribution, then what is your estimate of the variance of the means from one brand to the next?
e. Is the actual variance of the sample means consistent with this estimate?
f. What is the value of Fisher's F-statistic?
g. Do these data show any statistically significant differences among the three brands?

• **16.12**   In Exercise 16.9, you made an F test of the null hypothesis that the expected stock return in an even year is the same as in an odd year. Make a t test of this same hypothesis in the manner described in Chapter 12. Do your answers agree?

•• **16.13**   (*continuation*) Is the agreement or disagreement found in the preceding exercise a fluke or a lesson? To see which is the case, compare the formulas for the F-statistic and t-statistic.

16.2 THE MEAN SUM OF SQUARES

There is an alternative way to calculate the value of the F-statistic that is simpler, although the underlying logic is not quite as apparent. Let's number the k treatments $1, 2, \ldots, k$. There are n observations of the effects of each of these treatments. These effects might be plant heights, test scores, or something else. We'll label the measured effects Y_i, as shown in Table 16.3. Because there are n observations on each of k treatments, there are nk values of Y in all. For the first treatment, the average value of Y is $\overline{Y}_1$ and the variance is s_1^2. Similarly, for the second treatment, Y has a mean $\overline{Y}_2$ and a variance of s_2^2. The overall average value of Y will be labeled $\overline{Y}$:

$$\overline{Y} = \frac{Y_1 + Y_2 + \cdots + Y_{kn}}{kn}$$

Now let's look at the total sum of squared deviations of Y about its mean $\overline{Y}$:

$$\text{total sum of squares} = \sum_{i=1}^{kn} (Y_i - \overline{Y})^2$$

It can be shown that this total sum of squares consists of two factors:

$$n(\text{squared deviations of means}) = n\sum_{i=1}^{k} (\overline{Y}_i - \overline{Y})^2$$

Table 16.3   *A general format for the analysis of variance*

	k Treatments			
	1	*2*	. . .	k
n	Y_1	Y_{n+1}		
observed	Y_2	Y_{n+2}		
effects of	.	.		
each	.	.		
treatment	.	.		
	Y_n	Y_{2n}	. . .	Y_{kn}
Mean	$\overline{Y}_1$	$\overline{Y}_2$		$\overline{Y}_k$
Variance	s_1^2	s_2^2		s_k^2

$$\begin{matrix} \text{squared deviations} \\ \text{about the means} \end{matrix} = \left\{ \sum_{i=1}^{n} (Y_i - \overline{Y}_1)^2 + \cdots + \sum_{i=(k-1)n+1}^{kn} (Y_i - \overline{Y}_k)^2 \right\}$$

In particular,*

$$\begin{matrix} \text{total sum} \\ \text{of squares} \end{matrix} = n\left(\begin{matrix} \text{squared deviations} \\ \text{of means} \end{matrix} \right) + \begin{matrix} \text{squared deviations} \\ \text{about the means} \end{matrix}$$

For instance, in the fluorescein example, the overall average height is 27 inches and the total sum of squared deviations about this mean is

$$\begin{matrix} \text{total sum} \\ \text{of squares} \end{matrix} = (28 - 27)^2 + (33 - 27)^2 + (24 - 27)^2 + (27 - 27)^2$$

$$+ (27 - 27)^2 + (30 - 27)^2 + (23 - 27)^2 + (24 - 27)^2$$

$$= 1 + 36 + 9 + 0 + 0 + 9 + 16 + 9$$

$$= 80$$

The sample size ($n = 4$) multiplied by the squared deviations of the two sample means about the overall mean comes to

$$n\left(\begin{matrix} \text{squared} \\ \text{deviations} \\ \text{of means} \end{matrix} \right) = 4 \{(28 - 27)^2 + (26 - 27)\}^2$$

$$= 8$$

Within each sample, the squared deviations about that sample's mean sum to

$$\begin{matrix} \text{squared} \\ \text{deviations} \\ \text{about the means} \end{matrix} = (28 - 28)^2 + (33 - 28)^2 + (24 - 28)^2 + (27 - 28)^2$$

$$+ (27 - 26)^2 + (30 - 26)^2 + (23 - 26)^2 + (24 - 26)^2$$

$$= 0 + 25 + 16 + 1 + 1 + 16 + 9 + 4$$

$$= 72$$

Thus, as advertised, the squared deviations of the means plus the squared deviations about the means equals the total sum of squares.

The **total sum of squares** is a measure of the variation in Y. As shown, this variation can be split into two parts. The first part, the squared deviations of the

---

*Here's a sketch of a proof. The first of the nk squared deviations can be rewritten as

$$(Y_1 - \overline{Y})^2 = \{(\overline{Y}_1 - \overline{Y}) + (Y_1 - \overline{Y}_1)\}^2$$

$$= (\overline{Y}_1 - \overline{Y})^2 + (Y_1 - \overline{Y}_1)^2 + 2(\overline{Y}_1 - \overline{Y})(Y_1 - \overline{Y}_1)$$

The total sum of squares is the sum of nk such expressions. The sum of the first terms gives n sums of the k squared deviations of the means, and the sum of the second terms is the squared deviations about the k means. The sum of the third terms is zero, because each $\overline{Y}_i$ is the average of nY_i.

means, gauges how much the average value of Y varies from one treatment to the next; this is the variation **between treatments**. The second part, the squared deviations about the treatment means, tells us how much the individual values of Y vary about the mean of each treatment; this is the variation **within treatments**. Thus, another way to describe the total sum of squares is:

$$\text{total variation} = \frac{\text{variation between}}{\text{treatments}} + \frac{\text{variation within}}{\text{treatments}}$$

These words are reminiscent of our discussion of whether or not treatments matter, and indeed, as you will soon see, they provide another path to the F-statistic. Before we go down that road, however, let's look at one more set of labels that statisticians apply to this fundamental algebraic identity.

There are two reasons why Y varies. First, each treatment may have a different expected value for Y. Second, for any given treatment, there are other (unidentified) factors that cause Y to vary about its expected value. We could say that part of the variation in Y is "explained" by the different treatments and part is "unexplained," because it is caused by unknown factors. This logic leads to the following description:

$$\text{total variation in } Y = \frac{\text{variation explained}}{\text{by different treatments}} + \text{unexplained variation}$$

The ANOVA Table

The relationship between these various labels is shown in Table 16.4. This format is called an **ANOVA table**—an acronym for *AN*alysis *Of VA*riance. The first column says that we are separating the variation of Y into two parts: the between-treatment variation that is "explained" by the existence of the different treatments and the within-treatment variation that is left "unexplained." The second column gives the corresponding separation of the total sum of squares. In the third column, the degrees of freedom are separated, too. The k-squared deviations of the means have $k - 1$ degrees of freedom. The n-squared deviations about each mean have $n - 1$ degrees of freedom; with k means, this gives $k(n - 1)$ degrees of freedom. In total, there are nk-squared deviations about the overall mean, giving $nk - 1$ degrees of freedom.

In the fourth column, the sum of squares is divided by the appropriate degrees of freedom. As shown, the average "explained" sum of squares is equal to n times the variances of the sample means; the average "unexplained" sum of squares is equal to the mean of the sample variances.

The F-statistic can be calculated by computing the explained and unexplained sums of squares and dividing each by the appropriate degrees of freedom:

$$F = \frac{n(\text{sum of squared deviations of means})/(k - 1)}{(\text{sum of squared deviations about the means})/k(n - 1)}$$

Table 16.4 *The ANOVA format*

Source of variation	Sum of squares	Degrees of freedom	Mean sum of squares	
Explained (between treatments)	$n\left(\begin{array}{c}\text{Squared}\\\text{deviations}\\\text{of means}\end{array}\right)$	$k - 1$	$\dfrac{n\left(\begin{array}{c}\text{squared}\\\text{deviations}\\\text{of means}\end{array}\right)}{k - 1}$	$= n\left(\begin{array}{c}\text{variance}\\\text{of sample}\\\text{means}\end{array}\right)$
Unexplained (within treatments)	Squared deviations about the means	$k(n - 1)$	$\dfrac{\text{squared}\\\text{deviations}\\\text{about the means}}{k(n - 1)}$	$=$ mean of sample variances
	Total sum of squares	$nk - 1$		

$$F = \frac{n(\text{variance of sample means})}{(\text{mean of sample variances})}$$

$$= \frac{(\text{squared deviations of means})/(k - 1)}{(\text{squared deviations about the means})/k(n - 1)}$$

$$= \frac{\text{explained variance}}{\text{unexplained variance}}$$

There are at least four advantages of an ANOVA table. First, it provides a standard reporting format. Second, it gives a needed check on some tricky calculations. The explained and unexplained sums of squares must add up to the total sum of squares. If they don't, then there has been a computational error. Third, the sums of squares are easier to calculate and are often subject to less rounding error than the variances.* Fourth, it can be used to extend Fisher's F-test to data with unequal sample sizes.†

*If you do the calculations by hand (ugh!), then you should use the fact that the sum of the squared deviations about a mean is always equal to the sum of the squared values minus the number of observations times the mean squared. For example, the total sum of squares is

$$\sum_{i=1}^{kn} (Y_i - \bar{Y})^2 = \sum_{i=1}^{kn} (Y_i^2) - kn\bar{Y}^2$$

This shortcut was first given in Chapter 1 for calculating variances and standard deviations.

†Let's say that there are k samples of size $n_1, n_2, \ldots, n_k$. Two modifications are needed in our ANOVA calculations. First, the

$$n\left(\begin{array}{c}\text{squared}\\\text{deviations}\\\text{of means}\end{array}\right) = n_1(\bar{Y}_1 - \bar{Y})^2 + n_2(\bar{Y}_2 - \bar{Y})^2 + \cdots + n_k(\bar{Y}_k - \bar{Y})^2$$

Second, the "within" degrees of freedom is

$$(n_1 - 1) + (n_2 - 1) + \cdots + (n_k - 1)$$

Taste Tests of New Food Product

In developing a new "easy-to-prepare, nutritious, on-the run" food product, General Foods compared the taste of two versions of this product—one liquid and the other solid—to a competitive product that was already being sold successfully.[4] For this taste test, General Foods paid 75 males and 75 females to taste the products and be interviewed for their reaction. These 150 people were divided randomly into three groups of 50; each group was half male and half female. One group tasted the new liquid product, the second group tasted the new solid product, and the third group tasted the established product. Each person was asked to show his or her reaction to the product they tasted by marking a ballot showing faces ranging from delight to disgust. See Figure 1.

General Foods then assigned numerical scores to each face, going from +3 for delight to −3 for disgust. The results were as follows:*

	product		
score	*new liquid*	*new solid*	*established*
+3	7	5	1
+2	13	11	5
+1	16	19	15
0	11	13	17
−1	2	1	8
−2	1	1	3
−3	0	0	1
mean	1.18	1.06	0.22
variance	1.38	1.16	1.44

General Foods was naturally delighted to find its product more highly rated, on the average, than the established competitor. But the statistical question is whether this difference in the mean ratings can be explained by taste variations from one person to the next. Perhaps, by the luck of the draw, the established product was tasted by very fussy people who automatically give low ratings.

That sort of bad luck is always possible, but what we can do statistically is gauge the probability of such bad luck. The 1.33 average variance in the ratings for each product gauges the variation in people's ratings. If the ratings of these

---

*For the "new liquid," the mean is the sum of the scores divided by the number of observations,

$$\frac{7(+3) + 13(+2) + 16(+1) + 11(0) + 2(-1) + 1(-2) + 0(-3)}{50} = \frac{59}{50} = 1.18$$

while the variance is the sum of the squared deviations about the mean, divided by the number of observations minus one:

$$\frac{7(3 - 1.18)^2 + 13(2 - 1.18)^2 + \cdots + 0(-3 - 1.18)^2}{50 - 1} = \frac{67.38}{49} = 1.38$$

The other means and variances are calculated similarly.

Please check the box under the picture which expresses how you feel toward the product which you have just tasted.

Source: Elisabeth Street and Mavis G. Carroll, "Preliminary Evolution of a New Food Product", in Judith M. Tanur, et al., *Statistics: A Guide to the Unknown* (San Francisco: Holden-Day. 1972)

Figure 1 *Pictorial taste-test ballot (the scores $+3$ to -3 were assigned from left to right)*

three products came from a single distribution with that variance, the variance of the means for samples of size 50 would be $1.33/50 = 0.027$. The observed differences in the sample means, particularly for the established product, are much larger than this. The variance of these three sample means is 0.274 and the value of Fisher's F-statistic is

$$F = \frac{(50)(0.274)}{(1.33)} = 10.3$$

In an ANOVA format, we could report the results as shown in Table 1.

With $k = 3$ and $n = 50$, the degrees of freedom are $k - 1 = 2$ and $k(n - 1) = 147$, so that, according to Table 1, if the ratings came from a single distribution, then there would be about a 5 percent chance of observing an F-value greater than 3.0. The chance of an F-value greater than 10 is less than .001. Bad luck is always possible, but here that explanation for the differences in the ratings is not very plausible.

Table 1 *ANOVA table for General Foods taste test*

Source of variation	Sum of squares	Degrees of freedom	Mean sum of squares	F
Between ratings	27.36	2	13.68	
				10.3
Within ratings	194.76	147	1.32	
Total	222.12	149		

Table 16.5   *ANOVA table for fluorescein and plain water*

Source of variation	Sum of squares	Degrees of freedom	Mean sum of squares	F
Between treatments	8	1	8	
				0.67
Within treatments	72	6	12	
Total	80	7		

To illustrate an ANOVA table in action, let's take one more look at the fluorescein example. Earlier, we found that the total sum of squares is 80, the squared deviations of the means is 8, and the squared deviations about the means is 72. These calculations can be reported in an ANOVA format like Table 16.5. The variation is separated into "between treatment" and "within treatment," and it is up to the reader to recognize that the relative size of the between-treatment variation indicates whether or not there is a difference in the effects of the treatments; the within-treatment variation is the benchmark by which this between-treatment variation is judged. The ANOVA table shows the corresponding separation of the sum of squares and the degrees of freedom. The two sums of squares divided by the respective degrees of freedom give the mean sums of squares, and the ratio of these gives Fisher's *F*-statistic.

Exercises

16.14   The text gives some data on plant heights for 7 plants that were given a solution and 7 plants that were given plain water. See if the total sum of squares is equal to the squared deviations of the means plus the squared deviations about the means for these data.

16.15   Use the data in Table 16.1 to see if the total sum of squares is equal to the squared deviations of the means plus the squared deviations about the means.

• **16.16**   Show that, for $k = 2$ and $n = 3$, the total sum of squares is equal to the squared deviations of the means plus the squared deviations about the means for any values of Y.

16.17   A college consumer-protection group sponsored a beer-tasting, in which 30 students each drank a randomly assigned, unmarked pitcher of beer. Ten of these pitchers contained Spud beer, ten Filler, and ten Schultz. Each of the students was asked to rate the beer they drank on a scale from 1 to 10. The ratings turned out to be as follows:

Spud	Filler	Schultz
7.4	7.6	5.8
6.6	4.4	3.4
5.8	3.3	1.2
7.8	0.8	4.0
9.0	7.8	1.6

6.0	0.0	1.8
5.0	4.0	0.8
8.4	6.6	3.6
10.0	4.8	0.0
8.0	3.2	3.8

Why might we conclude that differences in ratings such as these are not statistically significant? If one beer gets higher ratings than another, doesn't that prove that it is the more popular beer? Are the differences in these particular ratings statistically significant? Use an ANOVA table to summarize your results.

16.18 The Educational Testing Service claims that its SAT tests are a useful predictor of college performance. To test this theory, data are collected on 30 students—10 from each of the following predicted freshman Grade Point Average (GPA) categories: 2.67–3.00, 3.00–3.33, and 3.33–3.67. The actual freshman-year GPAs are shown in the chart:

predicted GPA

2.33–2.67	2.67–3.00	3.00–3.33
2.53	2.43	2.40
2.90	3.20	3.07
2.43	2.57	3.40
2.37	2.80	2.76
2.60	2.10	3.27
2.16	3.50	3.83
2.03	3.00	2.86
2.80	2.70	3.60
3.17	3.30	3.17
2.70	2.90	3.50

What are the average freshman GPAs for each of these three groups? Are these differences statistically significant? What is the null hypothesis that you are testing? Use an ANOVA table to summarize your results.

16.19 Consumer Sports magazine tested the gasoline mileage of three subcompact cars by driving five of each make from Claremont, California to Brewster, Massachusetts. Their results were

miles per gallon (MPG)

Spiffy	Jiffy	Biffy
32.8	36.2	39.0
31.0	41.4	36.6
30.6	43.0	33.2
26.8	41.0	34.8
30.8	40.6	31.8

What are the average MPGs for each car? Use an ANOVA table to show whether the differences in MPGs are statistically significant.

16.20 A wholesaler makes deliveries at 20 retail stores each day. There are five different routes that look like they might be the fastest. Over a ten-week period, the firm tries each route 10 times and finds that the travel times (in hours) are

route 1	route 2	route 3	route 4	route 5
5.8	6.5	6.1	5.0	4.2
7.2	6.2	3.4	7.9	5.8
5.6	4.9	6.2	5.8	4.8
6.1	5.6	5.4	5.1	6.9
6.8	5.4	4.4	7.4	7.3
7.7	7.2	5.2	5.9	5.8
6.7	6.2	5.3	6.7	3.9
4.2	6.4	4.3	7.6	6.6
9.3	6.0	4.7	7.1	6.8
6.4	6.2	5.1	7.9	6.1

Why isn't one route consistently faster than the rest? What are the average travel times for each of these five routes? Are the differences in travel times statistically significant? What is the null hypothesis that is being tested? Use an ANOVA table to show your results.

16.3 A REGRESSION INTERPRETATION

The multiple regression model discussed in Chapter 15 is sufficiently general to encompass analysis of variance as a special case. The actual regression equation will have to be a bit different from those we have seen before, in that the explanatory variables we encountered in previous chapters all had numerical values. Income was $2000, $4000, or some other number; the unemployment rate was 5 percent, 10 percent, or another number. However, we can't say that one treatment is twice the size of another. All that we can say is that the treatments are different, and that as a consequence, their effects on Y may be different, too.

The treatments model introduced at the beginning of this chapter is

$$\text{treatment 1:} \quad Y = \alpha_1 + \epsilon$$

$$\text{treatment 2:} \quad Y = \alpha_2 + \epsilon$$

$$\cdot$$
$$\cdot$$
$$\cdot$$

$$\text{treatment } k: \quad Y = \alpha_k + \epsilon$$

We can't use the treatments themselves as typical explanatory variables, because the distinction between treatments is qualitative—"Treatment 4 was used, instead of the other treatments." To handle differences that are qualitative rather than quantitative, statisticians invented **0–1 dummy variables**, which are variables that are equal to 0 or 1, depending on whether or not a particular characteristic is true. Here, with k treatments, our regression model can be

$$Y = \alpha + \beta_1 D_1 + \beta_2 D_2 + \cdots + \beta_{k-1} D_{k-1} + \epsilon \qquad (16.3)$$

where

$$D_1 = 1 \text{ if treatment 1 is used, 0 otherwise}$$
$$D_2 = 1 \text{ if treatment 2 is used, 0 otherwise}$$
$$\cdot$$
$$\cdot$$
$$\cdot$$
$$D_{k-1} = 1 \text{ if treatment } k - 1 \text{ is used, 0 otherwise}$$

The parameters are

$$\alpha = \alpha_k$$
$$\beta_1 = \alpha_1 - \alpha_k$$
$$\beta_2 = \alpha_2 - \alpha_k$$
$$\cdot$$
$$\cdot$$
$$\cdot$$
$$\beta_{k-1} = \alpha_{k-1} - \alpha_k$$

Notice the clever slight of hand played by these 0–1 dummy variables. If the first treatment is used, then only D_1 is not equal to zero and Y will be

$$Y = \alpha + \beta_1 + \epsilon$$
$$= \alpha_k + (\alpha_1 - \alpha_k) + \epsilon$$
$$= \alpha_1 + \epsilon$$

If the second treatment is used, then only D_2 is not equal to zero and Y will be

$$Y = \alpha + \beta_2 + \epsilon$$
$$= \alpha_k + (\alpha_2 - \alpha_k) + \epsilon$$
$$= \alpha_2 + \epsilon$$

and so on. Thus, the multiple-variable Equation 16.3 has all of the k equations embedded in it.

The parameter α in Equation 16.3 gives the value of Y for the kth treatment, the one without a dummy variable. The $k - 1$ parameters β_i represent between-group differences—the extra effect on Y of using the ith treatment rather than treatment k. For instance, β_2 gives the difference in the expected values of Y for the second and kth treatments.

The k parameters α_i in Equation 16.3 can be estimated, as with any multiple regression; the only peculiarity is that the values of the explanatory variables are either 0 or 1. If, for instance, there were three treatments and four observations of the effects of each treatment, the data for the two explanatory variables would look like this:

treatment	D_1	D_2
1	1	0
1	1	0
1	1	0
1	1	0
2	0	1
2	0	1
2	0	1
2	0	1
3	0	0
3	0	0
3	0	0
3	0	0

It turns out, naturally enough, that such a multiple regression yields the estimates

$$a = \overline{Y}_k$$
$$b_1 = \overline{Y}_1 - \overline{Y}_k$$
$$b_2 = \overline{Y}_2 - \overline{Y}_k$$

and so on, giving the implicit estimates $a_i = \overline{Y}_i$. That is, the estimate of the expected value for each treatment is the observed sample mean for that treatment.

The null hypothesis that the treatment doesn't matter ($\alpha_1 = \alpha_2 = \cdots = \alpha_k$) can be written as

$$H_0 : \beta_1 = \beta_2 = \cdots = \beta_{k-1} = 0$$

Fisher has shown us that this composite hypothesis can be tested with his F-statistic. The lesson is, in fact, much more general: *Fisher's F-test can be used with any regression model to test any composite hypothesis!*

In general, the multiple regression model is

$$Y = \alpha + \beta_1 X_1 + \beta_2 X_2 + \cdots + \beta_k X_k + \epsilon$$

The predicted value of Y is given by

$$\hat{Y} = a + b_1 X_1 + b_2 X_2 + \cdots + b_k X_k$$

where a and the b_i are the estimated values of α and β_i. The variance of Y about its mean $\overline{Y}$ can be separated into two parts, the deviation of each prediction from the mean of Y and the prediction error $Y - \hat{Y}$:

$$Y - \overline{Y} = (\hat{Y} - \overline{Y}) + (Y - \hat{Y})$$

If we square this and sum it over the different values of Y, we get

$$\text{total sum} \atop \text{of squares} = {\text{prediction} \atop \text{sum of squares}} + {\text{sum of squared} \atop \text{prediction errors}}$$

or

$$\text{total sum} \atop \text{of squares} = {\text{explained} \atop \text{sum of squares}} + {\text{unexplained} \atop \text{sum of squares}}$$

The variation in the predictions is the "explained" sum of squares, because this is the variation in Y that is attributed to the explanatory variables. The prediction errors are the unexplained variation in Y. In ratio form,

$$1 = \frac{\text{explained}}{\text{total}} + \frac{\text{unexplained}}{\text{total}}$$

Because R-squared is 1 minus the ratio of the sum of squared prediction errors to the sum of squared deviations about the mean,

$$R^2 = 1 - \frac{\text{unexplained}}{\text{total}} = \frac{\text{explained}}{\text{total}}$$

Thus, R-squared can be thought of as the fraction of the variation in the dependent variable that is explained by the regression model.

A Generalized F Test

Fisher's F test can be applied to a wide variety of null hypotheses. A very general statement is as follows: Null hypotheses restrict the values of the parameters, so that some parameters are equal to each other or are equal to zero. To test such a hypothesis, the regression equation can be estimated twice, once with no restrictions and once imposing these restrictions. The resulting sums of the squared prediction errors are called "unrestricted unexplained" and "restricted unexplained," respectively. Because parameter restrictions necessarily increase the prediction errors, the question is whether this worsened fit is statistically significant—whether the parameter restrictions imposed by the null hypothesis increase the prediction errors sufficiently to persuade us to reject that hypothesis.

The null hypothesis can be tested by computing

$$F = \frac{\left({\text{restricted} \atop \text{unexplained}} - {\text{unrestricted} \atop \text{unexplained}} \right) / \text{NUM}}{\left({\text{unrestricted} \atop \text{unexplained}} \right) / \text{DEN}} \tag{16.4}$$

where the degrees of freedom for the numerator and denominator are

$$\text{NUM} = \text{number of restrictions imposed by null hypothesis}$$
$$\text{DEN} = \text{degrees of freedom for unrestricted regression}$$

For instance, in the treatments examples emphasized in this chapter, the unrestricted unexplained sum of squares is the squared deviations about the k means. With the $k - 1$ restrictions that the treatments have the same effects, the least squares predictor is the overall mean $\overline{Y}$ and the restricted unexplained sum of squares is equal to the total sum of the squared deviations about $\overline{Y}$. The degrees of freedom for the numerator is the number of restrictions, $k - 1$, and for the denominator it is the total number of observations kn less the number of parameters to be estimated k, giving $k(n - 1)$. Thus

$$F = \frac{\left(\begin{array}{c} \text{total} \\ \text{sum of} \\ \text{squares} \end{array} - \begin{array}{c} \text{squared} \\ \text{deviations} \\ \text{about means} \end{array}\right)/(k - 1)}{\left(\begin{array}{c} \text{squared} \\ \text{deviations} \\ \text{about means} \end{array}\right)/k(n - 1)}$$

the same as was derived earlier. The beauty of the present description of the F test is its generality. It can handle an incredible number of models and null hypotheses. The chapter will close with three brief examples.

First, let's analyze the fluorescein data once more, this time using the regression model

$$Y = \alpha + \beta D + \epsilon$$

where the dummy variable D is equal to 1 if plain water is used and equal to 0 if the fluorescein solution is applied. The parameter interpretation

$$\alpha = \alpha_2$$

$$\beta = \alpha_1 - \alpha_2$$

shows that this is indeed the original model

$$\text{plain water: } Y = \alpha_1 + \epsilon$$

$$\text{fluorescein: } Y = \alpha_2 + \epsilon$$

To estimate the regression model, we use the following data for Y and D:

treatment	Y	D
F	28	0
F	33	0
F	24	0
F	27	0
W	27	1
W	30	1
W	23	1
W	24	1

Ordinary least squares yields

$$\hat{Y} = 28.0 - 2.0\ D, \quad R^2 = .1$$
$$\quad [16.2] \quad [0.82]$$

[ ]: *t*-values

and the sum of squared prediction errors turn out to be

$$\frac{\text{unrestricted}}{\text{unexplained}} = 72$$

The restriction that fluorescein doesn't matter, $\beta = 0$, simplifies the model to

$$\hat{Y} = \bar{Y} = 27$$

with a sum of squared prediction errors

$$\frac{\text{restricted}}{\text{unexplained}} = 80$$

The unrestricted regression has DEN $= 8 - 2$ degrees of freedom since 8 observations are used to estimate 2 parameters. The null hypothesis $\beta = 0$ imposes NUM $= 1$ restriction on this regression.

The substitution of these various pieces of information into equation 16.4 gives

$$F = \frac{(80 - 72)/1}{72/(8-2)}$$

$$= .667$$

the same *F*-value obtained earlier in this chapter by a very different route. Thus, as advertised, analysis of variance is a special case of regression analysis.*

Now, to show the generality of Fisher's *F* test, let's go back to the example of using midterm scores X_1 and homework grades X_2 to predict final exam scores Y. The data in Table 15.2 yielded this regression equation

$$\hat{Y} = 5.80 + 0.51\ X_1 + 0.38\ X_2, \qquad \text{SEE} = 6.1, \qquad R^2 = .42$$
$$\quad [0.3] \quad [2.0] \qquad\quad [2.7]$$

[ ]: *t*-values

The reported *t*-values test the hypothesis $\beta_1 = 0$ or $\beta_2 = 0$, but what about the combined hypothesis, that both β_1 and β_2 are equal to 0? For this, we need an *F* test.

If β_1 and β_2 are zero, then allowing nonzero estimates shouldn't improve the predictions of Y very much. If, on the other hand, β_1 and β_2 are not equal to zero, then constraining their estimates to be zero should undermine the predictions. So,

---

*With a single restriction, the hypothesis $\beta = 0$ can also be tested by the 0.8 *t*-value. Exercises 16.29 and 16.30 show that the *t* and *F* tests coincide in this case.

the relevant question is how much difference these two restrictions make to the predictive accuracy. In the unrestricted equation, the sum of squared prediction errors happens to be 970.0. If we constrain β_1 and β_2 to be zero, then the estimated equation is just the average final exam score:

$$\hat{Y} = \bar{Y} = 81.34$$

and the sum of squared prediction errors is 1658.2. Thus, the appropriate F-statistic is

$$F = \frac{\left(\begin{array}{c}\text{restricted}\\\text{unexplained}\end{array} - \begin{array}{c}\text{unrestricted}\\\text{unexplained}\end{array}\right)/\text{NUM}}{\left(\begin{array}{c}\text{unrestricted}\\\text{unexplained}\end{array}\right)/\text{DEN}}$$

$$= \frac{(1658.2 - 970.0)/2}{970.0/(29 - 3)}$$

$$= 9.22$$

The numerator has 2 degrees of freedom, because we're imposing two restrictions. The denominator has $29 - 3 = 26$ degrees of freedom, because the unrestricted equation has 29 observations and 3 estimated parameters. Table 6 at the end of the book tells us that, were the null hypothesis true, there would be a .05 probability of F exceeding 3.37, and so the observed 9.22 F-value leads us to reject the hypothesis that both midterm scores and homework grades are of no value in predicting final exam scores. These results are displayed in the ANOVA Table 16.6.

For a third example, let's look again at using high school GPA X_1, verbal SAT score X_2, and math SAT score X_3 to predict freshman-year GPA Y. The estimated equation reported in Chapter 15 is

$$\hat{Y} = 0.437 + 0.361\ X_1 + 0.0014\ X_2 + 0.0007\ X_3, \qquad R^2 = .26$$
$$\qquad [20.3] \quad [6.23] \qquad [5.50] \qquad [2.64]$$

[　]: t-values

Table 16.6 *ANOVA table for predicting final exam scores*

Source of variation	Sum of squares	Degrees of freedom	Mean sum of squares	F
Explained by regression	688.2	2	344.1	
				9.22
Unexplained by regression	970.0	26	37.3	
Total	1658.2	28		

What if we want to test the hypothesis that verbal and math SAT scores affect freshman GPA equally: $\beta_2 = \beta_3$? Again, an F test can be devised. If we impose this restriction, then the equation to be estimated is

$$Y = \alpha + \beta_1 X_1 + \beta_2 (X_2 + X_3) + \epsilon$$

Under this null hypothesis, what matters is the total SAT score, not the division between verbal and math, because verbal and math scores count equally. Least squares estimation of this restricted equation yields

$$\hat{Y} = 0.407 + 0.358\, X_1 + 0.0021\, (X_2 + X_3), \qquad R^2 = .25$$

Using the unrestricted and restricted sums of squared prediction errors, the value of the F-statistic turns out to be

$$F = \frac{(59.31 - 58.91)/1}{58.91/(359 - 4)}$$

$$= 2.39$$

The numerator has 1 degree of freedom because the null hypothesis imposes one restriction, and the denominator has $359 - 4 = 355$ degrees of freedom because the unrestricted form uses data on 359 students to estimate 4 coefficients. Table 6 says that there is a .05 probability of $F > 3.9$, and thus, at the 5 percent level, we cannot reject the null hypothesis that math and verbal SAT scores have similar implications for college success.

Exercises

16.21   Use the data in Table 15.1 to estimate the equation

$$Y = \alpha + \beta_1 X_1 + \beta_2 X_2 + \beta_3 X_3 + \epsilon$$

where the dependent variable is fuel usage and the three independent variables are travel, horsepower, and speed. Make an F test of the hypothesis that $\beta_1 = \beta_2 = \beta_3 = 0$. Use an ANOVA table to show your results.

16.22   A certain technical analyst agrees that there is no simple relationship between stock returns from one month to the next, but argues that stock returns can be predicted from returns over the preceding two months. To test this theory, use the data in Table 16.2 to estimate the equation

$$Y = \alpha + \beta_1 X_1 + \beta_2 X_2 + \epsilon$$

where Y is the return this month, X_1 is the return the preceding month, and X_2 is the return the month before that. For example, the first observation is $Y = 0.30$, $X_1 = 5.85$, and $X_2 = -7.43$. Use an F test for the null hypothesis that $\beta_1 = \beta_2 = 0$.

16.23   In Exercise 15.47, you investigated how weight depends on age and height. Now use the data given there to estimate the equation

$$Y = \alpha_1 + \alpha_2 D_2 + \alpha_3 D_3 + \cdots + \alpha_6 D_6 + \beta_1 X + \epsilon$$

where Y is weight, X is height, and the D_i are five 0–1 dummy variables for age:

$$D_2 = 1 \text{ if } 25\text{–}34, 0 \text{ otherwise}$$
$$D_3 = 1 \text{ if } 35\text{–}44, 0 \text{ otherwise}$$
$$D_4 = 1 \text{ if } 45\text{–}54, 0 \text{ otherwise}$$
$$D_5 = 1 \text{ if } 55\text{–}64, 0 \text{ otherwise}$$
$$D_6 = 1 \text{ if } 65\text{–}74, 0 \text{ otherwise}$$

Interpret your estimates.

16.24 (*continuation*) What theoretical and empirical differences are there between this model and the model estimated in Exercise 15.47?

16.25 (*continuation*) Make an F test of the null hypothesis that all five of these dummy-variable coefficients equal zero. In plain English, what is the null hypothesis and what is your conclusion?

16.26 A political scientist claims that the relationship between the economy and election results has changed since World War II. Use the data in Table 14.5 for the years 1928 to 1980 to estimate the equation

$$Y = \alpha + \beta X + \epsilon$$

where Y is the incumbent percentage of the vote and X is the change in the unemployment rate. Now use 0–1 dummy variables to reestimate this equation, allowing for the possibility that the intercept α for 1928 to 1944 is not the same as the intercept for 1948 to 1980. What, in plain English, is this hypothesis? What are the results of an F test of the hypothesis?

● 16.27 (*continuation*) Now use 0–1 dummy variables to test the hypothesis that the slope β for 1928 to 1944 is not the same as the slope for 1948 to 1980. (Assume that the intercept is constant.) What, in plain English, is this hypothesis? What are the results of an F test?

● 16.28 (*continuation*) Now make an F test of the hypothesis that both the intercept and slope are different for 1928–1944 and 1948–1980.

16.29 Use the data given in Table 13.1 to estimate the equation $Y = \alpha + \beta X + \epsilon$, where Y is household spending and X is disposable income. To test the null hypothesis $\beta = 0$, do the following:

a. Calculate the t-statistic and compare it to the critical values given in Table 4 for both a 5 percent and 1 percent probability of Type I error.
b. Now calculate the F-statistic and compare it to the critical values given in Table 6 for both a 5 percent and 1 percent probability of Type I error.
c. Do these test results agree?

● 16.30 (*continuation*) Do you see any relationship between the numbers used for these t and F tests? To see if this is a quirk, use Appendix Tables 4 and 6 to compare the t-statistic with $n - 1$ degrees of freedom and the F-statistic with 1 degree of freedom for the numerator and $n - 1$ degrees of freedom for the denominator. What do you conclude?

16.4   SUMMARY

The analysis of variance is a powerful and, yet, quite general procedure. Entire books have been written on the details,[5] but the logic is relatively straightforward. We have a null hypothesis that the expected values of the effects of k treatments are equal. If the n observations of each treatment come from a single distribution, then the variance of the sample means should be σ^2/n. If the observed variance of the sample means is much greater than this, then the data indicate that the observed differences in the means are not reasonably attributed to chance variation, but must instead be caused by different expected values for the various treatments. To implement this procedure, we use the variation within each treatment to estimate σ. Fisher's F-statistic is

$$F = \frac{n(\text{variance of sample means})}{(\text{mean of sample variances})}$$

The F-value can also be calculated from sums of squared deviations,

$$F = \frac{n(\text{sum of squared deviations of } k \text{ means})/(k - 1)}{(\text{sum of squared deviations about the } k \text{ means})/k(n - 1)}$$

Part of its appeal is that, unlike many of our earlier statistical tests, analysis of variance can handle differences in more than two means. It can also handle more than the "one-way" ANOVA that I have shown you. For example, crop yields may depend not only on the watering solution, but also on the varieties planted. ANOVA can deal with this question and much more, but this Pandora's box is best left to a specialized course.

Fisher's F distribution does assume normality and equal variances for each treatment. Formal statistical tests for these assumptions are covered in more advanced courses; for now, all we can do is make a casual check for obvious violations. For normality, at least, we can appeal to the central limit theorem and hope that the variety of reasons for random variation cause Y to follow a normal distribution.

REVIEW EXERCISES

16.31   A new executive claims that female employees spend more time on the phone than male workers. To test this theory, 10 males and 10 females are selected at random and their calls are monitored for a week (without their knowledge). The results (in minutes):

females	males
960	540
420	640
280	500
540	220
260	140

240	480
220	400
560	700
140	780
500	300

Determine the following:

a. the mean times for females and males

b. the variances of the times for females and males

c. the mean of the variances

d. the variance of the means

e. the value of Fisher's F-statistic

f. if there is a statistically significant difference in the time females and males spend on the phone

16.32   General Stuff is introducing a new breakfast cereal and trying to decide whether to sell it in a package that measures $10 \times 6 \times 3$ inches or $10 \times 9 \times 2$ inches. The product is test marketed in 16 different cities, with the following sales results:

$10'' \times 6'' \times 3''$	$10'' \times 9'' \times 2''$
830	850
490	710
630	820
560	930
480	670
550	810
620	860
640	750

a. What are the mean sales for each package size?

b. What are the variances of sales for each size?

c. What is the mean of the variances?

d. What is the variance of the means?

e. What is the value of Fisher's F-statistic?

f. Is there a statistically significant difference in the sales of these two package sizes?

16.33   Farmer Jones claims that Gulp Feed makes pigs plumper than Glup Feed. To prove his claim, he raises nine pigs on Gulp and nine pigs on Glup. After two years, their weights are recorded:

Gulp	*Glup*
130	128
162	152
130	140
180	124
134	110
156	124
134	114
132	148
108	122

a. If Jones is right, why don't all of the pigs raised on Gulp weigh more than those on Glup?
b. What are the mean weights for each feed?
c. What are the variances of weights for each feed?
d. What is the mean of the variances?
e. What is the variance of the means?
f. What is the value of Fisher's F-statistic?
g. Is there a statistically significant difference in the pig weights?

16.34 A researcher wants to see if IQs are related to hair color. A random sample of 30 people yields the following data:

hair color

dark	*light*	*red*
120	80	120
85	105	80
100	115	115
95	100	110
115	115	105
105	105	100
105	110	85
115	80	85
90	95	125
110	85	115

a. What are the mean IQs for each hair color?
b. What are the variances of IQs for each hair color?
c. What is the mean of the variances?
d. What is the variance of the means?
e. What is the value of Fisher's F-statistic?
f. Is there a statistically significant difference in the IQs of people with different hair colors?

16.35 A marketing executive has been asked to select the color for a new soap box: red, yellow, green, or blue. This executive selects 20 stores at random (5 per color) to test market the product. The sales results are:

red	*yellow*	*green*	*blue*
510	525	320	365
605	500	280	350
580	360	300	325
590	460	260	335
580	450	230	355

Are these differences in sales statistically significant? What is the null hypothesis being tested?

16.36 Professor Jones is teaching a statistics class with 150 students. For her final examination, she prepares 50 copies of 3 different tests. These 150 exams are then shuffled and passed out randomly to her students. Their scores can be summarized as follows:

	test 1	test 2	test 3
mean	82.90	84.70	83.05
variance	89.87	102.41	107.72

Do the data indicate that the tests are equally difficult?

16.37 A large business wants to know if the number of employee absences varies with the days of the week. Data on the number of people absent each day for a 50-week period can be summarized as follows:

	Monday	Tuesday	Wednesday	Thursday	Friday
mean	730	620	635	615	670
variance	3690	4520	5300	4130	3870

Is there a statistically significant difference in the number of people that are absent on different days of the week?

16.38 ''Bite Back!,'' a consumer-protection television show, compared 3 brands of sandwich bags. Each brand was used to wrap 10 different sandwiches, and the weight loss after 2 days was recorded to gauge the moisture retention. The results were as follows:

	brands	
Plad	Clad	Blad
98	106	105
97	102	98
117	118	106
89	96	99
88	97	95
79	79	96
102	103	101
83	80	91
130	113	112
91	97	98

Why do the results vary from one sandwich to the next? If one bag were better, wouldn't it always have less weight loss? What is the value of Fisher's F-statistic here? Is there a statistically significant difference in the bags' moisture retention?

16.39 Three long jumpers at a track meet are each given 5 jumps. Their jumps were recorded:

Fred	Ned	Ed
23' 6"	24' 9"	25' 3"
22' 10"	24' 7"	26' 8"
24' 2"	23' 5"	25' 8"
24' 4"	25' 6"	24' 9"
23' 11"	25' 0"	26' 8"

Do these data indicate a statistically significant difference in their long-jumping abilities? What is the null hypothesis being tested here?

16.40 The investigation of daily stock patterns reported in the text was based on the Standard & Poor's 500 stock index. These researchers also looked at an index compiled by the Center for Research in Security Prices (CRSP):

	Monday	Tuesday	Wednesday	Thursday	Friday
mean	−.117	.010	.105	.047	.106
variance	.660	.518	.626	.469	.456

Does the F-value for these data reject the null hypothesis that the expected stock return is the same for each day of the week? (For simplicity, assume that the 4132 days reported are equally divided among these 5 days of the week.)

16.41 (*continuation*) The researchers used these data to estimate the equation

$$Y = \alpha_1 D_1 + \alpha_2 D_2 + \alpha_3 D_3 + \alpha_4 D_4 + \alpha_5 D_5 + \epsilon$$

where

$$D_1 = 1 \text{ if Monday, 0 otherwise}$$

$$D_2 = 1 \text{ if Tuesday, 0 otherwise}$$

$$D_3 = 1 \text{ if Wednesday, 0 otherwise}$$

$$D_4 = 1 \text{ if Thursday, 0 otherwise}$$

$$D_5 = 1 \text{ if Friday, 0 otherwise}$$

Can you guess what the values of their least-squares estimates turned out to be?

16.42 (*continuation*) To investigate whether Monday returns were significantly different from the other days of the week, they also regressed the equation

$$Y = \alpha + \beta_2 D_2 + \beta_3 D_3 + \beta_4 D_4 + \beta_5 D_5 + \epsilon$$

where the dummy variables are as defined in the preceding exercise. Can you guess what the values of these parameter estimates turned out to be? How would you test the hypothesis that the expected values of Monday and Tuesday returns are not same?

16.43 A statistics instructor believes that midterm scores are twice as important as homework in predicting final exam scores. Use the data in Table 15.2 to estimate the equation

$$Y = \alpha + \beta X_1 + \beta X_2 + \epsilon$$

where Y is the final exam score and the two explanatory variables are midterm and homework scores. Make an F test of the hypothesis that $\beta_1 = 2\beta_2$.

16.44 The value of F needed to reject the null hypothesis that the treatments are unimportant depends on the selected probability α of Type I error. Is this requisite F larger for $\alpha = .05$ or .01? Why?

•• **16.45** The value of F needed to reject the null hypothesis that the treatments are unimportant depends on the size of the sample n. Does this requisite F-value go up or down as n increases? Why?

•• **16.46** Consider the simple regression model $Y = \alpha + \beta X + \epsilon$. Use the estimation formulas given in Chapter 13 to show that the value of the F-statistic is always equal to the value of the t-statistic squared.

•• **16.47**   Show that the ratio of the variation between treatments to the total variation is the unadjusted R-squared. Is this a mathematical quirk, or does it make sense?

•• **16.48**   What is the relationship between Fisher's F-statistic and R-squared? See if you can find a simple equation relating the two. What is the value of F when R-squared $= 0$? When R-squared $= 1$?

• **16.49**   Two economists wanted to see if the relationship between the growth rates of money and GNP changed after the Federal Reserve changed its operating procedures in October 1979.[6] They used quarterly data for the second quarter of 1960 through the fourth quarter of 1982 to estimate the equation

$$Y = \alpha_0 + \alpha_1 D + \sum_{i=1}^{5} \beta_i X_i + \sum_{i=1}^{5} \gamma_i DX_i + \sum_{i=6}^{10} \beta_i X_i + \sum_{i=6}^{10} \gamma_i DX_i + \epsilon$$

where Y is the rate of growth of GNP, X_i for $i = 1$ to 5 are the rates of growth of $M1$ during the current and past four quarters, X_i for $i = 6$ to 10 are the rates of growth of high-employment government spending during the current and past four quarters, and D is a dummy variable equal to one up until the fourth quarter of 1979 and then equal to zero thereafter. How would you go about testing the null hypotheses that

a. $\gamma_1 = \gamma_2 = \gamma_3 = \gamma_4 = \gamma_5 = 0$?
b. α_1 and all ten γ_i equal zero?

•• **16.50**   (*continuation*) Critique their statistical conclusion that "the stability test for the coefficients on $M1$ growth is conducted by testing the joint hypothesis that all of the estimates [of γ_1, γ_2, γ_3, γ_4, and γ_5] are simultaneously equal to zero. The calculated F-statistic for this test is 2.01; the critical F-value is 2.72 for the 5 percent significance level. Consequently, the hypothesis that the coefficients on $M1$ growth have changed [since the fourth quarter of 1979] can be rejected at the 5% significance level."[6]

CHAPTER 17

Some Nonparametric Tests

Statistics, frankly, drive me nuts.

Larry Merchant
The National Football Lottery

TOPICS

Almost all of the many different statistical tests we have considered so far—involving *t*-statistics, *F*-statistics, and so on—assume that the random variation in the data conforms to a normal distribution. For tests about the value of a population mean, we assumed that the sample mean came from a normal distribution. In statistical tests of the parameters of the regression model, the error term is assumed to be normally distributed. In analysis-of-variance tests, the random variation within each treatment is assumed to follow a normal distribution.

We can appeal to the central limit theorem and a wide variety of empirical studies for theoretical and empirical support for this convenient normality assumption, but there are situations in which the samples are small and the data are very obviously not normally distributed. And even if there is a hint of normality, our enthusiasm may be restrained by a bit of prudent caution.

Statisticians have devised several alternative procedures for the researcher who is reluctant to assume normality. These procedures are intended to be appropriate *no matter what* the distribution of the data. They work for normal distributions, of course, but they also work for nonnormal distributions. For this reason, they are called **distribution-free** or **nonparametric** statistics.

If the data do, in fact, follow a normal distribution, then these nonparametric tests are not as powerful as *t* tests or *F* tests—which use the known implications of normal distributions. For any given probability of Type I error, the nonparametric tests will have higher probability of Type II error. A test that ignores information about the data, such as their normality, won't be as good as a test that uses this information. On the other hand, if the data do not come from a normal distribution, then nonparametric tests have a clear advantage over tests that make an erroneous assumption of normality. The seriousness of the error, and hence, the accuracy of *t* and *F* tests depends, of course, on how incorrect the normality assumption is. Because nonparametric tests are not sensitive to this assumption, they are said to be "robust."

There are many nonparametric tests that are used in widely varying degrees. We will look at a few popular tests in this chapter.

17.1 A SIGN TEST FOR THE MEDIAN

The mean can be a very misleading descriptive statistic. If 99 workers make $10,000 a year, while the boss makes $4,010,000 a year, then the $50,00 mean income does not accurately describe the average worker's pay. In such situations, the median is a popular alternative to the mean. Yet, most statistical tests apply to the mean, because the central limit theorem gives us the convenient result that a sample mean follows a normal distribution. There is no corresponding theorem for the median. With a bit of ingenuity, though, we can concoct a hypothesis test and even a confidence interval for the median.

Let's say that we are professors at a certain small college, which, like most small colleges, does not make faculty salaries public. The president of this college claims that the median salary is $30,000. How could we test this claim, short of finding out everyone's salary? Well, if $30,000 is the median, then half the salaries should be higher than this figure and half lower, so that if a faculty member is randomly selected, there should be a 50 percent chance that the salary will be above $30,000 and a 50 percent chance that it will be below $30,000. A random sample of 20 faculty members should turn up about half above the median and half below. If instead, we find that 17 out of 20 make less than $30,000, then the improbability of this outcome discredits the president's claim. The exact probabilities come from a binomial distribution with a success probability $\pi = .5$.

> For hypothesis tests of the median, the probability that a certain number of sample observations will be above the median and the rest below is given by the binomial distribution with $\pi = .5$.

If we sample 20 faculty members at random, Table 3 at the end of the book tells us that there is a .021 chance that at least 15 out of 20 will be below the population median and a .021 chance that at least 15 out of 20 will be above the median. These numbers provide the cutoffs for a two-tailed test. If the number below the purported median is greater than 14 or less than 6, we reject this claimed median; if the number below the claimed median is between 6 and 14, we accept the null hypothesis. The probability of Type I error is .042; this is not exactly 5 percent, but close enough.

Perhaps the sampled salaries (in $1000s) turn out as follows:

above $30,000		below $30,000	
48.0	29.0	29.0	28.5
43.5	28.5	28.0	28.0
38.5	27.5	27.5	27.0
34.0	27.0	26.5	26.0
31.0	25.5	24.0	23.0

Five are above $30,000, fifteen below $30,000. This result is sufficiently improbable to reject the null hypothesis that the median salary is $30,000.

This clever procedure is called a **sign test** because it focuses on the signs of the deviations from the purported median. Some data are above the median ($+$) and some are below ($-$). Were the null hypothesis true, the number above and below the claimed median should be divided about 50–50. (If an observation happens to be exactly on the claimed median, then it is discarded, because it doesn't provide any information about whether the number above is equal to the number below.)

With a little ingenuity, these sorts of median tests can be applied to a variety of situations. For instance, a farmer may claim that he can predict whether rainfall will be above or below historical average this year. If we are willing to assume that above and below average are equally likely, then a sign test can be constructed readily.

Similarly, a company's claim that a certain diet increases most people's IQ scores would be confirmed statistically if the data reject the null hypothesis that the diet has no effect on IQ scores. Assuming that, under the null hypothesis of "no effect," IQ scores are equally likely to go up or down, a sign test can be used. Perhaps 25 people are given an IQ test, placed on this diet, and then given an IQ test again. The null hypothesis is that scores are as likely to go down as up, and the competing one-sided alternative hypothesis is that scores are more likely to go up than down. If the null hypothesis is true, then the appropriate probabilities are given by the binomial distribution with $\pi = .5$. Table 3 tells us that there is a .054 probability of more than 16 successes in 25 trials, and hence, if 16 or fewer scores increase, we'll conclude that these data are consistent with the null hypothesis that scores are equally likely to increase or decrease. If more than 16 out of 25 scores increase, this is sufficiently improbable under the null hypothesis to call for its rejection.

Sign tests can also be used to compare two groups that are not necessarily before-and-after some event. For instance, the null hypothesis that men and women are paid equally well could be tested by a sample of pairs of men and women. If the null hypothesis is true, then the higher-paid person in each pair is equally likely to be the male or female. This is clearly a fitting candidate for a sign test, and you can set one up in Exercise 17.5.

A Confidence Interval

We can even use the logic underlying the sign test to construct a confidence interval for a median. To illustrate the reasoning, let's look again at the 20 faculty salaries listed earlier. We would like to use these data to pin down the median salary for the entire faculty. Although we can't know the exact median for certain unless we know all the salaries, we can calculate confidence intervals with a .95 chance of encompassing the population median.

Remember, a hypothesis test at the 5 percent level can be conducted by constructing a 95 percent confidence interval and seeing whether it includes the value specified by the null hypothesis. Any number inside the confidence interval would be accepted as a possible value for the parameter, while any value outside the interval would be rejected. Turning the logic around, we can construct a 95 percent confidence interval by seeing which parameter values would be accepted as null hypotheses at the 5 percent level.

For the median salary example, the table of binomial probabilities revealed that there is a .021 chance that 15 out of 20 sampled salaries will turn out to be below the median and a .021 chance that 15 out of 20 will be above the median. These probabilities provided a test with a .042 significance level. If the number of salaries below the purported median is greater than 14 or less than 6, the claimed median should be rejected; if the number below the median is between 6 and 14, the null hypothesis should be accepted. This rule implies that we can identify accepted and rejected hypotheses by finding the specific incomes in our data that

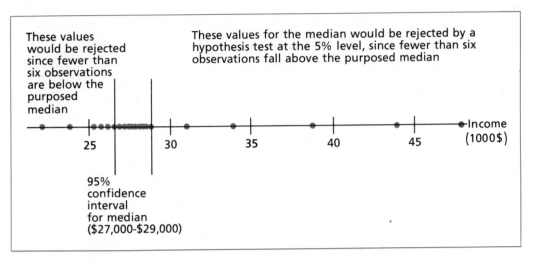

Figure 17.1 *A confidence interval for the median*

are sixth from the bottom and sixth from the top. These turn out to be $27,000 and $29,000. If we tested the null hypothesis that the median income is $26,999, we would reject it, because only 5 of the 20 observed salaries are lower than this. In contrast, $27,001 would be accepted as a possible value for the population median, because there are 6 salaries lower than this. At the other end of the scale, $28,999 would be accepted and $29,001 would be rejected. The usual practice is to draw the boundaries right on the borderline observations: $27,000 and $29,000. Thus, our 95 percent confidence interval for the median salary is $27,000 to $29,000. This logic is illustrated in Figure 17.1.

> With 20 observations, the boundaries for a 95 percent confidence interval for the median are the sixth observation from the bottom and the sixth from the top, because any values outside this range would be rejected as null hypotheses at the 5 percent level.

With a different number of observations, the table of binomial probabilities can be used to find how many observations we should count in from the bottom and top.

Exercises

17.1 A college dean claims that the median salary for full professors is $42,000. Cautious by nature, you use a random sample of 17 professors to test this claim. For a two-tailed test with approximately a .05 probability of Type I error, what outcomes would you consider persuasive evidence against the dean's claim? The data turn out to be (in $1000s): 45.0, 38.5, 41.5, 39.0, 43.0, 44.5, 37.5, 34.0, 54.0, 36.0, 37.5, 62.0, 35.5, 43.5, 38.0, 41.0, and 38.5. Do these data confirm or reject the dean's claim?

17.2   At graduation, a college president claims that the median starting salary for those seniors who have accepted jobs is $25,000. A dubious senior uses a random sample of 17 classmates to test this claim. Ruling out the possibility that this claimed median is too low, the senior constructs a one-tailed test at the 5 percent level. For a sample of size 17, what outcomes should be considered evidence against the president's claim? These 17 salaries (in $1000s) turn out to be: 22.5, 19.0, 28.0, 16.5, 23.5, 24.0, 18.5, 23.5, 29.0, 26.5, 24.5, 32.0, 26.0, 24.0, 26.5, 23.5, and 24.0. Do these data support or refute the president's claim?

17.3   (*continuation*) Is there any reason to think that the answers in this sort of survey may be biased one way or another? If there is a bias, will it increase the chances of incorrectly accepting or rejecting the president's claim? Some people decline to answer salary surveys. Could these nonresponses bias the results or can they be safely ignored?

17.4   An NFL executive claims that the median percentage increase in the salaries of veterans (5 or more years experience) was 24.5 percent last year. How would you structure a sign test of this claim? If you were to sample 50 veterans, what would be your criterion for accepting or rejecting this claim?

17.5   A large corporation claims that there is no systematic distinction between the salaries of its male and female executives. If you were to use a sign test based on a sample 20 males and 20 females, what would be your criterion for accepting or rejecting this claim?

17.6   A certain stockbroker claims that, in most years, her clients make more in the stock market than they would have made in a passbook savings account. How would you make a sign test of her claim? If you have 5 years of data, what would her record have to be to convince you that her claim is correct?

• 17.7   The text uses 20 faculty salaries to test a college president's claim that the median salary is $30,000. Use these data to make a *t* test of the null hypothesis that the mean salary is $30,000. Does your conclusion coincide with that given in the text? If there is any difference, explain how you would reconcile the results of these two tests.

•• 17.8   (*continuation*) If salaries are actually normally distributed with a mean of $28,000, what are the probabilities of Type II error for

a. a sign test of the null hypothesis that the median equals $30,000?
b. a *t* test of the null hypothesis that the mean is $30,000?

17.2   THE WILCOXON-MANN-WHITNEY RANK SUM TEST

Sometimes, we want to compare two populations, such as the income distributions in California and Texas. A random sample of 8 Texans and 10 Californians might give these data:

Texans *(yearly income $)*	Californians *(yearly income $)*
16,000	28,000
3,000	41,000
21,000	12,000
8,000	72,000
65,000	4,000
27,000	32,000
12,000	13,000
32,000	9,000
	22,000
	19,000

To put these numbers in perspective, let's arrange them in order, identifying which are from Texas (T) and California (C):

rank	income $
1	72,000 (C)
2	65,000 (T)
3	41,000 (C)
4.5	32,000 (T)
4.5	32,000 (C)
6	28,000 (C)
7	27,000 (T)
8	22,000 (C)
9	21,000 (T)
10	19,000 (C)
11	16,000 (T)
12	13,000 (C)
13.5	12,000 (T)
13.5	12,000 (C)
15	9,000 (C)
16	8,000 (T)
17	4,000 (C)
18	3,000 (T)

Notice that when there is a tie, we use the average of the ranks they would have had if they hadn't tied. Because the two $32,000 incomes tie for fourth and fifth, both are given ranks of 4.5.

One way to compare the rankings of the Californians and Texans is to compute their average rankings. The average rank of the Californians is

$$AR_1 = \frac{1 + 3 + 4.5 + 6 + 8 + 10 + 12 + 13.5 + 15 + 17}{10}$$

$$= \frac{90}{10}$$

$$= 9.0$$

while the average rank of the Texans is

$$AR_2 = \frac{2 + 4.5 + 7 + 9 + 11 + 13.5 + 16 + 18}{8}$$

$$= \frac{81}{8}$$

$$= 10.125$$

On the average, these 10 Californians tend to have higher incomes than these 8 Texans. The statistical question is whether the observed difference in their average ranks is sufficiently improbable to discredit the null hypothesis that they came from similar distributions. The answer requires knowledge of the distribution of the average ranks under the null hypothesis.

These probabilities have been tabulated and can be found in statistical reference books.[2] If the smaller of the two samples has at least 8–10 observations, then the average rank is approximately normally distributed,* and we can use our two-standard-deviations rule of thumb. The expected value of the average rank is

$$\mu_{AR} = \frac{n_1 + n_2 + 1}{2} \tag{17.1}$$

where n_1 and n_2 are the respective sizes of the two samples. In the California-Texas example, there are 18 observations in all and the expected value of the average rank is 9.5 if the data come from identical distributions. The standard deviation of the average rank depends on the relative sizes of the two samples. With a bit of work, it can be shown that the standard deviation of AR_1 is

$$\sigma_{AR_1} = \left\{ \frac{(n_1 + n_2 + 1) n_2}{12 \, n_1} \right\}^{1/2} \tag{17.2}$$

An analogous formula holds for the standard deviation of AR_2, but we need only look at one of the average ranks (it doesn't matter which one) to make our hypothesis test.

If the observed average rank is within (approximately) two standard deviations of its expected value, then we accept the null hypothesis that the data come from similar distributions; if the observed average rank is more than two standard deviations away, we reject the null hypothesis. This is called variously the Mann-

---

*Interestingly, while nonparametric statistics are designed for data that do not come from a normal distribution, the statistics themselves usually are normally distributed!

Whitney, Wilcoxon, or **Wilcoxon-Mann-Whitney rank sum test**. (Has anybody been left out?)†

In our California-Texas example, if we let California be number 1, then $n_1 = 10$, $n_2 = 8$, and

$$\mu_{AR} = \frac{(10 + 8 + 1)}{2} = 9.5$$

$$\sigma_{AR_1} = \left\{ \frac{(10 + 8 + 1)\, 8}{12\,(10)} \right\}^{1/2} = 1.125$$

Because two standard deviations is 2.25, if the income distributions in California and Texas were the same, then California's average rank should be within 2.25 of 9.5 about 95 percent of the time. The observed average rank of 9.0 is well within this range, and so it does not provide persuasive evidence for rejecting the null hypothesis that the income distributions are the same.

Matched-Pair Samples

In Chapter 12, we observed that sampling error in comparison tests can be reduced if some of the reasons for random variation can be controlled by choosing matched pairs—essentially twins who receive two different treatments. This sampling design is common in medical experiments, and can sometimes be used in business situations, too. Suppose we want to compare two word processors. We could select two people who seem equally competent and give each person the same ten assignments, with one person using one machine and the second person using the other machine. In this way, we have tried to control for some of the reasons for random variation—that some people are more productive and that some tasks are easier.

Perhaps the data turn out as shown in the first four columns of Table 17.1. If we are willing to assume normality, we can use these data for a matched-pair test, as was described in Chapter 12.* If, however, we are reluctant to assume normality,

---

†Equivalently, we can work with the total sum of ranks, SR, instead of the average value AR. The expected value and standard deviation are

$$\mu_{SR_1} = \frac{n_1(n_1 + n_2 + 1)}{2}$$

$$\sigma_{SR_1} = \left\{ \frac{n_1 n_2 (n_1 + n_2 + 1)}{12} \right\}^{1/2}$$

*Under the null hypothesis that there is no difference in the machines, the mean of a sample of n differences has an expected value of zero and a standard deviation $\sigma/\sqrt{n}$. The differences in the fourth column of Table 17.1 have a mean of 4.4 and a standard deviation of 4.88, giving an estimate for $\sigma/\sqrt{n}$ of $4.88/\sqrt{10} = 1.54$. Thus, the observed sample mean is nearly three standard deviations away from zero, leading to a rejection of the null hypothesis.

Table 17.1   *A comparison of two word processors*

Task	Number of minutes to complete task		Difference in working times	Absolute value of difference	Rank of absolute value	Signed rank
	Machine 1	*Machine 2*				
1	34	38	−4	4	5	−5
2	24	27	−3	3	4	−4
3	42	50	−8	8	8	−8
4	72	84	−12	12	10	−10
5	20	18	+2	2	2.5	+2.5
6	46	55	−9	9	9	−9
7	5	4	+1	1	1	+1
8	27	34	−7	7	7	−7
9	32	38	−6	6	6	−6
10	18	16	+2	2	2.5	+2.5
Total			−44			$S = -43$

then we can examine the ranks rather than the magnitudes of the differences. The fifth column gives the absolute values of the differences in working times, so that we can rank the size of the differences, as is shown in the sixth column. The seventh column then signs the rank, showing us that the second machine only beat the first in three cases, and each was a small margin of victory (a low rank).

If the machines were identical, the sum of the signed ranks, S, would come from an (approximate) normal distribution, with a zero expected value and the standard deviation shown here:

$$\mu_S = 0 \tag{17.3}$$

$$\sigma_S = \left\{ \frac{n(n + 1)(2n + 1)}{6} \right\}^{1/2} \tag{17.4}$$

A statistical test based on these facts is called a **Wilcoxon signed-rank sum test**. For $n = 10$, the standard deviation works out to be 19.6, so that the observed value $S = -43$ is two standard deviations away from zero and leads to the rejection of the null hypothesis that the machines are equal.

The Battle for Supermarket Shelves

A supermarket has a limited amount of shelf space and thousands upon thousands of products that it might stock. The supermarket manager must decide which products to carry and which to ignore. This is an important decision, because a store that carries the wrong products can lose sales and even customers. It is, of course, an even more important issue for the product manufacturers. A company can't sell its product if potential customers can't find it.

A second consideration is the particular shelves the products are displayed on. You've surely noticed that supermarkets put batteries, cigarettes, candy, magazines, and assorted specials by the checkout counters, where they are certain to be spotted by customers. With batteries and cigarettes, the store's intent is to remind us that we may be running out. Candy, magazines, and specials are "impulse" items—things that may not be on our shopping lists, but that we might buy if they catch our eye.

The same visibility issue arises on every aisle of the store: Which items are put at the end of the aisle, where every passing shopper sees them, and which are put in the middle of the aisle, where they will only be seen by shoppers who walk down the aisle? Another issue is which products get put at eye level, where they are easily spotted by hurried shoppers, and which products put are put down low or up high, where it takes some effort to find them?

Two researchers made a formal study of the effect of shelf location on sales.[1] In one of their experiments, they arranged for certain breakfast cereals to be displayed at different shelf heights in 24 stores. In 12 of the stores, the selected brand was displayed at eye level; in the other 12 stores, the brand was either above or below eye level. The stores were then ranked according to sales of this brand:

rank	sales	shelf
1	154	eye level
2	150	eye level
3	133	
4	130	eye level
5	126	
6	123	eye level
7	121	
8	112	eye level
9	111	eye level
10	109	
11	96	
12	93	
13	84	eye level
14.5	71	eye level
14.5	71	
16	67	eye level
17	62	eye level
18	58	
19	51	eye level
20	49	
21	38	eye level
22	37	
23	36	
24	27	

Table 17.2 *Matched-pair analysis of shelf height*

Sales in matched stores		Difference in sales	Absolute value of difference	Rank of absolute value	Signed rank
Eye-level shelf	*Other shelf*				
111	71	+40	40	10	+10
150	121	+29	29	9	+9
130	133	−3	3	2	−2
154	126	+28	28	8	+8
67	93	−26	26	6	−6
112	49	+63	63	12	+12
84	109	−25	25	5	−5
123	96	+27	27	7	+7
71	27	+44	44	11	+11
62	58	+4	4	3	+3
38	36	+2	2	1	+1
51	37	+14	14	4	+4
Total		+197			$S = +52$

Under the null hypothesis that shelf height is unimportant,

$$\mu_S = 0 \quad \text{and} \quad \sigma_S = \{n(n+1)(2n+1)/6\}^{1/2} = \{12(13)(25)/6\}^{1/2} = 25.5$$

The average rank is 10.875 for the displays at eye level and 14.125 for the displays at other levels.

If the level of the display is unimportant, the expected value of the average rank is

$$\mu_{AR} = \frac{n_1 + n_2 + 1}{2}$$

$$= \frac{(12 + 12 + 1)}{2} = 12.5$$

and the standard deviation is

$$\sigma_{AR_1} = \left\{ \frac{(n_1 + n_2 + 1)\, n_2}{12\, n_1} \right\}^{1/2}$$

$$= \left\{ \frac{(12 + 12 + 1)\, 12}{12\, (12)} \right\}^{1/2} = 1.44$$

Two standard deviations is 2.88. If the shelf level were unimportant, the average rank for eye-level displays would be 12.5 ± 2.88 in 95 percent of these experiments. Because the observed average rank of 10.875 is inside this range, this test, at least, does not reject the hypothesis that shelf height is unimportant.

Now, in fact, the 24 stores were not two independent random samples, but rather 12 matched pairs that were chosen for the similarity in their weekly sales figures. Thus, if the stores really are twins, the test just used overstates the necessary margin for sampling error. With matched pairs, the signed-rank test can be used, as is shown in Table 17.2. Using Equation 17.4, the standard deviation works out to be 25.5, so that the sum of the signed ranks, $S = 52$, is slightly more than two standard deviations away from zero.

This intriguing study is one of those borderline calls. If the stores were matched twins, as intended, then the data reject the null hypothesis that shelf height is unimportant at the 5 percent level. If, at the other extreme, the pairs are unrelated draws, then the observed sales differences are not sufficient to reject the null hypothesis. The conclusion then hinges on whether or not we believe the stores are matched pairs. The safest course, undoubtedly, is to gather some more data.

Exercises

17.9   The following income data have been collected for ten randomly selected families in California and Florida:

California (yearly income $)	Florida (yearly income $)
9,000	14,000
64,000	26,000
22,000	7,000
42,000	23,000
6,000	48,000
27,000	11,000
17,000	31,000
31,000	5,000
12,000	19,000
24,000	15,000

Make a rank sum test of the null hypothesis that the income distributions in California and Florida are the same.

17.10   The text applies a rank sum test to the incomes of ten California families and eight Texas families. The average ranks of the California families were used in the actual test. Redo the test calculations, this time using the average ranks of the Texas families. Is the result exactly the same? Does it matter, then, which group is used for a rank sum test?

17.11   A tire maker is experimenting with a new, less expensive manufacturing process. Tests of the durability (in miles) of the old and new processes turned up these data:

old	new
39,000	45,000
46,000	33,500
38,500	38,500
56,500	41,000
46,500	37,500
46,000	33,000
47,000	44,000
39,500	40,000

Make a rank sum test of the hypothesis that the new process has no effect on tire durability.

17.12 Here are birth-weight data on a random sample of black and white babies.

black	white
7 lb, 3 oz	7 lb, 10 oz
5 lb, 15 oz	6 lb, 14 oz
6 lb, 12 oz	5 lb, 8 oz
7 lb, 7 oz	8 lb, 12 oz
5 lb, 5 oz	7 lb, 2 oz
8 lb, 2 oz	7 lb, 8 oz
5 lb, 10 oz	7 lb, 10 oz
6 lb, 15 oz	6 lb, 2 oz
6 lb, 19 oz	7 lb, 13 oz
5 lb, 7 oz	7 lb, 5 oz
6 lb, 8 oz	6 lb, 5 oz
7 lb, 12 oz	8 lb, 9 oz
6 lb, 5 oz	6 lb, 12 oz
7 lb, 2 oz	8 lb, 6 oz
7 lb, 9 oz	7 lb, 14 oz

Make a rank sum test of the null hypothesis that these weights come from the same distribution.

17.13 A home inventor claims to have perfected a gizmo that increases gasoline mileage. Tests are conducted involving two similar cars, one with the gizmo and one without, that are driven over the same road at the same time and at approximately the same speeds. Ten such tests are conducted, with a variety of car models, roads, weather conditions, and speeds.

	miles per gallon	
test	with gizmo	without
1	27	24
2	32	30
3	26	29
4	18	22
5	19	26
6	38	34
7	33	37
8	45	43
9	32	28
10	36	35

Assuming these are matched pairs, calculate the sum of signed ranks and test the null hypothesis that the gizmo has no effect on gasoline mileage.

● **17.14** In Exercise 17.11, a rank sum test was used to compare the durability of tires manufactured by two different processes. Make an analysis-of-variance test using these same data. Do you get the same conclusion?

● **17.15** (*continuation*) Explain why you think that an analysis-of-variance test is either more or less appropriate than a rank sum test.

•• **17.16** (*continuation*) What third type of test could you use? Explain the advantages and disadvantages of the third test you chose and then apply this test to these tire data.

17.3 RANK CORRELATION TESTS

You have now seen several nonparametric counterparts to statistical tests that are based on the assumption of normality. Regression analysis provides yet another example. For the regression model

$$Y = \alpha + \beta X + \epsilon$$

the statistical test of the null hypothesis $\beta = 0$ assumes that the error term ϵ comes from a normal distribution. The reasonableness of this convenient approximation is based on the central limit theorem and the belief that the random variation in ϵ is the result of a great many separate influences.

As in the preceding section, the researcher who is reluctant to assume normality can work instead with rankings of the data. Here, for instance, are some midterm and final exam scores plucked from Table 14.1:

student	midterm exam score	midterm exam rank	final exam score	final exam rank
CC	75	3	84	1
JG	56	4	69	4
JL	25	5	49	5
SR	78	1	65	3
JV	76	2	83	2

Instead of estimating the parameters of a regression equation using the scores, we can use the ranks:

midterm rank (X)	final rank (Y)
3	1
4	4
5	5
1	3
2	2

The correlation coefficient R that comes from such a regression is called **Spearman's rank correlation coefficient**. As with any correlation coefficient, R is zero if there is no correlation and close to $+1$ or -1 if there is a close association; i.e., R-squared is close to 1.

With ranked data, the average value of each variable must be $(1 + 2 + \cdots + n)/n$ and, if there are no ties, the standard deviation can be figured out in advance, too. Because of these constraints on the data, Spearman's correlation coefficient simplifies to

$$R = 1 - \frac{6\Sigma(X_i - Y_i)^2}{n(n^2 - 1)}$$

where $\Sigma(X_i - Y_i)^2$ is the sum of the squared deviations between X and Y. For the midterm and final exam data,

$$\Sigma(X_i - Y_i)^2 = (3 - 1)^2 + (4 - 4)^2 + (5 - 5)^2 + (1 - 3)^2 + (2 - 2)^2 = 8$$

so that

$$R = 1 - \frac{6(8)}{5(25 - 1)} = .6$$

and R-squared is .36. There is a positive association between the rankings based on the midterm and final exam scores, but it is hardly a perfect correlation.

For small samples such as this one, the exact probability distribution for R can be worked out under the null hypothesis that the rankings are randomly determined independently of one another, and such tabulations are given in statistical reference books.[3] For $n = 5$, it turns out that R would have to exceed .9 for the correlation between the rankings to be statistically significant at the 5 percent level.

For larger samples of around size 20, a statistical test can be based on the fact that the distribution of R is—you guessed it—approximately normal, with expected value of zero under the null hypothesis of no correlation and standard deviation

$$\sigma_R = \left(\frac{1}{n - 1}\right)^{1/2}$$

Normality is so plausible for the regression model that researchers are seldom reluctant to assume it. As a consequence, Spearman's rank correlation coefficient is infrequently used, unless the only data that are available are rankings. For instance, instead of giving students numerical scores, a professor may rank them from best to worst. This is commonly done, by the way, by graduate school admissions committees. When two people rank the applicants, we can use Spearman's rank correlation coefficient to see there is a correlation between their rankings. If there isn't a strong positive correlation, then these two people are using different criteria, or else, the admissions process is pretty arbitrary!

Exercises

17.17   Rank all 25 of the midterm and final exam scores in Table 14.1 and then estimate the parameters of the regression equation $Y = \alpha + \beta X + \epsilon$, where Y is rank on the final exam and X is rank on the midterm. What is the value of Spearman's rank correlation coefficient? Interpret your results.

17.18   (*continuation*) Is this value of R statistically significant? What is the null hypothesis being tested?

17.19   (*continuation*) Compare and contrast these results with the regression equation estimated in Chapter 14. Why might the results disagree? If they did disagree, how would you choose between them?

17.20   Two vice presidents ranked ten prospective ventures:

	ranking	
venture	*Bob*	*Ray*
1	4	2
2	2	1
3	9	8
4	7	7
5	8	9
6	3	4
7	10	10
8	5	5
9	1	3
10	6	6

Gauge the correlation between these rankings by computing Spearman's rank correlation coefficient. Interpret your result.

17.21   Rank the income and consumption data in Table 13.1 and compute Spearman's rank correlation coefficient. Interpret your result.

17.22   Rank the unemployment and voting data in Table 14.5 and compute Spearman's rank correlation coefficient. Is the correlation between these rankings statistically significant?

● **17.23**   (*continuation*) Write a brief paragraph comparing and contrasting the results of Exercise 17.22 with the equation estimated on page 488 in Chapter 14.

17.4   RUNS TESTS

One of the foundations of probability and statistics is the Bernoulli-trial model, with its assumption that each outcome is independent of the others. The usual analogy is a coin flip, in which the probability of a head or tail does not depend on what happens on other flips. This independence is assumed in the central limit theorem, which underlies the normal distribution, and in the concept of a random sample, which underlies most statistical estimation, hypothesis tests, and confidence intervals.

There are many circumstances, though, in which we may suspect that the outcomes are not really independent. Statisticians have devised some tests for independence and I will show you one here—a **runs test**. Think of the coin-flip analogy again. I just flipped a coin 20 times:

T H H T H H T H T H H T T T T H H T H

Heads happened to come up exactly 10 times, which is, of course, far from guaranteed. (The binomial distribution tells us the chances of exactly 10 heads in 20 flips is .1762.) Ten heads in 20 flips are quite consistent with the natural assumption that, when a fair coin is flipped, heads and tails are equally likely. The assumption of interest here is that the outcomes are independent, in that the chances of a head are not influenced by the outcomes of other flips.

One thing to examine would be what happened after each flip of tails. Here, 6 of the tails were followed by heads and 4 were followed by another tail—nothing surprising there. We might also look at the heads: 5 were followed by tails, 4 by heads, and 1 by the end of the experiment. Again, there are no surprises. We could also look for more complicated patterns, such as the second flip after a flip of heads, or the third flip after a double heads. The possibilities are endless; this is not a pleasant prospect for researchers with better things to do. In addition, we know that determined data mining will lead eventually to some sort of pattern. So, if we look until we find a pattern, we will have shown nothing at all but a stubborn determination.

What we would like is a single test that covers the most common kinds of statistical dependence. To obtain one, let's think about the question from the other side. What are the most common kinds of dependence? There may be *momentum* in that when a head appears, this increases the chances of another head. If there were momentum in coin flips, the data might look like this:

H H H H H H T T T T T T T T T H H H H H

We start out with a head, which leads to heads on the next five throws. Then a tail appears, shifting momentum to the tails side. After 9 straight tails, momentum shifts back to heads for 5 more tosses. At the other extreme—*reaction*—coin flips might obey an extreme version of the naive law of averages: Whenever a head comes up, then a tail must follow, to balance things out:

H T H T H T H T H T H T H T H T H T H T

Notice the difference between these two contrasting kinds of statistical dependence. With momentum, a run of heads is followed by a long run of tails, and then back to a run of heads—three runs in all in 20 flips. With reaction, on the other hand, each run of heads or tails lasts but one flip, and then the coin comes up on the opposite side; in 20 tosses, there are 20 runs.

With *momentum,* the outcomes are characterized by a small number of long runs. With *reaction,* there are a large number of short runs.

Thus, a possible test for independence is to count the number of runs. If there are very few runs, then the data exhibit a surprising amount of momentum; if there are a large number of runs, then a surprising amount of reaction is shown.

With independence, the exact number of runs is a random variable that will vary from one experiment to the next. We could concoct a formal statistical test of independence, if only we could figure out the probability distribution for the number of runs. This is a formidable task! Well, some clever statisticians have already figured out these probabilities for us, and it turns out that, like so many things, the number of runs follows a normal distribution.

> If there are n independent trials, then the probability distribution for the number of runs R is approximately normal:

$$R \sim N[1 + n/2, (n - 1)^{1/2}/2] \tag{17.5}$$

(Both the expected value and standard deviation given here are approximations, which are more accurate the larger the sample.)

In the case of 20 independent coin flips, the expected number of runs is $1 + 20/2 = 11$ and the standard deviation is $(20 - 1)^{1/2}/2 = 2.18$. Ninety-five percent of the time, the number of runs in 20 coin flips should be 11 ± 4.36. More than 15 runs indicates reaction; fewer than 7 suggests momentum. In the actual data reported previously, there are 12 runs, providing no reason to question the assumption of independence.

Now, as you may have guessed, the runs test was not concocted for testing coin flips. There are lots of other, much more interesting situations in which there is a very serious question of whether or not independence holds. In each case, we want to phrase the question so that it parallels the coin-flip model and then apply a runs test. For instance, it has been argued that stock prices follow a random walk, in that, at any moment, they are equally likely to go up or down, regardless of their history. If we think of a price increase as "heads" and a decrease as "tails," then the runs test can be applied.

A slightly more sophisticated model recognizes that stocks, like almost all investments, do not have a zero expected return. Stock prices grow with the businesses they represent, and indeed they must for stocks to be an attractive investment. But still, we can postulate independence in the sense that whether the return on a stock is unusually high or low is unrelated to past performance. The coin-flip scenario assumes that heads and tails are equally likely. To apply a runs test to the annual returns on a stock, we need to determine the *median* annual return over the period studied, so that there is an equal chance that a return in any randomly selected year is higher or lower than this median. An above-average return is a "head" and a below-average return is a "tail." Now we can use a runs test to see whether there is momentum or reaction in stock prices.

Runs in Stock Prices

Technical analysts claim that they can find patterns in stock prices, and that by looking at where prices have been, they can tell where prices are going. Economic theorists dispute these claims. They argue that if any profitable pattern begins to appear, it will be exploited out of existence by technical analysts. If stock prices could be counted on to go up at any point in time, then eager buyers would jump the gun and bid prices up in advance, and others would anticipate this jumping the gun and buy even farther in advance. Still others would anticipate this anticipation, and so on. Chaos is the only sustainable pattern.

Part of the evidence against technical analysts is that they seem to make more money by selling their advice than by using it. There are so many hopeful technicians and so few who make money in the market, that good luck and bad luck seem the most plausible explanation of any success they enjoy. As a class, they don't seem any more successful than other investors.

Some other evidence is that technicians so often disagree in their advice. If there were recognizable patterns, you would think that people would at least agree on what these patterns were. Yet, whenever the market goes up, there are many technicians (those in the momentum camp) advising, "Buy. A body in motion tends to remain in motion." However, there are just as many reactionaries advising, "Sell. What goes up, must come down."

For some statistical evidence, here are the annual stock returns over the 20-year period 1961–1980:

year	% return	year	% return
1961	26.89	1971	14.31
1962	−8.73	1972	18.98
1963	22.80	1973	−14.66
1964	16.48	1974	−26.47
1965	12.45	1975	37.20
1966	−10.06	1976	23.84
1967	23.98	1977	−7.18
1968	11.06	1978	6.56
1969	−8.50	1979	18.44
1970	4.01	1980	32.42

Notice that stock returns were positive about twice as often as they were negative. Stocks usually do have a positive return.

The two middle returns are 12.45 and 14.31 percent. If we split the difference, then the median return is 13.38 percent. Now let's relabel these data in terms of above the median (+) or below the median (−):

year	% return	year	% return
1961	+	1971	+
1962	−	1972	+
1963	+	1973	−
1964	+	1974	−
1965	−	1975	+
1966	−	1976	+
1967	+	1977	−
1968	−	1978	−
1969	−	1979	+
1970	−	1980	+

As a check, you should always count the number of positive and negative signs to see that these are, as intended, equal. Here—barring a typographical error—there are 10 positive and 10 negative signs.

The question of interest is whether the number of runs seems unusually high or low. Equation 17.5 tells us that for $n = 20$, the number of runs is normally distributed with an expected value of 11 and a standard deviation of 2.18, just as in the case of 20 coin flips. If annual stock returns are independent, then there is a .95 probability that the number of runs over a 20-year period will be 11 ± 4.36, using our two-standard-deviations rule of thumb. If the number of runs is less than 7 or greater than 15, then the improbability of such an outcome casts doubt on the independence hypothesis. As it turns out, there are exactly 11 runs in the data (count them yourself), providing no evidence whatsoever against independence.

On the other hand, other empirical studies have found some evidence of momentum over very short time periods, although this momentum has been too slight to pay taxes, brokerage fees, and still make any money. (Or, as the joke goes, the government made money, the broker made money, and two out of three ain't bad.) For some evidence of brief momentum, reconsider Table 16.2, which shows 132 monthly stock returns over the eleven-year period 1970 through 1980. The median return is 0.34 percent. Table 17.3 shows the months in which the returns were above and below this median. Using Equation 17.5, the expected number of runs is $1 + 132/2 = 67$ and the standard deviation works out to be 5.7, so that a two-standard-deviations rule gives 67 ± 11.4 runs. If the monthly returns are independent, then there is only a 5 percent chance that the number of runs over a 132-month period will be fewer than 56 or more than 78. It turns out that a close inspection of Table 17.3 reveals only 55 runs, which is borderline evidence of momentum. It is left as an exercise for the student to determine whether or not this is profitable information.

Table 17.3 *Eleven years of monthly stock returns, above (+) or below (−) median*

Year	Jan	Feb	Mar	Apr	May	June	July	Aug	Sept	Oct	Nov	Dec
1970	−	+	−	−	−	−	+	+	+	−	+	+
1971	+	+	+	+	−	−	−	+	−	−	−	+
1972	+	+	+	+	+	−	+	+	−	+	+	+
1973	−	−	−	−	−	−	+	−	+	−	−	+
1974	−	−	−	−	−	−	−	−	−	+	−	−
1975	+	+	+	+	+	+	−	−	−	+	+	−
1976	+	−	+	−	−	+	−	−	+	−	−	+
1977	−	−	−	−	−	+	−	−	−	−	+	+
1978	−	−	+	+	+	−	+	+	−	−	+	+
1979	+	−	+	+	−	+	+	+	−	−	+	+
1980	+	−	−	+	+	+	+	+	+	+	+	−

Exercises

17.24   If a sequence contains a large number of runs, does this indicate momentum or reaction?

17.25   For each of the following sets of data, indicate whether you would expect to find a large or small number of runs:

a. whether the cars passing a certain point are traveling faster than 55 MPH
b. weekly win or loss by a college football team
c. which team scores in a college basketball game
d. daily pollution readings in Los Angeles
e. the monthly unemployment rate

17.26   With ten observations, how many runs would be considered evidence against the null hypothesis of independence? Flip a coin ten times, record your results, and count the number of runs. Do you accept or reject the hypothesis of independence?

17.27   Write down the results of 20 imaginary flips of a coin. Now use a runs test to see if these imaginary flips really were random.

17.28   Do you think that the success of political parties exhibits momentum, reaction, or randomness? The political parties of the 16 presidential election winners for 1920–1980 are shown here:

1920	Warren Harding, Republican
1924	Calvin Coolidge, Republican
1928	Herbert Hoover, Republican
1932	Franklin Roosevelt, Democrat
1936	Franklin Roosevelt, Democrat
1940	Franklin Roosevelt, Democrat
1944	Franklin Roosevelt, Democrat
1948	Harry Truman, Democrat
1952	Dwight Eisenhower, Republican
1956	Dwight Eisenhower, Republican
1960	John F. Kennedy, Democrat
1964	Lyndon Johnson, Democrat
1968	Richard Nixon, Republican
1972	Richard Nixon, Republican
1976	Jimmy Carter, Democrat
1980	Ronald Reagan, Republican

Use a runs test to see if these party results are random, or else show either significant momentum or reaction.

17.29   Here are some data on the interest rate on three-month Treasury bills:

	Jan	Feb	Mar	Apr	May	June	July	Aug	Sept	Oct	Nov	Dec
1975	6.49	5.58	5.54	5.69	5.32	5.19	6.16	6.46	6.38	6.08	5.47	5.50
1976	4.96	4.85	5.05	4.88	5.18	5.44	5.28	5.15	5.08	4.93	4.81	4.35
1977	4.60	4.66	4.61	4.54	4.94	5.00	5.15	5.50	5.77	6.19	6.16	6.06
1978	6.45	6.46	6.32	6.31	6.43	6.71	7.07	7.04	7.84	8.13	8.79	9.12

Find the median interest rate and then identify the monthly levels that are above (+) or below (−) this median. Count the number of runs and make a runs test of the hypothesis that the monthly interest rate levels are independent.

17.30 (*continuation*) Now compute the monthly changes in the Treasury bill rate. Find the median and record the monthly changes that are above (+) or below (−) this median. Make a runs test of the hypothesis that the monthly changes in the Treasury bill rate are independent.

17.5 SUMMARY

Many statistical tests assume that the random variation in the data follows a normal distribution. If there are doubts about the appropriateness of this assumption, then a nonparametric test can be used. These tests are "robust" in that they do not assume a particular probability distribution, but of course, they cannot be as powerful as tests that take advantage of (correct) knowledge about underlying probabilities.

The sign test for the median is based on the definition of the median: a random draw is equally likely to be above or below the population median. For a random sample of size n, the binomial distribution with a .5 "success" probability gives the chances that x of the outcomes will be above the median and $n - x$ below. A claimed value for the population median can be tested by seeing whether there is an improbable imbalance of outcomes, either above or below this median value. A confidence interval for the median can be constructed by locating the range of observed values that would be accepted as null hypotheses.

The Wilcoxon-Mann-Whitney rank sum test compares two population distributions by ranking the outcomes of samples from both distributions. If the populations are identical, then the average rank for each sample should be similar. For reasonably sized samples (at least 8 to 10 observations in the smaller sample), the average rank is approximately normally distributed with an expected value

$$\mu_{AR} = \frac{n_1 + n_2 + 1}{2}$$

The standard deviation of the average rank for the first sample is

$$\sigma_{AR} = \left\{ \frac{(n_1 + n_2 + 1)\, n_2}{12 n_1} \right\}^{1/2}$$

with a similar formula holding for the second sample. Either of the observed average ranks can be compared to its expected value and standard deviation to see if the deviation is large enough to cast doubt on the null hypothesis that the two populations are identical.

If the two samples are not independent, but are matched pairs, then the sum of the signed ranks, S, can be calculated as demonstrated in Table 17.1. Under the null hypothesis of identical populations (and a reasonably sized sample), S comes from an approximately normal distribution,

$$S \sim N[0, \{n(n + 1)(n + 2)/6\}^{1/2}]$$

If the observed value of S is more than two standard deviations away from zero, then this discredits the null hypothesis.

Spearman's rank correlation coefficient R is used in regression models when the data are ranks. It can be computed in the usual way, by estimating the regression equation and taking the square root of R-squared, or by the shortcut formula

$$\text{rank correlation:} \qquad R = 1 - \frac{6 \, \Sigma(X_i - Y_i)^2}{n \, (n^2 - 1)}$$

where the $X_i - Y_i$ are the observed differences in the ranks. The null hypothesis that the ranks are unrelated implies that R is normally distributed for large samples,

$$\text{rank correlation:} \qquad R \sim N[0, \, 1/(n - 1)^{1/2}]$$

and can be tested by seeing whether the observed value of R is more than two standard deviations from zero.

Runs tests are designed to test the null hypothesis that a sequence of outcomes is independent. There will be a few long runs if the outcomes exhibit momentum and many short runs if there is reaction. Under the null hypothesis of independence, the number of runs is approximately normal,

$$\text{runs:} \qquad R \sim N[1 + n/2, \, (n - 1)^{1/2}/2]$$

If the observed value of R is more than two standard deviations below $1 + n/2$, this indicates momentum; two standard deviations above indicates reaction.

REVIEW EXERCISES

17.31   An admissions officer at a small liberal arts college claims that the median parental income of its students is $26,100. To test this claim, a sample of 20 students yields the following parental incomes (in $1000s): 10.5, 14.5, 12.5, 48.5, 250.0, 23.5, 26.0, 34.0, 29.0, 30.3, 16.0, 21.5, 6.2, 18.0, 125.0, 65.0, 27.0, 32.0, 37.5, and 75.0.

Is the claim supported or refuted? What are your cutoffs for rejecting the admission officer's claim? For these data, what is a 95 percent confidence interval for the median?

17.32   An admissions officer at a small liberal arts college claims that the median parental contribution to the student's college expenses is $3010. To test this claim, a sample of 15 students yields the following data (in $1000s): 3.5, 0.4, 7.5, 12.5, 0.1, 9.0, 2.5, 12.5, 10.0, 1.0, 0.7, 0.0, 3.6, 8.0, and 3.0.

Is this claim supported or refuted? What is your decision rule for rejecting the admission officer's claim? Find a 95 percent confidence interval for the median parental contribution.

17.33   Dr. Quakk claims that older men weigh no more than older women; in particular, if a 65-year-old male and female are chosen at random, the female is, as often as not, the heavier of the two. Set up a sign test of this hypothesis that you could use if you had data for 25 males and 25 females.

17.34   (*continuation*) Use these weights (in pounds) to test Quakk's hypothesis:

males	females	males	females
155	161	225	135
155	145	142	151
127	151	147	129
137	123	155	175
175	149	155	159
177	123	131	157
161	141	177	141
204	175	163	141
145	155	153	173
181	161	141	167
181	137	155	125
141	151	147	123
		191	137

• **17.35**   (*continuation*) In Exercise 17.34, you made a sign test of Dr. Quakk's theory that older men weigh no more than older women. How would you make an *F* test of Quakk's theory using these same data? Do these two tests give the same conclusion? If they didn't, how would you choose between them?

17.36   A new all-potatoes diet claims to reduce most people's weight by 5 pounds within a week. How would you construct a sign test of this claim? If 30 people are tested, what would be your criterion for accepting the company's claim?

17.37   The nationwide median salary of full professors in a certain discipline is said to be $40,000. A random sample of 50 professors in a large state university system found that 30 earned more than $40,000. Does this show that the median salary in the system is greater than $40,000?

17.38   Here the are IQ scores of some randomly selected school children:

female	male
87	87
92	122
112	101
80	103
109	92
82	106
127	121
85	82
97	95
108	106

Make a rank sum test of the hypothesis that the distributions of male and female IQs are identical.

• **17.39**   (*continuation*) In Exercise 17.38, a rank sum test was used to test the hypothesis that the distributions of male and female IQs are the same. Make an analysis-of-variance test using these same data. What are the differences in these tests' assumptions and/or objectives? If the test results disagreed, which test would you find more persuasive?

17.40   A coach claims that the heights of soccer players are no different from the heights of nonplayers. A random sample of 21-year-old males yielded the following heights (in inches):

soccer players	nonplayers
72	66
70	74
67	70
63	68
75	72
71	76
66	73
71	70
69	67

Do these data support or refute the coach's claim?

17.41   A coach claims that the weights of soccer players are no different from the weights of nonplayers. A random sample of 18-year-old males yielded the following weights (in pounds):

soccer players	nonplayers
145	182
164	171
158	146
174	160
155	205
167	115
149	120
170	175
138	133

Do these data confirm or refute the coach?

17.42   Consumer Car magazine tested two new car models: a Sleek and a Boate. They purchased eight Sleeks and eight Boates, and calculated the miles per gallon for each in a 1000-mile test run:

Sleeks	Boates
43.5	34.5
41.0	29.5
37.5	35.5
36.5	31.0
44.0	38.5
41.0	35.0
43.0	41.0
40.0	37.5

Use a rank sum test to see if the observed differences in miles per gallon are statistically significant.

• **17.43** Is it possible to have a rank sum test find a difference in two distributions that is statistically significant but not substantial? Substantial, but not statistically significant? Make up some data to illustrate your arguments.

• **17.44** A technical analyst claims that the price of XYZ stock follows a regular cycle; it rises every day for a week, then falls every day the next week, and then rises again the week after that. If so, would a runs test using daily data show a large or small number of runs? (Be careful. This one is tricky.)

17.45 A traffic study recorded the speeds of cars passing a certain point on an expressway between 8:00 and 8:30 A.M. one morning. These speeds are listed horizontally in the chart; the first two speeds are 68 and 67:

68	67	62	54	59	64	65	58	65	54	60	80	70	70	70
65	60	65	55	55	50	48	52	50	46	46	45	42	40	42
40	40	38	40	40	41	38	40	42	42	42	42	40	42	42
43	45	40	40	39	40	41	42	42	42	38	40	40	42	42
42	40	42	44	42	41	43	45	48	50	44	46	44	44	44
43	45	45	50	45	44	47	48	47	50	46	46	48	46	48

Use a runs test to see if the speeds above and below the median are random.

17.46 Here are some monthly data on the unemployment rate:

	Jan	Feb	Mar	Apr	May	June	July	Aug	Sept	Oct	Nov	Dec
1975	8.1	8.1	8.6	8.8	9.0	8.8	8.6	8.4	8.4	8.4	8.3	8.2
1976	7.9	7.7	7.6	7.7	7.4	7.6	7.8	7.8	7.6	7.7	7.8	7.8
1977	7.5	7.6	7.4	7.2	7.0	7.2	6.9	7.0	6.8	6.8	6.8	6.4
1978	6.4	6.3	6.3	6.1	6.0	5.9	6.2	5.9	6.0	5.8	5.9	6.0
1979	5.9	5.9	5.8	5.8	5.7	5.7	5.7	6.0	5.8	6.0	5.9	6.0
1980	6.3	6.2	6.3	6.9	7.5	7.5	7.8	7.7	7.5	7.5	7.5	7.3

Find the median unemployment rate and then identify the monthly levels that are above (+) or below (−) this median. Count the number of runs and make a runs test of the hypothesis that the monthly levels of unemployment are independent.

17.47 (*continuation*) Now compute the monthly changes in the unemployment rate from Exercise 17.46: for example, 0.0 in February 1975 and 0.5 in March 1975. (You won't have an observation for January 1975.) Find the median change in the unemployment rate and record the monthly changes that are above (+) or below (−) this median. Make a runs test of the hypothesis that the monthly changes in the unemployment rate are independent.

•• **17.48** (*continuation*) Carefully explain the different questions asked by the tests in Exercises 17.46 and 17.47. Write down some hypothetical monthly figures to show how the levels could be independent while the changes are not, and how the changes could be independent while the levels are not.

• **17.49** The text applied a runs test to the monthly stock returns show in Table 16.2. Use these same data to estimate the equation $Y = \alpha + \beta X + \epsilon$, where Y is the percent return this month and X is the percent return the previous month. (You will not be able to use the January 1970 observation for Y, because you don't know the return the previous month.)

If you find a statistically significant relationship, what does this indicate? If the relationship is not statistically significant, what does this indicate? What differences are there in the assumptions and/or objectives of this regression model and the runs test?

•• **17.50** The text applied a runs test to the monthly stock return data in Table 17.3 and found some statistically significant momentum. Let's see if this momentum can be profitable. If momentum is present, then savvy investors may want to buy after a month in which the market has gone up and sell after a down month. First, compute the average return for those months in which the market went up the preceding month and the average return for those months in which the market went down the preceding month. Compare these two average returns. Second, compute the compounded return if an investor starts with $10,000 and buys stocks after the market has gone up, holds these stocks until after the market drops, and then buys in again after the market has gone up. Ignore taxes, but assume a 2 percent brokerage commission on each transaction.

CHAPTER **18**

Time Series Analysis and Indexes

The age of chivalry is gone; that of sophisters, economists, and calculators has succeeded.

Edmund Burke
Reflections on the Revolution in France

TOPICS

623

In some tests, data are collected at virtually identical times, or else, the time differences are unimportant; examples are the test scores of different students, the percentage returns this year on several different stocks, and product sales at somewhat different times in several different stores. In such cases, our interest is centered on how test scores vary across students, how returns differ from one stock to the next, and how sales vary from one store to another. The particular day, month, or year in which the data are collected is not of any special interest. There are other situations, though, in which our attention is focused on time, and in particular, how behavior changes as time passes. We might wonder how SAT scores have varied over the past 20 years, if a stock's return this year is correlated with its return in previous years, or how sales vary with the seasons of the year. These questions of how behavior varies as time passes can be answered with **time series analysis** and, if needed, **index numbers**.

18.1 A PICTURE IS WORTH 1000 WORDS

The most basic tool in time series analysis is a graph, with time on the horizontal axis and the variable of interest on the vertical axis. Figure 18.1 provides an example. Time is marked off in years, from 1970 through 1980. There are 11 annual observations of some hypothetical variable Y. The story told by this picture is that Y has been steadily increasing as time passes.

A persistent movement of a variable, either upward or downward, is called its **trend**.

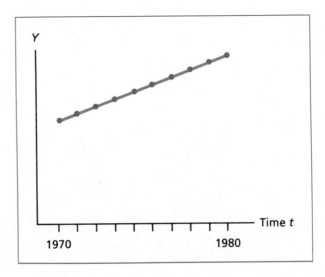

Figure 18.1 *A variable that grows over time*

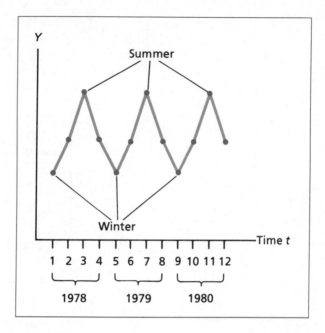

Figure 18.2 *A variable that goes up in the summer and down in the winter*

Figure 18.2 shows some monthly data on another hypothetical variable over the period 1978–1980. In this case, there is no apparent trend, but there is an obvious pattern to the fluctuations. This variable tends to go up in the summer and down in the winter; perhaps it is a graph of ice cream sales. Some variables show weekly patterns; for instance, there may be increased spending during the first week of the month, after the monthly paycheck is received, and decreased spending in the last week of the month, as funds run out. There are also daily patterns (movie attendance on Friday and job absenteeism on Monday). Other variables tend to be abnormally high or low on holidays, such as the sales of turkeys before Thanksgiving and Christmas.

> Short-term, regular fluctuations with the months, weeks, or days of the year are known as **seasonal variations**.

A variable can, of course, exhibit both a trend and seasonal patterns. Figure 18.3 shows a hypothetical example. This variable has been growing over time, but it also regularly increases during the last quarter of each year. This might be the sales of toys, books, or jewelry, which grow with the economy, and also predictably increase shortly before Christmas.

Some fluctuations are unrelated to time, and are just the haphazard consequence of a variety of events. Sales go up because a business decides to reduce the price it charges; sales go down because the Surgeon General declares that the product is hazardous to one's health. Other sales fluctuations may be due to no more than

Figure 18.3 *A variable with trend and seasonality*

Figure 18.4 *A randomly fluctuating variable*

Figure 18.5 *A variable with trend, seasonal, and random fluctuations*

when people happen to run out of a product or when they happen to find the time to go shopping. If sales are graphed versus time, as shown in Figure 18.4, these variations will seem to be just random wiggles and bumps, with no apparent trend or seasonal pattern.

> Fluctuations in a variable that are not related to time are called **random disturbances**.

A variable may have trend, seasonality, and random fluctuations, too. Figure 18.5 shows an example. The trick is to see through the random fluctuations and discover the trend and seasonal patterns.

Some Data

The graphs have so far been hypothetical, to ensure that the patterns are clear. Real data are seldom so well behaved, and the regularities are a bit harder to find, so that the untrained eye cannot always separate the trend, seasonal, and random influences. Let's try a few and then we will see how statistical procedures can be used to unravel time series data.

Figure 18.6   *Gross National Product, billions of 1972 dollars*

Figure 18.6 shows some annual data on U.S. Gross National Product (GNP), going back to the beginning of the century.* This graph was prepared by the Federal Reserve Board and they fitted a trend line, showing that GNP has tended to increase by about 3.1 percent a year over the long run. This long-run growth of the U.S. economy is caused by an expanding population, the accumulation of tools and equipment, and increasing productivity. The fluctuations about this trend line are booms and recessions, which are the business cycles that economists try to explain by looking at the behavior of consumers, businesses, and government. These business cycles appear to have some persistence to them, in that GNP seems to stay below the trend line for an extended period, and then go back above trend for a while.

Figure 18.7 shows U.S. output per hour over this same historical period. Here, the Federal Reserve Board fitted two trend lines, because the rate of growth of productivity seems to have increased since the 1930s. One of the advantages of a

---

*This graph uses a **ratio scale**, which is equivalent to graphing the logarithm of GNP. In the next section, you will see that if a variable grows at a constant percentage rate, then a graph of its logarithm versus time will be a straight line.

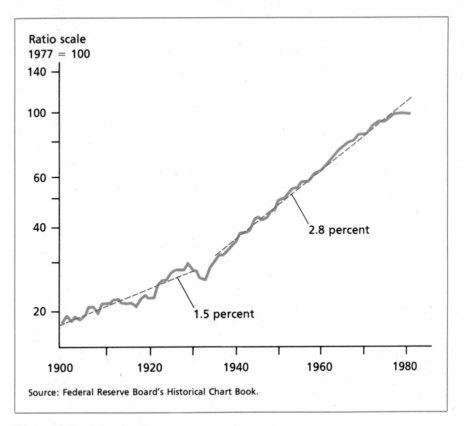

**Ratio scale
1977 = 100**

2.8 percent

1.5 percent

Source: Federal Reserve Board's Historical Chart Book.

Figure 18.7   *Output per hour*

graph is that it may uncover such changes. Figure 18.8 shows an even more dramatic example of how a single fitted trend line can be very misleading. In the first third of the century, the average workweek dropped dramatically, from 53 hours in 1900 to 40 hours in 1930. The workweek collapsed in the Great Depression, when many people had to settle for part-time work, and then jumped to 45 hours during World War II, as people worked overtime to arm the nation. After World War II, the average workweek went back to 40 hours and fluctuated around that level for the next 40 years. These differing historical periods would be masked by a single trend line.

These graphs use annual data going back to 1900 to show long-run trends. Short-term seasonal fluctuations would be lost in these graphs, in that any quarterly bumps and wiggles would be so small as to be indiscernible. Figure 18.9 puts a magnifying glass on quarterly GNP fluctuations by showing the shorter period, 1976–1982. It is apparent that output regularly increases in the fourth quarter and slumps in the first quarter of each year. This pattern may be related to the holiday season and to inhospitable weather during the first three months of the year.

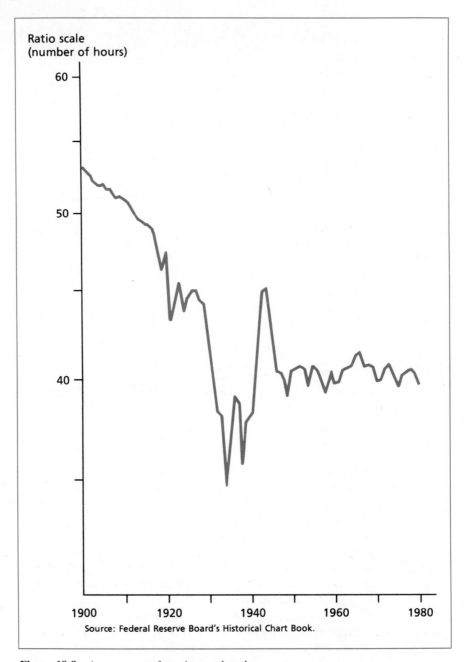

Figure 18.8 *Average manufacturing workweek*

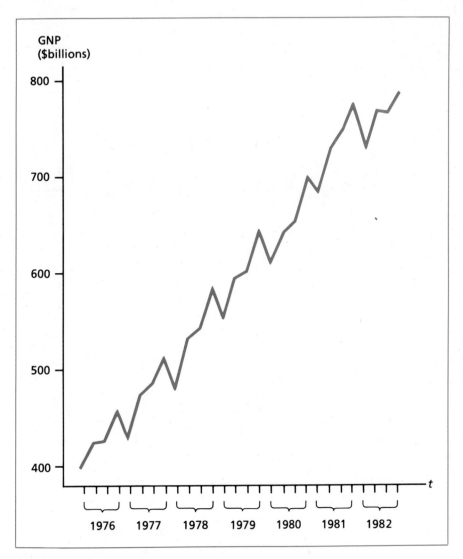

Figure 18.9 *Quarterly GNP, 1976–1982*

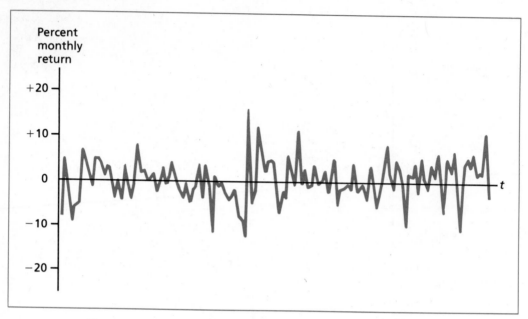

Figure 18.10   *Eleven years of monthly stock returns, 1970–1980*

Figure 18.10 shows some different data: monthly stock returns over the eleven-year period 1970–1980. Neither trend nor seasonality is very apparent here. Perhaps you can spot something, but I can't.

Exercises

18.1   Does the following graph show any trend or seasonality?

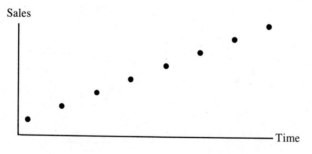

18.2 Does the following graph show any trend or seasonality?

Sales

18.3 Does the following graph show any trend or seasonality?

Sales

18.4 Does the following graph show any trend or seasonality?

Sales

18.2 MODELING A LONG-RUN TREND

The logic of a trend line is that a variable steadily grows or declines as time passes. The simplest model that captures this idea is to let the variable Y be a linear function of some measure of time t,

$$Y_t = \alpha + \beta t \tag{18.1}$$

The subscript t on the variable Y shows that this is the value of the dependent variable at time period t. With annual data, the natural units for t are years. We could let $t = 0$ in 1960, $t = 1$ in 1961, $t = 2$ in 1962, and so on, or we might let $t = 1960$ in 1960, and $t = 1961$ in 1961. The important point is that t increases by 1 each year, so that the annual increase in t records the passage of time. The annual increase in Y as time passes is given by β,

$$Y_t - Y_{t-1} = \beta$$

With monthly data, the most natural scheme is for t to increase by 1 each month; for weekly data, t could increase by 1 each week. In general, the units for t can be set to match the units for our data. The parameter α scales the data by giving the value of Y at $t = 0$,

$$Y_0 = \alpha$$

In this **linear model**, $Y_t = \alpha + \beta t$, the increase in Y each period is a constant β. An alternative assumption is that the *percentage* increase in Y is the same each period:

$$\frac{Y_t - Y_{t-1}}{Y_{t-1}} = g$$

If so,

$$Y_t - Y_{t-1} = g \, Y_{t-1}$$

or

$$Y_t = Y_{t-1}(1 + g)$$

Looking back t periods implies*

$$Y_t = Y_0 (1 + g)^t \tag{18.2}$$

where Y_0 is the value of Y at $t = 0$. (Remember that any number, such as $1 + g$, which is raised to the power 0 is equal to 1.) The parameter g is the constant percentage growth rate of Y as time passes.

Another way of writing this model is to take the logarithms of both sides of Equation 18.2:

$$\ln[Y_t] = \ln[Y_0] + \ln[1 + g] \, t$$

These could either be common logarithms (base 10) or, as shown here, natural logarithms (base $e = 2.71828$) denoted by ln.† Because $\ln[Y_0]$ and $\ln[1 + g]$ are

---

*The substitution of $Y_{t-1} = Y_{t-2}(1 + g)$ into $Y_t = Y_{t-1}(1 + g)$ gives $Y_t = Y_{t-2}(1 + g)^2$. Repeated substitutions yield Equation 18.2.

†The logarithm, base 10, of Y is that number X such that $10^X = Y$. The log of Y, base e, is the number Z such that $e^Z = Y$. The one property we use here is that $\ln[AB] = \ln[A] + \ln[B]$ and, hence, $\ln[(1 + g)^t] = t \ln[1 + g]$.

constants that do not vary with t, we can rewrite the equation as

$$\ln[Y_t] = \alpha + \beta t \tag{18.3}$$

Now compare this equation with the linear model Equation 18.1. In Equation 18.1, Y is a linear function of time t. If we plot Y versus t, we will get a straight line with slope β and intercept α. The slope is the constant *amount* by which Y increases each period. Equation 18.3 is said to be a **log-linear model**, because the logarithm of Y is a linear function of t. If the **log-linear model** is appropriate, then a graph of the logarithm of Y versus time t will yield a straight line. The slope of this line, β, is the logarithm of $(1 + g)$, where g is the constant *percentage* by which Y increases each period. For small values of g, the natural log of $1 + g$ is approximately equal to g:

g	ln[1 + g]
.00	0
.01	.0010
.02	.0198
.03	.0296
.04	.0392
.05	.0488
.06	.0583
.07	.0677
.08	.0770
.09	.0862
.10	.0953
.15	.1398
.20	.1823
.25	.2231

Thus, if natural logs are used, the slope of a fitted line is approximately equal to the percentage increase in Y each period.

The easiest way to make a log-linear graph is to buy some "semi-log" graph paper from your college bookstore. This special paper has a ratio scale, so that when you plot a number Y, you automatically get the logarithm $\ln[Y]$ (multiplied by some unimportant constant). Thus when you plot Y versus t on semi-log paper, you magically obtain a graph of $\ln[Y]$ versus t.

We can draw two conclusions so far:

If Y increases by a constant *amount* each period, then we can model this behavior by expressing Y as a linear function of time t.

If Y increases by a constant *percentage* each period, then the logarithm of Y is a linear function of t.

In practice, matters are never this simple. There are almost always factors other than the simple passage of time that affect Y. If we put these *deviations from trend* into an error term ϵ, then our two trend models become

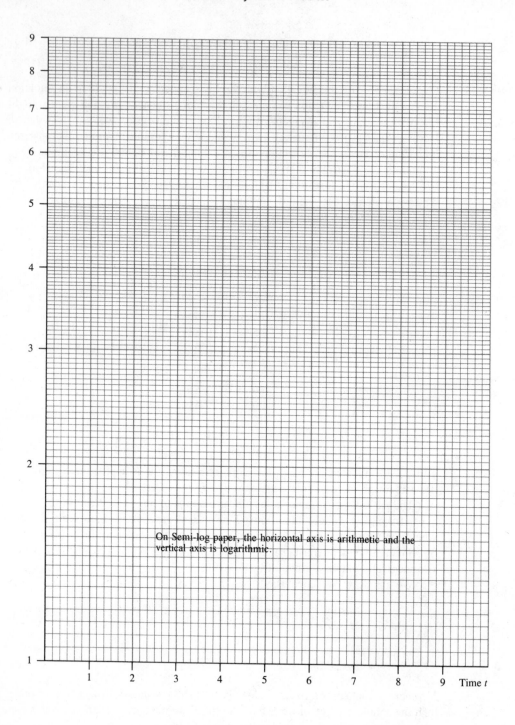

On Semi-log paper, the horizontal axis is arithmetic and the vertical axis is logarithmic.

$$Y_t = \alpha + \beta t + \epsilon \tag{18.4}$$

$$\ln[Y_t] = \alpha + \beta t + \epsilon \tag{18.5}$$

The parameters α and β can be estimated by a simple least squares regression.

To illustrate, let's use the annual GNP data for 1951–1981 that are shown in Table 18.1. (The 1982 and 1983 data will be used later in a forecasting test.) If I graph GNP versus time, as is shown in Figure 18.11, the relationship does not seem to be linear. Instead of a straight line, GNP curves upward, in that the annual *dollar* increase in GNP during the 1970s is generally larger than the *dollar* increase during the 1950s. Perhaps the annual *percentage* increases are comparable. To check this, Figure 18.12 uses semi-log paper to graph the log of GNP versus time. Now the relationship could be described by a straight line. Because the log-linear model seems the most appropriate, we'll use the 1951–1981 data to calculate the least squares estimates of Equation 18.5:

$$\ln[\hat{Y}_t] = -60.028 + 0.034\,t, \qquad R^2 = .991$$

where $t = 1951$ in 1951. The slope 0.034 is an estimate of $\ln[1 + g]$, and the implicit estimate of the annual growth rate g works out to be 0.035, or 3.5 percent per year:

$$g = e^{0.034} - 1 = 0.035$$

This is slightly different than the Federal Reserve's estimate because we used a slightly different time period.

The implicit fitted values of Y can be computed by taking the antilogarithm of $\ln[\hat{Y}_t]$,

$$Y_t = e^{\ln[\hat{Y}_t]}$$

Table 18.1 *Gross National Product, in billions of 1972 dollars*

Year	GNP	Year	GNP	Year	GNP
1951	579.4	1962	800.3	1973	1254.3
1952	600.8	1963	832.5	1974	1246.3
1953	623.6	1964	876.4	1975	1231.6
1954	616.1	1965	929.3	1976	1298.2
1955	657.5	1966	984.8	1977	1369.7
1956	671.6	1967	1011.4	1978	1438.6
1957	683.8	1968	1058.1	1979	1479.4
1958	680.9	1969	1087.6	1980	1475.0
1959	721.7	1970	1085.6	1981	1513.8
1960	737.2	1971	1122.4	1982	1485.4
1961	756.6	1972	1185.9	1983	1534.8

Figure 18.11   *A graph of annual GNP for 1951–1981 seems to curve upward*

In practice, this would be done with a computer program, or else by a hand calculator with a button marked e^x, exp, or something similar. To illustrate, for $t = 1960$, the predicted value of $\ln[Y]$ is $-60.027840 + 0.03401671(1970) = 6.985074$, which implies a prediction for Y of $e^{6.985074} = 1080.4$, as compared to the actual value, $Y = 1085.6$ (from Table 18.1).

Misleading Trends

One of the most bitter criticisms of statisticians is that, ''Figures don't lie, but liars figure.'' The complaint is that an unscrupulous statistician can prove anything by carefully choosing favorable data and conveniently ignoring conflicting evidence. Trend lines are a favorite vehicle for such chicanery. By a clever selection of the years to start and end a time-series analysis, a dishonest person may be able to force the trend line up or down, in whichever direction is desired.

If we are fitting a trend to a long series of relatively stable data, the specific

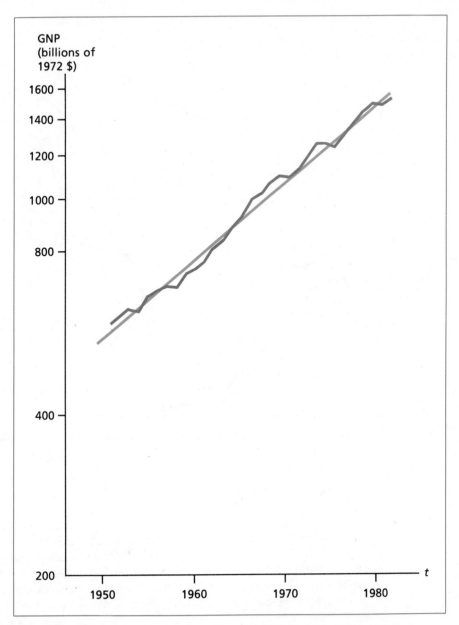

Figure 18.12   *A graph of the logarithm of annual GNP for 1951–1981 seems more nearly linear*

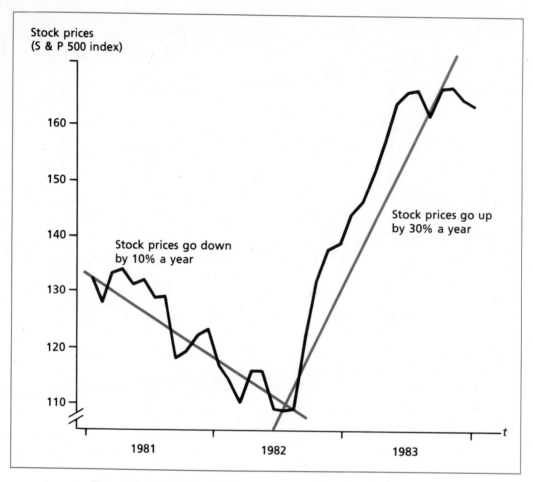

Figure 18.13 *Some trend line chicanery*

years used in the regression won't matter very much, but if we use a short series of volatile data, the chosen years can make all the difference in the world. Figure 18.13 illustrates this point with some data on stock prices. If we fit a trend line to the data for 1981 through mid-1982, then it appears that stock prices tend to fall by about 10 percent a year, but if we analyze the data for mid-1982 through 1983, stock prices seem to increase by about 30 percent a year. Which is correct? Well, both time periods are too short to show convincing trends for something as volatile as the stock market; a much longer perspective is needed. For instance, over the past 60 years, stock prices have increased by around 4.0 percent per year.[1]

Another source of misleading trends is fundamental changes in the underlying behavior. Recall Figure 18.8 on the average workweek. A line fitted to pre–World War II data would show a steep downward trend in the average workweek; a trend line fitted to the entire period 1900–1980 would show a less drastic downward trend; a line fitted to data for the 1930s and 1940s would show a steep upward trend; a line for 1940–1980 would show a steep downward trend; and a line for 1950–1980 data would show no trend at all. Any single trend line is misleading, because it ignores the fact that behavior during the years 1950–1980 was very different from 1900–1930 and that the 1930s and 1940s were exceptional periods with very unusual changes in the workweek.

The best antidotes for misleading trends are a visual inspection of the data and some common sense. A graph may reveal obvious breaks in the data, such as a change in behavior or an extraordinary deviation. Also, if the data appear to be volatile, then a bit of caution (and a longer perspective) may be in order. Finally, common sense can sometimes catch the problem. You may know that behavior now is much different than it used to be or that some unusual events may have occurred that give the appearance of a trend where there is none.

Time series analysis is essentially descriptive; it is a picture that is meant to tell a story. As with any story, bumblers may forget the punch line and dishonest people may lie. The conscientious person, though, can use time series analysis to describe, in a simple and yet accurate way, the behavior of a variable as time passes. There is room for mistakes and even chicanery, but there is also room for enlightenment. As with all statistics, time series analysis is an art as well as a science.

Exercises

18.5 Answer this student's question: "Why do we use time t as an explanatory variable for GNP when it is not time itself that causes GNP to change?"

18.6 Table 14.2 gives the annual returns for some selected stocks and for the stock market as a whole. See if these data show any trend in the market return by estimating the equation $Y = \alpha + \beta t + \epsilon$, where Y is the market rate of return and t is the year ($t = 1972$ in 1972, and so on).

18.7 Here are some data on the size of the U.S. population (in millions), from the U.S. census taken every ten years:

year t	population Y
1940	132
1950	151
1960	179
1970	203
1980	227

Plot these data, with Y on the vertical axis and t on the horizontal axis. Does there appear to be a linear relationship? Now, plot $\ln[Y]$ versus t; if you have semi-log paper, plot Y versus t. Does this relationship appear to be linear? Determine the least squares estimates of α and β in the model $\ln[Y] = \alpha + \beta t + \epsilon$. What is your estimate of the percentage growth rate g of population over this forty-year period?

18.8   Table 18.1 shows annual GNP for the years 1951–1983. Estimate the trend line $\ln[Y] = \alpha + \beta t + \epsilon$, where Y is annual GNP and $t = 1951$ in 1951, using data for

a. 1951–1960

b. 1961–1970

c. 1971–1980

In each case, what is the estimated growth rate of GNP? Are these three sets of estimates roughly consistent with each other? If there are substantial differences, explain why these specific differences occur.

18.9   (*continuation*) Acting out the role of unscrupulous data massager, select some consecutive years for which a trend-line regression gives a negative estimate of β.

18.10   The height of Lake Michigan varies from month to month and year to year. Here are the highest monthly mean levels (in feet) every ten years, for a hundred years:

year t	height Y
1860	583.3
1870	582.7
1880	582.1
1890	581.6
1900	580.7
1910	580.5
1920	581.0
1930	581.2
1940	579.3
1950	580.0

Find the least squares estimates of the equation $Y = \alpha + \beta t + \epsilon$, in order to determine if there was any statistically significant trend in the height of Lake Michigan. Why might you be cautious about extrapolating the trend equation forward 20,000 years or back 20,000 years?

18.11   Table 13.1 gives some data on household disposable income X and spending Y, for the five years 1977–1981. Use these data to see if there are any statistically significant trends in income, spending, and the fraction X/Y of income that is spent. In particular, make three graphs, plotting X, Y, and X/Y versus time t and then find the least squares estimates of the equations

$$X = \alpha_1 + \beta_1 t + \epsilon_1$$

$$Y = \alpha_2 + \beta_2 t + \epsilon_2$$

$$X/Y = \alpha_3 + \beta_3 t + \epsilon_3$$

(Set $t = 1977$ in 1977.) Which, if any, of these three variables shows a statistically significant trend? Explain.

• **18.12** In Exercise 18.7, you estimated the model

$$\ln[Y] = \alpha + \beta t + \epsilon, \text{ where } t = 1940 \text{ in } 1940$$

An alternative formulation is

$$\ln[Y] = \gamma + \delta T + \epsilon, \text{ where } T = 0 \text{ in } 1940$$

That is, $T = t - 1940$. What is the relationship between the parameters in these two formulations? Check your logic by using the data in Exercise 18.7 to estimate both equations.

18.3 MODELING SEASONAL REGULARITIES

One of the most important reasons for deviations about a trend line is seasonal fluctuations. The easiest way to account for these seasonal patterns is to use 0–1 dummy variables. Perhaps we believe that Y varies with the four quarters of the year. If so, we can use the model

$$Y_t = \alpha_1 + \alpha_2 D_2 + \alpha_3 D_3 + \alpha_4 D_4 + \epsilon \qquad (18.6)$$

where

$$Y_t = \text{quarterly value of } Y$$
$$D_2 = 1 \text{ in second quarter of each year, 0 otherwise}$$
$$D_3 = 1 \text{ in third quarter of each year, 0 otherwise}$$
$$D_4 = 1 \text{ in fourth quarter of each year, 0 otherwise}$$

The first quarter is selected arbitrarily as the reference quarter. In the first quarter, the three dummy variables are all equal to zero, and the equation simplifies to

$$\text{first quarter:} \quad Y_t = \alpha_1 + \epsilon$$

In the other three quarters, the equation changes to

$$\text{second quarter:} \quad Y_t = (\alpha_1 + \alpha_2) + \epsilon$$
$$\text{third quarter:} \quad Y_t = (\alpha_1 + \alpha_3) + \epsilon$$
$$\text{fourth quarter:} \quad Y_t = (\alpha_1 + \alpha_4) + \epsilon$$

The parameters α_2, α_3, and α_4 gauge the quarterly variations in Y. If α_2 is positive, then Y tends to be higher in the second quarter than in the first quarter, by an amount α_2. If α_2 is negative, then Y tends to be lower in the second quarter than the first, by an amount α_2. The parameters α_3 and α_4 similarly compare the third and fourth quarters with the first quarter. If these three parameters are not significantly different from zero, then there is no apparent systematic variation in Y from quarter to quarter.

The parameters of our seasonal dummy model, Equation 18.6 can be estimated by a least squares computer program. The procedure, called *multiple regression*, is explained in Chapter 15 and the actual calculations would be left to the computer.

With monthly data, we can use 11 monthly dummy variables; for weekly data, 51 weekly dummies could be used.

If there is both trend and seasonality, then a time variable can be included along with the seasonal dummy variables. For example, if we believe that Y grows by a constant percentage rate and also varies with the quarters of the year, then we can use least squares to estimate the model

$$\ln[Y_t] = \alpha_1 + \alpha_2 D_2 + \alpha_3 D_3 + \alpha_4 D_4 + \beta t + \epsilon \qquad (18.7)$$

Seasonal Adjustment

It is again important to recognize that these models are merely descriptive. They do not attempt to explain *why* there are long-run trends and short-run seasonality; they just try to identify the existence of such patterns. Similarly, they do not explain why there are fluctuations in addition to trend and seasonality, even though these "disturbances" are often fuel for the most interesting of questions—for example, why the economy has economic booms and recessions. The answer to such questions requires good theory and a regression model with true explanatory variables in place of the descriptive time variable. All that time series analysis offers are methods for describing the data.

The way these methods are often used in practice is to excise the trend and seasonality, so that we can more easily see the fluctuations that need to be explained by something else. For instance, the movements of GNP above and below the trend lines in Figures 18.6 and 18.12 allow us to identify periods of economic boom and recession. Most economic data are also **seasonally adjusted** to remove seasonal patterns.

The actual seasonal-adjustment calculations are quite complicated and are best left to a computer program. However, for a simple example of the logic involved, let's look at the quarterly GNP shown in Figure 18.9. (The data pictured in this graph are given in Table 18.2.) The graph seems to show a regular increase in output in the fourth quarter of each year, followed by a decline in the first quarter. To confirm and quantify this impression, I've estimated the equation

$$Y = \alpha_1 + \alpha_2 D_2 + \alpha_3 D_3 + \alpha_4 D_4 + \beta t + \epsilon$$

where

$$Y = \text{quarterly GNP}$$

$$D_2 = 1 \text{ in second quarter, 0 otherwise}$$

$$D_3 = 1 \text{ in third quarter, 0 otherwise}$$

$$D_4 = 1 \text{ in fourth quarter, 0 otherwise}$$

$$t = 0 \text{ in the first quarter of 1976, and}$$
$$\text{then increases by 1 each quarter}$$

The least squares estimates for 1976–1982 are

$$\hat{Y} = 382.85 + 24.34\,D_2 + 19.17\,D_3 + 37.46\,D_4 + 14.76\,t, \qquad R^2 = .992$$
$$\quad\ [68.7] \qquad [3.9] \qquad\ \ [3.0] \qquad\ \ \ [5.9] \qquad\ \ \ [53.0]$$

[ ]: *t*-values

The coefficients of the trend variable t and the three seasonal dummies are all statistically significant. According to the seasonal estimates, GNP tends to be about $24 billion higher in the second quarter than in the first quarter, $19 billion higher in the third quarter than in the first, and $37 billion higher in the fourth quarter than the first.

The trend term means that GNP increases by about $15 billion each quarter. The seasonal regularities imply that we shouldn't be surprised by seasonal fluctuations about this trend. Between the fourth quarter of each year and the first quarter of the next, we can expect quarterly GNP to drop by $22 billion (the usual $37 billion seasonal decline less the expected $15 billion trend increase). This is the expected pattern. If GNP drops by more than $22 billion, then we might become worried, because something bad may have occurred, beyond the usual first-quarter dip.

A more formal way of taking these expected seasonal patterns into account is to seasonally adjust the data. For any given year, let's label the unadjusted quarterly data

Table 18.2   *Quarterly GNP, in billions of dollars, 1976–1982*

Year	Quarter	GNP	Year	Quarter	GNP
1976	1	398.9	1980	1	616.1
	2	426.5		2	648.8
	3	430.8		3	661.0
	4	461.8		4	705.7
1977	1	436.9	1981	1	689.8
	2	476.6		2	733.7
	3	488.8		3	752.8
	4	515.6		4	777.7
1978	1	484.7	1982	1	733.6
	2	536.0		2	773.4
	3	547.6		3	772.5
	4	587.9		4	793.5
1979	1	559.8			
	2	598.5			
	3	607.1			
	4	649.8			

$$Y_1 = \text{first quarter GNP}$$

$$Y_2 = \text{second quarter GNP}$$

$$Y_3 = \text{third quarter GNP}$$

$$Y_4 = \text{fourth quarter GNP}$$

The seasonally adjusted data will be

$$S_1 = Y_1 + A_1$$

$$S_2 = Y_2 + A_2$$

$$S_3 = Y_3 + A_3$$

$$S_4 = Y_4 + A_4$$

where the A_i are the additive seasonal adjustments. (Multiplicative adjustments can also be used.)

Now, it would be nice if the annual values of the adjusted data coincided with the annual values of the unadjusted data:

$$S_1 + S_2 + S_3 + S_4 = Y_1 + Y_2 + Y_3 + Y_4$$

Thus, annual GNP for 1978 will be the same, regardless of whether we add up the seasonally adjusted or unadjusted quarterly data. For this to be true, the four seasonal adjustments must sum to zero:

$$A_1 + A_2 + A_3 + A_4 = 0$$

That is, if we add a few billion dollars here or there to make a seasonal adjustment, then we must take them away from somewhere else, to get the annual numbers to add up.

Our regression estimate is that seasonality causes GNP to be higher by a_2 (our estimate of α_2) if it is the second quarter rather than the first. Thus, if we add some amount A_1 to first quarter GNP, then we want to add $A_1 - a_2$ to second-quarter GNP. In this way, we can take into account the fact that we expect GNP to be higher in the second quarter than in the first. Similar adjustments for the third and fourth quarters give

$$A_2 = A_1 - a_2$$

$$A_3 = A_1 - a_3$$

$$A_4 = A_1 - a_4$$

This logic, along with the desire to have the four adjustments add up to zero, gives us our rules:

$$0 = A_1 + A_2 + A_3 + A_4$$

$$= A_1 + (A_1 - a_2) + (A_1 - a_3) + (A_1 - a_4)$$

$$= 4(A_1) - (a_2 + a_3 + a_4)$$

implies that

$$A_1 = (a_2 + a_3 + a_4)/4$$

$$A_2 = (a_2 + a_3 + a_4)/4 - a_2$$

$$A_3 = (a_2 + a_3 + a_4)/4 - a_3 \qquad (18.7)$$

$$A_4 = (a_2 + a_3 + a_4)/4 - a_4$$

Thus, we want to our seasonal adjustment to reduce: second-quarter GNP by a_2 relative to first-quarter GNP; third-quarter GNP by a_3 relative to first-quarter GNP; and fourth-quarter GNP by a_4 relative to first-quarter GNP. But we also want the adjustments to have no effect on annual GNP, so we make these three subtractions, but then add $(a_2 + a_3 + a_4)/4$ to each quarter.

The least squares estimates a_i for the quarterly GNP example yield

$$A_1 = 20.24$$

$$A_2 = -4.10$$

$$A_3 = 1.08$$

$$A_4 = -17.22$$

The seasonal regularity is that GNP typically rises by a little in the second quarter and by a lot in the fourth quarter, and falls by a lot in the first quarter and by a little in the third quarter. To offset this pattern, we add several billion dollars to first- and third-quarter GNP and subtract several billion dollars from second- and fourth-quarter GNP. As planned, the seasonal adjustments sum to zero and the difference between the first adjustment and each of the others is equal to the estimated coefficient of the relevant dummy variable.

Table 18.3   *Seasonally adjusted quarterly GNP, in billions of dollars, 1980–1982*

Year	Quarter	GNP	Seasonal adjustment	Adjusted GNP
1980	1	616.1	20.2	636.3
	2	648.8	−4.1	644.7
	3	661.0	1.1	662.1
	4	705.7	−17.2	688.5
1981	1	689.8	20.2	710.0
	2	733.7	−4.1	729.6
	3	752.8	1.1	753.9
	4	777.7	−17.2	760.5
1982	1	733.6	20.2	753.8
	2	773.4	−4.1	769.3
	3	772.5	1.1	773.6
	4	793.5	−17.2	776.3

Table 18.3 shows the seasonally adjusted data for the three-year period 1980–1982, with the adjusted and unadjusted data graphed together in Figure 18.14. Notice how the seasonally-adjusted data fluctuate less than the unadjusted data. This is because the seasonal adjustment is an attempt to correct for seasonal fluctuations, so that we can see other changes in GNP. Look, for example, at Table 18.3 at the fourth quarter of 1980 and the first quarter of 1981. In the unadjusted

Figure 18.14   *Seasonally adjusted and unadjusted quarterly GNP*

data, there is a $15.9 billion drop in GNP. But there is usually a $37.46 billion seasonal drop in GNP between the fourth and first quarters. (Remember, 37.46 is the estimated coefficient of the fourth-quarter dummy variable.) Because the observed $15.9 billion drop is $21.56 billion less than might be expected, the seasonally adjusted data show a $21.56 billion increase in GNP. The first quarter of 1981 was actually a relatively good quarter, because GNP did not drop as much as usual.

It has been said that, "With seasonally adjusted temperatures, you could eliminate winter in Canada."[2] That's funny, but not true unfortunately. Seasonal adjustment doesn't eliminate seasonal patterns; it merely takes them into account so that we can see if anything unusual is happening. Seasonally adjusted temperatures wouldn't eliminate winter, but they would tell us whether or not a particular winter was unusually cold.

These GNP data were deseasonalized, so that we could focus on GNP fluctuations that weren't simply due to seasonal patterns. In the same way, data can also be detrended, so that we abstract from increases in GNP that just represent normal growth. B, looking at deviations about the trend, we can identify periods in which GNP is increasing faster or slower than usual. Thus, when GNP increases, but not by as much as usual, this is a sign of economic weakness. The details of detrending are left as Exercise 18.20.

Monthly Stock Returns

Table 16.2 contains monthly stock returns over the eleven-year period 1970–1980. To see if there is any trend or seasonality in these data, I estimated the equation

$$Y = \alpha + \alpha_2 D_2 + \alpha_3 D_3 + \cdots + \alpha_{12} D_{12} + \beta t + \epsilon$$

where

Y is the monthly percentage return
D_i are 11 monthly dummy variables, with January as the reference month, and
t is time, with $t = 0$ in January, 1970 and increased by 1 each month
A least squares regression yielded these estimates:

$$\hat{Y} = 1.19 - 1.16D_2 - 1.34D_3 - 1.40D_4 - 2.15D_5 - 0.92D_6 - 1.46D_7$$
$$\quad [0.7] \quad [0.6] \quad\;\; [0.7] \quad\;\; [0.7] \quad\;\; [1.0] \quad\;\; [0.4] \quad\;\; [0.7]$$

$$\quad - 1.02D_8 - 2.22D_9 - 2.01D_{10} + 0.06D_{11} + 0.01D_{12} + 0.01t, \quad R^2 = .03$$
$$\quad\;\; [0.5] \quad\;\; [1.1] \quad\;\;\; [1.0] \quad\;\;\;\; [0.0] \quad\;\;\;\; [0.0] \quad\;\; [1.0]$$

[ ]: t-values

Not one of the seasonal dummies is statistically significant; nor is the time trend. There is no convincing evidence in these data of trend or seasonal patterns in stock returns. Government data collectors agree, in that securities prices are almost the only economic data that are not seasonally adjusted. The government statisticians can't find any seasonal patterns either!

Toys "R" Us

Toys "R" Us is the world's largest toy retailer, which operates some 150 toy supermarkets throughout the United States. Since 1978, their sales have increased by 30 percent per year, while their profits have grown by 40 percent per year. However, because they are in the toy business, these sales and profits are not evenly distributed throughout the year:

fiscal year begins	quarter	sales ($ millions)	earnings per share
1978	Feb 1–Apr 30	38.0	−0.08
	May 1–July 31	53.6	0.00
	Aug 1–Oct 31	57.5	0.02
	Nov 1–Jan 31	200.0	0.87
1979	Feb 1–Apr 30	56.5	−0.02
	May 1–July 31	75.8	0.08
	Aug 1–Oct 31	78.3	0.03
	Nov 1–Jan 31	269.7	1.13
1980	Feb 1–Apr 30	70.2	−0.02
	May 1–July 31	92.7	0.01
	Aug 1–Oct 31	101.8	0.00
	Nov 1–Jan 31	332.6	1.30
1981	Feb 1–Apr 30	97.3	0.03
	May 1–July 31	123.7	0.14
	Aug 1–Oct 31	132.9	0.14
	Nov 1–Jan 31	429.4	1.81
1982	Feb 1–Apr 30	138.3	0.11
	May 1–July 31	167.6	0.22
	Aug 1–Oct 31	189.9	0.25
	Nov 1–Jan 31	545.9	2.27

As you can see, more than half of their sales and almost all of their profits come during the Christmas season. We can formally describe this extreme seasonal pattern with the model*

$$Y = \alpha_1 + \alpha_2 D_2 + \alpha_3 D_3 + \alpha_4 D_4 + \beta t + \epsilon$$

where

$$D_2 = 1 \text{ in May–July quarter, 0 otherwise}$$

$$D_3 = 1 \text{ in Aug–Oct quarter, 0 otherwise}$$

$$D_4 = 1 \text{ in Nov–Jan quarter, 0 otherwise}$$

*Their growth is not really linear, but logarithms of profits can't be used, because of the zero and negative values. The linear trend model was used as a rough approximation, because I couldn't resist showing you the exceptional seasonality that buffets the world's largest toy seller.

Here, we will look at Y = earnings per share. The sales data are left as an exercise. The least squares estimation of this time-series equation gives

$$\hat{Y} = -0.25 + 0.55\, D_2 + 0.22\, D_3 + 1.38\, D_4 + 0.03t$$
$$\quad\;\; [2.0] \quad\;\; [0.4] \qquad [0.2] \qquad\;\; [9.7] \qquad [3.5]$$

[ ]: t-values

There is a statistically significant growth trend and a statistically significant difference between the fourth and first fiscal-quarter earnings. On average, fourth-quarter earnings tend to be about $1.40 higher than first-quarter earnings. Earnings also seem to be a bit higher in the second and third quarters than in the hapless first quarter, but these differences are not statistically significant, because the t-statistics are less than 2.

Table 1 shows the seasonal-adjustment calculations and Figure 1 depicts the seasonally adjusted and unadjusted data. Notice how the seasonal adjustment smooths out the data by abstracting from the regular seasonal fluctuations. Notice also, how

Table 1 *Seasonal adjustment of* Toys ''R'' Us *earnings*

Fiscal year begins	Quarter	Unadjusted earnings per share	Seasonal adjustment	Adjusted earnings per share
1978	Feb 1–Apr 30	−0.08	0.36	0.28
	May 1–July 31	0.00	0.31	0.31
	Aug 1–Oct 31	0.02	0.34	0.36
	Nov 1–Jan 31	0.87	−1.01	−0.14
1979	Feb 1–Apr 30	−0.02	0.36	0.34
	May 1–July 31	0.08	0.31	0.39
	Aug 1–Oct 31	0.03	0.34	0.37
	Nov 1–Jan 31	1.13	−1.01	0.12
1980	Feb 1–Apr 30	−0.02	0.36	0.34
	May 1–July 31	0.01	0.31	0.32
	Aug 1–Oct 31	0.00	0.34	0.34
	Nov 1–Jan 31	1.30	−1.01	0.29
1981	Feb 1–Apr 30	0.03	0.36	0.39
	May 1–July 31	0.14	0.31	0.45
	Aug 1–Oct 31	0.14	0.34	0.48
	Nov 1–Jan 31	1.81	−1.01	0.80
1982	Feb 1–Apr 30	0.11	0.36	0.47
	May 1–July 31	0.22	0.31	0.53
	Aug 1–Oct 31	0.25	0.34	0.59
	Nov 1–Jan 31	2.27	−1.01	1.26

the seasonally adjusted numbers sometimes tell a different story than the unadjusted data. Look at the fourth quarter of 1980, for instance. Earnings per share jumped from $0.0 to $1.30; however, taking into account the expected growth and the traditionally strong fourth-quarter results, this was actually a disappointing quarter. During the next three months, the first quarter of fiscal 1981, earnings slumped to $0.03 a share, but this was a much smaller drop than usual. On a seasonally adjusted basis, the $0.03 earnings in the first quarter of 1981 was actually more encouraging news than the $1.30 earnings in the fourth quarter of 1980.

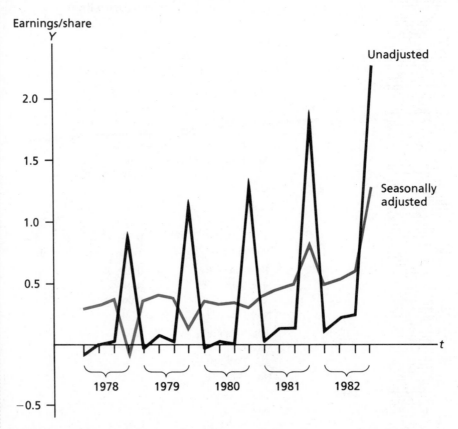

Figure 1   *Seasonally adjusted and unadjusted quarterly earnings per share for* Toys "R" Us

If there were seasonality in stock returns, extraordinary profits would be available to those who bought low and sold high. It is most likely that such profit incentives would cause the seasonality to disappear, in that the pressure of people trying to buy low would push prices up in the low quarters, while the pressure of sellers would pull prices down in the high quarters. In this way, any regular patterns would be destroyed by speculators. Such a self-destructive mechanism does not exist for quarterly GNP, because seasonality in GNP does not offer speculative profits. If consumers want to spend in the fourth quarter of each year, then businesses will produce more to meet this demand. There is no reason for them to produce three months early. If the weather is lousy in February, then home builders will wait for better weather. There is no reason for them to stop working in November in anticipation of February's dip. If anything, they will produce more in the fourth quarter, in a rush to finish before the weather turns nasty.

Exercises

18.13 Table 18.3 shows that in the first quarter of 1982 GNP fell by $44.1 billion, while seasonally adjusted GNP fell by only $6.7 billion. How can this be?

18.14 A business has estimated the following equation to identify seasonal fluctuations in its profits (in millions of dollars):

$$\hat{Y} = 20 + 10D_2 + 10D_3 + 10D_4$$

where

$$Y = \text{quarterly profits}$$
$$D_2 = 1 \text{ in second quarter, } 0 \text{ otherwise}$$
$$D_3 = 1 \text{ in third quarter, } 0 \text{ otherwise}$$
$$D_4 = 1 \text{ in fourth quarter, } 0 \text{ otherwise}$$

How should we interpret these estimates? Do profits tend to be higher in the first quarter or second quarter? Are profits usually higher in the second or third quarter? Make a rough sketch to show the usual seasonal pattern.

18.15 The text estimates the trend and seasonality in earnings per share for *Toys "R" Us*. Use the data given in this example to estimate the trend and seasonality in their sales:

$$\ln(Y) = \alpha_1 + \alpha_2 D_2 + \alpha_3 D_3 + \alpha_4 D_4 + \beta t + \epsilon$$

where

$$Y = \text{quarterly sales (in \$ millions)}$$
$$D_2 = 1 \text{ in May–July quarter, } 0 \text{ otherwise}$$
$$D_3 = 1 \text{ in Aug–Oct quarter, } 0 \text{ otherwise}$$
$$D_4 = 1 \text{ in Nov–Jan quarter, } 0 \text{ otherwise}$$

What is your estimate of the quarterly growth rate of their sales? What, if any, seasonal pattern is there in their sales?

18.16   (*continuation*) Use your estimated *Toys "R" Us* sales equation to calculate a seasonally adjusted sales series. Plot the adjusted and unadjusted sales data on the same graph, with time on the horizontal axis. (Use semi-log paper, if you have some.)

18.17   Determine the quarterly earnings per share over a ten-year period for a mythical Las Vegas, Inc. by rolling a pair of dice 40 times. For each of these 40 quarters, the earnings per share are equal to $9 minus the number that is rolled. Now see if there is any trend or seasonality in these data by estimating the equation

$$Y = \alpha_1 + \alpha_2 D_2 + \alpha_3 D_3 + \alpha_4 D_4 + \beta t + \epsilon$$

where

$$Y = \text{quarterly profits}$$

$$D_2 = 1 \text{ in second quarter, 0 otherwise}$$

$$D_3 = 1 \text{ in third quarter, 0 otherwise}$$

$$D_4 = 1 \text{ in fourth quarter, 0 otherwise}$$

$$t = 1 \text{ to 40, up by 1 each quarter}$$

18.18   (*continuation*) Redo these calculations using the same rolled numbers, but a different formula for calculating earnings. Let earnings at $t = 0$ be $2. Now, let the *change* in earnings each quarter equal $9 minus the number rolled.

18.19   Here are some monthly data on U.S. beer production (in thousands of barrels):

year

month	1975	1976	1977	1978
Jan	12,549	12,441	11,978	12,871
Feb	11,181	11,890	11,482	12,713
Mar	12,412	11,855	16,200	15,860
Apr	14,496	13,688	16,027	15,624
May	14,343	15,175	16,788	16,567
June	15,762	15,758	16,904	16,878
July	16,076	16,539	15,921	16,741
Aug	14,719	16,096	15,309	17,614
Sept	13,345	14,313	13,255	14,625
Oct	12,350	13,422	12,606	14,014
Nov	11,217	11,288	12,021	12,714
Dec	12,150	11,191	12,014	12,872

Do you discern any seasonal patterns in these data? Estimate the model

$$Y = \alpha_1 + \alpha_2 D_2 + \alpha_3 D_3 + \cdots + \alpha_{12} D_{12} + \epsilon$$

where the D_i are eleven seasonal dummies (with January as the reference month). In which, if any, months are there statistically significant differences in production, relative to January? Does this apparent seasonality make sense?

• **18.20**   The text uses the 1951–1981 GNP data shown in Table 18.1 to estimate a trend equation for GNP. Use these estimates to calculate a *detrended* GNP for 1971–1981. What does this detrended GNP measure?

18.4 FORECASTING

Many decisions by households, businesses, and government are based on forecasts of one sort or another. Your choice of a college major involves forecasts of how well you will do in your courses, what you want to do when you graduate, and what your career opportunities will be. You won't major in physics if you think that you can't pass physics courses; you probably won't major in education if you want to go to medical school; and you may be dissuaded from majoring in Latin by glum job prospects. Businesses routinely make forecasts of their sales, materials costs, interest rates, and a dizzying array of other things. Government policymakers forecast output, unemployment, inflation, interest rates, and so on.

Businesses and government often use time series analyses to make these forecasts, hoping that extrapolations of the past will yield accurate predictions of the future. For instance, the annual GNP data shown in Table 18.1 was used earlier in this chapter to estimate a trend equation for GNP,

$$\ln[\hat{Y}] = -60.0 + 0.0340\, t$$

where $t = 1951$ in 1951, $t = 1952$ in 1952, and so on. A projection of this estimated equation gives annual GNP forecasts into the future. Here is a sampling:

year	projected GNP billions of 1972 $
1982	1625.0
1983	1681.2
1990	2133.3
2000	2997.6

Of course, we know from Chapter 13 that least squares predictions have confidence intervals associated with them, and that these confidence intervals widen the farther one gets from the center of the available data. The computer program that I used to estimate this equation gave these confidence intervals:

year	projected GNP billions of 1972 $	95 percent confidence interval
1982	1625.0	1523.0 to 1733.9
1983	1681.2	1575.1 to 1794.5
1990	2133.3	1992.2 to 2284.3
2000	2997.6	2782.5 to 3229.4

As it turns out, the 1982 and 1983 projections were overly optimistic. In 1982, the Federal Reserve Board used a tight monetary policy to wring inflation out of the economy, and the United States suffered its most severe recession since the Great Depression in the 1930s. The unemployment rate averaged 9.7 percent and GNP came to $1485.4 billion, some $40 billion outside our 95 percent confidence interval. In 1983, it was more of the same, with a 9.6 percent unemployment rate and $1534.8 billion GNP. For the years 1990 and 2000, we'll just have to wait and see.

A Projection Gone Awry

International Business Machines (IBM) is the world's largest producer of computers and other data processing equipment. In early 1984, it had 600 million shares of stock outstanding that were valued at slightly over $100 a share, giving its stock a staggering aggregate market value of $60 billion. Stockholders have liked IBM for a long time because it earns a very healthy profit, pays a good dividend, and grows relentlessly. Throughout the 1940s and 1950s, IBM sales and profits grew by almost 30 percent per year, year after year. Some analysts cautioned that this phenomenal growth could not continue forever. The U.S. economy, as a whole, was only growing by about 3 percent per year as its population, equipment, and productivity slowly increased. If these respective growth rates continued much longer, IBM would soon produce almost all of the nation's gross national product. At that point, something would have to give: either the U.S. economy would start growing by 30 percent per year, or else IBM would slow to a more normal 3 percent growth rate.

Let's imagine that we are security analysts in 1978, and are trying to project IBM's profits per share over the next three years. A peek back over the previous thirteen years gives the following data:

year t	earnings per share Y
1966	$0.94
1967	1.16
1968	1.54
1969	1.64
1970	1.78
1971	1.88

It is important to recognize that time series forecasts are just mechanical extrapolations. Their justification is their simplicity and usefulness in describing the implications of the past. They provide no underlying rhyme or reason why things should continue as they have, just a computation of what will occur if recent trends continue. Time series analysis takes no account of real or imagined changes in behavior that may be occurring. To take such changes into account, we either have to make a subjective adjustment of our forecast or else construct a formal model that explains the effects of such changes.

For instance, an extrapolation may indicate that the unemployment rate will drop by 0.2 percent next month and by 0.5 percent next year. However, if we know that the Federal Reserve Board intends to tighten up the nation's money supply, then we may predict that unemployment won't decline at all and may even rise somewhat. The exact unemployment prediction that we come up with will be a subjective shading of the extrapolation, an adjustment based on our knowledge

1972	2.21
1973	2.70
1974	3.12
1975	3.34
1976	3.99
1977	4.58
1978	5.32

If we fit a time series trend model by ordinary least squares, we get

$$\ln[\hat{Y}] = -226.7 + 0.1357\, t, \qquad R^2 = .988$$
$$\quad\;\; [30.1] \qquad [30.2]$$

[ ]: t-values

The estimated coefficient of t is an estimate of $\ln[1 + g]$, and implies an annual growth rate $g = 0.145$ (14.5 percent per year). An extrapolation of this trend equation gives the following forecasts and associated 95 percent confidence intervals:

year	predicted IBM earnings per share	confidence interval
1979	$5.99	$5.20 to $6.90
1980	$6.86	$5.94 to $7.93
1981	$7.86	$6.77 to $9.13

Well, in 1979, IBM's uninterrupted growth was interrupted by a nasty combination of a weak world economy and increased competition in the computer industry. IBM's earnings per share fell to $5.16 in 1979, rebounded to $6.10 in 1980, and then fell again to $5.63 in 1981. The disappointing 1981 result was more than $2 below predicted earnings per share and well outside the computed confidence interval.

of the economy and the Federal Reserve Board. As another example, a business extrapolation of the sales of a product introduced two years ago may indicate a 20 percent increase in sales this year, but we know that, after two years of success, other firms usually start flooding the market with imitations that take away sales. Based on past experience, then, we may predict a slower growth or even a decline in sales.

In both of these cases, the alternative to subjective adjustments is a formal model that attempts to explain behavior, rather than merely extrapolate it. For their unemployment forecasts, government economists build regression models—several equations describing how unemployment depends on the state of the economy and how the state of the economy depends on the Federal Reserve's monetary policy. Each equation can be estimated by the least-squares procedures described in Chapters 13, 14, and 15. For sales forecasts, business economists build regression models that explain how sales depend on a product's price, on the existence of competing products, and on the numbers of years that a product has been on the market. Using data on experiences with similar products, these equations also can be estimated by least squares.

Those who build elaborate behavioral models can use a time-series model as a benchmark standard of comparison. The time-series model is a "naive extrapolation," that the person hopes to outforecast with a behavioral model that takes into account *why* things change. Time series models do best when the projections are short term and nothing dramatic occurs—when the future is just a simple extension of the past. Forecasts for one quarter ahead normally can't go too far off, but predictions five or ten years into a foggy future can be very wrong. The farther ahead we extrapolate, the more danger there is that a major turn of events will make the future unlike the past. In such circumstances, a time series model is bound to fail. A behavioral model may fail, too, but at least it has a chance.

Exercises

18.21   Explain why you either agree or disagree with this conclusion: "Because sales have increased steadily over the past five years, we can be certain that the trend will continue."

18.22   Use your results from Exercise 18.7 to predict the U.S. population in the years 2000, 2020, and 2030. Give a 95 percent confidence interval for each of these extrapolations.

18.23   In the text, IBM earnings-per-share data for 1966–1978 are extrapolated to predict earnings for 1979–1981, and these predictions are then compared with the actual values. Reestimate the trend equation, using all of the data for 1966–1981. Does the inclusion of the 1979–1981 data raise or lower the estimated growth rate? Why? Now extrapolate your equation to predict IBM's earnings per share for 1982, 1983, and 1984. Give 95 percent confidence intervals for each of these three predictions.

• **18.24**   (*continuation*) Go to a library and find out what IBM's earnings per share actually were in 1982, 1983, and 1984. How accurate are your predictions? Try to find out why IBM's earnings per share were higher or lower than your extrapolations.

18.25   The Democrats and Republicans are the two major political parties in the United States. Here is the ratio of the popular vote received by the Democratic party's presidential candidate to that of the Republican candidate:

election year t	$\dfrac{Democrat}{Republican}$ Y
1928	0.702
1932	1.447
1936	1.664
1940	1.222
1944	1.163
1948	1.099
1952	0.805

1956	0.733
1960	1.003
1964	1.587
1968	0.984
1972	0.618
1976	1.043
1980	0.808

See if there is any statistically significant trend in these data by estimating the model $Y = \alpha + \beta t + \epsilon$. Extrapolate your estimated equation to predict the 1984 election outcome. Is your extrapolation accurate? Why might this sort of extrapolation be an unsuccessful predictor?

18.5 INDEXES

We live in a complex society with more detailed statistical data than anyone could absorb or appreciate. Indexes are an attempt to summarize masses of data and show the general changes that take place as time passes. They are a statistical average, with the specific details of the averaging depending on the particular data being summarized. To illustrate the principles involved, we will look at two well-known indexes: the Consumer Price Index and the Dow Jones Average.

The Consumer Price Index

The Consumer Price Index (CPI) was started in the 1940s to determine whether workers' wages were staying ahead of prices, and today, it is still used by both sides in wage negotiations. In addition, many union contracts include formal escalator clauses, which automatically increase wages when the CPI goes up. Social Security benefits are also linked to the CPI, as are many rental leases, alimony agreements, and other contracts. The Congressional Budget Office reported in 1981 that

> . . . almost a third of federal expenditures is directly linked to the CPI or related price measures, and over half of the federal budget is affected if indirectly linked expenditures are added. A one percent increase in the CPI will automatically trigger nearly $2 billion of additional federal expenditures, at 1981 program levels.[3]

In addition to Social Security payments, federal CPI-indexed programs include military pay, food stamps, student loans, and dairy price supports. Government economic policies are also influenced by the rate of inflation, as measured by the CPI. If inflation seems rapid, Congress is likely to raise taxes and the Federal Reserve is almost certain to step on the monetary brakes, slowing the growth of the money supply. The last three economic recessions in the United States represented deliberate efforts to combat inflation by cooling off the economy.[4]

This is certainly a most important index, but how is the CPI actually computed?

The CPI is an ambitious attempt to keep track of the cost of living for typical U.S. households—the cost of buying food, clothing, shelter, VCRs, and the other necessities and luxuries we consume. Every ten years or so, the Bureau of Labor Statistics (BLS) makes an intensive survey of thousands of households to learn the details of their buying habits. In 1972–1973, they interviewed 40,000 households in 56 cities. Twenty of these cities—the 18 largest, plus one in Alaska and another in Hawaii—were included automatically, because the BLS wanted a separate price index for each of these 20 cities. The other 36 cities were randomly selected from those cities with more than 2500 people, and were grouped by size and geographic area. The 40,000 people surveyed in these 56 cities were also picked by random selection methods. Half were interviewed every three months for two years in order to keep track of their major expenses. The other half recorded their daily expenses in diaries for two weeks.

Based on this survey, the BLS constructs a market basket of 2000 goods and services. Each month thereafter, 250 BLS agents call or visit 20,000 stores in these 56 cities to collect current price data on about 400 of these goods and services. The 20,000 stores, 56 cities, 400 items, and the time of visit are all samples from much larger populations.

The resultant price data are then combined into price indexes, which measure the current cost of the market basket relative to the cost in a base period,

$$P = (100) \frac{\text{current cost of market basket}}{\text{cost of market basket in base period}} \tag{18.8}$$

The logic can best be demonstrated by an example. Table 18.4 shows some hypothetical data for a market basket of three items. This market basket cost $20 in 1975 and $30 in 1980, indicating a 50 percent increase ($30/$20 = 1.5). The CPI and most other price indexes are scaled to equal 100 in the base year; this is why there is a 100 in Equation 18.8. Thus, if 1975 is the base year for the data in Table 18.4, the price index would be set at $P = 100$ in 1975 and $P = 150$ in 1980. These numbers, 100 and 150, don't mean anything by themselves. The market basket didn't cost $100 or contain 150 loaves of bread. A price index only means

Table 18.4   *A price-index calculation*

		1975		1980	
	Quantity	*Price of one*	*Cost of basket*	*Price of one*	*Cost of basket*
Loaf of bread	10	$0.90	$9.00	$1.10	$11.00
Pound of meat	6	$1.50	$9.00	$2.50	$15.00
Gallon of milk	2	$1.00	$2.00	$2.00	$4.00
Total			$20.00		$30.00

This market basket cost $20 in 1975 and $30 in 1980, indicating a 50 percent increase.

something in comparison to its value in another period. Thus, a comparison of $P = 150$ in 1980 with $P = 100$ in 1975 tells us that prices increased by 50 percent over this 5-year period, in that this market basket cost 50 percent more in 1980 than in 1975.

Real Income

The most commonplace usage of price indexes is to see whether or not one's income is keeping ahead of prices. If prices increase by 50% and your income does too, then you are running fast but staying in the same place. You have 50% more dollars to spend but, since prices are up 50%, you can't buy any more now than you could before. Economists make such comparisons by calculating *real income:* nominal income divided by a price index.

Let's say that a person earned $20,000 in 1975 and $33,000 in 1980. Purchasing power could be calculated by dividing these incomes by the cost of the bundles shown in Table 18.4:

	dollar income	*cost of bundle*	*number of bundles*
1975	$20,000	$20	$20,000/$20 = 1000
1980	$33,000	$30	$33,000/$30 = 1100

In terms of purchasing power, this person's real income went up by 10%—they could purchase 10% more in 1980 than in 1975.

Economists usually express real income data relative to some base year. If 1975 is selected as the base year, we calculate prices relative to what they were in 1975 and then divide dollar income by this relative price calculation:

	dollar income	*price index*	*prices relative to 1975*	*real income (1975$)*
1975	$20,000	100	100/100 = 1.0	$20,000/1.0 = $20,000
1980	$33,000	150	150/100 = 1.5	$33,000/1.5 = $22,000

The division of dollar incomes by prices relative to 1975 gives real income in terms of 1975 dollars, indicated by the shorthand 1975$. Thus this person earned enough in 1980 to purchase what a $22,000 income bought in 1975. Since, in fact, $20,000 were earned in 1975, real income was 10% higher in 1980 than in 1975.

Alternatively, real incomes can be expressed in terms of 1980 dollars by using prices relative to 1980:

	dollar income	*price index*	*prices relative to 1980*	*real income (1980$)*
1975	$20,000	100	100/150 = 0.67	$20,000/0.67 = $30,000
1980	$33,000	150	150/150 = 1.0	$33,000/1.0 = $33,000

This person earned $20,000 in 1975, enough to buy what a $30,000 income in 1980 would purchase. The actual 1980 income of $33,000 was 10% higher than this.

Thus there are a variety of ways of telling the same story: this person's real income, taking into account the diminished purchasing power of the dollar, increased by 10% between 1975 and 1980.

Price-Index Weights

As is always the case, individual prices change by varying amounts. Some prices go up a lot, some go up a little, and some even go down. A price index is, implicitly, a weighted average of individual prices, where the weights are determined by consumer buying habits. (You will work out the details in Exercise 18.26.)

It Might Be Cheaper to Switch to Another Song

If you received the items listed in the song "The 12 Days of Christmas" today, be impressed—they cost a bundle.

Each year at this time Hugh Gee, publisher of Money Power Confidential, a San Francisco-based investor newsletter, issues his Christmas Index—the cost of the items in the song—and compares them with the year before. His findings:

A partridge costs $6 this year, compared with $5 in 1982, a 20% gain. Pear trees go for $15 vs. $10, up 50%. Two turtle doves sell for $20, unchanged from a year ago. Three French hens (a fancy name for chickens) can be purchased for $4.25 wholesale in Lodi, compared with $3.69 last year, up 15%.

Four calling birds (Gee picked rare grahlas) cost $2,000, unchanged from 1982. Five golden rings are a bargain this year at $1,875 vs $2,125, a 14% drop because the price of gold has eased. Six geese-a-laying (Canadian honkers) sell for $360 vs. $300, up 20%.

Seven swans-a-swimming cost $2,100, compared with $1,750, up 20% for the birds. And a 15-foot by 30-foot pool for them to do their swimming sells for $22,000 vs. $19,000, a 16% increase. For 8 maids-a-milking, Gee checked with several temporary help firms and found a place he could get them for $369.60, compared with $320, up 16%. Uniforms for the maids rent for $320 vs. $280, up 14%. Gee didn't list what the maids were supposed to milk, so you might assume they took turns milking the chickens.

Nine dancers dancing (at union rates) cost $1,485, compared with $1,323, up 12%. And because nude dancing is gauche at Christmas, it cost an extra $216 for costumes vs. $166.50, a 29% increase. Ten lords-a-leaping (real lords weren't available so Gee had to substitute union dancers willing to leap) cost $1,650, compared with $1,470, up 12%. Their lord suits rented for $400 vs. $350, a 14% gain.

Eleven pipers piping (at union rates) cost $1,045, compared with $891.88, a 17% increase. The fee for renting 11 flutes totaled $495 vs. $275, up 80% (apparently 1983 was a good year to be in the flute-rental business). And 12 drummers drumming cost $1,140 (no Shelley Manne at these rates), compared with $972.96, up 17%. Drum rentals added another $960 vs. $624, a 54% hike.

The total cost this year came to $36,460.85, up from last year's $31,887.03. In 1981 the total was a paltry $29,184.23. It seems that Christmas goods have bigger price mark-ups than everyday items because although the Christmas Index surged 14%, the government's Consumer Price Index rose a mere 3.5%.

©Ron W. Heinzel, *Los Angeles Times*, December 25, 1983. Reprinted by permission.

There are two inherent difficulties with all price indexes. The first is that purchases adjust to price changes. For example, gasoline consumption fell after its price soared. Should a price index's "typical market basket" reflect the quantities purchased before or after the price change? If before, then the price index overstates the change in the cost of living, because it ignores the fact that people will substitute less expensive items for more expensive ones. If after, then the price index understates the ill effects of the higher prices, because it ignores the lifestyle that people were forced to give up.

There is no good answer to this before-or-after question. Some indexes, called **Laspeyres indexes**, use the "before" quantities purchased in the base period. Others, called **Paasche indexes**, use the "after" quantities purchased each period.* Thus, the Laspeyres weights are fixed by base period spending habits, while the Paasche weights vary from year to year with spending habits. The CPI is a Laspeyres index, while the *consumption deflator* (another government index of consumer prices) is a Paasche index.

This distinction can make a big difference in the behavior of price indexes, particularly when relative prices have changed greatly and the base-period survey of spending habits was made several years ago. The major CPI surveys were made in 1934–1939, 1952, 1963, and 1972–1973. Many economists believe that the validity of the CPI in the late 1970s was undermined by significant changes in consumer buying patterns, such as the decrease in gasoline usage.

The CPI was also criticized in the late 1970s for its inclusion of home prices and mortgage rates. For people who already have homes, an increase in home prices is a benefit rather than a cost. Similarly, an increase in mortgage rates does not raise the expenses of people with old, fixed-rate mortgages. In addition, the CPI neglected the tax deductibility of interest payments and the fact that interest rates are a source of income as well as expense. In 1983, the Bureau of Labor Statistics responded to these criticisms by switching to rental costs as a measure of housing expenses.

The Commerce Department calculates a personal consumption deflator, which differs from the CPI in that it is a Paasche index (with weights that change with spending habits) and that it has always used rents to estimate housing costs. From the fourth quarter of 1969 to the fourth quarter of 1980, the CPI increased by about 130 percent, while the consumption deflator went up by 100 percent. The average annual percentage increases over these eleven years works out to be 7.8 percent for the CPI and 6.7 percent for the consumption deflator. There was inflation, no matter how we look at it, but how we look at it does affect our estimate of the severity of the inflation.

---

*Because the Paasche weights vary from year to year, changes in the index reflect quantity as well as price changes. A Paasche index can go up or down even if all prices are constant! An intermediate approach is a *chain index*, in which each period's computations use the market basket from the immediately preceding period. In an annual chain index, for example, a calculation of the average change in prices in 1980 would use 1979 spending habits, while the 1981 calculation would use 1980 spending habits.

Quality Adjustments

The second inherent difficulty with price indexes is that the quality of many items varies as time passes. When the price goes up 10 percent, but the box says ''new and improved,'' should we believe it? If the quality has in fact improved 10 percent, then there hasn't really been any inflation. It's like buying a 10 percent larger size; you simply paid more to get more. But how do you measure quality? Volkswagen Rabbits are very different from Beetles; they are roomier, they get better gas mileage, and they have front-wheel drive, water-cooled engines, fuel injection, and disc brakes. What is the percentage change in their quality? Many consumer goods, like personal computers, didn't even exist ten years ago. Another example is that of medical doctors; they have drugs and equipment that didn't exist 20 years ago, their fees are also much higher, and they don't make house calls. What is the percentage change in the quality of medical services?

The other side of this coin is ''candy bar inflation.'' For years, candy bar prices were constant, while the bars gradually became smaller and smaller. Many other products and services have similarly deteriorated. Their quality has gone down rather than up. Statisticians try to make quality adjustments in the price indexes, but this task is difficult and subjective. In the 1960s, many economists argued that quality improvements were underestimated to the extent that the reported annual increases in the CPI were about 1 to 2 percent too high.

In the 1970s, another quality issue emerged. The state and federal governments pushed for breathable air, drinkable water, and safe working environments. The costs of moving toward these objectives showed up in higher prices for automobiles, electricity, and other products, but the benefits weren't counted in any market basket. We paid more, but the price indexes didn't show that we were also getting more—better air, water, and so on. It is difficult to say how we could reasonably adjust price indexes for these sorts of changes in the quality of our living and working environments. All we can really say is that the neglect of environmental quality changes caused reported price indexes to understate inflation in the 1960s and to overstate inflation in the 1970s.

The Dow Jones Average

In 1880 Charles Dow and Edward Jones started a financial news service that they called Dow-Jones. Today, the most visible results are the *Wall Street Journal*, the most widely read newspaper in the United States, and the Dow Jones Industrial Average, the most widely reported stock market index.

The Dow Jones averages began as a barometer of economic activity. Dow was convinced that stock prices reflected informed opinion about future business conditions, and thus, that stock prices provided advance information about the economy. Two indexes were constructed: the Industrial Average would reflect production, while the Railroad Average would monitor commerce. The Railroad Average has always been the less prominent of the two indexes, an imbalance exacerbated by the decline of railroads in the United States. In 1969, 8 of the 20 railroad stocks were replaced by 6 airlines and 2 trucking firms, and it was renamed the Transportation Average; however, the Industrial Average still gets the headlines.

The Industrial Average began with 12 stocks in 1896 and grew to its present size, 30 stocks, by 1928. These select stocks represent the nation's industrial giants, the bluest of blue chips. It is a measure of economic evolution in the United States that only one company, General Electric, has been in the Dow Jones Industrial Average from the beginning (and even GE was dropped for awhile). The other 29 stocks have been added over time as other, once powerful companies faded. The

Table 18.5 *The 30 stocks in the Dow Jones Industrial Average*

Stock	Price per share (May 25, 1984)	Number of shares (millions)	Total market value ($ billions)
Allied Corp.	49 1/8	53.46	2.63
Aluminum Co.	32 3/4	80.94	2.65
American Brands	53 7/8	54.95	2.96
American Can	41 7/8	21.37	0.89
American Express	27 3/8	201.35	5.51
AT&T	15 5/8	936.70	14.64
Bethlehem Steel	46 3/4	46.25	0.96
DuPont	47	238.87	11.23
Eastman Kodak	64 5/8	165.57	10.70
Exxon	41 1/8	846.10	34.80
General Electric	52 1/4	454.63	23.75
General Foods	51	51.92	2.65
General Motors	63 1/4	316.54	20.02
Goodyear	23 3/4	105.43	2.50
Inco	10 3/4	97.46	1.05
IBM	107 1/4	610.72	65.50
International Harvester	6 3/8	40.58	0.26
International Paper	48	49.75	2.39
Merck	87 1/4	73.94	6.45
3-M	73 1/4	117.24	8.59
Owens-Illinois	34 3/8	27.75	0.95
Procter & Gamble	48	116.51	7.99
Sears Roebuck	30 3/4	351.41	10.81
Standard Oil of California	37	342.11	12.66
Texaco	36 3/4	233.37	8.58
Union Carbide	53 5/8	70.47	3.78
United Technologies	62 1/4	59.78	3.72
US Steel	26 7/8	104.64	2.81
Westinghouse	40 3/4	87.52	3.57
Woolworth	33 7/8	31.49	1.07

Great Depression was, of course, the blow that killed many of the mightiest. Twenty-five of the 30 blue chips in the Dow Jones Industrial Average were dropped in the 1930s and replaced with healthier companies. Another substitution was made in 1956, 4 more occurred in 1959, and 3–M was added in 1976 after the Anaconda copper company was taken over by Atlantic Richfield. The most recent substitutions occurred in 1979, when an ailing Chrysler and an unglamorous Esmark (formerly Swift & Company, a meatpacking firm) were replaced by Merck, a leading producer of health care products, and by IBM, the company with the largest market value of any company ($43 billion at the time and even more now). The current list of the ''biggest and best'' is shown in Table 18.5.

Originally, the Dow Jones Average was computed simply by adding together the prices of the 12 stocks and dividing by 12. This computation had to be modified as other companies were added or substitutions were made; otherwise, the Dow Jones Average would have jumped or plummeted for no real reason. Suppose, for instance, that all 12 of the original stocks were selling for $50 a share, giving a Dow Jones Average of 50, and another stock is added that happens to be selling for $10 a share. If we add up the 13 prices and divide by 13, we get a Dow Jones Average of

$$\frac{50 + 50 + \cdots + 50 + 10}{13} = \frac{610}{13} = 46.92$$

indicating that the average stock price dropped by more than 7 percent, when in fact, all that happened was the index was broadened from 12 stocks to 13. The same sort of false signal would be given if one stock was substituted for another that happened to be selling for a different price.

The same thing would happen whenever a stock splits. In a two-for-one split, each original share is replaced with two new shares, so that every owner of 100 old shares now has 200 new shares. For the company as a whole, the number of shares outstanding is doubled; this is a simple bookkeeping change that promptly halves the value of each share.*

The Dow Jones Averages allow for these cosmetic changes by adjusting the divisor. In our first example, if we don't want the inclusion of a thirteenth stock to shock the average, we can divide by some number k that keeps the average at 50:

$$\frac{50 + 50 + \cdots + 50 + 10}{k} = \frac{610}{k} = 50$$

*A shareholder with 100 out of 1 million old shares owned .01 percent of the company and received .01 percent of all the dividends distributed to shareholders. After a two-for-one split, this shareholder will have 200 out of 2 million new shares, still .01 percent of the company and its dividends. The market value of these 200 new shares should be the same as the value of the 100 old shares, implying a halving of the price per share. If the old shares were worth $4000 (100 shares at $40 per share), then the new shares should also be worth $4000 (200 shares at $20 per share).

implies $k = 610/50 = 12.2$, rather than 13. By the same logic, the divisor is adjusted when a substitution is made, and every time a stock splits. The cumulative effects of these adjustments have been to reduce the Dow Jones Industrial divisor to its present level of about 1.5.

> The Dow Jones Industrial Average is computed by adding up the per-share prices of 30 prominent companies and dividing by 1.5.

Thus, the Dow Jones Industrial Average is an average of 30 prices, with a rescaling to provide historical continuity. If you want, you can think of it as 30 prices divided by 30, but then multiplied by $30/1.5$ to keep the scale consistent with the averages computed in the past. With this periodic rescaling, we have a logically consistent daily index of stock prices running all the way back to 1896.

There are two primary criticisms of the Dow Jones Industrial Average. One is that it only includes 30 stocks. Admittedly, these 30 are among the biggest and the best, but still, every other stock is ignored completely. At present, these 30 companies are so prominent that they represent one-fourth of the total market value of the more than 1000 stocks traded on the New York Stock Exchange. It is impressive that 3 percent of the companies have 25 percent of the market value, but it may be misleading to ignore the other 75 percent—particularly because the excluded companies are quite different from those that are included. The 30 stocks in the Dow Jones Industrial Average are not a random sample. They are chosen because they are large, well-established companies, the bluest of the blue chips, and as such, their performance may not be representative of other, smaller and less prominent companies. The excluded companies may grow faster and are certainly riskier than the giants, and there may well be systematic differences in the behavior of their prices. Indeed, some security analysts compare movements in the Dow Jones Industrial Average with broader averages, such as the New York Stock Exchange (NYSE) Composite Index, to gauge the mood of the market. If the broader averages are soaring while the Dow is slumbering, this is interpreted as a signal that the speculators are loose again, gambling on risky stocks.

In addition, in the long run, it can make all the difference in the world which particular 30 are annointed the biggest and the best. IBM was originally added to the big 30 in 1932, replacing National Cash Register, but then was dropped mysteriously in 1939 in favor of AT&T. If IBM hadn't been left out for forty years, from 1939 to 1979, the Dow would have grown much faster and the stock market would have seemed much healthier. By 1979, the Dow would have been twice as high, at 1700 rather than 850.

The second criticism is that the Dow Jones Averages reflect per-share prices instead of market values. We've seen how per-share prices are dramatically affected by stock splits. The more general lesson is that the per-share price depends on how many shares the company happens to have issued. If one of two equally profitable companies has twice as many shares as the other, it will also have a per-share price that's half the size of the other. This is unimportant for the company and its shareholders, but it makes a big difference to the Dow Averages, in that a company's influence on the Dow Average depends on how many shares it happens to have issued!

Look at Table 18.5 again. For many years, DuPont was the highest-priced stock in the Dow Industrials, selling for around $120 a share. But in 1979, DuPont was split three-for-one and its price dropped to $40 a share and its importance to the Dow dropped, too. Before the split, a 10 percent drop in the price of DuPont (from $120 to $108) would drop the numerator of the Dow Jones Average by 12, causing the Dow to drop by $12/1.5 = 8$ points. In contrast, the bankruptcy of International Harvester, which sold for $6 a share, would only drop the Dow by 4 points. But after the split, DuPont lost its premiere position, in that for DuPont to change the Dow by 8 points, the price of its stock would have to change by 30 percent ($12/40$) instead of just 10 percent.

> The Dow Jones Industrial Average treats a $1 change in any of the 30 stock prices the same, regardless of whether it is a $1 change in a stock selling for $6, $40, or $120 a share.

The Dow Jones Average does not pay attention to how many shareholders are affected by price changes. In May 1984, American Can and Exxon were both selling for $41 and change, so that a $4 increase in either price would mean a 10 percent gain for shareholders, but Exxon had 40 times as many shares outstanding as American Can. A $4 per-share increase means $85 million in capital gains to American Can shareholders, but $3.4 billion in capital gains to Exxon shareholders. The Dow treats the two events as being identical, while they are, in fact, quite different—both as a barometer of the economy and in their implications for consumer spending.

It is for just these reasons that most analysts prefer an index of stock prices based on market values

$$\text{market value index} = \Sigma \begin{pmatrix} \text{number} \\ \text{of} \\ \text{shares} \end{pmatrix} \begin{pmatrix} \text{price} \\ \text{per} \\ \text{share} \end{pmatrix}$$

For an example, consider an index based on just three stocks—American Can, Exxon, and DuPont:

$$(41\ 7/8)(21.37) + (41\ 1/8)(846.10) + (47)(238.87) = 46.92$$

(The index would, of course, be scaled to equal 100 in a chosen base period.) In a market value index, a 10 percent change in the value of the index represents a 10 percent change in the aggregate market value of the companies included in the index. The Standard and Poor's 500, the NYSE Composite, and most other stock indexes are based on market value, but the Dow has its long tradition and an entrenched spot in the newspaper headlines. When the Dow is up 20 points, people can interpret that statistic readily as meaning very good news about the stock market, simply because they are used to hearing the Dow reported and remember that the Dow seldom goes up as much as 20 points in a single day. If they were to read that the NYSE Composite was up 2 points, they wouldn't know what to make of that statistic, even though it is describing the same events and probably describing them more accurately. As one securities analyst put it,

> Statistically [the Dow] isn't very good, but I follow it avidly. It's a kind of love-hate relationship. When you get down to it, it's the most convenient shorthand for the market.[5]

Exercises

18.26 Mr. Bunker lives on beer and pretzels. In 1970, he bought 1000 six-packs of beer at $1.00 each and 500 bags of pretzels at $0.50 each. In 1980, Bunker's beer cost $1.50 and his pretzels cost $1.00.

a. One way to calculate Bunker's rate of inflation is

$$\frac{\text{Bunker's inflation}}{\text{from 1970 to 1980}} = \frac{\text{cost of 1000 6-packs and 500 bags in 1980}}{\text{cost of 1000 6-packs and 500 bags in 1970}}$$

What was the percentage increase in Bunker's cost of living from 1970 to 1980? If we calculated a Bunker Price Index (BPI) and scaled this BPI to equal 100 in 1970, what would be the 1980 value of the BPI?

b. Another way to calculate Bunker's rate of inflation is

$$\begin{array}{l}\text{Bunker's inflation} \\ \text{from 1970 to 1980}\end{array} = \left(\begin{array}{c}\text{\% increase in} \\ \text{price of beer}\end{array}\right)\left(\begin{array}{c}\text{fraction of 1970 budget} \\ \text{spent on beer}\end{array}\right)$$

$$+ \left(\begin{array}{c}\text{\% increase in} \\ \text{pretzel prices}\end{array}\right)\left(\begin{array}{c}\text{fraction of 1970 budget} \\ \text{spent on pretzels}\end{array}\right)$$

What was Bunker's inflation rate using this approach?

c. Bunker earned $2 an hour in 1970 and $3 an hour in 1980. Did his wages win or lose the race against prices?

• **18.27** *Business Conditions Digest* reported the following CPI data:

year	CPI (P = 100.0 in 1967)
1975	161.2
1976	170.5
1977	181.5

The United Nations *Statistical Bulletin* reported this CPI data:

year	CPI (P = 100.0 in 1975)
1978	121.2
1979	135.1
1980	153.1

How much did prices increase between 1977 and 1978? Now put all six years of data together on the same scale, $P = 100.0$ in 1967. How would you recalibrate these data so that $P = 100.0$ in 1980? Which of the following CPI facts are the most important: levels, first differences, or ratios?

18.28 It has been alleged that statisticians do not fully take into account quality improvements in what we buy. If so, will their estimates of inflation and real income be too high or too low?

18.29 In July 1979, IBM (at $70 a share) and Merck (at $68) replaced Chrysler and Esmark (at $9 and $26, respectively) in the Dow Jones Industrial Average. To keep the Dow Jones index at 850, did the divisor of 1.443 have to be adjusted up or down? What was the new value of the divisor?

18.30 In a market value stock index, how must the divisor be adjusted for stock splits? Use the index for American Can, Exxon, and DuPont given in the text and assume that DuPont splits two-for-one, doubling the number of shares and halving its price.

18.6 SUMMARY

Time series analysis and index numbers are statistical efforts to describe behavior as time passes. Time series analysis focuses on the identification of trend and seasonal patterns, while indexes are concerned with aggregating excessive detail. The two most popular trend models are linear and log-linear

$$Y_t = \alpha + \beta t + \epsilon$$

$$\ln[Y_t] = \alpha + \beta t + \epsilon$$

Seasonality can be taken into account by adding seasonal dummies. The parameter estimates provide a statistical description of the behavior of Y, and also predictions of how Y will behave if past trend and seasonal patterns continue. In practice, time series models are used for two primary purposes. First, they can be used to detrend and deseasonalize data, so that we can identify events of interest. Periods when GNP is below trend indicate an economic recession; a January when *Toys "R" Us* sales didn't collapse would be phenomenal. The second usage is to provide a benchmark forecast that can be adjusted for other information that, it is hoped, will improve the forecasts.

Time series analysis is descriptive. It identifies trends and seasonal patterns in the data and tells what will happen if these continue. It does not explain why these patterns occur, why they should continue, or, most interesting, why there are fluctuations about these patterns.

Indexes are attempts to summarize masses of data and describe "average" behavior as time passes. The CPI, for instance, shows changes in the cost of buying a market basket purchased by typical households. Although the Dow Jones Industrial Average is an important exception, most stock indexes show changes in the market value of stocks.

REVIEW EXERCISES

18.31   A business has estimated the following equation to identify seasonal fluctuations in its sales:

$$\hat{Y} = 450 + 50D_2 + 50D_3 + 150D_4$$

where

Y = quarterly sales

D_2 = 1 in second quarter, 0 otherwise

D_3 = 1 in third quarter, 0 otherwise

D_4 = 1 in fourth quarter, 0 otherwise

How should we interpret these estimates? Do sales tend to be higher in the first quarter or second quarter? In the second or third quarter? In the third or fourth quarter? Make a rough sketch to show the usual seasonal pattern.

18.32   Gordon Jewelry is a leading retail jeweler. Its earnings per share during the fiscal years 1978–1982 are shown in the chart. (Often, the *fiscal* year that a particular business uses for accounting purposes does not begin on January 1.)

			fiscal year ends		
quarter	1978	1979	1980	1981	1982
Sept 1–Nov 30	0.32	0.34	0.45	0.57	0.21
Dec 1–Feb 28	1.29	1.77	2.15	2.19	1.97
Mar 1–May 31	0.37	0.56	0.55	0.54	0.25
June 1–Aug 31	0.32	0.60	−0.40	−0.15	0.32

Plot these data versus time and see if any seasonal trend is apparent. Now find the least squares estimates of the equation

$$Y = \alpha_1 + \alpha_2 D_2 + \alpha_3 D_3 + \alpha_4 D_4 + \beta t + \epsilon$$

where

Y = quarterly earnings per share

D_2 = 1 in Dec–Feb quarter, 0 otherwise

D_3 = 1 in Mar–May quarter, 0 otherwise

D_4 = 1 in June–Aug quarter, 0 otherwise

Interpret your estimates. Are there any statistically significant seasonal or trend patterns? If so, carefully explain them in language that a nonstatistician can understand.

18.33   Here are some data on quarterly earnings per share for Carter Hawley, which operates a variety of department stores and specialty shops, including Broadway, Neiman-Marcus, and Waldenbook:

fiscal year beginning

quarter	1978	1979	1980	1981	1982
Feb 1–Apr 30	0.19	0.21	0.21	0.21	0.17
May 1–July 31	0.29	0.31	0.29	0.23	0.08
Aug 1–Oct 31	0.39	0.45	0.37	0.24	0.20
Nov 1–Jan 31	1.65	1.70	1.24	0.87	1.20

Plot these data versus time and see if any seasonal trend is apparent. Now find the least squares estimates of the equation

$$Y = \alpha_1 + \alpha_2 D_2 + \alpha_3 D_3 + \alpha_4 D_4 + \beta t + \epsilon$$

where

$$Y = \text{quarterly earnings per share}$$

$$D_2 = 1 \text{ in May–July quarter, 0 otherwise}$$

$$D_3 = 1 \text{ in Aug–Oct quarter, 0 otherwise}$$

$$D_4 = 1 \text{ in Nov–Jan quarter, 0 otherwise}$$

Summarize the trend and seasonal patterns in these earnings data. Extrapolate your estimated equation to predict Carter Hawley earnings per share for the fiscal years 1983–1985.

18.34 Here are some data on quarterly earnings per share for the R.H. Macy company, which operates Macy's and Bamberger's department stores:

fiscal year ends

quarter	1978	1979	1980	1981	1982
Aug 1–Oct 31	0.41	0.42	0.72	0.72	0.75
Nov 1–Jan 31	1.21	1.29	1.74	1.84	1.89
Feb 1–Apr 30	0.12	0.17	0.23	0.42	0.48
May 1–July 31	0.31	0.55	0.55	0.70	0.78

Plot these data versus time and see if any seasonal trend is apparent. Now find the least squares estimates of the equation

$$Y = \alpha_1 + \alpha_2 D_2 + \alpha_3 D_3 + \alpha_4 D_4 + \beta t + \epsilon$$

where

$$Y = \text{quarterly earnings per share}$$

$$D_2 = 1 \text{ in May–July quarter, 0 otherwise}$$

$$D_3 = 1 \text{ in Aug–Oct quarter, 0 otherwise}$$

$$D_4 = 1 \text{ in Nov–Jan quarter, 0 otherwise}$$

Summarize the trend and seasonal patterns in these earnings data.

18.35 (*continuation*) Write a brief paragraph comparing the seasonal and trend patterns in the earnings of Carter Hawley and R.H. Macy over this period.

18.36 Here are some data on quarterly earnings per share for Molson, one of Canada's two largest brewers:

fiscal year beginning

quarter	1979	1980	1981	1982	1983
Apr 1–June 30	1.12	1.14	1.16	1.38	1.35
July 1–Sept 30	1.24	0.78	1.40	1.50	1.65
Oct 1–Dec 31	0.98	0.66	0.80	0.95	1.10
Jan 1–Mar 31	0.31	0.26	0.39	0.42	0.55

Plot these data versus time and see if any seasonal trend is apparent. Now find the least squares estimates of the equation

$$Y = \alpha_1 + \alpha_2 D_2 + \alpha_3 D_3 + \alpha_4 D_4 + \epsilon$$

where

$Y =$ quarterly earnings per share

$D_2 = 1$ in July–Sept quarter, 0 otherwise

$D_3 = 1$ in Oct–Dec quarter, 0 otherwise

$D_4 = 1$ in Jan–Mar quarter, 0 otherwise

Use these estimates to calculate seasonally adjusted values for Molson's quarterly earnings per share over this period, 1979–1983.

18.37 (*continuation*) What do you think will happen if you reestimate the model

$$Y = \alpha_1 + \alpha_2 D_2 + \alpha_3 D_3 + \alpha_4 D_4 + \epsilon$$

this time, using your seasonally adjusted values of Y? Check your logic by doing just that.

18.38 Here are some data on quarterly earnings per share for General Cinema, the largest U.S. theatre chain:

fiscal year ends

quarter	1979	1980	1981	1982	1983
Nov 1–Jan 31	0.45	0.50	0.60	0.78	1.00
Feb 1–Apr 30	0.57	0.56	0.69	1.19	1.05
May 1–July 31	0.95	0.98	1.45	1.70	2.10
Aug 1–Oct 31	0.27	0.68	1.25	1.48	1.75

Plot these data versus time and see if any trend or seasonal pattern is apparent. Now find the least squares estimates of the equation

$$Y = \alpha_1 + \alpha_2 D_2 + \alpha_3 D_3 + \alpha_4 D_4 + \beta t + \epsilon$$

where

$Y =$ quarterly earnings per share

$D_2 = 1$ in Feb–Apr quarter, 0 otherwise

$D_3 = 1$ in May–July quarter, 0 otherwise

$D_4 = 1$ in Aug–Oct quarter, 0 otherwise

Use these estimates to calculate seasonally adjusted values for General Cinema's quarterly earnings per share over this period, 1979–1983. Now extrapolate your estimated equation to predict General Cinema's (seasonally unadjusted) earnings per share for the fiscal years 1984–1985.

18.39   Here are some monthly data on the residential use of electric power (in millions of kilowatt-hours):

month	1975	1976	1977	1978
Jan	53,299	59,088	64,516	64,624
Feb	50,716	54,530	61,705	64,283
Mar	48,595	48,656	52,686	59,283
Apr	46,036	45,365	47,118	49,722
May	42,424	42,786	44,086	46,764
June	45,741	45,262	49,481	51,533
July	52,275	53,312	59,748	60,266
Aug	55,310	57,556	61,541	62,366
Sept	53,057	53,746	57,687	60,883
Oct	44,430	47,296	50,599	52,656
Nov	43,824	48,582	47,568	49,440
Dec	50,442	56,893	55,611	57,458

Use these data to estimate the trend and seasonal patterns in residential use of electricity,

$$Y = \alpha_1 + \alpha_2 D_2 + \alpha_3 D_3 + \cdots + \alpha_{12} D_{12} + \beta t + \epsilon$$

where the D_i are eleven seasonal dummies (with January as the reference month). In which, if any, months are there statistically significant differences in electric power usage, relative to January? Do these seasonal patterns make sense to you?

•• **18.40**   In the text, estimates are reported for the following time series model of quarterly GNP:

$$\ln[Y] = \alpha_1 + \alpha_2 D_2 + \alpha_3 D_3 + \alpha_4 D_4 + \epsilon$$

where

$$Y = \text{quarterly GNP}$$

$$D_2 = 1 \text{ in second quarter, 0 otherwise}$$

$$D_3 = 1 \text{ in third quarter, 0 otherwise}$$

$$D_4 = 1 \text{ in fourth quarter, 0 otherwise}$$

An alternative formulation is

$$\ln[Y] = \beta_4 + \beta_1 D_1 + \beta_2 D_2 + \beta_3 D_3 + \epsilon$$

where

$$Y = \text{quarterly GNP}$$

$$D_1 = 1 \text{ in first quarter, 0 otherwise}$$

$$D_2 = 1 \text{ in second quarter, 0 otherwise}$$

$$D_3 = 1 \text{ in third quarter, 0 otherwise}$$

What is the relationship between the parameters in these two formulations? Check your logic by using the data in Table 18.2 to estimate both equations.

•• **18.41**   (*continuation*) Yet another formulation is

$$\ln[Y] = \gamma_1 D_1 + \gamma_2 D_2 + \gamma_3 D_3 + \gamma_4 D_4 + \epsilon$$

What is the relationship between the parameters in this equation and the two equations in the preceding exercise? Check your logic by using the data in Table 18.2 to estimate the third equation and to compare your results with the first two equations.

18.42 Use the GNP data for 1951–1983 shown in Table 18.1 to estimate the trend equation $\ln[Y] = \alpha + \beta t + \epsilon$. Now extrapolate this equation to predict GNP for the years 1984, 1985, and 1986. Give 95 percent confidence intervals for each of these predictions.

• **18.43** (*continuation*) Go to a library and find out what the actual GNP (in 1972 $) was in 1984. Explain why your prediction was too low, too high, or just about right.

18.44 The annual production of electrical power (in billions of kilowatt-hours) by U.S. electric utilities is as follows:

year	production	year	production
1948	283	1961	792
1949	291	1962	852
1950	329	1963	914
1951	371	1964	984
1952	399	1965	1055
1953	443	1966	1144
1954	472	1967	1214
1955	547	1968	1329
1956	601	1969	1442
1957	632	1970	1492
1958	645	1971	1612
1959	710	1972	1750
1960	753	1973	1861

Use these data to estimate the trend equation $\ln[Y] = \alpha + \beta t + \epsilon$, where Y is electricity production and t is time.

Now extrapolate this estimated equation to predict production in 1974. Actual production in 1974 turned out to be 1867 billion kilowatt-hours. What is the size of your prediction error? Why is there such a prediction error?

18.45 Critically evaluate this economic commentary:

When it comes to measuring inflation, the average consumer can do a far better job than the economics experts . . . Over the years I have been using a system which is infallible. . . . The Phindex [short for the Phillips index] merely requires you to divide the total dollar cost of a biweekly shopping trip by the number of brown paper bags into which the purchases are crammed. You thus arrive at the average cost per bagful.

When I started this system some 10 years ago, we would walk out of the store with about six bags of groceries costing approximately $30—or an average of $5 per bag. . . .

On our most recent shopping trip, we emerged with nine bagsful of stuff and nonsense, totaling the staggering sum of $114. . . . the Phindex shows a rise from the initial $5 to almost $13, a whopping 153 percent.

Why is the government worrying about double-digit inflation when the Phindex clearly shows that over a relatively short time we have already escalated into triple digits?[6]

18.46   Explain the error in this interpretation of inflation data:

In the 12-month period ending in December of 1980, consumer prices rose by 12.4 percent—after a 13.3 percent increase the year before. Similar measures of inflation over the next three years were 8.9 percent, 3.9 percent, and 3.8 percent. . . . We are certainly paying less for what we buy than we were at the end of the Carter years.[7]

18.47   Under what circumstances would you expect to find a significant difference between Laspeyres and Paasche price indexes? Which index would increase more in these circumstances?

18.48   The Standard & Poor's 500 (S&P 500) is an index of the prices of 500 stocks. Could the Dow Jones Industrial Average and the S&P 500 ever move in opposite directions? If so, how would you tell the story in words that is being told by these indexes in numbers?

18.49   Here are some Sotheby Index data, based on auctions affiliated with Sotheby Parke Bernet:[8]

	1975	*1982*	*1983*
old master paintings	100	199	217
Chinese ceramics	100	460	445
continental silver	100	134	156

a. Do Chinese ceramics cost more than continental silver?

b. Which of these three would have been the best investment between 1975 and 1982? between 1982 and 1983?

● 18.50   Monthly CPI data can be found in *Business Conditions Digest*. (Check their end pages to find the issue which has historical data.) Use these data for 1971–1980 to see whether consumer prices display trend and/or seasonality by estimating the equation

$$\ln[Y] = \alpha + \beta_1 t + \sum_{i=2}^{12} \beta_i D_i + \epsilon$$

where the D_i are 11 seasonal dummies for the months February through December. Write a one-paragraph report summarizing your findings.

APPENDIX

Tables

Table 1 Binomial Probabilities
Table 2 Standardized Normal Distribution
Table 3 Random Digits
Table 4 Student t Distribution
Table 5 Chi-Square Distribution
Table 6 F Distribution

Table 1 *Binomial Probabilities*

These are the probabilities of x successes in n Bernoulli trials, each with probability π of success: $P[x] = \binom{n}{x} \pi^x(1 - \pi)^{n-x}$. For instance, with a $\pi = .20$ success probability, the probability of $x = 2$ successes in $n = 5$ trials is .2048. (*Note*: For $\pi > .5$, use the probability of $n - x$ successes with success probability $1 - \pi$. For instance, the probability of 4 successes in 6 trials when $\pi = .75$ is the same as the probability of 2 successes when $\pi = .25$, i.e., .2966.)

n	x	.01	.05	.10	.15	.20	.25	.30	.35	.40	.45	.50
1	0	.9900	.9500	.9000	.8500	.8000	.7500	.7000	.6500	.6000	.5500	.5000
	1	.0100	.0500	.1000	.1500	.2000	.2500	.3000	.3500	.4000	.4500	.5000
2	0	.9801	.9025	.8100	.7225	.6400	.5625	.4900	.4225	.3600	.3025	.2500
	1	.0198	.0950	.1800	.2550	.3200	.3750	.4200	.4550	.4800	.4950	.5000
	2	.0001	.0025	.0100	.0225	.0400	.0625	.0900	.1225	.1600	.2025	.2500
3	0	.9703	.8574	.7290	.6141	.5120	.4219	.3430	.2746	.2160	.1664	.1250
	1	.0294	.1354	.2430	.3251	.3840	.4219	.4410	.4436	.4320	.4084	.3750
	2	.0003	.0071	.0270	.0574	.0960	.1406	.1890	.2389	.2880	.3341	.3750
	3	.0000	.0001	.0010	.0034	.0080	.0156	.0270	.0429	.0640	.0911	.1250
4	0	.9606	.8145	.6561	.5220	.4096	.3164	.2401	.1785	.1296	.0915	.0625
	1	.0388	.1715	.2916	.3685	.4096	.4219	.4116	.3845	.3456	.2995	.2500
	2	.0006	.0135	.0486	.0975	.1536	.2109	.2646	.3105	.3456	.3675	.3750
	3	.0000	.0005	.0036	.0115	.0256	.0469	.0756	.1115	.1536	.2005	.2500
	4	.0000	.0000	.0001	.0005	.0016	.0039	.0081	.0150	.0256	.0410	.0625
5	0	.9510	.7738	.5905	.4437	.3277	.2373	.1681	.1160	.0778	.0503	.0312
	1	.0480	.2036	.3280	.3915	.4096	.3955	.3602	.3124	.2592	.2059	.1562
	2	.0010	.0214	.0729	.1382	.2048	.2637	.3087	.3364	.3456	.3369	.3125
	3	.0000	.0011	.0081	.0244	.0512	.0879	.1323	.1811	.2304	.2757	.3125
	4	.0000	.0000	.0004	.0022	.0064	.0146	.0284	.0488	.0768	.1128	.1562

Table 1   *(continued)*

n	x	.01	.05	.10	.15	.20	π .25	.30	.35	.40	.45	.50
	5	.0000	.0000	.0000	.0001	.0003	.0010	.0024	.0053	.0102	.0185	.0312
6	0	.9415	.7351	.5314	.3771	.2621	.1780	.1176	.0754	.0467	.0277	.0156
	1	.0571	.2321	.3543	.3993	.3932	.3560	.3025	.2437	.1866	.1359	.0938
	2	.0014	.0305	.0984	.1762	.2458	.2966	.3241	.3280	.3110	.2780	.2344
	3	.0000	.0021	.0146	.0415	.0819	.1318	.1852	.2355	.2765	.3032	.3125
	4	.0000	.0001	.0012	.0055	.0154	.0330	.0595	.0951	.1382	.1861	.2344
	5	.0000	.0000	.0001	.0004	.0015	.0044	.0102	.0205	.0369	.0609	.0938
	6	.0000	.0000	.0000	.0000	.0001	.0002	.0007	.0018	.0041	.0083	.0156
7	0	.9321	.6983	.4783	.3206	.2097	.1335	.0824	.0490	.0280	.0152	.0078
	1	.0659	.2573	.3720	.3960	.3670	.3115	.2471	.1848	.1306	.0872	.0547
	2	.0020	.0406	.1240	.2097	.2753	.3115	.3177	.2985	.2613	.2140	.1641
	3	.0000	.0036	.0230	.0617	.1147	.1730	.2269	.2679	.2903	.2918	.2734
	4	.0000	.0002	.0026	.0109	.0287	.0577	.0972	.1442	.1935	.2388	.2734
	5	.0000	.0000	.0002	.0012	.0043	.0115	.0250	.0466	.0774	.1172	.1641
	6	.0000	.0000	.0000	.0001	.0004	.0013	.0036	.0084	.0172	.0320	.0547
	7	.0000	.0000	.0000	.0000	.0000	.0001	.0002	.0006	.0016	.0037	.0078
8	0	.9227	.6634	.4305	.2725	.1678	.1002	.0576	.0319	.0168	.0084	.0039
	1	.0746	.2793	.3826	.3847	.3355	.2670	.1977	.1373	.0896	.0548	.0312
	2	.0026	.0515	.1488	.2376	.2936	.3115	.2965	.2587	.2090	.1569	.1094
	3	.0001	.0054	.0331	.0839	.1468	.2076	.2541	.2786	.2787	.2568	.2188
	4	.0000	.0004	.0046	.0185	.0459	.0865	.1361	.1875	.2322	.2627	.2734
	5	.0000	.0000	.0004	.0026	.0092	.0231	.0467	.0808	.1239	.1719	.2188
	6	.0000	.0000	.0000	.0002	.0011	.0038	.0100	.0217	.0413	.0403	.1094
	7	.0000	.0000	.0000	.0000	.0001	.0004	.0012	.0033	.0079	.0164	.0312
	8	.0000	.0000	.0000	.0000	.0000	.0000	.0001	.0002	.0007	.0017	.0039
9	0	.9135	.6302	.3874	.2316	.1342	.0751	.0404	.0207	.0101	.0046	.0020
	1	.0830	.2985	.3874	.3679	.3020	.2253	.1556	.1004	.0605	.0339	.0176
	2	.0034	.0629	.1722	.2597	.3020	.3003	.2668	.2162	.1612	.1110	.0703
	3	.0001	.0077	.0446	.1069	.1762	.2336	.2668	.2716	.2508	.2119	.1641
	4	.0000	.0006	.0074	.0283	.0661	.1168	.1715	.2194	.2508	.2600	.2461
	5	.0000	.0000	.0008	.0050	.0165	.0389	.0735	.1181	.1672	.2128	.2461
	6	.0000	.0000	.0001	.0006	.0028	.0087	.0210	.0424	.0743	.1160	.1641
	7	.0000	.0000	.0000	.0000	.0003	.0012	.0039	.0098	.0212	.0407	.0703
	8	.0000	.0000	.0000	.0000	.0000	.0001	.0004	.0013	.0035	.0083	.0176
	9	.0000	.0000	.0000	.0000	.0000	.0000	.0000	.0001	.0003	.0008	.0020
10	0	.9044	.5987	.3487	.1969	.1074	.0563	.0282	.0135	.0060	.0025	.0010
	1	.0914	.3151	.3874	.3474	.2684	.1877	.1211	.0725	.0403	.0207	.0098
	2	.0042	.0746	.1937	.2759	.3020	.2816	.2335	.1757	.1209	.0763	.0439
	3	.0001	.0105	.0574	.1298	.2013	.2503	.2668	.2522	.2150	.1665	.1172
	4	.0000	.0010	.0112	.0401	.0881	.1460	.2001	.2377	.2508	.2384	.2051
	5	.0000	.0001	.0015	.0085	.0264	.0584	.1029	.1536	.2007	.2340	.2461
	6	.0000	.0000	.0001	.0012	.0055	.0162	.0368	.0689	.1115	.1596	.2051

Table 1 *(continued)*

n	x	.01	.05	.10	.15	.20	π .25	.30	.35	.40	.45	.50
	7	.0000	.0000	.0000	.0001	.0008	.0031	.0090	.0212	.0425	.0746	.1172
	8	.0000	.0000	.0000	.0000	.0001	.0004	.0014	.0043	.0106	.0229	.0439
	9	.0000	.0000	.0000	.0000	.0000	.0000	.0001	.0005	.0016	.0042	.0098
	10	.0000	.0000	.0000	.0000	.0000	.0000	.0000	.0000	.0001	.0003	.0010
11	0	.8953	.5688	.3138	.1673	.0859	.0422	.0198	.0088	.0036	.0014	.0005
	1	.0995	.3293	.3835	.3248	.2362	.1549	.0932	.0518	.0266	.0125	.0054
	2	.0050	.0867	.2131	.2866	.2953	.2581	.1998	.1395	.0887	.0513	.0269
	3	.0002	.0137	.0710	.1517	.2215	.2581	.2568	.2254	.1774	.1259	.0806
	4	.0000	.0014	.0158	.0536	.1107	.1721	.2201	.2428	.2365	.2060	.1611
	5	.0000	.0001	.0025	.0132	.0388	.0803	.1321	.1830	.2207	.2360	.2256
	6	.0000	.0000	.0003	.0023	.0097	.0268	.0566	.0985	.1471	.1931	.2256
	7	.0000	.0000	.0000	.0003	.0017	.0064	.0173	.0379	.0701	.1128	.1611
	8	.0000	.0000	.0000	.0000	.0002	.0011	.0037	.0102	.0234	.0462	.0806
	9	.0000	.0000	.0000	.0000	.0000	.0001	.0005	.0018	.0052	.0126	.0269
	10	.0000	.0000	.0000	.0000	.0000	.0000	.0000	.0002	.0007	.0021	.0054
	11	.0000	.0000	.0000	.0000	.0000	.0000	.0000	.0000	.0000	.0002	.0005
12	0	.8864	.5404	.2824	.1422	.0687	.0317	.0138	.0057	.0022	.0008	.0002
	1	.1074	.3413	.3766	.3012	.2062	.1267	.0712	.0368	.0174	.0075	.0029
	2	.0060	.0988	.2301	.2924	.2835	.2323	.1678	.1088	.0639	.0339	.0161
	3	.0002	.0173	.0852	.1720	.2362	.2581	.2397	.1954	.1419	.0923	.0537
	4	.0000	.0021	.0213	.0683	.1329	.1936	.2311	.2367	.2128	.1700	.1208
	5	.0000	.0002	.0038	.0193	.0532	.1032	.1585	.2039	.2270	.2225	.1934
	6	.0000	.0000	.0005	.0040	.0155	.0401	.0792	.1281	.1766	.2124	.2256
	7	.0000	.0000	.0000	.0006	.0033	.0115	.0291	.0591	.1009	.1489	.1934
	8	.0000	.0000	.0000	.0001	.0005	.0024	.0078	.0199	.0420	.0762	.1208
	9	.0000	.0000	.0000	.0000	.0001	.0004	.0015	.0048	.0125	.0277	.0537
	10	.0000	.0000	.0000	.0000	.0000	.0000	.0002	.0008	.0025	.0068	.0161
	11	.0000	.0000	.0000	.0000	.0000	.0000	.0000	.0001	.0003	.0010	.0029
	12	.0000	.0000	.0000	.0000	.0000	.0000	.0000	.0000	.0000	.0001	.0002
13	0	.8775	.5133	.2542	.1209	.0550	.0238	.0097	.0037	.0013	.0004	.0001
	1	.1152	.3512	.3672	.2774	.1787	.1029	.0540	.0259	.0113	.0045	.0016
	2	.0070	.1109	.2448	.2937	.2680	.2059	.1388	.0836	.0453	.0220	.0095
	3	.0003	.0214	.0997	.1900	.2457	.2517	.2181	.1651	.1107	.0660	.0349
	4	.0000	.0028	.0277	.0838	.1535	.2097	.2337	.2222	.1845	.1350	.0873
	5	.0000	.0003	.0055	.0266	.0691	.1258	.1803	.2154	.2214	.1989	.1571
	6	.0000	.0000	.0008	.0063	.0230	.0559	.1030	.1546	.1968	.2169	.2095
	7	.0000	.0000	.0001	.0011	.0058	.0186	.0442	.0833	.1312	.1775	.2095
	8	.0000	.0000	.0001	.0001	.0011	.0047	.0142	.0336	.0656	.1089	.1571
	9	.0000	.0000	.0000	.0000	.0001	.0009	.0034	.0101	.0243	.0495	.0873
	10	.0000	.0000	.0000	.0000	.0000	.0001	.0006	.0022	.0065	.0162	.0349
	11	.0000	.0000	.0000	.0000	.0000	.0000	.0001	.0003	.0012	.0036	.0095
	12	.0000	.0000	.0000	.0000	.0000	.0000	.0000	.0000	.0001	.0005	.0016
	13	.0000	.0000	.0000	.0000	.0000	.0000	.0000	.0000	.0000	.0000	.0001

Table 1 *(continued)*

n	x	.01	.05	.10	.15	.20	π .25	.30	.35	.40	.45	.50
14	0	.8687	.4877	.2288	.1028	.0440	.0178	.0068	.0024	.0008	.0002	.0001
	1	.1229	.3593	.3559	.2539	.1539	.0832	.0407	.0181	.0073	.0027	.0009
	2	.0081	.1229	.2570	.2912	.2501	.1802	.1134	.0634	.0317	.0141	.0056
	3	.0003	.0259	.1142	.2056	.2501	.2402	.1943	.1366	.0845	.0462	.0222
	4	.0000	.0037	.0349	.0998	.1720	.2202	.2290	.2022	.1549	.1040	.0611
	5	.0000	.0004	.0078	.0352	.0860	.1468	.1963	.2178	.2066	.1701	.1222
	6	.0000	.0000	.0013	.0093	.0322	.0734	.1262	.1759	.2066	.2088	.1833
	7	.0000	.0000	.0002	.0019	.0092	.0280	.0618	.1082	.1574	.1952	.2095
	8	.0000	.0000	.0000	.0003	.0020	.0082	.0232	.0510	.0918	.1398	.1833
	9	.0000	.0000	.0000	.0000	.0003	.0018	.0066	.0183	.0408	.0762	.1222
	10	.0000	.0000	.0000	.0000	.0000	.0003	.0014	.0049	.0136	.0312	.0611
	11	.0000	.0000	.0000	.0000	.0000	.0000	.0002	.0010	.0033	.0093	.0222
	12	.0000	.0000	.0000	.0000	.0000	.0000	.0000	.0001	.0005	.0019	.0056
	13	.0000	.0000	.0000	.0000	.0000	.0000	.0000	.0000	.0001	.0002	.0009
	14	.0000	.0000	.0000	.0000	.0000	.0000	.0000	.0000	.0000	.0000	.0001
15	0	.8601	.4633	.2059	.0874	.0352	.0134	.0047	.0016	.0005	.0001	.0000
	1	.1303	.3658	.3432	.2312	.1319	.0668	.0305	.0126	.0047	.0016	.0005
	2	.0092	.1348	.2669	.2856	.2309	.1559	.0916	.0476	.0219	.0090	.0032
	3	.0004	.0307	.1285	.2184	.2501	.2252	.1700	.1110	.0634	.0318	.0139
	4	.0000	.0049	.0428	.1156	.1876	.2252	.2186	.1792	.1268	.0780	.0417
	5	.0000	.0006	.0105	.0449	.1032	.1651	.2061	.2123	.1859	.1404	.0916
	6	.0000	.0000	.0019	.0132	.0430	.0917	.1472	.1906	.2066	.1914	.1527
	7	.0000	.0000	.0003	.0030	.0138	.0393	.0811	.1319	.1771	.2013	.1964
	8	.0000	.0000	.0000	.0005	.0035	.0131	.0348	.0710	.1181	.1647	.1964
	9	.0000	.0000	.0000	.0001	.0007	.0034	.0116	.0298	.0612	.1048	.1527
	10	.0000	.0000	.0000	.0000	.0001	.0007	.0030	.0096	.0245	.0515	.0916
	11	.0000	.0000	.0000	.0000	.0000	.0001	.0006	.0024	.0074	.0191	.0417
	12	.0000	.0000	.0000	.0000	.0000	.0000	.0001	.0004	.0016	.0052	.0139
	13	.0000	.0000	.0000	.0000	.0000	.0000	.0000	.0001	.0003	.0010	.0032
	14	.0000	.0000	.0000	.0000	.0000	.0000	.0000	.0000	.0000	.0001	.0005
	15	.0000	.0000	.0000	.0000	.0000	.0000	.0000	.0000	.0000	.0000	.0000
16	0	.8515	.4401	.1853	.0743	.0281	.0100	.0033	.0010	.0003	.0001	.0000
	1	.1376	.3706	.3294	.2097	.1126	.0535	.0228	.0087	.0030	.0009	.0002
	2	.0104	.1463	.2745	.2775	.2111	.1336	.0732	.0353	.0150	.0056	.0018
	3	.0005	.0359	.1423	.2285	.2463	.2079	.1465	.0888	.0468	.0215	.0085
	4	.0000	.0061	.0514	.1311	.2001	.2252	.2040	.1553	.1014	.0572	.0278
	5	.0000	.0008	.0137	.0555	.1201	.1802	.2099	.2008	.1623	.1123	.0667
	6	.0000	.0001	.0028	.0180	.0550	.1101	.1649	.1982	.1983	.1684	.1222
	7	.0000	.0000	.0004	.0045	.0197	.0524	.1010	.1524	.1889	.1969	.1746
	8	.0000	.0000	.0001	.0009	.0055	.0197	.0487	.0923	.1417	.1812	.1964
	9	.0000	.0000	.0000	.0001	.0012	.0058	.0185	.0442	.0840	.1318	.1746
	10	.0000	.0000	.0000	.0000	.0002	.0014	.0056	.0167	.0392	.0755	.1222
	11	.0000	.0000	.0000	.0000	.0000	.0002	.0013	.0049	.0142	.0337	.0667

Table 1 *(continued)*

n	x	.01	.05	.10	.15	.20	π .25	.30	.35	.40	.45	.50
	12	.0000	.0000	.0000	.0000	.0000	.0000	.0002	.0011	.0040	.0115	.0278
	13	.0000	.0000	.0000	.0000	.0000	.0000	.0000	.0002	.0008	.0029	.0085
	14	.0000	.0000	.0000	.0000	.0000	.0000	.0000	.0000	.0001	.0005	.0018
	15	.0000	.0000	.0000	.0000	.0000	.0000	.0000	.0000	.0000	.0001	.0002
	16	.0000	.0000	.0000	.0000	.0000	.0000	.0000	.0000	.0000	.0000	.0000
17	0	.8429	.4181	.1668	.0631	.0225	.0075	.0023	.0007	.0002	.0000	.0000
	1	.1447	.3741	.3150	.1893	.0957	.0426	.0169	.0060	.0019	.0005	.0001
	2	.0117	.1575	.2800	.2673	.1914	.1136	.0581	.0260	.0102	.0035	.0010
	3	.0006	.0415	.1556	.2359	.2393	.1893	.1245	.0701	.0341	.0144	.0052
	4	.0000	.0076	.0605	.1457	.2093	.2209	.1868	.1320	.0796	.0411	.0182
	5	.0000	.0010	.0175	.0668	.1361	.1914	.2081	.1849	.1379	.0875	.0472
	6	.0000	.0001	.0039	.0236	.0680	.1276	.1784	.1991	.1839	.1432	.0944
	7	.0000	.0000	.0007	.0065	.0267	.0668	.1201	.1685	.1927	.1841	.1484
	8	.0000	.0000	.0001	.0014	.0084	.0279	.0644	.1134	.1606	.1883	.1855
	9	.0000	.0000	.0000	.0003	.0021	.0093	.0276	.0611	.1070	.1540	.1855
	10	.0000	.0000	.0000	.0000	.0004	.0025	.0095	.0263	.0571	.1008	.1484
	11	.0000	.0000	.0000	.0000	.0001	.0005	.0026	.0090	.0242	.0525	.0944
	12	.0000	.0000	.0000	.0000	.0000	.0001	.0006	.0024	.0081	.0215	.0472
	13	.0000	.0000	.0000	.0000	.0000	.0000	.0001	.0005	.0021	.0068	.0182
	14	.0000	.0000	.0000	.0000	.0000	.0000	.0000	.0001	.0004	.0016	.0052
	15	.0000	.0000	.0000	.0000	.0000	.0000	.0000	.0000	.0001	.0003	.0010
	16	.0000	.0000	.0000	.0000	.0000	.0000	.0000	.0000	.0000	.0000	.0001
	17	.0000	.0000	.0000	.0000	.0000	.0000	.0000	.0000	.0000	.0000	.0000
18	0	.8345	.3972	.1501	.0536	.0180	.0056	.0016	.0004	.0001	.0000	.0000
	1	.1517	.3763	.3002	.1704	.0811	.0338	.0126	.0042	.0012	.0003	.0001
	2	.0130	.1683	.2835	.2556	.1723	.0958	.0458	.0190	.0069	.0022	.0006
	3	.0007	.0473	.1680	.2406	.2297	.1704	.1046	.0547	.0246	.0095	.0031
	4	.0000	.0093	.0700	.1592	.2153	.2130	.1681	.1104	.0614	.0291	.0117
	5	.0000	.0014	.0218	.0787	.1507	.1988	.2017	.1664	.1146	.0666	.0327
	6	.0000	.0002	.0052	.0301	.0816	.1436	.1873	.1941	.1655	.1181	.0708
	7	.0000	.0000	.0010	.0091	.0350	.0820	.1376	.1792	.1892	.1657	.1214
	8	.0000	.0000	.0002	.0022	.0120	.0376	.0811	.1327	.1734	.1864	.1669
	9	.0000	.0000	.0000	.0004	.0033	.0139	.0386	.0794	.1284	.1694	.1855
	10	.0000	.0000	.0000	.0001	.0008	.0042	.0149	.0385	.0771	.1248	.1669
	11	.0000	.0000	.0000	.0000	.0001	.0010	.0046	.0151	.0374	.0742	.1214
	12	.0000	.0000	.0000	.0000	.0000	.0002	.0012	.0047	.0145	.0354	.0708
	13	.0000	.0000	.0000	.0000	.0000	.0000	.0002	.0012	.0045	.0134	.0327
	14	.0000	.0000	.0000	.0000	.0000	.0000	.0000	.0002	.0011	.0039	.0117
	15	.0000	.0000	.0000	.0000	.0000	.0000	.0000	.0000	.0002	.0009	.0031
	16	.0000	.0000	.0000	.0000	.0000	.0000	.0000	.0000	.0000	.0001	.0006
	17	.0000	.0000	.0000	.0000	.0000	.0000	.0000	.0000	.0000	.0000	.0001
	18	.0000	.0000	.0000	.0000	.0000	.0000	.0000	.0000	.0000	.0000	.0000

Table 1 *(continued)*

n	x	.01	.05	.10	.15	.20	π .25	.30	.35	.40	.45	.50
19	0	.8262	.3774	.1351	.0456	.0144	.0042	.0011	.0003	.0001	.0000	.0000
	1	.1586	.3774	.2852	.1529	.0685	.0268	.0093	.0029	.0008	.0002	.0000
	2	.0144	.1787	.2852	.2428	.1540	.0803	.0358	.0138	.0046	.0013	.0003
	3	.0008	.0533	.1796	.2428	.2182	.1517	.0869	.0422	.0175	.0062	.0018
	4	.0000	.0112	.0798	.1714	.2182	.2023	.1491	.0909	.0467	.0203	.0074
	5	.0000	.0018	.0266	.0907	.1636	.2023	.1916	.1468	.0933	.0497	.0222
	6	.0000	.0002	.0069	.0374	.0955	.1574	.1916	.1844	.1451	.0949	.0518
	7	.0000	.0000	.0014	.0122	.0443	.0974	.1525	.1844	.1797	.1443	.0961
	8	.0000	.0000	.0002	.0032	.0166	.0487	.0981	.1489	.1797	.1771	.1442
	9	.0000	.0000	.0000	.0007	.0051	.0198	.0514	.0980	.1464	.1771	.1762
	10	.0000	.0000	.0000	.0001	.0013	.0066	.0220	.0528	.0976	.1449	.1762
	11	.0000	.0000	.0000	.0000	.0003	.0018	.0077	.0233	.0532	.0970	.1442
	12	.0000	.0000	.0000	.0000	.0000	.0004	.0022	.0083	.0237	.0529	.0961
	13	.0000	.0000	.0000	.0000	.0000	.0001	.0005	.0024	.0085	.0233	.0518
	14	.0000	.0000	.0000	.0000	.0000	.0000	.0001	.0006	.0024	.0082	.0222
	15	.0000	.0000	.0000	.0000	.0000	.0000	.0000	.0001	.0005	.0022	.0074
	16	.0000	.0000	.0000	.0000	.0000	.0000	.0000	.0000	.0001	.0005	.0018
	17	.0000	.0000	.0000	.0000	.0000	.0000	.0000	.0000	.0000	.0001	.0003
	18	.0000	.0000	.0000	.0000	.0000	.0000	.0000	.0000	.0000	.0000	.0000
	19	.0000	.0000	.0000	.0000	.0000	.0000	.0000	.0000	.0000	.0000	.0000
20	0	.8179	.3585	.1216	.0388	.0115	.0032	.0008	.0002	.0000	.0000	.0000
	1	.1652	.3774	.2702	.1368	.0576	.0211	.0068	.0020	.0005	.0001	.0000
	2	.0159	.1887	.2852	.2293	.1369	.0669	.0278	.0100	.0031	.0008	.0002
	3	.0010	.0596	.1901	.2428	.2054	.1339	.0716	.0323	.0123	.0040	.0011
	4	.0000	.0133	.0898	.1821	.2182	.1897	.1304	.0738	.0350	.0139	.0046
	5	.0000	.0022	.0319	.1028	.1746	.2023	.1789	.1272	.0746	.0365	.0148
	6	.0000	.0003	.0089	.0454	.1091	.1686	.1916	.1712	.1244	.0746	.0370
	7	.0000	.0000	.0020	.0160	.0545	.1124	.1643	.1844	.1659	.1221	.0739
	8	.0000	.0000	.0004	.0046	.0222	.0609	.1144	.1614	.1797	.1623	.1201
	9	.0000	.0000	.0001	.0011	.0074	.0271	.0654	.1158	.1597	.1771	.1602
	10	.0000	.0000	.0000	.0002	.0020	.0099	.0308	.0686	.1171	.1593	.1762
	11	.0000	.0000	.0000	.0000	.0005	.0030	.0120	.0336	.0710	.1185	.1602
	12	.0000	.0000	.0000	.0000	.0001	.0008	.0039	.0136	.0355	.0727	.1201
	13	.0000	.0000	.0000	.0000	.0000	.0002	.0010	.0045	.0146	.0366	.0739
	14	.0000	.0000	.0000	.0000	.0000	.0000	.0002	.0012	.0049	.0150	.0370
	15	.0000	.0000	.0000	.0000	.0000	.0000	.0000	.0003	.0013	.0049	.0148
	16	.0000	.0000	.0000	.0000	.0000	.0000	.0000	.0000	.0003	.0013	.0046
	17	.0000	.0000	.0000	.0000	.0000	.0000	.0000	.0000	.0000	.0002	.0011
	18	.0000	.0000	.0000	.0000	.0000	.0000	.0000	.0000	.0000	.0000	.0002
	19	.0000	.0000	.0000	.0000	.0000	.0000	.0000	.0000	.0000	.0000	.0000
	20	.0000	.0000	.0000	.0000	.0000	.0000	.0000	.0000	.0000	.0000	.0000

Table 1 *(continued)*

n	x	.01	.05	.10	.15	.20	π .25	.30	.35	.40	.45	.50
25	0	.7778	.2774	.0718	.0172	.0038	.0008	.0001	.0000	.0000	.0000	.0000
	1	.1964	.3650	.1994	.0759	.0236	.0063	.0014	.0003	.0000	.0000	.0000
	2	.0238	.2305	.2659	.1607	.0708	.0251	.0074	.0018	.0004	.0001	.0000
	3	.0018	.0930	.2265	.2174	.1358	.0641	.0243	.0076	.0019	.0004	.0001
	4	.0001	.0269	.1384	.2110	.1867	.1175	.0572	.0224	.0071	.0018	.0004
	5	.0000	.0060	.0646	.1564	.1960	.1645	.1030	.0506	.0199	.0063	.0016
	6	.0000	.0010	.0239	.0920	.1633	.1828	.1472	.0908	.0442	.0172	.0053
	7	.0000	.0001	.0072	.0441	.1108	.1654	.1712	.1327	.0800	.0381	.0143
	8	.0000	.0000	.0018	.0175	.0623	.1241	.1651	.1607	.1200	.0701	.0322
	9	.0000	.0000	.0004	.0058	.0294	.0781	.1336	.1635	.1511	.1084	.0609
	10	.0000	.0000	.0000	.0016	.0118	.0417	.0916	.1409	.1612	.1419	.0974
	11	.0000	.0000	.0000	.0004	.0040	.0189	.0536	.1034	.1465	.1583	.1328
	12	.0000	.0000	.0000	.0000	.0012	.0074	.0268	.0650	.1140	.1511	.1550
	13	.0000	.0000	.0000	.0000	.0003	.0025	.0115	.0350	.0760	.1236	.1550
	14	.0000	.0000	.0000	.0000	.0000	.0007	.0042	.0161	.0434	.0867	.1328
	15	.0000	.0000	.0000	.0000	.0000	.0002	.0013	.0064	.0212	.0520	.0974
	16	.0000	.0000	.0000	.0000	.0000	.0000	.0004	.0021	.0088	.0266	.0609
	17	.0000	.0000	.0000	.0000	.0000	.0000	.0001	.0006	.0031	.0115	.0322
	18	.0000	.0000	.0000	.0000	.0000	.0000	.0000	.0001	.0009	.0042	.0143
	19	.0000	.0000	.0000	.0000	.0000	.0000	.0000	.0000	.0002	.0013	.0053
	20	.0000	.0000	.0000	.0000	.0000	.0000	.0000	.0000	.0000	.0001	.0016
	21	.0000	.0000	.0000	.0000	.0000	.0000	.0000	.0000	.0000	.0000	.0004
	22	.0000	.0000	.0000	.0000	.0000	.0000	.0000	.0000	.0000	.0000	.0001
30	0	.7397	.2146	.0424	.0076	.0012	.0002	.0000	.0000	.0000	.0000	.0000
	1	.2242	.3389	.1413	.0404	.0093	.0018	.0003	.0000	.0000	.0000	.0000
	2	.0328	.2586	.2277	.1034	.0337	.0086	.0018	.0003	.0000	.0000	.0000
	3	.0031	.1270	.2361	.1703	.0785	.0269	.0072	.0015	.0003	.0000	.0000
	4	.0002	.0451	.1771	.2028	.1325	.0604	.0208	.0056	.0012	.0002	.0000
	5	.0000	.0124	.1023	.1861	.1723	.1047	.0464	.0157	.0041	.0008	.0001
	6	.0000	.0027	.0474	.1368	.1795	.1455	.0829	.0353	.0115	.0029	.0006
	7	.0000	.0005	.0180	.0828	.1538	.1662	.1219	.0652	.0263	.0081	.0019
	8	.0000	.0001	.0058	.0420	.1106	.1593	.1501	.1009	.0505	.0191	.0055
	9	.0000	.0000	.0016	.0181	.0676	.1298	.1573	.1328	.0823	.0382	.0133
	10	.0000	.0000	.0004	.0067	.0355	.0909	.1416	.1502	.1152	.0656	.0280
	11	.0000	.0000	.0001	.0022	.0161	.0551	.1103	.1471	.1396	.0976	.0509
	12	.0000	.0000	.0000	.0006	.0064	.0291	.0749	.1254	.1474	.1265	.0806
	13	.0000	.0000	.0000	.0001	.0022	.0134	.0444	.0935	.1360	.1433	.1115
	14	.0000	.0000	.0000	.0000	.0007	.0054	.0231	.0611	.1101	.1424	.1354
	15	.0000	.0000	.0000	.0000	.0002	.0019	.0106	.0351	.0783	.1242	.1445
	16	.0000	.0000	.0000	.0000	.0000	.0006	.0042	.0177	.0489	.0953	.1354
	17	.0000	.0000	.0000	.0000	.0000	.0002	.0015	.0079	.0269	.0642	.1115
	18	.0000	.0000	.0000	.0000	.0000	.0000	.0005	.0031	.0129	.0379	.0806
	19	.0000	.0000	.0000	.0000	.0000	.0000	.0001	.0010	.0054	.0196	.0509

Table 1 *(continued)*

n	x	.01	.05	.10	.15	.20	.25 (π)	.30	.35	.40	.45	.50
	20	.0000	.0000	.0000	.0000	.0000	.0000	.0000	.0003	.0020	.0088	.0280
	21	.0000	.0000	.0000	.0000	.0000	.0000	.0000	.0001	.0006	.0034	.0133
	22	.0000	.0000	.0000	.0000	.0000	.0000	.0000	.0000	.0002	.0012	.0055
	23	.0000	.0000	.0000	.0000	.0000	.0000	.0000	.0000	.0000	.0003	.0019
	24	.0000	.0000	.0000	.0000	.0000	.0000	.0000	.0000	.0000	.0001	.0006
	25	.0000	.0000	.0000	.0000	.0000	.0000	.0000	.0000	.0000	.0000	.0001
40	0	.6690	.1285	.0148	.0015	.0001	.0000	.0000	.0000	.0000	.0000	.0000
	1	.2703	.2706	.0657	.0106	.0013	.0001	.0000	.0000	.0000	.0000	.0000
	2	.0532	.2777	.1423	.0365	.0065	.0009	.0001	.0000	.0000	.0000	.0000
	3	.0068	.1851	.2003	.0816	.0205	.0037	.0005	.0001	.0000	.0000	.0000
	4	.0006	.0901	.2059	.1332	.0475	.0113	.0020	.0003	.0000	.0000	.0000
	5	.0000	.0342	.1647	.1692	.0854	.0272	.0061	.0010	.0001	.0000	.0000
	6	.0000	.0105	.1068	.1742	.1246	.0530	.0151	.0031	.0005	.0000	.0000
	7	.0000	.0027	.0576	.1493	.1513	.0857	.0315	.0080	.0015	.0002	.0000
	8	.0000	.0006	.0264	.1087	.1560	.1179	.0557	.0179	.0040	.0006	.0001
	9	.0000	.0001	.0104	.0682	.1386	.1397	.0849	.0342	.0095	.0018	.0002
	10	.0000	.0000	.0036	.0373	.1075	.1444	.1128	.0571	.0196	.0047	.0008
	11	.0000	.0000	.0011	.0180	.0733	.1312	.1319	.0838	.0357	.0105	.0021
	12	.0000	.0000	.0003	.0077	.0443	.1057	.1366	.1090	.0576	.0207	.0051
	13	.0000	.0000	.0001	.0029	.0238	.0759	.1261	.1265	.0827	.0365	.0109
	14	.0000	.0000	.0000	.0010	.0115	.0488	.1042	.1313	.1063	.0575	.0211
	15	.0000	.0000	.0000	.0003	.0050	.0282	.0774	.1226	.1228	.0816	.0366
	16	.0000	.0000	.0000	.0001	.0019	.0147	.0518	.1031	.1279	.1043	.0572
	17	.0000	.0000	.0000	.0000	.0007	.0069	.0314	.0784	.1204	.1205	.0807
	18	.0000	.0000	.0000	.0000	.0002	.0029	.0172	.0539	.1026	.1260	.1031
	19	.0000	.0000	.0000	.0000	.0001	.0011	.0085	.0336	.0792	.1194	.1194
	20	.0000	.0000	.0000	.0000	.0000	.0004	.0038	.0190	.0554	.1025	.1254
	21	.0000	.0000	.0000	.0000	.0000	.0001	.0016	.0097	.0352	.0799	.1194
	22	.0000	.0000	.0000	.0000	.0000	.0000	.0006	.0045	.0203	.0565	.1031
	23	.0000	.0000	.0000	.0000	.0000	.0000	.0002	.0019	.0106	.0362	.0807
	24	.0000	.0000	.0000	.0000	.0000	.0000	.0001	.0007	.0050	.0210	.0572
	25	.0000	.0000	.0000	.0000	.0000	.0000	.0000	.0003	.0021	.0110	.0366
	26	.0000	.0000	.0000	.0000	.0000	.0000	.0000	.0001	.0008	.0052	.0211
	27	.0000	.0000	.0000	.0000	.0000	.0000	.0000	.0000	.0003	.0022	.0109
	28	.0000	.0000	.0000	.0000	.0000	.0000	.0000	.0000	.0001	.0008	.0051
	29	.0000	.0000	.0000	.0000	.0000	.0000	.0000	.0000	.0000	.0003	.0021
	30	.0000	.0000	.0000	.0000	.0000	.0000	.0000	.0000	.0000	.0001	.0008
	31	.0000	.0000	.0000	.0000	.0000	.0000	.0000	.0000	.0000	.0000	.0002
	32	.0000	.0000	.0000	.0000	.0000	.0000	.0000	.0000	.0000	.0000	.0001
50	0	.6050	.0769	.0052	.0003	.0000	.0000	.0000	.0000	.0000	.0000	.0000
	1	.3056	.2025	.0286	.0026	.0002	.0000	.0000	.0000	.0000	.0000	.0000
	2	.0756	.2611	.0779	.0113	.0011	.0001	.0000	.0000	.0000	.0000	.0000
	3	.0122	.2199	.1386	.0319	.0044	.0004	.0000	.0000	.0000	.0000	.0000
	4	.0015	.1360	.1809	.0661	.0128	.0016	.0001	.0000	.0000	.0000	.0000

Table 1   *(continued)*

n	x	.01	.05	.10	.15	.20	π .25	.30	.35	.40	.45	.50
	5	.0001	.0658	.1849	.1072	.0295	.0049	.0006	.0000	.0000	.0000	.0000
	6	.0000	.0260	.1541	.1419	.0554	.0123	.0018	.0002	.0000	.0000	.0000
	7	.0000	.0086	.1076	.1575	.0870	.0259	.0048	.0006	.0000	.0000	.0000
	8	.0000	.0024	.0643	.1493	.1169	.0463	.0110	.0017	.0002	.0000	.0000
	9	.0000	.0006	.0333	.1230	.1364	.0721	.0220	.0042	.0005	.0000	.0000
	10	.0000	.0001	.0152	.0890	.1398	.0985	.0386	.0093	.0014	.0001	.0000
	11	.0000	.0000	.0061	.0571	.1271	.1194	.0602	.0182	.0035	.0004	.0000
	12	.0000	.0000	.0022	.0328	.1033	.1294	.0838	.0319	.0076	.0011	.0001
	13	.0000	.0000	.0007	.0169	.0755	.1261	.1050	.0502	.0147	.0027	.0003
	14	.0000	.0000	.0002	.0079	.0499	.1110	.1189	.0714	.0260	.0059	.0008
	15	.0000	.0000	.0001	.0033	.0299	.0888	.1223	.0923	.0415	.0116	.0020
	16	.0000	.0000	.0000	.0013	.0164	.0648	.1147	.1088	.0606	.0207	.0044
	17	.0000	.0000	.0000	.0005	.0082	.0432	.0983	.1171	.0808	.0339	.0087
	18	.0000	.0000	.0000	.0001	.0037	.0264	.0772	.1156	.0987	.0508	.0160
	19	.0000	.0000	.0000	.0000	.0016	.0148	.0558	.4048	.1109	.0700	.0270
	20	.0000	.0000	.0000	.0000	.0006	.0077	.0370	.0875	.1146	.0888	.0419
	21	.0000	.0000	.0000	.0000	.0002	.0036	.0227	.0673	.1091	.1038	.0598
	22	.0000	.0000	.0000	.0000	.0001	.0016	.0128	.0478	.0959	.1119	.0788
	23	.0000	.0000	.0000	.0000	.0000	.0006	.0067	.0313	.0778	.1115	.0960
	24	.0000	.0000	.0000	.0000	.0000	.0002	.0032	.0190	.0584	.1026	.1080
	25	.0000	.0000	.0000	.0000	.0000	.0001	.0014	.0106	.0405	.0873	.1123
	26	.0000	.0000	.0000	.0000	.0000	.0000	.0006	.0055	.0259	.0687	.1080
	27	.0000	.0000	.0000	.0000	.0000	.0000	.0002	.0026	.0154	.0500	.0960
	28	.0000	.0000	.0000	.0000	.0000	.0000	.0001	.0012	.0084	.0336	.0788
	29	.0000	.0000	.0000	.0000	.0000	.0000	.0000	.0005	.0043	.0208	.0598
	30	.0000	.0000	.0000	.0000	.0000	.0000	.0000	.0002	.0020	.0119	.0419
	31	.0000	.0000	.0000	.0000	.0000	.0000	.0000	.0001	.0009	.0063	.0270
	32	.0000	.0000	.0000	.0000	.0000	.0000	.0000	.0000	.0003	.0031	.0160
	33	.0000	.0000	.0000	.0000	.0000	.0000	.0000	.0000	.0001	.0014	.0087
	34	.0000	.0000	.0000	.0000	.0000	.0000	.0000	.0000	.0000	.0006	.0044
	35	.0000	.0000	.0000	.0000	.0000	.0000	.0000	.0000	.0000	.0002	.0020
	36	.0000	.0000	.0000	.0000	.0000	.0000	.0000	.0000	.0000	.0001	.0008
	37	.0000	.0000	.0000	.0000	.0000	.0000	.0000	.0000	.0000	.0000	.0003
	38	.0000	.0000	.0000	.0000	.0000	.0000	.0000	.0000	.0000	.0000	.0001

Table 2   *Standardized Normal Distribution*

$P[Z > \text{cutoff}]$
For instance, $P[Z > 1.96] = .025$

Cutoff	.00	.01	.02	.03	.04	.05	.06	.07	.08	.09
0.0	.5000	.4960	.4920	.4880	.4840	.4801	.4761	.4721	.4681	.4641
0.1	.4602	.4562	.4522	.4483	.4443	.4404	.4364	.4325	.4286	.4247
0.2	.4207	.4168	.4129	.4090	.4052	.4013	.3974	.3936	.3897	.3859
0.3	.3821	.3783	.3745	.3707	.3669	.3632	.3594	.3557	.3520	.3483
0.4	.3446	.3409	.3372	.3336	.3300	.3264	.3228	.3192	.3156	.3121
0.5	.3085	.3050	.3015	.2981	.2946	.2912	.2877	.2843	.2810	.2776
0.6	.2743	.2709	.2676	.2643	.2611	.2578	.2546	.2514	.2483	.2451
0.7	.2420	.2389	.2358	.2327	.2296	.2266	.2236	.2206	.2177	.2148
0.8	.2119	.2090	.2061	.2033	.2005	.1977	.1949	.1922	.1894	.1867
0.9	.1841	.1814	.1788	.1762	.1736	.1711	.1685	.1660	.1635	.1611
1.0	.1587	.1562	.1539	.1515	.1492	.1469	.1446	.1423	.1401	.1379
1.1	.1357	.1335	.1314	.1292	.1271	.1251	.1230	.1210	.1190	.1170
1.2	.1151	.1131	.1112	.1093	.1075	.1056	.1038	.1020	.1003	.0985
1.3	.0968	.0951	.0934	.0918	.0901	.0885	.0869	.0853	.0838	.0823
1.4	.0808	.0793	.0778	.0764	.0749	.0735	.0722	.0708	.0694	.0681
1.5	.0668	.0655	.0643	.0630	.0618	.0606	.0594	.0582	.0571	.0559
1.6	.0548	.0537	.0526	.0516	.0505	.0495	.0485	.0475	.0465	.0455
1.7	.0446	.0436	.0427	.0418	.0409	.0401	.0392	.0384	.0375	.0367
1.8	.0359	.0352	.0344	.0336	.0329	.0322	.0314	.0307	.0301	.0294
1.9	.0287	.0281	.0274	.0268	.0262	.0256	.0250	.0244	.0239	.0233
2.0	.0228	.0222	.0217	.0212	.0207	.0202	.0197	.0192	.0188	.0183
2.1	.0179	.0174	.0170	.0166	.0162	.0158	.0154	.0150	.0146	.0143
2.2	.0139	.0136	.0132	.0129	.0125	.0122	.0119	.0116	.0113	.0110
2.3	.0107	.0104	.0102	.0099	.0096	.0094	.0091	.0089	.0087	.0084
2.4	.0082	.0080	.0078	.0075	.0073	.0071	.0069	.0068	.0066	.0064
2.5	.0062	.0060	.0059	.0057	.0055	.0054	.0052	.0051	.0049	.0048
2.6	.0047	.0045	.0044	.0043	.0041	.0040	.0039	.0038	.0037	.0036
2.7	.0035	.0034	.0033	.0032	.0031	.0030	.0029	.0028	.0027	.0026
2.8	.0026	.0025	.0024	.0023	.0023	.0022	.0021	.0021	.0020	.0019
2.9	.0019	.0018	.0017	.0017	.0016	.0016	.0015	.0015	.0014	.0014
3.0	.0013	.0013	.0013	.0012	.0012	.0011	.0011	.0011	.0010	.0010
4.0	.000 031 7									
5.0	.000 000 287									
6.0	.000 000 000 987									
7.0	.000 000 000 001 28									
8.0	.000 000 000 000 001									

Table 3 *Random Digits*

10 09 73 25 33	76 52 01 35 86	34 67 35 48 76	80 95 90 91 71	39 29 27 49 45
37 54 20 48 05	64 89 47 42 96	24 80 52 40 37	20 63 61 04 02	00 82 29 16 65
08 42 26 89 53	19 64 50 93 03	23 20 90 25 60	15 95 33 47 64	35 08 03 36 06
99 01 90 25 29	09 37 67 07 15	38 31 13 11 65	88 67 67 43 97	04 43 62 76 59
12 80 79 99 70	80 15 73 61 47	64 03 23 66 53	98 95 11 68 77	12 17 17 68 33
66 06 57 47 17	34 07 27 68 50	36 69 73 61 70	65 81 33 98 85	11 19 92 91 70
31 06 01 08 05	45 57 18 24 06	35 30 34 26 14	86 79 90 74 39	23 40 30 97 32
85 26 97 76 02	02 05 16 56 92	68 66 57 48 18	73 05 38 52 47	18 62 38 85 79
63 57 33 21 35	05 32 54 70 48	90 55 35 75 48	28 46 82 87 09	83 49 12 56 24
73 79 64 57 53	03 52 96 47 78	35 80 83 42 82	60 93 52 03 44	35 27 38 84 35
98 52 01 77 67	14 90 56 86 07	22 10 94 05 58	60 97 09 34 33	50 50 07 39 98
11 80 50 54 31	39 80 82 77 32	50 72 56 82 48	29 40 52 42 01	52 77 56 78 51
83 45 29 96 34	06 28 89 80 83	13 74 67 00 78	18 47 54 06 10	68 71 17 78 17
88 68 54 02 00	86 50 75 84 01	36 76 66 79 51	90 36 47 64 93	29 60 91 10 62
99 59 46 73 48	87 51 76 49 69	91 82 60 89 28	93 78 56 13 68	23 47 83 41 13
65 48 11 76 74	17 46 85 09 50	58 04 77 69 74	73 03 95 71 86	40 21 81 65 44
80 12 43 56 35	17 72 70 80 15	45 31 82 23 74	21 11 57 82 53	14 38 55 37 63
74 35 09 98 17	77 40 27 72 14	43 23 60 02 10	45 52 16 42 37	96 28 60 26 55
69 91 62 68 03	66 25 22 91 48	36 93 68 72 03	76 62 11 39 90	94 40 05 64 18
09 89 32 05 05	14 22 56 85 14	46 42 75 67 88	96 29 77 88 22	54 38 21 45 98
91 49 91 45 23	68 47 92 76 86	46 16 28 35 54	94 75 08 99 23	37 08 92 00 48
80 33 69 45 98	26 94 03 68 58	70 29 73 41 35	53 14 03 33 40	42 05 08 23 41
44 10 48 19 49	85 15 74 79 54	32 97 92 65 75	57 60 04 08 81	22 22 20 64 13
12 55 07 37 42	11 10 00 20 40	12 86 07 46 97	96 64 48 94 39	28 70 72 58 15
63 60 64 93 29	16 50 53 44 84	40 21 95 25 63	43 65 17 70 82	07 20 73 17 90
61 19 69 04 46	26 45 74 77 74	51 92 43 37 29	65 39 45 95 93	42 58 26 05 27
15 47 44 52 66	95 27 07 99 53	59 36 78 38 48	82 39 61 01 18	33 21 15 94 66
94 55 72 85 73	67 89 75 43 87	54 62 24 44 31	91 19 04 25 92	92 92 74 59 73
42 48 11 62 13	97 34 40 87 21	16 86 84 87 67	03 07 11 20 59	25 70 14 66 70
23 52 37 83 17	73 20 88 98 37	68 93 59 14 16	26 25 22 96 63	05 52 28 25 62
04 49 35 24 94	75 24 63 38 24	45 86 25 10 25	61 96 27 93 35	65 33 71 24 72
00 54 99 76 54	64 05 18 81 59	96 11 96 38 96	54 69 28 23 91	23 28 72 95 29
35 96 31 53 07	26 89 80 93 54	33 35 13 54 62	77 97 45 00 24	90 10 33 93 33
59 80 80 83 91	45 42 72 68 42	83 60 94 97 00	13 02 12 48 92	78 56 52 01 06
46 05 88 52 36	01 39 09 22 86	77 28 14 40 77	93 91 08 36 47	70 61 74 29 41
32 17 90 05 97	87 37 92 52 41	05 56 70 70 07	86 74 31 71 57	85 39 41 18 38
69 23 46 14 06	20 11 74 52 04	15 95 66 00 00	18 74 39 24 23	97 11 89 63 38
19 56 54 14 30	01 75 87 53 79	40 41 92 15 85	66 67 43 68 06	84 96 28 52 07
45 15 51 49 38	19 47 60 72 46	43 66 79 45 43	59 04 79 00 33	20 82 66 95 41
94 86 43 19 94	36 16 81 08 51	34 88 88 15 53	01 54 03 54 56	05 01 45 11 76
98 08 62 48 26	45 24 02 84 04	44 99 90 88 96	39 09 47 34 07	35 44 13 18 80
33 18 51 62 32	41 94 15 09 49	89 43 54 85 81	88 69 54 19 94	37 54 87 30 43
80 95 10 04 06	96 38 27 07 74	20 15 12 33 87	25 01 62 52 98	94 62 46 11 71
79 75 24 91 40	71 96 12 82 96	69 86 10 25 91	74 85 22 05 39	00 38 75 95 79
18 63 33 25 37	98 14 50 65 71	31 01 02 46 74	05 45 56 14 27	77 93 89 19 36
74 02 94 39 02	77 55 73 22 70	97 79 01 71 19	52 52 75 80 21	80 81 45 17 48
54 17 84 56 11	80 99 33 71 43	05 33 51 29 69	56 12 71 92 55	36 04 09 03 24
11 66 44 98 83	52 07 98 48 27	59 38 17 15 39	09 97 33 34 40	88 46 12 33 56
48 32 47 79 28	31 24 96 47 10	02 29 53 68 70	32 30 75 75 46	15 02 00 99 94
69 07 49 41 38	87 63 79 19 76	35 58 40 44 01	10 51 82 16 15	01 84 87 69 38

Reproduced by permission from The RAND Corporation, ''A Million Random Digits,'' Glencoe, Illinois: 1955.

Table 4 *Student* t *distribution*

$P[t > \text{cutoff}]$
For instance, with 10 degrees of
freedom, $P[t > 1.812] = .05$

Degrees of Freedom	Probability of a t-value larger than indicated cutoff				
	.10	*.05*	*.025*	*.01*	*.005*
1	3.078	6.314	12.706	31.821	63.657
2	1.886	2.920	4.303	6.965	9.925
3	1.638	2.353	3.182	4.541	5.841
4	1.533	2.132	2.776	3.747	4.604
5	1.476	2.015	2.571	3.365	4.032
6	1.440	1.943	2.447	3.143	3.707
7	1.415	1.895	2.365	2.998	3.499
8	1.397	1.860	2.306	2.896	3.355
9	1.383	1.833	2.262	2.821	3.250
10	1.372	1.812	2.228	2.764	3.169
11	1.363	1.796	2.201	2.718	3.106
12	1.356	1.782	2.179	2.681	3.055
13	1.350	1.771	2.160	2.650	3.012
14	1.345	1.761	2.145	2.624	2.977
15	1.341	1.753	2.131	2.602	2.947
16	1.337	1.746	2.120	2.583	2.921
17	1.333	1.740	2.110	2.567	2.898
18	1.330	1.734	2.101	2.552	2.878
19	1.328	1.729	2.093	2.539	2.861
20	1.325	1.725	2.086	2.528	2.845
21	1.323	1.721	2.080	2.518	2.831
22	1.321	1.717	2.074	2.508	2.819
23	1.319	1.714	2.069	2.500	2.807
24	1.318	1.711	2.064	2.492	2.797
25	1.316	1.708	2.060	2.485	2.787
26	1.315	1.706	2.056	2.479	2.779
27	1.314	1.703	2.052	2.473	2.771
28	1.313	1.701	2.048	2.467	2.763
29	1.311	1.699	2.045	2.462	2.756
30	1.310	1.697	2.042	2.457	2.750
40	1.303	1.684	2.021	2.423	2.704
60	1.296	1.671	2.000	2.390	2.660
120	1.290	1.661	1.984	2.358	2.626
∞	1.282	1.645	1.960	2.326	2.576

Taken from Table III of Fisher and Yates: *Statistical Tables for Biological, Agricultural, and Medical Research* published by Longmans Group Ltd. London (previously published by Oliver and Boyd Ltd., Edinburgh) by permission of the authors and publishers.

Table 5 *Chi-square distribution*

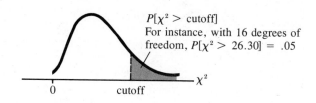

$P[\chi^2 > \text{cutoff}]$
For instance, with 16 degrees of
freedom, $P[\chi^2 > 26.30] = .05$

Degrees of freedom	Probability of a chi-square value larger than indicated cutoff				
	.10	.05	.025	.01	.005
1	2.71	3.84	5.02	6.63	7.88
2	4.61	5.99	7.38	9.21	10.60
3	6.25	7.81	9.35	11.34	12.84
4	7.78	9.49	11.14	13.28	14.86
5	9.24	11.07	12.83	15.09	16.75
6	10.64	12.59	14.45	16.81	18.55
7	12.02	14.07	16.01	18.48	20.28
8	13.36	15.51	17.53	20.09	21.96
9	14.68	16.92	19.02	21.67	23.59
10	15.99	18.31	20.48	23.21	25.19
11	17.28	19.68	21.92	24.72	26.76
12	18.55	21.03	23.34	26.22	28.30
13	19.81	22.36	24.74	27.69	29.82
14	21.06	23.68	26.12	29.14	31.32
15	22.31	25.00	27.49	30.58	32.80
16	23.54	26.30	28.85	32.00	34.27
17	24.77	27.59	30.19	33.41	35.72
18	25.99	28.87	31.53	34.81	37.16
19	27.20	30.14	32.85	36.19	38.58
20	28.41	31.41	34.17	37.57	40.00
21	29.62	32.67	35.48	38.93	41.40
22	30.81	33.92	36.78	40.29	42.80
23	32.01	35.17	38.08	41.64	44.18
24	33.20	36.42	39.36	42.98	45.56
25	34.38	37.65	40.65	44.31	46.93
26	35.56	38.89	41.92	45.64	48.29
27	36.74	40.11	43.19	46.96	49.64
28	37.92	41.34	44.46	48.28	50.99
29	39.09	42.56	45.72	49.59	52.34
30	40.26	43.77	46.98	50.89	53.67
40	51.81	55.76	59.34	63.69	66.77
50	63.17	67.50	71.42	76.15	79.49
60	74.40	79.08	83.30	88.38	91.95
70	85.53	90.53	95.02	100.43	104.22
80	96.58	101.88	106.63	112.33	116.32
90	107.57	113.14	118.14	124.12	128.30
100	118.50	124.34	129.56	135.81	140.17

Abridged from Catherine M. Thompson, "Table of percentage points of the x^2 distribution," *Biometrika,* Vol. 32, 1942, p. 187. Reprinted by permission of the Biometrika Trust.

Table 6   F *Distribution*

$P[F > \text{cutoff}]$
For instance, with 4 degrees of freedom
for the numerator and 20 for the
denominator, $P[F > 2.87] = .05$

Cutoffs for 5 percent probabilities

Degrees of freedom for denominator	Degrees of freedom for numerator									
	1	2	3	4	5	6	7	8	9	10
1	161	200	216	225	230	234	237	239	241	242
2	18.5	19.0	19.2	19.2	19.3	19.3	19.4	19.4	19.4	19.4
3	10.1	9.55	9.28	9.12	9.01	8.94	8.89	8.85	8.81	8.79
4	7.71	6.94	6.59	6.39	6.26	6.16	6.09	6.04	6.00	5.96
5	6.61	5.79	5.41	5.19	5.05	4.95	4.88	4.82	4.77	4.74
6	5.99	5.14	4.76	4.53	4.39	4.28	4.21	4.15	4.10	4.06
7	5.59	4.74	4.35	4.12	3.97	3.87	3.79	3.73	3.68	3.64
8	5.32	4.46	4.07	3.84	3.69	3.58	3.50	3.44	3.39	3.35
9	5.12	4.26	3.86	3.63	3.48	3.37	3.29	3.23	3.18	3.14
10	4.96	4.10	3.71	3.48	3.33	3.22	3.14	3.07	3.02	2.98
11	4.84	3.98	3.59	3.36	3.20	3.09	3.01	2.95	2.90	2.85
12	4.75	3.89	3.49	3.26	3.11	3.00	2.91	2.85	2.80	2.75
13	4.67	3.81	3.41	3.18	3.03	2.92	2.83	2.77	2.71	2.67
14	4.60	3.74	3.34	3.11	2.96	2.85	2.76	2.70	2.65	2.60
15	4.54	3.68	3.29	3.06	2.90	2.79	2.71	2.64	2.59	2.54
16	4.49	3.63	3.24	3.01	2.85	2.74	2.66	2.59	2.54	2.49
17	4.45	3.59	3.20	2.96	2.81	2.70	2.61	2.55	2.49	2.45
18	4.41	3.55	3.16	2.93	2.77	2.66	2.58	2.51	2.46	2.41
19	4.38	3.52	3.13	2.90	2.74	2.63	2.54	2.48	2.42	2.38
20	4.35	3.49	3.10	2.87	2.71	2.60	2.51	2.45	2.39	2.35
25	4.24	3.39	2.99	2.76	2.60	2.49	2.40	2.34	2.28	2.24
30	4.17	3.32	2.92	2.69	2.53	2.42	2.33	2.27	2.21	2.16
40	4.08	3.23	2.84	2.61	2.45	2.34	2.25	2.18	2.12	2.08
60	4.00	3.15	2.76	2.53	2.37	2.25	2.17	2.10	2.04	1.99
120	3.92	3.07	2.68	2.45	2.29	2.18	2.09	2.02	1.96	1.91
∞	3.84	3.00	2.60	2.37	2.21	2.10	2.01	1.94	1.88	1.83

Extracted from M. Merrington and C.M. Thompson, "Tables of Percentage Points of the Inverted Beta (*F*) Distribution," *Biometrika*, Vol. 33, 1943, pp. 73–88. Reprinted by permission of the Biometrika Trust.

Table 6 *(continued)*

Cutoffs for 1 percent probabilities

Degrees of freedom for denominator	Degrees of freedom for numerator									
	1	*2*	*3*	*4*	*5*	*6*	*7*	*8*	*9*	*10*
1	4052	5000	5403	5625	5764	5859	5928	5982	6022	6056
2	98.5	99.0	99.2	99.2	99.3	99.3	99.4	99.4	99.4	99.4
3	34.1	30.8	29.5	28.7	28.2	27.9	27.7	27.5	27.3	27.2
4	21.2	18.0	16.7	16.0	15.5	15.2	15.0	14.8	14.7	14.5
5	16.3	13.3	12.1	11.4	11.0	10.7	10.5	10.3	10.2	10.1
6	13.7	10.9	9.78	9.15	8.75	8.47	8.26	8.10	7.98	7.87
7	12.2	9.55	8.45	7.85	7.46	7.19	6.99	6.84	6.72	6.62
8	11.3	8.65	7.59	7.01	6.63	6.37	6.18	6.03	5.91	5.81
9	10.6	8.02	6.99	6.42	6.06	5.80	5.61	5.47	5.35	5.26
10	10.0	7.56	6.55	5.99	5.64	5.39	5.20	5.06	4.94	4.85
11	9.65	7.21	6.22	5.67	5.32	5.07	4.89	4.74	4.63	4.54
12	9.33	6.93	5.95	5.41	5.06	4.82	4.64	4.50	4.39	4.30
13	9.07	6.70	5.74	5.21	4.86	4.62	4.44	4.30	4.19	4.10
14	8.86	6.51	5.56	5.04	4.70	4.46	4.28	4.14	4.03	3.94
15	8.68	6.36	5.42	4.89	4.56	4.32	4.14	4.00	3.89	3.80
16	8.53	6.23	5.29	4.77	4.44	4.20	4.03	3.89	3.78	3.69
17	8.40	6.11	5.19	4.67	4.34	4.10	3.93	3.79	3.68	3.59
18	8.29	6.01	5.09	4.58	4.25	4.01	3.84	3.71	3.60	3.51
19	8.19	5.93	5.01	4.50	4.17	3.94	3.77	3.63	3.52	3.43
20	8.10	5.85	4.94	4.43	4.10	3.87	3.70	3.56	3.46	3.37
25	7.77	5.57	4.68	4.18	3.86	3.63	3.46	3.32	3.22	3.13
30	7.56	5.39	4.51	4.02	3.70	3.47	3.30	3.17	3.07	2.98
40	7.31	5.18	4.31	3.83	3.51	3.29	3.12	2.99	2.89	2.80
60	7.08	4.98	4.13	3.65	3.34	3.12	2.95	2.82	2.72	2.63
120	6.85	4.79	3.95	3.48	3.17	2.96	2.79	2.66	2.56	2.47
∞	6.63	4.61	3.78	3.32	3.02	2.80	2.64	2.51	2.41	2.32

References

Chapter 1

Opening quotation: Walter Bagehot.

1. Edward O. Thorpe, *Beat the Dealer,* revised, New York: Random House, 1966.
2. For some real numbers, see Maxine Brady, *The Monopoly Book,* New York: David McKay, 1976.
3. W. Allen Wallis and Harry V. Roberts, *Statistics: A New Approach,* New York: The Free Press, 1956, p. 192.
4. This example is from Harold Jacobs, *Mathematics: A Human Endeavor,* second edition, San Francisco: W.H. Freeman and Company, 1982, p. 562.
5. G. Udny Yule and M.G. Kendall, *An Introduction to the Theory of Statistics,* London: Charles Griffin, 1948, p. 100.
6. Quoted in "Scorecard," Jerry Kirshenbaum, ed., *Sports Illustrated,* February 1984.
7. Francis Galton, *Natural Inheritance,* London: Macmillan, 1889.
8. *The Way Things Work Book of the Computer: An Illustrated Encyclopedia of Information Science, Cybernetics and Data Processing,* New York: Simon and Schuster, 1974.
9. Mark Kac, "Probability," *Scientific American,* September 1964, pp. 92–108.
10. Gertrude E. Pearse, *Biometrika,* Vol. 20A, 1928, p. 336.
11. S.J. Pretorius, "Skew Bivariate Frequency Surfaces," *Biometrika,* Vol. 22, 1930–1931, p. 210.

Chapter 2

Opening quotation: E.W. Howe, *Sinner Sermons,* 1926.

1. Translation published in 1953 by Princeton University Press. Later reprinted by Holt, Rinehart, and Winston, translated by Sidney Henry Gould.
2. Here's a sampling: Oswald Jacoby, *Oswald Jacoby on Poker,* New York: Doubleday, 1981; and Maxine Brady, *The Monopoly Book,* New York: David McKay, 1976.

3. John Maynard Keynes, *A Treatise on Probability,* London: Macmillan, 1921, pp. 362–363.
4. "U.S. Operators find 1,004 Fields in 1977," *Oil and Gas Journal,* July 3, 1978, pp. 32–33.
5. Roger G. Ibbotson and Rex A. Sinquefield, *Stocks, Bonds, Bills, and Inflation: Historical Returns (1926–1978),* Charlottesville, Virginia: The Financial Analysts Research Foundation, 1979.
6. Richard Scammon, *Odds: On Virtually Everything,* New York: Putnam, 1980, p. 135.
7. Leo Gould, *You Bet Your Life,* Marcel Rodd, 1946.
8. Horace W. Brock, *The Future World Price of Gold,* supplement to *Optima,* vol. 30, No. 2, 1981.
9. Richard Scammon, p. 8.
10. Norman Dash, *Great Betting Systems,* Los Angeles: Price/Stern/Sloan and Ravenna Books, 1968, pp. 155–156.
11. Norman Dash, pp. 164–165.
12. Leo Gould.

Chapter 3

Opening quotation: Charles Sanders Peirce.

1. Unfortunately, many classic works are not in English; e.g., A.N. Kolmogorov, *Grundbegriffe der Wahrscheinlichkeitsrechnung,* Berlin: Springer, 1933. For a modern English discussion, see Paul G. Hoel, *Introduction to Mathematical Statistics,* fourth edition, New York: John Wiley, 1971, Ch. 2.
2. Clement McQuaid, ed., *Gambler's Digest,* Northfield, Illinois: Digest Books, 1971, pp. 24–25.
3. Norman Dash, *Great Betting Systems,* Los Angeles: Price/Stern/Sloan and Ravenna Books, 1968, pp. 155–156.
4. John Fisher, *Never Give a Sucker an Even Break,* New York: Pantheon Books, 1976.
5. P.S. Laplace, *A Philosophical Essay on Probabilities,* 1812, reprinted New York: Dover, 1951, p. 189.
6. T. Bayes, "Thomas Bayes Essay Toward Solving a Problem in the Doctrine of Chances," 1763, reprinted in *Biometrika,* Vol. 45, 1958, p. 297.
7. From the magazine *California Highways,* cited by Darrell Huff in *How to Take a Chance,* New York: Norton, 1959, p. 110.
8. Leo Gould, *You Bet Your Life,* Marcel Rodd, 1946.

Chapter 4

Opening quotation: James Thurber, "The Fairly Intelligent Fly," in *Fables for Our Time,* New York: Harper & Row, 1939, p. 13.

1. This example is from Joseph Newman, *Management Applications of Decision Theory,* New York: Harper & Row, 1971, pp. 32–61.
2. Richard Scammon, *Odds: On Virtually Everything,* New York: Putnam, 1980, p. 4.
3. M.E. Bitterman, "The Evolution of Intelligence," *Scientific American,* January 1965.
4. Milton Friedman and Leonard Savage, "The Utility Analysis of Choices Involving Risk," *Journal of Political Economy,* August 1948, pp. 279–304.
5. Roger G. Ibbotson and Rex A. Sinquefield, *Stocks, Bonds, Bills, and Inflation: Historical Returns (1926–1978),* Charlottesville, Virginia: The Financial Analysts Research Foundation, 1979.

6. Adam Smith, *The Wealth of Nations* (1776), reprinted London: Methuen, 1920, Vol. 1, Ch. 10, p. 109.

7. William J. Peters, "The Psychology of Risk in Consumer Decisions," in George Fisk, ed., *The Frontiers of Management & Psychology*, New York: Harper, 1964.

Chapter 5

Opening quotation: J.M. Keynes, *A Tract on Monetary Reform*, London: Macmillan, 1923, p. 65.

1. More elaborate tables can be found in the *Harvard Computation Laboratory Tables of the Cumulative Binomial Distribution*, Cambridge: Harvard University Press, 1955 and Sol Weintraub, *Tables of the Cumulative Binomial Probability Distribution for Small Values of p*, New York: Free Press of Glencoe, 1963.

2. For example, Marek Fisz, *Probability Theory and Mathematical Statistics*, third edition, New York: John Wiley and Sons, 1963, p. 131.

3. Quoted in *Gambler's Digest*, Clement McQuaid, ed., Northfield, Illinois: Digest Books, 1971, p. 287.

4. W. Allen Wallis and Harry V. Roberts, *Statistics: A New Approach*, New York: The Free Press, 1956, p. 322.

5. Clement McQuaid, ed., *Gambler's Digest*, p. 287.

6. Edgar Allen Poe, "The Mystery of Marie Roget," in *Murders in the Rue Morgue*, Girard, Kansas: Haldeman-Julius Co.

Chapter 6

Opening quotation: Sir Francis Galton.

1. Marek Fisz, *Probability Theory and Mathematical Statistics*, third edition, New York: John Wiley and Sons, 1963, pp. 196–202.

2. H.P. Bowditch, "The Growth of Children," Report of the Board of Health of Massachusetts, VIII, 1877.

3. A discussion of several limit theorems is given in Fisz, Ch. 6.

4. Mercer and Hall, "The Experimental Error of Field Trials," *Journal of Agricultural Science*, Vol. 4, 1911, p. 107.

5. George Gamow, *One Two Three . . . Infinity*, New York: Viking Press, 1947, pp. 214–215.

6. Edward Kasner and James Newman, *Mathematics and the Imagination*, New York: Simon & Schuster, 1940.

7. J.E. Littlewood, *A Mathematician's Miscellany*, London: Methuen, 1953, p. 110.

8. Eugene F. Fama, "Efficient Capital Markets: A Review of Theory and Empirical Work," *Journal of Finance*, May 1970, pp. 383–417.

9. Paul Samuelson, "Proof that Properly Anticipated Prices Fluctuate Randomly," *Industrial Management Review*, Spring 1965, pp. 41–49.

10. A very readable source of further details is Burton Malkiel, *A Random Walk Down Wall Street*, second edition, New York: Norton, 1978.

11. Roger G. Ibbotson and Rex A. Sinquefield, *Stocks, Bonds, Bills, and Inflation: Historical Returns (1926–1978)*, Charlottesville, Virginia: The Financial Analysts Research Foundation, 1979.

Chapter 7

Opening quotation: Lord Kelvin.

1. Michael S. Rozeff and William R. Kinney, "Capital Market Seasonability: the Case of Stock Market Returns," *Journal of Financial Economics,* October 1976.
2. Final Report of the Anthropometric Committee to the British Association, 1883, p. 256; cited in G. Udny Yule and M.G. Kendall, *An Introduction to the Theory of Statistics,* London, Charles Griffin, 1948, p. 94.
3. Harold Jacobs, *Mathematics: A Human Endeavor,* San Francisco, W.H. Freeman, 1982, p. 570.

Chapter 8

Opening quotation: Sir Arthur Conan Doyle, "The Adventure of the Copper Beeches," *Adventures of Sherlock Holmes,* New York: Harper and Brothers, 1892, p. 289.

1. This example is from Paul Meier, "The Biggest Public Health Experiment Ever: The 1954 Field Trial of the Salk Poliomyelitis Vaccine," in Judith Tanur *et al., Statistics: A Guide to the Unknown,* San Francisco: Holden-Day, 1972, pp. 2–13.
2. This example is from Michael Wheeler, *Lies, Damn Lies, and Statistics,* New York: Dell, 1976, Ch. 10.
3. The RAND Corporation, *A Million Random Digits With 100,000 Normal Deviates,* New York: The Free Press, 1955.
4. This example is from John Neter, "How Accountants Save Money By Sampling," in Tanur, *et al.,* pp. 203–211.
5. W. Allen Wallis and Harry V. Roberts, *Statistics: A New Approach,* New York: The Free Press, 1956, pp. 479–480.
6. "Coke-Pepsi Slugfest," *Time,* July 26, 1976, pp. 64–65.
7. "Down on the Farm," *Newsweek,* May 2, 1949, pp. 47–48.
8. L.L. Bairds, *The Graduates,* Princeton, New Jersey: ETS, 1973.
9. Earl W. Kintner, *A Primer on the Law of Deceptive Practices,* New York: Macmillan, 1971, p. 153.
10. F.F. Stephan and P.J. McCarthy, *Sampling Opinions,* New York: Wiley, 1958, p. 286.
11. Darrell Huff, *How to Lie With Statistics,* New York: Norton, 1954, p. 26.
12. Michael Wheeler, p. 88.
13. Michael Wheeler, p. 90.
14. Darrell Huff, p. 24.
15. Cited in Lucy Horwitz and Lou Ferleger, *Statistics for Social Change,* Boston: South End Press, 1980, pp. 181–182.
16. Michael Wheeler, p. 15.
17. Darrell Huff, *How to Take a Chance,* New York: Norton, 1959, pp. 115–117.
18. Stanley L. Warner, "Randomized Response: A Survey Technique for Eliminating Evasive Answer Bias," *Journal of the American Statistical Association,* Vol. 60, 1965, pp. 63–69.
19. Michael Wheeler, p. 289.
20. *University of Chicago Magazine,* April 1952, p. 10.
21. *Civil Liberties,* December 1952.
22. Ben Wattenberg, "Women Are Getting What They Want, Surprisingly Fast," *Los Angeles Times,* May 24, 1983.
23. U.S. Department of Commerce, *Statistical Abstract,* Washington, D.C.: U.S. Government Printing Office, 1981, Table 202, p. 123.
24. Michael Wheeler, p. 297.

25. Robert Reno, "Poll Shows Strong Work Ethic," *Newsday*, July 1983.
26. David Fay Smith and John Kochevar, "How Computers Are Changing Lives," *Dial*, June 1984, pp. 26–33, 55.
27. "More Children Equal Less Divorce," *Look*, February 13, 1951, p. 80.

Chapter 9

Opening quotation: Sir Arthur Conan Doyle, *A Study in Scarlet*, Philadelphia: J.B. Lippincott, 1893, p. 136.

1. Leonid F. Maistrov, *Probability Theory*, translated and edited by Samuel Kotz, New York: Academic Press, 1974, p. 153.
2. R. Clay Sprowls, *Elementary Statistics for Students of Social Science and Business*, New York: McGraw Hill, 1955, p. 104.
3. Robert J. Samuelson, "The Strange Case of the Missing Jobs," *Los Angeles Times*, October 27, 1983.
4. This example is from W. Allen Wallis and Harry V. Roberts, *Statistics: A New Approach*, New York: The Free Press, 1956, p. 471.
5. Lisa Birnbach, ed., *The Official Preppy Handbook*, New York: Workman, 1980, p. 85.
6. W. Allen Wallis and Harry V. Roberts, p. 100.

Chapter 10

Opening quotation: Sherlock Holmes.

1. Edward Leamer, "Let's Take the Con Out of Econometrics," *American Economic Review*, March 1983, p. 36.
2. From Harley Tinkham, "Morning Briefing," *Los Angeles Times*, November 26, 1983.
3. Lester Kauffman, "Statistical Quality Control at the St. Louis Division of American Stove Company," cited in Acheson Duncan, *Quality Control and Industrial Statistics*, Homewood, Illinois: Irwin, 1959.
4. E. Yehle, "Accuracy in Clerical Work," *Systems & Procedures: A Handbook for Business and Industry*, second edition, Victor Lazzaro, ed., Englewood Cliffs, New Jersey: Prentice-Hall, 1968.
5. William R. Simpson, "A Probabilistic Formulation of Murphy Dynamics as Applied to the Analysis of Operational Research Problems" in *The Best of the Journal of Irreproducible Results*, New York: Workman, 1983, pp. 120–123.
6. Kenneth B. Clark and Mamie P. Clark, "Racial Identification and Preference in Negro Children" in *Readings in Social Psychology*, Eleanor E. Macoby, Theodore M. Newcomb, and Eugene L. Hartley, eds., third edition, New York: Holt, Rinehart, and Winston, 1958, pp. 602–611.
7. R.A. Fisher, *Experiments in Plant Hybridization*, Edinburgh: Oliver and Boyd, 1965, p. 53. This book put Mendel's original paper together with comments by Fisher, based on a 1936 paper.
8. Roger C. Vergin and Michael Scriabin, "Winning Strategies for Wagering on National Football League Games," *Management Science*, Vol. 24, April 1978, pp. 809–818.
9. P.K. Whelpton and Clyde V. Kiser, *Social and Psychological Factors Affecting Fertility*, Vol. I, New York: Milbank Memorial Fund, 1950, p. 109.
10. Roger C. Vergin and Michael Scriabin, p. 812.
11. Frederick Mosteller, Robert E.K. Rourke, and George B. Thomas, Jr., *Probability with Statistical Applications*, Reading, Mass.: Addison-Wesley, 1961, p. 17.

Chapter 11

Opening quotation: Ronald H. Coase.

1. Arthur Melton, ed., *Journal of Experimental Psychology,* Vol. 64, 1962, 553–557.
2. Darrell Huff, *How to Lie With Statistics* New York: Norton, 1954, pp. 58–59.
3. F. Arcelus and A.H. Meltzer, "The Effect of Aggregate Economic Variables on Congressional Elections," *American Political Science Review,* Vol. 69, 1975, 1232–1239.
4. F. Mosteller and R. Rourke, *Sturdy Statistics,* Reading, Mass.: Addison-Wesley, 1971, p. 68.
5. *N.Y. Times,* Jan. 18, 1976.
6. Lucy Horwitz, and Lou Ferleger, *Statistics for Social Change,* Boston: South End Press, 1980, p. 177.
7. *Parade,* Oct. 8, 1972.
8. Cited by Martin Gardner in *Fads and Fallacies in the Name of Science,* New York: Dover, 1957, p. 305.
9. Norman Bloom, *The New World,* July 4, 1973.
10. "Pickles and Humbug," cited in Barry Siegel, "World May End With a Splash," *Los Angeles Times,* October 9, 1982.
11. Roger C. Vergin and Michael Scriabin, "Winning Strategies for Wagering on National Football League Games," *Management Science,* Vol. 24, April 1978, p. 814.
12. "News Briefs," *Cape Cod Times*, July 5, 1984.
13. *Newsweek,* February 4, 1974.

Chapter 12

Opening quotation: Maurice G. Kendall, "On the Reconciliation of Theories of Probability," 1949.

1. Donna Alcosser explained this test to me.
2. The poll results are summarized "A Look at the Opposite Sex," *Newsweek on Campus,* April 1984, p. 21. The numbers used in the text are approximations, since the article does not give the fractions of the 523 people polled who were male and female.
3. *Journal of the American Medical Association,* January 20, 1984.
4. Marion Gillim, "Physical Measurements of Mount Holyoke College Freshmen in 1918 and 1943," *Journal of the American Statistical Association,* March 1944, pp. 53–56.
5. Georg De Leon, "The Baldness Experiment," *Psychology Today,* October 1977, pp. 62–66.
6. See reference 2.
7. *New England Journal of Medicine,* January 1974.
8. David P. Phillips, "Deathday and Birthday: An Unexpected Connection," in Judith M. Tanur, et al., *Statistics: A Guide to the Unknown,* San Francisco: Holden-Day, 1972, pp. 52–65.
9. Karl Pearson, "On a Certain Double Hypergeometrical Series and Its Representation by Continuous Frequency Surfaces," *Biometrika,* Vol. 16, 1924, pp. 172–188.
10. P.L. Yu, C. Wrather, and G. Kozmetsky, "Auto Weight and Public Safety, a Statistical Study of Transportation Hazards," Research Report 233, Center for Cybernetic Studies, University of Texas, Austin, 1975.
11. Reported in G. Udny Yule and M.G. Kendall, *An Introduction to the Theory of Statistics,* London: Charles Griffin, 1948, p. 419.
12. Lester Kauffman, "Statistical Quality Control at the St. Louis Division of American Stove Company," cited in Acheson Duncan, *Quality Control and Industrial Statistics,* Homewood, Illinois: Irwin, 1959.

13. Dennis Lendrem, "Should John McEnroe Grunt?," *New Scientist,* July 21, 1983. Professor Lendrem was kind enough to send me his original data.

14. Joan R. Rosenblatt and James J Filliben, "Randomization and the Draft Lottery," *Science,* 171 (1971), pp. 306–308. Interestingly, there was also a draft lottery in 1940, in which the capsules apparently were not very well mixed. See the statement by Samuel Stouffer and Walter Bartky in the *Chicago Tribune,* November 2, 1940, p. 4.

15. Harriet H. Imrey, "Smoking Cigarettes: A Risk Factor For Sexual Activity Among Adolescent Girls," *Journal of Irreproducible Results,* Nov/Dec 1983, p. 11.

16. See reference 2.

17. Leo A. Goodman and William H. Kruskal, "Measures of Association for Cross Classifications," *Journal of the American Statistical Association,* 1954, pp. 732–764.

18. Thomas H. Wonnacott and Ronald J. Wonnacott, *Introductory Statistics for Business and Economics,* third edition, New York: John Wiley & Sons, 1977, pp. 306–308.

19. Robert Wiltsey, *Doctoral Use of Foreign Languages: A Survey,* Part II, Educational Testing Service, 1972, p. 61.

20. D. Weiss, B. Whitten, and D. Leddy, "Lead Content of Human Hair (1871–1971)," *Science,* 1972, pp. 69–70.

21. *Science,* June 10, 1977.

22. Karl Pearson, "On the Laws of Inheritance in Man, II," *Biometrika,* Vol. 3, 1904, pp. 131–190.

Chapter 13

Opening quotation: Edward Leamer, "Let's Take the Con Out of Econometrics," *American Economic Review,* March 1983, p. 37.

1. John Maynard Keynes, *The General Theory of Employment, Interest, and Prices* (1936), reprinted New York: Harcourt Brace Jovanovich, 1964, p. 96.

2. See Arthur Okun, *The Political Economy of Prosperity,* New York: Norton, 1970, p. 132 and, for an update, Gary Smith, "Okun's Law Revisited," *Quarterly Review of Economics and Business,* Winter 1975, pp. 37–54.

3. Dorothy S. Brady, "Family Saving, 1888 to 1950," in *A Study of Saving in the United States,* Vol. 3, by Raymond W. Goldsmith, Dorothy S. Brady, and Horst Medershausen, Princeton, N.J.: Princeton University Press, 1956, p. 183.

4. Joel Dean, "Statistical Cost Functions of a Hosiery Mill," *Journal of Business,* 1941, Supplement, 2, pp. 1–51.

5. These data are from Roger G. Ibbotson and Rex A. Sinquefield, *Stocks, Bonds, Bills, and Inflation: Historical Returns (1926–1978),* Charlottesville, Virginia: The Financial Analysts Research Foundation, 1979.

6. James Shields, *Monozygotic Twins,* London: Oxford University Press, 1962.

Chapter 14

Opening quotation: Lewis Carroll, *Alice in Wonderland,* New York: Heritage Press, 1941.

1. Securities and Exchange Commission (SEC), *Institutional Investor Study Report,* 1971, Vol. 2, pp. 325–347.

2. SEC, Institutional Investor Study Report, 1971, Vol. 4, p., 333. For some other studies, see Fischer Black, Michael Jensen, and Myron Scholes, "The Capital Asset Pricing Model: Some Empirical Tests," and Merton Miller and Myron Scholes, "Rates of Return in Relation to Risk: A Re-examination of Some Recent Findings," both in *Studies in the Theory of Capital Markets,* Michael Jensen, ed., New York: Praeger, 1972, pp. 47–127.

3. James B. Cloonan, American Association of Individual Investors *Journal*, October 1983, p. 37.
4. Ray C. Fair, "The Effect of Economic Events on Votes for President," *The Review of Economics and Statistics*, Vol. 60 (May 1978), pp. 159–173; Gerald H. Kramer, "Short-Term Fluctuations in U.S. Voting Behavior, 1896–1964," *The American Political Science Review*, Vol. 65 (March 1971), pp. 131–143.
5. Charles Osterberg, "Unsafe at Zero Speed." *Journal of Irreproducible Results*, Sept/Oct 1983, p. 19.
6. Mark Twain, *Life on the Mississippi*, 1874.
7. Christopher Jencks and others, *Inequality*, New York: Basic Books, 1972, p. 59.
8. Harold Hotelling, review of Horace Secrist, "The Triumph of Mediocrity in Business," *Journal of the American Statistical Association*, Vol. 28, 1933, pp. 463–465. Secrist and Hotelling debated this further in the 1934 volume of this journal, pp. 196–199.
9. These baseball statistics are from *Esquire*, April 1981.
10. Darrell Huff, *How to Take a Chance*, New York: W.W. Norton, 1959, p. 141.
11. Edward Ames and Stanley Reiter, "Distributions of Correlation Coefficients in Economic Time Series," *Journal of the American Statistical Association*, Vol. 56, September 1961, 636–656.
12. R.J. Hoyle, "Decline of Language as a Medium of Communication," *The Best of the Journal of Irreproducible Results*, George H. Scherr, ed., New York: Workman, 1983, pp. 134–135.
13. *Sports Illustrated*, "Scorecard," March 18, 1974.
14. Gary Pomerantz, "Getting to the Top Is Easier Than Staying There," *Washington Post*, July, 1983.
15. Albert Ando and Franco Modigliani, "The 'Permanent Income' and 'Life-Cycle' Hypotheses of Saving Behavior: Comparisons and Tests," in I. Friend and R. Jones, eds., *Consumption and Saving*, Vol. II, 1960, p. 154.

Chapter 15

Opening quotation: Anonymous.

1. Frank A Haight, "Do Speed Limits Reduce Traffic Accidents?," in Judith M. Tanur *et al.*, *Statistics: A Guide to Business and Economics*, San Francisco: Holden-Day, 1976, pp. 130–136.
2. Burton G. Malkiel and John G. Cragg, "Expectations and the Structure of Share Prices," *American Economic Review*, September 1970, pp. 601–617.
3. Haim Levy and Marshall Sarnat, *Investment and Portfolio Analysis*, New York: John Wiley, 1972, pp. 244–248.
4. Samuel Bowles and Henry Levin, "The Determinants of Scholastic Achievement—An Appraisal of Some Recent Evidence," *Journal of Human Resources*, Winter 1968, p. 15. Also see Bowles and Levin, "More on Multicollinearity and the Effectiveness of Schools," *Journal of Human Resources*, Summer 1968, pp. 393–400; and G. Cain and H. Watts, "Problems in Making Policy Inferences from the Coleman Report," *American Sociological Review*, April 1970, pp. 228–249.
5. An economist did estimate this sort of equation! See D.A. Katz, "Faculty Salaries, Promotions, and Productivity at a Large University," *American Economic Review*, June 1973.
6. Lawrence Fisher, "Determinants of Risk Premiums on Corporate Bonds," *Journal of Political Economy*, 67, June 1959, 217–237. The actual regression equation uses the logarithms of the variables.

Chapter 16

Opening quotation: Thomas Fuller.

1. W.J. Youden, "Chance, Uncertainty, and Truth in Science," *Journal of Quality Technology,* 1972.
2. Mark Gibbons and Patrick Hess, "Day of the Week Effects and Asset Returns," *Journal of Business,* October 1981, pp. 579–595.
3. O.L. Davies, *The Design and Analysis of Industrial Experiments,* London: Oliver and Boyd, 1956, p. 164.
4. Elisabeth Street and Mavis B. Carroll, "Preliminary Evaluation of a New Food Product," in Judith M. Tanur, *et al., Statistics: A Guide to Business and Economics,* San Francisco: Holden-Day, 1976, pp. 103–112.
5. Henry Scheffe, *The Analysis of Variance,* New York: John Wiley, 1959.

Chapter 17

Opening quotation: Larry Merchant, *The National Football Lottery,* New York: Holt, Rinehart, and Winston, 1963.

1. Ronald Frank and William Massy, "Shelf Position and Space Effects on Sales," *Journals of Marketing Research,* February 1970, pp. 59–66.
2. For example, William Beyer, ed., *Handbook of Tables for Probability and Statistics,* second edition, Cleveland, Ohio: Chemical Rubber Company, 1972.
3. William Beyer.

Chapter 18

Opening quotation: Edmund Burke, *Reflections on the Revolution in France,* 1790.

1. Roger G. Ibbotson and Rex A. Sinquefield, *Stocks, Bonds, Bills, and Inflation: Historical Returns (1926–1978),* Charlottesville, Virginia: The Financial Analysts Research Foundation, 1979.
2. Robert Stansfield, *N.Y. Times,* February 21, 1971.
3. Congressional Budget Office, *Indexing with the Consumer Price Index: Problems and Alternatives,* Washington, D.C.: U.S. Government Printing Office, June 1981.
4. A good reference is Gary Smith, *Macroeconomics,* New York: W.H. Freeman, 1985.
5. David Upshaw, of Drexel Burnham Lambert, quoted in Jack Egan, "Dow and the Law of Averages," *New York,* May 21, 1979, p. 12.
6. Lil Phillips, "Phindex shows horrific inflation," *Cape Cod Times,* July 10, 1984.
7. John A. Johnson, "Sharing Some Ideas," *Cape Cod Times,* July 12, 1984.
8. *Barrons,* July 30, 1984.

Numerical Answers to Selected Odd-numbered Exercises

Chapter 1

1.3 5000

1.5 .4858 males and .5142 females

1.9 Using $10,000 units for the histogram widths:

Income group	Relative frequency	Histogram height
low	.719	.288
middle	.156	.156
upper	.083	.005

1.11 4.6, 2.4, and −6.3.

1.13 10.08 and 5.77.

1.15 3.55, 3.5, and 3

1.21

Test scores	Ave. abs. deviation	Variance	Standard deviation
second	3.5	65.6	8.1
third	17.3	328.2	18.1

1.39 a. 30
   b. 26.67

1.45 24–27, 29.34, and 27.3

1.47 $38,004 and $12,500

Chapter 2

2.1 .4, .4, .2

2.3 a. .4
   b. .4
   c. .48
   d. .88
   e. 0

2.9 59,319 combinations, .0000169 probability

2.11 .0000002756

2.15 .1646

2.23 .667

2.29 .25, .667

2.31 .4167

2.35 .0851, .1702

2.47 a. 39,916,800
    b. 3,113,510,400
    c. 239,500,800

Chapter 3

3.3 .0385

3.5 .6

3.6 .5, .5, 1/3, 1/3, 1/6, no

3.13 .2857

3.17 .2637
3.19 .94235, .99981
3.21 .0586, .2378, .4950
3.23 2/3
3.25 .5
3.35 a. .6651
    b. .6187
    c. .5973

Chapter 4

4.1

x	$p[x]$
1	1/6
2	1/6
3	1/6
4	1/6
5	1/6
6	1/6

4.5 $500 per wager
4.7 2.75, 1.558, and 1.043
4.9 $250
4.13 -16.2% and -13.9%
4.15 .545
4.19 expected value = $1.028,
    expected cost = $1028
4.21 a. $0.75x
    b. $0.6875x
    c. $0.5x
4.25 10% and 5%
4.29 14, 18, and 1

Chapter 5

5.3 $P[2 \text{ heads}] = .375$
5.5 a. .2963
    b. .4444
    c. .2222
    d. .0370
5.9 .1921
5.15 .377, .252, .0284, .0568
5.17 .736
5.21 .5 and .375
5.27 a. .2461

b. .2051
c. .1172
d. .3770
e. .3438
5.31 .4040
5.35 .0499
5.49 a. .00111
    b. .00286
    c. .001234
    d. .008166
    e. .9999993

Chapter 6

6.1 a. discrete
    b. continuous
    c. continuous
    d. continuous
    e. discrete
    f. discrete
    g. discrete
    h. continuous
6.5 a. 1
    b. 0
    c. .25
    d. .75
    e. .4375
6.7 2.5 and 1.118. $Z = -1.342, -.447,$
    $+.447, +1.342$ with mean 0 and
    standard deviation 1
6.13 a. .5, 1, 5
    b. .5, .7071, .158114
    c. $-3.162, -2.530, -1.897, -1.265,$
       $-.632, 0, .632, 1.265, 1.897,$
       2.530, 3.162
    d. binomial
6.21 each is $0
6.23 $P[d \text{ feet to right}]$ is given by binomial
    with $d = 2x - 360$, where x is the
    number of successful steps to the right
6.27 The dollar change is $.5x - 2.5$, where x
    is the number of heads, and the
    probability distribution of x is binomial.
6.31 a. 1
    b. .5
    c. .5
    d. .375
    e. .75

Chapter 7

7.1 a. .5
  b. .1587
  c. .0228
  d. .0013
  e. .1587
7.3 a. 0
  b. 1.96
  c. −1.96
7.5 1. 50
  b. 15.87
  c. 97.72
7.13 1096, 6216, 164
7.15 .984, .001
7.17 .9437, .9757, >.999
7.19 .174
7.25 a. 867,600
  b. 243,333
  c. 30,200
  d. 2,000
  e. 60
7.29 .3286, .0465, .0018
7.45 800, .5, .5

Chapter 8

8.9 ratings: 20%, 18%, and 22%
  shares: 30%, 27%, and 33%
8.11 a. $246 gain
  b. $4246
  c. $4000
8.27 .2
8.50 .40, .24, .18, .10, .06, .02

Chapter 9

9.1 a. .5
  b. .0228
  c. .5
  d. .0000317
9.3 .1587, .000000287
9.9 .0062, 2.1 to 2.9
9.11 186,269.552 to 186,270.448
9.15 .000000287, 63.87 to 68.13
9.17 11.91 to 16.45
9.21 a. .2119

  b. .0352
  c. .0021
9.23 a. .5
  b. .1112
  c. .0073
  d. about .0000003
  e. .003
9.33 a. 4
  b. 16
  c. 2213 (using 1.96 std. devs.)
9.37 9,604 (using 1.96 std. devs.)

Chapter 10

10.3 .0578, .0735
10.5 .440, .560
10.9 a. >.999
  b. <.001
  c. virtually zero
10.17 reject if <97.06 or <102.94
10.19 .1977, .3085
10.21 P-value of .055
10.25 .0000047
10.29 a. .0000187
  b. .000000000000004
10.33 17.95
10.35 $Z = -2$, $P = .0228$, 1701 to 1799

Chapter 11

11.1 reject. $P = .693$
11.9 P-value = .006
11.17 .0228. .9641, .5. <.001, virtually 0
11.21 with cutoff of 8:
  a. .0547
  b. .0517
  c. .0489
  d. 1
11.23 .034
11.41 cutoffs: 133, 117
11.43 .59, .172
11.45 .5, .001 P-value
11.47 .012
11.49 a. 2
  b. 1
  c. 3

Chapter 12

12.1   95% confidence interval is -0.6 to 0.2
12.3   95% confidence interval is $-.2$ to $-.5$
12.5   95% confidence interval is $-.17$ to $.01$
12.11 4.43 chi-square value
12.15 408.1 chi-square value
12.21 38.6 chi-square value
12.27 1073.5 chi-square value
12.33 difference is 2.2 std. dev. from zero
12.41 difference is 1.5 std. dev. from zero.
12.49 1411.9 chi-square value

Chapter 13

13.7 $a = 23.87$, $b = .709$
13.9 $a = 830.65$, $b = .520$
13.11 cannot be estimated
13.15 a. 2.83
       c. $t = 2.07$
       e. $.09$ to 5.57
13.17 $t = 1.22$
13.21 $a = -126.7$, $b = 4.07$, $t = 7.45$
13.23 .63
13.27 $a = 15.91$, $b = .270$, SEE $= .2309$,
       $R^2 = .995$
13.31 a. $b = .039$, $t = 4.7$
       b. $b = -.167$, $t = 6.9$
       c. $b = .008$, $t = 1.0$
13.41 approaches the std. dev. of the error
       term

Chapter 14

14.1   a. $a = 15.72$, $b = .109$
       b. SEE $= 9.28$, $R^2 = .54$
14.5   a. $a = -167.8$, $b = 4.74$
       b. SEE $= 8.25$, $R^2 = .77$
       c. $t = 5.2$
       d. 2.90 to 6.58
14.7 $a = 1.32$, $b = 2.88$
14.11 e.g., 59.6% in Kloof and 40.4% in
       Consolidated
14.19 -1.67 to $-.65$
14.23 a. 16.81
       b. 2.31

14.31 a. 622.0
       b. 969.5
14.33 $2.16 for 500-pound breaking strength
14.35 $30.81
14.49 $t = 5.1$

Chapter 15

15.9   106.6
15.19 est. coeff.: -1.14, $.01$, $-.42$
15.23 est. coeff.: -404.3, $.947$, $.086$.
       t-values: 1.5, 16.1, 1.3
15.31 $R^2 = 1$
15.33 a. $32,750
       b. $50
       c. $50
15.35 -1201.1
15.37 BG: 113.0, HS: 164.7
15.41 est. coeff.: -3.93, $.10$, 7.4
15.47 est. coeff.: -150, 4.5, $.23$
15.49 no unique solution

Chapter 16

16.3   b. 110
       c. 5.5
       d. 128
       e. 23.28
16.9 $F = 1.5$
16.11 $F = 4.8$
16.15 total $= 13291.39$
16.19 means $= 30.4$, 40.44, 35.08. $F = 19.6$
16.21 $F = 14.3$
16.29 a. 12.2
       b. 148.8
16.31 a. 412, 470
       b. 58595.56, 43222.22
       c. 50908.89
       d. 1682.00
16.33 $F = 1.8$
16.35 $F = 49.4$

Chapter 17

17.1   reject if fewer than 5 above or below
       claimed median

17.7   mean = 30, std dev. = 6.4
17.9   average ranks = 9.55 and 11.45
17.11 average ranks = 6.06 and 10.94
17.17 R = .544
17.21 R = 1
17.29 5 runs
17.31 confidence interval: 18.0 to 34.0
17.45 11 runs

18.15 est. coeff.: 3.651, .199, .207, 1.316,
       .071
18.25 a = 14.36, b = −.00681
18.27 7.6% increase between 1977 and 1978
18.29 1.564
18.31 2nd, equal, 4th
18.33 est. coeff.: .359, .06, .168, 1.188,
       −.018

Chapter 18

18.7 a = −39.22, b = .0226
18.13 $37.4 billion seasonal difference

Index

In the beginning,
good always overpowered the evil of all man's sins.
But in time,
Our nations grew weak and our cities fell to slums
while evil stood strong.
In the dusts of hell lurked the blackest of hates,
for he who you fear awaits you.

Now, many, many, lifetimes later,
by beaten, destroyed, only corpses of rebels,
ashes of dreams and bloodstained streets.
It has been written
that those who have the youth have the future.
So, come now Children of the Beast
Be Strong and SHOUT AT THE DEVIL!

Table 2 Standardized Normal Distribution

$P[Z > \text{cutoff}]$
For instance, $P[Z > 1.96] = .025$

Cutoff	∞	.01	.02	.03	.04	.05	.06	.07	.08	.09
0.0	.5000	.4960	.4920	.4880	.4840	.4801	.4761	.4721	.4681	.4641
0.1	.4602	.4562	.4522	.4483	.4443	.4404	.4364	.4325	.4286	.4247
0.2	.4207	.4168	.4129	.4090	.4052	.4013	.3974	.3936	.3897	.3859
0.3	.3821	.3783	.3745	.3707	.3669	.3632	.3594	.3557	.3520	.3483
0.4	.3446	.3409	.3372	.3336	.3300	.3264	.3228	.3192	.3156	.3121
0.5	.3085	.3050	.3015	.2981	.2946	.2912	.2877	.2843	.2810	.2776
0.6	.2743	.2709	.2676	.2643	.2611	.2578	.2546	.2514	.2483	.2451
0.7	.2420	.2389	.2358	.2327	.2296	.2266	.2236	.2206	.2177	.2148
0.8	.2119	.2090	.2061	.2033	.2005	.1977	.1949	.1922	.1894	.1867
0.9	.1841	.1814	.1788	.1762	.1736	.1711	.1685	.1660	.1635	.1611
1.0	.1587	.1562	.1539	.1515	.1492	.1469	.1446	.1423	.1401	.1379
1.1	.1357	.1335	.1314	.1292	.1271	.1251	.1230	.1210	.1190	.1170
1.2	.1151	.1131	.1112	.1093	.1075	.1056	.1038	.1020	.1003	.0985
1.3	.0968	.0951	.0934	.0918	.0901	.0885	.0869	.0853	.0838	.0823
1.4	.0808	.0793	.0778	.0764	.0749	.0735	.0722	.0708	.0694	.0681
1.5	.0668	.0655	.0643	.0630	.0618	.0606	.0594	.0582	.0571	.0559
1.6	.0548	.0537	.0526	.0516	.0505	.0495	.0485	.0475	.0465	.0455
1.7	.0446	.0436	.0427	.0418	.0409	.0401	.0392	.0384	.0375	.0367
1.8	.0359	.0352	.0344	.0336	.0329	.0322	.0314	.0307	.0301	.0294
1.9	.0287	.0281	.0274	.0268	.0262	.0256	.0250	.0244	.0239	.0233
2.0	.0228	.0222	.0217	.0212	.0207	.0202	.0197	.0192	.0188	.0183
2.1	.0179	.0174	.0170	.0166	.0162	.0158	.0154	.0150	.0146	.0143
2.2	.0139	.0136	.0132	.0129	.0125	.0122	.0119	.0116	.0113	.0110
2.3	.0107	.0104	.0102	.0099	.0096	.0094	.0091	.0089	.0087	.0084
2.4	.0082	.0080	.0078	.0075	.0073	.0071	.0069	.0068	.0066	.0064
2.5	.0062	.0060	.0059	.0057	.0055	.0054	.0052	.0051	.0049	.0048
2.6	.0047	.0045	.0044	.0043	.0041	.0040	.0039	.0038	.0037	.0036
2.7	.0035	.0034	.0033	.0032	.0031	.0030	.0029	.0028	.0027	.0026
2.8	.0026	.0025	.0024	.0023	.0023	.0022	.0021	.0021	.0020	.0019
2.9	.0019	.0018	.0017	.0017	.0016	.0016	.0015	.0015	.0014	.0014
3.0	.0013	.0013	.0013	.0012	.0012	.0011	.0011	.0011	.0010	.0010
4.0	.000 031 7									
5.0	.000 000 287									
6.0	.000 000 000 987									
7.0	.000 000 000 001 28									
8.0	.000 000 000 000 001									